Study Guide

Avi J. Cohen
York University

Harvey B. King
University of Regina

ECONOMICS
Canada in the Global Environment

Eighth Edition

Michael Parkin   Robin Bade

PEARSON

Acquisitions Editor: Claudine O'Donnell
Developmental Editor: Karen Townsend
Lead Project Manager: Söğüt Y. Güleç
Manufacturing Manager: Susan Johnson
Production Editor: Leanne Rancourt
Copy Editor: Leanne Rancourt
Cover Design: Anthony Leung
Cover Image: Getty Images

If you purchased this book outside the United States or Canada, you should be aware that it has been imported without the approval of the publisher or the author.

10 9 8 7 6 5 4 3   EBM

ISBN 978-0-321-79893-0

Contents

Acknowledgments

This eighth edition of the *Study Guide* has benefited from students who pointed out mistakes and ambiguities they found in using the *Study Guide*. Thanks to Josh Atwal, Rabia Sajun, Ashish Shah, Tony Tran, and Fan Zhang for helping us in this area. Thanks also to Robin Bade and Michael Parkin for their dedication to the continuous improvement of the textbook, the *Study Guide*, and the teaching of economics.

Harvey King dedicates this edition to Morgan and Harrison (who weren't even born for the first edition and are now in university and keeping me alert and sharp), and to Tracy for all her love and patience. Avi Cohen dedicates this edition to Robert Cohen, my father, whose extraordinary qualities as a teacher make him my role model.

Harvey King
Avi Cohen
March 2012

The moment you know

It's that inspired moment when something makes perfect sense.
MyEconLab for **Parkin and Bade**, *Economics: Canada in the Global Environment*, **Eighth Edition**

MyEconLab is a dynamic online tool that helps you reach that moment, time and again.

- Chapter tests generate your personal study plan and an assignment tool lets your instructor guide your learning toward those moments of true understanding.

- Practise problems directly from the textbook's Review Quiz and end-of-chapter Problems and Applications in your personal Study Plan with links to online learning resources.

- "Help-Me-Solve-This" breaks down a problem and guides you through the steps to solve it.

- Links to the eText guide you to revisit a concept or explanation when needed.

- Animated graphs with audio explanations reinforce your reading.

- The graphing tool enables you to build and manipulate graphs to understand how concepts, numbers, and graphs connect.

- Unlimited Practice: Hundreds of practice questions ensure that you get as much practice as you need, and as you work on each exercise, instant feedback helps you understand and apply the concepts.

Study on the Go
Scan the QR code at the end of each chapter to link to resources you can use on your smartphone. Study on the Go provides a convenient and unprecedented integration between text and online content:

- Glossary flashcards
- Audio summaries
- Quizzes to make the most of your time when you're on the move

Introduction

Before You Begin …

Our experience has taught us that what first-year economics students want most from a *Study Guide* is help in mastering course material to do well on examinations. We have developed this *Study Guide* to respond specifically to that demand. Using this *Study Guide* alone, however, is not enough to guarantee that you will do well in your course. In order to help you overcome the problems and difficulties that most first-year students encounter, we have some general advice on how to study, as well as some specific advice on how to best use this *Study Guide*.

Some Friendly Advice

The study of economics requires a different style of thinking from what you may encounter in other courses. Economists make extensive use of assumptions to break down complex problems into simple, analytically manageable parts. This analytical style, while not ultimately more demanding than the styles of thinking in other disciplines, feels unfamiliar to most students and requires practice. As a result, it is not as easy to do well in economics simply on the basis of your raw intelligence and high school knowledge as it is in many other first-year courses. Many students who come to our offices are frustrated and puzzled by the fact that they are getting A's and B's in their other courses but only a C or worse in economics. They have not recognized that the study of economics is different and requires practice. In order to avoid a frustrating visit to your instructor after your first test, we suggest you do the following.

Don't rely solely on your high school economics. If you took high school economics, you will have seen the material on demand and supply, which your instructor will lecture on in the first few weeks. Don't be lulled into feeling that the course will be easy. Your high school knowledge of economic concepts will be very useful, but it will not be enough to guarantee high marks on exams. Your college or university instructors will demand much more detailed knowledge of concepts and ask you to apply them in new circumstances.

Keep up with the course material on a weekly basis. Read the appropriate chapter in the textbook before your instructor lectures on it. In this initial reading, don't worry about details or arguments you can't quite follow—just try to get a general understanding of the basic concepts and issues. You may be amazed at how your instructor's ability to teach improves when you come to class prepared. As soon as your instructor has finished covering a chapter, complete the corresponding *Study Guide* chapter. Avoid cramming the day before or even just the week before an exam. Because economics requires practice, cramming is an almost certain recipe for failure.

Keep a good set of lecture notes. Good lecture notes are vital for focusing your studying. Your instructor will only lecture on a subset of topics from the textbook. The topics your instructor covers in a lecture should usually be given priority when studying. Also give priority to studying the figures and graphs covered in the lecture.

Instructors do differ in their emphasis on lecture notes or the textbook, so early on in the course ask which is more important in reviewing for exams—lecture notes or the textbook. If your instructor answers that both are important, then ask the following, typically economic question: at the margin, which will be more beneficial— spending an extra hour rereading your lecture notes or an extra hour rereading the textbook? This question assumes that you have read each textbook chapter twice (once before lecture for a general understanding, and then later for a thorough understanding); that you have prepared a good set of lecture notes; and that you have worked through all of the problems in the appropriate *Study Guide* chapters. By applying this style of analysis to the problem of efficiently allocating your study time, you are already beginning to think like an economist!

Use your instructor and/or teaching assistants for help. When you have questions or problems with course material, come to the office to ask questions. Remember, you are paying for your education and instructors are there to help you learn. We are often amazed at how few students come to see us during office hours. Don't be shy. The personal contact that comes from one-on-one tutoring is professionally gratifying for us as well as (hopefully) beneficial to you.

Form a study group. A very useful way to motivate your studying and to learn economics is to discuss the course material and problems with other students. Explaining the answer to a question out loud is a very effective way of discovering how well you understand the question. When you answer a question only in your head, you often skip steps in the chain of reasoning without realizing it. When you are forced to explain your reasoning aloud, gaps and mistakes quickly appear, and you (with your fellow group members) can quickly correct your reasoning. The true/false and explain questions in the *Study Guide* and the questions at the end of each textbook chapter are good study-group material. You might also get together after having worked the *Study Guide* problems, but before looking at the answers, and help each other solve unsolved problems.

Work old exams. One of the most effective ways of studying is to work through exams your instructor has given in previous years. Old exams give you a feel for the style of questions your instructor may ask, and give you the opportunity to get used to time pressure if you force yourself to do the exam in the allotted time. Studying from old exams is not cheating, as long as you have obtained a copy of the exam legally. Some institutions post old exams online; others keep them in the library, the department, or at the student union. Upper-year students who have previously taken the course are usually a good source as well. Remember, though, that old exams are a useful study aid only if you use them to understand the reasoning behind each question. If you simply memorize answers in the hopes that your instructor will repeat the identical question, you are likely to fail. From year to year, instructors routinely change the questions or change the numerical values for similar questions.

MyEconLab

MyEconLab's powerful assessment and tutorial system works hand-in-hand with *Economics: Canada in the Global Environment*. With comprehensive homework, quiz, test, Gradebook, and tutorial options, instructors can manage all assessment needs in one program. *Economics in the News* is a turn-key solution to bringing daily news into the classroom. Every week during the academic year, two relevant news articles (one micro, one macro) are uploaded with links for further information questions that may be used for homework or classroom discussion.

Using the *Study Guide*

You should only attempt to complete a chapter in this *Study Guide* after you have read the corresponding textbook chapter and listened to your instructor lecture on the material. Each *Study Guide* chapter contains the following sections.

Key Concepts This first section is a one-to-two-page summary, in point form, of all key definitions, concepts, and material from the textbook chapter. The summary is organized using the same major section headings from the textbook chapter. Key terms from the textbook appear in bold. This section is designed to focus you quickly and precisely on the core material that you must master. It is an excellent study aid for the night before an exam. Think

of it as crib notes that will serve as a final check of the key concepts you have studied.

Helpful Hints When you encounter difficulty in mastering concepts or techniques, you will not be alone. Many students find certain concepts difficult and often make the same kinds of mistakes. We have seen these common mistakes often enough to have learned how to help students avoid them. The hints point out these mistakes and offer tips to avoid them. The hints focus on the most important concepts, equations, and techniques for problem solving. They also review crucial graphs that appear on every instructor's exams. We hope that this section will be very useful, since instructors always ask exam questions designed to test these possible mistakes in your understanding.

Self-Test This should be one of the most useful sections of this *Study Guide*. The questions are designed to give you practice and to test skills and techniques you must master to do well on exams. You are encouraged to write directly in the *Study Guide*. There are plenty of the multiple-choice questions (25 for each chapter) you are most likely to encounter on course tests and exams. There are also other types of questions, described below, each with a specific pedagogical purpose.

Before we describe the three parts of the Self-Test section, here are some tips that apply to all parts:

Use a pencil. This will allow you to erase your mistakes and have neat, completed pages from which to study. Draw graphs wherever applicable. Some questions will ask explicitly for graphs; many others will not, but will require a chain of reasoning that involves shifts of curves on a graph. *Always draw the graph.* Don't try to work through the reasoning in your head—you are much more likely to make mistakes that way. Whenever you draw a graph, even in the margins of this *Study Guide*, label the axes. You may think that you can keep the labels in your head, but you will be confronting many different graphs with many different variables on the axes. Avoid confusion: label! As an added incentive, remember that on exams where graphs are required, instructors will deduct marks for unlabelled axes.

Do the Self-Test questions as if they were real exam questions, which means do them without looking at the answers. This is the single most important tip we can give you. Struggling for the answers to questions that you find difficult is one of the most effective ways to learn. The athletic adage "No pain, no gain" applies equally to studying. You will learn the most from right answers you had to struggle for and from your wrong answers and mistakes. Only after you have attempted all the questions should you look at the answers. When you finally do check the answers, be sure to understand where you went wrong and why the right answer is right.

If you want to impose time pressure on yourself to simulate the conditions of a real exam, allow two minutes for each true/false and multiple-choice question. The short answer problems vary considerably in their time requirements, so it is difficult to give time estimates for them. However, we believe that such time pressure is probably not a good idea for *Study Guide* questions. A state of relaxed concentration is best. If you want practice with time pressure, use old exams, or use the Part Wrap Up Midterm Examinations (see description on page x).

There are many questions in each chapter, and it will take you somewhere between two and four hours to answer all of them. If you get tired (or bored), don't burn yourself out by trying to work through all of the questions in one sitting. Consider breaking up your Self-Test over two (or more) study sessions.

One other tip about the Self-Test: *Before* you jump in and do the questions, be sure to read through the Key Concepts and Helpful Hints. This will save you frustration at getting wrong answers to questions. When you do get wrong answers, you will often find an explanation of the right answers in the Key Concepts or Helpful Hints.

The three parts of the Self-Test section are as follows:

True/False and Explain These questions test basic knowledge of chapter concepts and your ability to apply the concepts. Some challenge your understanding, to see if you can identify mistakes in statements using basic concepts. These questions will quickly identify gaps in your knowledge and are useful to answer out loud in a study group. There are 15 of these questions, organized using the same major section headings from the textbook. The Test Bank that your instructor will likely use to make up tests and exams also contains true/false questions like those in the Self-Test.

When answering, identify each statement as *true* or *false*. Explain your answer in one sentence. The space underneath each question should be sufficient in every case for writing your answer.

Multiple-Choice These more difficult questions test your analytical abilities by asking you to apply concepts to new situations, manipulate information, and solve numerical and graphical problems.

This is the most frequently used type of test and exam question, and the Self-Test contains 25 of them for each chapter organized using the same major section headings from the textbook. Your instructor's Test Bank contains all of the *Study Guide* multiple-choice questions, numerous questions that closely parallel the *Study Guide* questions, plus many similar questions.

Before you answer, read each question and all five choices carefully. Many of the choices will be plausible and will differ only slightly. You must choose the one *best* answer. A useful strategy is to first eliminate any obviously wrong choices and then focus on the remaining alternatives. Be aware that sometimes the correct answer will be "none of the above." Don't get frustrated or think that you are dim if you can't immediately see the correct answer. These questions are designed to make you work to find the correct choice.

Short Answer Problems The best way to learn to do economics is to do problems. Problems are also a popular type of test and exam question—practise them as much as possible! Each Self-Test concludes with eight short answer, numerical, or graphical problems, often based on economic policy issues. In many chapters, this is the most challenging part of the Self-Test. It is also likely to be the most helpful for deepening your understanding of the chapter material. We have, however, designed the questions to teach as much as to test. We have purposely arranged the parts of each multipart question to lead you through the problem-solving analysis in a gradual and sequential fashion, from easier to more difficult parts.

Problems that require critical thinking are marked with the symbol ℮, to alert you to the need for extra time and effort. This symbol gives you the same indication you would have on a test or exam from the number of marks or minutes allocated to a problem.

Answers The Self-Test is followed by a section that gives answers to all the questions. But do not look at any answer until you have attempted the question.

When you finally do look, use the answer to understand where you went wrong, and think about why the answer is right. Every true/false and multiple-choice answer includes a brief, point-form explanation to suggest where you might have gone wrong and the economic reasoning behind the answer. At the end of each answer are page references to the textbook, so you can read a more complete explanation.

Answers to critical thinking questions are marked with ℮ to indicate why you might have struggled with that question! (We purposely did not mark which true/false and multiple-choice questions were critical thinking, to stay as close as possible to a real test or exam format. In an exam, all multiple-choice questions, for example, are worth the same number of marks, and you would have no idea which questions are the more difficult ones requiring critical thinking.)

The detailed answers to the short answer problems should be especially useful in clarifying and illustrating typical chains of reasoning involved in economic analysis. Answers to critical thinking problems are marked with ℮. If the answers alone do not clear up your confusion, go back to the appropriate sections of the textbook and to the Key Concepts and Helpful Hints in this *Study Guide*. If that still does not suffice, go to your instructor's or teaching assistants' office, or to your study-group members for help and clarification.

Part Wrap Up Problem and Midterm Examination
Every few chapters, at the end of each of the ten Parts of the textbook, you will find a special multipart problem (and answer). These problems draw on material from all chapters in the Part, and emphasize policy and real-world questions (e.g., the impact of cigarette smuggling on tax revenues). They will help you integrate concepts from different chapters that may seem unrelated but actually are. We often design exam questions similar to these problems.

Each Wrap Up also contains a Midterm Examination, consisting of four or more multiple-choice questions from each chapter in the textbook part. The midterm is set up like a real examination or test, with a scrambled order and a time limit for working the questions. Like the other multiple-choice questions, there are answers with point-form explanations as well as page references to the textbook so you can go find more complete explanations.

If you effectively combine the use of the textbook, the *Study Guide*, MyEconLab, and all other course resources, you will be well prepared for exams. Equally importantly, you will also have developed analytical skills and powers of reasoning that will benefit you throughout life and in whatever career you choose.

Do You Have Any Friendly Advice for Us?

We have attempted to make this *Study Guide* as clear and as useful as possible, and to avoid errors. No doubt, we have not succeeded entirely, and you are the only judges who count in evaluating our attempt. If you discover errors, or if you have other suggestions for improving the *Study Guide*, please write to us. In future editions, we will try to acknowledge the names of all students whose suggestions help us improve this supplement. Send your correspondence or email to either of us:

Professor Avi J. Cohen
Department of Economics
Vari Hall, York University
Toronto, Ontario M3J 1P3
avicohen@yorku.ca

Professor Harvey B. King
Department of Economics
University of Regina
Regina, Saskatchewan S4S 0A2
Harvey.King@uregina.ca

Should the Study of Economics Be Part of Your Future?

By Harvey King (University of Regina) and
Robert Whaples (Wake Forest University)

Should You Take More Economics Courses?

Soon you will learn about supply and demand, utility and profit maximization, employment and unemployment. First, however, let's take a moment to look to the future.

- Should you take more classes or maybe even major in economics?

- What about graduate school in economics?

Economists generally assume that people try to make rational choices to maximize their own well-being. The purpose of this chapter is help you make that rational maximizing choice by providing low-cost information. Let us assess the benefits and see whether they outweigh the costs of studying economics.

Benefits from Studying Economics

Knowledge, Enlightenment, and Liberation

As John Maynard Keynes, a famous British economist, said, "The ideas of economists … both when they are right and when they are wrong, are more powerful than is commonly understood. Indeed the world is ruled by little else. Practical men, who believe themselves to be quite exempt from any intellectual influences, are usually the slaves of some defunct economist." Studying economics is a liberating and enlightening experience. You don't want to be the slave of a defunct economist, do you? Liberate yourself. It's better to bring your ideas out in the open, to confront and understand them, rather than to leave them buried.

Knowledge, Understanding, and Satisfaction

Many of the most important problems in the world are economic. Studying economics gives you a practical set of tools to understand and solve them. Every day, on television and in the newspapers, we hear and read about big issues such as economic growth, inflation, unemployment, health-care reform, welfare reform, the environment, and the transition away from Communism. Your introduction to economics will let you watch the news or pick up a newspaper and better understand these issues. As an added bonus, economics helps you understand smaller, more immediate concerns, such as: How much Spam should I buy? Is skipping class today a good idea? Should I put my retirement funds in government bonds or in the stock market? After all, as George Bernard Shaw put it, "Economy is the art of making the most of life." Mick Jagger, who dropped out of the London School of Economics, complains that he "can't get no satisfaction." Maybe he should have studied more economics! The economic way of thinking will help you maximize your satisfaction.

Career Opportunities

All careers are not equal. While the wages in many occupations have not risen much lately, the wages of "symbolic analysts" who "solve, identify, and broker problems by manipulating symbols" are soaring.[1] These people "simplify reality into abstract images that can be rearranged, juggled, experimented with, communicated to other specialists, and then, eventually, transformed back into reality." Their wages have been rising as the globalization of the economy increases the demand for their insights and as technological developments (especially computers) have enhanced their productivity. Economists are the quintessential symbolic analysts, as we manipulate ideas about abstractions such as supply and demand, cost and benefits, and equilibrium. You can think of your training in economics as an exercise regimen—a workout for your brain.

You will use many of the concepts you will learn in introductory economics during your career, but it is the practice in abstract thinking that will really pay off. In fact, most economics majors do not go on to become economists. They enter fields that use their analytical abilities, including business, management, insurance, finance, real estate, marketing, law, education, policy analysis, consulting, government, planning, and even medicine, journalism, and the arts.

A recent survey of 100 former economics majors at one university included all of these careers. If you want to verify that economics majors graduate to successful and rewarding careers, just ask your professors or watch what happens to economics majors from your school as they graduate.

Statistics from the 2006 Canadian census show that economics majors earn a healthy salary. Table 1 shows the average yearly earnings for selected occupations, with those occupations that generally require a reasonable understanding of economics highlighted in italics.

TABLE 1	AVERAGE YEARLY EARNINGS, 2005, BOTH SEXES, SELECTED OCCUPATIONS
Occupation	**Average Yearly Earnings**
Judges	$176,719
Senior managers, financial	*$175,497*
Senior managers	$139,443
Specialist physicians	$116,560
Dentists	$102,377
Managers in financial services	*$96,798*
*Lawyers and Quebec notaries**	*$89,606*
General practitioners	$84,783
Government managers in economic analysis	*$82,474*
Financial managers in administrative services	*$80,854*
*University professors**	*$70,146*
Economists and economic policy researchers and analysts	*$67,676*
Average income, all occupations	$38,226

* Clearly, not all professors or lawyers require an understanding of economics! The point is that becoming a professor or lawyer is a high-paying option for an economics major.

Source: *Statistics Canada*, "Wage and Salary Statistics (4) in Constant (2005) Dollars, Work Activity in the Reference Year (3), Highest Certificate, Diploma or Degree (5), Age Groups (5A), Occupation - National Occupational Classification for Statistics 2006 (720B) and Sex (3) for the Paid Workers 15 Years and Over With Wages and Salaries of Canada, Provinces, Territories, 2000 and 2005 - 20% Sample Data," accessed March 1, 2009 from http://www12.statcan.gc.ca/english/census06/data/topics/RetrieveProductTable.cfm?Temporal=2006&PID=96285&GID=614135&METH=1&APATH=3&PTYPE=88971%2C97154&THEME=75&AID=&FREE=0&FOCUS=&VID=0&GC=99&GK=NA&RL=0&TPL=RETR&SUB=0&d1=0&d2=0&d3=0&d4=0&d5=231

The Costs of Studying Economics

Since the "direct" costs of studying economics (tuition, books, supplies) aren't generally any higher or lower than the direct costs of other courses, indirect costs will be the most important of the costs to studying economics.

Forgone Knowledge

If you study economics, you can't study something else. This forgone knowledge could be very valuable.

Time and Energy

Economics is a fairly demanding major. Although economics courses do not generally take as much time as courses in English and history (in which you have to read a lot of long books) or anatomy and physiology (in which you have to spend hours in the lab and hours memorizing

things), they do take a decent amount of time. In addition, some people find the material "tougher" than most subjects because memorizing is not the key. In economics (like physics), analysing and solving are the keys.

Grades

As Table 2 shows, grades in introductory economics courses are generally lower than grades in some other majors, including other social sciences and the humanities. On the other hand, grades in economics are similar to grades in some sciences and math.

TABLE 2	AVERAGE GRADES AND GRADE DISTRIBUTION IN INTRODUCTORY COURSES AT SEVEN ONTARIO UNIVERSITIES		
Department	**Mean Grade***	**% (A + B)**	**% (D + F)**
Music	3.02	72.1	9.7
English	2.76	64.0	9.4
French	2.69	61.1	12.4
Philosophy	2.54	57.6	15.3
Biology	2.52	54.5	19.7
Sociology	2.51	52.8	14.2
Political Science	2.49	55.6	14.1
Psychology	2.40	48.4	20.6
Physics	2.38	46.1	28.4
Mathematics	2.19	44.4	33.9
Chemistry	2.18	42.9	30.9
Economics	2.18	41.6	30.7
*A = 4, B = 3, C = 2, D = 1, F = 0.			

Source: Paul Anglin and Ronald Meng, "Evidence on Grades and Grade Inflation at Ontario's Universities," *University of Windsor Working Paper*, November 1999. Used with permission.

Caveat Emptor (Buyer Beware): Interpreting Your Grades Is Not Straightforward

High grades provide direct satisfaction to most students, but they also act as a signal about the student's ability to learn the subject material. Unfortunately, because the grade distribution is not uniform across departments, you may be confused and misled by your grades. You may think that you are exceptionally good at a subject because of a high grade, when in fact nearly everyone gets a high grade in that subject. The important point here is that you should be informed about your own school's grade distribution. Just because you got a B in economics and an A in history does not necessarily mean that your comparative advantage is in learning history rather than economics. Everyone—or virtually everyone—may receive an A in history. Earning a B or a C in economics might mean that it is the best major for you, because high grades are much harder to earn in economics. It is fun to have a high GPA in university, but maximizing GPA should not be your goal. Maximizing your overall well-being is probably your goal, and this might be obtained by trading off a tenth or so of your GPA for a more rewarding major—perhaps economics.

Potential Side Effects from Studying Economics

Studying economics has some potential side effects. We're not sure whether they are costs or benefits and will let you decide.

Changing Ideas About What Is Fair

One study compared students at the beginning and end of the semester in an introductory economics course.[2] It found that by the end of the semester, significantly more of the students thought that the functioning of the market is "fair." This was especially true for female students. The results were consistent across a range of professors who fell across the ideological spectrum.

For example, the proportion of students who regarded it as unfair to increase the price of flowers on a holiday fell almost in half. The proportion that favoured government control over flower prices, rather than market determination, fell by over 60 percent. The study argues that these responses do not reflect changes in deep values, but instead represent the discovery of previous inconsistencies and their modification in the light of new information learned during the semester.

Changing Behaviour

Many people believe that the study of economics changes students' values and behaviour. Some think that it changes them for the worse. Others disagree. In particular, it is argued that economics students become more self-interested and less likely to cooperate, perhaps because they spend so much time studying economic models, which often assume that people are self-interested. For example, one study reports experimental evidence that economics students are more likely than nonmajors to behave self-interestedly in prisoners' dilemma games and ultimatum bargaining games.[3]

This need not mean that studying economics will change you, however. Another study compares beginning first-year and third- or fourth-year economics students and concludes that economics students "are already different when they begin their study of economics."[4] In other words, students signing up for economics courses are already different; studying economics doesn't change them. However, there are reasons to question both of these conclusions, because it is not clear whether these laboratory experiments using economic games reflect reality. One experiment asked students whether they

would return money that had been lost. It found that economics students were more likely than others to say that they would keep the cash.

However, what people say and what they do are sometimes at odds. In a follow-up experiment, this theory was tested by dropping stamped, addressed envelopes containing $10 in cash in different campus classrooms. To return the cash, the students had only to seal the envelopes and mail them. The results were that 56 percent of the envelopes dropped in economics classes were returned, while only 31 percent of the envelopes dropped in history, psychology, and business classes were sent in.[5] Perhaps economics students are less selfish than others!

Obviously, no firm conclusions have been reached about whether or how studying economics changes students' behaviour.

Cost versus Benefits

Suppose that you've weighed the costs and benefits of studying economics and you've decided that the benefits are greater than or equal to the costs. Obviously, then, you should continue to take economics courses. If you can't decide whether the benefits outweigh the costs, then you should probably collect more information—especially if it is good but inexpensive. In either case, read the rest of this section.

The Economics Major

The study of economics is like a tree. The introductory microeconomics and macroeconomics courses you begin with are the tree's roots. Most colleges and universities require that you master this material before you go on to any other courses. The way of thinking, the language, and the tools that you acquire in the introductory course are usually reinforced in intermediate microeconomics and macroeconomics courses before they are applied in more specialized courses that you take. The intermediate courses are the tree's trunk. Among the specialized courses that make up the branches of economics are econometrics (statistical economics), financial economics, labour economics, resource economics, international trade, industrial organization, public finance, public choice, economic history, the history of economic thought, mathematical economics, current economic issues, and urban economics. The branches of the tree vary from department to department, but these are common. It will pay to check your school calendar and discuss these courses with professors and other students.

Graduate School in Economics

Preparing for Graduate School in Economics

You can prepare for graduate school in economics by taking several math classes. This would probably include one year of calculus plus a couple of courses in probability and statistics and linear/matrix algebra. Ask your adviser about the particular courses to take at your university. In addition, the mathematical economics and econometrics courses in the economics department are essential. (*Hint:* Even if you aren't going to graduate school, these mathematical courses can be valuable to you, just as more economics courses can be valuable for nonmajors.)

If your school offers graduate level economics courses, you might want to sit in on a few to get accustomed to the flavour of graduate school.

Most graduate programs require strong grades in economics, a good score on the Graduate Record Examination (GRE) for U.S. schools, and solid letters of recommendation. It is a good idea to get to know a few professors very well and to go above and beyond what is expected so that they can write glowing letters about you.

Financing Graduate School

Unlike some other graduate and professional degree programs, you probably won't need to pile up a massive amount of debt while pursuing an M.A. or Ph.D. in economics. Most graduate programs hire their economics graduate students as teaching or research assistants. Teaching assistants begin by grading papers and running review sessions and can advance to teaching classes on their own. Research assistants generally do data collection, statistical work, and library research for professors and often jointly write papers with them. Most assistantships will pay for tuition and provide you with enough money to live on.

Where Should You Apply?

The best graduate school for you depends on a lot of things, especially your ability level, geographical location, areas of research interests, and, of course, financing. You should talk with your professors about ability level and areas of research. They are good judges of your ability, the level of different schools, and finding a good match for you.

What You Will Do in Graduate School

Most students who go on to graduate school do only an M.A. These degrees typically take one year for the non-thesis route and about two years for the thesis route.

Course work will include 2–4 courses in economic theory, plus 4–6 courses in specific subfields.

Most Ph.D. programs in economics begin with a year of theory courses in macroeconomics and microeconomics. After a year you will probably take a series of tests to show that you have mastered this core theory. If you pass these tests, in the second and third year of courses you will take more specialized subjects and perhaps take lengthy examinations in a couple of subfields. After this you will be required to write a dissertation—original research that will contribute new knowledge to one of the fields of economics. These stages are intertwined with work as a teaching and/or research assistant, and the dissertation stage can be quite drawn out. In the social sciences the median time it takes for a student to complete the Ph.D. degree is about 7.5 years.[6] Be aware that a high percentage (roughly 50 percent) of students do not complete their doctoral degree.

What Is Graduate School Like?

Graduate school in economics comes as a surprise to many students. The material and approach are distinctly different from what you will learn as an undergraduate. The textbooks and journal articles you will read in graduate school are often very theoretical and abstract. A good source of information is sitting in on courses or reading the reflections of recent students. See especially *The Making of an Economist* by Arjo Klamer and David Colander (Boulder, CO: Westview Press, 1990).

The Committee on Graduate Education in Economics (COGEE) undertook an important review of graduate education in economics and reported its findings in the September 1991 issue of the *Journal of Economic Literature*. COGEE asked faculty members, graduate students, and recent Ph.D.s to rank the most important skills needed to be successful in the study of graduate economics. At the top of the list were analytical skills and mathematics, followed by critical judgment, the ability to apply theory, and computational skills. At the bottom of the list were creativity and the ability to communicate. If you are interested in economic issues but do not have the characteristics required by graduate economics departments, there are other economics-related fields to consider, such as graduate school in public policy. Many economics majors go to business schools to obtain an MBA and are often better prepared than students who have undergraduate degrees in business.

Economics Reading

If you decide to make studying economics part of your future, or if you're hungry for more economics, you should immediately begin reading the economic news and books by economists. Life is short. Why waste it watching TV?

The easiest way to get your daily recommended dose of economics is to keep up with current economic events. Here are a few sources to pick up at the newsstand, bookstore, or library over your summer or winter break.

The Globe and Mail *or* The National Post

Many undergraduates subscribe to *The Globe and Mail* or *The National Post* at low student rates. Join them! Not only are these well-written business newspapers, but they also have articles on domestic and international news, politics, the arts, travel, and sports, as well as lively editorial pages. Reading one of these papers is one of the best ways to tie the economics you are studying to the real world and to prepare for your career.

Magazines and Journals

The Economist, a weekly magazine published in England, is available at a student discount rate. Pick up a copy at your school library and you will be hooked by its informative, sharp writing. *Business Week* is also well worth the read.

Also recommended are *Challenge* magazine and *The Public Interest*, two quarterlies that discuss economic policy, as well as *Policy Options*, a bimonthly publication of the Institute for Research on Public Policy. Finally, there is the *Journal of Economic Perspectives*, which is published by the American Economic Association and written to be accessible to undergraduate economics students.

Books by Economists

Below is a list of suggested readings, compiled from asking other professors and from our own readings.

Steven Levitt and Stephen Dubner, *Freakonomics: A Rogue Economist Explores the Hidden Side of Everything.*

Milton Friedman, *Capitalism and Freedom.*

Robert Heilbroner, *The Worldly Philosophers: The Lives, Times, and Ideas of the Great Economic Thinkers.*

Jared Diamond, *Guns, Germs, and Steel: The Fates of Human Societies.*

Diane Coyle, *Sex, Drugs and Economics: An Unconventional Introduction to Economics.*

Patrick Luciani, *Economics Myths: Making Sense of Canadian Policy Issues.*

Hernando deSoto, *The Mystery of Capital: Why Capitalism Triumphed in the West and Failed Everywhere Else.*

Tyler Cowen, *The Great Stagnation: How America Ate all the Low-Hanging Fruit of Modern History, Got Sick and Will (Eventually) Feel Better.*

Adam Smith's *The Wealth of Nations* is a must-read for every student of economics. It was written in 1776, yet it is the most influential work of economics ever and its insights are still valuable.

Endnotes

1. This term is used by Robert Reich in *The Work of Nations*. The quote is from p. 178.

2. Robert Whaples, "Changes in Attitudes About the Fairness of Free Markets Among College Economics Students," *Journal of Economic Education*, vol. 26, no. 4 (Fall 1995).

3. Robert H. Frank, Thomas Gilovich, and Dennis T. Regan, "Does Studying Economics Inhibit Cooperation?" *Journal of Economic Perspectives*, vol. 7, no. 2 (Spring 1993), pp. 159–171.

4. John R. Carter and Michael D. Irons, "Are Economists Different, and if So, Why?" *Journal of Economic Perspectives*, vol. 5, no. 2 (Spring 1991), pp. 171–177.

5. "Economics Students Aren't Selfish, They're Just Not Entirely Honest," *Wall Street Journal*, January 18, 1995, B1.

6. See Ronald Ehrenberg, "The Flow of New Doctorates," *Journal of Economic Literature*, vol. 30, June 1992, pp. 830–875. If breaks in school attendance are included, this climbs to 10.5 years. Of course, some students attend only part time, and most have some kind of employment while completing their degrees.

Chapter 1
What Is Economics?

Definition of Economics

All economic questions arise from **scarcity**.

- ◆ Because wants exceed the resources available to satisfy them, we cannot have everything we want and must make choices.

  - • Choices depend on **incentives**—rewards that encourage actions and penalties that discourage action.

- ◆ **Economics** is the social science that studies the choices people make to cope with scarcity.

  - • **Microeconomics** studies choices of individuals and businesses.

  - • **Macroeconomics** studies national and global economies.

Two Big Economic Questions

Two questions summarize the scope of economics:

- ◆ How do choices determine *what*, *how*, and *for whom* **goods and services** are produced, and in what quantities?

- ◆ How can choices made in the pursuit of self-interest also promote the social interest?

The **factors of production** used to produce goods and services are

- ◆ **land** (shorthand for all natural resources), which earns **rent**.

- ◆ **labour** (includes **human capital**—knowledge and skills from education, training, experience), which earns **wages**.

- ◆ **capital** (machinery), which earns **interest**.

- ◆ **entrepreneurship,** which earns **profit**.

Choices made in **self-interest** are best for the person making them. Choices that are in the **social interest** are best for society as a whole. Society achieves **efficiency** when available resources are used to produce goods and services at the lowest cost.

- ◆ Markets often provide incentives so that the pursuit of our self-interest also promotes the social interest; but self-interest and social interest sometimes conflict.

- ◆ Economic principles allow us to understand when self-interest promotes the social interest, when they conflict, and policies to reduce those conflicts.

The Economic Way of Thinking

A choice is a **tradeoff**—we give up one thing to get something else—and the **opportunity cost** of any action is the highest-valued alternative forgone. Opportunity cost is the single most important concept for making choices.

- ◆ A **rational choice** compares costs and benefits and achieves the greatest benefit over cost.

- ◆ **Benefit**—gain or pleasure of a choice, is determined by a person's **preferences**—likes and dislikes and their intensity.

- ◆ The **big tradeoff** is between equality and efficiency. Government redistribution using taxes and transfers weaken incentives, so a more equally shared pie results in a smaller pie.

We make choices in small steps, or at the **margin**, and choices are influenced by incentives.

- ◆ Economic choices are made by comparing the *additional* benefit—**marginal benefit**—and *additional* opportunity cost—**marginal cost**—of a small increase in an activity. If marginal benefit exceeds marginal cost, we choose to increase the activity.

- ◆ By choosing only activities that bring greater benefits than costs, we use our scarce resources in the way that makes us as well off as possible.

Economics as Social Science and Policy Tool

Economics, as a social science, distinguishes between

- *positive* statements—statements about what *is;* they can be tested by checking them against the facts.

- *normative* statements—statements about what *ought* to be; they depend on values and cannot be tested.

Economics attempts to understand the economic world and is concerned with positive statements. Economists try to discover positive statements that are consistent with observed facts by

- unscrambling cause and effect.

- creating **economic models**—a simplified description of the economic world that includes only features needed for purpose of explanation.

- testing economic models, comparing predictions with the facts, using

  - natural experiments—where one factor is different in real world; other things are equal.

  - statistical investigations—correlations between variables.

  - economic experiments—putting people in decision-making situations and changing one variable to see the response.

Economics is a useful toolkit for

- personal decisions

- advising businesses on economic policy

- advising government on economic policy

For any *normative* policy objective, economics provides a method of evaluating alternative solutions—evaluate marginal benefits and marginal costs to find solutions that make the best use of resources.

HELPFUL HINTS

1   The definition of economics (explaining the choices we make using limited resources to try to satisfy unlimited wants) leads us directly to two important economic concepts: choice and opportunity cost. If wants exceed resources, we cannot have everything we want and therefore must make *choices* among alternatives. In making a choice, we forgo other alternatives, and the *opportunity cost* of any choice is the highest-valued alternative forgone.

2   Marginal analysis is a fundamental tool economists use to predict people's choices. The key to understanding marginal analysis is to focus on *additional*, rather than total, benefits and costs. For example, to predict whether or not Taejong will eat a fourth Big Mac, the economist compares Taejong's *additional* benefit or satisfaction from the fourth Big Mac with its *additional* cost. The total benefits and costs of all four Big Macs are not relevant. Only if the marginal benefit exceeds the marginal cost will Taejong eat a fourth Big Mac.

3   In attempting to understand how and why something works (e.g., an airplane, a falling object, an economy), we can try to use description or theory. A description is a list of facts about something. But it does not tell us which facts are essential for understanding how an airplane works (the shape of the wings) and which facts are less important (the colour of the paint).

   Scientists use theory to abstract from the complex descriptive facts of the real world and focus only on those elements essential for understanding. Those essential elements are fashioned into models—highly simplified representations of the real world.

   In physics and some other natural sciences, if we want to understand the essential force (gravity) that causes objects to fall, we use theory to construct a simple model and then test it by performing a controlled experiment. We create a vacuum to eliminate less important forces like air resistance.

   Economic models are also attempts to focus on the essential forces (competition, self-interest) operating in the economy, while abstracting from less important forces (whims, advertising, altruism). Unlike physicists, economists cannot easily perform controlled experiments to test their models. As a result, it is difficult to conclusively prove or disprove a theory and its models. Economists rely on naturally occurring experiments, statistical investigations of correlations between variables, and artificial laboratory economic experiments about choices.

4   Models are like maps, which are useful precisely because they abstract from real-world detail. A map that reproduced all of the details of the real world (street lamps, fireplugs, electric wires) would be useless. A useful map offers a

simplified view that is carefully selected according to the purpose of the map. Remember that economic models are not claims that the real world is as simple as the model. Models claim to capture the simplified effect of some real force operating in the economy. Before drawing conclusions about the real economy from a model, we must be careful to consider whether, when we reinsert all of the real-world complexities the model abstracted from, the conclusions will be the same as in the model.

5   The most important purpose of studying economics is not to learn what to think about economics but rather *how* to think about economics. The "what"—the facts and descriptions of the economy—can always be found in books. The value of an economics education is the ability to think critically about economic problems and *to understand how* an economy works. This understanding of the essential forces governing how an economy works comes through the mastery of economic theory and model-building.

S E L F - T E S T

True/False and Explain

Definition of Economics

1   Economics explains how we use unlimited resources to satisfy limited wants.

2   Economics studies the choices people make to cope with scarcity and the institutions that influence and reconcile choices.

Two Big Economic Questions

3   In economics, the definition of "land" includes nonrenewable resources but excludes renewable resources.

4   In economics, the definition of "capital" includes financial assets like stocks and bonds.

5   Entrepreneurs bear the risks arising from the business decisions they make.

6   "How do choices determine *what*, *how*, and *for whom* goods and services are produced?" is one of the big economic questions.

7   "When do choices made in the pursuit of the social interest also promote self-interest?" is one of the big economic questions.

8   Choices made in the pursuit of self-interest always promote the social interest.

The Economic Way of Thinking

9   When the opportunity cost of an activity increases, the incentive to choose that activity increases.

10   Tradeoffs and opportunity costs are the key concepts for understanding the economic way of thinking.

11   Economists assume that it is human nature for all people to act selfishly.

Economics as Social Science and Policy Tool

12   A positive statement is about what is, while a normative statement is about what will be.

CHAPTER 1

13 Economists test positive statements about how the world works to weed out those that are wrong.

14 The main economics policy tool is to compare total costs and total benefits to find the solution with the greatest gain.

15 Economics is a useful policy tool for governments and businesses, but not for individuals.

Multiple-Choice

Definition of Economics

1 The fact that human wants cannot be fully satisfied with available resources is called the problem of
   a opportunity cost.
   b scarcity.
   c normative economics.
   d what to produce.
   e who will consume.

2 The problem of scarcity exists
   a only in economies with government.
   b only in economies without government.
   c in all economies.
   d only when people have not optimized.
   e now, but will be eliminated with economic growth.

3 Scarcity differs from poverty because
   a resources exceed wants for the rich.
   b wants exceed resources even for the rich.
   c the rich do not have to make choices.
   d the poor do not have any choices.
   e the poor do not have any wants.

4 The branch of economics that studies the choices of individual households and firms is called
   a macroeconomics.
   b microeconomics.
   c positive economics.
   d normative economics.
   e home economics.

5 Microeconomics studies all of the following *except* the
   a decisions of individual firms.
   b effects of government safety regulations on the price of cars.
   c global economy as a whole.
   d prices of individual goods and services.
   e effects of taxes on the price of beer.

Two Big Economic Questions

6 The two big economic questions
   a arise from scarcity.
   b summarize the scope of economics.
   c describe choices we make.
   d examine incentives that influence choices.
   e are all of the above.

7 The first big economic question about goods and services includes all of the following *except*
   a *what* to produce.
   b *why* produce.
   c *how* to produce.
   d *what* quantities to produce.
   e *who* gets what is produced.

8 The trends over the past 60 years in what we produce show that _____ has expanded and _____ has shrunk.
   a manufacturing; services
   b manufacturing; agriculture
   c agriculture; services
   d agriculture; manufacturing
   e services; agriculture

9 All of the following are resources *except*
   a natural resources.
   b tools.
   c entrepreneurship.
   d government.
   e land.

10 The knowledge and skill obtained from education and training is
   a labour.
   b human capital.
   c physical capital.
   d entrepreneurship.
   e technological know-how.

11 Which statement about incomes earned by factors of production is *false*?
   a Land earns rent.
   b Natural resources earn rent.
   c Labour earns wages.
   d Capital earns profit.
   e Entrepreneurship earns profit.

12 When boats fish in international waters, that is certainly a(n)
  a self-interested choice.
  b altruistic choice.
  c globalization choice.
  d factor of production choice.
  e choice in the social interest.

The Economic Way of Thinking

13 When the government chooses to use resources to build a dam, those resources are no longer available to build a highway. This illustrates the concept of
  a a market.
  b macroeconomics.
  c opportunity cost.
  d a "how" tradeoff.
  e the big tradeoff.

14 The opportunity cost of attending university
  a depends on what you expect to earn with your degree.
  b must be greater than the money cost of attending university.
  c must be less than the money cost of attending university.
  d depends on your major.
  e depends on what you could earn now.

15 Renata has the chance to either attend an economics lecture or play tennis. If she chooses to attend the lecture, the value of playing tennis is
  a greater than the value of the lecture.
  b not comparable to the value of the lecture.
  c equal to the value of the lecture.
  d the opportunity cost of attending the lecture.
  e zero.

16 Which of the following sayings best describes opportunity cost?
  a "Make hay while the sun shines."
  b "Money is the root of all evil."
  c "Boldly go where no one has gone before."
  d "There's no such thing as a free lunch."
  e "Baseball has been very good to me."

17 Marginal benefit is the
  a total benefit of an activity.
  b additional benefit of a decrease in an activity.
  c additional benefit of an increase in an activity.
  d opportunity cost of a decrease in an activity.
  e opportunity cost of an increase in an activity.

18 Monika will choose to eat a seventh pizza slice if
  a the marginal benefit of the seventh slice is greater than its marginal cost.
  b the marginal benefit of the seventh slice is less than its marginal cost
  c the total benefit of all seven slices is greater than their total cost.
  d the total benefit of all seven slices is less than their total cost.
  e she is training to be a Sumo wrestler.

19 Economists assume that
  a self-interested actions are all selfish actions.
  b consumers and producers pursue their self-interest while politicians and public servants pursue the social interest.
  c incentives are key in reconciling self-interest and the social interest.
  d all people pursue the social interest.
  e human nature changes as incentives change.

Economics as Social Science and Policy Tool

20 A positive statement is
  a about what ought to be.
  b about what is.
  c always true.
  d capable of evaluation as true or false by observation and measurement.
  e **b** and **d**.

21 Which of the following is a positive statement?
  a Low rents will restrict the supply of housing.
  b High interest rates are bad for the economy.
  c Housing costs too much.
  d Owners of apartment buildings ought to be free to charge whatever rent they want.
  e Government should control the rents that apartment owners charge.

22 A normative statement is a statement regarding
  a what is usually the case.
  b the assumptions of an economic model.
  c what ought to be.
  d the predictions of an economic model.
  e what is.

23 Which of the following statements is normative?
   a Scientists should not make normative statements.
   b Warts are caused by handling toads.
   c As compact disc prices fall, people will buy more of them.
   d If income increases, sales of luxury goods will fall.
   e None of the above.

24 Which of the following statements is *false*? An economic model
   a is tested by comparing predictions with the facts.
   b is difficult to test because of the simultaneous operation of many factors.
   c tests only positive economic statements.
   d can be tested using natural and economic experiments
   e includes all aspects of the economic world.

25 The common element to making personal, business, and government policy decisions is to evaluate
   a total benefits and total costs to find greatest gain.
   b marginal benefits and marginal costs to find greatest gain.
   c marginal benefits and marginal costs to find highest marginal benefit.
   d marginal benefits and marginal costs to find lowest marginal costs.
   e average benefits and average costs to find greatest gain.

Short Answer Problems

1 "If all people would only economize, the problem of scarcity would be solved." Agree or disagree, and explain why.

2 Ashley, Doug, and Mei-Lin are planning to travel from Halifax to Sydney. The trip takes one hour by airplane and five hours by train. The air fare is $100 and train fare is $60. They all have to take time off from work while travelling. Ashley earns $5 per hour in her job, Doug $10 per hour, and Mei-Lin $12 per hour.

   Calculate the opportunity cost of air and train travel for each person. Assuming they are all economizers, how should each of them travel to Sydney?

3 Suppose the government builds and staffs a hospital to provide "free" medical care.

   a What is the opportunity cost of the free medical care?

   b Is it free from the perspective of society as a whole?

4 Branko loves riding the bumper cars at the amusement park, but he loves the experience a little less with each successive ride. In estimating the benefit he receives from the rides, Branko would be willing to pay $10 for his first ride, $7 for his second ride, and $4 for his third ride. Rides actually cost $5 apiece for as many rides as Branko wants to take. This information is summarized in Table 1.1.

TABLE **1.1**

Ride	1st	2nd	3rd
Marginal benefit	10	7	4
Marginal cost	5	5	5

   a If Branko chooses by comparing total benefit and total cost, how many rides will he take?

   b If Branko chooses by comparing marginal benefit and marginal cost, how many rides will he take?

   c Is Branko better off by choosing according to total or marginal benefit and cost? Explain why.

5 Assume Branko's benefits are the same as in Short Answer Problem 4. Starting fresh, if the price of a bumper car ride rises to $8, how many rides will Branko now take? Explain why.

6 Indicate whether each of the following statements is positive or normative. If it is normative (positive), rewrite it so that it becomes positive (normative).

   a The government ought to reduce the size of the deficit to lower interest rates.

   b Government imposition of a tax on tobacco products will reduce their consumption.

7   Perhaps the biggest economic question is "How can we organize our lives so that when each of us makes choices in our self-interest, these choices also promote the social interest?" When Nike builds a factory in Malaysia and pays workers far less than North American wages, it is acting in its own corporate self-interest. What questions do you need to ask to decide if this is also in the social interest?

℮ 8   Suppose your friend, who is a history major, claims that economic models are useless because they are so unrealistic. He claims that since the models leave out so many descriptive details about the real world, they can't possibly be useful for understanding how the economy works. How would you defend your decision to study economics?

A N S W E R S

True/False and Explain

1   **F**   Limited resources and unlimited wants. (1–2)

2   **T**   This is the full definition of economics—the institutional aspect is often omitted for brevity. (1–2)

3   **F**   "Land" includes all natural resources, whether nonrenewable (oil) or renewable (forests). (3–7)

4   **F**   "Capital" only consists of physical equipment like tools and buildings used in production. (3–7)

5   **T**   Entrepreneurs earn profits in return for bearing the risks of organizing labour, land, and capital. (3–7)

6   **T**   See text discussion. (3–7)

7   **F**   When do choices made in the pursuit of self-interest also promote the social interest? (3–7)

8   **F**   Markets often provide incentives so that pursuit of self-interest also promotes social interest, but self-interest and social interest sometimes conflict. (3–7).

9   **F**   Incentive decreases because activity is now more expensive. (8–9)

10   **T**   Scarcity requires choice, choice involves tradeoffs, and tradeoffs involve opportunity cost. (8–9)

11   **F**   Economists assume people act in their self-interest, but self-interested actions are not necessarily selfish actions, if what makes you happy is to help others. (10)

12   **F**   Normative statements are about what *ought* to be. (10)

13   **T**   Test *positive* statements. (10)

14   **F**   Compare *marginal* benefits and *marginal* costs. (10)

15   **F**   Useful for personal, business, government policy. (10)

Multiple-Choice

1   **b**   Definition. (1–2)

2   **c**   With infinite wants and finite resources, scarcity will never be eliminated. (1–2)

3   **b**   Poverty is a low level of resources. But wants exceed resources for everyone, necessitating choice. (1–2)

4   **b**   Definition. (1–2)

5   **c**   Macroeconomic topic. (1–2)

6   **e**   Economics explains choices created by scarcity and incentives that help reconcile self-interest and social interest. (3–7)

7   **b**   *Why* is not part of first big question. (3–7)

8   **e**   Services have expanded; agriculture and manufacturing have shrunk. See Text Fig. 1.1. (3–7)

9   **d**   Government is a social institution. (3–7)

10   **b**   Definition. (3–7)

11   **d**   Capital earns interest. (3–7)

℮ 12   **a**   Certainly in the fishing company's self-interest; not altruistic or in social interest depending on benefits and costs. (3–7)

13   **c**   Highway is forgone alternative. (8–9)

14   **e**   What you must give up, *not* what you will earn. May be more or less than money cost. (8–9)

15   **d**   Choosing lecture means its value > tennis. Tennis = (highest-valued) forgone alternative to lecture. (8–9)

16 **d** Every choice involves a cost. (8–9)

17 **c** Definition; **e** is marginal cost, **b** and **d** are nonsense. (8–9)

18 **a** Choices are made at the margin, when marginal benefit exceeds marginal cost. (8–9)

19 **c** Assume human nature is given and all people pursue self-interest. When self-interested choices are not in the social interest, there are wrong incentives. (8–9)

20 **e** Definition. (10)

21 **a** While **a** may be evaluated as true or false, other statements are matters of opinion. (10)

22 **c** Key word for normative statements is *ought*. (10)

23 **a** Key word is *should*. Even statement **b** is positive. (10)

24 **e** Includes only relevant aspects and ignores others. (10)

25 **b** See text discussion. (10)

Short Answer Problems

1 Disagree. If everyone economized, then we would be making the best possible use of our resources and would be achieving the greatest benefits or satisfaction possible, given the limited quantity of resources. But this does not mean that we would be satisfying all of our limitless needs. The problem of scarcity can never be "solved" as long as people have infinite needs and finite resources for satisfying those needs.

2 The main point is that the total opportunity cost of travel includes the best alternative value of travel time as well as the train or air fare. The total costs of train and air travel for Ashley, Doug, and Mei-Lin are calculated in Table 1.2.

On the basis of the cost calculation in Table 1.2, Ashley should take the train, Mei-Lin should take the plane, and Doug could take either.

TABLE **1.2**

Traveller	Train	Plane
Ashley		
(a) Fare	$ 60	$100
(b) Opportunity cost of travel time at $5/hr	$ 25	$ 5
Total cost	$ 85	$105
Doug		
(a) Fare	$ 60	$100
(b) Opportunity cost of travel time at $10/hr	$ 50	$ 10
Total cost	$110	$110
Mei-Lin		
(a) Fare	$ 60	$100
(b) Opportunity cost of travel time at $12/hr	$ 60	$ 12
Total cost	$120	$112

3 **a** Even though medical care may be offered without charge ("free"), there are still opportunity costs. The opportunity cost of providing such health care is the highest-valued alternative use of the resources used in the construction of the hospital, and the highest-valued alternative use of the resources (including human resources) used in the operation of the hospital.

b These resources are no longer available for other activities and therefore represent a cost to society.

4 **a** If Branko rides as long as total benefit is greater than total cost, he will take 3 rides.

Total benefit (cost) can be calculated by adding up the marginal benefit (cost) of all rides taken. Before taking any rides, his total benefit is zero and his total cost is zero. The first ride's marginal benefit is $10, which when added to 0 yields a total benefit of $10. The first ride's marginal cost is $5, which when added to zero yields a total cost of $5. Total cost is less than total benefit, so Branko takes the first ride. For the first and second rides together, total benefit is $17, which is greater than total cost of $10. For all 3 rides together, total benefit is $21, which is greater than total cost of $15.

b If Branko compares the marginal benefit of each ride with its marginal cost, he will only take 2 rides. He will take the first ride because its marginal benefit ($10) is greater than its marginal cost ($5). After the first ride, he will still choose to take the second ride because its marginal benefit ($7) is greater than its marginal cost ($5). But he will quit after the second ride. The third ride would add a benefit of $4, but it costs $5, so Branko would be worse off by taking the third ride.

c The marginal rule for choosing will make Branko better off. It would be a mistake to pay $5 for the third ride when it is only worth $4 to Branko. He would be better off taking that final $5 and spending it on something (the roller coaster?) that gives him a benefit worth at least $5.

You will learn much more about applying marginal analysis to choices like Branko's in Chapters 2 and 5.

5 If the price of a bumper car rises to $8, Branko now takes only 1 ride. He will take the first ride because its marginal benefit ($10) is greater than its marginal cost ($8). After the first ride, he will quit. The marginal benefit of the second ride ($7) is now less than its marginal cost ($8).

6 a The given statement is normative. The following is positive: If the government reduces the size of the deficit, interest rates will fall.

b The given statement is positive. The following is normative: The government ought to impose a tax on tobacco products.

7 Questions must identify benefits and costs that need to be compared. Some of the many possible questions are: Even though the Malaysian workers earn less than North Americans, are they better off or worse off with these jobs? As consumers in North America, are we better off or worse off with shoes being produced more cheaply in Malaysia? Are workers in North America better off or worse off with the Malaysian Nike plant? How do we define the social interest when people from many countries are involved?

You don't yet have enough information to answer these questions, but economics provides a way of thinking about them that makes it easier to come to a well-reasoned conclusion.

8 A brief answer to your friend's challenge appears in Helpful Hint **3**. Models are like maps, which are useful precisely because they abstract from real-world detail. A useful map offers a simplified view, which is carefully selected according to the purpose of the map. No mapmaker would claim that the world is as simple as her map, and economists do not claim that the real economy is as simple as their models. What economists claim is that their models isolate the simplified effect of some real forces (like optimizing behaviour) operating in the economy, and yield predictions that can be tested against real-world data.

Another way to answer your friend would be to challenge him to identify what a more realistic model or theory would look like. You would do well to quote Milton Friedman (a Nobel Prize winner in economics) on this topic: "A theory or its 'assumptions' cannot possibly be thoroughly 'realistic' in the immediate descriptive sense.... A completely 'realistic' theory of the wheat market would have to include not only the conditions directly underlying the supply and demand for wheat but also the kind of coins or credit instruments used to make exchanges; the personal characteristics of wheat-traders such as the color of each trader's hair and eyes, ... the number of members of his family, their characteristics,... the kind of soil on which the wheat was grown,... the weather prevailing during the growing season;... and so on indefinitely. Any attempt to move very far in achieving this kind of 'realism' is certain to render a theory utterly useless." From Milton Friedman, "The Methodology of Positive Economics," in *Essays in Positive Economics* (Chicago: University of Chicago Press, 1953), p. 32.

Chapter 1
Appendix: Graphs in Economics

Graphing Data

Graphs represent quantity as a distance. On a two-dimensional graph,

- horizontal line is *x-axis*.
- vertical line is *y-axis*.
- intersection (0) is the *origin*.

A **scatter diagram** shows the relationship between two variables, one measured on the *x*-axis, the other measured on the *y*-axis. Correlation between variables does not necessarily imply causation.

Misleading graphs often break the axes or stretch/compress measurement scales to exaggerate or understate variation. Always look closely at the values and labels on axes before interpreting a graph.

Graphs Used in Economic Models

Graphs showing relationships between variables fall into four categories:

- **Positive (direct) relationship**—variables move together in same direction: upward-sloping.
- **Negative (inverse) relationship**—variables move in opposite directions: downward-sloping.
- Relationships with a maximum/minimum:
  - Relationship slopes upward, reaches a maximum (zero slope), and then slopes downward.
  - Relationship slopes downward, reaches a minimum (zero slope), and then slopes upward.
- Unrelated (independent) variables—one variable changes while the other remains constant; graph is a vertical or horizontal straight line.

The Slope of a Relationship

Slope of a relationship is change in value of a variable on *y*-axis divided by change in value of a variable on *x*-axis.

- Δ means "change in."
- Formula for slope is $\Delta y / \Delta x$ = rise/run.
- Straight line (**linear relationship**) has a constant slope.
  - A positive, upward-sloping relationship has a positive slope.
  - A negative, downward-sloping relationship has a negative slope.
- A curved line has a varying slope, calculated
  - *at a point*—draw straight line tangent to curve at that point and calculate slope of the line.
  - *across an arc*—draw straight line across two points on curve and calculate slope of the line.

Graphing Relationships Among More Than Two Variables

Relationships among more than two variables can be graphed by holding constant the values of all variables except two. This is done by making a *ceteris paribus* assumption—"other things remain the same."

1 Throughout the text, relationships among economic variables will almost invariably be represented and analyzed graphically. An early, complete understanding of graphs will greatly facilitate your mastery of the economic analysis in later chapters. Avoid the common mistake of assuming that a superficial understanding of graphs will be sufficient.

2 If you have limited experience with graphical analysis, this appendix is crucial to your ability to understand later economic analysis. You will likely find significant rewards in occasionally returning to this appendix for review. If you are experienced in constructing and using graphs, this appendix may be "old hat." Even so, you should skim it and work through the Self-Test in this *Study Guide*.

3 Slope is a *linear* concept since it is a property of a straight line. For this reason, the slope is constant along a straight line but is different at different points on a curved (nonlinear) line. For the slope of a curved line, we actually calculate the slope of a straight line. The text presents two alternatives for calculating the slope of a curved line: (1) slope at a point and (2) slope across an arc. The first of these calculates the slope of the *straight line* that just touches (is tangent to) the curve at a point. The second calculates the slope of the *straight line* formed by the arc between two points on the curved line.

4 A straight line on a graph can also be described by a simple equation (see Text Mathematical Note, pages 24–25). The general form for the equation of a straight line is

$$y = a + bx$$

If you are given such an equation, you can graph the line by finding the y-intercept (where the line intersects the vertical y-axis), finding the x-intercept (where the line intersects the horizontal x-axis), and then connecting those two points with a straight line:

To find the y-intercept, set $x = 0$.
$$y = a + b(0)$$
$$y = a$$
To find the x-intercept, set $y = 0$.
$$0 = a + bx$$
$$x = -a/b$$

Connecting these two points (($x = 0$, $y = a$) and ($x = -a/b$, $y = 0$)) or (0, a) and ($-a/b$, 0) allows you to graph the straight line. For any straight line with the equation of the form $y = a + bx$, the slope of the line is b. Figure A1.1 illustrates a line where b is a *negative* number, so there is a *negative* relationship between the variables x and y.

FIGURE **A1.1**

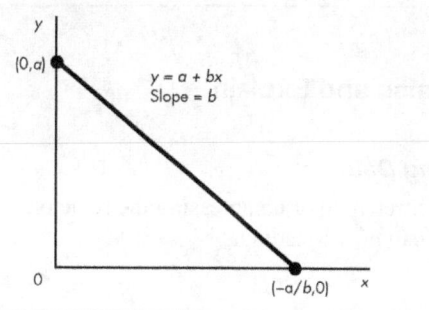

To see how to apply this general equation, consider this example:
$$y = 6 - 2x$$
To find the y-intercept, set $x = 0$.
$$y = 6 - 2(0)$$
$$y = 6$$
To find the x-intercept, set $y = 0$.
$$0 = 6 - 2x$$
$$x = 3$$

Connecting these two points, (0, 6) and (3, 0), yields the line in Fig. A1.2.

FIGURE **A1.2**

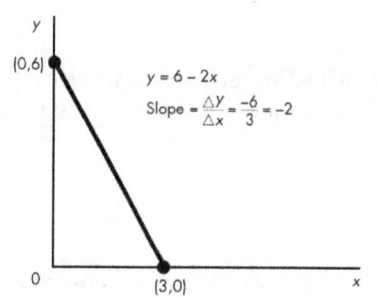

The slope of this line is –2. Since the slope is negative, there is a negative relationship between the variables x and y.

SELF-TEST

True/False and Explain

Graphing Data

1 Stretching or compressing the scale on an axis can be misleading.

2 A graph with a break in the axes must be misleading.

3 If a scatter diagram shows a clear relationship between variables x and y, then x must cause y.

Graphs Used in Economic Models

4 If the graph of the relationship between two variables slopes upward (to the right), the graph has a positive slope.

5 The graph of the relationship between two variables that are in fact unrelated is always vertical.

6 In Fig. A1.3, the relationship between y and x is first negative, reaches a minimum, and then becomes positive as x increases.

FIGURE **A1.3**

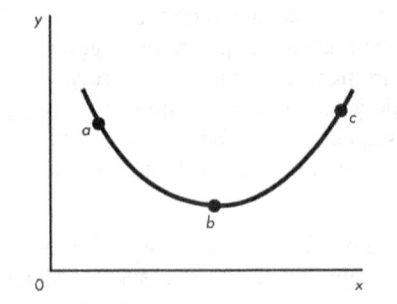

7 In Fig. A1.3, the value of x is a minimum at point b.

The Slope of a Relationship

8 In Fig. A1.3, the slope of the curve is increasing as we move from point b to point c.

9 In Fig. A1.3, the slope of the curve is approaching zero as we move from point a to point b.

10 The slope of a straight line is calculated by dividing the change in the value of the variable measured on the horizontal axis by the change in the value of the variable measured on the vertical axis.

11 For a straight line, if a small change in y is associated with a large change in x, the slope is large.

12 For a straight line, if a large change in y is associated with a small change in x, the line is steep.

13 The slope of a curved line is not constant.

Graphing Relationships Among More Than Two Variables

14 *Ceteris paribus* means "other things change."

15 Relationships between three variables can be displayed on a two-dimensional graph.

Multiple-Choice

Graphing Data

1 A point with a negative *x-coordinate* must be
 a below the horizontal axis.
 b above the horizontal axis.
 c to the left of the vertical axis.
 d to the right of the vertical axis.
 e below the vertical axis.

2 A point's position on a graph is best described by its
 a slope.
 b coordinates.
 c origin.
 d causation.
 e correlation.

3 Which of the following statements is *false*?
 a The intersection of the *x-axis* and *y-axis* is the origin.
 b Breaks in a graph's axes can be misleading.
 c Breaks in a graph's axes can highlight a relationship.
 d A causal relationship must imply a correlation.
 e A correlation must imply a causal relationship

Graphs Used in Economic Models

4 From the data in Table A1.1, it appears that
 a x and y have a negative relationship.
 b x and y have a positive relationship.
 c there is no relationship between x and y.
 d there is first a negative and then a positive relationship between x and y.
 e there is first a positive and then a negative relationship between x and y.

TABLE **A1.1**

Year	x	y
2004	6.2	143
2005	5.7	156
2006	5.3	162

5 If variables x and y move up and down together, they are said to be
 a positively related.
 b negatively related.
 c conversely related.
 d unrelated.
 e trendy.

6 The relationship between two variables that move in opposite directions is shown graphically by a line that is
 a positively sloped.
 b relatively steep.
 c relatively flat.
 d negatively sloped.
 e curved.

The Slope of a Relationship

7 In Fig. A1.4 the relationship between x and y as x increases is
  a positive with slope decreasing.
  b negative with slope decreasing.
  c negative with slope increasing.
  d positive with slope increasing.
  e positive with slope first increasing then decreasing.

FIGURE **A1.4**

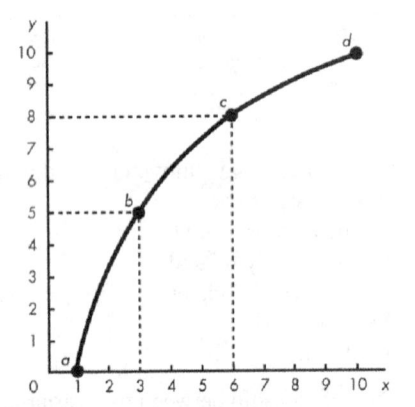

8 What is the slope across the arc between b and c in Fig. A1.4?
  a 1/2
  b 2/3
  c 1
  d 2
  e 3

9 In Fig. A1.4, consider the slopes of arc ab and arc bc. The slope at point b is difficult to determine exactly, but it must be
  a greater than 5/2.
  b about 5/2.
  c between 5/2 and 1.
  d about 1.
  e less than 1.

10 In Table A1.2, suppose that w is the independent variable measured along the horizontal axis. The slope of the line relating w and u is
  a positive with a decreasing slope.
  b negative with a decreasing slope.
  c positive with an increasing slope.
  d negative with a constant slope.
  e positive with a constant slope.

TABLE **A1.2**

w	2	4	6	8	10
u	15	12	9	6	3

11 Refer to Table A1.2. Suppose that w is the independent variable measured along the horizontal axis. The slope of the line relating w and u is
  a +3.
  b −3.
  c −2/3.
  d +3/2.
  e −3/2.

12 In Fig. A1.5, if household income increases by $1,000, household expenditure will
  a increase by $1,333.
  b decrease by $1,333.
  c remain unchanged.
  d increase by $1,000.
  e increase by $750.

FIGURE **A1.5**

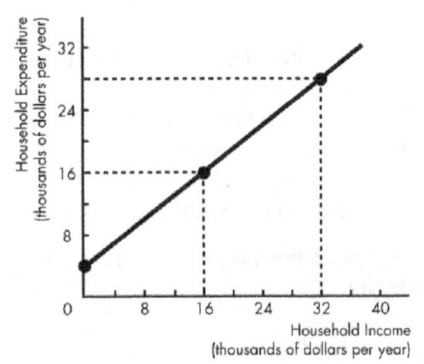

13 In Fig. A1.5, if household income is zero, household expenditure is
  a 0.
  b −$4,000.
  c $4,000.
  d $8,000.
  e impossible to determine from the graph.

14 In Fig. A1.5, if household expenditure is $28,000, household income is
a $36,000.
b $32,000.
c $28,000.
d $25,000.
e   none of the above.

15 At all points along a straight line, slope is
a   positive.
b   negative.
c   constant.
d   zero.
e   none of the above.

16 What is the slope of the line in Fig. A1.6?
a   2
b   1/2
c   3
d   1/3
e   −3

FIGURE **A1.6**

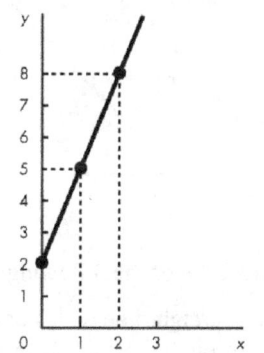

17 If the line in Fig. A1.6 were to continue down to the x-axis, what would the value of x be when y is zero?
a   0
b   2
c   2/3
d   −2/3
e   −3/2

18 If the equation of a straight line is $y = 6 + 3x$, the slope is
a   −3 and the y-intercept is 6.
b   −3 and the y-intercept is −2.
c   3 and the y-intercept is 6.
d   3 and the y-intercept is −2.
e   3 and the y-intercept is −6.

19 If the equation of a straight line is $y = 8 - 2x$, then the slope is
a   −2 and the x-intercept is −4.
b   −2 and the x-intercept is 4.
c   −2 and the x-intercept is 8.
d   2 and the x-intercept is −4.
e   2 and the x-intercept is 4.

Graphing Relationships Among More Than Two Variables

20 To graph a relationship among more than two variables, what kind of assumption is necessary?
a   normative
b   positive
c   linear
d   independence of variables
e   *ceteris paribus*

21 Given the data in Table A1.3, holding income constant, the graph relating the price of strawberries (vertical axis) to the purchases of strawberries (horizontal axis)
a   is a vertical line.
b   is a horizontal line.
c   is a positively sloped line.
d   is a negatively sloped line.
e   reaches a minimum.

TABLE **A1.3**

Weekly Family Income ($)	Price per Box of Strawberries ($)	Number of Boxes Purchased per Week
300	$1.00	5
300	$1.25	3
300	$1.50	2
400	$1.00	7
400	$1.25	5
400	$1.50	4

22 Given the data in Table A1.3, suppose family income decreases from $400 to $300 per week. Then the graph relating the price of strawberries (vertical axis) to the purchases of strawberries (horizontal axis) will
a   become negatively sloped.
b   become positively sloped.
c   shift rightward.
d   shift leftward.
e   no longer exist.

23 Given the data in Table A1.3, holding price constant, the graph relating family income (vertical axis) to the purchases of strawberries (horizontal axis) is a

  a vertical line.

  b horizontal line.

  c positively sloped line.

  d negatively sloped line.

  e positively or negatively sloped line, depending on the price that is held constant.

24 In Fig. A1.7, x is

  a positively related to y and negatively related to z.

  b positively related to both y and z.

  c negatively related to y and positively related to z.

  d negatively related to both y and z.

  e greater than z.

FIGURE **A1.7**

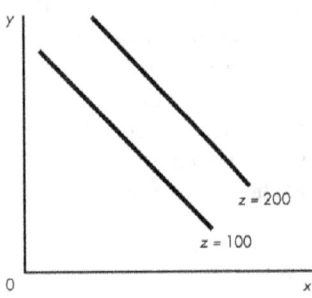

25 In Fig. A1.7, a decrease in the value of z will cause, *ceteris paribus*,

  a a decrease in the value of x.

  b an increase in the value of x.

  c an increase in the value of y.

  d no change in the value of y.

  e no change in the value of x.

Short Answer Problems

1 Draw a graph of variables x and y that illustrates each of the following relationships:

  a x and y move up and down together.

  b x and y move in opposite directions.

  c as x increases y reaches a maximum.

  d as x increases y reaches a minimum.

  e x and y move in opposite directions, but as x increases y decreases by larger and larger increments for each unit increase in x.

  f y is unrelated to the value of x.

  g x is unrelated to the value of y.

2 What does it mean to say that the slope of a line is $-2/3$?

3 Compute the slopes of the lines in Fig. A1.8(a) and (b).

FIGURE **A1.8**

(a)

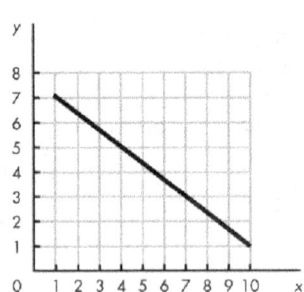

(b)

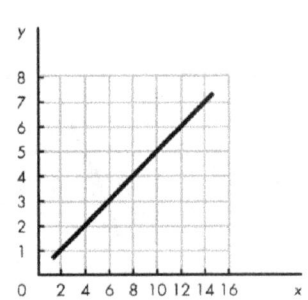

4 Draw each of the following:

  a a straight line with slope -10 and passing through the point (2, 80).

  b a straight line with slope 2 and passing through the point (6, 10).

5 The equation for a straight line is $y = 4 - 2x$.

  a Calculate the y-intercept, the x-intercept, and the slope.

  b Draw the graph of the line.

6 Explain two ways to measure the slope of a curved line.

7 Use the graph in Fig. A1.9 on the next page to compute the slope

  a across the arc between points a and b.

  b at point b.

  c at point c, and explain your answer.

FIGURE **A1.9**

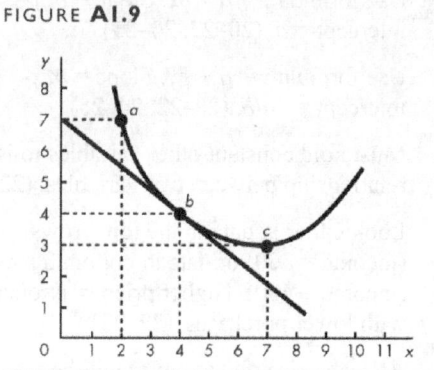

TABLE **A1.4**

Umbrellas Sold per Month (x)	Price per Umbrella (y)	Average Number of Rainy Days per Month (z)
120	$10	4
140	$10	5
160	$10	6
100	$12	4
120	$12	5
140	$12	6
80	$14	4
100	$14	5
120	$14	6

8 In Table A1.4, *x* represents the number of umbrellas sold per month, *y* represents the price of an umbrella, and *z* represents the average number of rainy days per month.

   a On the same diagram, graph the relationship between *x* (horizontal axis) and *y* (vertical axis) when *z* = 4, when *z* = 5, and when *z* = 6.

   b On average, it rains six days per month. This implies a certain average relationship between monthly umbrella sales and umbrella price. Suppose that the "greenhouse effect" reduces the average monthly rainfall to four days per month. What happens to the graph of the relationship between umbrella sales and umbrella prices?

   c On a diagram, graph the relationship between *x* (horizontal axis) and *z* (vertical axis) when *y* = $10 and when *y* = $12. Is the relationship between *x* and *z* positive or negative?

   d On a diagram, graph the relationship between *y* (horizontal axis) and *z* (vertical axis) when *x* = 120 and when *x* = 140. Is the relationship between *y* and *z* positive or negative?

ANSWERS

True/False and Explain

1 **T** Can exaggerate or hide relationships. (13–16)

2 **F** Breaks in the axes may be misleading, or may bring information into clearer view. (13–16)

3 **F** *x* and *y* are correlated, but correlation does not guarantee causation. (13–16)

4 **T** Upward-sloping curves/lines have positive slopes. (16–19)

5 **F** A graph of unrelated variables may be vertical or horizontal. (16–19)

6 **T** Arc *ab* would have negative slope, arc *bc* positive slope. (16–19)

7 **F** Value of *y* is minimum at point *b*. (16–19)

8 **T** Curve becomes steeper, meaning Δy is increasing faster than Δx, so slope is increasing. (20–22)

9 **T** At *b*, tangent has slope = 0, since $\Delta y = 0$ along the horizontal line through *b*. (20–22)

10 **F** Slope = (Δ variable on vertical (*y*) axis)/(Δ variable on horizontal (*x*) axis). (20–22)

11 **F** Large slope means large Δy associated with small Δx. (20–22)

12 **T** The steep line has a large slope, meaning large Δy is associated with small Δx. (20–22)

13 **T** Slope of a straight line is constant. (20–22)

14 **F** "Other things remain the same." Only variables being studied are allowed to change. (22–23)

15 **T** See Text Fig. A1.12. A *ceteris paribus* assumption holds one variable constant, allowing the other two variables to be plotted in two dimensions. (22–23)

Multiple-Choice

1 **c** Where x values are less than 0. Depending on *y-coordinate*, may be above or below the horizontal axis. (13–16)

2 **b** Combination of *x-coordinate* and *y-coordinate*. (13–16)

3 **e** A high correlation may be a coincidence. (13–16)

4 **a** Higher values x (6.2) associated with lower values y (143). (16–19)

5 **a** Definition. (16–19)

6 **d** Graph may be steep, flat, or curved, but must have a negative slope. (16–19)

7 **a** Slope of arc ab = +2.5. Slope of arc bc = +1. (20–22)

8 **c** $\Delta y = 3(8 - 5)$; $\Delta x = 3(6 - 3)$. (20–22)

9 **c** 5/2 is slope of ab, while 1 is slope of bc. (20–22)

10 **d** As w increases, u decreases. $\Delta u/\Delta w$ is constant. (20–22)

11 **e** Between any two points, $\Delta u = 3$, $\Delta w = -2$. (20–22)

12 **e** Slope $(\Delta y/\Delta x)$ = 3/4. If Δx (Δ household income) = \$1,000, then Δy (Δ household expenditure) = \$750 = ¾ of \$1,000. (20–22)

13 **c** Where the line intersects the household expenditure (y) axis. (20–22)

14 **b** From \$28,000 on vertical (expenditure) axis, move across to line, then down to \$32,000 on horizontal (income) axis. (20–22)

15 **c** Along straight line, the slope may or may not be **a**, **b**, or **d**. (20–22)

16 **c** Between any two points, $\Delta y = 3$ and $\Delta x = 1$. (20–22)

ⓔ 17 **d** Equation of line is $y = 2 + 3x$. Solve for x-intercept (set $y = 0$). (20–22, 24–25)

18 **c** Use formula $y = a + bx$. Slope = b, y-intercept = a. (20–22, 24–25)

19 **b** Use formula $y = a + bx$. Slope = b, x-intercept = $-a/b$. (20–22, 24–25)

20 **e** Must hold constant other variables to isolate relationship between two variables. (22–23)

21 **d** Look either at data in the top 3 rows (income = 300) or data in bottom 3 rows (income = 400). Higher price is associated with lower purchases. (22–23)

ⓔ 22 **d** At each price, fewer boxes will be purchased. (22–23)

ⓔ 23 **c** For $P = 1$, two points on line are (5 boxes, \$300) and (7 boxes, \$400). Same relationship for other prices. (22–23)

24 **c** Increased y causes decreased x holding z constant. Increased z causes increased x holding y constant. (22–23)

ⓔ 25 **a** Decreased z causes decreased x holding y constant. Decreased z causes decreased y holding x constant. (22–23)

Short Answer Problems

1 Figures A1.10(a) through (g) on the next page illustrate the desired graphs.

2 The negative sign in the slope of $-2/3$ means that there is a negative relationship between the two variables. The value of 2/3 means that when the variable measured on the vertical axis decreases by 2 units (the rise or Δy), the variable measured on the horizontal axis increases by 3 units (the run or Δx).

3 To find the slope, pick any two points on a line and compute $\Delta y/\Delta x$. The slope of the line in Fig. A1.8(a) is $-2/3$, and the slope of the line in Fig. A1.8(b) is 1/2.

FIGURE **AI.I0**

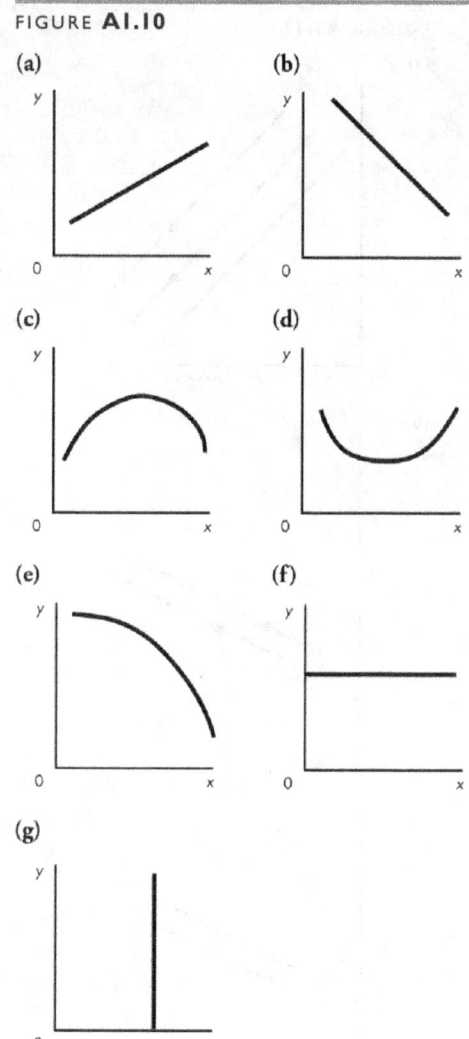

(a)   (b)

(c)   (d)

(e)   (f)

(g)

FIGURE **AI.II**

(a)

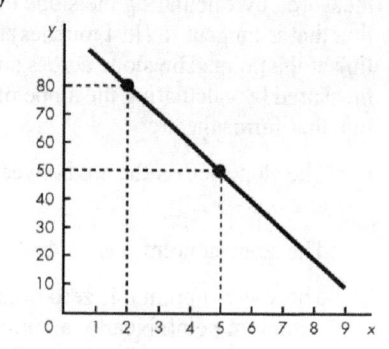

(b)

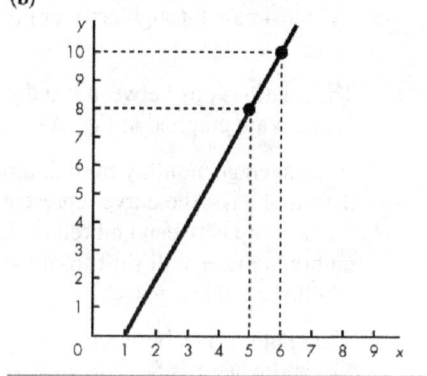

4 a   The requested straight line is graphed in Fig.
A1.11(a). First plot the point (2, 80). Then
pick a second point whose y-coordinate
decreases by 10 for every 1 unit increase in
the x-coordinate, for example, (5, 50). The
slope between the two points is $-30/3 = -10$.

b   The requested straight line is graphed in Fig.
A1.11(b). First plot the point (6, 10). Then
pick a second point whose y-coordinate
decreases by 2 for every 1 unit decrease in
the x-coordinate, for example, (5, 8). The
slope between the two points is $-2/-1 = 2$.

5 a   To find the y-intercept, set $x = 0$.
$$y = 4 - 2(0)$$
$$y = 4$$
To find the x-intercept, set $y = 0$.
$$0 = 4 - 2x$$
$$x = 2$$
The slope of the line is -2, the value of the
"b" coefficient on x.

b   The graph of the line is shown in Fig. A1.12.

FIGURE **AI.I2**

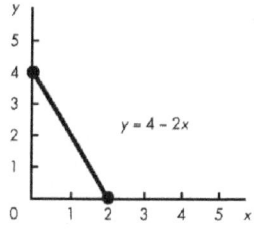

$y = 4 - 2x$

6 The slope of a curved line can be measured at a point or across an arc. The slope at a point is measured by calculating the slope of the straight line that is tangent to (just touches) the curved line at the point. The slope across an arc is measured by calculating the slope of the straight line that forms the arc.

7 a The slope across the arc between points *a* and *b* is –3/2.

b The slope at point *b* is –3/4.

c The slope at point *c* is zero because it is a minimum point. Nearby a minimum point the slope changes from negative to positive and must pass through zero, or no slope, to do so.

8 a The relationships between *x* and *y* for $z = 4$, 5, and 6 are graphed in Fig. A1.13(a).

b If the average monthly rainfall drops from 6 days to 4 days, the curve representing the relationship between umbrella sales and umbrella prices will shift from the curve labelled $z = 6$ to $z = 4$.

c The relationships between *x* and *z* when *y* is $10 and when *y* is $12 are graphed in Fig. A1.13(b). The relationship between *x* and *z* is positive.

d The relationships between *y* and *z* when $x = 120$ and when $x = 140$ are graphed in Fig. A1.13(c). The relationship between *y* and *z* is positive.

FIGURE **A1.13**

(a)

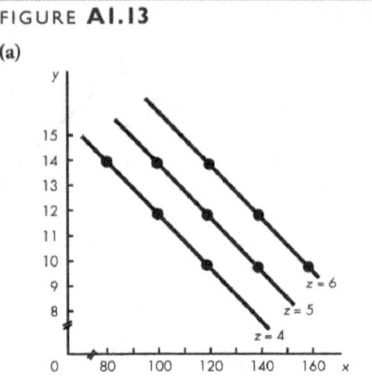

(b)

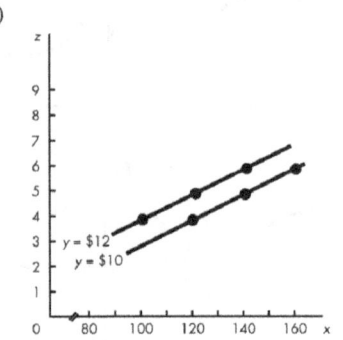

(c)

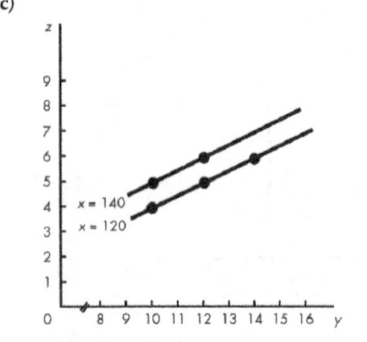

Chapter 2
The Economic Problem

Production Possibilities and Opportunity Cost

The production possibility frontier (*PPF*)

- ♦ is the boundary between unattainable and attainable production possibilities.

- ♦ shows maximum combinations of outputs (goods and services) that can be produced with given resources and technology.

PPF characteristics:

- ♦ points on *PPF* represent **production efficiency**—outputs produced at the lowest possible cost.

- ♦ points inside *PPF* are inefficient—attainable, but not maximum combinations of outputs; they represent unused or misallocated resources.

- ♦ points on *PPF* are preferred to points inside *PPF*.

- ♦ points outside *PPF* are unattainable.

- ♦ choosing among efficient points on *PPF* involves an **opportunity cost** (highest-valued opportunity foregone) and a *tradeoff*.

*PPF*s are generally bowed outward (concave), reflecting increasing opportunity costs as more of a good is produced.

- ♦ *PPF* is bowed outward because resources are not equally productive in all activities (nonhomogeneous). Resources most suitable for a given activity are the first to be used.

- ♦ Outward-bowed shape of *PPF* represents increasing opportunity cost—opportunity cost of good increases as its quantity produced increases.

- ♦ In moving between two points on *PPF* more of good *X* can be obtained only by producing less of good *Y*. Opportunity cost on *PPF* of additional *X* is amount of *Y* forgone.

- ♦ There is no opportunity cost in moving from point inside *PPF* to point on *PPF*.

Using Resources Efficiently

To choose among points on *PPF*, compare

- ♦ **marginal cost**—the opportunity cost of producing one more unit of a good.

  - • marginal cost curve slopes upwards because of *increasing opportunity cost*.

- ♦ **marginal benefit**—the benefit (measured in willingness to forgo other goods) from consuming one more unit of a good. Depends on **preferences**—likes, dislikes, and intensity of feelings.

  - • **marginal benefit curve** slopes downwards because of *decreasing marginal benefit*.

We choose a point on *PPF* of **allocative efficiency** where

- ♦ outputs are produced at lowest possible cost, and in quantities providing greatest possible benefit

- ♦ marginal benefit = marginal cost.

Economic Growth

Economic growth is the expansion of production possibilities—an outward shift of *PPF*.

- ♦ *PPF* shifts from changes in resources or technology.

- ♦ **Capital accumulation** and **technological change** shift *PPF* outward—economic growth.

- ♦ Opportunity cost of increased goods and services in future (economic growth through capital accumulation and technological progress) is decreased consumption today.

Gains from Trade

Production increases if people *specialize* in the activity in which they have a comparative advantage.

- ♦ Person has **comparative advantage** in producing a good if she can produce at a lower opportunity cost than anyone else.

- ♦ When each person specializes in producing a good at which she has comparative advantage and exchanges for other goods, there are gains from trade.

- ♦ Specialization and exchange allow consumption (not production) at points outside *PPF*.

- ♦ Person has **absolute advantage** in producing a good if, using the same quantity of resources, she can produce more than anyone else.

  - • Absolute advantage is irrelevant for specialization and gains from trade.

  - • Even a person with an absolute advantage in producing all goods gains by specializing in an activity in which she has a comparative advantage and trading.

Economic Coordination

Gains from trade and specialization require coordination. Decentralized coordination through markets depends on the social institutions of

- ♦ **firms**—hire and organize factors of production to produce and sell goods and services. Firms coordinate much economic activity, but the efficient size of a firm is limited.

- ♦ **markets**—coordinating buying and selling decisions through price adjustments.

- ♦ **property rights**—governing ownership, use, and disposal of resources, goods, and services.

- ♦ **money**—any generally acceptable means of payment; makes trading more efficient.

HELPFUL HINTS

1 This chapter reviews the absolutely critical concept of opportunity cost—the best alternative forgone—that was introduced in Chapter 1. Opportunity cost is a *ratio*. A helpful formula for opportunity cost, which works well in solving problems, especially problems that involve moving up or down a production possibility frontier (*PPF*), is:

$$\text{Opportunity Cost} = \frac{\text{Give Up}}{\text{Get}}$$

Opportunity cost equals the quantity of goods you must give up divided by the quantity of goods you will get. This formula applies to all *PPF*s, whether they are bowed out as in Text Fig. 2.1 or linear as in Text Fig. 2.6. To illustrate, look again at the bowed-out *PPF:*

FIGURE 2.1 Production Possibilities Frontier

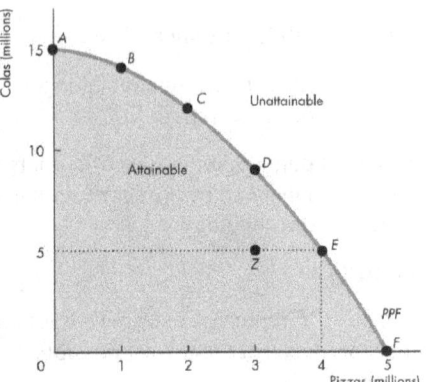

First, consider an example of moving down the *PPF*. In moving from *C* to *D*, what is the opportunity cost of an additional pizza? This economy must give up 3 colas (12 − 9) to get 1 pizza (3 − 2). Substituting into the formula, the opportunity cost is:

$$\frac{3 \text{ colas}}{1 \text{ pizza}} = 3 \text{ colas per pizza}$$

Next, consider an example of moving up the *PPF*. In moving from *D* to *C*, what is the opportunity cost of an additional cola? We must give up 1 pizza (3 − 2) to get 3 colas (12 − 9). Substituting into the formula, the opportunity cost is:

$$\frac{1 \text{ pizza}}{3 \text{ colas}} = \frac{1}{3} \text{ pizza per colas}$$

Opportunity cost is always measured in the units of the forgone good.

2 Opportunity cost can also be related to the slope of the *PPF*. As we move down between any two points on the *PPF*, the opportunity cost of an additional unit of the good on the horizontal axis is:

$$|\,\text{slope of } PPF\,|$$

The slope of the *PPF* is negative, but economists like to describe opportunity cost in terms of a positive quantity of forgone goods. Therefore, we must use the absolute value of the slope to calculate the desired positive number.

As we move up between any two points on the *PPF*, the opportunity cost of an additional unit of the good on the vertical axis is:

$$\left|\frac{1}{\text{slope of } PPF}\right|$$

This is the *inverse* relation we saw between possibilities *C* and *D*. The opportunity cost of an additional pizza (on the horizontal axis) between *C* and *D* is 3 colas. The opportunity cost of an additional cola (on the vertical axis) between *D* and *C* is 1/3 pizza.

3 All points on a *PPF* achieve production efficiency in that they fully employ all resources. But how do we pick a point on the *PPF* and decide *what* combination of goods we want? The *PPF* provides information about resources and *costs*. But choosing what goods we want also requires information about *benefits*.

This choice, like all economic choices, is made at the margin. To decide what goods we want, compare the marginal cost (*MC*) and marginal benefit (*MB*) of different combinations. Marginal cost is the opportunity cost of producing one more unit. The marginal cost of producing more of any good increases as we move along the *PPF*. Marginal benefit is the benefit received from consuming one more unit. Marginal benefit decreases as we consume more of any good.

If the marginal cost of a good exceeds the marginal benefit, we decrease production of the good. If the marginal benefit exceeds the marginal cost, we increase production. When marginal cost equals marginal benefit for every good, we have chosen the goods that we value most highly. The decision rule of *MB* = *MC* yields an *efficient* allocation of resources.

Text Fig. 2.4 is crucial for explaining all economic decisions. Make sure you spend time reviewing it even though it may be hard to fully understand. You will understand Text Fig. 2.4 better after we spend time in future chapters elaborating on the concepts of marginal cost and marginal benefit.

4 The colas and pizza production possibility frontier assumes that resources are *not* equally productive in all activities. Resources with such differences are also called nonhomogeneous resources. As a result of this assumption, opportunity cost increases as we increase the production of either good. In moving from possibility *C* to *D*, the opportunity cost per unit of pizza is 3 colas. But in increasing pizza production from *D* to *E*, the opportunity cost per unit of pizza increases to 4 colas. In producing the first 1 (million) pizzas, we use the resources best suited to pizza production. As we increase pizza production, however, we must use resources that are less well suited to pizza production—hence increasing opportunity cost. A parallel argument accounts for the increasing opportunity cost of increasing cola production.

It is also possible to construct an even simpler model of a *PPF* that assumes resources are equally productive in all activities, or homogeneous resources. As a result of this assumption, opportunity cost is constant as we increase production of either good. Constant opportunity cost means that the *PPF* will be a straight line (rather than bowed out). As you will see in some of the following exercises, such a simple model is useful for illustrating the principle of comparative advantage, without having to deal with the complications of increasing opportunity cost.

5 This chapter gives us our first chance to develop and use economic models. It is useful to think about the nature of these models in the context of the general discussion of models in Chapter 1. For example, one model in this chapter is a representation of the production possibilities in the two-person and two-good world of Liz and Joe. The model abstracts greatly from the complexity of the real world in which there are billions of people and numerous different kinds of goods and services. The model allows us to explain a number of phenomena that we observe in the world such as specialization and exchange.

The production possibilities model also has some implications or predictions. For example, countries that devote a larger proportion of their resources to capital accumulation will have more rapidly expanding production possibilities. The model can be subjected to "test" by comparing these predictions to the facts we observe in the real world.

S E L F - T E S T

True/False and Explain

Production Possibilities and Opportunity Cost

Refer to the production possibility frontier (*PPF*) in Fig. 2.2 for Questions **1** to **4**.

FIGURE **2.2**

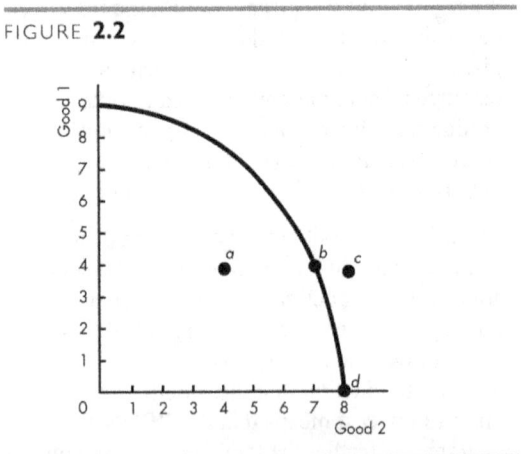

1 Point *a* is not attainable.

2 The opportunity cost of increasing the production of good 2 from 7 to 8 units is 4 units of good 1.

3 Point *c* is not attainable.

4 In moving from point *b* to point *d*, the opportunity cost of increasing the production of good 2 equals the absolute value of the slope of the *PPF* between *b* and *d*.

Using Resources Efficiently

5 The marginal cost of the 4th pizza is the cost of producing all 4 pizzas.

6 The marginal benefit of good *X* is the amount of good *Y* a person is willing to forgo to obtain one more unit of *X*.

7 The principle of decreasing marginal benefit states that the more we have of a good, the *less* we are willing to pay for an additional unit of it.

8 All points on a *PPF* represent both production efficiency and allocative efficiency.

Economic Growth

9 Economic growth, by shifting out the *PPF*, eliminates the problem of scarcity.

10 In a model where capital resources can grow, points on the *PPF* that have more consumption goods yield faster growth.

Gains from Trade

11 With specialization and trade, a country can produce at a point outside its *PPF*.

12 Canada has no incentive to trade with a cheap-labour country like Mexico.

13 Nadim definitely has a comparative advantage in producing skateboards if he can produce more than Elle.

Economic Coordination

14 The incentives for specialization and exchange do not depend on property rights but only on differing opportunity costs.

15 Price adjustments coordinate decisions in goods markets but not in factor markets.

Multiple-Choice

Production Possibilities and Opportunity Cost

1 If Harold can increase production of good X without decreasing the production of any other good, he
  a   is producing on his *PPF*.
  b   is producing outside his *PPF*.
  c   is producing inside his *PPF*.
  d   must have a linear *PPF*.
  e   must prefer good X to any other good.

2 The bowed-out (concave) shape of a *PPF*
  a   is due to the equal usefulness of resources in all activities.
  b   is due to capital accumulation.
  c   is due to technological change.
  d   reflects the existence of increasing opportunity cost.
  e   reflects the existence of decreasing opportunity cost.

3 The economy is at point b on the *PPF* in Fig. 2.3. The opportunity cost of producing one more unit of X is
  a   1 unit of Y.
  b   20 units of Y.
  c   1 unit of X.
  d   8 units of X.
  e   20 units of X.

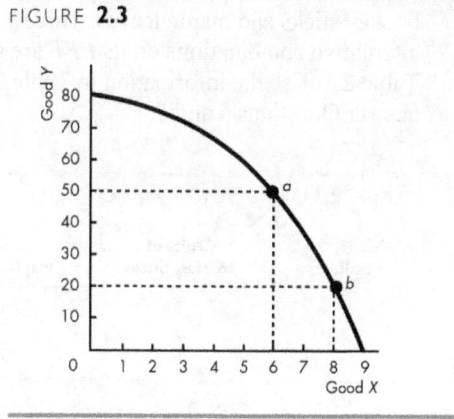

FIGURE **2.3**

4 Refer to the *PPF* in Fig. 2.3. Which of the following statements is *false*?
  a   Resources are not equally productive in all activities.
  b   Points inside the frontier represent unemployed resources.
  c   Starting at point a, an increase in the production of good Y will shift the frontier out.
  d   The opportunity cost of producing good Y increases as production of Y increases.
  e   Shifts in preferences for good X or good Y will not shift the frontier.

5 Refer to Fig. 2.4, which shows the *PPF* for an economy without discrimination operating at maximum efficiency. If discrimination against women workers is currently occurring in this economy, the elimination of discrimination would result in a(n)
  a   movement from a to b.
  b   movement from b to c.
  c   movement from a to c.
  d   outward shift of the *PPF*.
  e   inward shift of the *PPF*.

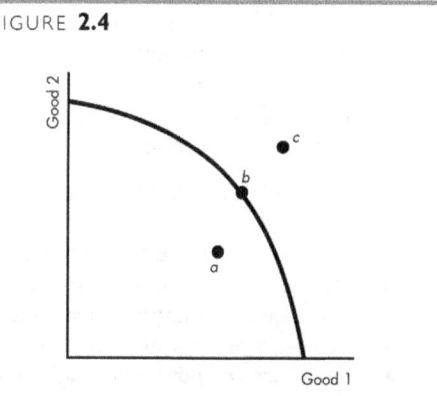

FIGURE **2.4**

Suppose a society produces only two goods—hockey sticks and maple leaves. Three alternative combinations on its *PPF* are given in Table 2.1. Use the information in Table 2.1 to answer Questions **6** and **7**.

TABLE **2.1** PRODUCTION POSSIBILITIES

Possibility	Units of Hockey Sticks	Units of Maple Leaves
a	3	0
b	2	3
c	0	9

6 In moving from combination *c* to combination *b*, the opportunity cost of producing one additional hockey stick is
  a 2 maple leaves.
  b 1/2 a maple leaf.
  c 6 maple leaves.
  d 1/6 a maple leaf.
  e 3 maple leaves.

7 According to this *PPF*
  a resources are equally productive in all activities.
  b a combination of 3 hockey sticks and 9 maple leaves is attainable.
  c a combination of 3 hockey sticks and 9 maple leaves would not employ all resources.
  d the opportunity cost of producing hockey sticks increases as more hockey sticks are produced.
  e the opportunity cost of producing hockey sticks decreases as more hockey sticks are produced.

Using Resources Efficiently

8 The marginal benefit curve for a good
  a shows the benefit a firm receives from producing one more unit.
  b shows the amount a consumer is willing to pay for one more unit.
  c is upward sloping.
  d is bowed out.
  e is none of the above.

9 With increasing production of food, its marginal benefit
  a increases and marginal cost increases.
  b increases and marginal cost decreases.
  c decreases and marginal cost increases.
  d decreases and marginal cost decreases.
  e decreases and marginal cost is constant.

10 Suppose the *PPF* for skirts and pants is a straight line. As the production of skirts increases, the marginal benefit of skirts
  a increases and marginal cost is constant.
  b is constant and marginal cost increases.
  c decreases and marginal cost decreases.
  d decreases and marginal cost increases.
  e decreases and marginal cost is constant.

11 With allocative efficiency, for each good produced, marginal
  a benefit equals marginal cost.
  b benefit is at its maximum.
  c benefit exceeds marginal cost by as much as possible.
  d cost exceeds marginal benefit by as much as possible.
  e cost is at its minimum.

Economic Growth

12 The *PPF* for wine and wool will shift if there is a change in
  a the price of resources.
  b the unemployment rate.
  c the quantity of resources.
  d preferences for wine and wool.
  e all of the above.

13 A movement *along* a given *PPF* will result from
  a technological change.
  b change in the stock of capital.
  c change in the labour force.
  d all of the above.
  e none of the above.

14 The opportunity cost of pushing the *PPF* outward is
  a capital accumulation.
  b technological change.
  c reduced current consumption.
  d the gain in future consumption.
  e all of the above.

15 In general, the higher the proportion of resources devoted to technological research in an economy, the
  a greater will be current consumption.
  b faster the *PPF* will shift outward.
  c faster the *PPF* will shift inward.
  d closer it will come to having a comparative advantage in the production of all goods.
  e more bowed out the shape of the *PPF* will be.

16 Refer to the *PPF* in Fig. 2.5. A politician who argues that "if our children are to be better off, we must invest now for the future" is recommending a current point like

a *a.*
b *b.*
c *c.*
d *d.*
e *e.*

FIGURE **2.5**

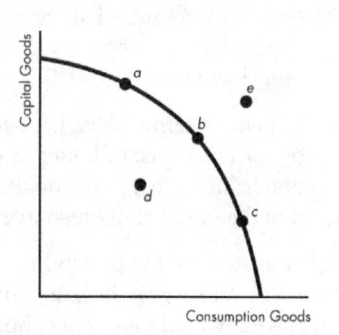

17 Refer to the *PPF* in Fig. 2.5. The statement that "unemployment is a terrible waste of human resources" refers to a point like

a *a.*
b *b.*
c *c.*
d *d.*
e *e.*

Gains from Trade

In an eight-hour day, Andy can produce either 24 loaves of bread or 8 kilograms of butter. In an eight-hour day, Rolfe can produce either 8 loaves of bread or 8 kilograms of butter. Use this information to answer Questions **18** and **19**.

18 Which of the following statements is *true*?

a Andy has an absolute advantage in butter production.
b Rolfe has an absolute advantage in butter production.
c Andy has an absolute advantage in bread production.
d Andy has a comparative advantage in butter production.
e Rolfe has a comparative advantage in bread production.

19 Andy and Rolfe

a can gain from exchange if Andy specializes in butter production and Rolfe specializes in bread production.
b can gain from exchange if Andy specializes in bread production and Rolfe specializes in butter production.
c cannot gain from exchange.
d can exchange, but only Rolfe will gain.
e can exchange, but only Andy will gain.

20 Mexico and Canada produce both oil and apples using labour only. A barrel of oil is produced with 4 hours of labour in Mexico and 8 hours of labour in Canada. A bushel of apples is produced with 8 hours of labour in Mexico and 12 hours of labour in Canada. Canada has

a an absolute advantage in oil production.
b an absolute advantage in apple production.
c a comparative advantage in oil production.
d a comparative advantage in apple production.
e none of the above.

21 In Portugal, the opportunity cost of a bale of wool is 3 bottles of wine. In England, the opportunity cost of 1 bottle of wine is 3 bales of wool. Given this information,

a England has an absolute advantage in wine production.
b England has an absolute advantage in wool production.
c Portugal has a comparative advantage in wine production.
d Portugal has a comparative advantage in wool production.
e no trade will occur.

22 To gain from comparative advantage, countries must not only trade, they must also

a save.
b invest.
c engage in research and development.
d engage in capital accumulation.
e specialize.

23 It takes Mom 30 minutes to cook dinner. In the same time she can iron 6 of your shirts. Dad takes an hour to cook dinner and 30 minutes to iron a single shirt. In this situation
  a Dad has an absolute advantage in cooking dinner.
  b Dad has an absolute advantage in ironing shirts.
  c Mom should not cook dinner, as her opportunity cost is 6 shirts.
  d there are no gains from trade.
  e Mom should cook dinner, even though the opportunity cost is 12 shirts.

Economic Coordination

24 Trade is organized using the social institutions of
  a firms.
  b property rights.
  c money.
  d markets.
  e all of the above.

25 Markets
    1 enable buyers and sellers to get information.
    2 are defined by economists as geographical locations where trade occurs.
    3 coordinate buying and selling decisions through price adjustments.
  a 1 only
  b 3 only
  c 1 and 3 only
  d 2 and 3 only
  e 1, 2, and 3

Short Answer Problems

1 Why is a *PPF* negatively sloped? Why is it bowed out?

2 Suppose that an economy has the *PPF* shown in Table 2.2.

TABLE **2.2** PRODUCTION POSSIBILITIES

Possibility	Maximum Units of Butter per Week	Maximum Units of Guns per Week
a	200	0
b	180	60
c	160	100
d	100	160
e	40	200
f	0	220

  a On graph paper, plot these possibilities, label the points, and draw the *PPF*. (Put guns on the *x*-axis.)
  b If the economy moves from possibility *c* to possibility *d*, the opportunity cost *per unit of guns* will be how many units of butter?
  c If the economy moves from possibility *d* to possibility *e*, the opportunity cost *per unit of guns* will be how many units of butter?
  d In general terms, what happens to the opportunity cost of guns as the output of guns increases?
  e In general terms, what happens to the opportunity cost of butter as the output of butter increases? What do the results in parts **d** and **e** imply about resources?
  f If (instead of the possibilities given) the *PPF* were a straight line joining points *a* and *f*, what would that imply about opportunity costs and resources?
  g Given the original *PPF* you have plotted, is a combination of 140 units of butter and 130 units of guns per week attainable? Would you regard this combination as an efficient one? Explain.
  h Given the original *PPF*, is a combination of 70 units of butter and 170 units of guns per week attainable? Does this combination achieve productive efficiency? Explain.

3 If the following events occurred (each is a separate event, unaccompanied by any other event), what would happen to the *PPF* in Short Answer Problem **2**?
  a A new, easily exploited energy source is discovered.
  b A large number of skilled workers immigrate into the country.
  c The output of butter increases.
  d A new invention increases output per person in the butter industry but not in the guns industry.
  e A new law is passed compelling workers, who could previously work as long as they wanted, to retire at age 60.

4 The Borg produce only two goods—cubes and transwarp coils—and want to decide where on their *PPF* to operate. Table 2.3 shows the marginal benefit and marginal cost of cubes, measured in the number of transwarp coils per cube.

TABLE **2.3**

Borg Cubes	Marginal Benefit	Marginal Cost
1	12	3
2	10	4
3	8	5
4	6	6
5	4	7
6	2	8

a If the Borg are efficient (and they are!), what quantity of cubes will they produce?

b If the Borg were to produce one more cube than your answer in **a**, why would that choice be inefficient?

5 Suppose the country of Quark has historically devoted 10 percent of its resources to the production of new capital goods. Use *PPF* diagrams like Text Figures on pages 36–37 to compare the consequences (costs and benefits) of each of the following:

a Quark continues to devote 10 percent of its resources to the production of capital goods.

b Quark begins now to permanently devote 20 percent of its resources to the production of capital goods.

6 Lawyers earn $200 per hour while secretaries earn $15 per hour. Use the concepts of absolute and comparative advantage to explain why a lawyer who is a better typist than her secretary will still specialize in doing only legal work and will trade with the secretary for typing services.

7 France and Germany each produce both wine and beer, using a single, homogeneous input—labour. Their production possibilities are:

• France has 100 units of labour and can produce a maximum of 200 bottles of wine or 400 bottles of beer.

• Germany has 50 units of labour and can produce a maximum of 250 bottles of wine or 200 bottles of beer.

a Complete Table 2.4.

TABLE **2.4**

	Bottles Produced by 1 Unit of Labour		Opportunity Cost of 1 Additional Bottle	
	Wine	Beer	Wine	Beer
France				
Germany				

Use the information in part **a** to answer the following questions.

b Which country has an absolute advantage in wine production?

c Which country has an absolute advantage in beer production?

d Which country has a comparative advantage in wine production?

e Which country has a comparative advantage in beer production?

f If trade is allowed, describe what specialization, if any, will occur.

8 Tova and Ron are the only two remaining inhabitants of the planet Melmac. They spend their 30-hour days producing widgets and woggles, the only two goods needed for happiness on Melmac. It takes Tova 1 hour to produce a widget and 2 hours to produce a woggle, while Ron takes 3 hours to produce a widget and 3 hours to produce a woggle.

a For a 30-hour day, draw an individual *PPF* for Tova, then for Ron.

b What does the shape of the *PPF*s tell us about opportunity costs? about resources?

c Assume initially that Tova and Ron are each self-sufficient. Define self-sufficiency. Explain what the individual consumption possibilities are for Tova, then for Ron.

d Who has an absolute advantage in the production of widgets? of woggles?

e Who has a comparative advantage in the production of widgets? of woggles?

f Suppose Tova and Ron each specialize in producing only the good in which she or he has a comparative advantage (one spends 30 hours producing widgets, the other spends 30 hours producing woggles). What will be the total production of widgets and woggles?

g Suppose Tova and Ron exchange 7 widgets for 5 woggles. On your *PPF* diagrams, plot the new point of Tova's consumption, then of Ron's consumption. Explain how these points illustrate the gains from trade.

A N S W E R S

True/False and Explain

1 **F** Attainable but not an efficient point. (30–32)

2 **T** Moving from *b* to *d*, production good 1 decreases by 4 units. (30–32)

3 **T** Outside *PPF*. (30–32)

4 **T** See Helpful Hint **2**. (30–32)

5 **F** Marginal cost is the *additional* cost of producing the 4th pizza alone. (33–35)

6 **T** Marginal benefit is also the amount a person is willing to pay for one more unit, but payment in money ultimately represents an opportunity cost in goods forgone. (33–35)

7 **T** The more we have of a good, the smaller is the marginal benefit and hence the willingness to pay for it. (33–35)

8 **F** All points represent productive efficiency (efficient use of resources). But allocative efficiency only occurs at the single point (combination of goods) that we prefer above all others (where $MB = MC$). (33–35)

9 **F** Cost of growth is forgone current consumption. (36–37)

10 **F** Points with more capital goods yield faster growth. (36–37)

11 **F** Can *consume* at a point outside the *PPF*. (38–40)

12 **F** Mutually beneficial trade depends on comparative advantage, not absolute advantage. (38–40)

13 **F** Nadim has absolute advantage in skateboard production, but without information about

opportunity costs, we don't know if he has comparative advantage. (38–40)

14 **F** Property rights are a prerequisite for specialization and exchange. (41–43)

15 **F** Price adjustments coordinate buying and selling decisions in all markets. (41–43)

Multiple-Choice

1 **c** For 0 opportunity cost, there must be unemployed resources. (30–32)

2 **d** **a** would be true if *un*equal resources; **b** and **c** shift the *PPF*. (30–32)

3 **b** To increase quantity *X* to 9, must decrease quantity *Y* from 20 to 0. (30–32)

4 **c** Increased production of *Y* moves up *along* the *PPF*. (30–32)

5 **a** Discrimination causes underemployment of resources. Women are not allowed to produce up to their full abilities. (30–32)

6 **e** Give up 6 maple leaves to get 2 hockey sticks: 6/2 = 3 maple leaves per hockey stick. (30–32)

7 **a** Constant opportunity cost means resources are equally productive for producing all goods—see Helpful Hint **4**. (30–32)

8 **b** Benefits apply to consumers; the curve is downward sloping. (33–35)

9 **c** Principles of diminishing marginal benefit and increasing marginal cost. (33–35)

10 **e** Diminishing marginal benefit, but a linear *PPF* means constant opportunity and marginal costs. (33–35)

11 **a** Whenever $MB \neq MC$, efficiency improves by reallocating resources to produce more goods with high marginal benefits, causing a decrease in their marginal benefit and increase in marginal cost. (33–35)

12 **c** Only changes in resources or technology shift the *PPF*. (36–37)

13 **e** **a**, **b**, and **c** all shift the *PPF*. (36–37)

14 **c** **a** and **b** cause an outward shift of the *PPF*, not opportunity cost; **d** is an effect of an outward shift in the *PPF*. (36–37)

15 **b** Technological change shifts *PPF* outward at the cost of current consumption. (36–37)

16 a Producing more capital goods now, shifts the *PPF* outward in the future. (36–37)

17 d Points inside the *PPF* represent unemployed resources, whether labour, capital, or land. (36–37)

18 c Andy produces 3 loaves bread per hour; Rolfe produces 1 loaf per hour—see Helpful Hint **5**. (38–40)

19 b Andy has comparative advantage (lower opportunity cost) in bread, Rolfe has comparative advantage in butter production. (38–40)

20 d Opportunity cost of oil in bushels of apples—Canada 2/3, Mexico 1/2. Opportunity cost of apples in barrels of oil—Canada 3/2, Mexico 2. (38–40)

21 c Opportunity cost of wine in bales of wool—Portugal 1/3, England 3. Opportunity cost of wool in bottles of wine—Portugal 3, England 1/3. (38–40)

22 e Gains from trade require specialization based on comparative advantage. **a–d** may increase productivity and absolute advantage, but not necessarily comparative advantage. (38–40)

23 c Dad has a comparative advantage cooking. (38–40)

24 e All 4 institutions are required for gains from trade and specialization through decentralized coordination. (41–43)

25 c 2 is the ordinary meaning of markets, not the economist's definition. (41–43)

Short Answer Problems

1 The negative slope of the *PPF* reflects opportunity cost: in order to have more of one good, some of the other must be forgone. It is bowed out because the existence of resources not equally productive in all activities creates increasing opportunity cost as we increase the production of either good.

2 a The graph of the *PPF* is given in Fig. 2.6.

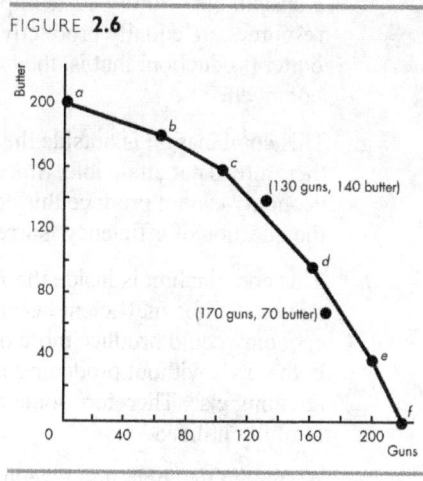

FIGURE **2.6**

(130 guns, 140 butter)

(170 guns, 70 butter)

b In moving from *c* to *d*, in order to gain 60 units of guns, we must give up 160 – 100 = 60 units of butter. The opportunity cost per unit of guns is

$$\frac{60 \text{ units butter}}{60 \text{ units guns}} = 1 \text{ unit butter per unit of guns}$$

c In moving from *d* to *e*, in order to gain 40 units of guns, we must give up 100 – 40 = 60 units of butter. The opportunity cost per unit of guns is

$$\frac{60 \text{ units butter}}{40 \text{ units guns}} = 1.5 \text{ unit butter per unit of guns}$$

d The opportunity cost of producing more guns increases as the output of guns increases.

e Likewise, the opportunity cost of producing more butter increases as the output of butter increases. Increasing opportunity costs imply that resources are not equally productive in gun and butter production; that is, they are nonhomogeneous.

f Opportunity costs would always be constant, regardless of the output of guns or butter. The opportunity cost per unit of guns would be

$$200/220 = 10/11 \text{ units of butter}$$

The opportunity cost per unit of butter would be

$$220/200 = 1.1 \text{ units of guns}$$

Constant opportunity costs imply that resources are equally productive in gun and butter production; that is, they are homogeneous.

g This combination is outside the *PPF* and therefore is not attainable. Since the economy cannot produce this combination, the question of efficiency is irrelevant.

h This combination is inside the *PPF* and is attainable. It is inefficient because the economy could produce more of either or both goods without producing less of anything else. Therefore some resources are not fully utilized.

3 a Assuming that both goods require energy for their production, the entire *PPF* shifts out to the northeast as in Fig. 2.7(a).

b Assuming that both goods use skilled labour in their production, the entire *PPF* shifts out to the northeast.

c The *PPF* does not shift. An increase in the output of butter implies a movement along the *PPF* to the left, not a shift of the *PPF* itself.

d The new invention implies that for every level of output of guns, the economy can now produce more butter. The *PPF* swings to the right, but remains anchored at point *f* as in Fig. 2.7(b).

e The entire *PPF* shifts in toward the origin.

4 a At the efficient quantity of output, marginal benefit = marginal cost. The Borg will produce 4 cubes (*MB* = *MC* = 4 transwarp coils/cube).

b At 5 cubes, marginal benefit = 4 and marginal cost = 7. Since *MC* > *MB*, the Borg could better use their resources by shifting production out of cubes and into transwarp coils.

5 a The situation for Quark is depicted in Fig. 2.8. Suppose Quark starts on *PPF*₁. If it continues to devote only 10 percent of its resources to the production of new capital goods, it is choosing to produce at a point like *a*. This will shift the *PPF* out in the next period, but only to the curve labelled 2 (where, presumably, Quark will choose to produce at point *b*).

FIGURE **2.7**

(a)

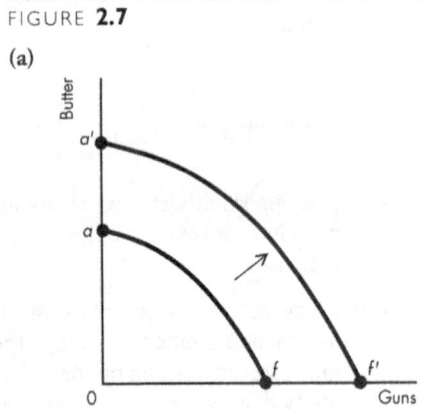

(b)

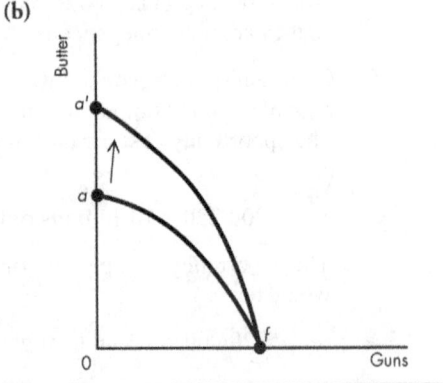

FIGURE **2.8**

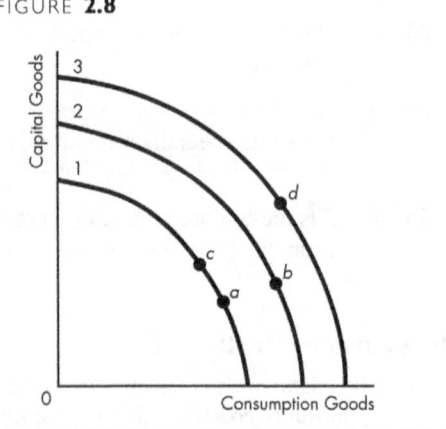

b Starting from the same initial *PPF*, if Quark now decides to increase the resources devoted to the production of new capital to 20 percent, it will be choosing to produce at a point like *c*. In this case, next period's *PPF* will shift further—to curve 3, and a point like *d*, for example.

Thus in comparing points *a* and *c*, we find the following costs and benefits: point *a* has the benefit of greater present consumption but at a cost of lower future consumption; point *c* has the cost of lower present consumption, but with the benefit of greater future consumption.

6   The lawyer has an absolute advantage in producing both legal and typing services relative to the secretary. Nevertheless, she has a comparative advantage in legal services, and the secretary has a comparative advantage in typing. To demonstrate these comparative advantages, we can construct Table 2.6 of opportunity costs.

TABLE **2.6**

	Opportunity Cost of 1 Additional Hour ($)	
	Legal Services	**Typing**
Lawyer	200	200
Secretary	>200	15

Consider first the lawyer's opportunity costs. The lawyer's best forgone alternative to providing 1 hour of legal services is the $200 she could earn by providing another hour of legal services. If she provides 1 hour of typing, she is also forgoing $200 (1 hour) of legal services. What would the secretary have to forgo to provide 1 hour of legal services? He would have to spend 3 years in law school, forgoing 3 years of income in addition to the tuition he must pay. His opportunity cost is a very large number, certainly greater than $200. If he provides 1 hour of typing, his best forgone alternative is the $15 he could have earned at another secretarial job.

Thus Table 2.6 shows that the lawyer has a lower opportunity cost (comparative advantage) of providing legal services, and the secretary has a lower opportunity cost (comparative advantage) of providing typing services. It is on the basis of comparative advantage (not absolute advantage) that trade will take place from which both parties gain.

7   a   The completed table is shown here as Table 2.4 Solution.

TABLE **2.4**   SOLUTION

	Bottles Produced by 1 Unit of Labour		Opportunity Cost of 1 Additional Bottle	
	Wine	**Beer**	**Wine**	**Beer**
France	2	4	2.0 beer	0.50 wine
Germany	5	4	0.8 beer	1.25 wine

b   Germany, which can produce more wine (5 bottles) per unit of input, has an absolute advantage in wine production.

c   Neither country has an absolute advantage in beer production, since beer output (4 bottles) per unit of input is the same for both countries.

d   Germany, with the lower opportunity cost (0.8 beer), has a comparative advantage in wine production.

e   France, with the lower opportunity cost (0.5 wine), has a comparative advantage in beer production.

f   The incentive for trade depends only on differences in comparative advantage. Germany will specialize in wine production and France will specialize in beer production.

8   a   The individual *PPF*s for Tova and Ron are given by Fig. 2.9(a) and (b), respectively.

FIGURE **2.9**

(a)

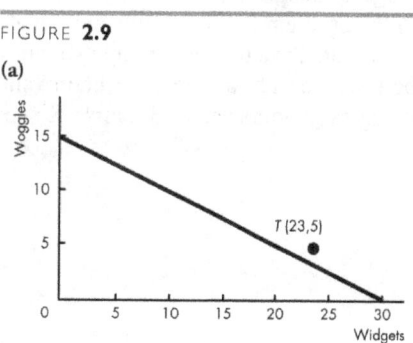

(b)

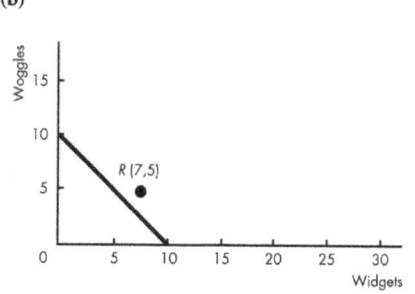

b   The linear shape of the *PPF*s tells us that opportunity costs are constant along each frontier and that resources are equally productive in all activities, or are homogeneous.

These linear *PPF*s with constant opportunity costs abstract from the complexity of the real world. The world generally has increasing opportunity costs, but that fact is not essential for understanding the gains from trade, which is the objective of this problem. Making the model more complex by including increasing opportunity costs would not change our results, but it would make it more difficult to see them.

c   Individuals are self-sufficient if they consume only what they produce. This means there is no trade. Without trade, Tova's (maximum) consumption possibilities are exactly the same as her production possibilities—points along her *PPF*. Ron's (maximum) consumption possibilities are likewise the points along his *PPF*.

d   Tova has an absolute advantage in the production of both widgets and woggles. Her absolute advantage can be defined either in terms of greater output per unit of inputs or fewer inputs per unit of output. A comparison of the *PPF*s in Fig. 2.9 shows that, for given inputs of 30 hours, Tova produces a greater output of widgets than Ron (30 versus 10) and a greater output of woggles than Ron (15 versus 10). The statement of the problem tells us equivalently that, per unit of output, Tova uses fewer inputs than Ron for both widgets (1 hour versus 3 hours) and woggles (2 hours versus 3 hours). Since Tova has greater productivity than Ron in the production of all goods (widgets and woggles), we say that overall she has an absolute advantage.

e   Tova has a comparative advantage in the production of widgets, since she can produce them at lower opportunity cost than Ron (1/2 woggle versus 1 woggle). On the other hand, Ron has a comparative advantage in the production of woggles, since he can produce them at a lower opportunity cost than Tova (1 widget versus 2 widgets).

f   Tova will produce widgets and Ron will produce woggles, yielding a total production between them of 30 widgets and 10 woggles.

g   After the exchange, Tova will have 23 widgets and 5 woggles (point *T*). Ron will have 7 widgets and 5 woggles (point *R*). These new post-trade consumption possibility points lie outside Tova's and Ron's respective pre-trade consumption (and production) possibilities. Hence trade has yielded gains that allow the traders to improve their consumption possibilities beyond those available with self-sufficiency.

Part 1 Wrap Up
Understanding the Scope of Economics

PROBLEM

The economy is a mechanism that allocates scarce resources among competing uses. But how do those allocation decisions get made? In the Canadian economy, markets are the primary institutions that coordinate individual decisions through price adjustments.

Suppose, for simplicity, the Canadian economy produced only two outputs—child-care services and televisions. The production possibility frontier (*PPF*) for the economy appears in Fig. P1.1 below. The economy is operating at point *a*, producing Q^0_{cc} units of child-care services and Q^0_{tv} televisions.

FIGURE **P1.1**

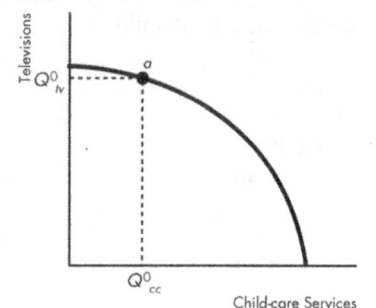

a What does the bowed-out (concave) shape of the *PPF* imply about resources? opportunity costs?

b As more women enter the labour force, there is increased demand for child-care services. As a result, the price and quantity of child-care services both increase. At the same time, the demand for televisions falls (perhaps to save money to pay for the additional child-care services). As a result, the price and quantity of televisions both decrease.

On the *PPF* in Fig. P1.1, label as point *b* a new combination of child-care services and televisions reflecting the changes in demand.

c Explain how the economy came to produce these new quantities in response to the changing demands of households.

d What determines the distance of the *PPF* from the origin? What determines the precise point on the *PPF* at which the economy operates? What is the true cost of moving from point *a* to point *b* on the *PPF*?

MIDTERM EXAMINATION

You should allocate 30 minutes for this examination (15 questions, 2 minutes per question). For each question, choose the one *best* answer.

1 A *PPF* shows that
  a there is a limit to the production of any one good.
  b to produce more of one good, we must produce less of another good.
  c there are limits to total production with given resources and technology.
  d all of the above are true.
  e none of the above is true.

2 Which of the following equations describes a straight line with a *y*-intercept of -2 and a slope of -5?
  a $y = -2 - 5x$
  b $y = -2 + 5x$
  c $y = -5 - 2x$
  d $x = -2 - 5y$
  e $x = -5 - 2y$

Suppose a society produces only two goods—guns and butter. Three alternative combinations on its *PPF* are given in Table P1.1. Use the information in Table P1.1 to answer Questions **3** and **4**.

TABLE **P1.1** PRODUCTION POSSIBILITIES

Possibility	Units of Butter	Units of Guns
a	8	0
b	6	1
c	0	3

3 In moving from combination *b* to combination *c*, the opportunity cost of producing *one* additional unit of guns is
  a 2 units of butter.
  b 1/2 unit of butter.
  c 6 units of butter.
  d 1/6 unit of butter.
  e 3 units of butter.

4 According to this *PPF*
  a a combination of 6 butter and 1 gun would not employ all resources.
  b a combination of 0 butter and 4 guns is attainable.
  c resources are equally productive in all activities.
  d the opportunity cost of producing guns increases as more guns are produced.
  e the opportunity cost of producing guns decreases as more guns are produced.

5 Which of the following is a normative statement?
  a Pollution is an example of an external cost.
  b Pollution makes people worse off.
  c Firms that pollute should be forced to shut down.
  d Pollution imposes opportunity costs on others.
  e None of the above.

6 The graph of the relationship between two variables that are negatively related
  a is horizontal.
  b slopes upward to the right.
  c is vertical.
  d slopes downward to the right.
  e is linear.

7 In Fig. P1.2, the slope of the line is
  a 1.50.
  b 1.25.
  c 1.00.
  d 0.75.
  e 0.50.

FIGURE **P1.2**

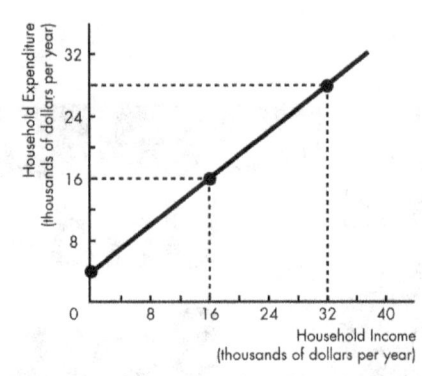

8 Other things being equal, which of the following statements is correct?

  1 If unemployment increases, the opportunity cost of attending university decreases.

  2 If men generally earn more than women in the labour market, the opportunity cost of attending university is higher for men than for women.

  a 1 only
  b 2 only
  c 1 and 2
  d Neither 1 nor 2
  e Impossible to judge without additional information

9 The economy is at point *b* on the *PPF* in Fig. P1.3. The opportunity cost of increasing the production of *Y* to 50 units is
  a 2 units of *X*.
  b 6 units of *X*.
  c 8 units of *X*.
  d 20 units of *Y*.
  e 30 units of *Y*.

FIGURE **P1.3**

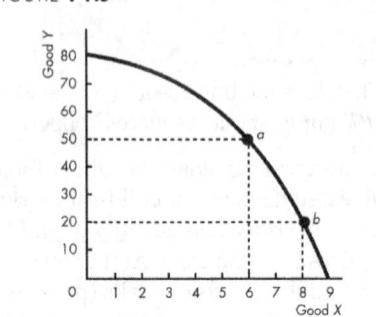

10 Because productive resources are scarce, we must give up some of one good in order to acquire more of another. This is the essence of the concept of
  a specialization.
  b monetary exchange.
  c comparative advantage.
  d absolute advantage.
  e opportunity cost.

11 The scarcity of resources implies that the *PPF* is
  a bowed inward (convex).
  b bowed outward (concave).
  c positively sloped.
  d negatively sloped.
  e linear.

12 If additional units of any good can be produced at a constant opportunity cost, the *PPF* is
  a bowed inward (convex).
  b bowed outward (concave).
  c positively sloped.
  d perfectly horizontal.
  e linear.

13 Marginal cost is the
  a total cost of an activity.
  b additional benefit of a decrease in an activity.
  c additional benefit of an increase in an activity.
  d opportunity cost of a decrease in an activity.
  e opportunity cost of an increase in an activity.

14 If variables *x* and *y* move in opposite directions, they are said to be
  a positively related.
  b negatively related.
  c intimately related.
  d unrelated.
  e siblings.

15 *Ceteris paribus* is a Latin term meaning
  a "Unscrambling cause and effect."
  b "Correlation shows causation."
  c "Causation shows correlation."
  d "Other relevant things remain the same."
  e "Your place or mine."

ANSWERS

Problem

a The bowed-out shape of the *PPF* implies that resources are not equally productive in all activities; they are nonhomogeneous. With nonhomogeneous resources, there are increasing opportunity costs as production increases of either child-care services or televisions.

b See Fig. P1.1 Solution.

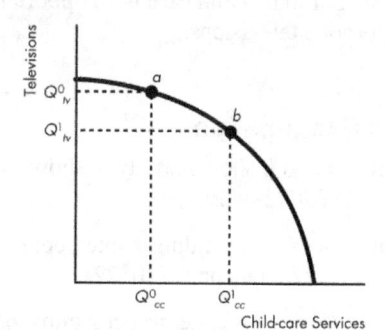

FIGURE **P1.1** SOLUTION

c The increased demand for child-care services puts upward pressure on the price of child-care services, making it more profitable to produce them. The higher price serves as a signal to firms to shift additional resources to producing child-care services.

    Those additional resources come from the television market. The decreased demand for televisions puts downward pressure on the price of televisions, making it less profitable to produce them. The lower price serves as a signal to firms to shift resources to more profitable uses (in child care).

    Thus the market economy responds to the changing demands of households by reallocating resources into child-care services from television production. Prices are the signals that coordinate the demand decisions of households with the resource allocation decisions of firms. The market—operating through a combination of price signals, self-interest, and competition—acts like an "invisible hand" to guide resources to the uses that households desire.

d   The distance of the *PPF* from the origin is determined by the quantities of resources and the technology in the economy. The *PPF* shows maximum combinations of outputs (goods and services) that can be produced with given resources and technology.

The precise point on the *PPF* at which the economy operates (e.g., the combination at point *a* of child-care services and televisions) is determined by the demands of households.

The true cost of moving from point *a* to point *b* is the televisions that must be forgone as scarce resources are shifted to produce more child-care services. In other words, the true cost of additional child care is an opportunity cost—forgone televisions.

Midterm Examination

1   d   **a** and **b** show scarcity, **c** shows opportunity cost. (29–32)

2   a   Set $x = 0$, yielding y-intercept $= -2$; slope is coefficient on x. (20–22)

3   e   Give up 6 butter to get 2 guns: $6/2 = 3$ butter per gun. (29–32)

4   d   Opportunity cost gun between *a* and $b = 2$ butter; between *b* and $c = 3$ butter. *a* on *PPF*, *b* outside *PPF*. (29–32)

5   c   **a** is a true statement (definition); **d** and **b** are positive statements that can be tested. (10)

6   d   As x increases, y decreases. (16–19)

7   d   For example, using points (0, 4) and (16, 16): $\Delta y = 12$ ($16 - 4$), $\Delta x = 16$ ($16 - 0$). (20–22)

8   c   Unemployment decreases expected average income from working. Higher opportunity cost for men may not be fair, but is a fact. (8–9)

9   a   To move from *b* to *a*, quantity *X* decreases from 8 to 6. (29–32)

10   e   Definition. (29–32)

11   d   Scarcity implies opportunity cost, which involves a negative relationship—to get more of *X* you must give up *Y*. (29–32)

12   e   Constant opportunity cost yields constant slope *PPF*. (29–32)

13   e   Definition; **c** is marginal benefit, **b** and **d** are nonsense. (8–9)

14   b   Definition. (16–19)

15   d   Definition. (22–23)

Chapter 3
Demand and Supply

Markets and Prices

Competitive market—many buyers and sellers so no one can influence prices.

Relative price of a good is

- ♦ its *opportunity cost*—the other goods that must be forgone to buy it.

- ♦ ratio of its **money price** to the money price of another good.

- ♦ determined by demand and supply.

Demand

The **quantity demanded** of a good is the amount consumers plan to buy during a given time period at a particular price. The **law of demand** states: "Other things remaining the same, the higher the price of a good, the smaller is the quantity demanded." Higher price reduces quantity demanded for two reasons:

- ♦ *substitution effect*—with an increase in the relative price of a good, people buy less of it and more of substitutes for the good.

- ♦ *income effect*—with an increase in the relative price of a good and unchanged incomes, people have less money to spend on all goods, including the good whose price increased.

The **demand curve** represents the inverse relationship between quantity demanded and price, *ceteris paribus*. The demand curve also is a willingness-and-ability-to-pay curve, which measures marginal benefit.

- ♦ A change in price causes movement along the demand curve. This is called a **change in the quantity demanded**. The higher the price of a good, the lower the quantity demanded.

- ♦ A shift of the demand curve is called a **change in demand**. The demand curve shifts from changes in

  - prices of related goods.

  - expected future prices.

  - income.

  - expected future income and credit.

  - population.

  - preferences.

- ♦ Increase in demand—demand curve shifts rightward.

- ♦ Decrease in demand—demand curve shifts leftward.

- ♦ For an increase in

  - price of a **substitute**—demand shifts rightward.

  - price of a **complement**—demand shifts leftward.

  - expected future prices—demand shifts rightward.

  - income (**normal good**)—demand shifts rightward.

  - income (**inferior good**)—demand shifts leftward.

  - expected future income or credit (**normal good**)—demand shifts rightward.

  - expected future income or credit (**inferior good**)—demand shifts leftward

  - population—demand shifts rightward.

  - preferences—demand shifts rightward.

Supply

The **quantity supplied** of a good is the amount producers plan to sell during a given time period at a particular price. The **law of supply** states: "Other things remaining the same, the higher the price of a good, the greater is the quantity supplied." Higher price increases quantity supplied because marginal cost increases with increasing quantities. Price must rise for producers to be willing to increase production and incur higher marginal cost.

The **supply curve** represents the positive relationship between quantity supplied and price, *ceteris paribus*. The supply curve is also a minimum-supply-price curve, showing the lowest price at which a producer is willing to sell another unit.

- A change in price causes movement along the supply curve. This is called a **change in the quantity supplied**. The higher the price of a good, the greater the quantity supplied.

- A shift of the supply curve is called a **change in supply**. The supply curve shifts from changes in

  - prices of factors of production.
  - prices of related goods produced.
  - expected future prices.
  - number of suppliers.
  - technology.
  - state of nature.

- Increase in supply—supply curve shifts rightward.

- Decrease in supply—supply curve shifts leftward.

- For an increase in

  - prices of factors of production—supply shifts leftward.
  - price of a *substitute in production*—supply shifts leftward.
  - price of a *complement in production*—supply shifts rightward.
  - expected future prices—supply shifts leftward.
  - number of suppliers—supply shifts rightward.
  - technology—supply shifts rightward.
  - state of nature—supply shifts rightward.

Market Equilibrium

The **equilibrium price** is where the demand and supply curves intersect—where quantity demanded equals quantity supplied.

- Above the equilibrium price, there is a surplus (quantity supplied > quantity demanded), and price will fall.

- Below the equilibrium price, there is a shortage (quantity demanded > quantity supplied), and price will rise.

- Only in equilibrium is there no tendency for the price to change. The **equilibrium quantity** is the quantity bought and sold at the equilibrium price.

Predicting Changes in Price and Quantity

For a single change *either* in demand *or* in supply, *ceteris paribus*, when

- demand increases, P rises and Q increases.

- demand decreases, P falls and Q decreases.

- supply increases, P falls and Q increases.

- supply decreases, P rises and Q decreases.

When there is a simultaneous change *both* in demand *and* supply, we can determine the effect on either price or quantity. But without information about the relative size of the shifts of the demand and supply curves, the effect on the other variable is ambiguous. *Ceteris paribus*, when

- both demand and supply increase, P may rise/fall/remain constant and Q increases.

- both demand and supply decrease, P may rise/fall/remain constant and Q decreases.

- demand increases and supply decreases, P rises and Q may rise/fall/remain constant.

- demand decreases and supply increases, P falls and Q may rise/fall/remain constant.

H E L P F U L   H I N T S

1   When you are first learning about demand and supply, think of specific examples to help you understand how to use the concepts. For example, in analysing complementary goods, think about hamburgers and french fries; in analysing substitute goods, think of hamburgers and hot dogs. This will reduce the "abstractness" of the economic theory and make concepts easier to remember.

2 The statement "Price is determined by demand and supply" is a shorthand way of saying that price is determined by all of the factors affecting demand (prices of related goods, expected future prices, income, expected future income and credit, population, preferences) and all of the factors affecting supply (prices of factors of production, prices of related goods produced, expected future prices, number of suppliers, technology, state of nature). The benefit of using demand and supply curves is that they allow us to systematically sort out the influences on price of each of these separate factors. Changes in the factors affecting demand shift the demand curve and move us up or down the given supply curve. Changes in the factors affecting supply shift the supply curve and move us up or down the given demand curve.

Any demand and supply problem requires you to sort out these influences carefully. In so doing, *always draw a graph*, even if it is just a small graph in the margin of a true/false or multiple-choice problem. Graphs are a very efficient way to "see" what happens. As you become comfortable with graphs, you will find them to be effective and powerful tools for systematically organizing your thinking.

Do not make the common mistake of thinking that a problem is so easy that you can do it in your head, without drawing a graph. This mistake will cost you dearly on examinations. Also, when you do draw a graph, be sure to label the axes. As the course progresses, you will encounter many graphs with different variables on the axes. It is easy to become confused if you do not develop the habit of labelling the axes.

3 Another common mistake among students is failing to *distinguish* correctly between *a shift in a curve* and *a movement along a curve*. This distinction applies both to demand and to supply curves. Many questions in the Self-Test are designed to test your understanding of this distinction, and you can be sure that your instructor will test you heavily on this. The distinction between "shifts in" versus "movements along" a curve is crucial for systematic thinking about the factors influencing demand and supply, and for understanding the determination of equilibrium price and quantity.

Consider the example of the demand curve. The quantity of a good demanded depends on its own price, the prices of related goods, expected future prices, income, expected future income and credit, population, and preferences. The term "demand" refers to the relationship between the price of a good and the quantity demanded, holding constant all of the other factors on which the quantity demanded depends. This demand relationship is represented graphically by the demand curve. Thus, the effect of a change in price on quantity demanded is already reflected in the slope of the demand curve; the effect of a change in the price of the good itself is given by a movement along the demand curve. This is referred to as a **change in quantity demanded**.

On the other hand, if one of the other factors affecting the quantity demanded changes, the demand curve itself will shift; the quantity demanded *at each price* will change. This shift of the demand curve is referred to as a **change in demand**. The critical thing to remember is that a change in the price of a good will not shift the demand curve; it will only cause a movement along the demand curve. Similarly, it is just as important to distinguish between shifts in the supply curve and movements along the supply curve.

To confirm your understanding, consider the effect (draw a graph!) of an increase in household income on the market for energy bars. First note that an increase in income affects the demand for energy bars and not supply. Next we want to determine whether the increase in income causes a shift in the demand curve or a movement along the demand curve. Will the increase in income increase the quantity of energy bars demanded even if the price of energy bars does not change? Since the answer to this question is yes, we know that the demand curve will shift rightward. Note further that the increase in the demand for energy bars will cause the equilibrium price to rise. This price increase will be indicated by a movement along the supply curve (an increase in the quantity supplied) and will not shift the supply curve itself.

Remember: It is shifts in demand and supply curves that cause the market price to change, not changes in the price that cause demand and supply curves to shift.

4 When analysing the shifts of demand and supply curves in related markets (for substitute goods like beer and wine), it often seems as though the feedback effects from one market to the other can go on endlessly. To avoid confusion, stick to the rule that each curve (demand and supply) for

42   CHAPTER 3

a given market can shift a maximum of *once*. (See Short Answer Problems **4** and **6** for further explanation and examples.)

5   The relationships between price and quantity demanded and supplied can be represented in three equivalent forms: demand and supply schedules, curves, and equations. Text Chapter 3 illustrates schedules and curves, but demand and supply equations are also powerful tools of economic analysis. The Mathematical Note to Chapter 3 (pages 76–77) provides the general form of these equations. The purpose of this Helpful Hint and the next is to further explain the equations and how they can be used to determine the equilibrium values of price and quantity.

Fig. 3.1 presents a simple demand and supply example in three equivalent forms: (a) schedules, (b) curves, and (c) equations. The demand and supply schedules in (a) are in the same format as Text Fig. 3.7. The price-quantity combinations from the schedules are plotted on the graph in (b), yielding linear demand and supply curves. What is new about this example is the representation of those curves by the equations in (c).

If you recall (Chapter 1 Appendix) the formula for the equation of a straight line ($y = a + bx$), you can see that the demand equation is the equation of a straight line. Instead of y, P is the dependent variable on the vertical axis, and instead of x, Q_D is the independent variable on the horizontal axis. The intercept on the vertical axis a is +5, and the slope b is –1. The supply equation is also linear and graphed in the same way, but with Q_S as the independent variable. The supply curve intercept on the vertical axis is +1, and the slope is +1. The negative slope of the demand curve reflects the law of demand, and the positive slope of the supply curve reflects the law of supply.

You can demonstrate the equivalence of the demand schedule, curve, and equation by substituting various values of Q_D from the schedule into the demand equation, and calculating the associated prices. These combinations of quantity demanded and price are the coordinates (Q_D, P) of the points on the demand curve. You can similarly demonstrate the equivalence of the supply schedule, curve, and equation.

FIGURE **3.1**

(a) Demand and Supply Schedules

Price ($)	Q_D	Q_S	Shortage (–)/ Surplus (+)
1	4	0	–4
2	3	1	–2
3	2	2	0
4	1	3	+2
5	0	4	+4

(b) Demand and Supply Curves

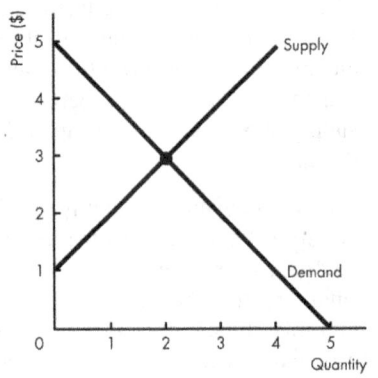

(c) Demand and Supply Equations

Demand: $P = 5 - 1Q_D$
Supply: $P = 1 + 1Q_S$

The demand and supply equations are very useful for calculating the equilibrium values of price and quantity. As the schedules and curves both show, two things are true in equilibrium: (1) the price is the same for consumers (the highest price they are willing to pay for the last unit) and producers (the lowest price they are willing to accept for the last unit) and (2) the quantity demanded equals the quantity supplied, so that there are no surpluses or shortages. In terms of the demand and supply equations, this means that, *in equilibrium,*

(1)   the price in both equations is the same. We will denote the equilibrium price as P^*.

(2) $Q_D = Q_S$ = the equilibrium quantity bought and sold. We will denote the equilibrium quantity as Q^*.

In equilibrium, the equations become

Demand: $P^* = 5 - 1Q^*$

Supply: $P^* = 1 + 1Q^*$

These equilibrium equations constitute a simple set of simultaneous equations. Since there are two equations (demand and supply) and two unknowns (P^* and Q^*), we can solve for the unknowns.

Begin the solution by setting demand equal to supply:

$$5 - 1Q^* = 1 + 1Q^*$$

Collecting like terms, we find

$$4 = 2Q^*$$
$$2 = Q^*$$

Once we have Q^* (equilibrium quantity), we can solve for the equilibrium price using either the demand or the supply equations. Look first at demand:

$$P^* = 5 - 1Q^*$$
$$P^* = 5 - 1(2)$$
$$P^* = 5 - 2$$
$$P^* = 3$$

Alternatively, substituting Q^* into the supply equation yields the same result:

$$P^* = 1 + 1Q^*$$
$$P^* = 1 + 1(2)$$
$$P^* = 1 + 2$$
$$P^* = 3$$

Once you have solved for Q^*, the fact that substituting it into either the demand or the supply equation yields the correct P^* provides a valuable check on your calculations. If you make a mistake in your calculations, when you substitute Q^* into the demand and supply equations, you will get two different prices. If that happens, you know to recheck your calculations. If you get the same price when you substitute Q^* into the demand and supply equations, you know your calculations are correct.

6 Economists have developed the convention of graphing quantity as the independent variable (on the horizontal x-axis) and price as the dependent variable (on the vertical y-axis), and the foregoing equations reflect this. Despite this convention, economists actually consider real-world prices to be the independent variables and quantities the dependent variables. In that case, the equations would take the form

Demand: $Q_D = 5 - 1P$
Supply: $Q_S = -1 + 1P$

You can solve these equations for yourself to see that they yield exactly the same values for P^* and Q^*. (*Hint:* First solve for P^* and then for Q^*.) Whichever form of the equations your instructor may use, the technique for solving the equations will be similar and the results identical.

SELF-TEST

True/False and Explain

Markets and Prices

1 In a competitive market, every single buyer and seller influences price.

2 The relative price of a good is the other goods that must be forgone to buy it.

3 A good's relative price can fall even when its money price rises.

Demand

4 The law of demand tells us that as the price of a good rises, demand decreases.

5 The demand curve is a willingness-and-ability-to-pay curve that measures marginal cost.

6 Hamburgers and fries are complements. If Burger Bar reduces the price of fries, the demand for hamburgers increases.

7 A decrease in income always shifts the demand curve leftward.

Supply

8 A supply curve shows the maximum price at which the last unit will be supplied.

9 If *A* and *B* are substitutes, an increase in the price of *A* always shifts the supply curve of *B* leftward.

10 When a cow is slaughtered for beef, its hide becomes available to make leather. Thus beef and leather are substitutes in production.

11 If the price of beef rises, there will be an increase in both the supply of leather and the quantity of beef supplied.

Market Equilibrium

12 When the actual price is above the equilibrium price, a shortage occurs.

Predicting Changes in Price and Quantity

13 If the expected future price of a good increases, there will always be an increase in equilibrium price and a decrease in equilibrium quantity.

14 Suppose new firms enter the steel market. *Ceteris paribus*, the equilibrium price of steel will always fall and the quantity will rise.

15 Suppose the demand for PCs increases while the cost of producing them decreases. The equilibrium quantity of PCs will rise and the price will always fall.

Multiple-Choice

Markets and Prices

1 A relative price is
  a the ratio of one price to another.
  b an opportunity cost.
  c a quantity of a "basket" of goods and services forgone.
  d determined by demand and supply.
  e all of the above.

Demand

2 If an increase in the price of good *A* causes the demand curve for good *B* to shift leftward,
  a *A* and *B* are substitutes in consumption.
  b *A* and *B* are complements in consumption.
  c *A* and *B* are complements in production.
  d *B* is an inferior good.
  e *B* is a normal good.

3 Which of the following could *not* cause an increase in demand for a commodity?
  a an increase in income
  b a decrease in income
  c a decrease in the price of a substitute
  d a decrease in the price of a complement
  e an increase in preferences for the commodity

4 Some sales managers are talking shop. Which of the following quotations refers to a movement along the demand curve?
  a "Since our competitors raised their prices our sales have doubled."
  b "It has been an unusually mild winter; our sales of wool scarves are down from last year."
  c "We decided to cut our prices, and the increase in our sales has been remarkable."
  d "The Green movement has sparked an increase in our sales of biodegradable products."
  e None of the above.

5   If Hamburger Helper is an inferior good, then, *ceteris paribus*, a decrease in income will cause
    a   a leftward shift of the demand curve for Hamburger Helper.
    b   a rightward shift of the demand curve for Hamburger Helper.
    c   a movement up along the demand curve for Hamburger Helper.
    d   a movement down along the demand curve for Hamburger Helper.
    e   none of the above.

6   A decrease in quantity demanded is represented by a
    a   rightward shift of the supply curve.
    b   rightward shift of the demand curve.
    c   leftward shift of the demand curve.
    d   movement upward and to the left along the demand curve.
    e   movement downward and to the right along the demand curve.

7   Which of the following "other things" are *not* held constant along a demand curve?
    a   income
    b   prices of related goods
    c   the price of the good itself
    d   preferences
    e   all of the above

Supply

8   The fact that a decline in the price of a good causes producers to reduce the quantity of the good supplied illustrates
    a   the law of supply.
    b   the law of demand.
    c   a change in supply.
    d   the nature of an inferior good.
    e   technological improvement.

9   A shift of the supply curve for rutabagas will be caused by
    a   a change in preferences for rutabagas.
    b   a change in the price of a related good that is a substitute in consumption for rutabagas.
    c   a change in income.
    d   a change in the price of rutabagas.
    e   none of the above.

10 If a factor of production can be used to produce either good *A* or good *B*, then *A* and *B* are
    a   substitutes in production.
    b   complements in production.
    c   substitutes in consumption.
    d   complements in consumption.
    e   normal goods.

11 Which of the following will shift the supply curve for good *X* leftward?
    a   a decrease in the wages of workers employed to produce *X*
    b   an increase in the cost of machinery used to produce *X*
    c   a technological improvement in the production of *X*
    d   a situation where quantity demanded exceeds quantity supplied
    e   all of the above

12 Some producers are chatting over a beer. Which of the following quotations refers to a movement along the supply curve?
    a   "Wage increases have forced us to raise our prices."
    b   "Our new, sophisticated equipment will enable us to undercut our competitors."
    c   "Raw material prices have skyrocketed; we will have to pass this on to our customers."
    d   "We anticipate a big increase in demand. Our product price should rise, so we are planning for an increase in output."
    e   "New competitors in the industry are causing prices to fall."

13 If an increase in the price of good *A* causes the supply curve for good *B* to shift rightward,
    a   *A* and *B* are substitutes in consumption.
    b   *A* and *B* are complements in consumption.
    c   *A* and *B* are substitutes in production.
    d   *A* and *B* are complements in production.
    e   *A* is a factor of production for making *B*.

Market Equilibrium

14 If the market for Twinkies is in equilibrium,
    a   Twinkies must be a normal good.
    b   producers would like to sell more at the current price.
    c   consumers would like to buy more at the current price.
    d   there will be a surplus.
    e   equilibrium quantity equals quantity demanded.

15 The price of a good will tend to fall if
    a   there is a surplus at the current price.
    b   the current price is above equilibrium.
    c   the quantity supplied exceeds the quantity demanded at the current price.
    d   all of the above are true.
    e   none of the above is true.

16 A surplus can be eliminated by
    a   increasing supply.
    b   government raising the price.
    c   decreasing the quantity demanded.
    d   allowing the price to fall.
    e   allowing the quantity bought and sold to fall.

17 A shortage is the amount by which quantity
    a   demanded exceeds quantity supplied.
    b   supplied exceeds quantity demanded.
    c   demanded increases when the price rises.
    d   demanded exceeds the equilibrium quantity.
    e   supplied exceeds the equilibrium quantity.

Predicting Changes in Price and Quantity

18 Which of the following will definitely cause an increase in the equilibrium price?
    a   an increase in both demand and supply
    b   a decrease in both demand and supply
    c   an increase in demand combined with a decrease in supply
    d   a decrease in demand combined with an increase in supply
    e   none of the above

19 Coffee is a normal good. A decrease in income will
    a   increase the price of coffee and increase the quantity demanded of coffee.
    b   increase the price of coffee and increase the quantity supplied of coffee.
    c   decrease the price of coffee and decrease the quantity demanded of coffee.
    d   decrease the price of coffee and decrease the quantity supplied of coffee.
    e   cause none of the above.

20 An increase in the price of Pepsi (a substitute for coffee) will
    a   increase the price of coffee and increase the quantity demanded of coffee.
    b   increase the price of coffee and increase the quantity supplied of coffee.
    c   decrease the price of coffee and decrease the quantity demanded of coffee.
    d   decrease the price of coffee and decrease the quantity supplied of coffee.
    e   cause none of the above.

21 A technological improvement lowers the cost of producing coffee. At the same time, preferences for coffee decrease. The *equilibrium quantity* of coffee will
    a   rise.
    b   fall.
    c   remain the same.
    d   rise or fall depending on whether the price of coffee falls or rises.
    e   rise or fall depending on the relative shifts of demand and supply curves.

22 Since 1980, there has been a dramatic increase in the number of working mothers. On the basis of this information alone, we can predict that the market for child-care services has experienced a(n)
    a   increase in demand.
    b   decrease in demand.
    c   increase in quantity demanded.
    d   decrease in quantity supplied.
    e   increase in supply.

23 If A and B are complementary goods (in consumption) and the cost of a factor of production used in the production of A decreases, the price of
    a   both A and B will rise.
    b   both A and B will fall.
    c A will fall and the price of B will rise.
    d A will rise and the price of B will fall.
    e A will fall and the price of B will remain unchanged.

24 The demand curve for knobs is $P = 75 - 6Q_D$ and the supply curve for knobs is $P = 35 + 2Q_S$. What is the equilibrium price of a knob?
    a $5
    b $10
    c $40
    d $45
    e   none of the above

25 The demand curve for tribbles is $P = 300 - 6Q_D$. The supply curve for tribbles is $P = 20 + 8Q_S$. If the price of a tribble was set at $120, the tribble market would experience
    a   equilibrium.
    b   excess demand causing a rise in price.
    c   excess demand causing a fall in price.
    d   excess supply causing a rise in price.
    e   excess supply causing a fall in price.

Short Answer Problems

⊕ 1 A tax on crude oil would raise the cost of the primary resource used in the production of gasoline. A proponent of such a tax has claimed that it will not raise the price of gasoline using the following argument: While the price of gasoline may rise initially, that price increase will cause the demand for gasoline to decrease, which will push the price back down. What is wrong with this argument?

2 Brussels sprouts and carrots are substitutes in consumption and, since they can both be grown on the same type of land, substitutes in production too. Suppose there is an increase in the demand for brussels sprouts. Trace the effects on price and quantity traded in both the brussels sprout and the carrot market. (Keep in mind Helpful Hint **4**.)

3 The information given in Table 3.1 is about the behaviour of buyers and sellers of fish at the market on a particular Saturday.

TABLE **3.1** DEMAND AND SUPPLY SCHEDULES FOR FISH

Price (per fish)	Quantity Demanded	Quantity Supplied
$0.50	280	40
$1.00	260	135
$1.50	225	225
$2.00	170	265
$2.50	105	290
$3.00	60	310
$3.50	35	320

a On graph paper, draw the demand curve and the supply curve. Be sure to label the axes. What is the equilibrium price?

b We will make the usual *ceteris paribus* assumptions about the demand curve so that it does not shift. List six factors that we are assuming do not change.

c We will also hold the supply curve constant by assuming that six factors do not change. List them.

d Explain briefly what would happen if the price was initially set at $3.

e Explain briefly what would happen if the price was initially set at $1.

f Explain briefly what would happen if the price was initially set at $1.50.

4 A newspaper reported, "Despite a bumper crop of cherries this year, the price drop for cherries won't be as much as expected because of short supplies of plums and peaches."

a Use a demand and supply graph for the cherry market to explain the effect of the bumper crop alone.

b On the same graph, explain the impact on the cherry market of the short supplies of plums and peaches.

5 The market for wine in Canada is initially in equilibrium with supply and demand curves of the usual shape. Beer is a close substitute for wine; cheese and wine are complements. Use demand and supply diagrams to analyse the effect of each of the following (separate) events on the equilibrium price and quantity in the Canadian wine market. Assume that all of the *ceteris paribus* assumptions continue to hold except for the event listed. For both equilibrium price and quantity you should indicate in each case whether the variable rises, falls, remains the same, or moves ambiguously (may rise or fall).

a The income of consumers falls (wine is a normal good).

b Early frost (state of nature) destroys a large part of the world grape crop.

c A new churning invention reduces the cost of producing cheese.

d A new fermentation technique is invented that reduces the cost of producing wine.

e A new government study is published that links wine drinking and increased heart disease.

f Costs of producing both beer and wine increase dramatically.

6 Table 3.2 lists the demand and supply schedules for cases of grape jam.

TABLE **3.2** DEMAND AND SUPPLY SCHEDULES FOR GRAPE JAM PER WEEK

Price (per case)	Quantity Demanded (cases)	Quantity Supplied (cases)
$70	20	140
$60	60	120
$50	100	100
$40	140	80
$30	180	60

a On the graph in Fig. 3.2, draw the demand and supply curves for grape jam. Be sure to properly label the axes. Label the demand and supply curves D_0 and S_0 respectively.

FIGURE **3.2**

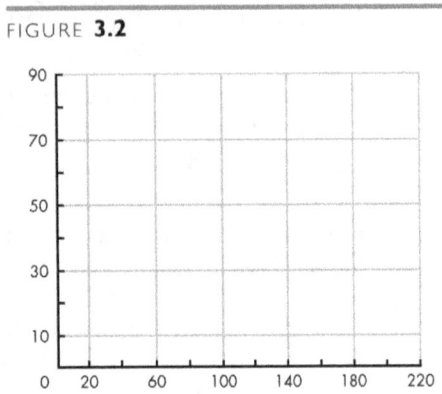

b What are the equilibrium price and quantity in the grape jam market? On your diagram, label the equilibrium point a.

c Is there a surplus or shortage at a price of $40? How much?

d The demand and supply schedules can also be represented by the following demand and supply equations:

Demand: $P = 75 - 0.25Q_D$

Supply: $P = 0.5Q_S$

Use these equations to solve for the equilibrium quantity (Q^*); equilibrium price (P^*). (*Hint:* Your answers should be the same as those in **6b**.)

e Suppose the population grows sufficiently that the demand for grape jam increases by 60 cases per week at every price.

i Construct a table (price, quantity demanded) of the new demand schedule.

ii Draw the new demand curve on your original graph and label it D_1.

iii Label the new equilibrium point b. What are the new equilibrium price and quantity?

iv What is the new demand equation? (*Hints:* What is the new slope? What is the new price-axis intercept?)

7 The demand equation for dweedles is

$$P = 8 - 1Q_D$$

The supply equation for dweedles is

$$P = 2 + 1Q_S$$

where P is the price of a dweedle in dollars, Q_D is the quantity of dweedles demanded, and Q_S is the quantity of dweedles supplied. The dweedle market is initially in equilibrium and income is $300.

a What is the equilibrium quantity (Q^*) of dweedles?

b What is the equilibrium price (P^*) of a dweedle?

c As a result of an increase in income to $500, the demand curve for dweedles shifts (the supply curve remains the same). The new demand equation is

$$P = 4 - 1Q_D$$

Use this information to calculate the new equilibrium quantity of dweedles; calculate the new equilibrium price of a dweedle.

d On the graph in Fig. 3.3, draw and label: (1) the supply curve, (2) the initial demand curve, (3) the new demand curve.

e Are dweedles a normal or inferior good? How do you know?

FIGURE **3.3**

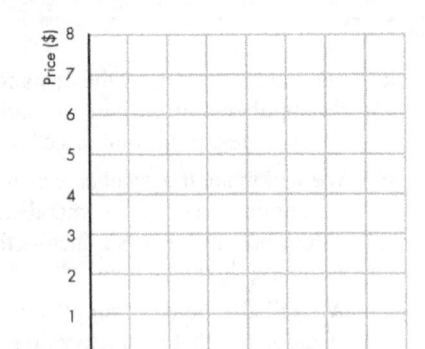

8 The demand equation for flubits is

$$P = 80 - 2Q_D$$

The supply equation for flubits is

$$P = 50 + 1Q_S$$

where P is the price of a flubit in dollars, Q_D is the quantity of flubits demanded, and Q_S is the quantity of flubits supplied. Assume that there are no changes in *ceteris paribus* assumptions.

a If the price of flubits was set at $56, calculate the exact surplus or shortage of flubits.

b Explain the adjustment process that will bring the situation above to equilibrium.

c What is the equilibrium quantity (Q^*) of flubits?

d What is the equilibrium price (P^*) of a flubit?

e Now assume that as a result of technological advances, the supply curve for flubits shifts (the demand curve remains the same). The new supply equation is

$$P = 20 + 1Q_S$$

Use this information to calculate the new equilibrium quantity of flubits; calculate the new equilibrium price of a flubit.

ANSWERS

True/False and Explain

1 F No single buyer or seller influences price. (55–56)

2 T Relative price is an opportunity cost. (55–56)

3 T If money prices of other goods rise even more, a good's relative price falls. If the price of gum rises from $1 to $2, but the price of coffee rises from $1 to $4, the opportunity cost of a pack of gum falls from 1 to 0.5 coffee forgone. (55–56)

4 F As price rises, *quantity demanded* decreases. (57–61)

5 F Measures marginal benefit. (57–61)

6 T Combined meal of hamburger and fries is now cheaper. (57–61)

7 F Leftward shift for normal good, rightward shift for inferior good. (57–61)

8 F Supply curve shows minimum price at which last unit supplied. (62–65)

9 F True if A and B are substitutes in production, but false if they are substitutes in consumption. (62–65)

10 F Beef and leather are complements in production because they are produced together of necessity. (62–65)

11 T For complements in production, a higher price for one good causes increased quantity supplied and increase in supply of the other good. (62–65)

12 F At $P >$ equilibrium P, there is surplus (quantity supplied > quantity demanded). (66–67)

13 F Higher expected future prices cause a rightward shift in demand and leftward shift in supply. Price rises, but Δ quantity depends on relative magnitude of shifts. (68–75)

14 T Increased number of firms causes rightward shift in supply, leading to a fall in price and increased quantity. (68–75)

15 F Quantity will increase but Δ price depends on the relative magnitude of the shifts in demand and supply. (68–75)

Multiple-Choice

1 e Definitions. (55–56)

2 b For example, higher-priced fries cause decreased demand for hamburgers. (57–61)

3 c Both income answers could be correct if the commodity were normal (**a**) or inferior (**b**). (57–61)

4 c The other answers describe shifts of the demand curve. (57–61)

5 b Changes in income shift the demand curve rather than causing movement along the demand curve. (57–61)

6 d Decreased quantity demanded is movement up along the demand curve. Could also be caused by a leftward shift in supply. (57–61)

ⓔ **7 c**   "Other things" shift the demand curve. Only price can change along a fixed demand curve. (57–61)

8 a   Question describes movement down along the supply curve. (62–65)

ⓔ **9 e**   Answers **a**, **b**, and **c** shift demand, while **d** causes movement along the supply curve. (62–65)

10 a   Definition of a substitute in production. (62–65)

11 b   Higher-priced factors of production shifts supply leftward. (62–65)

12 d   The other answers describe shifts of the supply curve. (62–65)

13 d   Definition of complements in production. Price changes of related goods in consumption shift demand. (62–65)

14 e   At equilibrium price, plans producers and consumers match; quantity demanded = quantity supplied. (66–67)

15 d   All answers describe price above the equilibrium price. (66–67)

16 d   Other answers make surplus (excess quantity supplied) larger. (66–67)

17 a   Shortage is horizontal distance between the demand and supply curves at a price below the equilibrium price. (66–67)

18 c   Answers **a** and **b** have an indeterminate effect on price, while **d** causes a lower price. (68–75)

19 d   Demand shifts leftward. (68–75)

20 b   Demand shifts rightward. (68–75)

21 e   Supply shifts rightward, demand shifts leftward, price definitely falls. (68–75)

22 a   More working mothers increases preferences for child care, causing increased demand for child-care services. (68–75)

ⓔ **23 c**   Supply A shifts rightward causing lower-priced A. This increases demand for B, causing higher-priced B. (68–75)

ⓔ **24 d**   See Helpful Hint **5**. Set demand equal to supply, solve for $Q^* = 5$. Substitute $Q^* = 5$ into either demand or supply equation to solve for P^*. (68–77)

ⓔ **25 b**   At $P = \$120$, $Q_D = 30$, and $Q_S = 12.5$. There is excess demand so price will rise. (68–77)

Short Answer Problems

ⓔ **1**   This argument confuses a movement along an unchanging demand curve with a shift in the demand curve. The proper analysis is as follows. The increase in the price of oil (the primary factor of production in the production of gasoline) will shift the supply curve of gasoline leftward. This will cause the equilibrium price of gasoline to increase and thus the quantity demanded of gasoline will decrease. Demand itself will not decrease—that is, the demand curve will not shift. The decrease in supply causes a movement along an unchanged demand curve.

2   The answer to this question requires us to trace through the effects on the two graphs in Fig. 3.4 on the next page: (a) for the brussels sprout market and (b) for the carrot market. The sequence of effects occurs in order of the numbers on the graphs.

Look first at the market for brussels sprouts. The increase in demand shifts the demand curve rightward from D_0 to D_1 (1), and the price of brussels sprouts rises. This price rise has two effects (2) on the carrot market. Since brussels sprouts and carrots are substitutes in consumption, the demand curve for carrots shifts rightward from D_0 to D_1. And, since brussels sprouts and carrots are substitutes in production, the supply curve of carrots shifts leftward from S_0 to S_1. Both of these shifts in the carrot market raise the price of carrots, causing feedback effects on the brussels sprout market. But remember the rule (Helpful Hint **4**) that each curve (demand and supply) for a given market can shift a maximum of *once*. Since the demand curve for brussels sprouts has already shifted, we can only shift the supply curve from S_0 to S_1 (3) because of the substitutes in production relationship. Each curve in each market has now shifted once and the analysis must stop. We can predict that the net effects are increases in the equilibrium prices of both brussels sprouts and carrots, and indeterminate changes in the equilibrium quantities in both markets.

FIGURE **3.4**

(a) Brussel Sprout Market

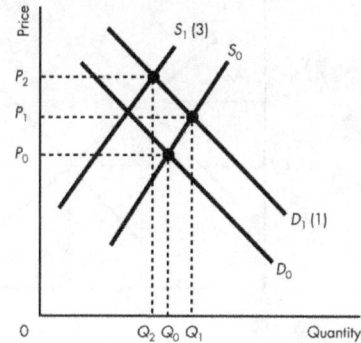

(b) Carrot Market

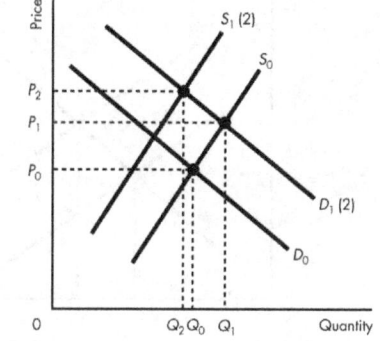

3 a The demand and supply curves are shown in Fig. 3.5. The equilibrium price is $1.50 per fish.

FIGURE **3.5**

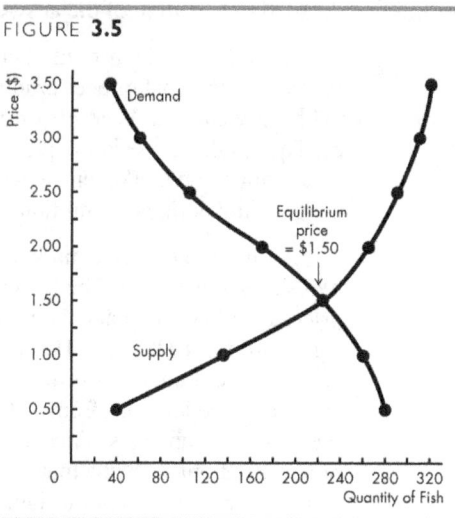

b Prices of related goods; expected future prices; income; expected future income and credit; population; preferences.

c Prices of productive resources; prices of related goods produced; expected future prices; number of suppliers; technology; state of nature.

d At a price of $3, quantity supplied (310) exceeds quantity demanded (60). Fish sellers find themselves with surplus fish. Rather than be stuck with unsold fish (which yields no revenue), some sellers cut their price in an attempt to increase the quantity of fish demanded. Competition forces other sellers to follow suit, and the price falls until it reaches the equilibrium price of $1.50, while quantity demanded increases until it reaches the equilibrium quantity of 225 units.

e At a price of $1, the quantity demanded (260) exceeds the quantity supplied (135)—there is a shortage. Unrequited fish buyers bid up the price in an attempt to get the "scarce" fish. Prices continue to be bid up as long as there is excess demand, so the quantity supplied increases in response to higher prices. Price and quantity supplied both rise until they reach the equilibrium price ($1.50) and quantity (225 units).

f At a price of $1.50, the quantity supplied exactly equals the quantity demanded (225). There is no excess demand (shortage) or excess supply (surplus), and therefore no tendency for the price or quantity to change.

4 a The demand and supply curves for the cherry market are shown in Fig. 3.6.

FIGURE **3.6**

Cherry Market

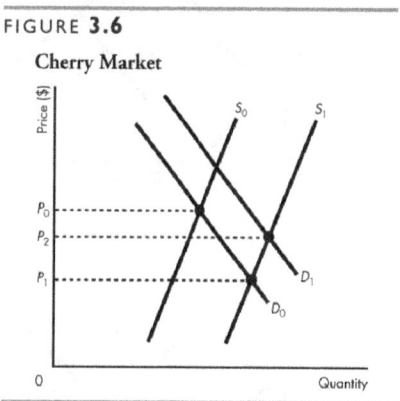

Suppose D_0 and S_0 represent the demand and supply curves for cherries last year. This year's bumper crop increases supply to S_1. Other things being equal, the price of cherries would fall from P_0 to P_1.

b But other things are not equal. Short supplies of plums and peaches (their supply curves have shifted leftward) drive up their prices. The increase in the prices of plums and peaches, which are substitutes in consumption for cherries, increases the demand for cherries to D_1. The net result is that the price of cherries only falls to P_2 instead of all the way to P_1.

5 The demand and supply diagrams for parts **a** to **e** are shown in Fig. 3.7.

FIGURE **3.7**

(a)

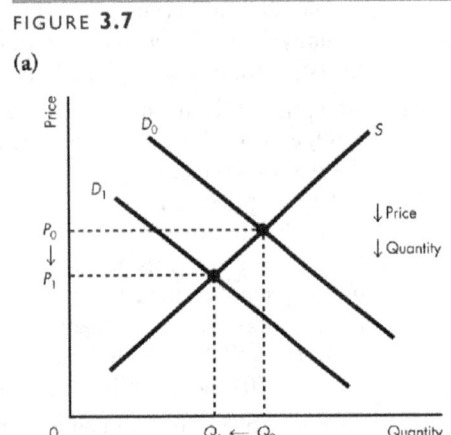

(b)

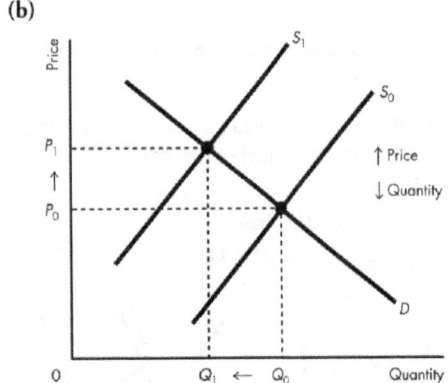

(c)

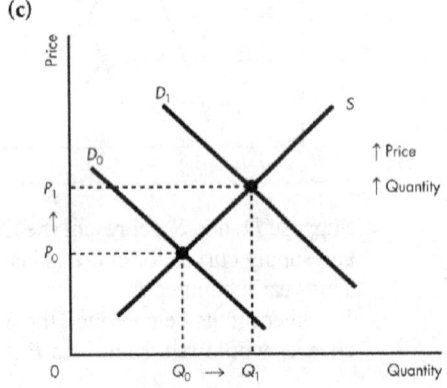

(d)

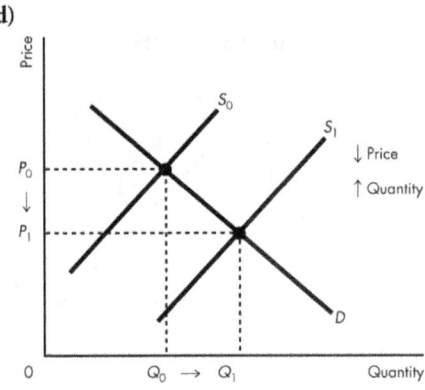

(e)

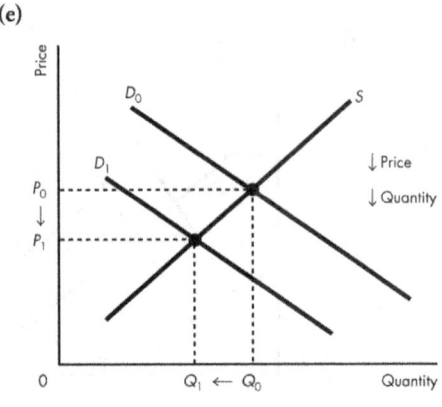

f Questions like this require the examination of two separate but related markets—the beer and wine markets. Since this kind of question often causes confusion for students, Fig. 3.8 on the next page gives a more detailed explanation of the answer.

Look first at the beer market. The increase in the cost of beer production shifts the supply curve of beer leftward from S_0 to S_1. The resulting rise in the price of beer affects the wine market since beer and wine are substitutes (in consumption).

Turning to the wine market, there are two shifts to examine. The increase in beer prices causes the demand for wine to shift rightward from D_0 to D_1. The increase in the cost of wine production shifts the supply curve of wine leftward from S_0 to S_1. This is the end of the analysis, since the question only asks about the wine market. The final result is a rise in the equilibrium price of wine and an ambiguous change in the quantity of wine. Although the diagram shows $Q_1 = Q_0$, Q_1 may be $\geq$ or $\leq Q_0$.

FIGURE **3.8**

(a) Beer Market

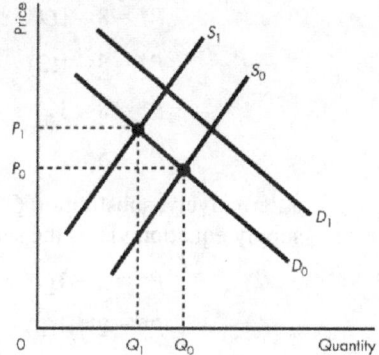

(b) Wine Market

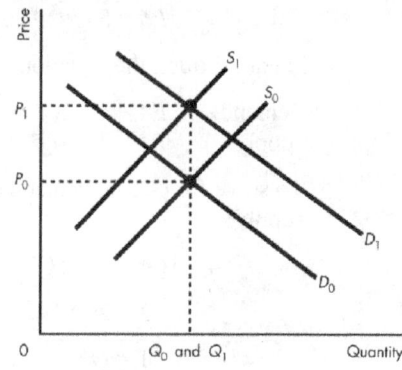

Many students rightfully ask, "But doesn't the rise in wine prices then shift the demand curve for beer rightward, causing a rise in beer prices and an additional increase in the demand for wine?" This question, which is correct in principle, is about the dynamics of adjustment, and these graphs are only capable of analysing once-over shifts of demand or supply. We could shift the demand for beer rightward, but the resulting rise in beer prices would lead us to shift the demand for wine a *second time*. In practice, stick to the rule that each curve (demand and supply) for a given market can shift a maximum of *once*.

6 a   The demand and supply curves for grape jam are shown in Fig. 3.2 Solution.

FIGURE **3.2** SOLUTION

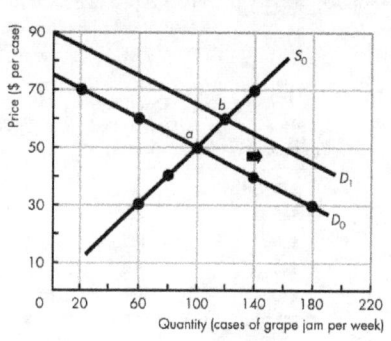

Quantity (cases of grape jam per week)

b   The equilibrium is given at the intersection of the demand and supply curves (labelled point *a*). The equilibrium price is $50 per case and the equilibrium quantity is 100 cases per week.

c   At a price of $40 there is a shortage of 60 cases per week.

d   In equilibrium, the equations become:

Demand: $P^* = 75 - 0.25Q^*$

Supply: $P^* = 0.5Q^*$

To solve for Q^*, set demand equal to supply:

$$75 - 0.25Q^* = 0.5Q^*$$
$$75 = 0.75Q^*$$
$$100 = Q^*.$$

To solve for P^*, we can substitute Q^* into either the demand or supply equations. Look at demand first:

$$P^* = 75 - 0.25Q^*$$
$$P^* = 75 - 0.25(100)$$
$$P^* = 75 - 25$$
$$P^* = 50$$

Alternatively, substituting Q^* into the supply equation yields the same result:

$$P^* = 0.5Q^*$$
$$P^* = 0.5(100)$$
$$P^* = 50$$

e   **i**   Table 3.3 also contains the (unchanged) quantity supplied, for reference purposes.

TABLE **3.3**   NEW DEMAND AND UNCHANGED SUPPLY SCHEDULES FOR GRAPE JAM PER WEEK

Price (per case)	Quantity Demanded (cases)	Quantity Supplied (cases)
$70	80	140
$60	120	120
$50	160	100
$40	200	80
$30	240	60

ii   The graph of the new demand curve, D_1, is shown in Fig. 3.2 Solution.

iii   The new equilibrium price is $60 per case and the quantity is 120 cases of grape jam per week.

iv   The new demand equation is $P = 90 - 0.25Q_D$. Notice that the slope of the new demand equation is the same as the slope of the original demand equation. An increase in demand of 60 cases at every price results in a rightward *parallel* shift of the demand curve. Since the two curves are parallel, they have the same slope. The figure of 90 is the price-axis intercept of the new demand curve, which you can see on your graph. *Remember:* The demand equation is the equation of a straight line ($y = a + bx$)—in this case, $a = 90$.

If you want additional practice in the use of demand and supply equations for calculating equilibrium values of price and quantity, you can use the new demand curve equation together with the supply curve equation to calculate the answers you found in **e iii**.

7   In equilibrium, the equations become

Demand: $P^* = 8 - 1Q^*$
Supply: $P^* = 2 + 1Q^*$

a   To solve for Q^*, set demand equal to supply:

$$8 - 1Q^* = 2 + 1Q^*$$
$$6 = 2Q^*$$
$$3 = Q^*$$

b   To solve for P^*, we can substitute Q^* into either the demand or supply equations. Look first at demand:

$$P^* = 8 - 1Q^*$$
$$P^* = 8 - 1(3)$$
$$P^* = 8 - 3$$
$$P^* = 5$$

Alternatively, substituting Q^* into the supply equation yields the same result:

$$P^* = 2 + 1Q^*$$
$$P^* = 2 + 1(3)$$
$$P^* = 2 + 3$$
$$P^* = 5$$

c   In equilibrium, the equations are

Demand: $P^* = 4 - 1Q^*$
Supply: $P^* = 2 + 1Q^*$

To solve for Q^*, set demand equal to supply:

$$4 - 1Q^* = 2 + 1Q^*$$
$$2 = 2Q^*$$
$$1 = Q^*$$

To solve for P^*, we can substitute Q^* into either the demand or supply equations. Look first at demand:

$$P^* = 4 - 1Q^*$$
$$P^* = 4 - 1(1)$$
$$P^* = 4 - 1$$
$$P^* = 3$$

Alternatively, substituting Q^* into the supply equation yields the same result:

$$P^* = 2 + 1Q^*$$
$$P^* = 2 + 1(1)$$
$$P^* = 2 + 1$$
$$P^* = 3$$

d   The supply curve, initial demand curve, and new demand curve for dweedles are shown in Fig. 3.3 Solution.

FIGURE **3.3** SOLUTION

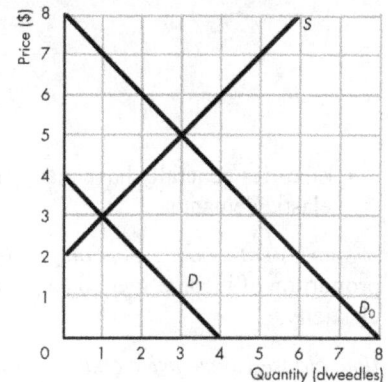

e   Dweedles are an inferior good. An increase in income (from $300 to $500) caused a decrease in demand—the demand curve for dweedles shifted leftward.

8 a   Substitute the price of $56 into the demand and supply equations to calculate the quantities demanded and supplied at that price. This is the mathematical equivalent of what you do on a graph when you identify a price on the vertical axis, move your eye across to the demand (or supply) curve, and then move your eye down to read the quantity on the horizontal axis.

Substituting into the demand equation, we find

$$P = 80 - 2Q_D$$
$$56 = 80 - 2Q_D$$
$$2Q_D = 24$$
$$Q_D = 12.$$

Substituting into the supply equation,

$$P = 50 + 1Q_S$$
$$56 = 50 + 1\,Q_S$$
$$6 = Q_S$$

Quantity demanded exceeds quantity supplied by 6 (12 − 6), so there is a shortage of 6 flubits.

b   A shortage means the price was set below the equilibrium price. Competition between consumers for the limited number of flubits will bid up the price and increase the quantity supplied until we reach the equilibrium price and quantity.

c   In equilibrium, the equations are

Demand: $P^* = 80 - 2Q^*$

Supply: $P^* = 50 + 1Q^*$

To solve for Q^*, set demand equal to supply:

$$80 - 2Q^* = 50 + 1Q^*$$
$$30 = 3Q^*$$
$$10 = Q^*$$

d   To solve for P^*, substitute Q^* into the demand equation:

$$P^* = 80 - 2Q^*$$
$$P^* = 80 - 2(10)$$
$$P^* = 80 - 20$$
$$P^* = 60$$

You can check this answer yourself by substituting Q^* into the supply equation.

e   The new equilibrium equations are

Demand: $P^* = 80 - 2Q^*$

Supply: $P^* = 20 + 1Q^*$

To solve for Q^*, set demand equal to supply:

$$80 - 2Q^* = 20 + 1Q^*$$
$$60 = 3Q^*$$
$$20 = Q^*$$

To solve for P^*, substitute Q^* into the supply equations:

$$P^* = 20 + 1Q^*$$
$$P^* = 20 + 1(20)$$
$$P^* = 20 + 20$$
$$P^* = 40$$

You can check this answer yourself by substituting Q^* into the demand equation.

Chapter 4
Elasticity

Price Elasticity of Demand

Price elasticity of demand (η) measures responsiveness of quantity demanded to change in price.

♦ η is a units-free measure of responsiveness.

$$\eta = \left| \frac{\% \, \Delta \text{ quantity demanded}}{\% \, \Delta \text{ price}} \right| = \left| \frac{\Delta Q / Q_{ave}}{\Delta P / P_{ave}} \right|$$

♦ Elasticity is *not* equal to slope. Moving down along a linear demand curve, slope ($\Delta P / \Delta Q$) is constant, but elasticity decreases as P_{ave} falls and Q_{ave} increases.

♦ | *When* | *Demand Is* |
| --- | --- |
| $\eta = \infty$ | **perfectly elastic** (horizontal) |
| $1 < \eta < \infty$ | **elastic** |
| $\eta = 1$ | **unit elastic** |
| $0 < \eta < 1$ | **inelastic** |
| $\eta = 0$ | **perfectly inelastic** (vertical) |

Elasticity and **total revenue** ($P \times Q$)—the **total revenue test**:

♦ | *When Demand Is* | *Price Cut Causes* |
| --- | --- |
| elastic ($\eta > 1$) | increased total revenue |
| unit elastic ($\eta = 1$) | no change total revenue |
| inelastic ($\eta < 1$) | decreased total revenue |

Elasticity of demand depends on

♦ *closeness of substitutes*—closer substitutes for a good yield higher elasticity.

• Goods that are defined more narrowly have higher elasticity.

• Necessities generally have poor substitutes and inelastic demands.

• Luxuries generally have many substitutes and elastic demands.

♦ *proportion of income spent on good*—the greater proportion of income spent on a good yields higher elasticity.

♦ *time elapsed since price change*—longer time lapse yields higher elasticity.

• Short-run demand describes responsiveness to a change in price *before* there is sufficient time for all substitutions to be made.

• Long-run demand describes responsiveness to a change in price *after* there is sufficient time for all substitutions to be made.

• Short-run demand is usually less elastic than long-run demand.

More Elasticities of Demand

Cross elasticity of demand (η_x) measures the *responsiveness* of quantity demanded of good *A* to a change in price of good *B*.

♦ $\eta_x = \dfrac{\% \, \Delta \text{ quantity demanded good } A}{\% \, \Delta \text{ price good } B}$

♦ $\eta_x > 0$ Goods are substitutes.

♦ $\eta_x = 0$ Goods are independent.

♦ $\eta_x < 0$ Goods are complements.

Income elasticity of demand (η_y) measures *responsiveness* of demand to a change in income.

♦ $\eta_y = \dfrac{\% \, \Delta \text{ quantity demanded}}{\% \, \Delta \text{ income}}$

♦ | *When* | *Demand Is* |
| --- | --- |
| $\eta_y > 1$ | income elastic (normal good) |
| $0 < \eta_y < 1$ | income inelastic (normal good) |
| $\eta_y < 0$ | negative income elasticity (inferior good) |

Elasticity of Supply

Elasticity of supply (η_s) measures *responsiveness* of quantity supplied to change in price.

◆ $\eta_s = \dfrac{\% \, \Delta \text{ quantity supplied}}{\% \, \Delta \text{ price}}$

◆

When	*Supply Is*
$\eta_s = \infty$	perfectly elastic (horizontal)
$1 < \eta_s < \infty$	elastic
$\eta_s = 1$	unit elastic
$0 < \eta_s < 1$	inelastic
$\eta_s = 0$	perfectly inelastic (vertical)

Elasticity of supply depends on

◆ *resources substitution possibilities*—the more common the productive resources used, the higher η_s.

◆ *time frame for supply decision*—the longer the time elapsed, from momentary to short-run to long-run supply, the higher η_s.

- Momentary supply describes responsiveness of quantity supplied immediately following a price change.

- Short-run supply describes responsiveness of quantity supplied to a price change when *some* technologically possible adjustments to production have been made.

- Long-run supply describes responsiveness of quantity supplied to a price change when *all* technologically possible adjustments to production have been made.

HELPFUL HINTS

1 There are many elasticity formulas in this chapter, but they are all based on the same simple, intuitive principle—*responsiveness*. All of the demand and supply elasticity formulas measure the *responsiveness* (sensitivity) *of quantity* (demanded or supplied) to changes in something else. Thus percentage change in quantity is always in the numerator of the relevant formula. As you come to understand how quantity responds to changes in price, income, and prices of related goods, you will be able to work out each elasticity formula, even if you have temporarily forgotten it.

2 The complete formula (see Text Fig. 4.2, page 85) for calculating the price elasticity of demand between two points on the demand curve is

$$\eta = \dfrac{\% \, \Delta \text{ quantity demanded}}{\% \, \Delta \text{ price}}$$

$$= \left| \left(\dfrac{\Delta Q}{Q_{ave}} \right) \Big/ \left(\dfrac{\Delta P}{P_{ave}} \right) \right|$$

The law of demand assures us that price and quantity demanded always move in opposite directions along any demand curve. Thus without the absolute value sign, the formula for the price elasticity of demand would yield a negative number. Because our main interest is in the *magnitude* of the response in quantity demanded to a change in price, for simplicity's sake we take the absolute value to guarantee a positive number. Whenever you see the often-used shorthand term "*elasticity* of demand," remember that it means the absolute value of the *price* elasticity of demand.

3 Elasticity is *not* the same as slope (although they are related). Along a straight-line demand curve the slope is constant, but the elasticity varies from infinity to zero as we move down the demand curve. To see why, look at the formula below, which is just a rearrangement of the elasticity formula in Helpful Hint **2**.

$$\eta = \left| \left(\dfrac{\Delta Q}{\Delta P} \right) \times \left(\dfrac{P_{ave}}{Q_{ave}} \right) \right|$$

The term in the first parentheses is simply the inverse of the slope. Since the slope is constant everywhere along a straight-line demand curve, so is the inverse of the slope. Consider, however, what happens to the term in the second parentheses as we move down the demand curve. At the "top" of the demand curve, P_{ave} is very large and Q_{ave} is very small, so the term in the second parentheses is large. As we move down the demand curve, P_{ave} becomes smaller and Q_{ave} becomes larger, so the term in the second parentheses falls in value. The net result is that the absolute value of the price elasticity of demand falls as we move down the demand curve.

4 One of the most practical and important uses of the concept of price elasticity of demand is that it allows us to predict the effect on total revenue of a change in price. A fall in price will increase total revenue if demand is elastic, leave total revenue unchanged if demand is unit elastic, and decrease total revenue if demand is inelastic. Because price and quantity demanded always

move in opposite directions along a demand curve, a fall in price will cause an increase in quantity demanded. Since total revenue equals price times quantity, the fall in price will tend to decrease total revenue, while the increase in quantity demanded will increase total revenue. The net effect depends on which of these individual effects is larger.

The concept of price elasticity of demand conveniently summarizes the net effect. For example, if demand is elastic, the percentage change in quantity demanded is greater than the percentage change in price. Hence, with a fall in price, the quantity effect dominates and total revenue will increase. If, however, demand is inelastic, the percentage change in quantity demanded is less than the percentage change in price. Hence, with a fall in price, the price effect dominates and total revenue will decrease.

5 Two other important elasticity concepts are the income elasticity of demand and the cross elasticity of demand.

Income elasticity of demand:

$$\eta_y = \frac{\% \Delta \text{ quantity demanded}}{\% \Delta \text{ income}}$$

$$= \left(\frac{\Delta Q}{Q_{ave}} \right) \Big/ \left(\frac{\Delta Y}{Y_{ave}} \right)$$

Cross elasticity of demand:

$$\eta_x = \frac{\% \Delta \text{ quantity demanded good } A}{\% \Delta \text{ price good } B}$$

$$= \left(\frac{\Delta Q^A}{Q^A_{ave}} \right) \Big/ \left(\frac{\Delta P^B}{P^B_{ave}} \right)$$

Notice that these two elasticity formulas do *not* have absolute value signs and can take on either positive or negative values. While these formulas measure responsiveness, both the magnitude *and the direction* of the response are important. In the case of income elasticity of demand, the response of quantity demanded to an increase in income will be positive for a normal good and negative for an inferior good. In the case of cross elasticity of demand, the response of the quantity demanded of good A to an increase in the price of good B will be positive if the goods are substitutes and negative if the goods are complements.

In calculating an income elasticity or a cross elasticity, be alert to the fact that the *price of the good in the numerator* of the formula *is assumed constant*. Income elasticity measures the quantity response to a change in income, *ceteris paribus*. Cross elasticity measures the quantity response of good A to a change in the price of good B, *ceteris paribus*. This means that we cannot simply read numerical values for calculating these elasticities from the equilibrium positions of a set of demand and supply curves. For example, when income increases, demand shifts rightward (for a normal good), and the new equilibrium quantity will also have a higher equilibrium price. To calculate income elasticity correctly, we compare the income and quantity demanded of the initial equilibrium with the new income and quantity demanded. To obtain the correct new quantity demanded, we must use the new demand curve, but must calculate the quantity demanded that would have prevailed at the *initial*, unchanged price. (See Short Answer Problems **7** and **8** for examples.)

S E L F - T E S T

True/False and Explain

Price Elasticity of Demand

1 The price elasticity of demand measures how responsive prices are to changes in demand.

2 Price elasticity of demand is constant along a linear demand curve.

3 If a decrease in supply causes total revenue to increase, demand must be inelastic.

4 If a 9 percent increase in price leads to a 5 percent decrease in quantity demanded, total revenue has decreased.

5   If you like Pepsi cola and Coca-Cola about the same, your demand for Pepsi is likely to be elastic.

6   The more narrowly we define a good, the more elastic its demand.

7   If your expenditures on toothpaste are a small proportion of your total income, your demand for toothpaste is likely to be inelastic.

8   The demand for gasoline is likely to become more inelastic with the passage of time after a price increase.

More Elasticities of Demand

9   An inferior good has a negative cross elasticity of demand.

10 If a 10 percent increase in the price of widgets causes a 6 percent increase in the quantity of woozles demanded, then widgets and woozles must be complements.

11 We would expect a negative cross elasticity of demand between hamburgers and hamburger buns.

Elasticity of Supply

12 Elasticity of supply equals the change in quantity supplied divided by the change in price.

13 A horizontal supply curve is perfectly elastic.

14 Goods produced with rare resources have a low elasticity of supply.

15 Supply is generally more inelastic in the long run than in the short run.

Multiple-Choice

Price Elasticity of Demand

1   There are two points on the demand curve for volleyballs, as shown in Table 4.1.

TABLE **4.1**

Price per Volleyball	Quantity Demanded
$19	55
$21	45

What is the elasticity of demand between these two points?
a   2.5
b   2.0
c   0.5
d   0.4
e   none of the above

2   If the price elasticity of demand is 2, a 1 percent decrease in price will
a   double the quantity demanded.
b   reduce the quantity demanded by half.
c   increase the quantity demanded by 2%.
d   reduce the quantity demanded by 2%.
e   increase the quantity demanded by 0.5%.

3   If price elasticity of demand is zero, then as the price falls
a   total revenue does not change.
b   quantity demanded does not change.
c   quantity demanded falls to zero.
d   total revenue increases from zero.
e   none of the above occurs.

4 A perfectly vertical demand curve has a price elasticity of
- **a** zero.
- **b** greater than zero but less than one.
- **c** one.
- **d** greater than one.
- **e** infinity.

5 A union leader who claims that "higher wages increase living standards without causing unemployment" believes that the demand for labour is
- **a** income elastic.
- **b** income inelastic.
- **c** perfectly elastic.
- **d** perfectly inelastic.
- **e** unit elastic.

6 Business people talk about price elasticity of demand without using the actual term. Which of the following statements reflects elastic demand for a product?
- **a** "A price cut won't help me. It won't increase sales, and I'll just get less money for each unit that I was selling before."
- **b** "I don't think a price cut will make any difference to my bottom line. What I may gain from selling more I would lose on the lower price."
- **c** "My customers are real bargain hunters. Since I set my prices just a few cents below my competitors', customers have flocked to the store and sales are booming."
- **d** "With the recent economic recovery, people have more income to spend and sales are booming, even at the same prices as before."
- **e** None of the above.

7 A technological breakthrough lowers the cost of photocopiers. If the demand for photocopiers is price inelastic, we predict that photocopier sales will
- **a** fall and total revenue will rise.
- **b** fall and total revenue will fall.
- **c** rise and total revenue will rise.
- **d** rise and total revenue will fall.
- **e** rise but changes in total revenue will depend on elasticity of supply.

8 A decrease in tuition fees will decrease the university's total revenue if the price elasticity of demand for university education is
- **a** negative.
- **b** greater than zero but less than one.
- **c** equal to one.
- **d** greater than one.
- **e** less than the price elasticity of supply.

9 If the demand for orange juice is price elastic, a severe frost that destroys large quantities of oranges will likely
- **a** reduce the equilibrium price of juice, but increase total consumer spending on it.
- **b** reduce the equilibrium quantity of juice as well as total consumer spending on it.
- **c** reduce both the equilibrium quantity and the price of juice.
- **d** increase the equilibrium price of juice as well as total consumer spending on it.
- **e** increase the equilibrium price of juice, but leave total consumer spending on it constant.

10 If a 4 percent rise in the price of peanut butter causes total revenue to fall by 8 percent, demand for peanut butter
- **a** is elastic.
- **b** is inelastic.
- **c** is unit elastic.
- **d** has an elasticity of 1/2.
- **e** has an elasticity of 2.

11 Tina and Brian work for the same recording company. Tina claims that they would be better off by increasing the price of their CDs while Brian claims that they would be better off by decreasing the price. We can conclude that
- **a** Tina thinks the demand for CDs has price elasticity of zero, and Brian thinks price elasticity equals one.
- **b** Tina thinks the demand for CDs has price elasticity equal to one, and Brian thinks price elasticity equals zero.
- **c** Tina thinks the demand for CDs is price elastic, and Brian thinks it is price inelastic.
- **d** Tina thinks the demand for CDs is price inelastic, and Brian thinks it is price elastic.
- **e** Tina and Brian should stick to singing and forget about economics.

12 Given the relationship shown in Fig. 4.1 on the next page between total revenue from the sale of a good and the quantity of the good sold,
- **a** this is an inferior good.
- **b** this is a normal good.
- **c** the elasticity of demand is zero.
- **d** the elasticity of demand is infinity.
- **e** the elasticity of demand is one.

FIGURE **4.1**

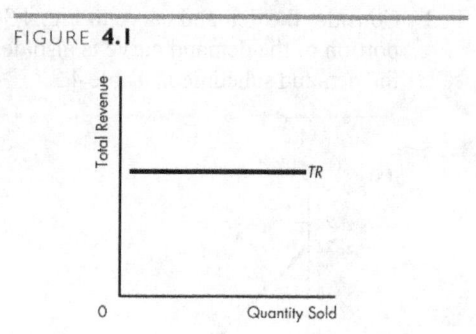

13 If the Jets decrease ticket prices and find that total revenue does not change, the price elasticity of demand for tickets is
a zero.
b greater than zero, but less than one.
c equal to one.
d greater than one.
e inferior.

14 The fact that butter has margarine as a close substitute in consumption
a makes the supply of butter more elastic.
b makes the supply of butter less elastic.
c makes the demand for butter more elastic.
d makes the demand for butter less elastic.
e does not affect butter's elasticity of supply or demand.

15 A given percentage increase in the price of a good is likely to cause a larger percentage decline in quantity demanded
a the shorter the passage of time.
b the larger the proportion of income spent on it.
c the harder it is to obtain good substitutes.
d all of the above.
e none of the above.

More Elasticities of Demand

16 A negative value for
a price elasticity of supply implies an upward-sloping supply curve.
b cross elasticity of demand implies complementary goods.
c price elasticity of demand implies an inferior good.
d income elasticity of demand implies a normal good.
e income elasticity of demand implies an error in your calculation.

17 The cross elasticity of the demand for white tennis balls with respect to the price of yellow tennis balls is probably
a negative and high.
b negative and low.
c positive and high.
d positive and low.
e zero.

18 If a 10 percent increase in income causes a 5 percent increase in quantity demanded (at a constant price), what is the income elasticity of demand?
a 0.5
b −0.5
c 2.0
d −2.0
e none of the above

19 Luxury goods tend to have income elasticities of demand that are
a greater than one.
b greater than zero but less than one.
c positive.
d negative.
e first positive and then negative as income increases.

20 If a 4 percent decrease in income (at a constant price) causes a 2 percent decrease in the consumption of dweedles,
a the income elasticity of demand for dweedles is negative.
b dweedles are a necessity and a normal good.
c dweedles are a luxury and a normal good.
d dweedles are an inferior good.
e a and d are true.

Elasticity of Supply

21 When price goes from $1.50 to $2.50, quantity supplied increases from 9,000 to 11,000 units. What is the price elasticity of supply?
a 0.4
b 0.8
c 2.5
d 4.0
e none of the above

22 Preferences for brussels sprouts increase. The price of brussels sprouts will not change if the price elasticity of
a demand is 0.
b demand is 1.
c supply is 0.
d supply is 1.
e supply is infinity.

23 A sudden end-of-summer heat wave increases the demand for air conditioners and catches suppliers with no reserve inventories. The momentary supply curve for air conditioners is
  a perfectly elastic.
  b perfectly inelastic.
  c elastic.
  d upward sloping.
  e horizontal.

24 The long-run supply curve is likely to be
  a more elastic than momentary supply, but less elastic than short-run supply.
  b less elastic than momentary supply, but more elastic than short-run supply.
  c less elastic than both momentary and short-run supply curves.
  d more elastic than both momentary and short-run supply curves.
  e vertical.

25 Long-run elasticity of supply of a good is greater than short-run elasticity of supply because
  a more substitutes in consumption for the good can be found.
  b more complements in consumption for the good can be found.
  c more technological ways of adjusting supply can be exploited.
  d income rises with more elapsed time.
  e the long-run supply curve is steeper.

Short Answer Problems

1 Why does supply tend to be more elastic in the long run?

2 In Fig. 4.2, which demand curve (D_A or D_B) is more elastic in the price range P_1 to P_2? Explain why. (*Hint:* Use the formula for price elasticity of demand.)

FIGURE **4.2**

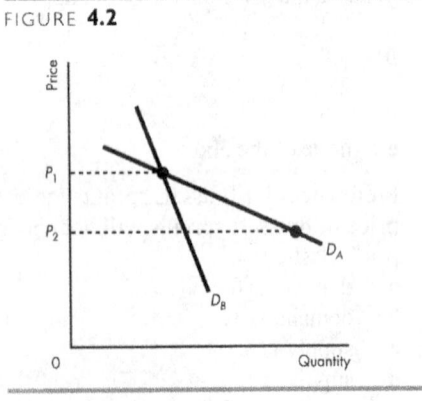

3 Consider the demand curve in Fig. 4.3(a). A portion of the demand curve is also described by the demand schedule in Table 4.2.

FIGURE **4.3**

(a)

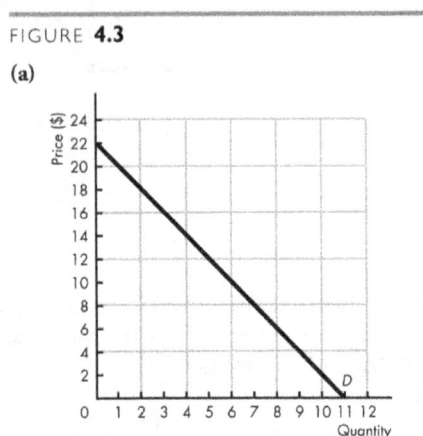

(b)

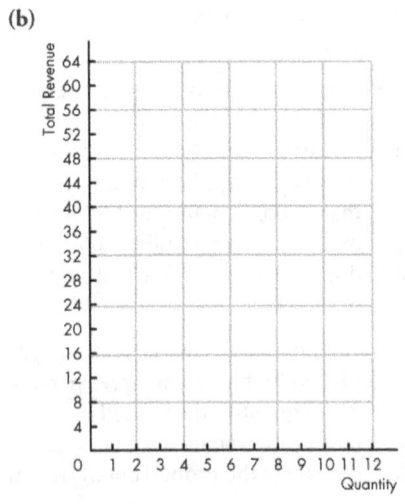

TABLE **4.2**

Price ($)	Quantity Demanded	Total Revenue
22	0	
20	1	
18	2	
16	3	
14	4	
12	5	
10	6	
8	7	
6	8	

Fill in the numbers for total revenue in the last column of Table 4.2, and graph your results on Fig. 4.3(b). Describe the shape of the total revenue curve as quantity increases (price decreases).

4 Using the same information for the demand curve in Short Answer Problem **3**:

a Complete the second and third columns of Table 4.3: η (the price elasticity of demand) and ΔTR (the change in total revenue) as the price falls from the higher price to the lower price. Describe the relationship between elasticity and change in total revenue as price falls (moving down the demand curve).

TABLE **4.3**

$\Delta P(\$)$	η	$\Delta TR(\$)$	η'	$\Delta TR'(\$)$
16 — 14				
14 — 12				
12 — 10				
10 — 8				
8 — 6				

b Suppose income increases from $10,000 to $14,000, causing an increase in demand: at every price, quantity demanded increases by 2 units. Draw the new demand curve on Fig. 4.3(a) and label it D'. Use this new demand curve to complete the last two columns of Table 4.3 for η' (the new price elasticity of demand) and $\Delta TR'$ (the new change in total revenue).

c Using the price range between $16 and $14, explain why D' is more inelastic than D.

d Calculate the income elasticity of demand, assuming the price remains constant at $12. Is this a normal or inferior good? Explain why you could have answered the question even without calculating the income elasticity of demand.

5 The demand equation for woozles is $P = 60 - 2Q_D$. The supply equation for woozles is $P = 32 + 5Q_S$, where P is the price of a woozle in dollars, Q_D is the quantity of woozles demanded, and Q_S is the quantity of woozles supplied.

a Calculate the price elasticity of demand for woozles between $Q_D = 4$ and $Q_D = 6$.

b Initially, the woozle market is in equilibrium with $P^* = 52$ and $Q^* = 4$. Then, the supply curve shifts (the demand curve remains constant) yielding a new equilibrium price of $P^* = 48$.

Using all of the relevant information above, show *two separate methods* for determining whether total revenue increases, decreases, or remains constant in moving from the initial equilibrium to the new equilibrium.

6 Suppose Jean loses his present job and his monthly income falls from $10,000 to $6,000, while his monthly purchases of grits increase from 200 to 400.

a Calculate his income elasticity of demand for grits.

b Are grits a normal or inferior good? Explain why.

7 The demand equation for tribbles is $P = 50 - 1Q_D$. The supply equation for tribbles is $P = 20 + 0.5Q_S$, where P is the price of a tribble in dollars, Q_D is the quantity of tribbles demanded, and Q_S is the quantity of tribbles supplied. The tribble market is initially in equilibrium, and income is $180.

a What is the equilibrium quantity (Q^*) of tribbles?

b What is the equilibrium price (P^*) of a tribble?

c As a result of a decrease in income to $120, the demand curve for tribbles shifts (the supply curve remains the same). The new demand equation is:

$$P = 110 - 1Q_D$$

Use this information to calculate the new equilibrium quantity of tribbles; calculate the new equilibrium price of a tribble.

d Calculate the income elasticity of demand for tribbles. Are tribbles a normal or inferior good? (*Hint*: In your calculation be sure to (1) use the information about the *initial* equilibrium conditions [price, quantity, and income] and (2) keep in mind that price is assumed *constant* in calculating income elasticity; only income and quantity change.)

8 Table 4.4 gives the demand schedules for good *A* when the price of good *B* (P_B) is $8 and $12. Complete the last column of the table by computing the cross elasticity of demand between goods *A* and *B* for each of the three prices of *A*. Are *A* and *B* complements or substitutes?

TABLE **4.4** DEMAND SCHEDULES FOR GOOD *A*

	$P_B = \$8$	$P_B = \$12$	
P_A	Q_A	Q'_A	η_x
$8	2,000	4,000	
$7	4,000	6,000	
$6	6,000	8,000	

ANSWERS

True/False and Explain

1 **F** It measures the responsiveness of quantity demanded to ΔP. (84–90)

2 **F** Slope is constant; η falls as we move down the demand curve. (84–90)

3 **T** Decreased *S* causes increased *P* and increased total revenue, so demand is inelastic. (84–90)

4 **F** (% increase *P*) > (% decrease *Q*), so total revenue ($P \times Q$) increases. (84–90)

5 **T** Colas are substitutes for you. (84–90)

6 **T** With narrower definition, there are more substitutes. (84–90)

7 **T** Lower proportion of income spent on good, more inelastic is demand. (84–90)

8 **F** Elasticity increases with elapsed time. (84–90)

9 **F** An inferior good has negative income elasticity; the cross elasticity sign depends on whether substitute or complement. (91–93)

10 **F** η_x is positive so goods are substitutes. (91–93)

11 **T** η_x is negative for complements. (91–93)

12 **F** η_s equals *percentage* change in quantity supplied divided by *percentage* change in price. (94–97)

13 **T** η_s = infinity. (94–97)

14 **T** $\eta_s < 1$. (94–97)

15 **F** Supply is more elastic in the long run. (94–97)

Multiple-Choice

1 **b** $|(-10/50)/(2/20)| = 2$. (84–90)

2 **c** $\eta = |(\% \Delta Q_D)/(\% \Delta P)| = |(1/5)/(1/10)| = 2$. Q_D and *P* are always inversely related on the demand curve. (84–90)

3 **b** Demand curve is vertical, so lower *P* does not Δ quantity demanded. (84–90)

4 **a** Definition. (84–90)

5 **d** Labour demand curve would be vertical. (84–90)

6 **c** Small fall in *P* causes large increase in quantity demanded. **a** inelastic, **b** unit elastic, **d** on income elasticity. (84–90)

7 **d** Rightward shift in supply causes increased quantity sold and lower *P*; with inelastic demand causes decreased total revenue. (84–90)

8 **b** Lower *P* causes decreased total revenue when $\eta < 1$. η is never negative. (84–90)

9 **b** Decreased *S* causes decreased Q_D and higher *P*. Since $\eta > 1$, higher *P* causes decreased expenditure. (84–90)

10 **a** If higher *P* causes decreased total revenue, η must be > 1. Must know (% ΔQ_D) to precisely calculate η. (84–90)

11 **d** Better off means increased total revenue. By definition of relation between higher *P*, η, and total revenue. (84–90)

12 **e** Note total revenue (*TR*) on *y*-axis. Since *TR* is constant as increased *Q* (and presumably lower *P*), $\eta = 1$. **a**, **b** depend on η_y. (84–90)

13 **c** Total revenue test. (84–90)

14 **c** Closer substitutes yield higher elasticity of demand. (84–90)

15 **b** η increases with increased proportion of income spent on a good. η increases when longer time passage and easier to obtain substitutes. (84–90)

16 **b** η_s and η are never negative. η_y is negative for an inferior good. (91–93)

17 **c** Close substitutes, so η_x is positive and very elastic (high). (91–93)

18 **a** $\eta_y = (\% \, \Delta Q_D)/(\% \, \Delta \text{ income}) = 5/10 = 0.5$. (91–93)

19 **a** See answer to **20** below. **c** is correct, but **a** is the best answer. (91–93)

20 **b** $\eta_y > 0$ so it is a normal good. Necessities tend to have $\eta_y < 1$, while luxuries tend to have $\eta_y > 1$. (91–93)

21 **a** $\eta_s = (\% \, \Delta Q_S)/(\% \, \Delta P) = (2{,}000/10{,}000)/(1/2) = 0.4$. (94–97)

22 **e** Increased D causes no ΔP if the supply curve is horizontal ($\eta_s = $ infinity). (94–97)

23 **b** Definition. (94–97)

24 **d** Definition. Momentary supply curve is the most vertical. (94–97)

25 **c** Definition. **a, b, d** affect demand, not supply. Long-run supply curve is flatter than short-run. (94–97)

Short Answer Problems

1 Supply is more elastic in the long run, because the passage of time allows producers to find better (more efficient) ways of producing that are not available in the short run. The responsiveness of production to an increase in price will increase as firms have time to discover and implement new technologies or to increase the scale of operation.

2 D_A is more elastic than D_B. To see why, look at the formula for price elasticity of demand:

$$\eta = \left| \frac{\% \, \Delta \text{ quantity demanded}}{\% \, \Delta \text{ price}} \right|$$

The percentage change in price is the same for the two demand curves. But the percentage change in quantity is greater for D_A. At P_1, the initial quantity demanded is the same for both demand curves (Q_1). With the fall in price to P_2, the increase in quantity demanded is greater for D_A (to Q_{2A}) than for D_B (to Q_{2B}). Therefore D_A is more elastic than D_B. See Fig. 4.2 Solution.

FIGURE **4.2** SOLUTION

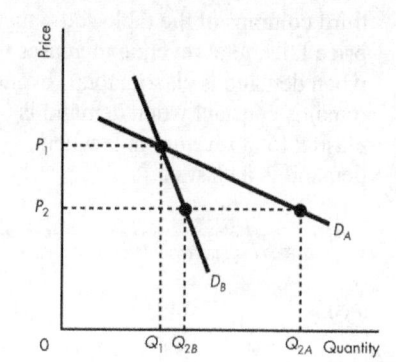

3 The numbers for total revenue are shown in Table 4.2 Solution. The total revenue curve is shown in Fig. 4.3(b) Solution. The total revenue curve first increases (at a diminishing rate—its slope is decreasing as we move up the curve), then reaches a maximum between $Q = 5$ and $Q = 6$, then decreases. We will encounter this pattern of changing total revenue again in studying monopoly in Chapter 13.

TABLE **4.2** SOLUTION

Price ($)	Quantity Demanded	Total Revenue
22	0	0
20	1	20
18	2	36
16	3	48
14	4	56
12	5	60
10	6	60
8	7	56
6	8	48

FIGURE **4.3(b)** SOLUTION

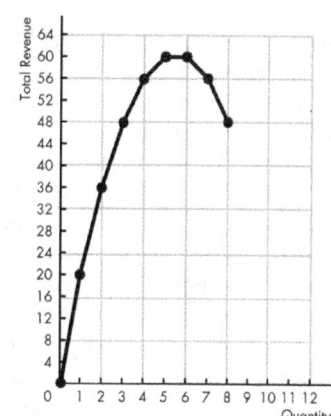

4 a The completed columns are shown in Table 4.3 Solution. The second and third columns of the table show that as price falls, total revenue increases when demand is elastic; total revenue remains constant when demand is unit elastic; total revenue falls when demand is inelastic.

TABLE **4.3** SOLUTION

ΔP ($)	η	ΔTR ($)	η'	$\Delta TR'$ ($)
16 — 14	2.14	+8	1.36	+4
14 — 12	1.44	+4	1.00	0
12 — 10	1.00	0	0.73	−4
10 — 8	0.69	−4	0.53	−8
8 — 6	0.47	−8	0.37	−12

b The new demand curve is labelled D' in Fig. 4.3(a) Solution. The last two columns of the table have been completed on the basis of the new demand curve.

FIGURE **4.3(a)** SOLUTION

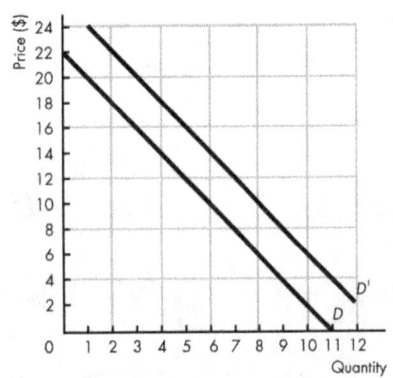

c Since they are parallel, D' and D have exactly the same slope. Thus we know that for a given change in price, the change in quantity demanded will be the same for the two curves. However, elasticity is determined by *percentage* changes, and the percentage change in quantity demanded is different for the two curves, although the percentage change in price will be the same. For a given percentage change in price, the percentage change in quantity demanded will always be less for D'. For example, as the price falls from $16 to $14 (a 13 percent change), the quantity demanded increases from 5 to 6 units along D', but from 3 to 4

units along D. The percentage change in quantity demanded is only 18 percent along D' and 29 percent along D. Since the percentage change in price is the same for both curves, D' is more inelastic than D.

d Income increases from $10,000 to $14,000. At a constant price of $12, the increase in income, which shifts out the demand curve to D', increases the quantity consumers will demand from 5 units to 7 units. Substituting these numbers into the formula for the income elasticity of demand yields

$$\eta_y = \left(\frac{\Delta Q}{Q_{ave}}\right)\Big/\left(\frac{\Delta Y}{Y_{ave}}\right)$$
$$= \left(\frac{2}{6}\right)\Big/\left(\frac{4,000}{12,000}\right) = +1$$

The income elasticity of demand is a positive number, since both ΔQ and ΔY are positive. Therefore this is a normal good. We already knew that from the information in part **b**, which stated that the demand curve shifted rightward with an increase in income. If this were an inferior good, the increase in income would have shifted the demand curve leftward and the income elasticity of demand would have been negative.

5 a In order to calculate price elasticity of demand, we need to know two points (each point a combination of price and quantity demanded) on the demand curve. We are given only the quantity demanded coordinate of each point. By substituting $Q_D = 4$ and $Q_D = 6$ into the demand equation, we can solve for the two price coordinates:

At $Q_D = 4$; $P = 60 - 2(4) = 52$

At $Q_D = 6$; $P = 60 - 2(6) = 48$

These price and quantity demanded coordinates can now be substituted into the formula for the price elasticity of demand:

$$\eta = \left|\left(\frac{\Delta Q}{Q_{ave}}\right)\Big/\left(\frac{\Delta P}{P_{ave}}\right)\right|$$
$$= \left|\left(\frac{-2}{5}\right)\Big/\left(\frac{4}{50}\right)\right| = 5$$

b One method is simply to compare total revenue ($P \times Q$) at each equilibrium:

- Initial equilibrium:

Total revenue $= (P \times Q) = (52 \times 4) = 208$.

- New equilibrium:

If $P^* = 48$, Q^* can be calculated by substituting P^* into the demand equation:

$$48 = 60 - 2Q^*$$

$$2Q^* = 12$$

$$Q^* = 6$$

So total revenue $= (P \times Q) = (48 \times 6) = 288$. In moving from the initial to the new equilibrium, total revenue has increased.

A second method is to use the information from part **a** on the price elasticity of demand. We know that between $Q_D = 4$ and $Q_D = 6$ on the demand curve, demand is elastic. These two points correspond to the initial equilibrium and, after the shift of the supply curve, the new equilibrium. Since demand here is elastic, we know that the fall in price from $P = 52$ to $P = 48$ will increase total revenue.

6 a Using the formula for income elasticity of demand:

$$\eta_y = \left(\frac{\Delta Q}{Q_{ave}}\right)\Big/\left(\frac{\Delta Y}{Y_{ave}}\right)$$

$$= \left(\frac{200 - 400}{\frac{1}{2}(200 + 400)}\right)\Big/\left(\frac{10{,}000 - 6{,}000}{\frac{1}{2}(10{,}000 + 6{,}000)}\right)$$

$$= \left(\frac{-200}{300}\right)\Big/\left(\frac{4{,}000}{8{,}000}\right) = -\frac{4}{3}$$

b Grits are an inferior good because the income elasticity of demand is negative.

7 a The initial equilibrium quantity (Q^*) of tribbles is 20. (Refer to *Study Guide* Chapter 3 if you need help in solving demand and supply equations.)

b The initial equilibrium price (P^*) of a tribble is $30. (Refer to *Study Guide* Chapter 3 if you need help in solving demand and supply equations.)

c The new equilibrium quantity of tribbles is 60. The new equilibrium price of a tribble is $50.

d At the initial income of $180 and price of $30, the quantity of tribbles demanded is 20. In order to find the new quantity demanded at income of $120, we have to use the new demand equation. But since *price* is assumed constant in calculating income elasticity, we have to substitute $P = 30$ into the new demand equation to get the appropriate new quantity. It would be *incorrect* to use the new equilibrium quantity, because that quantity corresponds to a *different price* ($50).

$$P = 110 - 1Q_D$$

$$30 = 110 - 1Q_D$$

$$Q_D = 80$$

We now have appropriate information about the initial quantity demanded (20) and income ($180), and about the new quantity demanded (80) and income ($120). Substituting this information into the formula for income elasticity of demand yields

$$\eta_y = \left(\frac{\Delta Q}{Q_{ave}}\right)\Big/\left(\frac{\Delta Y}{Y_{ave}}\right)$$

$$= \left(\frac{-60}{50}\right)\Big/\left(\frac{60}{150}\right) = -3$$

Since the income elasticity of demand for tribbles is negative, tribbles are an inferior good.

8 The cross elasticities of demand between A and B are in Table 4.4 Solution. Since the cross elasticities are positive, we know that A and B are substitutes.

TABLE **4.4** SOLUTION
DEMAND SCHEDULES FOR GOOD A

	$P_B = \$8$	$P_B = \$12$	
P_A	Q_A	Q'_A	η_x
$8	2,000	4,000	1.67
$7	4,000	6,000	1.00
$6	6,000	8,000	0.71

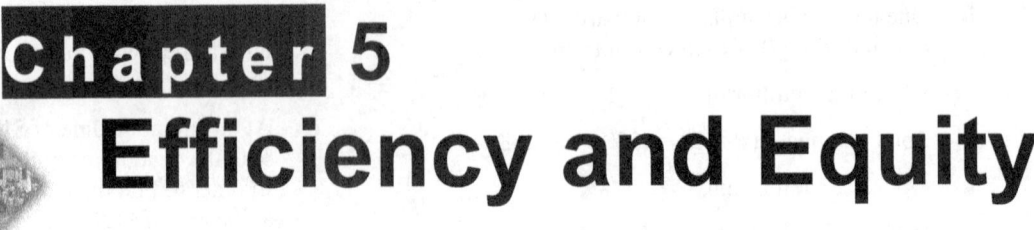

Chapter 5
Efficiency and Equity

Resource Allocation Methods

Alternative methods for allocating scarce resources are market price (resources go to those most willing and able to pay); **command system** (by order of authority); majority rule; contest; first-come, first-served; lottery; personal characteristics; force.

Benefit, Cost, and Surplus

Value is what consumers are willing to pay; price is what consumers actually pay.

   ♦ Demand curve is a marginal benefit curve.

   • Marginal benefit = value = maximum willing to pay for an additional unit.

Individual demand and market demand:

   ♦ *individual demand*—relationship between quantity demanded and price for a single individual.

   ♦ *market demand*—sum of individual demands; relationship between total quantity demanded and price.

   ♦ *market demand curve*—horizontal sum of individual demand curves.

   • Market demand curve is the economy's marginal social benefit (*MSB*) curve.

   ♦ **Consumer surplus** is the marginal benefit of a good minus its price, summed over the quantity bought. It is the triangular area under the demand curve, but above the market price (see Text Fig. 5.2, p. 109).

Opportunity cost is what producers pay; price is what producers receive.

   ♦ Supply curve is a marginal cost curve.

   • Marginal cost = minimum producers must receive to produce an additional unit.

Individual supply and market supply:

   ♦ *individual supply*—relationship between quantity supplied and price for a single producer.

   ♦ *market supply*—sum of individual supplies; relationship between total quantity supplied and price.

   ♦ *market supply curve*—horizontal sum of individual supply curves.

   • Market supply curve is the economy's marginal social cost (*MSC*) curve.

   ♦ **Producer surplus** is the price of a good minus its marginal cost, summed over the quantity sold. It is the triangular area below the market price, but above the supply curve (see Text Fig. 5.4, p. 111).

Is the Competitive Market Efficient?

In competitive equilibrium

   ♦ marginal social benefit = marginal social cost.

   ♦ resource allocation is efficient.

   ♦ *total surplus* (consumer surplus + producer surplus) is maximized.

Market failure—when markets deliver inefficient outcomes (from underproduction or overproduction); is measured by **deadweight loss**—decrease in total surplus below efficient levels.

Sources of market failure:

   ♦ price and quantity regulations, taxes, subsidies (Chapter 6).

   ♦ *externalities*—the cost or benefit affecting others besides the buyers and sellers of a good (Chapter 16).

- Competitive markets overproduce goods and services that have external costs.

- Competitive markets underproduce goods and services that have external benefits.

♦ *public goods*—consumed simultaneously by all, even if they don't pay for it (Chapter 17).

- Competitive markets produce less than the efficient quantity of public goods because of the free-rider problem.

♦ *monopolies*—firms that restrict output and raise price, creating deadweight loss (Chapter 13).

♦ high **transactions costs**—opportunity costs of making trades in a market—lead to underproduction.

Is the Competitive Market Fair?

Ideas about fairness divide into two approaches:

♦ Fair results—there should be equality of incomes.

- **Utilitarianism**—result should be the "greatest happiness for the greatest number." Requires income transfers from rich to poor.

- Income transfers create the "**big tradeoff**" between efficiency and fairness. Transfers use scarce resources and weaken incentives, so a more equally shared pie results in a smaller pie.

- Modified utilitarianism—after incorporating costs of income transfers, result should make the poorest person as well off as possible.

♦ Fair rules—people in similar situations should be treated similarly.

- **Symmetry principle.**

- Equality of opportunity.

- Requires property rights and voluntary exchange.

H E L P F U L   H I N T S

1 This chapter provides important tools for analysing economic policies. Policy analysis involves judgments of efficiency and fairness (or equity). The concepts of consumer and producer surplus allow us to evaluate efficiency—efficient outcomes maximize total surplus—the sum of consumer and producer surplus. Efficiency is a positive concept. The outcomes of different policies can be measured and compared objectively (at least in principle) to see which is more efficient.

Fairness is another important aspect of any economic policy. Fairness is a normative concept, depending on value judgments about which reasonable people can differ. But policymakers must make decisions, and it is helpful to be explicit about what ideas of fairness are used to judge policy. The two main normative ideas developed in this chapter are fair results and fair rules.

2 There are two ways to interpret or "read" a demand curve—as a demand curve and as a marginal benefit curve. Both readings are correct, but each provides slightly different information. You can see the two readings in Text Figures 5.1 and 5.2 on pages 108 and 109.

The first reading (Fig. 5.1) starts with price. For a given price, the demand curve tells us the quantity demanded. Pick a price on the vertical axis. To find quantity demanded, we go "over" to the demand curve and "down" to the quantity axis. This is the standard demand curve of Chapter 3.

The second reading (Fig. 5.2) starts with quantity. For a given quantity, the demand curve tells us the maximum price people are willing to pay. Pick a quantity on the horizontal axis. To find the maximum price people are willing to pay, we go "up" to the demand curve and "over" to the price axis. This is a reading of the demand curve as a marginal benefit curve. For a given quantity, the marginal benefit curve tells us the value (equals the maximum price people are willing to pay) of that unit of the good.

We read a demand curve "over and down." But we read a marginal benefit curve "up and over." Each reading is helpful, depending on the problem you are trying to solve or the issue you are trying to analyse. If you get stuck with a demand or marginal benefit curve problem, you may not be using the most suitable reading. Try reading the curve both ways and see which one is most helpful.

3 As with the demand curve, there are two ways to interpret or "read" a supply curve—as a supply curve and as a marginal cost curve. Both readings are correct, but each provides slightly different information. You can see the two readings in Text Figures 5.3 and 5.4 on pages 110 and 111.

The first reading (Fig. 5.3) starts with price. For a given price, the supply curve tells us the quantity supplied. Pick a price on the vertical axis. To find quantity supplied, we go "over" to the supply curve and "down" to the quantity axis. This is the standard supply curve of Chapter 3.

The second reading (Fig. 5.4) starts with quantity. For a given quantity, the supply curve tells us the minimum price producers are willing to accept. Pick a quantity on the horizontal axis. To find the minimum price producers are willing to accept, we go "up" to the supply curve and "over" to the price axis. This is a reading of the supply curve as a marginal cost curve. For a given quantity, the marginal cost curve tells us the opportunity cost of producing that unit of the good.

Thus we read a supply curve "over and down," while we read a marginal cost curve "up and over." Each reading is helpful, depending on the problem you are trying to solve or the issue you are trying to analyse. If you get stuck with a supply or marginal cost curve problem, you may not be using the most suitable reading. Try reading the curve both ways and see which one is most helpful.

4   The market demand curve is a marginal social benefit curve and the market supply curve is a marginal social cost curve *as long as there are no external benefits or costs*. Once you think of demand and supply curves as marginal social benefit and cost curves, the concepts of consumer surplus and producer surplus follow directly. Consumer surplus is the difference between the maximum amount people are willing to pay and the price actually paid. At any price, consumer surplus for the market is the area below the demand (marginal social benefit) curve but above the horizontal line at market price. Producer surplus is the difference between the minimum amount producers are willing to accept and the price actually received. At any price, producer surplus for the market is the area above the supply (marginal social cost) curve but below the horizontal line at market price.

5   An efficient allocation of resources occurs at the quantity of output that maximizes total surplus (consumer surplus + producer surplus). Total surplus is maximized at the quantity where marginal social benefit (MSB) equals marginal social cost (MSC). To see why the $MSB = MSC$ condition signals maximum efficiency, consider outputs less than and greater than the efficient quantity of output.

If output is less than the efficient quantity (to the left), MSB is greater than MSC. Resources are creating more value (MSB) than they cost (MSC). By shifting more resources into production of this good and out of production of other goods where MSB is only equal to or less than MSC, total surplus will increase.

Similarly, if output is greater than the efficient quantity (to the right), MSC is greater than MSB. Resources cost more (MSC) than the value (MSB) that they are creating. By shifting more resources out of production of this good and into production of other goods where MSB is at least equal to or greater than MSC, total surplus will increase.

Only at the output where $MSB = MSC$ is total surplus at a maximum, and no reallocation of resources can increase the sum of consumer surplus and producer surplus.

6   Fairness is a normative issue. But note that the tradeoff between economic efficiency and fairness (the "big tradeoff") is a positive issue. Income transfers to achieve fairness norms have real impacts on economic output due to administrative costs and incentive effects. The loss of output and reduced efficiency can be measured. Even though fairness has a cost, policymakers may still come to the conclusion that improved fairness or equity is worth the loss in efficiency. That is the normative issue.

True/False and Explain

Resource Allocation Methods

1   A command system can work well to allocate resources when it is easy to monitor activities.

Benefit, Cost, and Surplus

2   The value of a good is its consumer benefit.

3   The market demand curve is the horizontal sum of all individual demand curves.

4 The market demand curve is formed by adding the willingness to pay for each individual at each price.

5 Consumer surplus is the marginal benefit of a good minus the price paid for it.

6 Consumer surplus equals the area above the demand curve, but below market price.

7 The market supply curve is the vertical sum of the individual firm supply curves.

8 The opportunity cost of producing a given quantity of a good is the area under the supply curve.

9 Producer surplus is the marginal cost of producing a good minus its price.

Is the Competitive Market Efficient?

10 Adam Smith's "invisible hand" suggests that competitive markets send resources to their highest-valued use.

11 Markets always use resources efficiently.

12 Deadweight loss is a loss to consumers and a gain to producers.

Is the Competitive Market Fair?

13 Utilitarianism is an example of a fair results idea.

14 If we think of the total income of a society as a pie, a more equally shared pie results in a larger pie.

15 In economic life, the symmetry principle translates into equality of outcomes.

Multiple-Choice

Resource Allocation Methods

1 An efficient method to allocate resources when the efforts of the participants are hard to monitor and reward directly is a
  a command system.
  b lottery.
  c contest.
  d first-come, first-served rule.
  e market price.

Benefit, Cost, and Surplus

2 The maximum price a consumer is willing to pay for a good is known as the
  a consumer surplus.
  b value of a good.
  c relative price of a good.
  d money price of a good.
  e marginal cost of a good.

3 Market demand is the
   a   sum of the prices that each individual is willing to pay for each quantity demanded.
   b   sum of the quantities demanded by each individual at each price.
   c   sum of the consumer surplus of each individual.
   d   difference between the maximum amount each individual is willing to pay for a good and the market price.
   e   difference between the market price and the maximum amount each individual is willing to pay for a good.

4 Consumer surplus is the
   a   difference between the maximum price consumers are willing to pay and the minimum price producers are willing to accept.
   b   difference between the marginal benefit of a good and the price paid for the good.
   c   total value to consumers of a good.
   d   area under the demand curve.
   e   total amount paid for the good.

5 Consider the demand curve in Fig. 5.1. What is the value of the first unit of the good?

FIGURE **5.1**

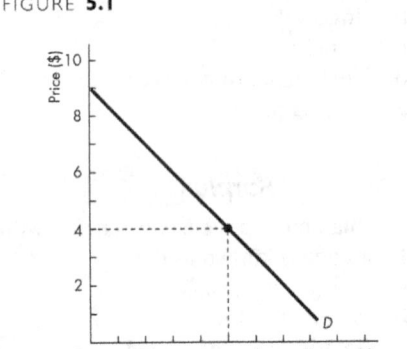

Quantity

   a $10
   b $9
   c $8
   d $5
   e $4

6 Consider the demand curve in Fig. 5.1. If the price of the good is $4, what is the total consumer surplus?
   a $32.50
   b $25.00
   c $20.00
   d $12.50
   e   none of the above

7 The marginal cost of a service is
   a   the opportunity cost of the first unit produced.
   b   the maximum price producers must receive to induce them to supply an additional unit of the service.
   c   the value of all alternatives forgone.
   d   increasing with increased output.
   e   decreasing with increased output.

8 A supply curve is
   a   a marginal cost curve.
   b   a minimum supply-price curve.
   c   an opportunity cost of production curve.
   d   all of the above.
   e   none of the above.

9 Producer surplus is the
   a   difference between the maximum price consumers are willing to pay and the minimum price producers are willing to accept.
   b   difference between producers' revenues and opportunity costs of production.
   c   opportunity cost of production.
   d   area under the supply curve.
   e   total amount paid for the good.

10 Consider the demand and supply curves in Fig. 5.2. Which area in the diagram indicates the opportunity cost of production?
   a   *abc*
   b   *aec*
   c   *ebc*
   d   0*bcd*
   e   0*ecd*

FIGURE **5.2**

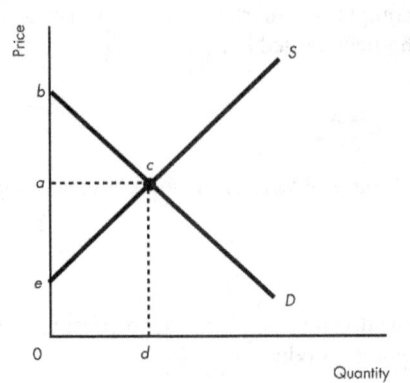

Quantity

11 Consider the demand and supply curves in Fig. 5.2. Which area in the diagram indicates producer surplus?
a   *abc*
b   *aec*
c   *ebc*
d   *0bcd*
e   *0ecd*

Is the Competitive Market Efficient?

12 At current output, the marginal benefit of Furbys is greater than marginal cost. To achieve an efficient allocation,
1 Furby output must increase.
2 Furby output must decrease.
3 the marginal benefit of Furbys will rise.
4 the marginal cost of Furbys will fall.
a   1 and 3
b   1 and 4
c   2 and 3
d   2 and 4
e   1 only

13 If production is not at an efficient level, which of the following *must* be true?
a   Marginal benefit exceeds marginal cost.
b   Marginal cost exceeds marginal benefit.
c   Production will increase.
d   Production will decrease.
e   None of the above.

14 In competitive equilibrium, which of the following statements is *false*?
a   Marginal social benefit equals marginal social cost.
b   Willingness to pay equals opportunity cost.
c   The sum of consumer surplus and producer surplus is maximized.
d   Deadweight loss is maximized.
e   Resources are used efficiently to produce goods and services that people value most highly.

15 If resources are allocated efficiently,
a   consumer surplus exceeds producer surplus.
b   producer surplus exceeds consumer surplus.
c   the sum of consumer surplus and producer surplus is maximized.
d   marginal social benefit is maximized.
e   marginal social cost is minimized.

16 Markets may not achieve an efficient allocation of resources when there are
a   public goods.
b   external benefits.
c   monopolies.
d   subsidies.
e   all of the above.

17 The overproduction of a good means that
a   deadweight loss has been eliminated.
b   the sum of consumer surplus and producer surplus is greater than the sum for an efficient allocation.
c   marginal social cost exceeds marginal social benefit.
d   marginal social benefit exceeds marginal social cost.
e   this is a public good.

18 Deadweight loss is
a   borne entirely by consumers.
b   gained by producers.
c   the social loss from inefficiency.
d   not a problem with overproduction.
e   all of the above.

19 Consider the demand and supply curves in Fig. 5.3. Which area in the diagram indicates the deadweight loss from underproduction?
a   *eacf*
b   *acd*
c   *abd*
d   *bcd*
e   *kaci*

FIGURE **5.3**

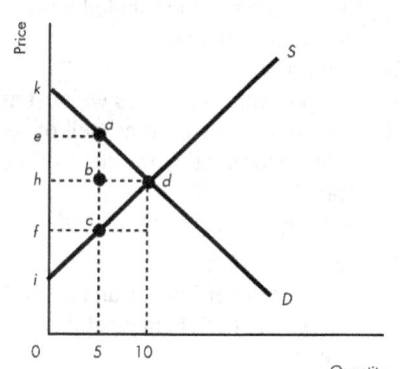

20 Consider the demand and supply curves in Fig. 5.3. Which area in the diagram indicates the loss in consumer surplus from underproduction?
  a *eacf*
  b *acd*
  c *abd*
  d *bcd*
  e *kaci*

Is the Competitive Market Fair?

21 Which of the following applies to the *results* principle of fairness?
  a symmetry principle
  b equality of opportunity
  c the big tradeoff
  d protection of private property
  e purely voluntary exchange

22 A principle of fairness that emphasizes equality of opportunity is
  a fair results.
  b fair rules.
  c fair incomes.
  d utilitarianism.
  e modified utilitarianism.

23 According to the "big tradeoff,"
  a income transfers reduce efficiency.
  b efficiency requires income transfers.
  c a more equally shared pie results in a larger pie.
  d property rights and voluntary exchange ensure equality of opportunity.
  e income transfers should make the poorest person as well off as possible.

24 According to Rawls' modified utilitarianism, income should be redistributed until
  a incomes are equal.
  b opportunities are equal.
  c the poorest person is as well off as possible.
  d the poorest person is as well off as possible, after incorporating the costs of income transfers.
  e the big tradeoff is eliminated.

25 Economists tend to
  a agree about efficiency and about fairness.
  b agree about efficiency but disagree about fairness.
  c disagree about efficiency but agree about fairness.
  d be more agreeable than philosophers about fairness.
  e be more disagreeable than philosophers about fairness.

Short Answer Problems

1 Table 5.1 gives the demand schedules for broccoli for three individuals: Tom, Jana, and Ted.

TABLE **5.1**   INDIVIDUAL DEMAND FOR BROCCOLI

Price ($ per kilogram)	Quantity Demanded (kilograms per week)		
	Tom	Jana	Ted
0.50	10	4	10
0.75	9	2	7
1.00	8	0	4
1.25	7	0	1

  a Calculate the market demand schedule.

  b On a single diagram, draw the individual demand curves for Tom, Jana, and Ted, as well as the market demand curve.

Fig. 5.4 shows the market for champagne. Note that the demand curve is also a marginal social benefit curve, and the supply curve is also a marginal social cost curve. Use this information to answer Questions 2–5.

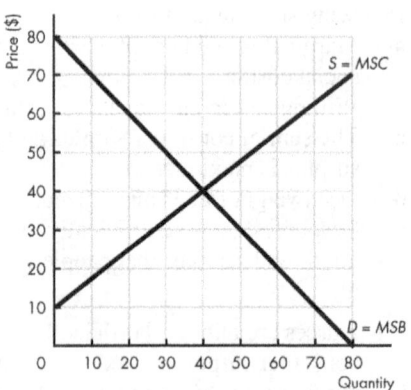

FIGURE **5.4**   THE CHAMPAGNE MARKET

2 a If the price of a bottle of champagne is $60, what is the quantity demanded? the quantity supplied?

  b At the price of $60, is there a shortage or a surplus of champagne? Explain the forces that will move the market toward equilibrium.

c If the quantity sold of champagne is 20 bottles, what is the marginal social benefit of the 20th bottle to consumers? the marginal social cost to producers?

d At the quantity of 20 bottles, what is the relationship between the value of the 20th bottle of champagne and the value of the resources forgone to make it? Explain the forces that will move the market toward an efficient allocation of resources.

3 Suppose the champagne market in Fig. 5.4 is in equilibrium.

a Calculate the consumer surplus.

b Calculate the producer surplus.

c What is the sum of consumer surplus and producer surplus?

d What is the condition for economic efficiency?

4 Suppose now that that there is underproduction in the champagne market in Fig. 5.4 and output is restricted to 20 bottles.

a List three kinds of obstacles to efficiency that might cause underproduction.

b Calculate the deadweight loss.

c What is the sum of consumer surplus and producer surplus?

d How does the sum compare to the sum in Short Answer Problem **3c**? Is the output of 20 bottles efficient?

5 Suppose instead that there is overproduction in the champagne market and output increases to 60 bottles.

a List one kind of obstacle to efficiency that might cause overproduction.

b Calculate the deadweight loss.

c What is the sum of consumer surplus and producer surplus?

d How does the sum compare to the sum in Short Answer Problem **3c**? Is the output of 60 bottles efficient?

6 There appears to be a contradiction between the Chapter 1 claim that the basic economic problem is scarcity and the Chapter 5 claim that there can be a problem of "overproduction." When the basic problem is that there is too little to meet our wants, how can there be too much of a good?

7 Ideas about fairness divide into two groups—fair results and fair rules.

a What is the basic principle of fair-results ideas? What is the basic principle of fair-rules ideas?

b What is utilitarianism? Explain why it is a fair-results or fair-rules idea.

8 Suppose two political parties are vying for your vote in an upcoming election. The "Rights" advocate a more privatized health-care system, where the market sets the price for medical services and individuals pay more of their own bills. The "Lefts" advocate more government subsidies in health care, which would extend free coverage to preventative dental care and prescription drugs.

a As an intelligent and economically informed citizen, use the concepts of efficiency and fairness (equity) to evaluate the likely pros and cons of each party's policy.

b Which policy would you likely support? What does this say about your personal valuation of efficiency versus equity?

ANSWERS

True/False and Explain

1 **T** Works badly when there are many, difficult-to-monitor activities. (106–107)

2 **F** Value = MB. (108–111)

3 **T** Definition. (108–111)

4 **F** Adding the quantities demanded by each individual at each price. (108–111)

5 **T** Definition. (108–111)

6 **F** The area under the demand curve, but above the market price. (108–111)

7 **F** Horizontal sum of individual firm supply curves. (108–111)

8 **T** That area sums the opportunity cost of production for each unit of good produced. (108–111)

9 **F** Price of a good minus its marginal cost of production. (108–111)

10 **T** Competitive markets are "led by an invisible hand" to promote efficient resource use, which benefits all. (112–115)

11 F Not when there are obstacles to efficiency like price and quantity regulations, externalities, monopoly, high transaction costs. (112–115)

12 F Social loss borne by entire society. (112–115)

13 T For utilitarianism, only equality of results is fair, bringing "the greatest happiness for the greatest number." (116–119)

14 F A more equally shared pie results in a smaller pie because of the "big tradeoff" between efficiency and fairness. (116–119)

15 F The symmetry principle—treat others as you would like to be treated—translates into equality of *opportunity*. (116–119)

Multiple-Choice

1 c Only a few end up with a big prize, but many work harder trying to win. (106–107)

2 b Value = marginal benefit. (108–111)

3 b See text discussion. (108–111)

4 b Definition. Area under the demand curve but above the market price. (108–111)

5 c From $Q = 1$, go up to demand curve to read over to maximum price willing to pay. (108–111)

6 d Area of triangle ($1/2ba$) below demand and above $P = 4$. (108–111)

7 d Principle of increasing marginal cost; $MC =$ value of *best* alternative forgone. (108–111)

8 d All definitions of supply curve. (108–111)

9 b Definition. Area below the market price but above the supply curve. (108–111)

10 e Area below the supply curve. (108–111)

11 b Area below the market price but above the supply curve. (108–111)

12 e With increasing Q, MSB must fall and MSC rise. (112–115)

13 e If production is below efficient level, **a** and **c** are true; if production is above efficient level, **b** and **d** are true. (112–115)

14 d No deadweight loss. All other answers are definitions of competitive equilibrium. (112–115)

15 c Definition where marginal benefit equals marginal cost. No other necessary relation between consumer and producer surplus. (112–115)

16 e All change quantity produced above (**d**) or below (**a**, **b**, **c**) efficient quantity. (112–115)

17 c Production beyond efficient level creates deadweight loss, reducing total surplus. (112–115)

18 c Borne by consumers and producers when there is underproduction or overproduction. (112–115)

19 b Decrease in consumer and producer surplus compared to efficient quantity (10) of production. (112–115)

20 c Area subtracted from consumer surplus at efficient quantity (10) of production (*hkd*). (112–115)

21 c Other answers apply to *rules* principle of fairness. (116–119)

22 b Other answers apply to *results* principle of fairness. (116–119)

23 a Tradeoff between equity (which requires income transfers) and efficiency. (116–119)

24 d Rawls' idea incorporates the effects of the big tradeoff in trying to redistribute income more equally, but not totally equally. (116–119)

25 b Efficiency is a positive issue; fairness is a normative issue. (116–119)

Short Answer Problems

1 a The market demand schedule is obtained by adding the quantities demanded by Tom, Jana, and Ted at each price (see Table 5.2).

TABLE **5.2**	MARKET DEMAND SCHEDULE FOR BROCCOLI
Price ($ per kilogram)	**Quantity Demanded (kilograms per week)**
0.50	24
0.75	18
1.00	12
1.25	8

b Fig. 5.5 illustrates the individual demand curves for Tom, Jana, and Ted as well as the market demand curve.

FIGURE **5.5**

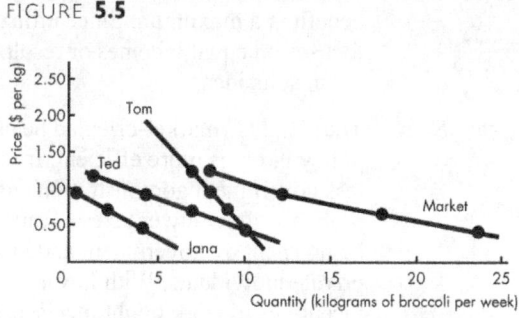

2 a Quantity demanded is 20 bottles; quantity supplied is approximately 67 bottles. We find these quantities by starting with the price of $60 and reading "over" to each curve and "down" to the quantity.

b There is a surplus because quantity supplied exceeds quantity demanded. Producers have excess supplies, so they will cut prices rather than be stuck with unsold goods. Quantity demanded will increase as price falls, until we end up at the equilibrium price of $40/bottle and the equilibrium quantity of 40 bottles.

c Marginal social benefit is $60; marginal social cost is $25. We find these values by starting with the quantity of 20 bottles and reading "up" to each curve and "over" to the marginal social benefit and cost (measured in prices).

d The 20th bottle of champagne is valued by consumers at $60, but uses only $25 worth of resources to make. With marginal social benefit exceeding marginal social cost, consumers would happily pay more than $25 for an additional bottle of champagne and will bid up the price. Producers will increase the quantity supplied until the market reaches the equilibrium price of $40/bottle and the equilibrium quantity of 40 bottles. Producers increase champagne output by transferring resources from other uses. Resources, which were being used elsewhere to create value just equal to their cost, are now being used more efficiently in that they create more value in champagne production than their cost.

3 a Consumer surplus is the triangular area under the demand curve but above the horizontal line at the market price of $40. The formula for the area of a triangle is 1/2(base)(altitude), so consumer surplus = 1/2(40)(40) = 800.

b Producer surplus is the triangular area above the supply curve but below the horizontal line at the market price of $40. Producer surplus = 1/2(40)(30) = 600.

c The sum of consumer and producer surplus is 800 + 600 = 1,400.

d Economic efficiency occurs when the sum of consumer surplus and producer surplus is maximized. Is this specific outcome efficient? We can't be sure if 1,400 is a maximum until we compare other situations in the champagne market.

4 a Price and quantity regulations, taxes, external benefits, public goods, monopoly, and high transactions costs all might cause output to be restricted.

b Deadweight loss is the decrease in consumer surplus and producer surplus that results from an inefficient level of production. It is equal to the triangular area between the demand and supply curves from quantity = 20 to quantity = 40. Deadweight loss = 1/2(35)(20) = 350.

c The new sum of consumer and producer surplus is the original amount of 1,400 minus the deadweight loss: 1,400 – 350 = 1,050.

d The sum of consumer and producer surplus (1,050) is less than the equilibrium sum in Short Answer Problem **3c** at an output of 40 bottles. Since an efficient output maximizes the sum of consumer and producer surplus, the output of 20 bottles is not efficient.

5 a Subsidies to producers or external costs can cause overproduction.

b Deadweight loss is equal to the triangular area between the demand and supply curves from quantity = 40 to quantity = 60. Deadweight loss = 1/2(35)(20) = 350. (It is just a coincidence that this deadweight loss from overproduction happens to be equal to the deadweight loss from underproduction. In general these losses are not necessarily equal.)

c   The new sum of consumer and producer surplus is the original amount of 1,400 minus the deadweight loss:
$1,400 - 350 = 1,050$.

d   The sum of consumer and producer surplus (1,050) is less than the equilibrium sum in Short Answer Problem **3c** at an output of 40 bottles. Since an efficient output maximizes the sum of consumer and producer surplus, the output of 60 bottles is not efficient.

6   Because wants *in general* exceed the resources available to satisfy them, we cannot have everything we want and must make choices. This basic problem leads to economizing behaviour— choosing the best or optimal use of available resources. But *specific* wants can be satisfied. Each of us has relatively limited wants, for example, for salt, for heat in our houses during the winter, or for nail clippers. If these or other goods are produced beyond the point where the marginal benefit equals the marginal cost, there is a problem of overproduction.

Overproduction is a problem because the resources could be *better used* to produce different goods that could meet still-unsatisfied wants. The money invested in excessive salt production could be diverted to health research to find a cure for cancer, or to schools to allow more demands for education to be satisfied. Because wants *in general* are unlimited, producing too much of a good to satisfy a *specific* want actually prevents us from making optimal use of available resources. So the ideas of scarcity and overproduction are not contradictory. In fact, overproduction of a *specific* good is a problem precisely because there is a problem of scarcity in satisfying wants *in general*.

7   **a**   Fair-results ideas are based on the principle that results are most important, and that the fairest economic result is equal incomes for all. Fair-rules ideas are based on the symmetry principle—that people in similar situations should be treated similarly. This principle translates into equality of opportunity in economic life.

b   Utilitarianism is based on the principle that the fairest system is one in which incomes are equal. Utilitarians argue that transferring income from the rich to the poor will result in "the greatest happiness for the greatest number," since the marginal benefit of an additional dollar to the poor person is greater than the benefit to the rich person. Only at equal incomes for all is total social benefit at a maximum. Since utilitarianism focuses on equal incomes or results, it is a fair-results idea.

8   **a**   The "Rights" market-oriented health-care policy likely is more efficient. It requires less government administration and would probably allow lower taxes because less is being spent by government and more by private individuals. With lower taxes, incentives to work might increase, and the size of the economic pie might be larger.

With lower government subsidies, the price of health care to individuals will rise. Health care may become unaffordable to some members of society, so the "Rights" policy may be less fair from a "fair results" perspective. From a "fair rules" perspective, the "Rights" policy is fair as long as everyone faces the same opportunities.

The "Lefts" subsidized health-care policy likely is less efficient, because it would require subsidies to health-care providers and require more government administration and higher taxes to pay for the policy. With higher taxes, incentives to work might decrease, and the size of the economic pie might be smaller. On the other hand, with a healthier population, productivity might increase because fewer work days would be lost to illness. So the net effect on efficiency is unclear.

More health-care services will become available to a greater number of people, so the "Lefts" policy may be fairer from a fair-results perspective. From a fair-rules perspective, the "Lefts" policy may be less fair if, to pay for the policy, individuals with higher incomes are taxed more than those with lower incomes.

b   There is obviously no single correct answer to this question. The important thing is to think explicitly about your personal valuation of efficiency versus equity, and which idea of fairness appeals most to you.

Chapter 6
Government Actions in Markets

A Housing Market with a Rent Ceiling

In a government-regulated housing market

♦ a **rent ceiling** (a **price ceiling** applied to rents) makes it illegal to raise rents.

♦ housing stocks are lower than in an unregulated market both in the short and long run; no incentive to economize on space or build new housing.

♦ shortages cause excess demand and

  • **search activity** (time spent looking for someone with whom to do business).

  • **black markets** (illegal markets where prices exceed ceilings).

Unregulated markets allocate housing resources efficiently, while rent ceilings create inefficiencies (deadweight loss) without necessarily improving fairness.

A Labour Market with a Minimum Wage

A **minimum wage** (a **price floor** applied to wages) makes it illegal to hire labour below a specified wage.

♦ Minimum wages create excess supply of labour (unemployment) and lower the quantity of labour demanded and hired.

♦ Unemployed workers willing to work at a lower wage spend more time searching for work.

♦ Minimum wage benefits those who keep jobs, but makes the unemployed worse off.

Taxes

A tax on sellers shifts the supply curve up by a vertical distance equal to the amount of the tax. A tax on buyers shifts the demand curve down by a vertical distance equal to the amount of the tax. Results are the same.

Tax incidence—division of the burden of a tax between buyers and sellers—depends on elasticities of supply and demand.

Supply elasticity and tax division:

♦ Perfectly inelastic supply—sellers pay all.

♦ More inelastic supply—sellers pay more.

♦ More elastic supply—buyers pay more.

♦ Perfectly elastic supply—buyers pay all.

Demand elasticity and tax division:

♦ Perfectly inelastic demand—buyers pay all.

♦ More inelastic demand—buyers pay more.

♦ More elastic demand—sellers pay more.

♦ Perfectly elastic demand—sellers pay all.

Taxes decrease the quantity produced and consumed, creating deadweight loss.

Fairness of taxes can be evaluated by

♦ *benefits principle*—fairness is people paying taxes equal to benefits they receive from government services

♦ *ability-to-pay principle*—fairness is people paying taxes according to their ability to pay (rich pay more than poor)

Production Quotas and Subsidies

Government can take actions in markets for farm products by setting

- ◆ **production quotas** (quantity restrictions on production), which increase market price, decrease Q grown, and create inefficient underproduction.

- ◆ **subsidies** (payments by governments to producers), which increase supply, decrease market price (but farmers receive market price plus subsidy), and create inefficient overproduction.

Markets for Illegal Goods

Penalizing dealers for selling illegal goods increases the cost of selling goods and decreases supply. Penalizing buyers for consuming illegal goods decreases willingness to pay and decreases demand.

- ◆ When (sellers' penalties > buyers' penalties), Q decreases, P rises.

- ◆ When (sellers' penalties < buyers' penalties), Q decreases, P falls.

- ◆ Taxing (decriminalized) goods can achieve the same consumption levels as prohibition.

HELPFUL HINTS

1　In the real world, governments often regulate markets using price constraints, so it is important to study the effects of such regulation. Another benefit of studying government regulation is to understand how markets work when, by contrast, the government does *not* affect the normal operation of markets.

　　Whenever something disturbs an equilibrium in an unregulated (free) market, the desires of buyers and sellers are brought back into balance by price movements. If prices are controlled by government regulation, however, the price mechanism can no longer serve this purpose. Thus *balance* must be restored in some other way. In the case of price ceilings, black markets are likely to arise. If black markets cannot develop because of strict enforcement of price ceilings, demanders will be forced to bear the costs of increased search activity, waiting in line, or something else.

2　This chapter discusses government price constraints in three markets: rental housing, labour, and farm products. The basic principles, however, can be generalized to other markets.

　　In any market with a legal price ceiling set below the market-clearing price, we will observe excess quantity demanded, because price cannot increase to eliminate it. As a consequence, the marginal benefit of the last unit of the good available will exceed the controlled price. Demanders are willing to engage in costly activities up to the marginal benefit of that last unit (search activity, waiting lines, and black market activity) to obtain the good.

　　Furthermore, if price is allowed to increase in response to a decrease in supply or an increase in demand, there are incentive effects for suppliers to produce more and demanders to purchase less (movements along the supply and demand curves). Indeed, it is the response to these incentives that restores equilibrium in markets with freely adjusting prices. If the price cannot adjust, these price-induced incentive effects do not have a chance to operate. In the case of rent ceilings, the inability of rents (price) to rise means that (1) there is no inducement to use the current stock of housing more intensively in the short run, and (2) there is no incentive to construct new housing in the long run. Similarly, the effects on any market in which a minimum price (price floor) is set above the market-clearing (equilibrium) price will be similar to those discussed in the text for the labour market under minimum wage or price floors in agricultural markets.

3　The division of the burden of a tax is called tax incidence. Who pays a sales tax imposed on producers depends on the elasticities of demand and supply. The general principles of tax incidence are

- • more inelastic demand—consumers pay more.

- • more elastic demand—producers pay more.

- • more inelastic supply—producers pay more.

- • more elastic supply—consumers pay more.

True/False and Explain

A Housing Market with a Rent Ceiling

1 In an unregulated housing market, higher rents increase the short-run quantity of housing supplied.

2 When rents in an unregulated housing market rise due to a decrease in supply, people who are unable to pay the higher rents will not get housing.

3 If a rent ceiling exceeds people's willingness to pay, search activity and black markets will increase.

A Labour Market with a Minimum Wage

4 In an unregulated labour market, a decrease in the demand for labour causes the wage rate to rise.

5 An increase in the minimum wage will reduce the number of workers employed.

6 Most economists believe that raising the minimum wage has no effect on unemployment.

7 Minimum wage laws increase the amount of time people spend searching for work.

Taxes

8 The more elastic demand is for a product, the larger the fraction of a sales tax paid by consumers.

9 A sales tax always creates deadweight loss.

10 The deadweight loss from a sales tax equals the tax revenue collected by government.

Production Quotas and Subsidies

11 Farm subsidies like those in Canada are a major source of tension between rich and developing nations.

12 A production quota creates inefficiency through overproduction.

13 A subsidy paid to producers shifts the demand curve for a good rightward.

Markets for Illegal Goods

14 The statement "If we legalize and tax drugs, tax revenues could be used to finance more drug education programs" is normative.

15 If penalties are imposed on both sellers and buyers in a market for prohibited goods, the price may rise, fall, or remain constant, while the quantity bought always decreases.

Multiple-Choice

A Housing Market with a Rent Ceiling

1 The short-run supply curve for rental housing is positively sloped because
   a   the supply of housing is fixed in the short run.
   b   the current stock of buildings will be used more intensively as rents rise.
   c   the cost of constructing new buildings increases as the number of buildings increases.
   d   the cost of constructing a new buildings is about the same regardless of the number of buildings in existence.
   e   new buildings will be constructed as rents rise.

2 Rent ceilings imposed by governments
   a   keep rental prices below the unregulated market price.
   b   keep rental prices above the unregulated market price.
   c   keep rental prices equal to the unregulated market price.
   d   increase the stock of rental housing.
   e   increase the intensity of use of the current stock of rental housing.

3 A price ceiling set below the equilibrium price will result in
   a   excess supply.
   b   excess demand.
   c   the equilibrium price.
   d   an increase in supply.
   e   a decrease in demand.

4 Which of the following is *not* a likely outcome of rent ceilings?
   a   a black market for rent-controlled housing
   b   long waiting lists of potential renters of rent-controlled housing
   c   a short-run shortage of housing
   d   black market prices below the rent ceiling prices
   e   increased search activity for rent-controlled housing

A Labour Market with a Minimum Wage

5 If the minimum wage is set at $2 per hour in Fig. 6.1, what is the level of unemployment in millions of hours?
   a   50
   b   40
   c   20
   d   10
   e   0

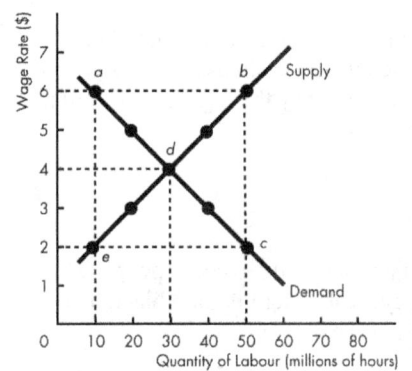

FIGURE **6.I**

6 In Fig. 6.1, if the minimum wage is set at $6 per hour, what is the level of unemployment in millions of hours?
   a   50
   b   40
   c   20
   d   10
   e   0

7 In Fig. 6.1, if the minimum wage is set at $6 per hour, what is the area of deadweight loss?
   a   *abd*
   b   *bcd*
   c   *cde*
   d   *ade*
   e   0

Taxes

8 Figure 6.2 on the next page shows the market for frisbees before and after a sales tax is imposed. The sales tax on each frisbee is
   a $0.40.
   b $0.60.
   c $1.00.
   d $5.60.
   e $6.60.

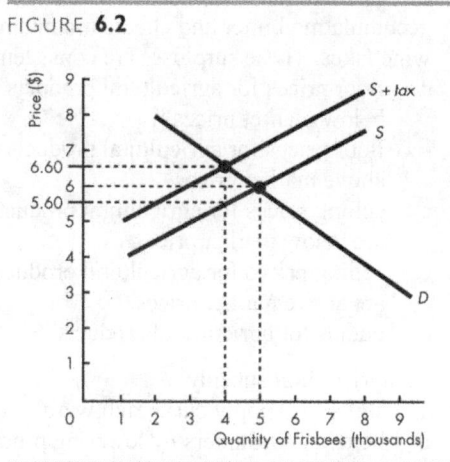

FIGURE **6.2**

9 Refer to Fig. 6.2. For each frisbee, the sellers' share of the tax is
   a $0.40.
   b $0.60.
   c $1.00.
   d $5.60.
   e $6.60.

10 Refer to Fig. 6.2. For each frisbee, the buyers' share of the tax is
   a $0.40.
   b $0.60.
   c $1.00.
   d $5.60.
   e $6.60.

11 Refer to Fig. 6.2. Government revenue from the tax is
   a $4,000.
   b $5,000.
   c $22,400.
   d $26,400.
   e $30,000.

12 From Fig. 6.2 we can deduce that between 4,000 and 5,000 units, the demand for frisbees is
   a inelastic.
   b unit elastic.
   c elastic.
   d more elastic than the supply (*S*) of frisbees.
   e soaring.

13 Refer to Fig. 6.2. Deadweight loss from the tax is
   a $500.
   b $1,000.
   c $3,600.
   d $4,000.
   e $5,000.

14 A tax on buyers
   a shifts the demand curve up by a vertical distance equal to the tax.
   b shifts the supply curve up by a vertical distance equal to the tax.
   c has the same effect on price and quantity as a tax on sellers.
   d has a different effect on price and quantity as a tax on sellers.
   e increases the price received by sellers.

15 If the price of a good is not affected by a sales tax,
   a supply is perfectly elastic.
   b demand is perfectly elastic.
   c elasticity of supply is greater than elasticity of demand.
   d elasticity of demand is greater than elasticity of supply.
   e none of the above.

16 Which of the following statement(s) about taxes and fairness is/are *true*?
   a The benefits principle of fairness is people paying taxes equal to the benefits they receive from government services
   b For the ability-to-pay principle of fairness, the rich should pay more taxes than the poor.
   c High fuel taxes to pay for highways are justified by the benefits principle.
   d Tax cuts to the rich are unfair according to the ability-to-pay principle.
   e All of the above are true.

Production Quotas and Subsidies

17 A production quota set above the equilibrium quantity will cause
   a a decrease in supply.
   b a rise in price.
   c inefficient underproduction.
   d all of the above.
   e none of the above.

18 Figure 6.3 on the next page illustrates the short-run demand and supply curves in the wheat bran market. If the Wheat Marketing Board sets a quota of 50 million bushels, the market-clearing price of a bushel of wheat bran is
   a $1.
   b $3.
   c $5.
   d two scoops of raisins.
   e none of the above.

FIGURE **6.3**

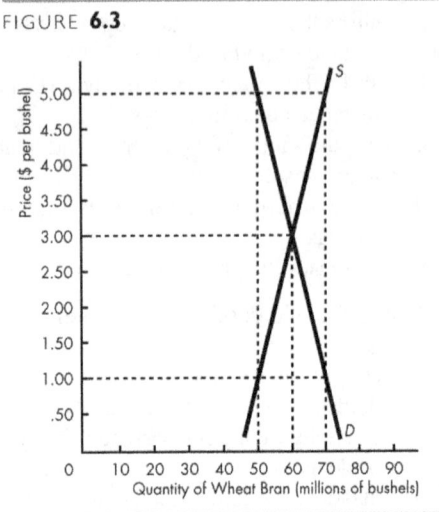

19 Refer to Fig. 6.3. With the quota of 50 million bushels, farmers have an incentive to
  a decrease output because the market-clearing price is below cost of production.
  b decrease output because there is a surplus at the market-clearing price.
  c increase output because the market-clearing price is above cost of production.
  d increase output because there is a shortage at the market-clearing price.
  e stick to the quota.

20 Refer to Fig. 6.3. Suppose the marketing board develops a new kind of subsidy called a direct payment plan. Farmers are told, "We will guarantee you $5 per bushel, but everything you produce at this price must be sold on the market for whatever buyers will pay; then we will give you (at taxpayers' expense) the difference between the market price and $5 per bushel." How many bushels of wheat bran will be sold?
  a 20 million
  b 50 million
  c 60 million
  d 70 million
  e none of the above

21 Refer to Fig. 6.3. The amount of taxpayers' money that the marketing board pays to farmers in Question **20** is
  a zero.
  b $70 million.
  c $250 million.
  d $280 million.
  e $350 million.

22 European Union (EU) countries have been accumulating butter and cheese mountains and wine lakes. These surpluses are consistent with
  a floor prices for agricultural products that are below market prices.
  b floor prices for agricultural products that are above market prices.
  c ceiling prices for agricultural products that are below market prices.
  d ceiling prices for agricultural products that are above market prices.
  e quotas for agricultural products.

23 An agricultural subsidy
  a shifts the supply curve rightward.
  b benefits consumers by lowering product prices.
  c benefits farmers by raising the price they receive.
  d imposes major costs on taxpayers.
  e does all of the above.

Markets for Illegal Goods

24 If enforcement is aimed at sellers of a prohibited good,
  a price and quantity bought will decrease.
  b price and quantity bought will increase.
  c price will increase and quantity bought will decrease.
  d price will decrease and quantity bought will increase.
  e price change will be uncertain and quantity bought will decrease.

25 Which of the following statements about prohibited goods is *true*?
  a Taxes are more effective in changing preferences than prohibition.
  b Prohibition is more effective in generating revenue than an equivalent tax.
  c Taxes and penalties cannot be set so as to yield equivalent outcomes.
  d Taxes generate revenues, while prohibition generates more enforcement expenses.
  e None of the above is true.

Short Answer Problems

1 Suppose that the market for rental housing is initially in long-run equilibrium. Use graphs to answer the following:

  a Explain how an unregulated market for rental housing would adjust if there is a sudden significant increase in demand. What will happen to rent and the quantity of units rented in the short run and in the long run? Be sure to discuss the effect on incentives (in both the short and the long run) as the market-determined price (rent) changes.

b Now explain how the market would adjust to the increase in demand if rent ceilings are established at the level of the initial equilibrium rent. What has happened to supplier incentives in this case?

2 The demand for and supply of gasoline are given in Table 6.1.

TABLE **6.1**

Price ($ per litre)	Quantity Demanded (millions of litres per day)	Quantity Supplied (millions of litres per day)
1.40	8	24
1.30	10	22
1.20	12	20
1.10	14	18
1.00	16	16
0.90	18	14

a What are the equilibrium price and quantity of gasoline?

b Suppose that the quantity of gasoline supplied suddenly declines by 8 million litres per day at every price. Construct a new table of price, quantity demanded, and quantity supplied, and draw a graph of the demand curve and the initial and new supply curves. Assuming that the market for gasoline is unregulated, use either your table or your graph to find the new equilibrium price and quantity of gasoline.

c How has the change in price affected the behaviour of demanders? the behaviour of suppliers?

3 Suppose that the government imposes a price ceiling of $1 per litre of gasoline at the same time as the decrease in supply reported in Short Answer Problem **2b**.

a What is the quantity of gasoline demanded? quantity supplied?

b What is the quantity of gasoline actually sold?

c What is the excess quantity of gasoline demanded?

d For the last litre of gasoline sold, what is the marginal benefit? marginal cost?

e Is this an efficient outcome? Explain.

4 Governments tend to put high sales taxes (often called "sin" taxes) on liquor and cigarettes. Aside from moral and health reasons, why are these goods chosen as a source of tax revenue?

5 The Ministry of Treasury has been authorized to levy a $0.15 per unit excise (sales) tax on one of two goods—comic books or dog biscuits. As a summer student at the Ministry, you are given an assignment by the Director of Taxes, Dr. More. You must choose the good that meets two objectives: (1) it will yield the greatest tax revenue and (2) the major burden of the tax will fall on consumers. Ministry researchers have estimated the supply and demand curves (without the tax) for each market. The comic book market is shown in Fig. 6.4 and the dog biscuit market in Fig. 6.5. The following questions will help you complete your assignment.

FIGURE **6.4** COMIC BOOK MARKET

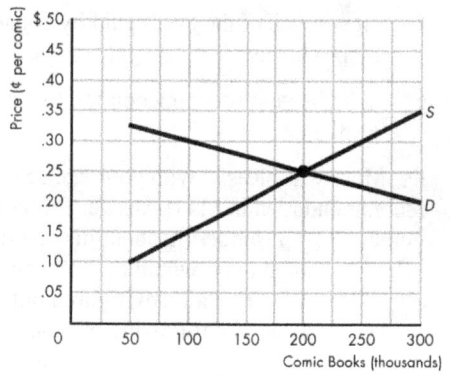

a For the comic book market, shift the appropriate curve to reflect the tax and draw it on Fig. 6.4. Label the curve either "S + tax" or "D + tax." Identify the new equilibrium price and quantity. Compare the total expenditure in the original and new equilibriums.

b Calculate the total tax revenue collected, and indicate it as an area on Fig. 6.4.

c How much of the tax is paid by consumers? by producers?

FIGURE **6.5** DOG BISCUIT MARKET

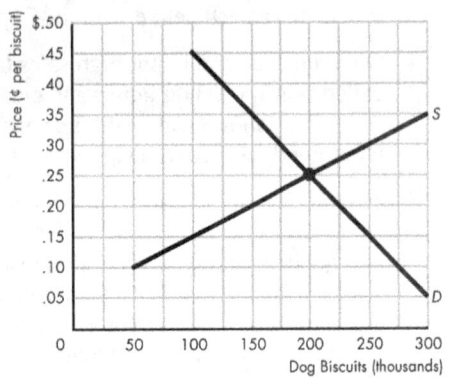

d Now perform the same analysis on the dog biscuit market. Shift the appropriate curve to reflect the tax and draw it on Fig. 6.5. Label the curve either "*S + tax*" or "*D + tax*." Identify the new equilibrium price and quantity. Compare the total expenditure in the original and new equilibriums.

e Calculate the total tax revenue collected and indicate it as an area on Fig. 6.5.

f How much of the tax is paid by consumers? by producers?

g What is your recommendation to Dr. More? Explain.

ⓔ **6** Dr. More was pleased with your excise tax recommendation in Short Answer Problem **5**, but you can't stop wondering about his comment, "Hmm, I thought you would do it the other way." If you haven't already figured out to what he was referring, the following questions will help.

a For the comic book market, calculate the elasticity of demand between the original and new equilibrium points. Is demand elastic or inelastic?

b Perform the same calculation for the dog biscuit market. Is demand elastic or inelastic?

c What do you know about demand elasticities that would have allowed you to complete your assignment "the other way" and predict which market would yield maximum tax revenue, and which market would place most of the tax burden on consumers?

7 After spending so much time on Dr. More's tax assignment in Short Answer Problems **5** and **6**, you realize you have one last chance to impress the boss. While your previous tax assignment had two important policy objectives—maximum tax revenue and appropriate tax burden—no one asked you about the relative efficiency loss of a tax on comic books versus dog biscuits. If the policy objective is to minimize deadweight loss, which good do you recommend be taxed?

8 Questions about the fairness of taxes are normative questions that depend on value judgments. If we arrange political parties in Canada on a spectrum from left (NDP) to right (Conservatives), which party is most likely to use the benefits principle to justify tax policy? Which party is most likely to use the ability-to-pay principle? Explain you answers.

ANSWERS

True/False and Explain

1 **T** Higher rents create incentives to use current buildings more intensively. (128–130)

2 **T** At equilibrium rent, all who can afford housing get it, but not necessarily those who need housing. (128–130)

3 **F** Ceiling is above market price so search activity won't increase and black markets won't arise. (128–130)

4 **F** Leftward shift in demand causes the wage rate to fall. (131–133)

5 **T** Raising the minimum wage decreases the quantity of labour demanded. (131–133)

6 **F** Exceptions are economists Card and Krueger. (131–133)

7 **T** Compared to an unregulated market, increased job search by labour in excess supply at minimum wage. (131–133)

8 **F** More elastic demand means more substitutes available and consumers are better able to escape tax by not buying. (133–138)

ⓔ **9** **F** Usually true; false if demand or supply is perfectly inelastic. (133–138)

10 **F** See Text Fig. 6.10 (p. 137). Tax revenue and deadweight loss come from lost surplus, but they are not equal. (133–138)

11 T See "Economics in Action." (141)

12 F Creates inefficiency through underproduction. (139–141)

13 F Shifts supply rightward. (139–141)

℮ 14 F Positive statement; can be verified by observation. (142–143)

℮ 15 T Effect on P depends on the relative magnitude of penalties. (142–143)

Multiple-Choice

1 b **c, d,** and **e** refer to long run. (128–130)

2 a Definition. **d** and **e** are the result of higher rent in an unregulated market. (128–130)

3 b Draw graph. No Δ *ceteris paribus* assumptions, so no shift in supply or demand. (128–130)

4 d Black market prices will be above ceiling. (128–130)

℮ 5 e Floor below equilibrium P doesn't prevent market from reaching equilibrium. (131–133)

6 b Quantity supplied (50) > quantity demanded (10). (131–133)

7 d Half of loss is consumer surplus, half is producer surplus. (131–133)

8 c Equals the vertical distance between the two supply curves. (133–138)

9 a Original P = $6, new P = $6.60. Sellers pay $1 tax and get $0.60 more from buyers, so sellers pay $0.40. (133–138)

10 b See previous answer. (133–138)

11 a $1 per frisbee × 4,000 units sold. (133–138)

℮ 12 c Rise in P ($6 to $6.60) decreases total revenue ($30,000 to $26,400). **d** is wrong: η = 2.3 and η_s = 3.2. (133–138)

13 a Area of triangle ($1/2ba$) with base = $1 ($6.60 – $5.60) and altitude = 1,000 (5,000 – 4,000). (133–138)

14 c See Text Fig. 6.6. Shifts demand curve down by vertical distance tax and decreases price received by sellers. (133–138)

15 b **a** would raise P by full amount of tax. **c** and **d** affect P but amounts uncertain. (133–138)

16 e The two principles are conflicting, but one can justify every statement. (133–138)

17 e **d** is true if quota is *below* equilibrium quantity. (139–141)

18 c Where vertical supply curve at 50 million bushels intersects demand. (139–141)

℮ 19 c Farmers receiving $5 but willing to supply this quantity at (their cost of) $1. (139–141)

℮ 20 d Quantity supplied at P = $5. (139–141)

℮ 21 d 70 million bushels sell for $1 per bushel. Taxpayers make up the difference of $4 per bushel × 70 million. (139–141)

22 b Floor above market P creates excess supply. (139–141)

23 e Definition. (139–141)

24 c Supply shifts leftward as penalties are added to other costs. (142–143)

25 d Reverse taxes and prohibition to make **a** and **b** true. (142–143)

Short Answer Problems

1 a Figure 6.6 on the next page corresponds to an unregulated market for rental housing. The initial demand, short-run supply, and long-run supply curves are D_0, SS_0, and LS. The market is initially in long-run equilibrium at point a corresponding to rent R_0 and quantity of rental units Q_0. Demand then increases to D_1, creating excess quantity demanded of $Q_2 - Q_0$ at the initial rent. In the short run, in an unregulated market, rent rises to R_1 to clear the markets and the equilibrium quantity of housing rented is Q_1 (point b). As the rent rises, the quantity of rental housing supplied increases (movement from point a to point b along supply curve SS_0) as the existing stock of housing is used more intensively. The quantity of housing demanded decreases (movement from point c to point b along demand curve D_1). Together, these movements eliminate the excess quantity demanded. The higher rent also provides an incentive to construct new housing in the long run—the shift in the supply curve from SS_0 to SS_1. The new long-run equilibrium is at point c, with rent restored to its original level and the number of units rented equal to Q_2.

FIGURE **6.6**

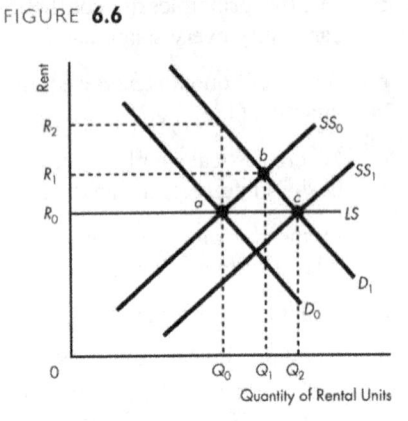

FIGURE **6.7**

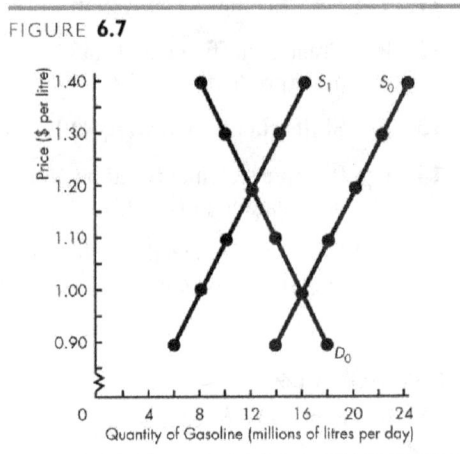

b We can also use Fig. 6.6 to discuss the behaviour of a market with a rent ceiling set at R_0. Start in the same long-run equilibrium at point a. Once again we observe an increase in demand from D_0 to D_1. In this case, however, the rent cannot rise to restore equilibrium. There will be no incentive to use the existing stock of housing more intensively in the short run or to construct new housing in the long run. The quantity of rental housing supplied will remain at Q_0. Since the last unit of rental housing is valued at R_2, but rent is fixed at R_0, demanders of rental housing will be willing to bear additional costs up to $R_2 - R_0$ (in the form of additional search activity or illegal payments) in order to obtain rental housing.

2 a The equilibrium price of gasoline is $1 per litre, since at that price the quantity of gasoline demanded is equal to the quantity supplied (16 million litres per day). The equilibrium quantity of gasoline is 16 million litres per day.

b The new table and graph are shown in Table 6.2 and Fig. 6.7.

TABLE **6.2**

Price	Quantity Demanded (millions of litres per day)	Quantity Supplied (millions of litres per day)
1.40	8	16
1.30	10	14
1.20	12	12
1.10	14	10
1.00	16	8
0.90	18	6

The new equilibrium price is $1.20 per litre, since at that price the quantity of gasoline demanded equals the new quantity supplied (12 million litres per day). The new equilibrium quantity is 12 million litres of gasoline per day.

c The increase in price has caused the quantity of gasoline demanded to decrease by 4 million litres per day (from 16 to 12 million). Given the new supply curve S_1, the increase in price from $1 to $1.20 per litre increases the quantity of gasoline supplied by 4 million litres per day (from 8 to 12 million).

3 a At the ceiling price of $1, quantity demanded is 16 million litres per day, quantity supplied is 8 million litres per day.

b The quantity of gasoline actually sold is 8 million litres per day. When, at a given price, quantity demanded and quantity supplied differ, whichever quantity is *less* determines the quantity actually sold.

c The excess quantity of gasoline demanded is 8 million litres per day.

d The marginal benefit of the 8-millionth litre per day of gasoline sold is $1.40. You can obtain this answer from your graph by imagining a vertical line from the quantity 8 million litres up to where it intersects the demand curve at $1.40. The demand curve is also a marginal benefit curve, showing the highest price consumers are willing to pay for each additional litre.

The marginal cost of the 8-millionth litre per day of gasoline sold is $1. The imaginary vertical line from the quantity 8 million litres intersects the supply curve S_1 at $1. The supply curve is also a marginal cost curve, showing the minimum producers must receive to produce an additional litre.

e Since marginal benefit ($1.40) > marginal cost ($1), the outcome is *not* efficient. The sum of consumer and producer surplus could be increased by allowing the price to rise, which would shift more resources into production of this good and out of production of other goods where marginal benefit is only equal to or less than marginal cost.

4 Because alcohol and nicotine are addictive, the demands for liquor and cigarettes are relatively inelastic. When liquor and cigarette prices are increased by "sin" taxes, the percentage fall in quantity demanded is less than the percentage increase in price. Thus total revenue increases as does tax revenue. To raise a fixed amount of revenue, it takes a much smaller per-unit tax on goods with inelastic demand than on goods with elastic demand. Inelastic demand also means, *ceteris paribus*, that a greater portion of the tax is borne by consumers rather than producers.

5 a See Fig. 6.4 Solution. In the comic book market, the supply curve shifts up vertically by an amount equal to the tax ($0.15). The original equilibrium price is $0.25 and quantity is 200,000. The new equilibrium price is $0.30 and quantity is 100,000. Total expenditure has decreased, from $50,000 ($0.25 × 200,000) to $30,000 ($0.30 × 100,000).

FIGURE **6.4** SOLUTION
COMIC BOOK MARKET

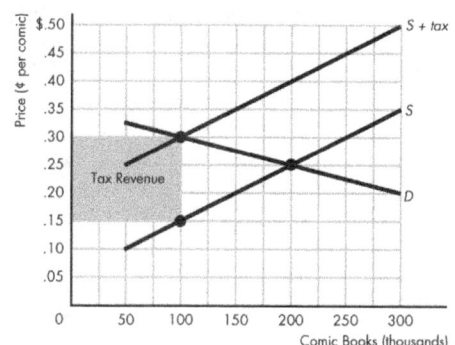

b Total tax revenue is $0.15 per comic book × 100,000 units sold = $15,000 and is indicated by the shaded area on Fig. 6.4 Solution.

c As a result of the tax, the price to consumers has gone up by $0.05 (from $0.25 to $0.30). Consumers' share of the tax burden is $5,000 ($0.05 × 100,000). Producers pay the $0.15 tax to government, but only get back $0.05 of it from consumers. Therefore, producers' share of the tax burden is $10,000 ($0.10 × 100,000).

d See Fig. 6.5 Solution. In the dog biscuit market, the supply curve shifts up vertically by an amount equal to the tax ($0.15). The original equilibrium price is $0.25 and quantity is 200,000. The new equilibrium price is $0.35 and quantity is 150,000. Total expenditure has increased, from $50,000 ($0.25 × 200,000) to $52,500 ($0.35 × 150,000).

FIGURE **6.5** SOLUTION
DOG BISCUIT MARKET

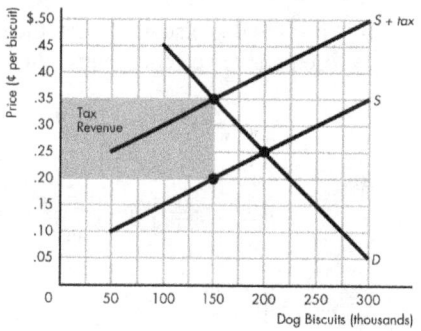

e Total tax revenue is $0.15 per dog biscuit × 150,000 units sold = $22,500 and is indicated by the shaded area on Fig. 6.5 Solution.

f As a result of the tax, the price to consumers has gone up by $0.10 (from $0.25 to $0.35). Consumers' share of the tax burden is $15,000 ($0.10 × 150,000). Producers pay the $0.15 tax to government, and get back $0.10 of it from consumers. Therefore, producers' share of the tax burden is $7,500 ($0.05 × 150,000).

g You confidently recommend to Dr. More that the Ministry tax dog biscuits. An excise tax on dog biscuits meets both objectives:

(1) it will raise more tax revenue than a tax on comic books ($22,500 versus $15,000) and (2) it will put more of the tax burden on consumers. In the dog biscuit market, consumers will pay $15,000, which is 67 percent of the tax burden. In the comic book market, consumers will pay only $5,000, which is 33 percent of the tax burden.

6 You are kicking yourself because you forgot that there is a relationship between elasticity of demand and both (1) a change in total revenue for a (tax-induced) increase in price, and (2) whether consumers or producers bear more of the burden of a tax.

a For the comic book market, the elasticity of demand (η) calculation is

$$\eta = \left|\left(\frac{\Delta Q}{Q_{ave}}\right) \Big/ \left(\frac{\Delta P}{P_{ave}}\right)\right|$$

$$= \left|\left(\frac{100-200}{150}\right) \Big/ \left(\frac{.30-.25}{.275}\right)\right|$$

$$= \left|\left(\frac{-.667}{.182}\right)\right| = 3.67$$

Demand is elastic.

b For the dog biscuit market, the elasticity of demand (η) calculation is

$$\eta = \left|\left(\frac{\Delta Q}{Q_{ave}}\right) \Big/ \left(\frac{\Delta P}{P_{ave}}\right)\right|$$

$$= \left|\left(\frac{150-200}{175}\right) \Big/ \left(\frac{.35-.25}{.30}\right)\right|$$

$$= \left|\left(\frac{-.286}{.333}\right)\right| = 0.86$$

Demand is inelastic.

c You forgot that an increase in price increases total expenditure when demand is inelastic, and decreases total expenditure when demand is elastic. Thus you could have used elasticity data to predict that expenditure would increase in the dog

biscuit market. An increase in expenditure is not the same as an increase in tax revenue, but if more money is being spent, there is more to be spent on taxes. You also forgot that the more inelastic demand is, the more of a tax consumers pay.

If you had thought of the elasticity approach without prompting, good for you! Dr. More will be calling on you again for advice. If you didn't think of it, time to return to Drs. Parkin and Bade for a refresher.

7 Deadweight loss can be calculated from Fig. 6.4 Solution and Fig. 6.5 Solution. The loss is the area of the triangle bordered by the three black dots. For comic books, the triangle has a base of $0.15 and altitude of 100,000, so the area = $1/2ba$ = 1/2($0.15)(100,000) = $7,500.

For dog biscuits, the triangle has a base of $0.15 and altitude of 50,000, so the area = $1/2ba$ = 1/2($0.15)(100,000) = $3,750.

Once again, your recommendation is to tax dog biscuits. Dr. More is impressed—you are offered full-time employment!

8 Political parties on the right are most likely to use the benefits principle, arguing for a fair exchange value between what the government takes in taxes and gives back in benefits. The rich should not pay more than the poor unless the rich receive greater benefits. This is also consistent with the fair-rules view in Chapter 5.

Political parties on the left are most likely to use the ability-to-pay principle, arguing that because the rich can afford to pay more than the poor, they should shoulder the extra burden. This is consistent with the fair-outcomes view in Chapter 5. If the rich pay more taxes than the poor, after-tax outcomes will be more equal.

There is no right answer here. As a citizen, you must decide which principle of fairness appeals most to you.

Chapter 7
Global Markets in Action

How Global Markets Work

Imports are goods and services we buy from other countries; **exports** are what we sell to other countries.

National comparative advantage drives international trade—a country exports goods/services that it can produce at a lower opportunity cost than any other nation, and imports goods/services that other nations can produce at a lower opportunity cost.

♦ For import goods, world price < pre-trade domestic price.

   • Quantity demanded (= quantity bought) increases with international trade.

   • Quantity supplied decreases with international trade and is lower than quantity demanded.

   • At world price, Canadian imports = Canadian quantity demanded – Canadian quantity supplied.

♦ For export goods, world price > pre-trade domestic price.

   • Quantity supplied increases with international trade.

   • Quantity demanded (= quantity bought) decreases with international trade and is lower than quantity supplied.

   • At world price, Canadian exports = Canadian quantity supplied – Canadian quantity demanded.

Winners, Losers, and the Net Gain from Trade

Winners and losers from international trade can be identified through consumer and producer surpluses.

For imports

♦ *lower* price for imported goods leads to *more* consumption by consumers and *higher* consumer surplus (area under demand curve and above price)—consumers of imported goods *gain* from international trade.

♦ *lower* price for imported goods leads to *less* production by producers and *lower* producer surplus (area above supply curve and below price)—producers of import-competing goods *lose* from international trade.

♦ consumer surplus gain > producer surplus loss—there is a higher total surplus for society from imported goods.

For exports

♦ *higher* price for exported goods leads to *less* consumption by consumers and *lower* consumer surplus—consumers of exported goods *lose* from international trade.

♦ *higher* price for exported goods leads to *more* production by producers and *higher* producer surplus—producers of exported goods *gain* from international trade.

International Trade Restrictions

Governments use four tools to influence international trade and protect domestic industries: tariffs, import quotas, other import barriers, and export subsidies.

Tariffs are taxes on imported goods, providing revenue for government, and benefiting import-competing industries.

- ◆ Higher domestic price = world price + tariff.

- ◆ Higher price means lower domestic quantity bought *and* higher domestic quantity produced— quantity imported shrinks.

- ◆ Government *gains* tariff revenue = tariff rate × quantity imported.

- ◆ Domestic producers *gain* producer surplus from higher price and higher production.

- ◆ Consumers *lose* consumer surplus from higher price and lower consumption.

- ◆ Society loses due to lower total surplus (= deadweight loss): Extra producer surplus + tariff revenue < lost consumer surplus.

- ◆ Tariffs have decreased due to **General Agreement on Tariffs and Trade** (**GAAT**) and other trade agreements.

- ◆ Recent attempts by the **World Trade Organization (WTO)** to lower barriers to trade in the **Doha Round** of trade talks has failed due to disputes between rich and developing nations.

Import quotas restrict import quantities, with quota licences distributed to importers.

- ◆ New supply curve = domestic supply curve + quota amount.

- ◆ Domestic price higher than world price—quantity demanded and bought falls, quantity supplied rises.

- ◆ Consumers lose consumer surplus from higher price.

- ◆ Domestic producers gain producer surplus from higher price.

- ◆ Importers gain profits from buying at world price and selling at higher domestic price.

- ◆ Society loses due to lower total surplus in a similar manner to effects of tariffs.

Other import barriers restrict supply of imports, increasing domestic price and domestic production.

- ◆ Examples include health, safety, and regulation barriers and voluntary export restraints (similar to a quota allocated to foreign exporters).

Export subsidies are payments from government to producers of exported goods.

- ◆ Export subsidies are illegal under international trade agreements, but agricultural subsidies to farmers increase domestic production, some of which is exported, creating deadweight loss.

The Case Against Protection

Trade restrictions are used despite losses of gains from trade for two somewhat credible reasons—to protect **infant industries** as they mature and to prevent foreign companies from **dumping** products on world markets at prices less than cost.

A country may restrict trade for less credible reasons:

- ◆ to save the jobs lost from free trade

- ◆ to compete with cheap foreign labour

- ◆ to penalize lax environmental standards

- ◆ to prevent rich countries from exploiting developing countries

One new worry is **offshoring** (hiring foreign labour or buying goods/services from abroad), especially **offshore outsourcing** (hiring foreign labour to produce in other countries).

- ◆ Lower transportation and communications costs have increased offshoring.

- ◆ Benefits, costs, winners, and losers from offshoring are similar to those for free trade, with losers concentrated in the domestic services industry.

The biggest problem with protection is that it invites retaliation from other countries (trade wars).

There are still trade restrictions because:

- ◆ tariff revenue is an attractive tax base for governments in developing countries.

- ◆ rent-seeking (lobbying) by groups/industries that suffer disproportionately under freer trade.

In Canada, employment insurance and interprovincial transfers provide some compensation for losses due to free trade, but in general losers are not compensated.

1   This chapter demonstrates that a country gains from trading internationally, both from exporting and from importing.

A country gains from exporting because the world price is higher than the domestic price. Producers gain surplus from selling internationally at this higher price. Even though consumers lose some of their surplus (due to the higher price), the producers' gains more than outweigh this loss, so the country's total surplus is higher.

Similarly, a country gains from importing because the world price is lower than the domestic price. Consumers gain surplus from buying at this lower price. Even though producers lose some of their surplus (due to the lower price), the consumers' gain more than outweighs this loss, and the country's total surplus is higher.

Note that an importing country even gains from buying a good that is dumped at below-cost on the world market by another country. In essence, the dumping country is giving the importing country a subsidy!

2   Given the considerable gains from free trade, why then do countries have such a strong tendency to impose trade restrictions? The key is that while free trade creates benefits to the economy as a whole, there are both winners and losers. The winners gain more in total than the losers lose, but the losers tend to be concentrated in a few industries.

Given this concentration, free trade will be resisted by some acting on the basis of rational self-interest. Even though the overwhelming majority will benefit while only a small minority are hurt, it is not surprising to see trade restrictions implemented. The cost of a given trade restriction to *each* of the majority will be individually quite small, while the benefit to *each* of the few will be individually large. Thus the minority will have a significant incentive to see that restriction takes place, while the majority will have little incentive to expend time and energy in resisting trade restriction.

3   To understand the source of pressures for trade restrictions, let's summarize the winners and losers from trade restrictions.

Under three forms of restrictions (tariffs, quotas, and voluntary export restraints) *consumers* lose, because the price of the imported good increases. *Domestic producers* of the imported good and their factors of production gain from all three, because the price of the imported good increases. *Foreign producers* and their factors of production lose under all three schemes, because their export sales decrease. Under quotas and voluntary export restraints, the *holders of import licences* gain from buying low and selling high (they may be foreign or domestic). *Government* gains tariff revenue under tariffs and, potentially, votes under other schemes.

Given this list, it is hardly surprising that the main supporters of trade restrictions are domestic producers and their factors of production.

True/False and Explain

How Global Markets Work

1   When a Canadian citizen stays in a hotel in France, Canada is exporting a service.

2   Countries will export goods and services that they can produce at a lower opportunity cost than other countries.

3   For a country to export a good, the world price must be lower than the domestic price.

4   If Canada starts importing widgets, the price of widgets in Canada will fall and the quantity bought will increase.

Winners, Losers, and the Net Gain from Trade

5 All parts of society gain from being able to export goods at a higher price than the domestic price.

6 Domestic producers gain from the introduction of imports.

7 Domestic consumers gain from the introduction of imports.

International Trade Restrictions

8 When governments impose import quotas, they increase their country's gains from trade.

9 A tariff on a good will raise its domestic price and reduce the domestic quantity traded.

10 An import quota will cause the domestic price of the imported good to decrease.

11 The government revenue plus the increase in producer surplus offsets the losses in consumer surplus from a tariff.

The Case Against Protection

12 Japan is dumping steel if it sells steel in Japan at a lower price than it sells it in Canada.

13 Since Mexican labour is paid so much less than Canadian labour, a free trade agreement guarantees Canada will lose jobs to Mexico.

14 Elected governments are slow to reduce trade restrictions because there would be more domestic losers than winners.

15 A trade agreement that increases both imports and exports will decrease jobs domestically.

Multiple-Choice

How Global Markets Work

1 Which of the following is a Canadian service export?
a A Canadian buys dinner while travelling in Switzerland.
b A Swiss buys dinner while travelling in Canada.
c A Canadian buys a clock made in Switzerland.
d A Swiss buys a computer made in Canada.
e A Canadian buys a Canadian computer in Switzerland.

2 If Canada imports widgets, it must be the case that
a Canada has a comparative advantage in widget production.
b widgets are cheaper in Canada than the rest of the world.
c the Canadian quantity supplied of widgets is greater than the Canadian quantity demanded for widgets at the world price.
d the Canadian quantity supplied of widgets is less than the Canadian quantity demanded for widgets at the world price
e there is no tariff on widgets.

3 Table 7.1 shows Glazeland's doughnut market before international trade. Glazeland opens up to international trade. If the world price is $0.60, then Glazeland will produce _____ doughnuts and will _____ _____ doughnuts.
   a 2 million; import 3 million
   b 4 million; import 1 million
   c 4 million; export 1 million
   d 5 million; import 3 million
   e 5 million; export 3 million

TABLE 7.1 Glazeland's Doughnut Market

Price (dollars per doughnut)	Glazeland's Supply (millions)	Glazeland's Demand (millions)
0.20	1	10
0.30	2	8
0.40	3	6
0.50	4	4
0.60	5	2
0.70	6	0

4 Table 7.1 shows Glazeland's doughnut market before international trade. Glazeland opens up to international trade. If the world price is $0.40, then Glazeland will produce _____ doughnuts and will _____ _____ doughnuts.
   a 3 million; import 3 million
   b 3 million; export 3 million
   c 4 million; import 1 million
   d 4 million; export 1 million
   e 6 million; export 3 million

5 If Canada starts exporting gadgets, then the domestic price of gadgets
   a decreases, leading to a decline in production and imports fill the gap.
   b decreases, leading to a decline in quantity demanded and the difference is exported.
   c stays the same, but Canada increases production in response to the world demand.
   d increases, quantity demanded declines, production increases and the difference is exported.
   e increases, quantity demanded increases and the difference is imported.

Winners, Losers, and the Net Gain from Trade

6 If the widget industry enters the world market, and the world price is higher than the domestic price, then the
   a higher price will make consumers better off.
   b higher price will make producers worse off.
   c increased production will make consumers better off.
   d decreased production will make producers worse off.
   e amount of exports will be positive.

7 Figure 7.1 shows a domestic import market. What is the area of *producer* surplus at the world price?
   a ABICDFGH
   b ABCF
   c FGHJ
   d FGJ
   e J

FIGURE 7.1

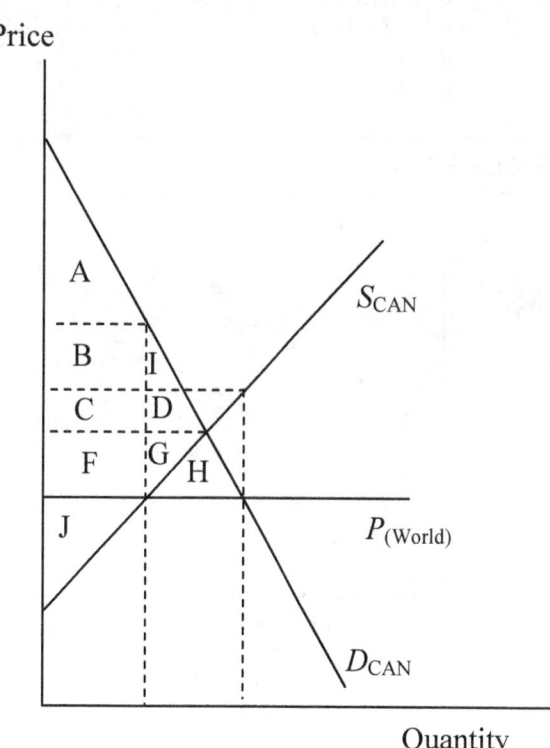

8 Figure 7.1 shows a domestic import market. What is the area of *consumer* surplus at the world price?
  a ABICDFGH
  b ABCF
  c FGHJ
  d FGJ
  e J

9 Figure 7.1 shows a domestic import market. What is the area of *increase* in *total* surplus from moving from the domestic price to the world price?
  a H
  b J
  c FGH
  d IDG
  e ABICDFGH

10 Figure 7.2 shows a domestic export market. What is the area of *producer* surplus at the world price?
  a ABI
  b ABICDE
  c CDEFGJ
  d FGJ
  e J

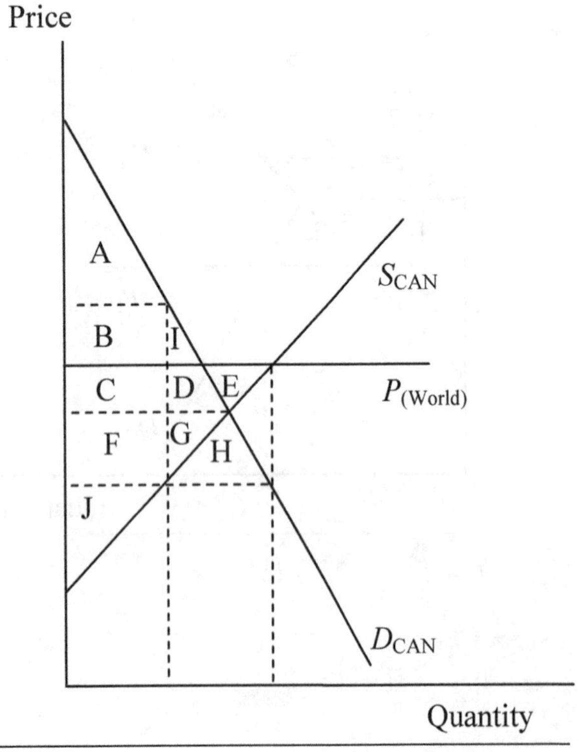

11 Figure 7.2 shows a domestic export market. What is the area of *consumer* surplus at the world price?
  a ABI
  b ABICD
  c ABCDFJ
  d FGJ
  e J

12 Figure 7.2 shows a domestic export market. What is the area of *increase* in *total* surplus from moving from the domestic price to the world price?
  a CD
  b CDE
  c E
  d CDEFGJ
  e H

International Trade Restrictions

13 When an *import quota* is imposed, the gap between the domestic price and the export price is captured by
  a consumers in the importing country.
  b the domestic producers of the good.
  c the government of the importing country.
  d foreign exporters.
  e the importers of the good.

14 When a *voluntary export restraint* agreement is reached, the gap between the domestic import price and the export price is captured by
  a consumers in the importing country.
  b the domestic producers of the good.
  c the government of the importing country.
  d foreign exporters.
  e the domestic importers of the good.

15 When a *tariff* is imposed, the gap between the domestic price and the export price is captured by
  a consumers in the importing country.
  b the domestic producers of the good.
  c the government of the importing country.
  d foreign exporters.
  e the domestic importers of the good.

FIGURE **7.2**

Price

Quantity

16 Table 7.2 shows the Canadian supply of and demand for widgets. Widgets are available on the world market for $7. If the Canadian government imposes a tariff of $1, the domestic selling price will be ___ and quantity bought will be ____.
   a $6; 48 million
   b $7; 44 million
   c $8; 16 million
   d $8; 24 million
   e $8; 40 million

TABLE **7.2** Canada's Market for Widgets

Price (dollars per widgets)	Canadian Supply (millions)	Canadian Demand (millions)
5	12	52
6	16	48
7	20	44
8	24	40
9	28	36
10	32	32
12	36	28

17 Table 7.2 shows the Canadian supply of and demand for widgets. Widgets are available on the world market for $7. If the Canadian government imposes a tariff of $1, how many widgets will Canada import?
   a   32 million
   b   24 million
   c   16 million
   d   24 million
   e   40 million

18 Table 7.2 shows the Canadian supply of and demand for widgets. Widgets are available on the world market for $7. Canadian widget producers convince their government to protect the domestic industry from cheap imports. If the Canadian government sets an import quota of 8 million widgets, the resulting price of a widget in Canada will be _____ and domestic production will be ____.
   a $6; 40 million
   b $7; 36 million
   c $8; 32 million
   d $9; 28 million
   e $10; 32 million

19 A tariff on watches imported by Atlantis will cause Atlantis's domestic price of watches to
   a   decrease and imports to increase.
   b   increase and watch production in Atlantis to increase.
   c   increase and watch production in Atlantis to decrease.
   d   decrease and watch production in Atlantis to increase.
   e   decrease and watch production in Atlantis to decrease.

20 The introduction of a tariff will
   a   increase consumer surplus, decrease producer surplus, and decrease total surplus.
   b   increase consumer surplus, increase producer surplus, and decrease total surplus.
   c   decrease consumer surplus, decrease producer surplus, and decrease total surplus.
   d   decrease consumer surplus, increase producer surplus, and decrease total surplus.
   e   decrease consumer surplus, increase producer surplus, and increase total surplus.

The Case Against Protection

21 Which of the following is *not* an argument for protectionism?
   a   to prevent dumping
   b   to save jobs in import-competing industries
   c   to gain a comparative advantage
   d   to allow infant industries to grow
   e   to prevent rich nations from exploiting poor nations

22 The biggest problem with protection is that
   a   it invites retaliation from trading partners.
   b   losers are not compensated.
   c   it worsens environmental standards.
   d   it can worsen national security.
   e   it lowers wages.

23 Why is international trade restricted?
   a   because government revenue is costly to collect via tariffs
   b   to get higher consumption possibilities
   c   to realize the gains from trade
   d   due to rent-seeking
   e   because free trade creates economic losses on average

24 The effects of offshoring from opening up call centres in India are similar to the effects from
   a   free trade.
   b   tariffs.
   c   import quotas.
   d   voluntary export restraints.
   e   export subsidies.

25 In Canada, when international trade hurts producers and reduces jobs in import-competing industries, the government response is to
   a   introduce tariffs.
   b   do absolutely nothing.
   c   fully compensate all losers.
   d   guarantee every job loser retraining.
   e   use employment insurance to help job losers with temporary relief.

Short Answer Problems

1 It is often argued by union leaders that tariffs are needed to protect domestic jobs. In light of the explanation in the textbook, evaluate this argument.

2 In a recent case, the U.S. government investigated Chinese bra manufacturers for suspected "dumping" of bras in the United States. The U.S. Department of Trade determined that the cost of making a bra in China was equivalent to $12 per bra, although they were being sold in the United States for $11 each. They then imposed dumping duties (tariffs) on Chinese bras of $1 per bra.

   a   Define dumping, and explain whether this is a case of dumping.

   b   Dumping duties are put in place to protect the U.S. economy from the "unfair" low price of the dumped imports. Did the dumping duties on bras make the U.S. economy better off?

3 Consider a simple world in which there are two countries, Atlantis and Beltran, each producing and consuming gadgets. The Atlantean gadget market is shown in Table 7.3, and the Beltranian market is given in Table 7.4. Both countries use the dollar as their currency.

TABLE 7.3 Atlantis' Market for Gadgets

Price (dollars per gadgets)	Atlantean Supply (millions)	Atlantean Demand (millions)
0	0	240
10	50	210
20	100	180
30	150	150
40	180	120
50	210	90
60	240	60
70	270	30
80	300	0

TABLE 7.4 Beltran's Market for Gadgets

Price (dollars per gadgets)	Beltranian Supply (millions)	Beltranian Demand (millions)
0	0	200
10	25	190
20	50	180
30	75	170
40	100	160
50	120	150
60	140	140
70	160	130
80	180	120

   a   Do the conditions exist for the two countries to trade in gadgets? Explain briefly.

   b   If they do trade, who will be the exporter and who will be the importer?

   c   Using the information in the tables, find the trading price of gadgets, and indicate how much will be exported from one country to another, and how much will be imported.

4 Suppose that Atlantis and Beltran engage in trade. (You should have been able to show in Short Answer Problem 3 that Atlantis will export gadgets to Beltran.) In a graph, show the Atlantis market for gadgets, indicating the pre-trade equilibrium and the free trade equilibrium. Indicate the change in consumer surplus, change in producer surplus, and change in total surplus for Atlantis. Indicate the winners and losers in Atlantis from free trade.

5 Suppose that Atlantis and Beltran engage in trade. (You should have been able to show in Short Answer Problem 3 that Atlantis will export gadgets to Beltran.) In a graph, show the Beltran market for gadgets, indicating the pre-trade equilibrium and the free trade equilibrium. Indicate the change in consumer surplus, change in producer surplus, and change in total surplus

for Beltran. Identify the winners and losers in Beltran from free trade.

6 Continue the analysis of Atlantis and Beltran trading gadgets. Suppose that the importing country (Beltran) introduces a tariff of $10. Show on your graph from Short Answer Problem **5** what this will do to the quantity demanded in Beltran, quantity produced, and amount imported. Indicate in words who will gain and who will lose from the tariff in Beltran. How much is the tariff revenue for Beltran?

ⓒⓣ **7** Continue the analysis of Atlantis and Beltran trading gadgets. What will the impact of the tariff introduced by Beltran be on the quantity exported from Atlantis, and what will be the impact on the domestic price of gadgets, quantity produced, and quantity demanded in Atlantis? Indicate in words who will gain and who will lose from the tariff in Atlantis. (It is likely easier to work with Table 7.3 instead of doing this graphically.)

8 Rich countries are often worried about the impact of offshoring of services (such as call centres for computers or software) to developing countries like India. Suppose that Canada was to ban the use of offshoring for call centres. Explain in words who would gain and who would lose from this ban in Canada, and in India.

A N S W E R S

True/False and Explain

1 **F** Canada is importing (using) a service. (152)

2 **T** Definition of national comparative advantage. (152)

3 **F** Must be higher to generate profits. (154)

4 **T** See Text Fig. 7.1. (153)

5 **F** Consumers lose surplus from higher price. (156)

6 **F** Imports lower prices for import-competing producers, reducing producer surplus. (155)

7 **T** Imports lower prices for import-competing goods, increasing consumer surplus. (155)

8 **F** Trade restrictions reduce gains from trade. (157–159)

9 **T** Tariff raises price paid inside the country, which decreases quantity traded. (157–159)

10 **F** Quota decreases supply, increasing domestic price—see Text Fig. 7.7. (160)

11 **F** There is deadweight loss—see Text Fig. 7.6. (159)

12 **F** Dumping is selling in Canada at a lower price than in Japan. (163)

13 **F** Must also examine productivity of workers in each country, and Canadian workers are more productive. (164)

14 **F** Because losers' losses are individually much greater than winners' gains. (166)

15 **F** More imports will likely decrease jobs, but more exports will increase them—net outcome is not clear. (164)

Multiple-Choice

1 **b** **a** and **c** are imports, **d** and **e** are exports of a *good*. (152)

2 **d** If we import, world price is lower and our supply is therefore too low compared to demand. Could still have a tariff. (153)

3 **e** Price = $0.60 implies supply of 5 million, but demand is only 2 million, so 3 million are exported. (153–154)

4 **a** Price = $0.40 implies supply of 3 million, but demand is 6 million, so 3 million are imported. (153–154)

5 **d** See Text Fig. 7.2. (154)

6 **e** Higher price and higher production increases producer surplus and lowers consumer surplus. (156)

7 **e** Area below price and above supply curve. (155)

8 **a** Area above price and below demand curve. (155)

9 **a** Gain in consumer surplus (FGH)—loss of producer surplus (FG). (155)

10 **c** Area below price and above supply curve. (156)

11 **a** Area above price and below demand curve. (156)

12 **c** Gain in producer surplus (CDE)—loss of consumer surplus (CD). (156)

13 e Under a quota, domestic government allocates the licences to import. (160)

14 d Because they have the right to export. (162)

15 c They collect tariff revenue = import price – world price. (157–159)

16 e New price is $1 + $7 = $8, so quantity bought (from demand curve) is 40 million. (157–159)

17 c Difference between quantity demanded and supplied at $8. (157–159)

18 d Equilibrium is price where quota of 8 million = import demand = quantity demanded – quantity supplied. (160–161)

19 b Tariff increases domestic price = export price + tariff, and domestic production increases in response. (157–159)

20 d See Text Fig. 7.6. (159)

21 c See text discussion. (163–167)

22 a See text discussion. (163–167)

23 d See text discussion. (163–167)

24 a Similar effect on domestic price of good, domestic production, imports, winners, and losers. (165)

25 e See text discussion. (166–167)

Short Answer Problems

1 This argument has some truth to it. As the textbook shows on pages 157–158, the tariff will lead an increase in domestic production of the protected good, which will lead to an increase in jobs in that industry. However, the same tariff could trigger a trade war, which would reduce foreign purchases of goods, reducing exports and export production, and reducing jobs in the export industry. The net effect on jobs is unclear.

2 a Dumping occurs when a foreign firm sells its exports at a lower price than the cost of production. Since the cost of production is higher than the export price, this is indeed a case of dumping.

b The dumping duties are exactly like a tariff, and as shown in Text Fig. 7.6 (p. 159), the effect of a tariff is to increase the domestic price of bras, reduce domestic bra consumption (and reduce consumer surplus) and increase domestic bra production (and increase producer surplus), and lower U.S.

total surplus. The U.S. economy is made worse off.

3 a The pre-trade price of gadgets in Atlantis would be $30, while the pre-trade price in Beltran would be $60. If a trading price between $30 and $60 could come about, both sides would gain. Therefore, the appropriate conditions exist for trade.

b The exporter would be Atlantis, with the lower price, and Beltran would be the importer with the higher price.

c We can find the trading price ($40) in a variety of manners. We could combine the two supply schedules into a "world" supply schedule, and combine the two demand schedules into a "world" demand schedule, and find the equilibrium world price. Such a schedule is shown below in Table 7.5, and world equilibrium occurs with a quantity of 280 million and price of $40.

TABLE **7.5** "World" Market for Gadgets

Price (dollars per gadgets)	World Supply (millions)	World Demand (millions)
0	0	440
10	75	400
20	150	360
30	225	320
40	280	280
50	330	240
60	380	200
70	430	160
80	480	120

We can also find the trading price ($40) by looking at Tables 7.3 and 7.4, and noting that at a price of $40, supply in Atlantis exceeds demand by 60 million, while supply in Beltran is short of demand by 60 million, indicating that sending 60 million from Atlantis to Beltran would create equilibrium. In summary, Atlantis exports 60 million gadgets and Beltran imports 60 million.

4 Figure 7.3 on the next page shows the Atlantean market. The initial pre-trade equilibrium occurs at a price of $30 and a quantity traded of 150 million. We have established the world price will be $40. At this price, Atlantis will demand only 120 million gadgets (read off the demand curve), and will produce 180 million gadgets (read off the supply curve), and will export the surplus of 60 million gadgets.

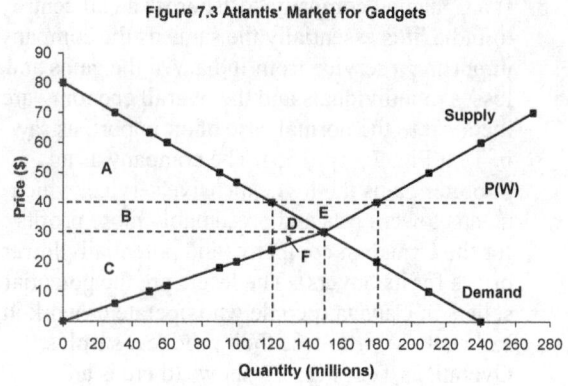

Figure 7.3 Atlantis' Market for Gadgets

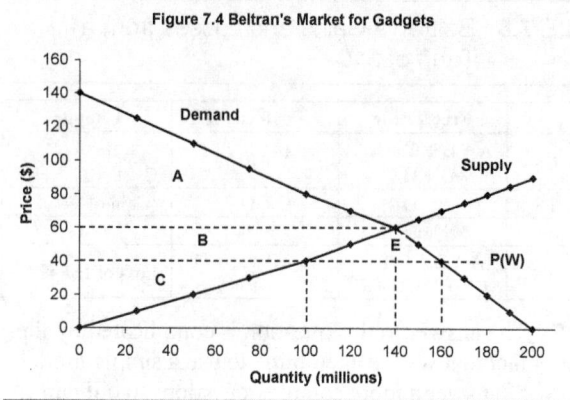

Figure 7.4 Beltran's Market for Gadgets

Table 7.6 below summarizes the amounts of consumer surplus (the area above the price and below the demand curve), producer surplus (the area below the price and above the supply curve), and total surplus (consumer surplus + producer surplus) in the two situations, as well as the change in each from pre-trade to the trade equilibrium.

TABLE 7.6 Atlantis' Gains and Losses from Free Trade

	Pre-Trade	Free Trade	Change
CS	A + B + D	A	Loss of B + D
PS	C + F	B + C + D + E + F	Gain of B + D + E
TS	A + B + C + D + F	A + B + C + D + E + F	Gain of E

Table 7.6 shows that consumers lose and producers win, with an overall gain for Atlantis.

5   Figure 7.4 shows the Beltran market. The initial pre-trade equilibrium occurs at a price of $60 and a quantity traded of 140 million. We have established the world price will be $40. At this price, Beltran will demand 160 million gadgets (read off the demand curve), and will produce only 100 million gadgets (read off the supply curve), and will import the shortage of 60 million gadgets.

Table 7.7 summarizes Beltran's amounts of consumer surplus (the area above the price and below the demand curve), producer surplus (the area below the price and above the supply curve), and total surplus (consumer surplus + producer surplus) in the two situations, as well as the change in each from pre-trade to the trade equilibrium.

TABLE 7.7 Beltran's Gains and Losses from Free Trade

	Pre-Trade	Free Trade	Change
CS	A	A + B + E	Gain of B + E
PS	B + C	C	Loss of B
TS	A + B + C	A + B + C + E	Gain of E

Table 7.7 shows that consumers win and producers lose, with an overall gain for Beltran.

6   Figure 7.5 below shows the impact of the tariff on Beltran's market. The tariff adds $10 to the world price, leading to a domestic price of $50. At this price, demand is only 150 million gadgets, and supply increases to 120 million gadgets, leading to a decreased amount of imports at 30 million units.

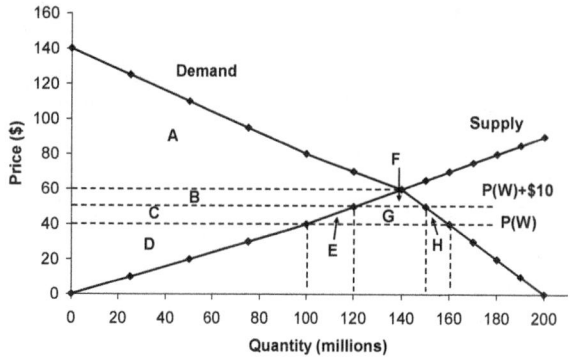

Figure 7.5 Impact of a Tariff on Beltran

Table 7.8 on the next page summarizes the gains and losses from the introduction of the tariff. Consumers lose consumer surplus, producers gain producer surplus, the government gains tariff revenue ($10 × 30 million gadget imports), but overall total surplus is lower.

TABLE **7.8** Beltran's Gains and Losses from a Tariff of $10

	Free Trade	Post-Tariff	Change
CS	A + B + C + E + F + G + H	A + B + F	Loss of C + E + G + H
PS	D	C + D	Gain of C
Tariff Rev.	None	G	G
TS	A + B + C + D + E + F + G + H	A + B + C + D + F + G	Loss of E + H

7   The answer to this question is complicated by the fact that we are attempting to use a simple model to answer a more complex question, so only an approximate answer is possible. Beltran is now importing only 30 million gadgets from Atlantis, instead of the previous 60 million units. Therefore, Atlantis will export only 30 million units. Looking at Table 7.3, we can see that this will occur at some price between $30 and $40 (we cannot exactly tell where without a mathematical model incorporating the tax, which is beyond the complexities of this model). Therefore, the impact of the Beltran tariff is to reduce the world price somewhat. Since the price received by Atlantean sellers will fall, they will lose some producer surplus. Since the price paid by Atlantean consumers will fall, they will gain some consumer surplus. The overall impact of the fall in world price for Atlantis will be a reduction in total surplus, which can be shown on Fig. 7.3 (the area E gets smaller).

8   If a Canadian company "offshores" a call centre to India, it is essentially the same as the company importing a service from India. All the gains and losses to individuals and the overall economy are identical to the normal case of an import, as saw in Text Fig. 7.3 (p. 155). The company as an importer gains the less expensive service, which means lower costs and presumably more profits for the Canadian company (and potentially lower prices for its buyers). The losers are the potential sellers in Canada (people who operate or work in call centres), who lose their producer surplus. Overall, as Text Fig. 7.3 shows, there is an increase in total surplus in Canada from being able to import the cheaper product.

Similarly, for India this is an export of a service, and as in Text Fig. 7.4 (p. 156), we can see that the Indian suppliers of the call centre services gain producer surplus, Indian consumers lose consumer surplus from the higher Indian price, and overall Indian total surplus is higher.

If the use of offshore call centres is banned, then all the gains and losses are reversed. The Canadian buyers of call centre services lose their consumer surplus (they face higher costs). The Canadian import-competing call centres gain back their lost producer surplus, but overall Canadian total surplus is lower. For India, the Indian suppliers lose producer surplus, the Indian consumers gain consumer surplus, and overall Indian total surplus is lower.

Part 2 Wrap Up
Understanding How Markets Work

PROBLEM

The finance minister has asked your boss at the finance department, Dr. Ina Lastic, to estimate the effects of levying a \$24-per-carton tax on cigarettes. Dr. Lastic predicts that the tax will raise significant tax revenues (at least \$30 million) because cigarette demand is inelastic.

Unfortunately, Dr. Lastic is unaware of a recent study you read in *The Globe and Mail* about past tax increases that found "Ottawa has not received the entire tax windfall it expected from increased cigarette levies because of growing tobacco smuggling."

She has asked you to perform the following detailed analysis for her predictions. The demand and supply curves (without taxes) for cigarettes are given in Fig. P2.1. The before-tax price is \$28 per carton, and the before-tax quantity is 2.25 million cartons per year.

a Draw the new "*S* + tax" curve on Fig. P2.1.

b According to Dr. Lastic's predictions, what is the after-tax equilibrium price? equilibrium quantity?

c Calculate her predicted tax revenues.

d Check to see if Dr. Lastic's claim that the demand for cigarettes is inelastic is correct by calculating η between the before-tax equilibrium and the after-tax equilibrium. Was she right?

FIGURE **P2.1** CANADIAN CIGARETTE MARKET

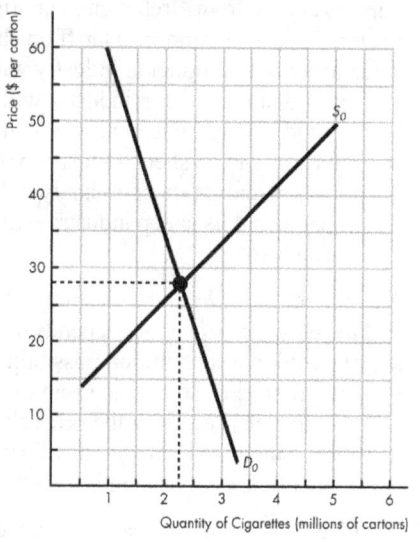

e Dr. Lastic gets high marks for economics so far. Nonetheless, you respectfully point out that her revenue prediction is wrong because she hasn't taken into account the effects of smuggling. Showing an uncharacteristic willingness to stretch herself, she replies, "I'm listening. What's *your* prediction of tax revenue?"

Here's your chance to impress the boss. You know that the supply curve of cigarettes in the United States is the same as the before-tax supply curve in Canada. You have estimated the cost of breaking the law (*CBL*) to suppliers at \$16 per carton and risk to consumers of buying smuggled cigarettes is so small that their *CBL* is effectively zero. Use this information to answer the following questions.

i Draw and label any appropriate new curve(s) on Fig. P2.1.

ii What is *your* prediction of the after-tax price of a carton of cigarettes? the quantity of cigarettes sold legally? the quantity of smuggled cigarettes sold illegally? (*Hint:* The price of legal and illegal cigarettes will be equal because they are perfect substitutes.)

iii What is your prediction of tax revenue?

MIDTERM EXAMINATION

You should allocate 40 minutes for this examination (20 questions, 2 minutes per question). For each question, choose the one *best* answer.

1 Acadia and Breton have free trade. Acadia imports cheese from Breton and exports sheep to Breton. If Acadia imposes a tariff on cheese, Acadia's cheese-producing industry will
  a expand, and its sheep industry will contract.
  b expand, and its sheep industry will expand.
  c contract, and its sheep industry will contract.
  d contract, and its sheep industry will expand.
  e expand, and its sheep industry will be unchanged.

2 The magnitude of *both* the elasticity of demand and the elasticity of supply depends on
  a the resource substitution possibilities.
  b the proportion of income spent on a good.
  c the time elapsed since the price change.
  d the technological conditions of production.
  e none of the above factors.

3 If an increase in price causes a decrease in total revenue, price elasticity of demand is
  a negative.
  b zero.
  c greater than zero but less than one.
  d equal to one.
  e greater than one.

4 The marginal benefit of a good is
  a the maximum amount a person is willing to pay for an additional unit.
  b the minimum amount a person is willing to pay for an additional unit.
  c equal to marginal cost.
  c greater than marginal cost.
  e less than marginal cost.

5 The proportion of a sales tax paid by consumers will be greater the more
  1 elastic is demand.
  2 inelastic is demand.
  3 elastic is supply.
  4 inelastic is supply.
  a 2 only
  b 1 and 3
  c 1 and 4
  d 2 and 3
  e 2 and 4

6 The "big tradeoff" is between
  a efficiency and fairness.
  b fair results and fair rules.
  c equality of income and equality of opportunity.
  d the symmetry principle and utilitarianism.
  e consumer surplus and producer surplus.

7 If both demand and supply increase, equilibrium price
  a will rise and quantity will increase.
  b will fall and quantity will increase.
  c could rise or fall and quantity will increase.
  d will rise and quantity could either increase or decrease.
  e will fall and quantity could either increase or decrease.

8 If turnips are an inferior good, then, *ceteris paribus*, a rise in the price of turnips will cause
  a a decrease in the demand for turnips.
  b an increase in the demand for turnips.
  c a decrease in the supply of turnips.
  d an increase in the supply of turnips.
  e none of the above.

9 In Fig. P2.2, if the minimum wage is set at $6 per hour, what is the level of unemployment in millions of hours?
  a 50
  b 40
  c 20
  d 10
  e 0

FIGURE **P2.2**

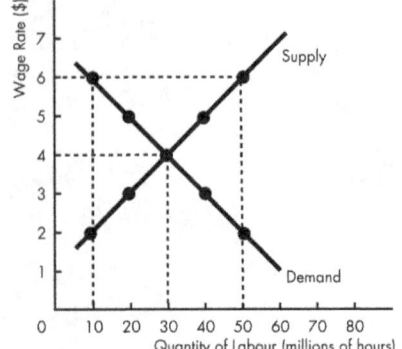

10 A demand curve is
   a   a consumer surplus curve.
   b   a marginal benefit curve.
   c   a minimum-willingness-to-pay curve.
   d   all of the above.
   e   none of the above.

11 If a 10 percent increase in income causes a 10 percent decrease in the consumption of widgets (at a constant price),
   a   the price elasticity of demand for widgets equals 1.
   b   the income elasticity of demand for widgets is negative.
   c   the income elasticity of demand for widgets equals 1.
   d   widgets are a normal good.
   e   none of the above is true.

12 A price floor set below the equilibrium price results in
   a   excess supply.
   b   excess demand.
   c   the equilibrium price.
   d   an increase in supply.
   e   a decrease in demand.

13 When there is underproduction of a good,
   a   the sum of consumer surplus and producer surplus is greater than the sum for an efficient allocation.
   b   the sum of consumer surplus and producer surplus is less than the sum for an efficient allocation.
   c   deadweight loss is less than for an efficient allocation.
   d   only consumer surplus is lost.
   e   only producer surplus is lost.

14 A decrease in the price of X from \$6 to \$4 causes an increase in the quantity of Y demanded (at the current price of Y) from 900 to 1,100 units. What is the cross elasticity of demand between X and Y?
   a   0.5
   b   −0.5
   c   2
   d   −2
   e   **a** or **b**, depending on whether X and Y are substitutes or complements

15 A decrease in quantity supplied is represented by a
   a   movement down the supply curve.
   b   movement up the supply curve.
   c   leftward shift of the supply curve.
   d   rightward shift of the supply curve.
   e   rightward shift of the demand curve.

16 At current output, the marginal benefit of shoehorns is less than marginal cost. To achieve an efficient allocation,
   1   shoehorn output must increase.
   2   shoehorn output must decrease.
   3   the marginal benefit of shoehorns will rise.
   4   the marginal cost of shoehorns will rise.
   a   1 and 3
   b   1 and 4
   c   2 and 3
   d   2 and 4
   e   1 only

17 Farmland can be used to produce either cattle or corn. If the demand for cattle increases,
   a   demand for corn will increase.
   b   supply of corn will increase.
   c   demand for corn will decrease.
   d   supply of corn will decrease.
   e   **b** and **c**.

18 Refer to Fig. P2.3. The opportunity cost of 1 beer in Partyland is _____, and the opportunity cost of 1 beer in Cowabunga is _____.
   a   dependent on where on the *PPF* we measure it; dependent on where on the *PPF* we measure it
   b   100 pizzas; 25 pizzas
   c   3 pizzas; 1 pizza
   d   1 pizza; 1 pizza
   e   1 pizza; 1/3 pizza

FIGURE **P2.3** PARTYLAND AND COWABUNGA—*PPF* FOR BEER AND PIZZA

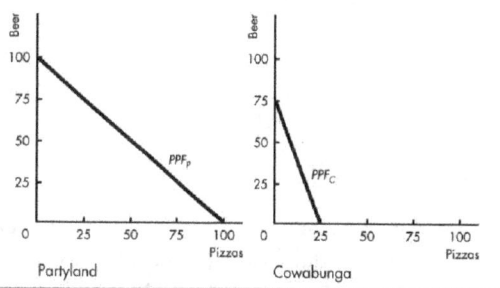

19 Refer to Fig. P2.3 on the previous page. The opportunity cost of 1 pizza in Partyland is _____, and the opportunity cost of 1 pizza in Cowabunga is _____.
   a dependent on where on the *PPF* we measure it; dependent on where on the *PPF* we measure it
   b 100 beers; 25 beers
   c 3 beers; 1 beer
   d 1 beer; 1 beer
   e 1 beer; 3 beers

20 Refer to Fig. P2.3 on the previous page. If trade occurs between Partyland and Cowabunga,
   a there will be a lot of drunk turtles.
   b Partyland will export both pizza and beer, because it has a comparative advantage in both.
   c Cowabunga will export both pizza and beer, because it has a comparative advantage in both.
   d Partyland will export pizza, and Cowabunga will export beer.
   e Partyland will export beer, and Cowabunga will export pizza.

ANSWERS

Problem

a See Fig. P2.1 Solution. Ignore the curve *S* + *CBL* for now.

b The after-tax equilibrium price is $46 per carton. The after-tax equilibrium quantity is 1.5 million cartons per year.

c Tax revenue is 1.5 million cartons × $24 per carton = $36 million per year.

d

$$\eta = \left| \frac{\frac{\Delta Q}{Q_{ave}}}{\frac{\Delta P}{P_{ave}}} \right|$$

$$\eta = \left| \frac{\frac{-.75}{1.875}}{\frac{18}{37}} \right| = \frac{.4}{.486} = .82$$

The demand curve is inelastic ($\eta < 1$) between the two equilibrium points. Dr. Lastic's predictions about tax revenue (without smuggling) and elasticity were correct.

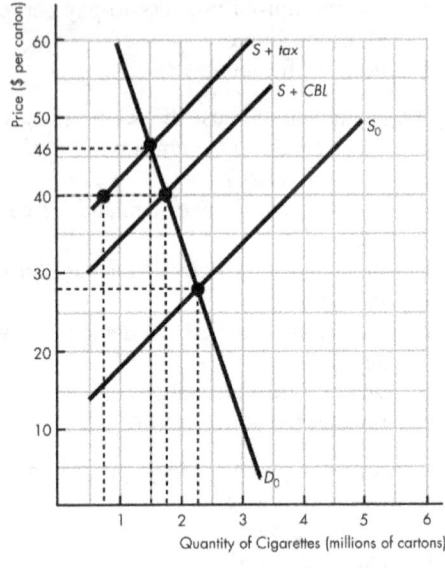

e i See Fig. P2.1 Solution. Since the *CBL* to consumers is zero, the demand curve does not shift. The smugglers' supply curve is *S* + *CBL*.

ii Since consumers can buy cigarettes from smugglers at a price of $40 per carton, no one is willing to buy at the higher legal price of $46. The legal price is bid down to $40. At that price, legal suppliers will supply 0.75 million cartons (read off of the *S* + *tax* curve), and total market demand is 1.75 million cartons. Smugglers supply the difference, 1 million cartons.

iii Tax revenue is 0.75 million cartons × $24 per carton = only $18 million per year.

Dr. Lastic is impressed. She says, "When I studied economics, we were taught that illegal activities were the business of law enforcement officials, not economists. What you have shown is that almost any activity can be analysed from an economic perspective. Well done. Let's draft our reply to the minister."

Midterm Examination

1 a Tariff increases domestic price of cheese, decreasing imports and increasing domestic production. Decreased imports = decreased exports in Breton, decreasing its income, decreasing its imports = decrease in

Acadia's exports, decreasing Acadia's sheep production. (157–162)

ⓔ **2** **c** **a** and **d** affect η_s only. **b** affects η only. (94–97)

3 **e** Total revenue test. (84–90)

4 **a** Definition. Relation to *MC* depends whether the allocation is efficient or not. (108–111)

5 **d** Definition. (133–138)

6 **a** Definition. (116--119)

7 **c** Rightward shifts in demand and supply must increase equilibrium quantity, but the effect on price is indeterminate. (68–73)

ⓔ **8** **e** Rise in *P* causes movement along the demand curve. (57–61)

9 **b** Quantity supplied (50) > quantity demanded (10). (131–133)

10 **b** Also a *maximum* willingness to pay curve. (108–111)

11 **b** $\eta_y = (\%\,\Delta Q_D)/(\%\,\Delta \text{ income}) = -10/10 = -1$; widgets are an inferior good. (91–93)

ⓔ **12** **c** Draw a graph. Floor doesn't prevent *P* rising from excess demand. (131–133)

13 **b** Deadweight loss reduces both consumer and producer surplus relative to an efficient allocation. (112–115)

14 **b** $\eta_x = (\%\,\Delta Q^Y_D)/(\%\,\Delta P^X) = (200/1{,}000)/(-2/5) = -0.5.$ (91–93)

15 **a** Illustration of law of supply. (62–65)

16 **c** With decreasing *Q*, *MB* must rise and *MC* fall. (112–115)

17 **d** Cattle and corn are substitutes in production. Increased demand for cattle raises the price of cattle, causing decreased supply of corn. (62–65)

18 **e** Opportunity cost of 1 more beer = lost pizza. For Partyland, going from 0 beer to 25 beers costs 25 pizzas (one for one). Do the same calculation for Cowabunga. (152–154)

19 **e** Same type of calculation as in **3**. (152–154)

20 **d** Each exports where they have a comparative advantage (lowest opportunity cost). (152–154)

Chapter 8
Utility and Demand

Consumption Choices

Household consumption choices are determined by consumption possibilities and preferences.

A budget line marks the boundary between affordable (points on the line or inside) and unaffordable (outside the line) choices.

♦ Income and prices (P) of goods and services are given.

Preferences (likes and dislikes) are based on **utility**—benefit or satisfaction from consumption.

♦ **Total utility** (TU) is the total benefit from consumption of goods and services. Increased consumption increases total utility.

♦ **Marginal utility** (MU) is the Δ in total utility from a one-unit increase in quantity good consumed. MU is positive, but due to **diminishing marginal utility**, decreases as consumption good increases.

Utility-Maximizing Choices

Consumers strive for utility maximization—maximum attainable benefit.

♦ Given income and the prices of goods and services, **consumer equilibrium** occurs when the consumer allocates income in a way that maximizes total utility.

♦ Total utility is maximized when all income is spent and **marginal utility per dollar** spent is equal for all goods. For substitute goods movies (M) and pop (P), this occurs when

$$\frac{MU_M}{P_M} = \frac{MU_P}{P_P}$$

The power of marginal analysis for predicting economic choices stems from a simple rule—if the marginal gain from an action exceeds the marginal loss, take the action.

♦ The rule applied to the utility maximization example is—if the marginal utility per dollar spent on movies exceeds the marginal utility per dollar spent on pop, buy more movies and less pop.

♦ The marginal gain from more movies exceeds the marginal loss from less pop.

Predictions of Marginal Utility Theory

Ceteris paribus, if P_M falls, Q_M consumed increases (movement down along the demand curve for movies); also causes a leftward shift in the demand curve for pop.

Ceteris paribus, if P_P rises, Q_P consumed decreases (movement up along the demand curve for pop); also causes a rightward shift in the demand curve for movies.

Movies and pop are normal goods. *Ceteris paribus*, increased income causes increased consumption of movies and pop (rightward shifts in both demand curves).

Marginal utility theory allows us to derive and predict the above results, which, in Chapter 3, were just *assumptions* about consumer demand.

Value is related to total utility or consumer surplus. Price is related to marginal utility. Distinction between total utility and marginal utility resolves the diamond–water paradox:

♦ Diamonds, though less useful (low TU and small consumer surplus) than water, have higher price (high MU).

♦ Water is more useful (high TU and large consumer surplus), but has lower price (low MU).

New Ways of Explaining Consumer Choices

Behavioural economics studies how limits on the human brain's ability to compute and implement rational decisions influences economic behaviour. Limits include bounded rationality, bounded willpower, and bounded self-interest.

Neuroeconomics uses neuroscience to study the effects of economic events and choices inside the human brain.

HELPFUL HINTS

1 Utility is a useful abstract concept for thinking clearly about consumer choice. The arbitrary units used to measure utility don't matter. All that marginal utility theory requires is that you can judge whether the additional satisfaction per dollar spent on good X is greater or less than the additional satisfaction per dollar spent on Y. If it is greater, then you choose more X. How much greater is irrelevant for the decision.

2 The marginal utility per dollar spent on good X can be written as MU_X/P_X, where MU_X is the marginal utility of the last unit of X consumed, and P_X is the price of a unit of good X. The consumer equilibrium (utility-maximizing) condition for goods X and Y can be written

$$\frac{MU_X}{P_X} = \frac{MU_Y}{P_Y}$$

This implies that, in consumer equilibrium, the ratio of marginal utilities equals the ratio of prices of the two goods:

$$\frac{MU_X}{MU_Y} = \frac{P_X}{P_Y}$$

This result is often useful.

3 If you are not in consumer equilibrium, then the above equation is not satisfied. For example, consider spending all of your income on a consumption plan where

$$\frac{MU_X}{P_X} > \frac{MU_Y}{P_Y}$$

or, equivalently,

$$\frac{MU_X}{MU_Y} > \frac{P_X}{P_Y}$$

Since P_X and P_Y are given, this means that MU_X is "too large" and MU_Y is "too small." Total utility can be increased by consuming more X (and thereby decreasing MU_X due to the principle of diminishing marginal utility) and less Y (and thereby increasing MU_Y due to diminishing marginal utility).

SELF-TEST

True/False and Explain

Consumption Choices

1 All points inside a consumer's budget line are unaffordable.

2 The principle of diminishing marginal utility means that as consumption of a good increases, total utility increases but at a decreasing rate.

Utility-Maximizing Choice

3 A household is maximizing utility if the marginal utility per dollar spent is equal for all goods and all its income is spent.

4 If the marginal utilities from consuming two goods are not equal, the consumer cannot be in equilibrium.

5 If the marginal utility per dollar spent on good X exceeds the marginal utility per dollar spent on good Y, total utility will increase by increasing consumption of X and decreasing consumption of Y.

6 If the marginal gain from an action exceeds the marginal loss, you should take the action.

Predictions of Marginal Utility Theory

7 When the price of good X rises, the marginal utility from the consumption of X decreases.

8 When income decreases, the marginal utility derived from a good will always increase.

9 When the price of one good rises, demand decreases for goods that are substitutes.

10 When income increases, the quantity demanded of all goods increases.

11 In consumer equilibrium, price is proportional to total utility.

12 A demand curve describes the quantity demanded at each price when marginal utility is maximized.

13 If a shift in supply decreases the price of a good, consumer surplus increases.

New Ways of Explaining Consumer Choice

14 Neuroeconomics studies how limits on the human brain's ability to compute and implement rational decisions influences economic behaviour.

15 All economists agree that it is important to explain what goes on inside people's heads.

Multiple-Choice

Consumption Choices

1 A household's consumption choices are determined by
  a prices of goods and services.
  b income.
  c preferences.
  d all of the above.
  e **a** and **b** only.

2 Total utility equals
  a the sum of the marginal utilities of each unit consumed.
  b the area below the demand curve but above the market price.
  c the slope of the marginal utility curve.
  d the marginal utility of the last unit divided by price.
  e the marginal utility of the last unit consumed multiplied by the total number of units consumed

3 Total utility is always
  a greater than marginal utility.
  b less than marginal utility.
  c decreasing when marginal utility is decreasing.
  d decreasing when marginal utility is increasing.
  e increasing when marginal utility is positive.

4 According to the principle of diminishing marginal utility, as consumption of a good increases, total utility
  a decreases and then eventually increases.
  b decreases at an increasing rate.
  c decreases at a decreasing rate.
  d increases at an increasing rate.
  e increases at a decreasing rate.

Maximizing Utility

5 If a consumer is in equilibrium,
   a total utility is maximized given the consumer's income and the prices of goods.
   b marginal utility is maximized given the consumer's income and the prices of goods.
   c marginal utility per dollar spent is maximized given the consumer's income and the prices of goods.
   d the marginal utility of each good will be equal.
   e none of the above is true.

6 Suppose that Ally spends her entire income of $10 on law books and miniskirts. Law books cost $2 and miniskirts cost $4 (see Table 8.1). The marginal utility of each good is independent of the amount consumed of the other good.

TABLE **8.1**   ALLY'S MARGINAL UTILITY

	Marginal Utility	
Quantity	Law Books	Miniskirts
1	12	16
2	10	12
3	8	8
4	6	4

If Ally is maximizing her utility, how many miniskirts does she buy?
   a 0
   b 1
   c 2
   d 3
   e 4

7 If potato chips were free, individuals would consume
   a an infinite quantity of chips.
   b the quantity of chips at which total utility from chips falls to zero.
   c the quantity of chips at which marginal utility from chips falls to zero.
   d zero chips, since this equates marginal utility and price.
   e none of the above.

8 In consumer equilibrium, a consumer equates the
   a total utility from each good.
   b marginal utility from each good.
   c total utility per dollar spent on each good.
   d marginal utility per dollar spent on each good.
   e total income spent on each good with total utility from each good.

9 Samir consumes apples and bananas and is in consumer equilibrium. The marginal utility of the last apple is 10 and the marginal utility of the last banana is 5. If the price of an apple is $0.50, what is the price of a banana?
   a $0.05
   b $0.10
   c $0.25
   d $0.50
   e $1.00

10 If Ms. Petersen is maximizing her utility in the consumption of goods A and B, which of the following statements must be *true*?
   a $MU_A = MU_B$
   b $\dfrac{MU_A}{P_A} = \dfrac{MU_B}{P_B}$
   c $\dfrac{MU_A}{P_B} = \dfrac{MU_B}{P_A}$
   d $TU_A = TU_B$
   e $\dfrac{TU_A}{P_A} = \dfrac{TU_B}{P_B}$

11 Squid costs $2 per kilogram and octopus costs $1 per kilogram. Jacques buys only octopus and gets 10 units of utility from the last kilogram he buys. Assuming that Jacques has maximized his utility, his marginal utility, in units, from the first kilogram of squid must be
   a more than 10.
   b less than 10.
   c more than 20.
   d less than 20.
   e zero.

12 If Soula is maximizing her utility and two goods have the same marginal utility, she will
   a buy only one.
   b buy equal quantities of both.
   c be willing to pay the same price for each.
   d get the same total utility from each.
   e do none of the above.

13 Sergio is maximizing his utility in his consumption of beer and bubblegum. If the price of beer is greater than the price of bubblegum, then we know with *certainty* that
 a Sergio buys more beer than bubblegum.
 b Sergio buys more bubblegum than beer.
 c the marginal utility of the last purchased beer is greater than the marginal utility of the last purchased bubblegum.
 d the marginal utility of the last purchased bubblegum is greater than the marginal utility of the last purchased beer.
 e the marginal utilities of the last purchased beer and bubblegum are equal.

14 Suppose that Madonna spends her entire income of $6 on purple nail polish and leather outfits. Nail polish costs $1 per unit and outfits cost $2 per unit (see Table 8.2). The marginal utility of each good is independent of the amount consumed of the other good.

TABLE **8.2** MADONNA'S MARGINAL UTILITY

Quantity	Marginal Utility	
	Nail Polish	**Outfits**
1	8	16
2	6	12
3	4	10
4	3	6

If Madonna is maximizing her utility, what is her *total* utility?
 a 19
 b 28
 c 38
 d 42
 e none of the above

Predictions of Marginal Utility Theory

15 Bikes and roller blades are substitutes. Marginal utility theory predicts that when the price of bikes increases due to a decrease in supply, the quantity demanded of bikes
 a decreases and the demand curve for roller blades shifts rightward.
 b decreases and the demand curve for roller blades shifts leftward.
 c decreases and the demand curve for roller blades will not shift.
 d increases and the demand curve for roller blades shifts rightward.
 e increases and the demand curve for roller blades shifts leftward.

16 Which of the following is *not* a prediction of marginal utility theory?
 a Other things remaining the same, the higher the price of a good, the lower the quantity demanded.
 b Other things remaining the same, the higher the price of a good, the higher the consumption of substitutes for that good.
 c Other things remaining the same, the lower the price of a good, the lower the consumption of substitutes for that good.
 d the law of demand
 e diminishing marginal utility

17 Chuck and Barry have identical preferences but Chuck has a much higher income. If each is maximizing his utility,
 a they will have equal total utilities.
 b Chuck will have lower total utility than Barry.
 c Chuck will have lower marginal utility than Barry for each normal good consumed.
 d Chuck will have higher marginal utility than Barry for each normal good consumed.
 e they will have equal marginal utilities for each normal good consumed.

18 The relative prices of beer to back bacon are 2:1. If Bob's current consumption is at a level where $MU_{BEER}/MU_{BACKBACON}$ is 1:2, to achieve maximum utility Bob must
 a consume more beer and less back bacon.
 b not change his current consumption of beer and back bacon.
 c consume less beer and more back bacon.
 d increase the price of beer.
 e consume twice as much beer and one-half as much back bacon.

19 Broomhilda is initially maximizing her utility in her consumption of goods X and Y. The price of good X doubles, *ceteris paribus*. For Broomhilda to once again maximize her utility, her *quantity* of X consumed must
 a rise until the marginal utility of X has doubled.
 b fall to one-half its previous level.
 c fall until the marginal utility of X has doubled.
 d fall until the marginal utility of X falls to one-half its previous level.
 e yield infinite bliss.

20 Beverly is currently in consumer equilibrium. An increase in her income will
   a increase her total utility.
   b decrease her total utility.
   c increase her marginal utility of all goods.
   d decrease her marginal utility of all goods.
   e increase her consumption of all goods.

21 Bill and Ted consume 15 chocolate bars each at the current price. If Bill's demand curve is more elastic than Ted's demand curve,
   a Bill's willingness to pay for the 15th chocolate bar is greater than Ted's.
   b Ted's willingness to pay for the 15th chocolate bar is greater than Bill's.
   c Bill's consumer surplus is greater than Ted's.
   d Ted's consumer surplus is greater than Bill's.
   e Bill's consumer surplus equals Ted's.

22 The high price of diamonds relative to the price of water reflects the fact that, at typical levels of consumption,
   a the total utility of water is relatively low.
   b the total utility of diamonds is relatively high.
   c the marginal utility of water is relatively high.
   d the marginal utility of diamonds is relatively low.
   e none of the above is true.

23 The principle of diminishing marginal utility means that the consumer surplus from the second slice of pizza is
   a greater than that from the first.
   b equal to that of the first
   c less than that of the first.
   d equal to that of the first divided by 2.
   e equal to that of the first multiplied by 2.

New Ways of Explaining Consumer Choices

24 Which of the following barriers to rational choices are studied by behavioural economics?
   a bounded rationality
   b bounded willpower
   c bounded self-interest
   d the endowment effect
   e all of the above

25 Neuroeconomics studies all of the following concepts *except*
   a the prefrontal cortex.
   b the hippocampus.
   c the hippopotamus.
   d dopamine.
   e anxiety and fear.

Short Answer Problems

1 Explain why the consumer equilibrium condition and the principle of diminishing marginal utility imply the law of demand.

2 Consider the following information for a consumer who is trying to allocate her income between goods X and Y so as to maximize utility. The price of X is $2 and the price of Y is $1 per unit. When all income is spent, the marginal utility of the last unit of X is 20 and the marginal utility of the last unit of Y is 16.

   a Why is the consumer not in equilibrium?

   b To increase utility, which good should this consumer consume more of and which less of?

3 A consumer is initially maximizing his utility in the consumption of goods A and B so that

$$\frac{MU_A}{P_A} = \frac{MU_B}{P_B}$$

The price of A then rises as a result of the shift in supply shown in Fig. 8.1.

FIGURE **8.1**

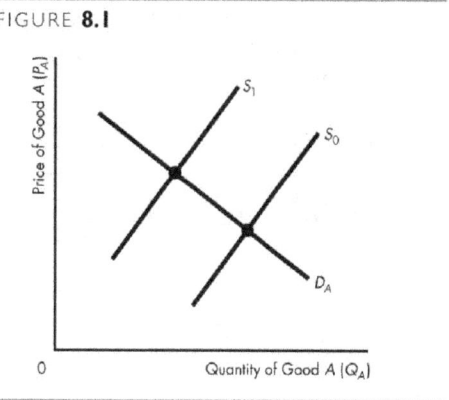

3 (continued) Use this condition for utility maximization to explain how the consumer will move to a new utility-maximizing equilibrium. Show the connection between your explanation and the change on the diagram.

4 Tables 8.3 and 8.4 give Amy's utility from the consumption of popcorn and candy bars during a week.

TABLE **8.3**   AMY'S UTILITY FROM POPCORN

Bags of Popcorn	Total Utility	Marginal Utility
1	20	
2	36	
3	50	
4		12
5	72	
6	80	

TABLE **8.4**   AMY'S UTILITY FROM CANDY BARS

Number of Candy Bars	Total Utility	Marginal Utility
1	14	
2	26	
3		10
4	44	
5	51	
6	57	

a   Complete the tables.

b   Suppose the price of a bag of popcorn is $1 and the price of a candy bar is $0.50. Given the information in Tables 8.3 and 8.4, complete Table 8.5 where MU/P means marginal utility divided by price, which is equivalent to marginal utility per dollar spent.

TABLE **8.5**   AMY'S MU/P

Bags of Popcorn	MU/P	Number of Candy Bars	MU/P
1		1	
2		2	
3		3	
4		4	
5		5	
6		6	

5 Amy's weekly allowance is $4. Using your answers to Short Answer Problem **4**, answer the following if Amy spends her entire allowance on popcorn and candy bars.

a   How much popcorn and how many candy bars will Amy consume each week if she maximizes her utility?

b   Show that the utility-maximizing condition is satisfied.

c   What is total utility?

d   If, instead, Amy consumed 3 bags of popcorn and 2 candy bars, explain why she would not be maximizing her utility using figures both for total utility and for the terms MU/P.

6 Suppose that Amy's preferences remain as they were in Short Answer Problem **4**, but the price of a candy bar doubles to $1.

a   Construct a new table (similar to Table 8.5) of MU/P for popcorn and candy bars.

b   Amy's allowance continues to be $4. After the price change, how much popcorn and how many candy bars will she consume each week?

c   Are popcorn and candy bars substitutes or complements for Amy? Why?

d   On the basis of the information you have obtained, draw Amy's demand curve for candy bars.

e   Suppose that both bags of popcorn and candy bars continue to sell for $1 each, but now Amy's allowance increases to $6 per week.

   i   How many candy bars and bags of popcorn will Amy choose to consume per week under the new situation?

   ii   Are popcorn and candy bars normal goods? Why or why not?

7 Suppose that Andre Agassi spends his entire income of $8 on razors and toy tennis rackets (see Table 8.6). The price of a razor is $2 and the price of a tennis racket is $4. The marginal utility of each good is independent of the amount consumed of the other good.

TABLE **8.6**   ANDRE'S MARGINAL UTILITY

Quantity	Marginal Utility	
	Razors	Rackets
1	20	36
2	18	32
3	16	20
4	8	16

a   If Andre is maximizing his utility, how many units of each good should he purchase?

b   If Andre's income rises to $24, how many units of each good should he purchase?

c   Using the information above, calculate Andre's income elasticity of demand for razors.

8   Suppose that Igor maximizes his utility by spending his entire income on bats and lizards (see Table 8.7). The marginal utility of each good is independent of the amount consumed of the other good.

TABLE **8.7**   IGOR'S MARGINAL UTILITY

Quantity	Marginal Utility	
	Bats	Lizards
1	20	45
2	18	40
3	16	25
4	8	20

Igor's income is $16. The price of a bat is $2, and he buys 3 bats. If the marginal utility of the last lizard he buys is 40, calculate the price of a lizard using two separate methods.

ANSWERS

True/False and Explain

1   **F**   Points on and inside the budget line are affordable. (180–182)

2   **T**   Because MU is positive but diminishing. (180–182)

3   **T**   Rules for maximizing total utility. (183–186)

4   **F**   Ratios of MU/P are crucial. If prices are unequal, marginal utilities are unequal in consumer equilibrium. (183–186)

ⓔ **5**   **T**   Increased consumption of X causes decreased MU_X. Decreased consumption of Y causes increased MU_Y. Moves ratios MU/P toward equality and total utility maximization. (183–186)

6   **T**   Rule for maximizing total utility. (183–186)

7   **F**   Rising P causes decreased Q and increased MU. (187–193)

ⓔ **8**   **F**   True for a normal good; may be false for an inferior good. (187–193)

9   **F**   Demand increases for substitutes because now they are relatively cheaper. (187–193)

ⓔ **10**   **F**   Quantity demanded increases for normal goods but decreases for inferior goods. (187–193)

11   **F**   Price is proportional to marginal utility. (187–193)

12   **F**   When *total* utility is maximized. (187–193)

13   **T**   With a fall in price and increased quantity consumed, more units with willingness-to-pay > price. (187–193)

14   **F**   This is the definition of behavioural economics. (194–195)

15   **F**   Most economists do not agree on importance of new areas of economics. (194–195)

Multiple-Choice

1   **d**   Consumption possibilities (constraints) and preferences. (180–182)

2   **a**   **b** is consumer surplus. For **c**, MU = slope of TU curve. **d** and **e** are nonsense. (180–182)

3   **e** TU is increasing when MU is positive, whether MU is decreasing or increasing. TU may be $\lesseqgtr MU$. (180–182)

ⓔ **4**   **e**   Because marginal utility is positive but diminishing with increased consumption. (180–182)

5   **a**   Consumers maximize TU. **c** and **d** are wrong because MU/P equal for TU maximization. (183–186)

6   **b**   Buys 1 miniskirt ($MU/P = 16/4$) and 3 books ($MU/P = 8/2$). (183–186)

ⓔ **7 c** Maximizes *TU*. With fewer chips, *MU* is still positive, so *TU* could increase. With more, *MU* turns negative so *TU* would decrease. (183–186)

8 d Definition. *MU/P* is key to utility maximization. (183–186)

9 c Solve $10/0.5 = 5/P_{BANANA}$ for P_{BANANA}. (183–186)

10 b Definition. (183–186)

ⓔ **11 d** For octopus, $MU_O/P_O = 10$. For squid, $MU_S/2$ would need to be < 10, so MU_S must be < 20. (183–186)

ⓔ **12 c** From maximum condition of equal *MU/P*. No necessary relation between *MU* and quantity or *TU*. (183–186)

13 c From maximum condition of equal *MU/P*. No necessary relation between *MU* and quantity. (183–186)

14 d Buys 2 polish and 2 outfits. $TU = 8 + 6 + 16 + 12$. (183–186)

15 a See text discussion. (187–193)

16 e Diminishing *MU* is *assumption* of theory. (187–193)

17 c Chuck consumes greater quantities of each good, so *MU* is lower. (187–193)

18 c To equalize *MU/P* must increase MU_{BEER} and decrease $MU_{BACKBACON}$. **d** is wrong because no control over prices. (187–193)

19 c From maximum condition of equal *MU/P*. No necessary relation between *MU* and quantity consumed. (187–193)

ⓔ **20 a** For inferior goods, consumption may decrease and *MU* increase. (187–193)

21 d Ted's steeper demand curve means greater willingness to pay for previous units. Willingness to pay for last unit is equal. (187–193)

22 e For diamonds: *TU* is relatively low, *MU* is relatively high. For water: *TU* is relatively high, *MU* is relatively low. (187–193)

23 c 2nd slice value is less than 1st because of diminishing marginal utility; consumer surplus is less. (187–193)

24 e All limits on rational choice. (194–195)

25 c See text discussion. (194–195)

Short Answer Problems

1 Suppose we observe an individual in consumer equilibrium consuming X_0 units of good *X* and Y_0 units of good *Y*, with the prices of *X* and *Y* given by P_X and P_Y respectively. This means that at consumption levels X_0 and Y_0, the marginal utility per dollar spent on *X* equals the marginal utility per dollar spent on *Y*. Now let the price of *X* increase to P^1_X. The marginal utility per dollar spent on *X* declines and thus is now less than the marginal utility per dollar spent on *Y*. To restore equilibrium, our consumer must increase the marginal utility of *X* and decrease the marginal utility of *Y*. From the principle of diminishing marginal utility we know that the only way to do this is to decrease the consumption of *X* and increase the consumption of *Y*. This demonstrates the law of demand, since an increase in the price of *X* has been shown to require a decrease in the consumption of *X* to restore consumer equilibrium.

2 a This consumer is not in equilibrium because the marginal utility per dollar spent is not the same for goods *X* and *Y*. The marginal utility per dollar spent on *X* is $MU_X/P_X = 20/2 = 10$, which is less than the marginal utility per dollar spent on *Y*: $MU_Y/P_Y = 16$.

b To equate the marginal utilities per dollar spent (and thus increase utility), this consumer should increase consumption of *Y* and decrease consumption of *X*. The principle of diminishing marginal utility implies that this will decrease the marginal utility of *Y* and increase the marginal utility of *X*.

3 When the price of *A* rises, *ceteris paribus*,

$$\frac{MU_A}{P_A} < \frac{MU_B}{P_B}$$

The consumer is no longer in equilibrium. In order to restore the equality in the equilibrium condition, the consumer must change his consumption to make MU_A rise and MU_B fall. (The consumer cannot change the prices of *A* and *B*.) Since marginal utility diminishes with increases in quantity consumed, the consumer must decrease consumption of *A* and increase consumption of *B*. Decreased consumption of *A* moves the consumer up to the left on the demand curve, from the initial intersection of *D* and S_0 to the new intersection of *D* and S_1. In the new consumer equilibrium, equality will be restored in the equilibrium condition.

4 a   The tables are completed in Table 8.3 Solution and Table 8.4 Solution.

TABLE **8.3**   SOLUTION
AMY'S UTILITY FROM POPCORN

Bags of Popcorn	Total Utility	Marginal Utility
1	20	20
2	36	16
3	50	14
4	62	12
5	72	10
6	80	8

TABLE **8.4**   SOLUTION
AMY'S UTILITY FROM CANDY BARS

Number of Candy Bars	Total Utility	Marginal Utility
1	14	14
2	26	12
3	36	10
4	44	8
5	51	7
6	57	6

b   The table is completed in Table 8.5 Solution.

TABLE **8.5**   SOLUTION
AMY'S *MU/P*

Bags of Popcorn	MU/P	Number of Candy Bars	MU/P
1	20	1	28
2	16	2	24
3	14	3	20
4	12	4	16
5	10	5	14
6	8	6	12

5 a   2 bags of popcorn and 4 candy bars.

b   The utility-maximizing condition is satisfied, since Amy spends all her income ($4), and the marginal utility per dollar spent is the same for popcorn and candy bars (16).

c   Total utility is the utility from the consumption of 2 bags of popcorn (36) plus the utility from the consumption of 4 candy bars (44) = 80.

d   If Amy consumed 3 bags of popcorn and 2 candy bars, total utility would be 76, which is less than 80, the total utility from the consumption of 2 bags of popcorn and 4 candy bars. For the combination of 3 bags of popcorn and 2 candy bars, *MU/P* for popcorn is 14 while *MU/P* for candy bars is 24. Since *MU/P* is not the same for both goods, this combination does not meet the condition for utility maximization.

6 a   See Table 8.8.

TABLE **8.8**   AMY'S *MU/P*

Bags of Popcorn	MU/P	Number of Candy Bars	MU/P
1	20	1	14
2	16	2	12
3	14	3	10
4	12	4	8
5	10	5	7
6	8	6	6

b   3 bags of popcorn and 1 candy bar. Amy spends all of her income ($4), and the marginal utility per dollar spent is the same for popcorn and candy bars (14).

c   Popcorn and candy bars are substitutes for Amy, since an increase in the price of a candy bar causes an increase in the demand for popcorn.

d   Amy's demand curve for candy bars is given in Fig. 8.2. Two points on the demand curve have been identified: when the price of a candy bar is $1, one candy bar will be demanded, and when the price is $0.50, 4 candy bars will be demanded. The demand curve is a line through these two points.

FIGURE **8.2**

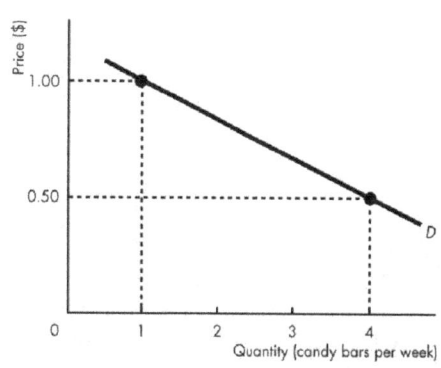

e i Now, Amy will choose to consume 4 bags of popcorn and 2 candy bars (instead of 3 bags of popcorn and 1 candy bar). Amy spends all of her income ($6) and the marginal utility per dollar spent is the same for popcorn and candy bars (12).

ii Popcorn and candy bars are both normal goods for Amy, since the increase in income (allowance) leads to increases in the demand for both goods.

7 a The utility-maximizing combination of goods is shown in Table 8.9.

TABLE **8.9**   ANDRE'S *MU/P*

| Quantity | MU/P | |
	Razors	Rackets
1	10	9
2	9	8
3	8	5
4	4	4

Andre should purchase 2 razors and 1 racket. Andre spends all of his income ($8), and the marginal utility per dollar spent is the same for razors and rackets (9).

b Andre should purchase 4 razors and 4 rackets. He spends all of his income ($24), and the marginal utility per dollar spent is the same for razors and rackets (4).

c The income elasticity of demand (η_y) for razors is

$$\eta_y = \frac{\dfrac{\Delta Q}{Q_{ave}}}{\dfrac{\Delta Y}{Y_{ave}}} = \frac{\dfrac{4-2}{\frac{1}{2}(4+2)}}{\dfrac{24-8}{\frac{1}{2}(24+8)}} = \frac{\dfrac{2}{3}}{\dfrac{16}{16}} = \frac{2}{3}$$

8 There are two methods for calculating the price of a lizard. One method is based on the fact that Igor spends all of his income on bats and lizards. This means that

$$Y = P_B Q_B + P_L Q_L$$

where Y = income, P_B = the price of a bat, Q_B = the quantity of bats purchased, P_L = the price of a lizard, and Q_L = the quantity of lizards purchased. We know $Y = 16$, $P_B = 2$, $Q_B = 3$, and if the marginal utility of the last lizard is 40, then $Q_L = 2$. Substituting these values, we can solve for P_L.

$$16 = 2(3) + P_L(2)$$
$$10 = P_L(2)$$
$$5 = P_L$$

The second method uses the condition for utility maximization:

$$\frac{MU_B}{P_B} = \frac{MU_L}{P_L}$$

We know that $MU_L = 40$, $P_B = 2$, and if Igor buys 3 bats $MU_B = 16$. Substituting these values, we can solve for P_L.

$$\frac{16}{2} = \frac{40}{P_L}$$
$$80 = 16P_L$$
$$5 = P_L$$

Chapter 9
Possibilities, Preferences, and Choices

KEY CONCEPTS

Consumption Possibilities

A **budget line** shows limits to household consumption, given income, and prices of goods and services. Consider the example of movies (horizontal axis) and pop (vertical axis).

♦ The budget equation is

$$Q_P = \frac{Y}{P_P} - \frac{P_M}{P_P}\, Q_M$$

♦ The magnitude of the slope of the budget equation (P_M/P_P) equals the **relative price** of movies in terms of pop.

♦ Intercepts measure a household's **real income** in movies (x-intercept) and pop (y-intercept).

♦ Higher P_M yields steeper budget line, fixed pop-intercept.

♦ Higher P_P yields flatter budget line, fixed movie-intercept.

♦ Higher Y yields rightward parallel shift budget line.

Preferences and Indifference Curves

An **indifference curve** maps household preferences, joining combinations of goods giving equal satisfaction.

♦ Indifference curves generally slope downward and bow toward the origin (convex).

♦ Indifference curves farther from the origin represent higher levels of satisfaction.

♦ Indifference curves never intersect.

♦ **Marginal rate of substitution** (*MRS*) is the magnitude of the slope of an indifference curve—the rate at which household gives up good y (pop) for additional unit of good x (movies) and remains indifferent (remains on same indifference curve).

♦ **Diminishing marginal rate of substitution** is the tendency for *MRS* to diminish as we move down along an indifference curve. Accounts for bowed-toward-the-origin shape of indifference curves.

  • More substitutability between goods yields straighter indifference curves.

  • Less substitutability between goods yields more tightly curved indifference curves.

Predicting Consumer Choices

Given income and prices of goods, a household allocates income to maximize satisfaction. Household chooses best affordable point, which is on the budget line and on the highest possible indifference curve. At the best affordable point,

♦ household spends all its income and achieves maximum possible satisfaction.

♦ budget line and indifference curve are tangent and have same slope—*MRS* equals the relative price.

Price effect is Δ consumption resulting from Δ price of a good. Price effect = substitution effect + income effect.

♦ **Substitution effect**—Δ in consumption resulting from Δ in price accompanied by (hypothetical) Δ in income leaving household indifferent between initial and new situations. For normal and inferior goods, substitution effect of falling price is increased consumption.

♦ **Income effect**—Δ in consumption resulting from (hypothetically) restoring original income but keeping prices constant at new level. For normal goods, income effect of (hypothetically) increased income is increased consumption. For inferior goods, (hypothetically) increased income yields decreased consumption.

♦ The downward-sloping demand curve is a consequence of the consumer choosing his best affordable combination of goods. The demand curve can be derived from the price effect—by tracing the best affordable quantity of a good as its price changes.

For normal goods, substitution and income effects work in the same direction, so falling price yields increased consumption.

For inferior goods, substitution and income effects work in opposite directions, but net effect of falling price usually yields (smaller) increased consumption.

HELPFUL HINTS

1 The consumer's basic problem is to do the best given her constraints. These constraints, which limit possible choices, depend on income and the prices of goods and are represented graphically by the budget line. Doing the best means finding the most preferred outcome consistent with those constraints. In this chapter, preferences are represented graphically by indifference curves.

   Graphically, the consumer problem is to find the highest indifference curve attainable given the budget line. To make graphical analysis easier, we examine choices between only two goods, but the same principles apply in the real world to many choices, including the choice between labour and leisure.

2 The budget equation for pop and movies on text page 205 is

$$Q_P = \frac{Y}{P_P} - \frac{P_M}{P_P} Q_M$$

This is the type of straight-line equation ($y = a + bx$) that we discussed in the Chapter 1 appendix. The differences are that Q_P is the dependent variable (instead of y) and Q_M is the independent variable (instead of x). We can use the budget equation to graph the budget line by finding the Q_P-intercept (where the line intersects the vertical Q_P-axis), finding the Q_M-intercept (where the line intersects the horizontal Q_M-axis), and then connecting those two points with a straight line.

To find the Q_P-intercept, set $Q_M = 0$.

$$Q_P = \frac{Y}{P_P} - \frac{P_M}{P_P} (0)$$

$$Q_P = \frac{Y}{P_P}$$

To find the Q_M-intercept, set $Q_P = 0$.

$$0 = \frac{Y}{P_P} - \frac{P_M}{P_P} Q_M$$

$$\frac{P_M}{P_P} Q_M = \frac{Y}{P_P}$$

$$Q_M = \frac{Y}{P_M}$$

The Q_P-intercept, $Q_P = Y/P_P$, is the consumer's real income in terms of pop. It tells us how much pop could be purchased if all income was spent on pop. The Q_M-intercept, $Q_M = Y/P_M$, is the consumer's real income in terms of movies. It tells us how many movies could be purchased if all income was spent on movies. These intercepts provide an easy method for drawing a budget line. Each of the two endpoints (the intercepts) is just income divided by the price of the good on that axis. Connecting those endpoints with a straight line yields the budget line.

The slope of the budget line provides additional information for the consumer's choice. The magnitude (absolute value) of the slope equals the relative price (or opportunity cost) of movies in terms of pop. In other words, the magnitude of the slope equals the number of units of pop it takes to buy one movie. More generally, the magnitude of the slope of the budget line (P_X/P_Y) equals the relative price (or opportunity cost) of the good on the horizontal x-axis in terms of the good on the vertical y-axis; or the number of units of vertical-axis goods it takes to buy one unit of the horizontal-axis good.

3 The marginal rate of substitution (*MRS*) is the rate at which a consumer gives up good Y for an additional unit of good X and still remains indifferent (on the same indifference curve). The *MRS* equals the magnitude of the slope of the indifference curve, $\Delta Q_Y/\Delta Q_X$.

   Because indifference curves are bowed toward the origin (convex), the magnitude of the slope and hence the *MRS* diminishes as we move down an indifference curve. The diminishing *MRS* means that the consumer is willing to give up less of good *Y* for each additional unit of good *X*. As the consumer moves down an indifference curve, she is coming to value good *Y* more and value good *X* less. This is easily explained by the principle of diminishing marginal utility, which underlies the following equation:

$$\text{Marginal rate of substitution} = \frac{MU_X}{MU_Y}$$

At the top of the indifference curve, the consumer is consuming little *X* and much *Y*, so the marginal utility of *X* (MU_X) is high and the marginal utility of *Y* (MU_Y) is low. Moving down the curve, as the quantity of *X* consumed increases, MU_X decreases; and as the quantity of *Y* consumed decreases, MU_Y increases. Thus the principle of diminishing marginal utility provides an intuitive understanding of why the *MRS* diminishes as we move down an indifference curve.

4 At the consumer's best affordable point, the budget line is just tangent to the highest-affordable indifference curve, so the magnitude of the slope of the budget line equals the magnitude of the slope of the indifference curve. Combining the information from Helpful Hint **2** (the magnitude of the slope of the budget line equals P_X/P_Y) and Helpful Hint **3** (the magnitude of the slope of the indifference curve equals MU_X/MU_Y) yields

$$\frac{P_X}{P_Y} = \frac{MU_X}{MU_Y}$$

Rearranging terms yields

$$\frac{MU_X}{P_X} = \frac{MU_Y}{P_Y}$$

This is the equation for utility maximization from Chapter 8. You can now see why the budget equation/indifference curve analysis of consumer choice developed in Chapter 9 complements the marginal utility analysis of Chapter 8.

5 Understanding the distinction between the income and substitution effects of a change in the price of a good is often challenging for students. Consider a decrease in the price of good *A*. This has two effects that will influence the consumption of *A*. First, the decrease in the price of *A* will reduce the relative price of *A*, and second, it will increase real income. The substitution effect is the answer to the question: How much would the consumption of *A* change as a result of the relative price decline if we also (hypothetically) reduce income by enough to leave the consumer indifferent between the new and original situations? The income effect is the answer to the question: How much more would the consumption of *A* change if we (hypothetically) restore the consumer's real income but leave relative prices at the new level?

SELF-TEST

True/False and Explain

Consumption Possibilities

1 The graph of a budget line will be bowed toward the origin.

2 At any point on a budget line, all income is spent.

3 *Ceteris paribus*, an increase in the price of goods means that real income falls.

4 An increase in income causes a leftward parallel shift of the budget line.

Preferences and Indifference Curves

5 We assume that more of any good is preferred to less of the good.

6 Higher indifference curves represent higher levels of income.

7 The principle of the diminishing marginal rate of substitution explains why indifference curves are bowed toward the origin.

8 Perfect substitutes will have L-shaped indifference curves.

9 The closer two goods are to perfect substitutes, the closer the marginal rate of substitution is to being constant.

10 If an indifference curve is steep, the marginal rate of substitution is low.

Predicting Consumer Choices

11 At the best affordable consumption point of movies and pop, the marginal rate of substitution equals the ratio of the price of movies to the price of pop.

12 When the relative price of a good decreases, the income effect always leads to increased consumption of the good.

13 When the relative price of a good increases, the substitution effect always leads to decreased consumption of the good.

14 The law of demand can be derived from an indifference curve model by tracing the impact on quantity demanded of an increase in price.

15 When the price of an inferior good falls, the substitution effect increases consumption and the income effect decreases consumption.

Multiple-Choice

Consumption Possibilities

1 Which of the following statements best describes a consumer's budget line?
a the amount of each good a consumer can purchase
b the limits to a consumer's set of affordable consumption choices
c the desired level of consumption for the consumer
d the consumption choices made by a consumer
e the set of all affordable consumption choices

2 Real income is measured in
a monetary units.
b price units.
c units of satisfaction.
d units of indifference.
e units of goods.

3 Consider the budget line and indifference curve in Fig. 9.1. If the price of good X is $2, what is the price of good Y?
a $0.37
b $0.67
c $1.50
d $2.67
e impossible to calculate without additional information

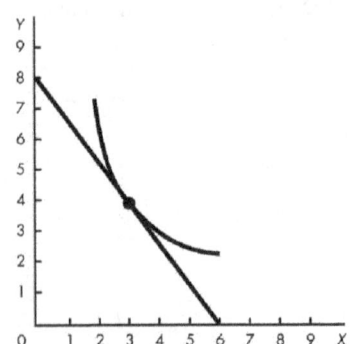

FIGURE **9.1**

4 The budget line depends on
a income only.
b prices only.
c income and prices.
d preferences only.
e preferences and prices.

5 Bill consumes apples and bananas. Suppose Bill's income doubles and the prices of apples and bananas also double. Bill's budget line will
   a shift left but not change slope.
   b remain unchanged.
   c shift right but not change slope.
   d shift right and become steeper.
   e shift right and become flatter.

6 The initial budget equation for pop and movies is $Q_P = 20 - 4Q_M$, and the price of pop (P_P) is $5. If the price of pop falls to $4, which of the following is the new budget equation?
   a $Q_P = 25 - 2Q_M$
   b $Q_P = 25 - 4Q_M$
   c $Q_P = 25 - 5Q_M$
   d $Q_P = 20 - 5Q_M$
   e none of the above

7 Zarina's income allows her to afford 3 tomatoes and no toothbrushes, or 2 toothbrushes and no tomatoes. The relative price of toothbrushes (price toothbrush/price tomato) is
   a 2/3.
   b 3/2.
   c 6/1.
   d 1/6.
   e impossible to calculate without additional information.

8 If the price of the good measured on the vertical axis increases, the budget line will
   a become steeper.
   b become flatter.
   c shift leftward but stay parallel to the original budget line.
   d shift rightward but stay parallel to the original budget line.
   e shift leftward and become steeper.

9 If income increases, the budget line will
   a become steeper.
   b become flatter.
   c shift leftward but stay parallel to the original budget line.
   d shift rightward but stay parallel to the original budget line.
   e stay parallel but shift leftward or rightward depending on whether a good is normal or inferior.

10 The budget equation for pop ($_P$) and movies ($_M$) is $Q_P = 10 - 5Q_M$, with movies on the horizontal axis and pop on the vertical axis. The price of pop (P_P) is $4. That means income ($Y$) is ____ and the price of movies (P_M) is ____.
   a $Y = 50; $P_M = 20
   b $Y = 200; $P_M = 20
   c $Y = 40; $P_M = 2
   d $Y = 40; $P_M = 20
   e none of the above combinations

Preferences and Indifference Curves

11 The shape of an indifference curve depends on
   a the prices of goods.
   b household income.
   c the substitutability between goods for the household.
   d the level of satisfaction for the household.
   e all of the above.

12 In general, as a consumer moves down an indifference curve increasing consumption of good X (measured on the horizontal axis),
   a more of Y must be given up for each additional unit of X.
   b a constant amount of Y must be given up for each additional unit of X.
   c less of Y must be given up for each additional unit of X.
   d the relative price of Y increases.
   e the relative price of Y decreases.

13 Which of the following statements is *false*?
   a Indifference curves are negatively sloped.
   b A preference map consists of a series of nonintersecting indifference curves.
   c Indifference curves are bowed out from the origin.
   d The marginal rate of substitution is the magnitude of the slope of an indifference curve.
   e The marginal rate of substitution increases with movement up an indifference curve.

14 In moving down along an indifference curve, the marginal rate of substitution (*MRS*) for complements will
   a increase faster than the *MRS* for substitutes.
   b increase more slowly than the *MRS* for substitutes.
   c be relatively constant.
   d decrease faster than the *MRS* for substitutes.
   e decrease more slowly than the *MRS* for substitutes.

15 If two goods are perfect substitutes, their
  a indifference curves are positively sloped straight lines.
  b indifference curves are negatively sloped straight lines.
  c indifference curves are L-shaped.
  d marginal rate of substitution is zero.
  e marginal rate of substitution is infinity.

Predicting Consumer Choices

16 When the price of an inferior good rises, the income effect
  a is always larger than the substitution effect.
  b decreases consumption of the good and the substitution effect increases consumption.
  c and the substitution effect both increase consumption of the good.
  d and the substitution effect both decrease consumption of the good.
  e increases consumption of the good and the substitution effect decreases consumption.

17 Which of the following statement(s) about Fig. 9.2 is *true*?
  a Point s is preferred to point q, but s is not affordable.
  b Points q and r yield the same utility, but q is more affordable.
  c Point t is preferred to point q, but t is not affordable.
  d Points q and s cost the same, but q is preferred to s.
  e All of the above statements are true.

FIGURE **9.2**

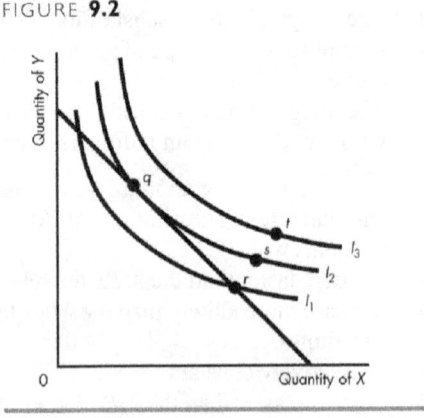

18 For a rise in price, the substitution effect
  a always increases consumption.
  b increases consumption for normal goods only.
  c decreases consumption for normal goods only.
  d decreases consumption for inferior goods only.
  e does none of the above.

19 The initial budget line labelled RS in Fig. 9.3 would shift to RT as a result of a(n)
  a rise in the price of good X.
  b fall in the price of good X.
  c decrease in preferences for good X.
  d rise in the price of good Y.
  e increase in real income.

FIGURE **9.3**

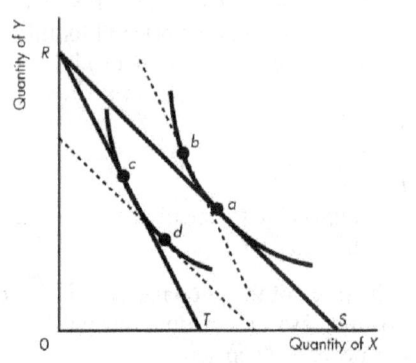

20 When the initial budget line labelled RS in Fig. 9.3 shifts to RT, the substitution effect is illustrated by the move from point
  a a to b.
  b a to c.
  c a to d.
  d b to d.
  e d to c.

21 When the initial budget line labelled RS in Fig. 9.3 shifts to RT, the income effect is illustrated by the move from point
  a a to b.
  b a to c.
  c a to d.
  d b to c.
  e b to d.

22 If the price of good *X* (measured on the horizontal axis) falls, the substitution effect is represented by a movement to a
a   higher indifference curve.
b   lower indifference curve.
c   steeper part of the same indifference curve.
d   flatter part of the same indifference curve.
e   flatter part of a higher indifference curve.

23 When Clark Gable took off his shirt in *It Happened One Night*, he was not wearing an undershirt. As a result, men's undershirt sales plummeted. *Ceteris paribus*, we can conclude that men's undershirt
a   preferences changed when prices changed.
b   preferences changed when income changed.
c   choices changed when preferences changed.
d   choices changed when prices changed.
e   choices changed when income changed.

24 When the price of an inferior good falls, the
1   income and substitution effects both move quantity demanded in the same direction.
2   income and substitution effects move quantity demanded in opposite directions.
3   income effect is usually larger than the substitution effect.
4   substitution effect is usually larger than the income effect.
a   1 and 2
b   1 and 4
c   2 and 3
d   2 and 4
e   none of the above

25 For a rise in price, the substitution effect
a   increases consumption for normal goods only.
b   always increases consumption.
c   decreases consumption for normal goods only.
d   decreases consumption for inferior goods only.
e   does none of the above.

Short Answer Problems

1 Explain why it is logically impossible for indifference curves to intersect each other by comparing points *a*, *b*, and *c* in Fig. 9.4.

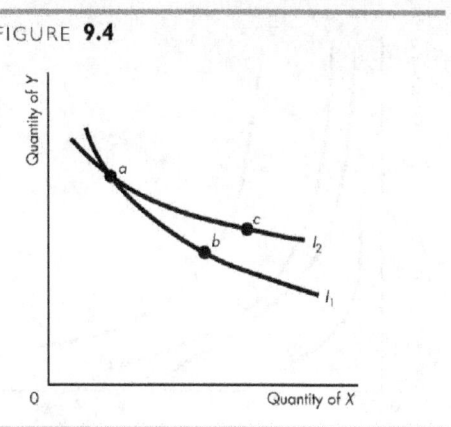

FIGURE **9.4**

2 For normal goods,

- an increase in income causes an *increase in demand* (demand curve shifts to the right).

- the income effect (due to a decrease in price) causes an *increase in quantity demanded*.

Explain why these two statements are or are not contradictory. Be sure to define clearly any important concepts.

3 Jan and Dan both like bread and peanut butter and have the same income. Since they face the same prices, they have identical budget lines. Currently, Jan and Dan consume exactly the same quantities of bread and peanut butter; they have the same best affordable consumption point. Jan, however, views bread and peanut butter as close (though not perfect) substitutes, while Dan considers bread and peanut butter to be quite (but not perfectly) complementary.

a   On the same diagram, draw a budget line and representative indifference curves for Jan and Dan. (Measure the quantity of bread on the horizontal axis.)

b   Now, suppose the price of bread declines. Graphically represent the substitution effects for Jan and Dan. For whom is the substitution effect greater?

4 Figure 9.5 illustrates a consumer's indifference map for food and clothing.

FIGURE **9.5**

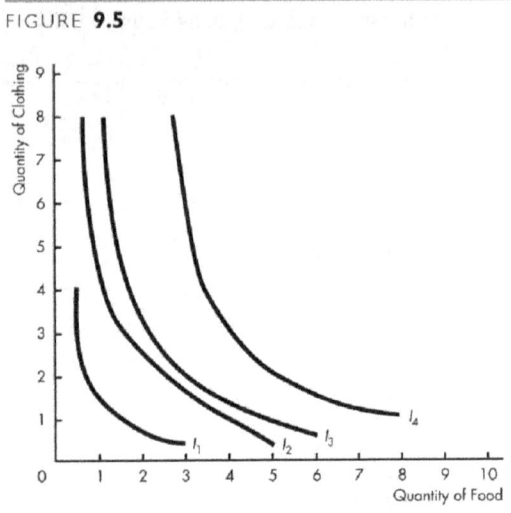

a   **i**   Initially, the price of a unit of clothing is $P_C = \$1$ and the price of a unit of food is $P_F = \$1.50$. If income is $Y = \$9$, draw the consumer's budget line on Fig. 9.5 and label the best affordable point as point a. What is the quantity of food consumed?

ii   What is the equation of the budget line in terms of P_C, P_F, and Y? What is the equation of the budget line in numerical terms? Express the magnitude (absolute value) of the slope of the budget line as a ratio of P_C and P_F.

iii   At point a, what is the value of the marginal rate of substitution (or equivalently, MU_F/MU_C)?

iv   Use your answers in parts **ii** and **iii** to derive the formula for utility maximization. Explain.

b   If P_F increases to $3 per unit while income and P_C remain unchanged, draw the new budget line and label the new best affordable point as point b. What is the new quantity of food consumed?

c   If P_F increases again to $4.50 per unit while income and P_C remain unchanged, draw the corresponding budget line and label the best affordable point as point c. What is the quantity of food consumed?

d   On a separate graph, plot and draw the demand curve for food that corresponds to

points a, b, and c. Be sure to clearly label the axes.

e   Suppose prices remain at their initial values ($P_C = \$1$, $P_F = \$1.50$) but income falls to $3. Draw the new budget line and label the best affordable point as point z. What is the quantity of food consumed? Is food a normal or inferior good? Explain. On your demand curve graph from part **d**, plot point z and roughly sketch a demand curve corresponding to the new income level.

5   Sharon, a fitness fanatic, plays squash and takes aerobics classes at her health club. Squash courts rent for $2 per hour and aerobics classes are $1 per hour. Sharon has decided to spend $12 per week for fitness activities. Figure 9.6 illustrates several indifference curves for squash and aerobics on Sharon's preference map.

FIGURE **9.6**

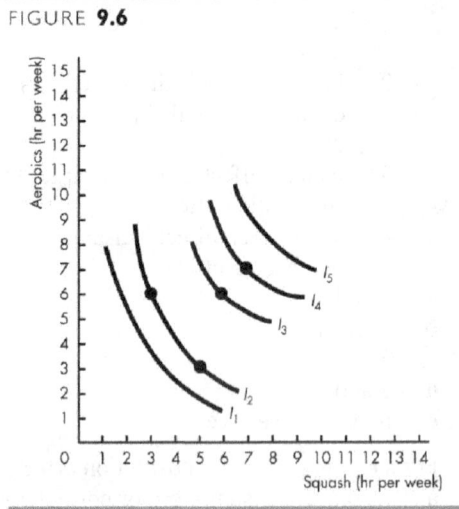

a   How many hours of squash and aerobics will Sharon consume at her best affordable point?

b   Suppose that squash rentals fall to $1 per hour.

i   How many hours of squash and aerobics will Sharon now consume? What is the increase in her hours of squash?

ii   Of the total increase in hours of squash, how many hours are due to the substitution effect of the price fall?

iii   Of the total increase in hours of squash, how many hours are due to the income effect of the price fall?

c On a separate graph, plot two points on Sharon's demand curve for squash and draw her straight-line demand curve.

d The price of squash continues to be $1 but Sharon's fitness budget increases to $14. How many hours of squash and aerobics will Sharon now consume?

ⓒ **6** Ms. Muffet consumes both curds and whey. The initial price of curds is $1 per unit, and the price of whey is $1.50 per unit. Ms. Muffet's initial income is $12.

a What is the relative price of curds?

b Derive Ms. Muffet's budget equation and draw her budget line on a graph. (Measure curds on the horizontal axis.)

c On your graph, draw an indifference curve so that the best affordable point corresponds to 6 units of curds and 4 units of whey.

d What is the marginal rate of substitution of curds for whey at this point?

e Show that any other point on the budget line is inferior.

7 Given the initial situation described in Short Answer Problem **6**, suppose Ms. Muffet's income now increases.

a Illustrate graphically how the consumption of curds and whey are affected if both goods are normal. (Numerical answers are not necessary. Just show whether consumption increases or decreases.)

b Draw a new graph showing the effect of an increase in Ms. Muffet's income if whey is an inferior good.

8 Return to the initial circumstances described in Short Answer Problem **6**. Now suppose the price of curds doubles to $2 a unit, while the price of whey remains at $1.50 per unit and income remains at $12.

a Draw the new budget line.

b Why is the initial best affordable point (label it point *r*) no longer the best affordable point?

c Using your graph, show the new best affordable point and label it *t*. What has happened to the consumption of curds?

d Decompose the effect on the consumption of *X* into the substitution effect and the income

effect. On your graph, indicate the substitution effect as movement from point *r* to point *s* (which you must locate) and indicate the income effect as movement from point *s* to point *t*.

ANSWERS

True/False and Explain

1 **F** Budget lines are straight. Indifference curves are bowed toward origin. (204–205)

2 **T** Expenditure = income along budget line. (204–205)

3 **T** Real income = income/price goods. (205)

4 **F** Rightward parallel shift. (206)

5 **T** See text discussion. (207–208)

6 **F** Represent higher levels of satisfaction. (207–208)

7 **T** See text discussion. (208–209)

8 **F** True for perfect complements. (209–210)

9 **T** Constant *MRS* is a straight line. (209–210)

10 **F** *MRS* is high. (209–210)

ⓒ **11** **T** Budget line is tangent to indifference curve. (210–211)

ⓒ **12** **F** True for normal goods, false for inferior goods. (213–214)

13 **T** The substitution effect for normal and inferior goods always works in the same direction. (213–214)

14 **T** See text discussion. (211–212)

15 **T** Income effect decreases consumption— higher real income means household can afford to buy higher-quality (normal) goods instead. (213–214)

Multiple-Choice

1 **b** **a** should be combinations of goods; **c** is about indifference curves; **d** is about the best affordable point; **e** includes the area inside the budget line. (204–205)

2 **e** Quantity of goods household can buy. (205)

3 **c** Income = $12 ($2 × 6 units *X*), so price *Y* = $12/8 units *Y*. (204–206)

4 c See text discussion. Indifference curves depend on preferences. (204–205)

5 b Numerators and denominators of both intercepts double, so intercepts do not change. (205–206)

6 c From $Q_P = (Y/P_P) - (P_M/P_P)Q_M$. If $P_P = \$5$, then $Y = \$100$ and $P_M = \$20$. Then recalculate Q_P equation for $P_P = \$4$. (205–206)

7 b (3 × price tomato) = (2 × price toothbrush). Divide both sides by price tomato and by 2. (204–206)

8 b y-intercept shifts down, x-intercept unchanged. (205–206)

9 d Increased income does not change slope but increases x- and y-intercepts. (205–206)

10 d From $Q_P = (Y/P_P) - (P_M/P_P)Q_M$. If $P_P = \$4$, and $(Y/P_P) = 10$, then $Y = \$40$. If $(P_M/P_P) = 5$, then $P_M = \$20$. (205–206)

11 c Budget line depends on **a** and **b**. At any level of satisfaction, indifference curve could be any shape. (207–210)

12 c Due to diminishing *MRS*. **d** and **e** are wrong since relative price relates to the budget line, not the indifference curve. (207–210)

13 c Indifference curves bow in toward the origin. (207–210)

14 d *MRS* is always diminishing moving down the indifference curve. Complements have more tightly curved indifference curves. (209–210)

15 b With constant slope = 1. (209–210)

16 e Rising price reduces real income, increasing consumption for inferior good. (209–210)

17 c t is on a higher indifference curve, but outside the budget line. s and q yield the same utility so **a**, **d** are wrong. q is preferred to r so **b** is wrong. (210–211)

18 e For rising price, the substitution effect always decreases consumption for both normal and inferior goods. (213–214)

19 a With the same income, less X can be purchased. **c** relates to indifference curves. Increase in real income is a move from point b to c. (211–212)

20 a Budget line with new prices is tangent to the original indifference curve. (213–214)

21 d Hypothetically restore original income (reverse the increase in real income) but keep prices constant at new level. (213–214)

22 d New budget line is flatter and drawn tangent to the same indifference curve. (213–214)

23 c Gable's influence caused decreased preference for undershirts. Combined with unchanged prices and incomes, this caused decreased consumption. (210–214)

24 d See text discussion. (213–214)

25 e Always decreases consumption. (213–214)

Short Answer Problems

1 The explanation takes the form of a proof by contradiction. Since points a and b are on the same indifference curve (I_1), the consumer is indifferent between them. Since points a and c are on the same indifference curve (I_2), the consumer is also indifferent between them. If the consumer is indifferent between a and b and between a and c, this implies an indifference between b and c. But indifference between points b and c is logically impossible, because we assume that more of any good is preferred to less of that good. Since point c has more of both good X and good Y than point b, the consumer cannot be indifferent between b and c. Indifference between b and c contradicts the assumption that more is preferred to less. Hence indifference curves cannot intersect.

2 These statements appear to be contradictory because an increase in income leads, in the first statement, to a shift of the demand curve but, in the second statement, to a movement along the demand curve. The reason the statements are *not* contradictory has to do with a crucial distinction between *nominal* income and *real* income.

The first statement (an *increase* in income causes an increase in *demand* [demand curve shifts rightward]) describes how an increase in *nominal* income shifts the demand curve. *Nominal* income is measured in dollars.

The second statement (the income effect [due to a decrease in price] causes an increase in *quantity demanded*) describes how an increase in *real* income causes a movement along the stationary demand curve.

Real income is measured in purchasing power, or the quantities of goods that nominal income can buy. When the price of a good decreases, your *real* income goes up because you can now purchase more of that good with the same, unchanged, *nominal* income. Because *nominal* income is unchanged in the second statement, the demand curve does not shift. But because *real* income has increased, the decrease in price leads to an increase in *quantity demanded*.

3 a   Initially, Jan and Dan are at point *c* on the budget line labelled *AB* in Fig. 9.7. Jan's indifference curve is I_J. Note that her indifference curve is close to a straight line, reflecting the fact that bread and peanut butter are close substitutes. On the other hand, since Dan considers bread and peanut butter to be complementary, his indifference curve, I_D, is more tightly curved.

FIGURE **9.7**

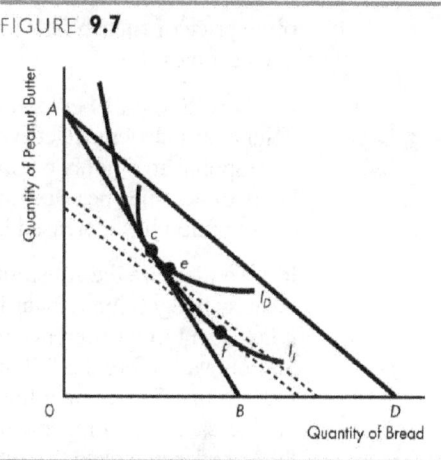

Quantity of Bread

b   If the price of bread declines, the budget line will become flatter, such as the line labelled *AD* in Fig. 9.7. In order to measure the substitution effect, find the point on the original indifference curve that has the same slope as the new budget line. Since Dan's indifference curve is more sharply curved, it becomes flatter quite rapidly as we move away from point *c*. Thus the substitution effect is quite small, from *c* to point *e*. Since Jan's indifference curve is almost a straight line, the substitution effect must be much larger, from *c* to point *f*.

4   The consumer's budget line is shown in Fig. 9.5 Solution.

FIGURE **9.5** SOLUTION

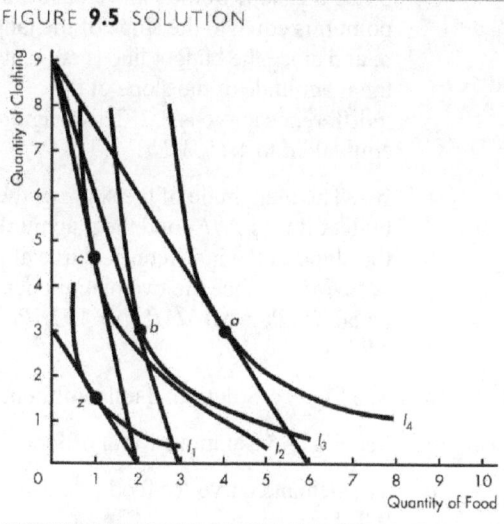

Quantity of Food

a   i   4 units of food.

ii   The consumer's budget is given by

$$P_C Q_C + P_F Q_F = Y$$

To obtain the budget equation, follow the calculation procedure on text page 205. Divide by P_C to obtain

$$Q_C + \frac{P_F}{P_C} Q_F = \frac{Y}{P_C}$$

Subtract $(P_F/P_C)Q_F$ from both sides to obtain

$$Q_C = \frac{Y}{P_C} - \frac{P_F}{P_C} Q_F$$

To obtain the budget equation in numerical terms, substitute in the values $P_C = \$1$, $P_F = \$1.50$, and $Y = \$9$.

$$Q_C = \frac{9}{1} - \frac{1.50}{1} Q_F$$

The magnitude (absolute value) of the slope of the budget line is 3/2, which is the ratio of P_F/P_C. Note that this price ratio cannot be read directly off the graph, since the axes measure quantities, not prices.

iii   The marginal rate of substitution at point *a* is defined as the magnitude of the slope of the indifference curve at point *a*.

Since the slope of the indifference curve at point a is equal to the slope of the tangent at a, and since the budget line is tangent at a, the magnitude of the slope of the indifference curve is 3/2. This magnitude is equivalent to MU_F/MU_C.

iv The magnitude of the slope of the budget line is P_F/P_C and the magnitude of the slope of the indifference curve at a is MU_F/MU_C. Since the two magnitudes are equal, $P_F/P_C = MU_F/MU_C$ or $MU_F/P_F = MU_C/P_C$.

b See Fig. 9.5 Solution: 2 units of food.

c See Fig. 9.5 Solution: 1 unit of food.

d The demand curve for food is shown in Fig. 9.8.

FIGURE **9.8**

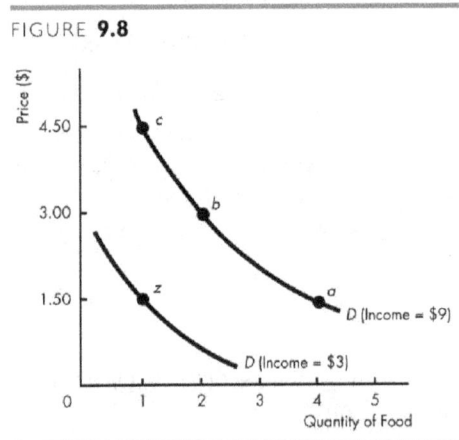

e See Fig. 9.5 Solution: 1 unit of food. Food is a normal good because a *decrease* in income (with prices constant) causes a decrease in food consumption (from 4 units to 1 unit). See Fig. 9.8 for the new demand curve (income = $3).

5 a In order to find Sharon's best affordable point, draw the budget line in Fig. 9.6 Solution. The initial budget line is labelled AB and Sharon's best affordable point is point c on indifference curve I_2. Thus Sharon consumes 3 hours of squash and 6 hours of aerobics per week.

FIGURE **9.6** SOLUTION

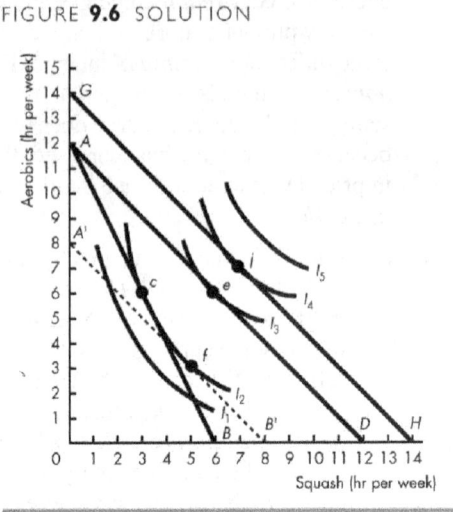

b If the price of squash falls to $1, the budget line becomes AD.

i Now Sharon's best affordable point is point e on indifference curve I_3. This corresponds to 6 hours of squash and 6 hours of aerobics per week. Her squash consumption has increased by 3 hours.

ii To measure the substitution effect, shift the new budget line leftward in parallel until it is tangent to indifference curve I_2, where Sharon was before the fall in the price of squash. In effect, budget line $A'B'$ removes the increase in real income due to the price fall in order to isolate the substitution effect of the price fall on Sharon's squash consumption. Point f is what Sharon would have consumed at the new prices if her income fell just enough to return her to her original indifference curve. The substitution effect of the fall in the price of squash is the movement from initial point c to point f, which is an increase in squash hours consumed of 2 (from 3 to 5 hours).

iii To measure the income effect, shift the budget line $A'B'$ rightward in parallel fashion until it is tangent to the indifference curve I_3, where Sharon was before we hypothetically reduced her real income. In effect, this shift isolates the income effect by restoring the increase in real income due to the price fall while keeping prices constant at their new values. The income effect of the fall in the price of squash is the movement from point f to point e, which is an increase in squash hours consumed of 1 (from 5 to 6 hours).

The results are summarized in Table 9.1.

TABLE **9.1**   PRICE EFFECT FROM FIGURE
9.6 SOLUTION

Effect	Move from Point	Δ Hours Squash
Substitution effect	c to f	2
+ Income effect	f to e	1
= Price effect	c to e	3

c   In parts **a** and **b**, income spent on fitness was
constant at $12 and the price of aerobics was
constant at $1 per hour. When the price of
squash was $2 per hour Sharon wanted to
consume 3 hours of squash, and when the
price of squash was $1 Sharon wanted to
consume 6 hours of squash. This gives us
two points on Sharon's demand curve for
squash, which are labelled *a* and *b* in Fig.
9.9. Drawing a line passing through these
points allows us to obtain her straight-line
demand curve, labelled *D*.

FIGURE **9.9**

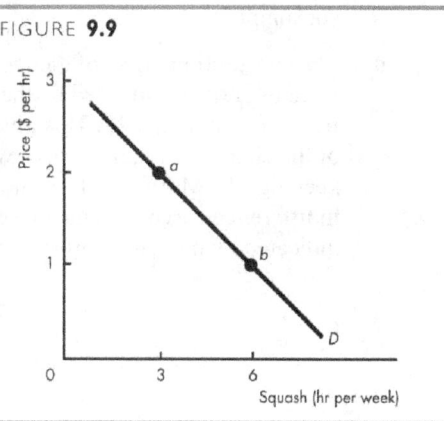

d   When Sharon's fitness budget increases to
$14, the budget line shifts right to the line
labelled *GH* in Fig. 9.6 Solution. Sharon's
best affordable point is now at *j*, which
corresponds to 7 hours of squash and 7
hours of aerobics consumed per week.

6 a   The relative price of curds is the price of
curds divided by the price of whey:

$1/$1.50 = 2/3

b   Let P_C = the price of curds, P_W = the price of
whey, Q_C = quantity of curds, Q_W = quantity
of whey, and Y = income. The budget
equation, in general form, is

$$Q_W = \frac{Y}{P_W} - \frac{P_C}{P_W} Q_C$$

Since P_C = $1, P_W = $1.50, and Y = $12,
Ms. Muffet's budget equation is specifically
given by

$$Q_W = 8 - 2/3 Q_C$$

The graph of this budget equation, the
budget line, is given by the line labelled *AB*
in Fig. 9.10.

FIGURE **9.10**   CURDS & WHEY NORMAL
GOODS

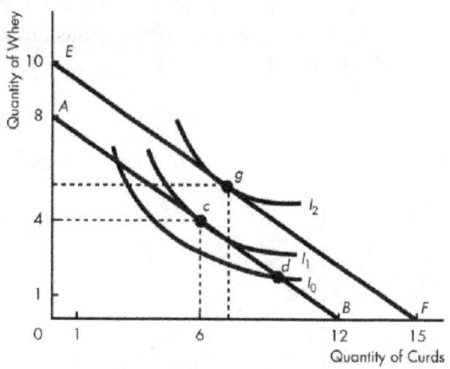

c   If the best affordable point corresponds to 6
units of curds and 4 units of whey, then the
relevant indifference curve must be tangent
to (just touch) the budget line *AB* at *c*, which
is indifference curve I_1.

d   The marginal rate of substitution is given by
the magnitude of the slope of the
indifference curve at point *c*. We do not
know the slope of the indifference curve
directly, but we can easily compute the slope
of the budget line. Since, at point *c*, the
indifference curve and the budget line have
the same slope, we can obtain the marginal
rate of substitution of curds for whey. Since
the slope of the budget line is –2/3, the
marginal rate of substitution is 2/3. For
example, Ms. Muffet is willing to give up 2
units of whey in order to receive 3 additional
units of curds and still remain indifferent.

e Since indifference curves cannot intersect each other and since indifference curve I_1 lies everywhere above the budget line (except at point c), we know that every other point on the budget line is on a lower indifference curve. For example, point d lies on indifference curve I_0. Thus every other point on the budget line is inferior to point c.

7 a An increase in income will cause a parallel rightward shift of the budget line, for example to EF in Fig. 9.10. If both curds and whey are normal goods, Ms. Muffet will move to a point like g at which the consumption of both goods has increased.

b If whey is an inferior good, its consumption will fall as income rises. This is illustrated in Fig. 9.11. Once again the budget line shifts from AB to EF, but Ms. Muffet's preferences are such that her new consumption point is a point like g' where the consumption of whey has actually declined.

FIGURE **9.11** WHEY AS INFERIOR GOOD

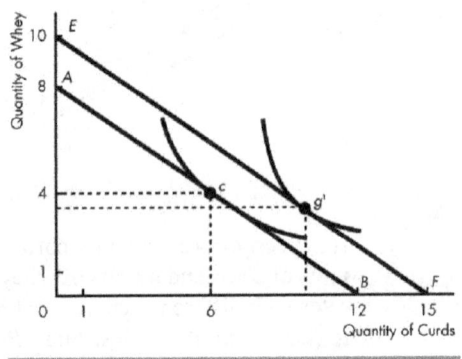

8 a Ms. Muffet's initial budget line is AB and the initial best affordable point is r in Fig. 9.12. Note that point r in Fig. 9.12 is the same as point c in Fig. 9.10. The new budget line following an increase in the price of curds to \$2 (income remains at \$12) is AH.

FIGURE **9.12**

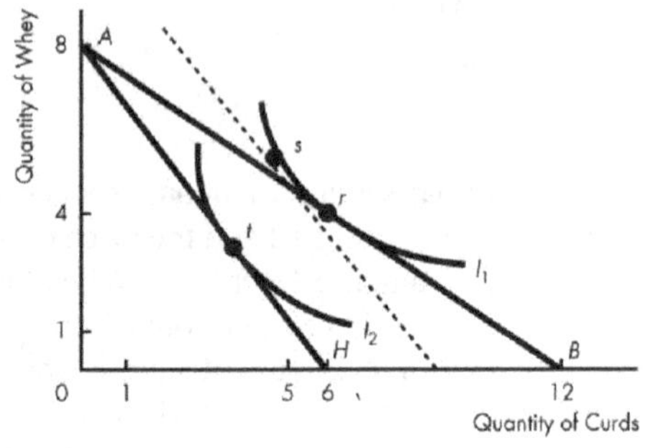

b After the price increase, point r is no longer the best affordable point, since it is no longer even affordable.

c The new best affordable point (labelled t in Fig. 9.12) indicates a decrease in the consumption of curds.

d The substitution effect of the increase in the price of curds is indicated by the movement from r to s in Fig. 9.12. This gives the effect of the change in relative prices while keeping Ms. Muffet on the same indifference curve. The income effect is indicated by movement from s to t.

Part 3 Wrap Up
Understanding Households' Choices

PROBLEM

Michael spends his income on only two goods—food and medicine. The indifference map and budget line in Fig. P3.1 show different combinations of food and medicine that Michael prefers given different incomes. The combinations can also be described as the points *a* to *f* in Table P3.1. Use this information to answer the following questions.

FIGURE **P3.1**

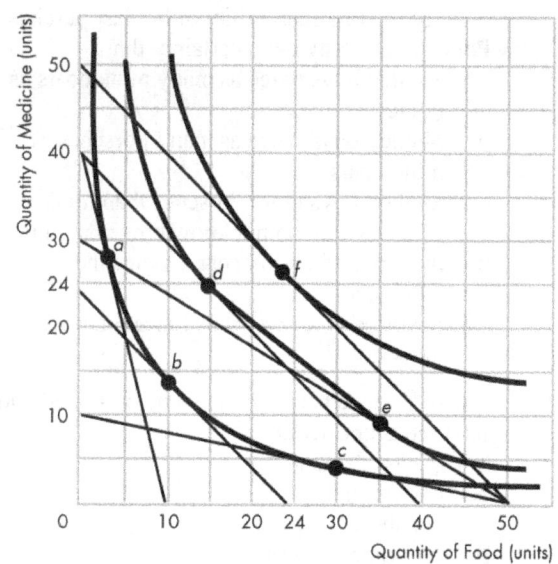

Quantity of Medicine (units) / Quantity of Food (units)

TABLE **P3.1**

Point	Quantity of Food (units)	Quantity of Medicine (units)
a	3	28
b	10	14
c	30	4
d	15	25
e	35	9
f	23	27

a Assume Michael's income is $300 and the price of food is $6 per unit. Using the information in Table P3.1, derive the coordinates (combinations of price and quantity) of three points on Michael's demand curve for medicine. Record the points in Table P3.2.

TABLE **P3.2** MICHAEL'S DEMAND CURVE FOR MEDICINE

Price ($)	Quantity (units)

b Now assume Michael's income is $600, the price of food is $12 per unit, and the price of medicine is $20 per unit. At Michael's best affordable point (consumer equilibrium), what is the ratio of $MU_{FOOD}/MU_{MEDICINE}$?

c Starting from Michael's best affordable point in part **b**, suppose the price of medicine then falls to $12 per unit and we want to separate the substitution and income effects of the price change.

  i The substitution effect moves Michael from point _____ to point _____ (fill in the blanks).

  ii The income effect moves Michael from point _____ to point _____ (fill in the blanks).

d Define the substitution effect and explain how your answer to part **c i** illustrates the substitution effect *alone*.

e Define the income effect and explain how your answer to part **c ii** illustrates the income effect *alone*.

f Is medicine a normal or inferior good for Michael? Explain your answer.

M I D T E R M
E X A M I N A T I O N

You should allocate 20 minutes for this examination (10 questions, 2 minutes per question). For each question, choose the one *best* answer.

1 Marginal utility equals
  a total utility divided by price.
  b total utility divided by the total number of units consumed.
  c the slope of the total utility curve.
  d the inverse of total utility.
  e the area below the demand curve but above market price.

2 A consumer maximizes his utility by purchasing 2 units of good X at $5/unit and 3 units of good Y at $7/unit. What is the ratio of the marginal utility of X to the marginal utility of Y?
  a 5/7
  b 7/5
  c 2/3
  d 3/2
  e 10/21

3 A change in the price of the good measured on the horizontal (x) axis changes which aspect(s) of the budget equation?
  a slope and y-intercept
  b slope and x-intercept
  c x- and y-intercepts but not slope
  d slope only
  e none of the above

4 Which of the following statements about the budget line is *false*? The budget line
  a divides affordable from unaffordable consumption points.
  b is based on fixed prices.
  c is based on fixed income.
  d is based on fixed quantities.
  e constrains consumer choices.

5 Suppose good X is measured on the horizontal axis and good Y on the vertical axis. The marginal rate of substitution is best defined as the
  a relative price of good X in terms of good Y.
  b relative price of good Y in terms of good X.
  c rate at which a person will give up good Y to get more of good X and remain indifferent.
  d rate at which a person will give up good X to get more of good Y and remain indifferent.
  e slope of the budget line.

6 When the price of a good changes, the change in consumption that leaves the consumer indifferent is called the
  a utility effect.
  b substitution effect.
  c income effect.
  d price effect.
  e inferior effect.

7 Shelley is maximizing her utility in her consumption of mink coats and Porsches. If the marginal utility of her last purchased mink coat is twice the marginal utility of her last purchased Porsche, we know with certainty that
  a Shelley buys twice as many mink coats as Porsches.
  b Shelley buys twice as many Porsches as mink coats.
  c Shelley buys more Porsches than mink coats, but we do not know how many more.
  d the price of a mink coat is twice the price of a Porsche.
  e the price of a Porsche is twice the price of a mink coat.

8 The difference between the value of a good and its price is known as
  a excess demand.
  b excess supply.
  c consumer surplus.
  d consumer excess.
  e marginal utility.

9 A change in income changes which aspect(s) of the budget equation?

a slope and y-intercept only

b slope and x-intercept only

c x- and y-intercepts but not slope

d slope only

e none of the above

10 When the price of a normal good rises, the income effect

a increases consumption of the good and the substitution effect decreases consumption.

b decreases consumption of the good and the substitution effect increases consumption.

c and the substitution effect both increase consumption of the good.

d and the substitution effect both decrease consumption of the good.

e is always larger than the substitution effect.

A N S W E R S

Problem

a If Michael spends his entire income of $300 on food (at $6 per unit), he can buy 50 units of food. This gives us the quantity-of-food intercept of his budget line. There are three alternative budget lines with that intercept. If Michael can also buy 50 units of medicine with $300, the price of a unit a medicine must be $6. That budget line is tangent to the highest indifference curve at point f, where Michael would consume 27 units of medicine. So one point on Michael's demand curve for medicine is (price = $6, quantity = 27 units). The other two points in Table P3.2 Solution (points e and c in Fig. P3.1) can be derived in the same way.

TABLE **P3.2** SOLUTION
MICHAEL'S DEMAND CURVE FOR
MEDICINE

Price ($)	Quantity (units)
6	27
10	9
30	4

b At the best affordable point (see Chapter 8's Helpful Hint **2**, page 109)

$$MU_{FOOD}/MU_{MEDICINE} = P_{FOOD}/P_{MEDICINE}$$

Since $P_{FOOD}/P_{MEDICINE} = 12/20$,

$$MU_{FOOD}/MU_{MEDICINE} = 12/20 = 3/5$$

c i The substitution effect moves Michael from point e to point d.

ii The income effect moves Michael from point d to point f.

d The substitution effect is the effect of a change in price on the quantity bought when the consumer (hypothetically) remains indifferent between the original and new situation.

In moving from point e to point d, the new price of medicine is reflected in the budget line tangent to the indifference curve at point d. This budget line eliminates the increase in real income that resulted from the decrease in the price of medicine. Michael is indifferent between the original (point e) and the new situation (point d) since both are on the same indifference curve.

e The income effect is the change in consumption resulting from (hypothetically) restoring the consumer's original income but keeping prices constant at the new level.

In moving from point d to point f, the prices of medicine (and food) stay constant at their new level, but Michael's real income is (hypothetically) restored to what it would have been as a result of the fall in the price of medicine.

f Medicine is a normal good for Michael because the income effect is positive—consumption of medicine increases from 25 to 27 units between points d and f.

Midterm Examination

1 c $MU = \Delta$ total utility/Δ quantity. (180–182)

2 a Quantities are irrelevant. Ratio of MUs must be equal to ratio of prices. (183–186)

3 b See Chapter 8 Helpful Hint **2** and analyse ΔP_M (movies on horizontal axis). (204–206)

4 d Quantities vary along the budget line. (204–206)

5 c Definition. **a** and **b** relate to slope of the budget line. MRS = **e** only at best affordable point. (207–210)

6 **b** Definition. (210–215)

7 **d** From maximum condition of equal MU/P. There is no necessary relation between MU and quantity. (183–186)

8 **c** See Text Fig. 8.7. (191)

9 **c** See Chapter 9 Helpful Hint **2**. Δ income (Y) does not change slope (P_M/P_P) but does Δ intercepts (Y/P_M) and (Y/P_P). (204–206)

10 **d** Both work in the same direction. Rising P causes decreased quantity consumed. (210–215)

Chapter 10
Organizing Production

The Firm and Its Economic Problem

A **firm** is an institution that hires and organizes factors of production to produce and sell goods and services. A firm's goal is profit maximization.

- Accounting costs = explicit costs + conventional depreciation

- Accounting profit = revenues – (explicit costs + conventional depreciation)

Opportunity costs of production consist of explicit costs (paid in money) and implicit costs (opportunities forgone but not paid in money). A firm's major implicit costs are

- **implicit rental rate**—the opportunity cost of using its own capital. Equals **economic depreciation** (change in market value of capital) + forgone interest.

- cost of owner's resources—(wage income forgone) + normal profit. **Normal profit** is the expected return to *entrepreneurial ability* and is part of a firm's opportunity costs of production. Normal profit is the average profit in the industry.

Economists' costs and profits:

- *opportunity costs* = explicit costs + implicit costs

- **economic profit** = revenues – (explicit costs + implicit costs)

- because normal profit is part of implicit costs, economic profit (when positive) is over and above normal profit.

- opportunity cost and economic profit are key to correctly predicting firm behaviour.

Limits to profit maximization are

- **technology** constraints—available resources and technology.

- information constraints—limited information and uncertainty about the firm's workforce, potential customers, and competitors.

- market constraints—limited demand for firm's output; marketing efforts of competitors.

Technological and Economic Efficiency

Technological efficiency—using least inputs to produce given output.

Economic efficiency—least cost of producing given output.

Information and Organization

Firms organize production by using

- **command systems** based on a managerial hierarchy.

- **incentive systems** to overcome problems of limited information and uncertainty.

With limited information, the **principal–agent problem** arises when *agents* (those employed by others) do not act in the best interests of the *principals* (employers of the agents).

- Strategies for coping with the principal–agent problem and inducing agents to act in the best interests of the principals include ownership, incentive pay, and long-term contracts.

- To cope with limited information and uncertainty, firms have devised different forms of business organization:

    - *sole proprietorship*—single owner with unlimited liability

- *partnership*—two or more owners with unlimited liability.

- *corporation*—owned by limited liability stockholders.

Markets and the Competitive Environment

Types of market structure:

- ◆ **perfect competition**—many firms; identical products; easy entry of new firms.

- ◆ **monopolistic competition**—many firms; slightly differentiated products (**product differentiation**); easy entry.

- ◆ **oligopoly**—few firms; identical or differentiated products; some barriers to entry.

- ◆ **monopoly**—single firm; product with no close substitutes; high barriers to new entry.

Market structure of most industries lies between the extremes of perfect competition and monopoly.

- ◆ To evaluate competitiveness of a market, economists use two measures of industrial concentration:

  - • **four-firm concentration ratio**—percentage of industry sales made by largest four firms.

  - • **Herfindahl–Hirschman Index** (HHI)—sum of squared market shares of the 50 largest firms in the industry.

- ◆ High concentration ratios usually indicate low degree of competition.

- ◆ Problems with concentration ratios:

  - • national, but many industries regional/global.

  - • no indication of entry barriers and turnover.

  - • firms operate in other industries.

Produce or Outsource? Firms and Markets

Firms coordinate economic activity when they perform tasks more efficiently than markets. Firms often have advantages of

- ◆ lower **transactions costs**—costs arising from finding someone with whom to do business.

- ◆ **economies of scale**—lower unit cost of producing good as output rate increases.

- ◆ economies of scope—lower unit cost from producing a range of goods and services.

- ◆ economies of team production—individuals in the production process specializing in mutually supportive tasks.

HELPFUL HINTS

1 In this chapter, we again meet our old friend opportunity cost. Here we look at the costs firms face and examine the differences between *opportunity cost* measures used by economists and *accounting cost* measures. Opportunity cost, which is the relevant cost concept for economic decisions, includes *explicit* and *implicit costs*. Important examples of implicit costs include economic depreciation, the owner's forgone interest and forgone wages, and normal profits. Accounting cost includes only explicit out-of-pocket costs and conventional depreciation. These differences in cost measures between accountants and economists also lead to the following differences in profit measures:

Economists

Opportunity costs = Explicit costs + Implicit costs

Economic profit = Revenues − (Explicit costs + Implicit costs)

Accountants

Accounting costs = Explicit costs + Conventional depreciation

Accounting profit = Revenues − (Explicit costs + Conventional depreciation)

Implicit costs, which economists include but accountants exclude, are the key difference between economists' and accountants' measures of cost and profit. Accounting profit does *not* subtract normal profits or other implicit costs, so accounting profit is generally greater than economic profit.

Because normal profit is part of implicit costs, economic profit is profit over and above normal profit. If we think of normal profit as average profit, economic profit is *above-average* profit. Economic profit is a signal to firms that they are earning a greater return on investment than could be earned on average elsewhere in the economy.

Economic profit can also be negative if revenues are less than opportunity costs. As we will see in Chapter 12, such an *economic loss* is a signal to firms that they are earning a lower return on investment than could be earned on average elsewhere.

2   The difference between *technological efficiency* and *economic efficiency* is critical since economic decisions are made only on the basis of economic efficiency. Technological efficiency is an engineering concept and occurs when the firm produces a given output using the least inputs. There is no consideration of input costs. Economic efficiency occurs when the firm produces a given output at least cost. All technologically efficient production methods are not economically efficient. But all economically efficient methods are also technologically efficient. Competition favours firms that choose economically efficient production methods and penalizes firms that do not.

3   This chapter introduces four types of market structure—perfect competition, monopolistic competition, oligopoly, and monopoly. These market structures will not mean much to you now, but you will learn more about them in Chapters 12–15. Pay attention to Text Table 10.6 (p. 240), which summarizes the characteristics of the different market structures and gives you a sense of how the structures differ. As you study each market structure in the following chapters, refer back to Table 10.6 to put it in perspective.

S E L F - T E S T

True/False and Explain

The Firm and Its Economic Problem

1   The goal of the firm is to maximize market share.

2   Normal profit is the expected return for supplying entrepreneurial ability.

3   Implicit costs include economic profit.

4   A firm's opportunity cost of using its own machine is lower than if it had rented the machine.

Technological and Economic Efficiency

5   Economically efficient production methods use relatively less of higher-cost resources and relatively more of lower-cost resources.

6   An economically efficient production process can become economically inefficient if the relative prices of inputs change.

7   All economically efficient production methods are also technologically efficient.

Information and Organization

8   Giving corporate managers stock in their companies is a strategy for coping with a principal–agent problem.

9   In a principal–agent relationship between the stockholders and managers of Scotiabank, the stockholders are agents and the managers are principals.

10   Owners of a corporation have limited liability.

Markets and the Competitive Environment

11   Product differentiation gives a monopolistically competitive firm some monopoly power.

12 A high concentration ratio always indicates a low degree of competition.

13 Concentration ratios measure barriers to entry in a market.

Produce or Outsource? Firms and Markets

14 Outsourcing is an example of firm coordination of economic activity.

15 Markets will coordinate economic activity in situations where there are economies of scale.

Multiple-Choice

The Firm and Its Economic Problem

1 Abdul operates his own business and pays himself a salary of $20,000 per year. He refused a job that pays $30,000 per year. What is the opportunity cost of Abdul's time in the business?
   a $10,000
   b $20,000
   c $30,000
   d $50,000
   e zero

2 Economic profit is revenues minus
   a explicit costs.
   b implicit costs.
   c opportunity costs.
   d accounting costs.
   e (explicit costs + conventional depreciation).

3 The rate of interest is 10 percent per year. You invest $50,000 of your own money in a business and earn *accounting* profit of $20,000 after one year. *Ceteris paribus*, what is your *economic* profit?
   a $20,000
   b $15,000
   c $5,000
   d $2,000
   e −$15,000

4 In general,
   1 opportunity cost is greater than accounting cost.
   2 opportunity cost is less than accounting cost.
   3 economic profit is greater than accounting profit.
   4 economic profit is less than accounting profit.
   a 1 only
   b 1 and 3
   c 1 and 4
   d 2 and 3
   e 2 and 4

5 A profit-maximizing firm is constrained by
   a demand for its product.
   b limited resources.
   c available technology.
   d limited information.
   e all of the above.

Technological and Economic Efficiency

6 In Table 10.1, which method(s) of making a photon torpedo is/are technologically efficient?
   a 1 only
   b 2 only
   c 3 only
   d all of the methods
   e 1 and 3 only

TABLE **10.1**   THREE METHODS OF MAKING ONE PHOTON TORPEDO

	Quantities of Inputs	
Method	Labour	Capital
1	5	10
2	10	7
3	15	5

7 Refer to Table 10.1. If the price of labour is $10 per unit and the price of capital is $20 per unit, which method(s) is/are economically efficient?
   a 1 only
   b 2 only
   c 3 only
   d all of the methods
   e 1 and 3 only

8 Which of the following statements is *true*?
a All technologically efficient methods are also economically efficient.
b All economically efficient methods are also technologically efficient.
c Technological efficiency changes with changes in relative input prices.
d Technologically efficient firms will be more likely to survive than economically efficient firms.
e None of the above

9 The business people are still talking over coffee. Which of their statements below describes *economic* efficiency?
a "The new production process we've installed uses less capital and labour than the old one."
b "The new assembly line has higher capital costs, but the fall in workers' hours has lowered overall costs."
c "The costs per unit fell dramatically as we increased the length of our production runs."
d "Despite the higher costs of negotiating the contracts, hiring the cleaning firm is much cheaper than using our own staff."
e "The computer servicing people we hired work well as an integrated problem-solving group."

10 To produce a unit of output, Alphaworks uses 10 hours of labour and 5 kilos of material, Betaworks uses 5 hours of labour and 10 kilos of material, and Gammaworks uses 10 hours of labour and 10 kilos of material. If labour costs \$10/hour and material costs \$5/kilo, which firm(s) is/are economically efficient?
a Alphaworks only
b Betaworks only
c Gammaworks only
d Alphaworks and Betaworks
e Alphaworks and Gammaworks

Information and Organization

11 Firms organize production using
a command systems only.
b incentive systems only.
c command and incentive systems.
d market systems only.
e principal–agent systems only.

12 The possibility that an employee may not work hard is an example of the
a limited liability problem.
b principal–agent problem.
c transactions cost problem.
d technological efficiency problem.
e partnership problem.

13 Firm strategies for coping with the principal–agent problem are
a ownership, incentive pay, and long-term contracts.
b proprietorship, partnership, and the corporation.
c economies of scale, scope, and team production.
d technology, information, and the market.
e none of the above.

14 A firm that has two or more owners with joint unlimited liability is
a a proprietorship.
b a partnership.
c a conglomerate.
d a corporation.
e none of the above.

15 What is a *disadvantage* of a corporation relative to a proprietorship or partnership?
a owners' unlimited liability
b profits are taxed twice as corporate profits and stockholders' dividends
c high cost of capital
d perpetual life
e none of the above

16 The majority of business revenues are accounted for by
a proprietorships.
b partnerships.
c corporations.
d cooperatives.
e not-for-profit organizations.

Markets and the Competitive Environment

17 The most extreme *absence* of competition is
a perfect competition.
b monopolistic competition.
c product differentiation.
d oligopoly.
e monopoly.

18 A market structure where a small number of firms compete is
a perfect competition.
b monopolistic competition.
c product differentiation.
d oligopoly.
e monopoly.

19 Product differentiation is an important feature of the market structure of
a perfect competition.
b monopolistic competition.
c oligopoly.
d monopoly.
e all of the above.

20 The four-firm concentration ratio measures the share of the largest four firms in total industry
a profits.
b sales.
c cost.
d capital.
e none of the above.

21 Which of the following statements is *false*? Concentration ratios
a are national measures, but firms in some industries operate in regional markets.
b are national measures, but firms in some industries operate in global markets.
c tell us nothing about barriers to entry in the industry.
d tell us nothing about how sales vary among firms in the industry.
e have difficulty classifying multi-product firms by industry.

Produce or Outsource? Firms and Markets

22 Which of the following statements is *false*?
a Firms and markets are institutions for coordinating economic activity.
b Firms organize productive resources to produce goods and services.
c Firms sell goods and services.
d Technologically efficient firms can eliminate scarcity.
e Firms use command systems to organize production.

23 Firms coordinate economic activity more efficiently than markets when firms have
a lower transactions costs.
b economies of scale.
c economies of scope.
d economies of team production.
e all of the above.

24 Economies of scale exist when
a transactions costs are high.
b transactions costs are low.
c hiring additional inputs does not increase the price of inputs.
d the cost of producing a unit of output falls as the output rate increases.
e the firm is too large and too diversified.

25 A firm with lower unit cost from producing a wider range of goods and services has economies of
a transactions costs.
b scale.
c scope.
d team production.
e market coordination.

Short Answer Problems

1 A year ago, Frank, the bricklayer, decided to start a business manufacturing doll furniture. Frank has two sisters; Angela is an accountant and Edith is an economist. (Both sisters are good with numbers, but Edith doesn't have enough personality to be an accountant.) Each of the sisters computes Frank's cost and profit for the first year using the following information:

1 Frank took no income from the firm. He has a standing offer to return to work as a bricklayer for $30,000 per year.

2 Frank rents his machinery for $9,000 a year.

3 Frank owns the garage in which he produces, but could rent it out at $3,000 per year.

4 To start the business, Frank used $10,000 of his own money and borrowed $30,000 at the market rate of interest of 10 percent per year.

5 Frank hires one employee at an annual salary of $20,000.

6 The cost of materials during the first year is $40,000.

7 Frank's entrepreneurial abilities are worth $14,000.

8 Frank's revenue for his first year is $100,000.

a Set up a table indicating how Angela and Edith would compute Frank's cost. Ignore any depreciation. What is Frank's cost as computed by Angela? by Edith?

b What is Frank's profit (or loss) as computed by Angela? by Edith?

2 According to your roommate, it is always more economically efficient to produce wheat using some machinery than using only labour. Suppose that there are two technologically efficient methods of producing one tonne of wheat:

- Method 1 requires 20 machine hours plus 20 hours of labour.

- Method 2 requires 100 hours of labour.

Country *A* has a highly developed industrial economy, while country *B* is less developed. In country *A* the price of an hour of labour (the wage rate) is $8, while the wage rate in country *B* is $4. The price of a machine hour is $20 in both countries. Which method is economically efficient in country *A*? in country *B*? Explain.

⊕ 3 Consider countries *A* and *B* described in Short Answer Problem **2**.

   a What wage rate in country *B* would make the two methods equally efficient in country *B*?

   b What price of a machine hour would make the two methods equally efficient in country *A*?

⊕ 4 Explain why an economically efficient production method must be technologically efficient.

5 The standard tip in a restaurant is 15 percent. Restaurants could raise their prices 15 percent, set a no-tipping policy, and pay servers the extra 15 percent. Use principal–agent analysis to explain why most restaurants prefer tipping.

6 The annual sales for firms in the Canadian thingamabob industry are reported in Table 10.2.

TABLE **10.2** THINGAMABOB INDUSTRY SALES

Firm	Sales ($)
Things 'R' Us	500
ThingMart	400
The Thing Club	350
Thingmania	250
All other firms	13,500

   a Calculate the four-firm concentration ratio for the thingamabob industry.

   b How competitive is the industry according to the ratio?

7 The U.S. yadayada industry consists of only five firms, whose markets shares are reported in Table 10.3.

TABLE **10.3** YADAYADA INDUSTRY MARKET SHARE

Firm	Market Share (%)
Jerry's Yadayadas	30
Elaine's Yadayadas	40
George's Yadayadas	20
Kramer's Yadayadas	5
Neuman's Yadayadas	5

   a Calculate the Herfindahl–Hirschman Index for the yadayada industry.

   b How competitive is the industry according to the index?

8 Considering the geographical scope of markets, how might a concentration ratio *understate* the degree of competitiveness in an industry? How might it *overstate* the degree of competitiveness?

ANSWERS

True/False and Explain

1 **F** Maximize profit. (228–230)

2 **T** Definition. (228–230)

3 **F** Implicit costs include normal profit. (228–230)

4 **F** Opportunity cost is equal for ownership or rental. Explicit cost is lower for ownership. (228–230)

5 **T** That achieves lowest per-unit cost. (231–232)

6 **T** Technological efficiency does not change with price changes, but economic efficiency can. (231–232)

7 **T** But the reverse is false—technological efficiency does not guarantee economic efficiency. (231–232)

8 **T** Makes managers' (agents) incentives same as shareholders' (principals). (233–236)

9 **F** Stockholders' (principals) profits depend on job done by managers (agents). (233–236)

10 T Liability only for value of investment. Sole proprietorship has unlimited liability. (234–236)

11 T Firm is sole producer of differentiated version of a good. (237–241)

12 F Often true, but depends on geographical scope of market, barriers to entry, and multi-product firms. (237–241)

13 F Small town with 4 restaurants has high concentration ratio but low entry barriers. (237–241)

14 F Example of market coordination. (242–243)

15 F Firms more efficient if economies of scale. (242–243)

Multiple-Choice

1 c Forgone income. (228–230)

2 c Definition. (228–230)

3 b Economic profit = accounting profit – implicit costs = $20,000 – (0.10 × $50,000). (228–230)

4 c See formulas in Helpful Hint **1**. (228–230)

5 e Technology, information, and market constraints. (228–230)

6 d No method has more of one input and the same amount of the other input, compared with the alternative method. (231–232)

7 b 2 costs $240 while 1 and 3 cost $250. (231–232)

8 b **c** is true for economic efficiency. Reverse of **d** is true. (231–232)

9 b Lowest cost. **c** describes economies of scale. **d** and **e** describe market coordination of production. (231–232)

10 b Costs are Alphaworks = $125, Betaworks = $100, Gammaworks = $150. (231–232)

11 c Principal–agent solutions are part of an incentive system. (233–236)

12 b See text discussion. (233–236)

13 a All create incentives for the agent to work in interests of the principal. **b** lists types of business organization, **c** lists advantages of firms over markets, **d** lists constraints on firms. (233–236)

14 b Definition. (234–236)

15 b See Text Table 10.4 (p. 235); **d** is an advantage, **a** and **c** are disadvantages of proprietorship and partnership. (233–236)

16 c See Text graphic. (233–236)

17 e Monopoly is least competition, perfect competition is the most. (237–241)

18 d Definition. (237–241)

19 b Many firms producing slightly differentiated products. (237–241)

20 b Definition. (237–241)

21 d Concentration ratios measure sales by size of firm. (237–241)

22 d Scarcity can never be eliminated. (242–243)

23 e See text discussion. (242–243)

24 d See text discussion. (242–243)

25 c Definition. (242–243)

Short Answer Problems

1 a Table 10.4 gives the cost as computed by Angela and Edith. The item numbers correspond to the item numbers in the problem.

TABLE **10.4**

Item Number	Angela's Accounting Computation (accounting cost)	Edith's Economic Computation (opportunity cost)
1.	$0	$30,000
2.	9,000	9,000
3.	0	3,000
4.	3,000	4,000
5.	20,000	20,000
6.	40,000	40,000
7.	0	$14,000
Total Cost	$72,000	$120,000

b Revenue is $100,000. Angela's accounting computation of profit uses this formula:

$$\text{Accounting profit} = \text{Revenues} - \text{Explicit costs}$$

$$= \$100,000 - \$72,000$$

$$= \$28,000$$

Edith's economic computation of profit uses this formula:

$$\begin{aligned} \text{Economic profit} &= \text{Revenues} - \text{Opportunity costs} \\ &= \$100{,}000 - \$120{,}000 \\ &= -\$20{,}000 \ (\text{an economic loss}) \end{aligned}$$

2 Both production methods are technologically efficient. The economically efficient production method has the lower cost of producing a tonne of wheat. In country A, the price of an hour of labour is $8 and the price of a machine hour is $20. The cost of producing a tonne of wheat is $560 using method 1 and $800 using method 2. Therefore method 1 is economically efficient for country A.

The price of an hour of labour is $4 in country B, and thus it will face different costs of producing a tonne of wheat. Under method 1, the cost will be $480 but under method 2, which uses only labour, the cost will be $400. So method 2 is economically efficient for country B.

The reason for this difference is that economic efficiency means producing at lowest cost. If the relative prices of inputs are different in two countries, there will be differences in the relative costs of production using alternative methods. Therefore, your roommate is wrong.

3 a If the wage rate in country B were to increase to $5 an hour, then production of a tonne of wheat would be $500 under either method. How did we obtain this answer? Express the cost under method 1 (C_1) and the cost under method 2 (C_2) as follows:

$$C_1 = 20P_m + 20P_h$$

$$C_2 = 100P_h$$

where P_m is the price of a machine hour and P_h is the price of an hour of labour (the wage rate). We are given that $P_m = \$20$ and asked to find the value of P_h that makes the two methods equally efficient; the value of P_h that makes $C_1 = C_2$. Thus we solve the following equation for P_h:

$$\begin{aligned} 20P_m + 20P_h &= 100P_h \\ 20(\$20) + 20P_h &= 100P_h \\ \$400 &= 80P_h \\ \$5 &= P_h \end{aligned}$$

b If the price of a machine hour is $32, production of a tonne of wheat would be $800 under either method in country A. This question asks: Given the wage rate of $8 ($P_h$) in country A, what value of P_m makes $C_1 = C_2$? Thus we solve the following equation for P_m:

$$\begin{aligned} 20P_m + 20P_h &= 100P_h \\ 20P_m + 20(\$8) &= 100(\$8) \\ 20P_m &= \$640 \\ P_m &= \$32 \end{aligned}$$

4 If a production method is economically efficient, then it is the least-cost method of producing a given level of output. Why does this imply that the method must also be technologically efficient—using the least inputs?

Try to imagine an economically efficient production method that is technologically *inefficient*. The method would *not* use the least inputs. No matter what the price of those inputs, there would always be a method that uses less inputs and therefore costs less. So a technologically inefficient method could *not* be economically efficient. Economic efficiency implies technological efficiency.

5 Restaurants face a classic principal–agent problem because servers may provide poor service to customers and drive away future business. Instead of having managers try to closely monitor each server, it is more efficient to delegate monitoring to customers. Customers tip on the basis of quality of service, creating an incentive for the server—the agent—to provide good service. This is exactly what the restaurant owner—the principal—wants.

6 a The four-firm concentration ratio is the percentage of the value of sales accounted for by the four largest firms in an industry. For thingamabobs, sales of the four largest firms are $500 + 400 + 350 + 250 = 1{,}500$. Total industry sales are $1{,}500 + 13{,}500 = 15{,}000$. So the ratio is $1{,}500/15{,}000 = 10$ percent.

b Since a ratio of less than 40 percent indicates a competitive market, the thingamabob industry is very competitive.

7 a The Herfindahl–Hirschman Index, for an industry of fewer than 50 firms, is the square of the percentage market share of each firm. For the yadayada industry, the index is

$$30^2 + 40^2 + 20^2 + 5^2 + 5^2 = 2,950$$

b Since an index of more than 1,800 indicates a concentrated market, the yadayada industry is very concentrated.

8 Concentration ratios are calculated from a national geographical perspective. If the actual scope of the market is not national, the concentration ratio will likely misstate the degree of competitiveness in an industry. If the actual market is global, the concentration ratio will understate the degree of competitiveness. A firm may have a concentration ratio of 100 as the only producer in the nation, but may face a great deal of international competition. When the scope of the market is regional, the concentration ratio will overstate the degree of competitiveness. The concentration ratio includes firms elsewhere in the nation that are not real competitors in the region.

Chapter 11
Output and Costs

Decision Time Frames

A firm has two decision time frames:

- **short run**—quantities of some resources are fixed; quantities of other resources are variable.

  - Fixed resources are called the firm's fixed *plant*—usually technology, buildings, capital, and management.

  - Variable resources—usually labour.

  - Short-run decisions are easily reversed.

- **Long run**—quantities of all resources are variable.

  - **Sunk cost**—*past* cost of buying a new plant. Firm's decisions depend only on short-run cost of changing labour input and long-run cost of changing plant. Sunk costs are irrelevant.

  - Long-run decisions are *not* easily reversed.

Short-Run Technology Constraint

Short-run production is described by

- **total product** curve (*TP*)—maximum attainable output with fixed quantity of capital as the quantity of labour varies.

- **marginal product** curve (*MP*)—ΔTP resulting from a one-unit increase in variable input.

- **average product** curve (*AP*)—*TP* per unit of variable input.

As variable input increases, *MP* increases (increasing marginal returns), reaches maximum, and then decreases (**diminishing marginal returns**). When $MP > AP$, *AP* is increasing. When $MP < AP$, *AP* is decreasing. When $MP = AP$, maximum *AP*.

- **Law of diminishing returns**—with given quantity of fixed inputs, as firm uses more variable input, its *MP* eventually diminishes.

Short-Run Cost

Short-run cost curves are determined by technology and prices of productive resources.

- **Total cost** (*TC*) = *TFC* + *TVC*

  - **Total fixed cost** (*TFC*)—cost of fixed inputs (including normal profit)

  - **Total variable cost** (*TVC*)—cost of variable inputs

- **Marginal cost** (*MC*)—ΔTC resulting from a one-unit increase in output

- **Average total cost** (*ATC*) = *AFC* + *AVC*

  - **Average fixed cost** (*AFC*)—total fixed cost per unit of output

  - **Average variable cost** (*AVC*)—total variable cost per unit of output

  - *AFC* curve decreases constantly as output increases.

  - *AVC*, *ATC*, and *MC* curves are U-shaped.

  - As output increases, *MC* decreases, reaches minimum, and then increases.

  - When $MC < ATC$, *ATC* decreases.

    When $MC > ATC$, *ATC* increases.

    When $MC = ATC$, minimum *ATC*.

    Same relation of *MC* and *AVC*.

Long-Run Cost

Long-run cost—cost of production when all inputs (capital and labour) are adjusted to economically efficient quantities.

♦ *Production function*—relationship between maximum attainable output and quantities of all inputs—describes long-run costs.

Long-run average cost curve (*LRAC*)—a planning curve that tells the firm the plant size and quantity of labour to use at each output to minimize cost. Consists of the segments of different short-run *ATC* curves along which average total cost is lowest.

♦ In the long run, when all inputs increase by the same percentage, increases in output can show three different returns to scale:

- **economies of scale** (increasing returns to scale)—percentage increase in firm's output > percentage increase in inputs. *LRAC* slopes downward.

- **constant returns to scale**—percentage increase in firm's output = percentage increase in inputs. *LRAC* is horizontal.

- **diseconomies of scale** (decreasing returns to scale)—percentage increase in firm's output < percentage increase in inputs. *LRAC* slopes upward.

♦ **Minimum efficient scale**—smallest quantity of output yielding minimum *LRAC*.

HELPFUL HINTS

1   Be sure to understand how economists use the terms *short run* and *long run*. These terms do *not* refer to calendar time. Think of them as planning horizons. The short run is a planning horizon short enough that while some resources are variable, at least one resource cannot be varied but is fixed. The long run refers to a planning horizon that is long enough that all resources can be varied.

2   This chapter introduces many new concepts and graphs and may at first appear overwhelming. Don't get lost among the trees and lose sight of the forest. There is a simple and fundamental relationship between product curves and cost curves.

The chapter explains the short-run product curves and concepts of total product, marginal product, and average product. This is followed by the short-run cost function and concepts of total cost, marginal cost, average variable cost, and average total cost.

But all of these seemingly separate concepts are related to the *law of diminishing returns*. The law states that as a firm uses more of a variable input, with a given quantity of fixed inputs, the marginal product of the variable input eventually diminishes. This law explains why the marginal product and average product curves eventually fall, and why the total product curve becomes flatter. When productivity falls, costs increase, and the law explains the eventual upward slope of the marginal cost curve. When marginal product falls, marginal cost increases.

The marginal cost curve, in turn, explains the U-shape of the average variable cost and average total cost curves. When the marginal cost curve is below the average variable (or total) cost curve, the average variable (or total) cost curve is falling. When marginal cost is above the average variable (or total) cost curve, the average variable (or total) cost curve is rising. The marginal cost curve intersects the average variable (or total) cost curve at the minimum point on the average variable (or total) cost curve.

Use the law of diminishing returns as the key to understanding the relationships between the many short-run concepts and graphs in the chapter. But all concepts and graphs are not equally important. Pay most attention to the unit-cost concepts and graphs—especially marginal cost, average variable cost, and average total cost—because these will be used the most in later chapters to analyse the behaviour of firms.

3   Be sure to thoroughly understand Fig. 11.1 (Text Fig. 11.5 on p. 259). It is the most important graph in the chapter and one of the most important graphs in all of microeconomics.

FIGURE **11.1**

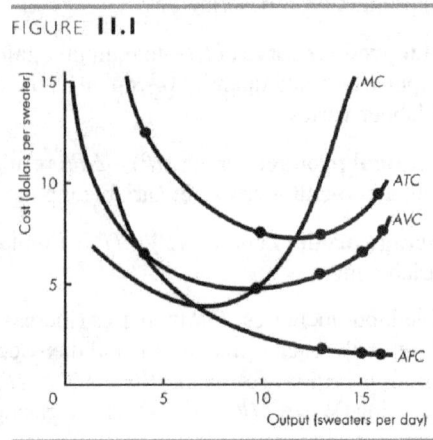

The curves for average total cost (*ATC*), average fixed cost (*AFC*), and average variable cost (*AVC*) are derived by taking the values for *TC*, *TFC*, and *TVC* and dividing by quantity of output. Since these are average values for a fixed quantity of output, they are plotted directly above the corresponding units of output.

On the other hand, marginal cost (*MC*) is the *change* in total cost (or equivalently, in total variable cost) resulting from a one-unit increase in output. It is plotted *midway* between the corresponding units of output. The *ATC*, *AVC*, and *MC* curves are crucially important. The *ATC* and *AVC* curves are both U-shaped. The *MC* curve is also U-shaped and intersects the *ATC* and *AVC* curves at their minimum points. The *MC* curve is below the *ATC* and *AVC* curves when *ATC* and *AVC* are falling, and above the *ATC* and *AVC* curves when they are rising. The less important *AFC* curve falls continuously as output increases.

4 You will probably draw a graph like the one in Fig. 11.1 at least a hundred times in this course. Here are some hints on drawing the graph quickly and easily:

- Be sure to label the axes: quantity of output (*Q*) on the horizontal axis and average cost on the vertical axis.

- Draw an upward-sloping marginal cost curve, as shown here in Fig. 11.2. The marginal cost curve can have a small downward-sloping section at first, but this is not important. Next, draw a shallow U-shaped curve that falls until it intersects the marginal cost curve, and then rises. Then pick a point further up the marginal cost curve. Draw another shallow U-shaped curve whose minimum point passes through your second point. Finally, label the curves.

Any time a test question (including those in the Self-Test) asks about these curves, *draw a graph* before you answer.

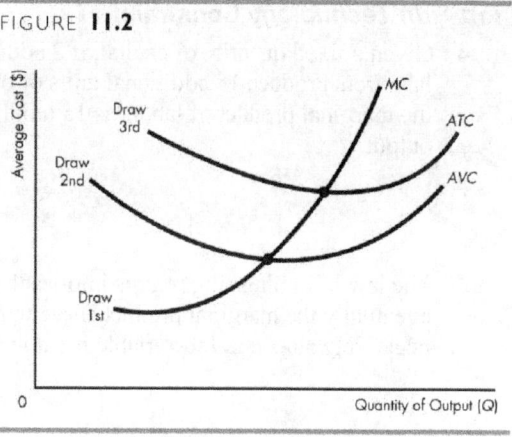

FIGURE **11.2**

5 The later sections of the chapter explain long-run costs using a production function where both labour and capital inputs are variable. While diminishing returns is the key for understanding short-run costs, the concept of *returns to scale* is the key for understanding long-run costs. Returns to scale are the increase in output relative to the increase in inputs when all inputs are increased by the same percentage. Returns to scale can be increasing, constant, or decreasing, and correspond to the downward-sloping, horizontal, and upward-sloping sections of the long-run average cost curve.

SELF-TEST

True/False and Explain

Decision Time Frames

1 All resources are fixed in the short run.

2 The firm's short-run decisions are easily reversed.

3 The firm's long-run decisions depend on sunk costs.

Short-Run Technology Constraint

4 Given a fixed quantity of capital, if 2 additional labourers produce 15 additional units of output, the marginal product of labour is 15 units of output.

5 The law of diminishing returns implies that eventually the marginal product curve will be negatively sloped as the variable input increases.

6 Marginal product is measured by the slope of the total product curve.

7 The law of diminishing returns implies that we will not observe a range of increasing marginal returns.

8 If the marginal product of labour is greater than the average product of labour, average product is increasing.

Short-Run Cost

9 Average variable cost reaches its minimum at the same level of output at which average product is a maximum.

10 If average variable cost is decreasing, then marginal cost must be decreasing.

11 The average total cost curve always intersects the minimum point of the marginal cost curve.

Long-Run Cost

12 No part of any short-run average total cost curve can lie below the long-run average cost curve.

13 Economies of scale means that the long-run average cost curve is positively sloped.

14 If a firm can double its output by building a second plant identical to its first plant, there are constant returns to scale.

15 Minimum efficient scale occurs at the minimum point on the average total cost curve.

Multiple-Choice

Decision Time Frames

1 In economics, the short run is a time period in which
 a one year or less elapses.
 b all resources are variable.
 c all resources are fixed.
 d some resources are variable but some resources are fixed.
 e all resources are variable but the technology is fixed.

2 Long-run decisions
 a are not easily reversed.
 b do not depend on sunk costs.
 c involve changes in a firm's plant.
 d can vary all resources of a firm.
 e are all of the above.

Short-Run Technology Constraint

3 The average product of labour is
 a the slope of the total product curve.
 b the slope of the marginal product curve.
 c the increase in total product divided by the increase in labour employed.
 d the total product divided by the quantity of labour employed.
 e none of the above.

4 When the marginal product of labour is less than the average product of labour,
  a the average product of labour is increasing.
  b the marginal product of labour is increasing.
  c the total product curve is negatively sloped.
  d the firm is experiencing diminishing returns.
  e none of the above is true.

5 Refer to Fig. 11.3 illustrating Swanky's short-run total product curve. Which of the following statements is *true*?
  a Points above the curve are attainable and inefficient.
  b Points below the curve are attainable and inefficient.
  c Points below the curve are unattainable and inefficient.
  d Points on the curve are unattainable and efficient.
  e Points on the curve all have equal marginal products.

FIGURE **11.3**

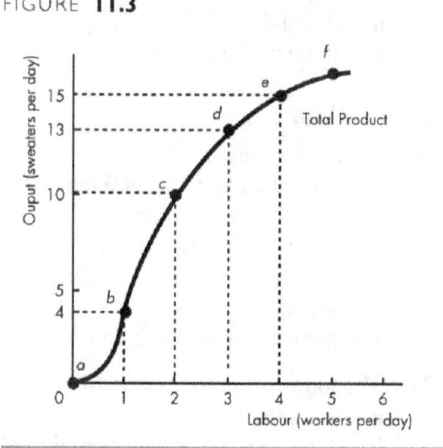

6 Refer to Fig. 11.3 illustrating Swanky's short-run total product curve. Marginal product reaches a maximum when you add which labourer?
  a 1st labourer
  b 2nd labourer
  c 3rd labourer
  d 4th labourer
  e 5th labourer

7 Which of the following statements by a restaurant owner refers to the law of diminishing returns?
  a "The higher the quality of the ingredients we use, the higher the cost of producing each meal."
  b "If we double the size of our premises and double everything else—kitchen staff, serving staff, equipment—we can increase the number of meals we serve, but not to double current levels."
  c "We can increase the number of meals we serve by just adding more kitchen staff, but each additional worker adds fewer meals than the previous worker because traffic in the kitchen will get worse."
  d "We can serve the same number of meals with fewer kitchen staff, but we would have to buy more labour-saving kitchen equipment."
  e "We can serve the same number of meals with less kitchen equipment, but we would have to hire more kitchen staff."

Short-Run Cost

8 The vertical distance between the *TC* and *TVC* curves is
  a decreasing as output increases.
  b increasing as output increases.
  c equal to *AFC*.
  d equal to *TFC*.
  e equal to *MC*.

9 Total cost is $20 at 4 units of output and $36 at 6 units of output. Between 4 and 6 units of output, marginal cost
  a is less than average total cost.
  b is equal to average total cost.
  c is equal to average variable cost.
  d is greater than average total cost.
  e cannot be compared with any average cost without additional information.

10 Marginal cost is the amount that
  a total cost increases when one more labourer is hired.
  b fixed cost increases when one more labourer is hired.
  c variable cost increases when one more labourer is hired.
  d total cost increases when one more unit of output is produced.
  e fixed cost increases when one more unit of output is produced.

11 A firm's fixed costs are $100. If total costs are $200 for one unit of output and $310 for two units, what is the marginal cost of the second unit?
a $100
b $110
c $200
d $210
e $310

12 If *ATC* is falling *MC* must be
a rising.
b falling.
c equal to *ATC*.
d above *ATC*.
e below *ATC*.

13 Which of the following does *not* cause decreasing *ATC*?
a decreasing marginal cost
b decreasing average variable cost
c decreasing average fixed cost
d increasing marginal product
e increasing returns to scale

14 The average variable cost curve will shift up if
a there is an increase in fixed costs.
b there is a technological advance.
c the price of a variable input decreases.
d the price of a variable input increases.
e the price of output increases.

15 The marginal cost (*MC*) curve intersects the
a *ATC*, *AVC*, and *AFC* curves at their minimum points.
b *ATC* and *AFC* curves at their minimum points.
c *AVC* and *AFC* curves at their minimum points.
d *ATC* and *AVC* curves at their minimum points.
e *TC* and *TVC* curves at their minimum points.

16 According to the law of diminishing returns,
1 marginal productivity eventually rises.
2 marginal productivity eventually falls.
3 marginal cost eventually rises.
4 marginal cost eventually falls.
a 1 and 3
b 1 and 4
c 2 and 3
d 2 and 4
e 4 only

17 Average variable cost is at a minimum at the same output where
a average product is at a maximum.
b average product is at a minimum.
c marginal product is at a maximum.
d marginal product is at a minimum.
e marginal cost is at a minimum.

18 A rise in the price of a fixed input will cause a firm's
a average variable cost curve to shift up.
b average total cost curve to shift up.
c average total cost curve to shift down.
d marginal cost curve to shift up.
e marginal cost curve to shift down.

19 A technological advance will shift
1 *TP*, *AP*, and *MP* curves up.
2 *TP*, *AP*, and *MP* curves down.
3 *TC*, *ATC*, and *MC* curves up.
4 *TC*, *ATC*, and *MC* curves down.
a 1 and 3
b 1 and 4
c 2 and 3
d 2 and 4
e none of the above

Long-Run Cost

20 In the long run,
a only the plant size is fixed.
b all inputs are variable.
c all inputs are fixed.
d a firm must experience diseconomies of scale.
e none of the above is true.

21 The long-run average cost curve
a is a planning curve.
b identifies the cost-minimizing plant size and quantity of labour for each output level.
c is the relation between lowest attainable *ATC* and output when both plant size and labour are variable.
d consists of the segments of different short-run *ATC* curves along which average total cost is lowest.
e is all of the above.

22 Constant returns to scale means that as all inputs are increased,
a total output remains constant.
b average total cost remains constant.
c average total cost increases at the same rate as inputs.
d long-run average cost remains constant.
e long-run average cost rises at the same rate as inputs.

23 If all inputs are increased by 10 percent and output increases by less than 10 percent, it must be the case that
a average total cost is decreasing.
b average total cost is increasing.
c the *LRAC* curve is negatively sloped.
d there are economies of scale.
e there are diseconomies of scale.

24 Minimum efficient scale is the smallest quantity of output at which
a the *LRAC* curve reaches it lowest level.
b the *ATC* curve reaches its lowest level.
c the *AFC* curve reaches its lowest level.
d economies of scale begin.
e diminishing returns begin.

25 A firm will always want to increase its scale of plant if
a it persistently produces on the upward-sloping part of its short-run average total cost curve.
b it persistently produces on the downward-sloping part of its short-run average total cost curve.
c it is producing below minimum efficient scale.
d marginal cost is below average total cost.
e marginal cost is below average variable cost.

Short Answer Problems

1 Why must the marginal cost curve intersect the average total cost curve at the minimum point of the average total cost curve?

2 Explain the connection, if any, between the U-shape of the average total cost curve and (a) fixed costs and (b) the law of eventually diminishing returns.

3 Use the concepts of marginal and average to answer the following question. Suppose the worst student at Hubertville High School transfers to Histrionic High School. Is it possible that the average grade-point of the students at each school rises? Explain.

4 What is the difference, if any, between diminishing returns and diseconomies of scale?

5 For a given scale of plant, Table 11.1 gives the total monthly output of golf carts attainable using varying quantities of labour.

TABLE **11.1** MONTHLY GOLF CART PRODUCTION

Labourers (per month)	Output (units per month)	Marginal Product	Average Product
0	0		
1	1		
2	3		
3	6		
4	12		
5	17		
6	20		
7	22		
8	23		

a Complete the table for the marginal product and average product of labour. (Note that marginal product should be entered *midway* between rows to emphasize that it is the result of *changing* inputs—moving from one row to the next. Average product corresponds to a fixed quantity of labour and should be entered on the appropriate row.)

b Label the axes and draw a graph of the total product curve (*TP*).

c On a separate piece of paper, label the axes and draw a graph of both marginal product (*MP*) and average product (*AP*). (Marginal product should be plotted *midway* between the corresponding units of labour, as in Text Fig. 11.2(b) on p. 255, while average product should be plotted directly above the corresponding units of labour, as in Text Fig. 11.3 on p. 256.)

6 Now let's examine the short-run costs of golf cart production. The first two columns of Table 11.1 are reproduced in the first two columns of Table 11.2 on the next page. The cost of 1 labourer (the only variable input) is $2,000 per month. Total fixed cost is $2,000 per month.

TABLE **11.2** SHORT-RUN COSTS (MONTHLY)

L	Q	TFC ($)	TVC ($)	TC ($)	MC ($)	AFC ($)	AVC ($)	ATC ($)
0	0	2,000						
1	1							
2	3							
3	6							
4	12							
5	17							
6	20							
7	22							
8	23							

a Given this information, complete Table 11.2 by computing total fixed cost (*TFC*), total variable cost (*TVC*), total cost (*TC*), marginal cost (*MC*), average fixed cost (*AFC*), average variable cost (*AVC*), and average total cost (*ATC*). Your completed table should look like the table in Text Fig. 11.5 on p. 259, with marginal cost entered *midway* between the rows.

b Label the axes and draw the *TC*, *TVC*, and *TFC* curves on a single graph.

c Label the axes and draw the *MC*, *ATC*, *AVC*, and *AFC* curves on a single graph. Be sure to plot *MC midway* between the corresponding units of output.

7 Now suppose that the price of a labourer increases to $2,500 per month. Construct a table for the new *MC* and *ATC* curves (output, *MC*, *ATC*) for golf cart production. Label the axes and draw a graph of the new *MC* and *ATC* curves. What is the effect of the increase in the price of the variable input on these curves?

8 Return to the original price of labour of $2,000 per month. Now suppose that we double the quantity of fixed inputs so that total fixed costs also double to $4,000 per month. This increases the monthly output of golf carts for each quantity of labour as indicated in Table 11.3.

TABLE **11.3** NEW MONTHLY PRODUCTION OF GOLF CARTS

Labourers (per month)	Output (units per month)
0	0
1	1
2	4
3	10
4	19
5	26
6	31
7	34
8	36

a Construct a table for the new *MC* and *ATC* curves (output, *MC*, *ATC*). Label the axes and draw a graph of the new *MC* and *ATC* curves.

b What is the effect on these curves (compared with the original *MC* and *ATC* curves in Short Answer Problem **6c**) of an increase in "plant size"? Are there economies of scale?

c Draw the long-run average cost (*LRAC*) curve if these are the only two plant sizes available.

ANSWERS

True/False and Explain

1 **F** Some resources fixed, some variable. (252)

2 **T** Firm can change output by changing quantity of labour hired. Long-run decisions are not easily reversed. (252)

3 **F** Sunk costs are past costs and are irrelevant to all firm decisions about the present or the future. (252)

4 **F** $\Delta TP/\Delta L = 15/2 = 7.5$. (253–256)

5 **T** *MP* must eventually diminish with increasing *L*. (253–256)

6 **T** $\Delta TP/\Delta L$. (253–256)

7 **F** *Eventually* diminishing returns. *MP* can initially increase. (253–256)

8 **T** See Text Fig. 11.3 and grade-point discussion for intuition. (253–256)

9 **T** $AVC = TVC/Q = WL/Q = W/(Q/L) = W/AP$. (257–261)

ⓔ **10** **F** MC must be below AVC, but MC may be increasing or decreasing. (257–261)

11 **F** MC intersects at minimum ATC. (257–261)

12 **T** $LRAC$ consists of lowest-cost segments of all average total cost curves. (262–265)

13 **F** Negatively sloped; falling long-run average costs as output increases. (262–265)

14 **T** All inputs increase by 100 percent and output increases by 100 percent. (262–265)

15 **F** Smallest Q at which $LRAC$ curve is at minimum. ATC is short-run. (262–265)

Multiple-Choice

1 **d** Definition. (252)

2 **e** From definition of long run. (252)

3 **d** Definition. (253–256)

ⓔ **4** **d** When $MP < AP$, MP is decreasing (diminishing returns), AP is decreasing, and TP is positively sloped. (253–256)

5 **b** Attainable but not maximum TP. (253–256)

6 **b** MP = slope TP curve = 6 for 2nd labourer. (253–256)

7 **c** MP decreases as the restaurant uses more variable resource (labour). (253–256)

8 **d** $TC = TFC + TVC$. Distance is constant. (257–258)

ⓔ **9** **d** $MC = 16/2 = 8$. ATC is \$5 at 4 units and \$6 at 6 units. (258)

10 **d** Definition; **b** and **e** are wrong because fixed costs don't change; **a** and **c** are wrong because MC can also decrease and may be affected by costs other than labour. (258)

11 **b** Fixed costs are irrelevant. $\Delta TC/\Delta Q =$ (\$310 – \$200)/(2 – 1). (257–258)

ⓔ **12** **e** MC could be increasing or decreasing below the ATC when ATC is decreasing. (258–261)

13 **e** Increasing returns to scale is a long-run concept; ATC is a short-run concept. (258–261)

14 **d** **a** and **e** don't affect AVC; **b** and **c** shift AVC down. (258–261)

15 **d** AFC always decreases, TC and TVC always increase. (257–259)

16 **c** Decreasing MP causes increasing MC. (258–261)

17 **a** AVC decreases as long as AP is increasing. See Text Fig. 11.6. (260)

18 **b** Won't affect AVC or MC. (260–261)

19 **b** Productivity increases, costs decrease. (260–261)

20 **b** Definition. All returns to scale are possible in the long run. (262–265)

21 **e** All definitions of the $LRAC$. (262–265)

22 **d** $LRAC$ is horizontal. (262–265)

23 **e** Definition. Since all resources are variable, **a** and **b** are irrelevant. (262–265)

24 **a** Definition of a long-run concept; **b**, **c**, **e** are short-run concepts; **d** would be correct if where economies of scale *end*. (262–265)

ⓔ **25** **a** Plant already too big in **b**; for **c**, sales may not justify a plant that big; **d** and **e** relate to short run. (262–265)

Short Answer Problems

1 The average total cost curve is U-shaped, first falling and then rising as output increases. When average total cost is falling, marginal cost must be less than average total cost, and when average total cost is rising, marginal cost must be greater than average total cost. Therefore, the marginal cost curve must intersect the average total cost curve at its minimum point. In order for average total cost to fall, it must have been *pulled down* by a smaller increase in cost from the last unit of output. Therefore, marginal cost is lower than average total cost. Similarly, when average total cost is rising, it must be that it has been *pulled up* by a higher marginal cost. When average total cost is at its minimum, it is neither falling nor rising, so marginal cost cannot be lower or higher than average total cost. Therefore, marginal cost must be equal to average total cost.

2 The U-shape of the average total cost (ATC) curve arises from the opposing forces of (a) spreading fixed costs over a larger output and (b) the law of eventually diminishing returns.

As output increases, fixed costs are spread over a larger output so average fixed cost (AFC) falls. Initially, as output increases, the marginal productivity of the variable resource rises, causing average variable cost (AVC) to fall.

Falling *AVC*, together with falling *AFC*, causes average total cost (*ATC*) to fall, contributing to the downward-sloping portion of *ATC*. Eventually, as output increases, diminishing returns set in, marginal productivity falls, and *AVC* rises. Eventually, *AVC* rises more quickly than *AFC* falls, contributing to the upward-sloping portion of the *ATC*.

3 Yes, it is possible that the average grade-point of the students at each school rises. Think of the transferring student as the *marginal* student. If his grade-point average, although the lowest at Hubertville High, is higher than the *average* grade-point at Histrionic High, then the results are: the *average* grade-point at Hubertville High rises with the elimination of the lowest grade-point, and the average grade-point at Histrionic High rises because the transferring (*marginal*) student's grade-point pulls up the *average* grade-point.

4 The law of diminishing returns states that as a firm uses more of a variable input, with a given quantity of fixed inputs, the marginal product of the variable input eventually diminishes. Diseconomies of scale occur when a firm increases all of its inputs by an equal percentage, and this results in a lower percentage increase in output. Diminishing (marginal) returns is a short-run concept since there must be a fixed input. Diseconomies of scale is a long-run concept since all inputs must be variable.

5 a The completed Table 11.1 is shown here as Table 11.1 Solution.

TABLE **11.1** SOLUTION
MONTHLY GOLF CART PRODUCTION

Labourers (per month)	Output (units per month)	Marginal Product	Average Product
0	0		0
		·········· 1	
1	1		1.00
		·········· 2	
2	3		1.50
		·········· 3	
3	6		2.00
		·········· 6	
4	12		3.00
		·········· 5	
5	17		3.40
		·········· 3	
6	20		3.33
		·········· 2	
7	22		3.14
		·········· 1	
8	23		2.88

b Figure 11.4 gives the graph of the total product curve.

FIGURE **11.4**

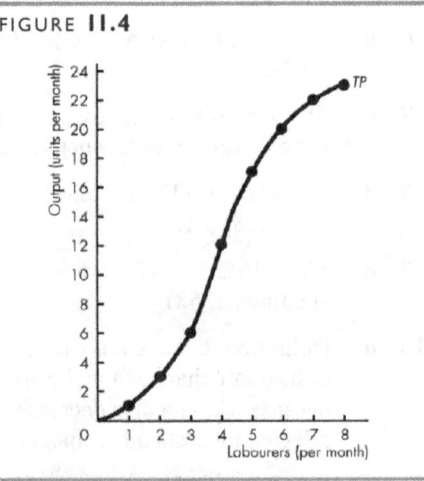

c Figure 11.5 on the next page gives the graphs of marginal product and average product.

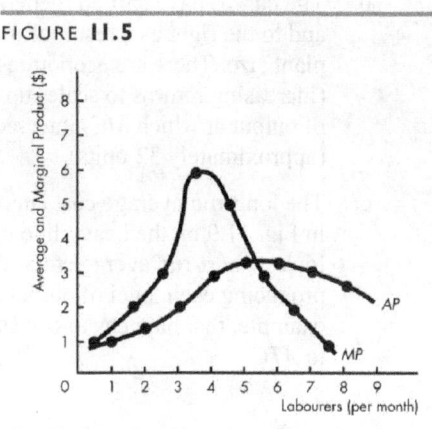

FIGURE **11.5**

6 a Completed Table 11.2 is shown here as Table 11.2 Solution.

TABLE **11.2** SOLUTION
SHORT-RUN COSTS (MONTHLY)

L	Q	TFC ($)	TVC ($)	TC ($)	MC ($)	AFC ($)	AVC ($)	ATC ($)
0	0	2,000	0	2,000		—	—	—
					2,000			
1	1	2,000	2,000	4,000		2,000	2,000	4,000
					1,000			
2	3	2,000	4,000	6,000		667	1,333	2,000
					667			
3	6	2,000	6,000	8,000		333	1,000	1,333
					333			
4	12	2,000	8,000	10,000		167	667	833
					400			
5	17	2,000	10,000	12,000		118	588	706
					667			
6	20	2,000	12,000	14,000		100	600	700
					1,000			
7	22	2,000	14,000	16,000		91	636	727
					2,000			
8	23	2,000	16,000	18,000		87	696	783

b The *TC, TVC,* and *TFC* curves are graphed in Fig. 11.6.

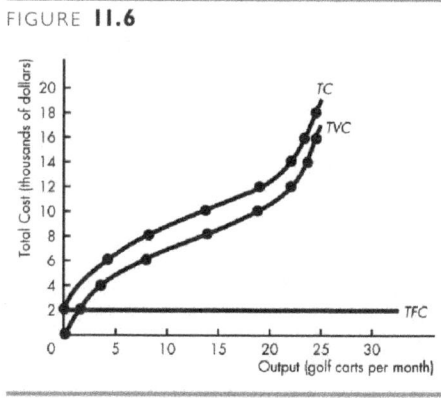

FIGURE **11.6**

c The *MC, ATC, AVC,* and *AFC* curves are graphed in Fig. 11.7.

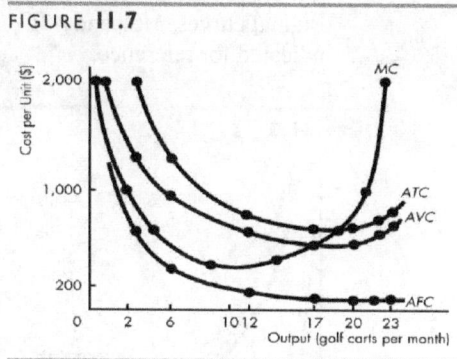

FIGURE **11.7**

7 The new *MC* and *ATC* curves (and the associated table) for golf cart production are given in Fig. 11.8. The original curves, MC_0 and ATC_0, are indicated for reference. The new curves are labelled MC_1 and ATC_1. Both curves have shifted up as a result of an increase in the price of labour.

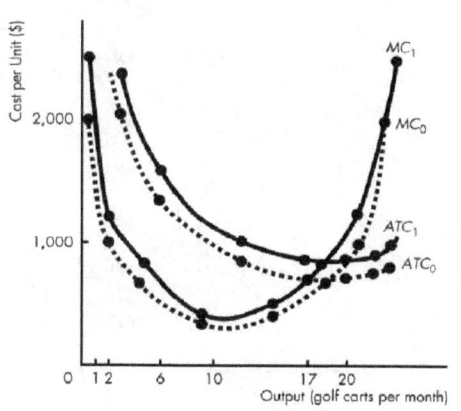

FIGURE **11.8**

Output	MC ($)	ATC ($)
0		0
	2,500	
1		4,500
	1,250	
3		2,333
	833	
6		1,583
	417	
12		1,000
	500	
17		853
	833	
20		850
	1,250	
22		886
	2,500	
23		957

8 a The new *MC* and *ATC* curves (and the associated table) are given in Fig. 11.9. The new curves are labelled MC_2 and ATC_2. The original curves, MC_0 and ATC_0, are indicated for reference.

b The curves have shifted (generally) down and to the right as a result of increasing the plant size. There are economies of scale (increasing returns to scale) up to the level of output at which MC_2 intersects ATC_2 (approximately 32 units).

c The long-run average cost curve is indicated in Fig. 11.9 by the heavy line tracing out the lowest short-run average total cost of producing each level of output. In this example, that happens to correspond entirely to *ATC*.

FIGURE **11.9**

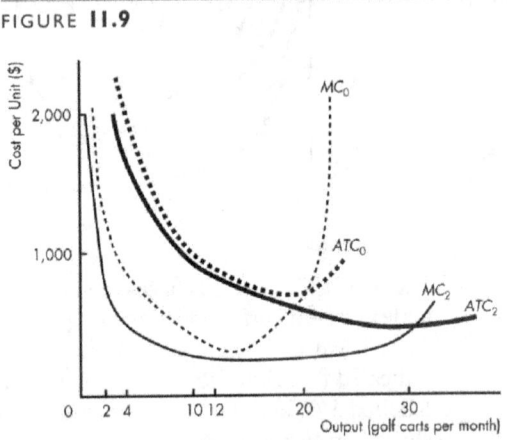

Output	MC ($)	ATC ($)
0		0
	2,000	
1		6,000
	667	
4		2,000
	333	
10		1,000
	222	
19		632
	286	
26		538
	400	
31		516
	667	
34		529

Chapter 12
Perfect Competition

What Is Perfect Competition?

Perfect competition is a model of market structure where the force of *competition* is extreme and firms have no *market power*. Assumptions include many firms; identical products; many buyers; free entry; no advantages for existing firms over new firms; complete information.

Perfect competition can arise when

♦ industry demand is *large* relative to the minimum efficient scale of a firm (smallest quantity of output yielding minimum *LRAC*).

♦ products of each firm are identical.

In perfect competition,

♦ each firm is a **price taker**.

♦ each firm faces a perfectly elastic demand curve at the market price.

The firm maximizes economic profit.

♦ Economic profit = total revenue – total cost (total cost includes normal profit)

♦ Normal profit = expected return to entrepreneurial ability

♦ **Total revenue** (*TR*)—price (*P*) × quantity (*Q*)

• Average revenue (*AR*)—*TR/Q*

• Marginal revenue (*MR*)—$\Delta TR/\Delta Q$

• In perfect competition, $AR = MR = P$

The Firm's Output Decision

In the short run, the firm decides what quantity to produce or to shut down.

♦ Economic profit is maximized at the quantity where $MR = MC$:

• If $MR > MC$, the firm increases Q to increase economic profit.

• If $MR < MC$, the firm decreases Q to increase economic profit.

♦ For a firm incurring economic loss:

• if $P > AVC$, firm will continue to produce.

• if $P < AVC$, firm will temporarily shut down.

• **shutdown point** is at minimum AVC.

The perfectly competitive firm's supply curve is its MC curve above minimum AVC.

Output, Price, and Profit in the Short Run

Short-run industry supply curve is the horizontal sum of individual firm's supply curves.

In the short run, the number of firms and their plant size are fixed.

Equilibrium market price and quantity are determined by industry demand and supply curves.

♦ Three possible short-run profit-maximizing outcomes for firms:

• $P (= AR = MR) > ATC$ yields economic profit.

• $P (= AR = MR) = ATC$ yields zero economic profit (*break-even point* at minimum ATC; firm just earning normal profit).

• $P (= AR = MR) < ATC$ yields economic loss (firm earning less than normal profit).

Output, Price, and Profit in the Long Run

In the long run, the number of firms in the industry and the plant size of each firm can adjust. Economic profit/loss are signals for firms to enter/exit the industry and cause reallocation of resources.

♦ Economic profit attracts new entry, causing a rightward shift of industry supply, causing falling P and the elimination of economic profit.

♦ Economic loss induces existing firms to exit, causing a leftward shift of industry supply, causing rising P and the elimination of economic loss.

In long-run competitive equilibrium,

♦ $MR = P = MC$; firms maximize short-run profit.

♦ P = minimum ATC; economic profit is zero; no incentive for firms to enter or exit industry.

♦ P = minimum $LRAC$; optimum plant size; no incentive for firm to change plant size.

Changing Tastes and Advancing Technology

For a permanent shift in demand,

♦ decreased demand causes falling P, economic loss and exit, decreased industry supply, causing rising P. In the long run, enough firms exit so remaining firms earn normal profit.

♦ increased demand causes rising P, economic profit and entry, increased industry supply, causing falling P. In the long run, enough firms enter so economic profit is eliminated and firms earn normal profit.

The change in long-run equilibrium price from a permanent shift in demand depends on

♦ **external economies**—factors beyond control of firm that lower costs as industry output increases.

♦ **external diseconomies**—factors beyond control of firm that raise costs as industry output increases.

The shape of the **long-run industry supply curve** depends on the existence of external economies or diseconomies. The long-run industry supply curve shows how industry quantity supplied varies as market price varies after all possible adjustments, including changes in plant size and number of firms. Shape may be

♦ horizontal for constant-cost industry.

♦ upward sloping for increasing cost industry with external diseconomies.

♦ downward sloping for decreasing cost industry with external economies.

New technology lowers costs, increases industry supply, causing falling P. New technology firms make economic profit and enter. Old technology firms incur economic loss and exit or switch to new technology. In the long run, all firms use new technology and earn zero economic profit (normal profit only).

Competition and Efficiency

Resource use is efficient when the most highly valued goods are produced; when no one can become better off without someone else becoming worse off; when marginal benefit equals marginal costs. Requires

♦ consumers to be on their demand = marginal social benefit curves and to be getting the most value from their resources.

♦ firms to be on their supply = marginal social cost curves and to be technologically efficient and economically efficient (lowest possible $LRAC$).

♦ equilibrium to be where price = marginal social benefit = marginal social cost; maximum gains from trade (consumer surplus + producer surplus).

Perfect competition achieves efficient use of resources at the market equilibrium price and quantity if there are no external benefits and external costs (Ch. 5).

HELPFUL HINTS

1 Although perfectly competitive markets are rare in the real world, there are three important reasons to develop a thorough understanding of their behaviour.

First, many markets closely approximate perfectly competitive markets. The analysis in this chapter gives direct and useful insights into the behaviour of these markets.

Second, the theory of perfect competition allows us to isolate the effects of competitive forces that are at work in *all* markets, even in those that do not match the assumptions of perfect competition.

Third, the perfectly competitive model serves as a useful benchmark for evaluating the relative efficiency of different market structures in subsequent chapters.

2 In the short run, a perfectly competitive firm cannot change the size of its plant—it has fixed inputs. The firm is also a price taker; it always sells at the market price, which it cannot influence. The only variable that the firm controls is its level of output. The short-run condition for profit maximization is to choose the level of output at which marginal revenue equals marginal cost. This is a general condition that, as we will see in subsequent chapters, applies to other market structures such as monopoly and monopolistic competition. Since for the perfectly competitive firm marginal revenue is equal to price, this profit-maximizing condition takes a particular form: choose the level of output at which price is equal to marginal cost ($P = MC$).

3 Many students have trouble understanding why a firm continues to operate at the break-even point, where economic profit is zero. The key to understanding lies in the definition of which costs are included in the average total cost curve. Recall from Chapter 10 that the economist defines a firm's total costs as *opportunity costs*, which include both explicit costs and *implicit costs*.

Implicit costs include forgone interest, forgone rent, and forgone cost of the owner's resources. Owners supply their time, which could have been used to earn income elsewhere. Owners also supply entrepreneurial ability. Normal profit is the expected return to entrepreneurial ability and is part of a firm's implicit costs.

At the break-even point where total revenue equals total cost (or, equivalently, average revenue equals average total cost), the owners of the firm are still earning a return on their investment, time, and entrepreneurial ability, which is equal to the best return that they could earn elsewhere. That is the definition of opportunity cost—the best alternative forgone. As the phrase "normal profit" implies, this profit could normally be earned as a return to entrepreneurial ability, on average, in any other industry. At the break-even point, the firm is earning normal profit even though its economic profit (sometimes called "extra-normal" or "above-average" profit) is zero. In earning normal profit, the firm is earning just as much profit as it could anywhere else, and is therefore totally content to continue producing in this industry.

4 When the price of output falls below the break-even point, but is above the shutdown point, the firm will continue to produce even though it is incurring economic losses. In this price range, the firm is no longer earning normal profit and theoretically could earn more by switching to another industry. Nonetheless, the firm will continue to operate in the short run because switching has costs. In order to switch industries, the firm must shut down, which entails still paying its total fixed costs.

As long as price is above the shutdown point (minimum average variable cost), a firm will decide to produce since it will be covering total variable cost and part of total fixed cost. Its loss will be less if it continues to produce at the output where $P = MC$ than if it shuts down.

If price falls below the shutdown point, a firm that produces output will not only lose its total fixed costs, it will lose *additional* money on every unit of output produced, since average revenue is less than average variable cost. Thus, when price is less than average variable cost, the firm will choose to minimize its loss by shutting down.

5 In the long run, fixed costs disappear, and the firm can switch between industries and change plant size without cost. Economic profit serves as the signal for the movement or reallocation of firm resources until long-run equilibrium is achieved. Firms will move out of industries with negative economic profit (economic loss) and into industries with positive economic profit. Only when economic profit is zero will there be no tendency for firms to exit or enter industries.

The fact that there are no restrictions on entry into the industry is what assures that economic profit will be zero and that firms will be producing at the minimum of their long-run average cost curves in long-run equilibrium.

6 In long-run equilibrium, three conditions are satisfied for each firm in an industry:

i $MR = P = MC$. This implies that profits are maximized for each firm.

ii $P = ATC$. This implies that economic profit is zero and each firm is just earning normal profit.

iii $P = $ minimum $LRAC$. This implies that production takes place at the point of minimum long-run average cost.

```
SELF-TEST
```

True/False and Explain

What Is Perfect Competition?

1 A firm in a perfectly competitive industry cannot influence price.

2 The industry demand curve in a perfectly competitive industry is horizontal.

3 The objective of firms in a competitive industry is to maximize revenue.

The Firm's Output Decision

4 Firms will incur an economic loss in the long run but not the short run.

5 At prices below minimum average total cost, a firm will always shut down.

Output, Price, and Profit in the Short Run

6 The supply curve of a perfectly competitive firm gives the quantities of output supplied at alternative prices as long as the firm earns economic profit.

Output, Price, and Profit in the Long Run

7 In long-run equilibrium, each firm in a perfectly competitive industry will choose the plant size associated with minimum long-run average cost.

8 Suppose a perfectly competitive industry is in long-run equilibrium when there is a substantial increase in total fixed costs. All firms will now incur economic losses and some firms will go out of business.

9 Suppose a perfectly competitive industry is in long-run equilibrium when there is an increase in demand. As new firms start entering the industry, the output of each existing firm will increase.

Changing Tastes and Advancing Technology

10 Suppose a perfectly competitive industry is in long-run equilibrium when there is a permanent increase in demand. In the short run, firms will earn an economic profit.

11 Suppose a perfectly competitive industry is in long-run equilibrium when there is a permanent decrease in demand. In the long run, firms will incur an economic loss.

12 In a perfectly competitive industry with external economies, the long-run industry supply curve is positively sloped.

Competition and Efficiency

13 Resource use is efficient as long as marginal benefit is greater than marginal cost.

14 Resource use is efficient as long as consumer surplus equals producer surplus.

15 A perfectly competitive industry will achieve efficiency if there are no external costs or external benefits.

Multiple-Choice

What Is Perfect Competition?

1 Which of the following is *not* a characteristic of a perfectly competitive industry?
 a downward-sloping industry demand curve
 b perfectly elastic demand curve for each individual firm
 c each firm decides its quantity of output
 d slightly differentiated products
 e many firms each supplying a small fraction of industry supply

2 For perfect competition to arise it is necessary that industry demand be
 a inelastic.
 b elastic.
 c perfectly elastic.
 d large relative to the minimum efficient scale of a firm.
 e small relative to the minimum efficient scale of a firm.

3 If a firm faces a perfectly elastic demand for its product,
 a it is not a price taker.
 b it will want to lower its price to increase sales.
 c it will want to raise its price to increase total revenue.
 d its marginal revenue curve is equal to the price of the product.
 e it will always earn zero economic profit.

The Firm's Output Decision

4 In a perfectly competitive industry, the market price is $10. An individual firm is producing the output at which $MC = ATC = \$15$. AVC at that output is $10. What should the firm do to maximize its short-run profits?
 a shut down
 b expand output
 c contract output
 d leave output unchanged
 e insufficient information to answer

5 In which of the following situations will a perfectly competitive firm earn economic profit?
 a $MR > AVC$
 b $MR > ATC$
 c $ATC > MC$
 d $ATC > AR$
 e $AR > AVC$

6 In the price range below minimum average variable cost, a perfectly competitive firm's supply curve is
 a horizontal at the market price.
 b vertical at zero output.
 c the same as its marginal cost curve.
 d the same as its average variable cost curve.
 e none of the above.

7 A firm in a perfectly competitive industry is maximizing its short-run profits by producing 500 units of output. At 500 units of output, which of the following *must be false*?
 a $MC < AVC$
 b $MC < ATC$
 c $MC > ATC$
 d $AR < ATC$
 e $AR > AVC$

8 If a profit-maximizing firm in perfect competition is earning economic profit, it must be producing a level of output where
 a price is greater than marginal cost.
 b price is greater than marginal revenue.
 c marginal cost is greater than marginal revenue.
 d marginal cost is greater than average total cost.
 e average total cost is greater than marginal cost.

Output, Price, and Profit in the Short Run

9 If a perfectly competitive firm in the short run is able to pay its variable costs and part, but not all, of its fixed costs, then it is operating in the range on its marginal cost curve that is anywhere
 a above the break-even point.
 b below the break-even point.
 c above the shutdown point.
 d below the shutdown point.
 e between the shutdown and break-even points.

10 The short-run industry supply curve is
a the horizontal sum of the individual firms' supply curves.
b the vertical sum of the individual firms' supply curves.
c vertical at the total level of output being produced by all firms.
d horizontal at the current market price.
e none of the above.

11 The supply curve for an individual firm in a perfectly competitive industry is $P = 1 + 2Q_S$. If the industry consists of 100 identical firms, then what is industry supply when $P = 7$?
a 300
b 400
c 600
d 800
e none of the above

12 Refer to Fact 12.1. If the price of fiddleheads last month was $15 per bag, Franklin
a should have shut down because total revenue did not cover total variable cost.
b incurred an economic loss of $135.
c earned zero economic profit.
d earned economic profit of $50.
e earned economic profit of $100.

FACT 12.1

Franklin is a fiddlehead farmer. He sold 10 bags of fiddleheads last month, with total fixed cost of $100 and total variable cost of $50.

---

13 Refer to Fact 12.1. If fiddlehead prices fell to $10 per bag while production and cost figures remained the same, Franklin would
a shut down immediately.
b break even because total revenues just cover total fixed costs.
c be indifferent between producing and shutting down because his loss of $50 just covers total variable costs.
d continue producing despite his loss of $50.
e continue producing despite his loss of $100.

14 Refer to Fact 12.1. Suppose the price of fiddleheads is expected to stay at $10 per bag, and Franklin's production and cost figures are expected to stay the same. His total fixed cost consists entirely of rent on land, and his five-year lease on the land runs out at the end of the month. Should Franklin renew the lease?
a Yes, because total revenue will still cover total fixed cost.
b Yes, because total revenue will still cover total variable cost and a portion of total fixed cost.
c No, because total revenue must cover all costs for resources to remain in fiddlehead farming in the long run.
d No, because in the long run, zero economic profit is a signal to move resources out of fiddlehead farming.
e There is insufficient information to answer.

Output, Price, and Profit in the Long Run

15 The maximum loss for a firm in long-run equilibrium is
a zero.
b its total cost.
c its total variable cost.
d its average total cost.
e none of the above.

16 For a perfectly competitive firm in long-run equilibrium, which of the following is *not* equal to price?
a short-run average total cost
b short-run average variable cost
c short-run marginal cost
d long-run average cost
e average revenue

17 When economic profit is zero
a the product will not be produced in the short run.
b the product will not be produced in the long run.
c firms will leave the industry.
d revenues are not covering implicit costs.
e none of the above will occur.

Changing Tastes and Advancing Technology

18 A perfectly competitive industry is in short-run equilibrium with price below average total cost. Which of the following is *not* a prediction of the long-run consequences of such a situation?
a Price will increase.
b The output of the industry will increase.
c Firms will leave the industry.
d The output of each remaining firm will increase.
e Economic profit will be zero.

19 Figure 12.1 illustrates the cost curves for a perfectly competitive firm. The current market price is $11 and the firm has the plant size shown by $SRAC_1$. The firm's short-run equilibrium output is
a 7 units.
b 9 units.
c 10 units.
d 17 units.
e 18 units.

FIGURE **12.1**

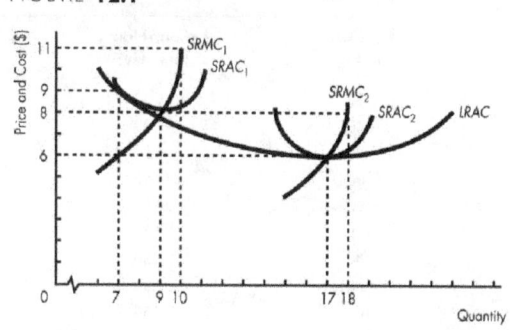

20 Refer to Fig. 12.1. The current market price is $11 and the firm has the plant size shown by $SRAC_1$. In the long run, the firm will
a exit from the industry.
b keep its current plant size, and other firms will enter the industry.
c keep its current plant size, and other firms will exit from the industry.
d increase its plant size, and other firms will enter the industry.
e increase its plant size, and other firms will exit from the industry.

21 Refer to Fig. 12.1. The long-run equilibrium price and quantity combination is
a $6 and 7 units.
b $6 and 17 units.
c $8 and 9 units.
d $8 and 18 units.
e $9 and 7 units.

22 If an industry experiences external economies as the industry expands in the long run, the long-run industry supply curve will
a be perfectly inelastic.
b be perfectly elastic.
c have a positive slope.
d have a negative slope.
e have allocative inefficiency.

23 Which of the following is *not* true of a new long-run equilibrium resulting from a new technology in a perfectly competitive industry?
a Price will be lower.
b Industry output will be greater.
c Firm profits will be greater.
d All firms in the industry will be using the new technology.
e Average total cost will be lower.

Competition and Efficiency

24 A long-run equilibrium in a perfectly competitive industry would *not* be efficient if
a firms are price takers.
b new technologies are developed.
c there are external economies or external diseconomies.
d there are external costs or external benefits.
e there is free entry to the industry.

25 Resources are used efficiently when
a consumers are on their marginal social benefit curves.
b firms are economically efficient.
c price = marginal social benefit = marginal social cost.
d there are no external benefits or external costs.
e all of the above are true.

Short Answer Problems

1 Why will a firm in a perfectly competitive industry choose *not* to charge a price either above or below the market price?

2 Why will economic profit tend to be zero in long-run equilibrium in a perfectly competitive industry?

3 Table 12.1 gives the total cost structure for one of many identical firms in a perfectly competitive industry.

TABLE 12.1

Quantity (units per day)	Total Cost ($)	Total Variable Cost ($)	Average Total Cost ($)	Average Variable Cost ($)	Marginal Cost ($)
0	12				
					...
1	24				
					...
2	32				
					...
3	42				
					...
4	54				
					...
5	68				
					...
6	84				

a Complete the table by computing total variable cost, average total cost, average variable cost, and marginal cost at each level of output. (*Remember:* As in the problems in Chapter 11, marginal cost should be entered *midway* between rows.)

b Complete Table 12.2 by computing the profit (per day) for the firm at each level of output if the price of output is $9; $11; $15.

TABLE 12.2

Quantity (units per day)	Profit P = $9	Profit P = $11	Profit P = $15
0			
1			
2			
3			
4			
5			
6			

c Consider the profit-maximizing output decision of the firm at alternative prices. How much will the firm produce if the price of output is $9? $11? $15? Explain each of your answers.

4 A firm will maximize profit if it produces every unit of output for which marginal revenue exceeds marginal cost. This is called the *marginal analysis* of profit maximization. Using marginal analysis, determine the profit-maximizing level of output for the firm in Short Answer Problem **3** when the price of output is $15. How does your answer here compare with your answer in Short Answer Problem **3c**?

5 This problem concerns a hypothetical pottery manufacturing firm that produces ceramic mugs for sale in a purely competitive market. With a plant of given size, the firm can turn out the quantities of ceramic mugs shown in Table 12.3 by varying the amount it uses of a single variable input, labour.

TABLE 12.3

Number of Mugs	Labour-Hours (per day)
20	6.50
40	11.00
60	14.50
80	17.50
100	20.50
120	23.75
140	27.50
160	32.00
180	37.50
200	44.50
220	53.50
240	65.00
260	79.50
280	97.50

Suppose the firm can hire all the labour it would ever want at the going wage of $8 per labour-hour. The firm's total fixed costs are $64 per day.

a Draw a table showing output, total variable cost (*TVC*), total cost (*TC*), average variable cost (*AVC*), average total cost (*ATC*), and marginal cost (*MC*). (*Remember:* Marginal cost should be entered *midway* between rows of output.)

b On a graph with *Mugs (per day)* on the horizontal axis, draw the three "per-unit" cost curves, *AVC*, *ATC*, and *MC*. (Note that the marginal cost values from your table should be plotted on the graph *midway* between the corresponding units of output.)

c Consider (separately) the following alternative market prices that the firm might face:

$P = \$3.20, P = \$2, P = \$1.65, P = \$1.40.$

Assuming that the firm wants to maximize its profit, for *each* of the above prices answer the following questions: Approximately how many mugs per day would the firm produce? How do you know? Is the firm making a profit at that price? And if so, approximately how much?

6 Suppose that the ceramic pottery mug industry consists of 60 firms, each identical to the single firm discussed in Short Answer Problem **5**. Table 12.4 represents some points on the industry demand schedule for ceramic pottery mugs.

TABLE **12.4**

Price ($)	Quantity Demanded
1.00	15,900
1.60	14,400
2.20	12,900
2.80	11,400
3.40	9,900
4.00	8,400
4.60	6,900
5.20	5,400
5.80	3,900
6.40	2,400
7.00	900

a On a new graph, draw the industry short-run supply curve. Draw the industry demand curve on the same graph.

b What is the short-run equilibrium price of ceramic pottery mugs?

c Is the ceramic pottery mug industry in long-run equilibrium? Explain your answer.

7 A perfectly competitive industry has 100 identical firms in the short run, each of which has the short-run cost curves listed in Table 12.5.

TABLE **12.5**

Output (units)	Average Total Cost ($)	Average Variable Cost ($)	Marginal Cost ($)
11	20.5	13.1	
			12
12	19.8	13.0	
			14
13	19.3	13.1	
			16
14	19.1	13.3	
			18
15	19.0	13.6	
			20
16	19.1	14.0	
			22
17	19.2	14.5	
			24
18	19.5	15.0	
			26
19	19.8	15.6	
			28
20	20.3	16.2	
			30
21	20.7	16.9	

This short-run average total cost curve touches the long-run average cost curve at the minimum point on the long-run average cost curve as the point "Long-run competitive equilibrium" in Text Fig. 12.12 on p. 291. The industry demand schedule is the same in the long and the short run. Table 12.6 represents some points on the demand schedule.

TABLE **12.6**

Price ($)	Quantity Demanded
11	3,200
13	3,000
15	2,800
17	2,600
19	2,400
21	2,200
23	2,000
25	1,800
27	1,600
29	1,400
31	1,200

a What is the quantity of output corresponding to the firm's break-even point? the shutdown point? Explain your answers.

b What is the short-run equilibrium price in this market? Show how you found your answer.

c What amount of profit or loss is being made by each firm at the short-run equilibrium price? Is this industry in long-run equilibrium at its present size? Why or why not?

d Exactly how many firms will exist in this industry in the long run? Explain your answer. How much economic profit will each firm earn in the long run?

8 Consider a perfectly competitive industry in long-run equilibrium. All firms in the industry are identical.

a Draw a two-part graph illustrating the long-run equilibrium for the industry—part (a) on the left—and for the typical firm—part (b) on the right. The graph of the firm should include the MC, ATC, MR, and $LRAC$ curves. Assume that the $LRAC$ curve is U-shaped as it is in Text Fig. 12.12 on p. 291. Label the equilibrium price P_0, the equilibrium industry quantity Q_0, and the output of the firm q_0.

b Now, suppose there is a decline in industry demand. Using your graphs from part **a**, show what happens to market price, firm output, firm profits, and industry equilibrium quantity in the short run (assume that the shutdown point is not reached).

Then show what happens to market price, firm output, firm profits, and industry equilibrium quantity in the long run (assume that there are no external economies or diseconomies). What has happened to the number of firms?

A N S W E R S

True/False and Explain

1 **T** Each firm is a price taker. (274–275)

2 **F** Individual firm demand curve is horizontal. Industry demand curve is downward sloping. (274–275)

3 **F** Maximize economic profit. (274–275)

4 **F** Losses in the short run but not the long run. (276–279)

5 **F** True if $P <$ minimum AVC. False if $P >$ minimum AVC but $<$ minimum ATC. (276–279)

6 **F** As long as $P >$ minimum AVC. (280–283)

7 **T** Otherwise the firm is driven out of business by lower-cost firms. (283–285)

8 **T** ATC shifts upward with no ΔMC. Economic losses cause exit. (283–285)

9 **F** As new firms enter, supply shifts rightward, price falls, and output of each existing firm decreases. (283–285)

10 **T** Price rises above ATC, creating economic profit. (286–289)

11 **F** Short-run economic losses cause firms to exit, shifting supply leftward, raising price until economic losses eliminated. (286–289)

12 **F** Negatively sloped. (286–289)

13 **F** Efficient when $MB = MC$. (290–291)

14 **F** Efficient when sum of consumer surplus and producer surplus is maximized. (290–291)

15 **T** $P = MB = MC$ and maximum sum of consumer and producer surpluses. (290–291)

Multiple-Choice

1 **d** Identical products. (274–275)

2 **d** So there is room for many (efficient) firms in the industry. (274–275)

3 **d** Firm can increase Q without ΔP, so MR from additional $Q = P$. (274–275)

4 **c** Draw graph. Firm should choose lower Q where $P = MC$. If AVC at current $Q = \$10$, minimum AVC must be $< \$10$, so new Q at $P >$ minimum AVC. (276–279)

5 **b** Since $MR = AR$, $AR > ATC$. Multiplying by Q yields $TR > TC$, so there is economic profit. (276–279)

6 **b** Firm stays shut down ($Q = 0$) until P reaches minimum AVC. (276–279)

7 **a** **a** implies shutdown. Other answers possible with losses (**b**, **d**) or profits (**c**, **e**). (276–279)

8 d $(MC = P =) AR > ATC$. **a, b, c** not consistent with profit maximization. **e** implies losses. (276–279)

9 e If the firm couldn't pay variable costs then below shutdown. If paying all variable and fixed costs, then breaking even. (280–283)

10 a Definition. **c** is momentary supply curve. **d** is demand curve facing individual firm. (280–283)

11 a For one firm: $7 = 1 + 2Q_S$; $2Q_S = 6$; $Q_S = 3$. For 100 firms, $3 \times 100 = 300$. (280–283)

12 c Profit $= TR$ ($\$15 \times 10$) $- TC$ ($\$100 + \$50$) $= 0$. (280–283)

13 d TR ($\$10 \times 10$) $- TC$ ($\$100 + \$50$) $= -\$50$. Shutting down would bring bigger loss of $\$100$ (fixed costs). (280–283)

14 c He is making a long-run decision. **a, b** refer to the short run. **d** is false because *losses* are a signal to move resources. (280–283)

15 a Definition of long-run equilibrium includes zero economic profit. (283–285)

16 b Long-run equilibrium is at intersection of ATC, MC, and $LRAC$ curves. (283–285)

17 e Product produced in short and long run, revenues exactly cover all costs (including implicit costs). (283–285)

18 b As firms exit, supply shifts left, decreasing industry Q and raising P. In response to higher P, remaining firms increase Q. (286–289)

19 c Choose Q where $P = MC$. (286–289)

20 d Economic profit attracts new entry, causing falling P and increased output creates incentive to build larger, lower-cost plant. (286–289)

21 b Long-run equilibrium is at intersection of $SRAC$, MC, and $LRAC$ curves. (286–289)

22 d Because decreasing costs as industry Q increases. (286–289)

23 c In long-run equilibrium, economic profit is always zero. (286–289)

24 d **a, e** are conditions of perfect competition. **b, c** affect the shape of the long-run supply curve but not efficiency. (290–291)

25 e When there are no external benefits or external costs, **a** and **b** are true; **c** is the equilibrium between demand and supply. (290–291)

Short Answer Problems

1 If a firm in a perfectly competitive industry charged a price even slightly higher than the market price, it would lose all of its sales. Thus it will not charge a price above the market price. Since it can sell all it wants at the market price, it would not be able to increase sales by lowering its price. Thus it would not charge a price below the market price since this would decrease total revenue and profits.

2 In a perfectly competitive industry, the existence of positive economic profit will attract the entry of new firms, shifting the industry supply curve rightward, causing the market price to fall and firm profits to decline. This tendency will exist as long as there is positive economic profit. Similarly, the existence of economic losses will cause firms to exit from the industry, shifting the industry supply curve leftward, causing the market price to rise and firm profits to rise (losses to decline). This tendency will exist as long as losses are being incurred. Thus, the only point of rest in the long run (the only equilibrium) occurs when economic profits are zero.

3 a Completed Table 12.1 is shown here as Table 12.1 Solution.

TABLE **12.1** SOLUTION

Quantity (units per day)	Total Cost ($)	Total Variable Cost ($)	Average Total Cost ($)	Average Variable Cost ($)	Marginal Cost ($)
0	12	0	—	—	
					… 12
1	24	12	24.00	12.00	
					… 8
2	32	20	16.00	10.00	
					… 10
3	42	30	14.00	10.00	
					… 12
4	54	42	13.50	10.50	
					… 14
5	68	56	13.60	11.20	
					… 16
6	84	72	14.00	12.00	

b Completed Table 12.2 is given here as Table 12.2 Solution. The values for profit are computed as total revenue minus total cost, where total revenue is price times quantity and total cost is given in Table 12.1.

TABLE **12.2** SOLUTION

Quantity (units per day)	Profit P = $9	Profit P = $11	Profit P = $15
0	−12	−12	−12
1	−15	−13	−9
2	−14	−10	−2
3	−15	**−9**	3
4	−18	−10	6
5	−23	−13	**7**
6	−30	−18	6

c If the price is $9, profit is maximized (actually, loss is minimized) when the firm shuts down and produces zero units. If the firm chooses to produce, its loss will be at least $14, which is greater than the fixed cost loss of $12. If the price is $11, the firm is still unable to make a positive economic profit. The loss is minimized (at $9) if the firm produces 3 units. At this price, all of variable cost and part of fixed cost can be recovered. At a price of $15, the firm will maximize profit (at $7) at an output of 5 units per day.

4 The marginal analysis of profit maximization states that the firm should produce all units of output for which marginal revenue exceeds marginal cost. For a perfectly competitive firm, marginal revenue equals price, so (equivalently) the firm should produce every unit for which price exceeds marginal cost. If the price of output is $15, we can see from Table 12.2 Solution that the firm should produce 5 units. Since the marginal cost of moving from the 4th to the 5th unit ($14) is less than price ($15), the 5th unit should be produced. The marginal cost of moving to the 6th unit ($16), however, is greater than price. It should not be produced. The answer here is the same as the answer in **3c**.

5 a With only one variable input (labour), AVC (for any level of output) = (labour hours × wage rate). The requested table is Table 12.7.

TABLE **12.7**

Output (per day)	TVC ($)	TC ($)	AVC ($)	ATC ($)	MC ($)
0	0	64	—	—	
					... 2.60
20	52	116	2.60	5.80	
					... 1.80
40	88	152	2.20	3.80	
					... 1.40
60	116	180	1.93	3.00	
					... 1.20
80	140	204	1.75	2.55	
					... 1.20
100	164	228	1.64	2.28	
					... 1.30
120	190	254	1.58	2.12	
					... 1.50
140	220	284	1.57	2.03	
					... 1.80
160	256	320	1.60	2.00	
					... 2.20
180	300	364	1.67	2.02	
					... 2.80
200	356	420	1.78	2.10	
					... 3.60
220	428	492	1.95	2.24	
					... 4.60
240	520	584	2.17	2.43	
					... 5.80
260	636	700	2.45	2.69	
					... 7.20
280	780	844	2.79	3.01	

b The graph appears in Fig. 12.2. It also illustrates the answers to part **c**.

FIGURE **12.2**

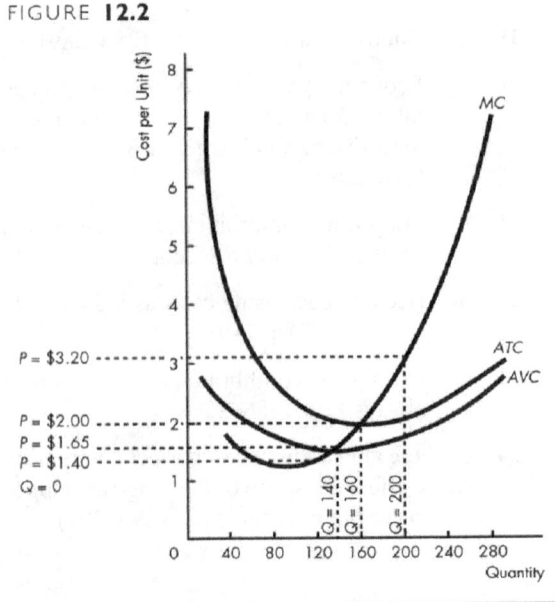

c   In every case, at the profit-maximizing
output, marginal revenue (which, for a price-
taking firm in a perfectly competitive
market, is the same as market price) is equal
to marginal cost, provided that price is
greater than average variable cost.

Profit "per unit of output" is the
difference between average revenue (price)
and average total cost at the level of output.
Total profit is "per unit profit" × number of
units of output. Economic profit might be
zero or negative (a loss) and still be the best
the firm can attain in the short run. The
calculations of total profit at each price
appear in Table 12.8.

TABLE **12.8**

Price ($)	Output Chosen	Per Unit Profit ($)	Total Profit ($)
3.20	200	1.10	220.00
2.00	160	0	0
1.65	140	−0.38	−53.20
1.40	0	0	−64.00

Note the following:

1. Marginal cost is $3.20 at approximately 200 units.

2. The per unit profit is $P - ATC$.

3. 160 units is the "break-even" level of output, where
    MC = minimum ATC and the firm is just covering all its
    opportunity costs.

4. At an output of 140 units, the firm continues to produce in
    the short run because it can more than cover its variable costs.
    If it produced zero units, its loss would be greater, $64, which
    is the amount of its fixed costs.

5. Any positive output increases losses when the price is below the
    shutdown price, which here is approximately $1.57. When
    price is less than minimum AVC, the firm would not only lose
    its fixed costs, it would also lose additional money on every
    unit it produced.

6   There are 60 identical price-taking firms.

For every possible price (above minimum
AVC of approximately $1.57), each firm will
supply the quantity at which $P = MC$. We can
derive (in Table 12.9) the industry supply
schedule from the MC curve of an individual
firm.

TABLE **12.9**

Price ($)	Quantity Supplied by 1 Firm	Quantity Supplied by 60 Firms
1.57	134	8,040
1.80	150	9,000
2.20	170	10,200
2.80	190	11,400
3.60	210	12,600
4.60	230	13,800
5.80	250	15,000
7.20	270	16,200

a   The graph of the industry supply curve
appears in Fig. 12.3, together with the
industry demand curve.

FIGURE **12.3**

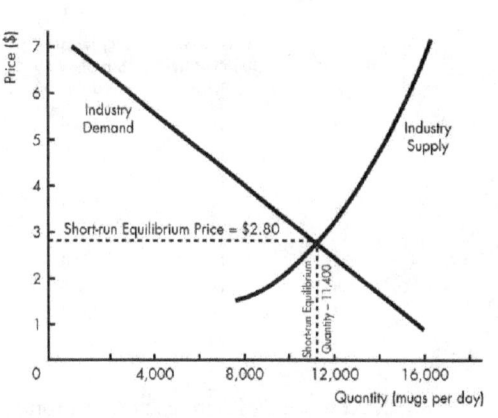

b   The short-run equilibrium price is $2.80
(where a total of 11,400 mugs per day are
supplied and sold; or 190 mugs per day
supplied by each firm at MC of $2.80).

c   At a price of $2.80 and output of 190, for
each firm, $P > ATC$ where ATC = $2.06. So
all existing firms are making an economic
profit after covering all opportunity costs
including a normal profit. (See Helpful Hint
3.) The industry will attract new entrants
because it offers more than normal profit.
Even though the industry is in short-run
equilibrium, it is *not* in long-run equilibrium
because the number of firms has not
"stabilized." New firms will enter the
industry, the industry supply curve will shift
rightward, and price will fall until no firm is
making economic profit.

⊕ **7 a** The break-even point occurs at 15 units of output. At this level of output, ATC is at its minimum ($19) and is equal to MC. Since the MC of moving from the 14th to the 15th unit is $18, and the MC of moving from the 15th to the 16th unit is $20, we can interpolate the MC exactly at 15 units as midway between $18 and $20, or as $19. The shutdown point occurs at 12 units of output. At this level of output, AVC is at its minimum ($13) and is equal to MC. The interpolated value of MC at exactly 12 units of output is midway between $12 and $14, or is $13.

b The short-run equilibrium price is $25. This is the price at which industry quantity supplied equals quantity demanded, as shown in Table 12.10.

TABLE **12.10**

P = MC ($)	Quantity Supplied by 1 Firm	Quantity Supplied by 100 Firms	Quantity Demanded
13	12	1,200	3,000
15	13	1,300	2,800
17	14	1,400	2,600
19	15	1,500	2,400
21	16	1,600	2,200
23	17	1,700	2,000
25	**18**	**1,800**	**1,800**
27	19	1,900	1,600
29	20	2,000	1,400

c At a price of $25, each firm produces 18 units of output. At 18 units, ATC is $19.50, so economic profit is being earned. The amount of profit is ($25 − $19.50 per unit =) $5.50 per unit. Total economic profit per firm is $5.50/unit × 18 units = $99. This means that new entrants will be attracted to the industry. We conclude that the industry is not in long-run equilibrium.

d Entry continues until economic profit is competed away, and all firms are operating at the minimum point of the $LRAC$ curve (which, in this problem, is also the minimum point of the given short-run average total cost curve).

Minimum ATC for each firm occurs at 15 units of output, when $ATC = MC = $19, so price in the long run must be $19. At a price of $19, consumers demand 2,400 units (from Table 12.10). It follows that when the industry is in long-run equilibrium, there must be 2,400 units/15 units per firm = 160 firms in the industry, each producing 15 units of output at zero economic profit.

8 a A long-run equilibrium in a perfectly competitive industry is illustrated in Fig. 12.4.

Part (a) illustrates industry equilibrium at the intersection of industry demand (D_0) and industry supply (S_0): point a. The equilibrium industry quantity is labelled Q_0 and the equilibrium market price is labelled P_0.

FIGURE **12.4**

(a) Industry

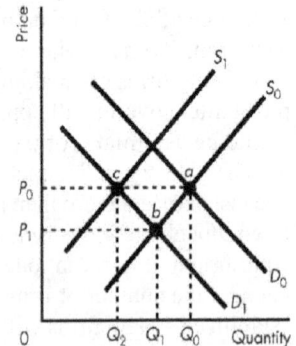

(b) Firm

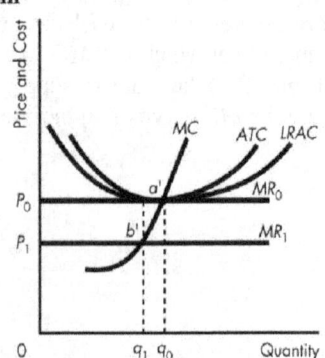

Part (b) illustrates the situation for a single firm in long-run equilibrium. The firm is at point a', the minimum point of both the short-run average total cost curve (ATC) and the long-run average cost curve ($LRAC$). The firm is producing the output labelled q_0 and earning zero economic profit.

b   The new short-run equilibrium is also illustrated in Fig. 12.4. The decrease in demand shifts the market demand curve leftward, from D_0 to D_1. The new market equilibrium is at point b. The price has fallen from P_0 to P_1 and the industry equilibrium quantity has fallen from Q_0 to Q_1. The fall in price induces firms to reduce output as shown by the move from point a' to point b' on the MC curve in part (b). Since P_1 is less than minimum ATC, firms are incurring losses in the new short-run equilibrium.

The new long-run equilibrium is also illustrated in Fig. 12.4. With short-run losses, firms will exit from the industry in the long run. This causes the industry supply curve to shift leftward, causing the price to rise and thus reducing losses. Firms continue to leave until the industry supply curve has shifted enough to eliminate losses, from S_0 to S_1. This gives a new long-run industry equilibrium at point c and the price has returned to its initial level, P_0, but industry quantity has fallen to Q_2.

As firms exit and the market price rises, remaining firms will increase their output (moving up the MC curve from point b' to point a') and their losses will be reduced. When sufficient firms have left the industry, the price will have risen (returned) to P_0 and firms will have returned to point a' in part (b). At this point, each firm is again earning zero economic profit and firm output has returned to q_0. But, since there are now fewer firms, industry equilibrium quantity is less.

Chapter 13
Monopoly

Monopoly and How It Arises

Monopoly is a model of market structure where the force of *competition* is absent and there is only one supplier with market power. Monopoly arises when there are

- ♦ no close substitutes for the product.

- ♦ **barriers to entry**—constraints protecting the firm from competition from potential new entrants.

  - Natural barriers to entry—a **natural monopoly** occurs when, due to economies of scale, one firm can supply the market at lower *LRAC* than multiple firms can.

  - Ownership barriers to entry—one firm owns a significant portion of a key resource.

  - Legal barriers to entry—for a **legal monopoly**, competition and entry are restricted by *public franchise*, *government licence*, *patent*, or *copyright*

Price-setting strategies depend on type of monopoly:

- ♦ **Single-price monopoly**—must sell each unit of output at the same price to all customers.

- ♦ **Price discrimination**—selling different units of output for different prices.

A Single-Price Monopoly's Output and Price Decision

Single-price monopoly charges the same price for every unit output.

- ♦ Monopoly's demand curve is industry demand curve.

- ♦ Marginal revenue (*MR*) < price (*P*). To sell additional output, must lower *P* on *all* output.

- ♦ In moving down the monopoly's demand curve

  - when total revenue (*TR*) is increasing, *MR* is positive, $\eta > 1$.

  - when *TR* maximum, *MR* is zero, $\eta = 1$.

  - when *TR* decreasing, *MR* is negative, $\eta < 1$.

- ♦ Monopoly's technology and costs are like a firm in perfect competition.

- ♦ Profit-maximizing monopoly chooses output at which *MR* = *MC*, charges maximum price consumers are willing to pay (on demand curve).

- ♦ Monopoly never operates in inelastic range of demand curve. Monopoly has no supply curve.

- ♦ Monopoly can make economic profit even in the long run because barriers prevent entry of new firms.

Single-Price Monopoly and Competition Compared

Output and price:

- ♦ Single-price monopoly Q < competitive Q.

- ♦ Single-price monopoly P > competitive P.

Efficiency:

- ♦ Single-price monopoly is inefficient compared to efficiency of perfect competition. Monopoly prevents gains from trade: restricts output, captures some consumer surplus, but creates *deadweight loss*—total loss of *consumer surplus* and *producer surplus* (revenue – opportunity cost production) below efficient levels.

♦ Social cost of monopoly is greater than deadweight loss because of **rent seeking**—attempt to capture **economic rent** (consumer surplus, producer surplus, or economic profit).

  • If no barriers to rent seeking, cost of resources used rent seeking = value monopoly profit (with no rent seeking), so no economic profit.

  • Social cost of monopoly = deadweight loss + resources used rent seeking

Price Discrimination

Price discrimination (selling different units of output for different prices) converts consumer surplus into economic profit for the monopoly. Examples include charging lower per-unit price on large order than small; discriminating among groups with different average willingness to pay.

Price discrimination requires:

♦ Product cannot be resold.

♦ Charge lower P to lower willingness-to-pay group. Charge higher P to higher willingness-to-pay group.

Perfect price discrimination—different price for each unit sold; obtains maximum price each consumer is willing to pay; converts *all* consumer surplus into economic profit.

♦ MR curve is the same as demand curve.

♦ Same output and efficiency (zero deadweight loss) of perfectly competitive industry, but

  • all consumer surplus is captured as economic profit.

  • rent seeking occurs that might eliminate economic profit.

Monopoly Regulation

Natural monopolies may be regulated to operate in the social interest: to achieve gains from monopoly (economies of scale) but avoid worst inefficiencies, higher prices, and restricted output.

♦ **Regulation**—government rules influencing prices, quantities, and entry.

♦ **Deregulation**—removing government regulation.

Two theories about how regulation works:

♦ **Social interest theory**—predicts regulations serve the social interest to eliminate deadweight loss and efficiently allocate resources.

♦ **Capture theory**—predicts regulations serve self-interest of producers, who "capture" the regulator, for maximum economic profit and deadweight loss.

Possible regulation rules:

♦ **Marginal cost pricing rule**—set price equal to marginal cost. Maximizes total surplus and is efficient, but not viable because firm incurs economic loss.

♦ **Average cost pricing rule**—set price equal to average total cost. Firm earns normal profit only. Inefficient, but better than unregulated monopoly.

♦ **Rate of return regulation**—set price to achieve target rate of return on capital.

  • Ideally, yields normal profit only; same outcome as average cost pricing rule.

  • But problem of incentives for firm to inflate cost (of capital) to yield economic profit.

♦ **Price cap regulation**—set price ceiling to achieve target rate of return on capital.

  • Gives firm incentive to keep costs under control. Replacing rate of return regulation.

  • Often combined with earnings sharing regulation that forces firms to share profits above a target level with consumers.

HELPFUL HINTS

1 The opposite extreme of perfect competition is monopoly. While in perfect competition there are many firms that can decide only on quantity produced but not on price, a monopoly is a single firm with the ability to set both quantity and price. These differences create differences in the revenue situation facing the monopoly. The cost curves for the two market structures are assumed to be the same.

   Because there is only one firm, the industry demand curve is also the firm demand curve. Facing a negatively sloped demand curve, if a single-price monopoly wants to sell one more unit of output, it must lower its price. This has two effects on revenue. First, the sale of an additional unit will increase revenue by the amount of the price. However, since the firm must also *drop the price on previous units*, revenue on these will decrease. The net change in revenue, the marginal revenue, will be less than price and the marginal revenue curve will lie below the demand curve.

Combining this new revenue situation with our familiar cost curves from Chapter 11 yields the important Text Fig. 13.4(b), which is reproduced below as Fig. 13.1. Notice the following points about this graph.

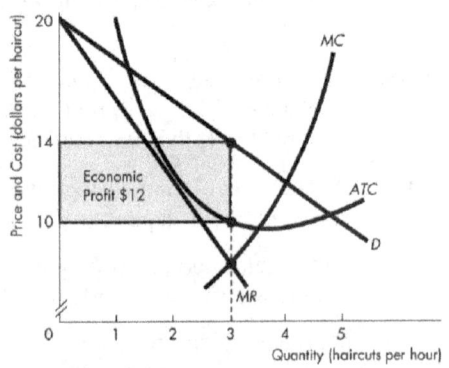

FIGURE **13.1** MONOPOLY OUTPUT & PRICE

The profit-maximization rule for a single-price monopoly is to find the quantity of output where $MR = MC$. This is the same rule that applies to a perfectly competitive firm.

For a perfectly competitive firm MR is also equal to price, so the intersection of MR and MC yields the profit-maximizing output and price. That is not true for the monopolist. MR is not equal to price, and once the profit-maximizing output is identified, the monopolist still has to set the price.

To find the profit-maximizing price, draw an imaginary vertical line up to the demand curve from the intersection of MR and MC. Then draw an imaginary horizontal line to the price axis to read the price.

Understanding what the vertical and horizontal distances of the economic profit area represent will make you less likely to make mistakes in drawing that area. The vertical distance is between the demand (or average revenue) curve and the average total cost curve. That distance measures average revenue minus average total cost, which equals average economic profit, or economic profit per unit. The horizontal distance is just the number of units produced. So the area of the rectangle (vertical distance × horizontal distance) = economic profit per unit × number of units = total economic profit. Do *not* make the mistake of drawing the vertical distance down to the intersection of MC and MR. That intersection has no economic meaning for the calculation of total economic profit.

2   There is an easy trick for drawing the marginal revenue curve corresponding to any linear demand curve. The price intercept (where $Q = 0$) is the same as for the demand curve, and the quantity intercept (where $P = 0$) is exactly *half* of the output of the demand curve. The marginal revenue curve is, therefore, a downward-sloping straight line whose slope is twice as steep as the slope of the demand curve.

3   Price discrimination can be profitable for a monopoly only if different consumer groups have different willingness to pay for the product. If such differences exist, the price-discriminating monopolist treats the groups as different markets. The profit-maximization rule for a price-discriminating monopoly is to find the quantity of output where *MR in each market* = MC. Then, in each market, charge the maximum price the consumer group is willing to pay for that output (on demand curve). Different willingness to pay translates into different elasticities of demand between groups, yielding different prices in the two markets.

4   The absence of entry barriers into a perfectly competitive industry is the basis for the prediction that any short-run economic profit in perfect competition will be competed away in the long run. Conversely, the presence of entry barriers in monopoly is the basis for the prediction that monopoly profits can persist in the long run. However, when rent-seeking activity is taken into account, there may be no long-run economic profit, even in monopoly. Rent seeking is any activity aimed at obtaining existing monopoly rights or creating new monopoly rights. Competition among rent seekers bids up the cost of rent seeking until it just equals the value of the potential monopoly profits, leaving the rent-seeker-turned-monopolist with little or no economic profit.

5   Figure 13.2 on the next page depicts revenue and marginal cost curves for an industry. Use this figure to think of regulation as determining the division of the potential total surplus (the area of triangle *abc*) among consumer surplus, producer surplus, and deadweight loss.

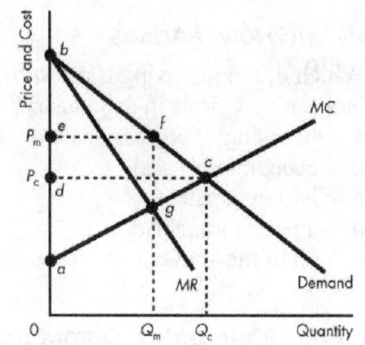

FIGURE 13.2

If the industry is perfectly competitive, then output will be Q_c and the market price will be P_c. Total surplus is maximized and is given by the area of triangle *abc*. Total surplus is equal to the sum of consumer surplus (triangle *dbc*) and producer surplus (triangle *adc*). There is no deadweight loss so efficiency is achieved.

If the industry is a profit-maximizing monopoly, output will be Q_m and the price will be P_m. In this case, total surplus is represented by the area of trapezoid *abfg*. Because of monopoly restriction of output, total surplus under monopoly is less than under competition. The difference is the deadweight loss from monopoly—the amount of total surplus that is lost when we go from competition to monopoly. The deadweight loss is given by the area of triangle *gfc*. Total surplus can be divided into consumer surplus (triangle *ebf*) and producer surplus (trapezoid *aefg*). Consumer surplus is quite small, but producer surplus is at a maximum.

Actual output is likely to be between these bounds. As output moves from Q_c to Q_m, consumer surplus decreases while producer surplus and the deadweight loss both increase. If this industry is regulated, the social interest theory of intervention predicts output will be close to Q_c, while the capture theory of intervention predicts output closer to Q_m.

SELF-TEST

True/False and Explain

Monopoly and How It Arises

1   Monopoly can arise when there are close substitutes for a product.

2   If one firm can supply the market at a lower cost than multiple firms can, then there are natural barriers to entry.

3   Barriers to entry are essential to a monopoly.

A Single Price Monopoly's Output and Price Decision

4   Over the output range where total revenue is decreasing, marginal revenue is positive.

5   The supply curve of a monopoly firm is its marginal cost curve.

6   Once a single-price monopoly chooses its output, average revenue always equals price.

Single-Price Monopoly and Competition Compared

7   In moving from perfect competition to single-price monopoly, part of the deadweight loss is due to a reduction in producer surplus.

8 When rent seeking is taken into account, economic profits from monopoly are guaranteed in the long run.

Price Discrimination

9 Price discrimination only works for goods that can be readily resold.

10 Price discrimination is an attempt by a monopolist to capture the producer surplus.

11 For a perfect price-discriminating monopolist, the demand curve is also the marginal revenue curve.

Monopoly Regulation

12 If a regulator applies an average total cost pricing rule, a natural monopoly will earn normal profits only.

13 According to the capture theory, government regulatory agencies eventually capture the profits of the industries they regulate.

14 Under rate of return regulation, firms can get closer to maximizing producer surplus if they inflate their costs.

15 Price cap regulation gives firms incentives to keep costs under control, and is replacing rate of return regulation

Multiple-Choice

Monopoly and How It Arises

1 Which of the following is a *natural* barrier to the entry of new firms in an industry?
a licensing of professions
b economies of scale
c issuing a patent
d a public franchise
e all of the above

A Single-Price Monopoly's Output and Price Decision

2 In order to increase sales from 7 units to 8 units, a single-price monopolist must drop the price from $7 per unit to $6 per unit. What is marginal revenue in this range?
a $48
b $6
c $1
d –$1
e none of the above

3 Four monopolists were overheard talking at an expensive restaurant. Which of their statements below is a correct strategy for maximizing profits?
a "In my company, we don't increase output unless we know that the larger output will raise total revenue."
b "I think cost minimization is the key to maximizing profits."
c "We try to make the most of our equipment by producing at maximum capacity."
d "I don't really keep close tabs on total profits, but I don't approve any business deal unless it increases my revenue more than it increases my costs."
e None of the above.

4 A profit-maximizing monopoly will never produce at an output level
a where it would incur economic losses.
b where marginal revenue is less than price.
c where average cost is greater than marginal cost.
d in the inelastic range of its demand curve.
e in the inelastic range of its marginal revenue curve.

5 For the single-price monopoly shown in Fig.
13.3, when profit is maximized, quantity is
  a 3 and price is $3.
  b 3 and price is $6.
  c 4 and price is $4.
  d 4 and price is $5.
  e 5 and price is $4.

FIGURE 13.3

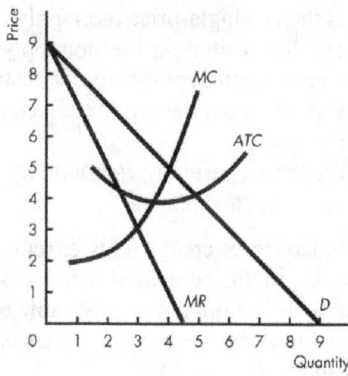

6 If the single-price monopoly shown in Fig. 13.3
is maximizing profit, what is total economic
profit?
  a $3
  b $4
  c $6
  d $9
  e none of the above

7 A single-price monopolist will maximize profits
if it produces the output where
  a price equals marginal cost.
  b price equals marginal revenue.
  c marginal revenue equals marginal cost.
  d average revenue equals marginal cost.
  e average revenue equals marginal revenue.

8 If a profit-maximizing monopoly is producing an
output at which marginal cost exceeds marginal
revenue, it
  a should raise price and lower output.
  b should lower price and raise output.
  c should lower price and lower output.
  d is incurring losses.
  e is maximizing profit.

Single-Price Monopoly and Competition Compared

9 Table 13.1 lists marginal costs for the XYZ firm.
If XYZ sells 3 units at a price of $6 each, what is
its producer surplus?
  a $2
  b $6
  c $7
  d $9
  e $12

TABLE 13.1

Quantity	Marginal Cost
1	2
2	3
3	4
4	5

10 Which of the following is true for a producing
single-price monopolist but not for a producing
perfect competitor?
  a The firm maximizes profit by setting
    marginal cost equal to marginal revenue.
  b The firm is a price taker.
  c The firm can sell any level of output at any
    price it sets.
  d The firm's marginal cost is less than average
    revenue.
  e None of the above.

11 Activity for the purpose of creating monopoly is
  a called rent seeking.
  b illegal in Canada.
  c called price discrimination.
  d called legal monopoly.
  e costless.

12 Taking rent-seeking activity into account, the
social cost of monopoly is equal to the
  a deadweight loss from monopoly.
  b monopoly profit.
  c deadweight loss plus monopoly profit.
  d deadweight loss minus monopoly profit.
  e consumer surplus lost plus producer surplus
    lost.

13 Consider the industry demand curve in Fig. 13.4. If the industry operates under perfect competition, which area in the diagram indicates consumer surplus?
a *aek*
b *dhk*
c *dik*
d *dih*
e none of the above

FIGURE **13.4**

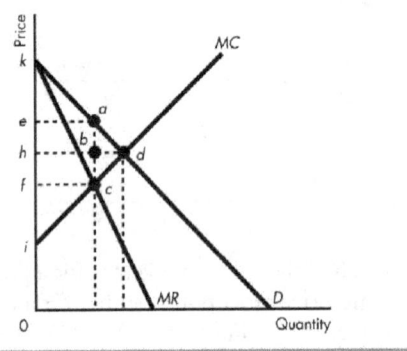

14 Consider the industry demand curve in Fig. 13.4. If the industry operates under perfect competition, which area in the diagram indicates producer surplus?
a *aek*
b *dhk*
c *dik*
d *dih*
e none of the above

15 Consider the industry demand curve in Fig. 13.4. Which area in the diagram indicates the deadweight loss from a single-price monopoly?
a *eacf*
b *acd*
c *abd*
d *bcd*
e none of the above

Price Discrimination

16 Which area in Fig. 13.4 indicates the deadweight loss from a perfect price-discriminating monopoly?
a *eacf*
b *acd*
c *abd*
d *bcd*
e none of the above

17 When perfect price discrimination occurs, which of the following statements is *false*?
a Buyers cannot resell the product.
b The firm can distinguish between buyers.
c The firm sets prices.
d The firm captures consumer surplus.
e Efficiency is worse than with a single-price monopoly.

18 The output of a (not perfect) price-discriminating monopoly will be
a less than a single-price monopoly.
b more than a single-price monopoly, but less than a perfectly competitive industry.
c the same amount as a perfectly competitive industry.
d more than a perfectly competitive industry.
e none of the above.

19 Many video stores charge a lower rental for Wednesday nights compared with weekends. This price discrimination is profitable only if the average willingness to pay for DVDs on Wednesdays is
a greater than the average willingness to pay for DVDs on weekends.
b less than the average willingness to pay for DVDs on weekends.
c positive and the average willingness to pay for DVDs on weekends is negative.
d negative and the average willingness to pay for DVDs on weekends is positive.
e equal to one.

Monopoly Regulation

20 A natural monopoly has
a low fixed cost and low marginal cost.
b low fixed cost and high marginal cost.
c high fixed cost and low marginal cost.
d high fixed cost and high marginal cost.
e high fixed cost and increasing marginal cost.

21 Figure 13.5 on the next page gives revenue and cost curves for an industry. This industry is a natural monopoly because
a one firm can supply the entire market at a lower price than can two or more firms.
b there are decreasing returns to scale over the entire range of demand.
c there are diseconomies of scale over the entire range of demand.
d even a single firm will be unable to earn a positive profit in this industry.
e all of the above are true.

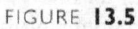

FIGURE **13.5**

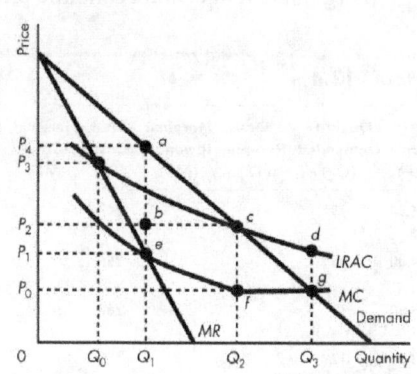

22 Consider the natural monopoly in Fig. 13.5. If regulators set a price just sufficient for the firm to earn normal profits, what output will it produce?
a 0, because the firm incurs economic losses when $P = MC$
b Q_0
c Q_1
d Q_2
e Q_3

23 Consider the natural monopoly in Fig. 13.5. If regulators use a marginal cost pricing rule, what line segment gives the amount of subsidy (per unit of output) required to keep the monopolist in business?
a ba
b ea
c fc
d gd
e eb

24 Consider the natural monopoly in Fig. 13.5. Under price cap regulation, regulators will set the price at
a P_0.
b P_1.
c P_2.
d P_3.
e P_4.

25 A monopolist under rate of return regulation has an incentive to
a inflate costs.
b produce more than the efficient quantity of output.
c charge a price equal to marginal cost.
d maximize consumer surplus.
e maximize shareholder profits.

Short Answer Problems

1 A single-price monopoly is the only seller of skyhooks in the Canadian market. The firm's total fixed cost is $112 per day. Its total variable costs and total costs (both in dollars per day) are shown in Table 13.2.

TABLE **13.2**

Quantity	Total Variable Cost (TVC)	Total Cost (TC)	Marginal Cost (MC)	Average Variable Cost (AVC)	Average Total Cost (ATC)
9	135	247			
10	144	256			
11	155	267			
12	168	280			
13	183	295			
14	200	312			
15	219	331			
16	240	352			
17	263	375			
18	288	400			
19	315	427			
20	344	456			

a Complete the table by computing marginal cost, average variable cost, and average total cost. (*Remember:* Marginal cost should be entered *midway* between rows of output.)

b Table 13.3 on the next page lists some points on the demand curve facing the firm, as well as the total cost information from part **a**. Complete the table by copying your values for marginal cost from Table 13.2 and by computing total revenue, marginal revenue, and economic profit. (*Remember:* Marginal revenue, like marginal cost, should be entered *midway* between rows of output.)

What is the firm's profit-maximizing quantity of output? At what price will it sell skyhooks? What will be its total economic profit? Explain your answers.

TABLE **13.3**

Price (P)	Quantity Demanded (Q_D)	Total Revenue (TR)	Marginal Revenue (MR)	Total Cost (TC)	Marginal Cost (MC)	Economic Profit (TR–TC)
57	9			247		
56	10			256		
55	11			267		
54	12			280		
53	13			295		
52	14			312		
51	15			331		
50	16			352		
49	17			375		
48	18			400		
47	19			427		
46	20			456		

computing the new values for total revenue, marginal revenue, and economic profit.

TABLE **13.4**

Price (P)	Quantity Demanded (Q_D)	Total Revenue (TR)	Marginal Revenue (MR)	Total Cost (TC)	Marginal Cost (MC)	Economic Profit (TR–TC)
24.50	9			247		
24.00	10			256		
23.50	11			267		
23.00	12			280		
22.50	13			295		
22.00	14			312		
21.50	15			331		
21.00	16			352		
20.50	17			375		
20.00	18			400		
19.50	19			427		
19.00	20			456		
18.50	21			487		

c On the graph in Fig. 13.6, plot the demand curve and the *MR*, *AVC*, *ATC*, and *MC* curves corresponding to the data in parts **a** and **b**. Show the equilibrium output and the area of economic profit on your diagram.

FIGURE **13.6**

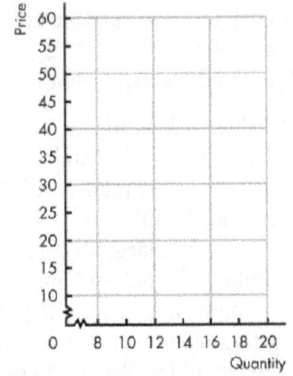

d The firm's cost curves are unchanged, but consumer demand shifts. Table 13.4 lists points on the new demand curve, as well as the total cost information from part **a**. Complete the table by copying your values for marginal cost from Table 13.2, and by

What is the firm's new profit-maximizing quantity of output? At what price will it now sell skyhooks? What will be its total economic profit? Explain.

e On the graph in Fig. 13.7, plot the new demand curve and *MR* curve. Copy the *AVC*, *ATC*, and *MC* curves from Fig. 13.6. Show the new equilibrium output and the area of economic profit on your diagram.

FIGURE **13.7**

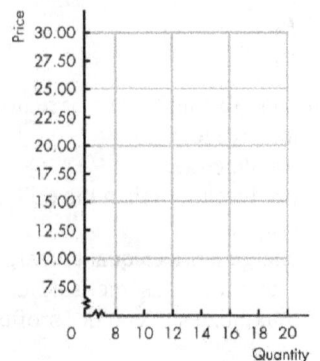

f Suppose demand falls even further so that the new demand curve equation is $P = 19 - 1/2Q_D$. On the graph in Fig. 13.8, plot this demand curve and copy the *AVC* curve from Fig. 13.8. Explain why the monopolist will shut down in the short run.

FIGURE **13.8**

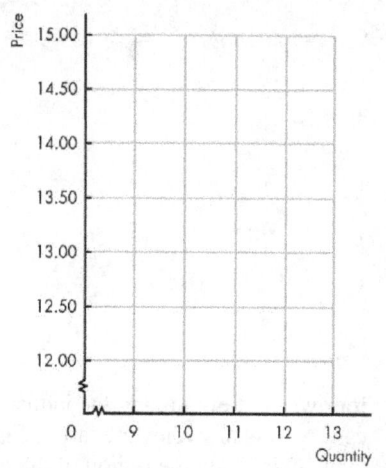

⊕ **2** You are given the following information about an industry consisting of 100 identical firms.

The demand curve facing the industry is

$$P = 36 - 0.01Q$$

The marginal revenue curve facing the industry is

$$MR = 36 - 0.02Q$$

The marginal cost curve of an individual firm is

$$MC = -12 + 2Q$$

The horizontal sum of the marginal cost curves of all of the firms in the industry is

$$MC = -12 + 0.02Q$$

Use this information to answer the following questions.

a Suppose all 100 firms are controlled by a single-price monopolist. Calculate the profit-maximizing quantity of output for the monopolist. Calculate the price per unit of output that the monopolist will charge.

b Suppose instead that the 100 firms operate independently as a perfectly competitive industry. Calculate the short-run equilibrium quantity of output for the industry as a whole. Calculate the short-run equilibrium price for the industry.

c *Without* using your answer about industry output in part **b**, calculate the short-run equilibrium output per firm.

d Compare the monopoly price and quantity outcomes with the perfect competition price and quantity outcomes.

⊕ **3** Before every Olympic Games, the International Olympic Committee (IOC) auctions off the monopoly rights to televise the Games to the highest bidder. NBC won the bid for the Summer 1996 Olympics, paying US$456 million. Yet analysts (correctly) predicted that NBC would not make a profit, since NBC did not profit from telecasts of the 1988 and 1992 Olympics. The questions below will help to understand this apparent paradox.

a What kind of monopoly does NBC have?

b NBC earns revenue by selling airtime to commercial sponsors. Assume that NBC faces a normal, downward-sloping demand curve in selling 30-second commercial spots. Let's ignore for the moment the payment to the IOC and assume that marginal cost and average total cost of delivering the airtime are equal and constant. Draw a diagram representing NBC's profit-maximizing decision. Although you do not have enough information to calculate precise numbers, indicate generally the quantity of commercial spots sold and the price per commercial spot.

c On your diagram, indicate the area representing economic profit. If the analysts' predictions were correct, what is the value of this area?

d Why did NBC fail to realize this economic profit?

4 Barney's Bistro has two kinds of customers for lunch: stockbrokers and retired senior citizens. The demand schedules for lunches for the two groups are given in Table 13.5 on the next page.

Barney decides to price discriminate between the groups by treating each demand separately and charging the price that maximizes profit in each of the two submarkets. Marginal cost and average total cost are equal and constant at $2 per lunch.

TABLE **13.5**

Price (P)	Stockbrokers				Senior Citizens			
	Quantity Demanded (Q_D)	Total Revenue (TR_{SB})	Marginal Revenue (MR_{SB})		Quantity Demanded (Q_D)	Total Revenue (TR_{SC})	Marginal Revenue (MR_{SC})	
8	0				0			
7	1				0			
6	2				0			
5	3				1			
4	4				2			
3	5				3			
2	6				4			
1	7				5			
0	8				6			

a Complete Table 13.5 by computing the total and marginal revenue associated with stockbroker demand (TR_{SB} and MR_{SB}) as well as the total and marginal revenue associated with senior citizen demand (TR_{SC} and MR_{SC}). (*Remember:* Marginal revenue should be entered *midway* between rows.)

b What are the profit-maximizing output and price for stockbrokers?

c What are the profit-maximizing output and price for senior citizens?

d What is total economic profit?

e Show that the total economic profit in part **d** is the maximum by comparing it with total economic profit if instead Barney served 1 additional lunch *each* to stockbrokers and senior citizens, and 1 less lunch *each* to stockbrokers and senior citizens.

f What is the consumer surplus for stockbrokers? for senior citizens? for all customers?

5 The price of the last unit sold and the quantity sold are exactly the same in an industry under perfect competition and under a perfect price-discriminating monopoly. Are consumers therefore indifferent between the two? Explain.

6 Figure 13.9 gives the demand, marginal revenue, and marginal cost curves for a certain industry. Your task is to illustrate how consumer and producer surplus are distributed under each of four ways of organizing the industry. In each case redraw any relevant part of Fig. 13.9 and then (1) indicate the region of the graph corresponding to consumer surplus by drawing horizontal lines through it; (2) indicate the region corresponding to producer surplus by drawing vertical lines through it; and (3) indicate the region (if any) corresponding to deadweight loss by putting dots in the area.

a The industry consists of many perfectly competitive firms.

b The industry is a single-price monopoly.

c The industry is a perfect price-discriminating monopoly.

FIGURE **13.9**

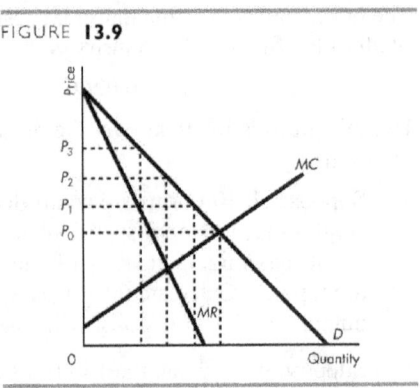

7 a Why is rate of return regulation equivalent to average cost pricing?

b Why is rate of return regulation being increasingly replaced by price cap regulation?

8 Figure 13.10 illustrates the industry demand, marginal revenue (*MR*), and marginal cost (*MC*) curves in a monopoly. The industry is regulated.

a What price and quantity are predicted by the public interest theory of regulation? Why?

b What price and quantity are predicted by the capture theory of regulation? Why?

FIGURE **13.10**

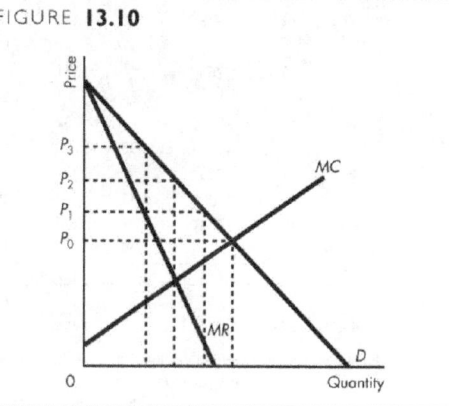

ANSWERS

True/False and Explain

1 **F** When there are *no* close substitutes. (300–301)

2 **T** Definition of natural monopoly. (300–301)

3 **T** Without barriers to entry, other firms will enter industry, creating competition. (300–301)

4 **F** *MR* is negative. (302–305)

5 **F** Monopolist has no supply curve. (302–305)

6 **T** Average of all (equal) prices of product = price. For any row in text Table 13.1, $AR = TR/Q = P$. (302–305)

7 **T** Area below competitive price and above *MC* for reduced output. (306–309)

8 **F** In equilibrium, economic profit may be totally eliminated by rent-seeking costs. (306–309)

9 **F** Can*not* be readily resold. (309–312)

10 **F** To capture consumer surplus and convert to economic profit. (309–312)

11 **T** Demand curve gives revenue for each successive unit sold (at different price). (309–312)

12 **T** $P = AR = ATC$. Outcome is inefficient because there is deadweight loss, but more efficient than an unregulated monopoly. (313–315)

13 **F** Industry captures more of total surplus. (313–315)

14 **T** Increased costs yield increased profits. (313–315)

15 **T** Specifies highest price firms are allowed to charge; used in electricity and telecommunications industries. (313–315)

Multiple-Choice

1 **b** Others are legal barriers. (300–301)

2 **d** $TR (P = \$7) = \$7 \times 7 = \$49$. $TR (P = \$6) = \$6 \times 8 = \$48$. $MR = \Delta TR = \$48 - \$49$. (302–305)

3 **d** *MR–MC* comparisons are key. Revenue **a** and cost **b** are important, but must be *compared* for profitability. (302–305)

4 **d** *TR* would be decreased needlessly. Monopolist could decrease *Q* and raise *P* to increase *TR*. (302–305)

5 **b** *Q* where *MR* = *MC*. Highest *P* consumers will pay for 3 units. (302–305)

6 **c** $(AR - ATC) \times Q = (\$6 - \$4) \times 3$. (302–305)

7 **c** Rule for choosing output. (302–305)

8 **a** Draw graph. $Q_{current} > Q$ corresponding to $MR = MC$. (302–305)

9 **d** Sum of $(P - MC)$ for each unit of output. (306–309)

10 **d** **a** is true for both. **b** is true for competitor only. **c** is false for both. (306–309)

11 **a** Definition. Activity has costs. (306–309)

12 **c** Monopoly profit = resources used rent seeking. (306–309)

13 **b** Area above price but below demand (willingness to pay). (306–309)

14 **d** Area below price but above *MC*. (306–309)

15 b Sum of lost producer (*bcd*) and consumer (*abd*) surplus compared to competitive outcome. (306–309)

16 e Deadweight loss is zero. (309–312)

17 e Efficiency the same as perfect competition. (309–312)

18 b **c** is true for perfect price discrimination. (309–312)

19 b Charge lower price with higher η and higher price with lower η. (309–312)

20 c Yielding an always downward-sloping *LRAC*. (313–315)

21 a Definition of natural monopoly. (313–315)

22 d Where *P* = *ATC*. (313–315)

23 d To cover loss per unit of output. (313–315)

24 c See Text Fig. 13.12. (313–315)

25 a To increase profits. (313–315)

Short Answer Problems

1 a Completed Table 13.2 is given here as Table 13.2 Solution.

TABLE **13.2** SOLUTION

Quantity	Total Variable Cost (TVC)	Total Cost (TC)	Marginal Cost (MC)	Average Variable Cost (AVC)	Average Total Cost (ATC)
9	135	247		15.00	27.44
			... 9		
10	144	256		14.40	25.60
			... 11		
11	155	267		14.09	24.27
			... 13		
12	168	280		14.00	23.33
			... 15		
13	183	295		14.08	22.69
			... 17		
14	200	312		14.29	22.29
			... 19		
15	219	331		14.60	22.07
			... 21		
16	240	352		15.00	22.00
			... 23		
17	263	375		15.47	22.06
			... 25		
18	288	400		16.00	22.22
			... 27		
19	315	427		16.58	22.47
			... 29		
20	344	456		17.20	22.80

b Completed Table 13.3 is shown here as Table 13.3 Solution.

TABLE **13.3** SOLUTION

Price (P)	Quantity Demanded (Q_D)	Total Revenue (TR)	Marginal Revenue (MR)	Total Cost (TC)	Marginal Cost (MC)	Economic Profit (TR–TC)
57	9	513		247		266
			... 47		...9	
56	10	560		256		304
			... 45		...11	
55	11	605		267		338
			... 43		...13	
54	12	648		280		368
			... 41		...15	
53	13	689		295		394
			... 39		...17	
52	14	728		312		416
			... 37		...19	
51	15	765		331		434
			... 35		...21	
50	16	800		352		448
			... 33		...23	
49	17	833		375		458
			... 31		...25	
48	18	864		400		464
			... 29		...27	
47	19	893		427		466
			... 27		...29	
46	20	920		456		464

Equilibrium output occurs where *MC* = *MR* = 28, *Q* = 19, *P* = $47, economic profit = $466 per day.

The profit-maximizing quantity of output occurs where marginal cost equals marginal revenue, at 19 units. The maximum price the firm can charge and still sell 19 units is $47. This combination of quantity and price yields a total economic profit of $466, which, as can be seen from the table, is the maximum possible profit.

c The requested diagram appears in Fig. 13.5 Solution.

FIGURE **13.5** SOLUTION

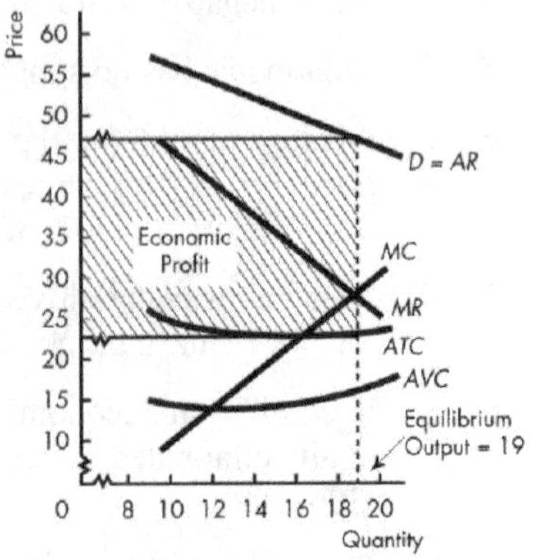

d Completed Table 13.4 is given here as Table 13.4 Solution.

TABLE **13.4** SOLUTION

Price (P)	Quantity Demanded (Q_D)	Total Revenue (TR)	Marginal Revenue (MR)	Total Cost (TC)	Marginal Cost (MC)	Economic Profit (TR–TC)
24.50	9	220.50		247		−26.50
			... 19.50		... 9	
24.00	10	240.00		256		−16.00
			... 18.50		... 11	
23.50	11	258.50		267		−8.50
			... 17.50		... 13	
23.00	12	276.00		280		−4.00
			... 16.50		... 15	
22.50	13	292.50		295		−2.50
			... 15.50		... 17	
22.00	14	308.00		312		−4.00
			... 14.50		... 19	
21.50	15	322.50		331		−8.50
			... 13.50		... 21	
21.00	16	336.00		352		−16.00
			... 12.50		... 23	
20.50	17	348.50		375		−26.50
			... 11.50		... 25	
20.00	18	360.00		400		−40.00
			... 10.50		... 27	
19.50	19	370.50		427		−56.50
			... 9.50		... 29	
19.00	20	380.00		456		−76.00

Equilibrium output occurs where $MC = MR = 16$, $Q = 13$, $P = \$22.50$, economic profit = −$2.50.

The profit-maximizing quantity of output occurs where marginal cost equals marginal revenue, now at 13 units. The maximum price the firm can charge and still sell 13 units is $22.50. This combination of quantity and price yields a total economic profit of −$2.50 (an economic loss). As can be seen from the table, this is the minimum possible loss. The firm will continue to produce in the short run, because this loss is less than its shutdown loss, which would be $112, the amount of its fixed cost.

e The requested diagram appears in Fig. 13.7 Solution.

FIGURE **13.7** SOLUTION

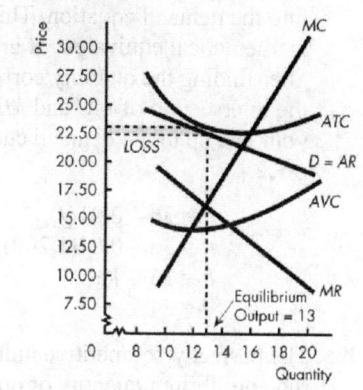

f The requested diagram appears in Fig. 13.8 Solution. Since the demand curve is everywhere below the *AVC* curve, no matter what quantity of output the firm might produce, price will be less than *AVC*. This means that the firm will lose money on every unit produced in addition to losing its total fixed cost. The monopolist will minimize loss in this case by shutting down and losing just its fixed cost ($112).

FIGURE **13.8** SOLUTION

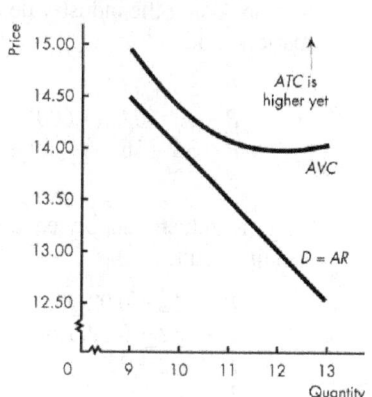

2 a The monopolist will choose the quantity of output where marginal revenue equals marginal cost. To calculate this quantity, set the equation for marginal revenue equal to the equation for industry marginal cost (since the monopolist controls all of the firms).

$$36 - 0.02Q = -12 + 0.02Q$$
$$48 = 0.04Q$$
$$1{,}200 = Q$$

188 CHAPTER 13

To calculate the price that the monopolist will charge, substitute the quantity 1,200 into the demand equation. This is the mathematical equivalent of graphically, after finding the quantity corresponding to the intersection of *MC* and *MR*, moving your eye up to the demand curve to read the price.

$$P = 36 - 0.01Q$$
$$P = 36 - 0.01(1,200)$$
$$P = 36 - 12$$
$$P = 24$$

b The perfectly competitive industry's short-run equilibrium quantity of output occurs where industry demand intersects industry supply. Set the industry demand equation equal to the industry supply equation, which is the horizontal sum of the marginal cost curves of all firms in the industry.

$$36 - 0.01Q = -12 + 0.02Q$$
$$48 = 0.03Q$$
$$1,600 = Q$$

To calculate the short-run equilibrium price for the industry, we can substitute the quantity 1,600 into either the industry demand equation or the industry supply equation. Using the industry demand equation yields

$$P = 36 - 0.01Q$$
$$P = 36 - 0.01(1,600)$$
$$P = 36 - 16$$
$$P = 20$$

Using the industry supply equation yields the same result:

$$P = -12 + 0.02Q$$
$$P = -12 + 0.02(1,600)$$
$$P = -12 + 32$$
$$P = 20$$

c If industry output is 1,600 units and there are 100 identical firms, then obviously the output per firm is 1,600 units/100 firms equals 16 units/firm. But the question specifically asks you *not* to use the information about industry output.

The other way to calculate the short-run equilibrium output per firm is to substitute the equilibrium price of 20 into the individual firm's marginal cost curve, which is also its short-run supply curve:

$$P = -12 + 2Q$$
$$20 = -12 + 2Q$$
$$32 = 2Q$$
$$16 = Q$$

d The monopoly price ($24) is higher than the perfect competition price ($20) and the monopoly quantity of output (1,200) is lower than the perfect competition quantity of output (1,600).

3 a NBC had a legal monopoly, based on a public franchise—an exclusive right granted to a firm to supply a good or service.

b The requested diagram is shown in Fig. 13.11. The quantity of commercial spots sold is Q_{CS} and the price is P_{CS}.

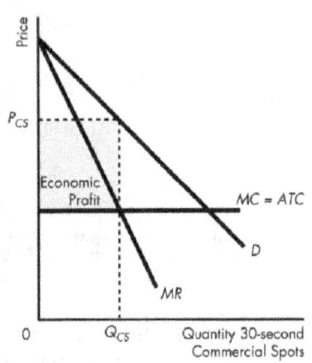

FIGURE **13.11**

c The shaded rectangle above *ATC* and below P_{CS} in Fig. 13.11 represents economic profit. That profit, which is based on costs that exclude the US$456 million payment to the IOC, will be US$456 million if the analysts are correct.

d NBC fails to make an economic profit because of the costs of rent seeking. NBC competes for the monopoly rights to televise the Olympics. Bidders continue to offer a higher price for those rights until the price equals the value of the economic profit to be earned from owning the rights

4 a The completed table is Table 13.5 Solution on the next page.

b The profit-maximizing output for stockbrokers occurs when $MC = \$2 = MR_{SB}$. This is at 3 lunches and the price is $5 per lunch to stockbrokers.

c The profit-maximizing output for senior citizens occurs when $MC = \$2 = MR_{SC}$. This occurs at 2 lunches and the price to senior citizens is $4 per lunch.

d Total revenue is $15 from stockbrokers, $8 from senior citizens, or $23. Since average total cost is $2 per lunch, total cost is $2 × 5 lunches = $10. Total economic profit is $13.

e If Barney served 1 more lunch each to stockbrokers and senior citizens, that would be 4 lunches for stockbrokers ($4 per lunch) and 3 lunches for senior citizens ($3 per lunch). Since average total cost is $2 per lunch, total cost is $2 × 7 lunches = $14. Total revenue is $16 from stockbrokers, $9 from senior citizens, or $25. Total economic profit is $11, less than the $13 in part **d**.

If Barney served 1 less lunch each to stockbrokers and senior citizens, that would be 2 lunches for stockbrokers ($6 per lunch) and 1 lunch for senior citizens ($5 per lunch). Since average total cost is $2 per lunch, total cost is $2 × 3 lunches = $6. Total revenue is $12 from stockbrokers, $5 from senior citizens, or $17. Total economic profit is $11, less than the $13 in part **d**.

f The consumer surplus of stockbrokers is

$$(\$7 - \$5) + (\$6 - \$5) + (\$5 - \$5) = \$3$$

The consumer surplus of senior citizens is

$$(\$5 - \$4) + (\$4 - \$4) = \$1$$

The consumer surplus of all customers is

$$\$3 + \$1 = \$4$$

TABLE **13.5** SOLUTION

	Stockbrokers			Senior Citizens		
Price (P)	Quantity Demanded (Q_D)	Total Revenue (TR_{SB})	Marginal Revenue (MR_{SB})	Quantity Demanded (Q_D)	Total Revenue (TR_{SC})	Marginal Revenue (MR_{SC})
8	0	0		0	0	
			7			0
7	1	7		0	0	
			5			0
6	2	12		0	0	
			3			5
5	3	15		1	5	
			1			3
4	4	16		2	8	
			−1			1
3	5	15		3	9	
			−3			−1
2	6	12		4	8	
			−5			−3
1	7	7		5	5	
			−7			−5
0	8	0		6	0	

5 While the quantity sold and the price charged to the last customer are the same for perfect competition and a perfect price discriminator, the distribution of consumer surplus is not the same. Since a perfect price discriminator charges each customer the most she is willing to pay, there is no consumer surplus. Any consumer surplus that would have occurred under perfect competition now accrues to the monopoly. Consumers would like to obtain more consumer surplus, and therefore pay less for the same amount.

Consequently, consumers prefer perfect competition.

6 a Under perfect competition, price equals marginal cost. The amount of consumer surplus is given by the area under the demand curve but above the price (P_0) while the amount of producer surplus is given by the area above the MC curve but below the price; see Fig. 13.9 Solution (a).

b If the industry is a single-price monopoly, price will be greater than MC and output will be less than under competition. Consumer surplus is still given by the area under the demand curve but above the price (P_2), while producer surplus is given by the area above the MC curve but below the price up to the monopoly level of output. The remaining part of the large triangle is a deadweight loss—the amount of surplus under competition that is lost under a single-price monopoly; see Fig. 13.9 Solution (b).

c   Under perfect price discrimination, all of the potential surplus is captured by the producer and there is no deadweight loss (or consumer surplus). See Fig. 13.9 Solution (c).

FIGURE **13.9** SOLUTION

(a)

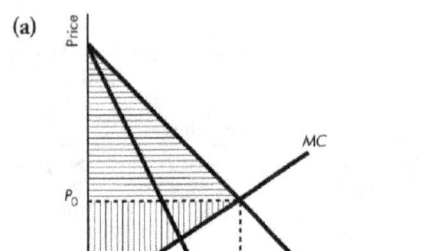

(b)

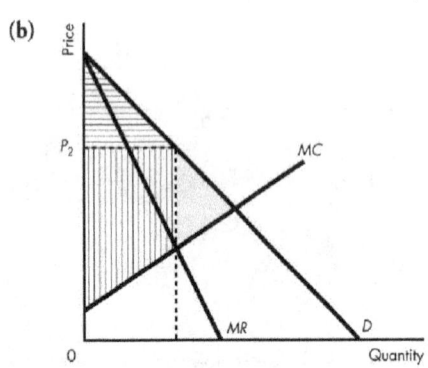

(c)

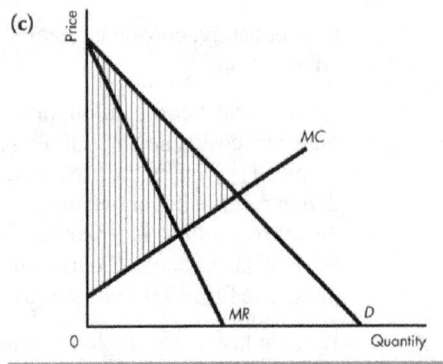

---

7   a   The key here is to recall that economic cost includes a normal rate of return. Because rate of return regulation sets a price that allows a normal rate of return, it is setting the price equal to average total cost.

b   Under rate of return regulation, firms have an incentive to inflate their costs, since they are guaranteed a normal rate of return on all costs. A price ceiling in price cap regulation gives firms an incentive to operate efficiently and keep costs under control. Regulators try and set a price ceiling that yields the same output as (uninflated) average cost pricing. In case the price is set too high, price cap regulation is often combined with earnings sharing regulation, so profits above a target level must be shared with firms' customers.

8   a   Social interest theory predicts that regulators set price and quantity to maximize total surplus. This means they choose quantity (and price) where MC is equal to demand. This corresponds to a quantity of 500 units and a price of $4 per unit.

b   Capture theory predicts that regulators choose quantity and price to maximize the profit of the industry. This is the quantity a profit-maximizing monopolist would choose, 300 units, where $MC = MR$. The highest price that could be charged and still sell that quantity can be read from the demand curve: $6 per unit.

Chapter 14
Monopolistic Competition

Monopolistic Competition

Monopolistic competition is a model of market structure in which many firms compete; there is **product differentiation** (firms make similar but slightly different products) giving firms some monopoly power; firms compete on product quality, price, and marketing; there is free entry and exit.

- ♦ Firm ignores other individual firms and collusion is impossible because all firms have a small market share.

- ♦ Firm faces a downward-sloping demand curve.

- ♦ Marginal revenue curve ≠ demand curve.

- ♦ Firm can choose price and output.

Price and Output and in Monopolistic Competition

Outcomes:

- ♦ Profit maximization (or loss minimization): choose Q where $MC = MR$, charge highest possible price (on demand curve).

- ♦ Short-run economic profit possible, attracts entry, causing leftward shift of demand (and MR) curves facing each firm.

- ♦ Short-run economic loss possible, some firms exit, causing rightward shift of demand (and MR) curves facing each remaining firm.

- ♦ Long-run economic profit = 0, $P = ATC$. But

  - • ATC not at minimum. Firm has **excess capacity**, producing *below* its **efficient scale** where ATC = minimum.

  - • $P > MC$ by amount of **markup**.

- ♦ Inefficiency of monopolistic competition must be weighed against gain of greater product variety.

Product Development and Marketing

To restore economic profits, monopolistically competitive firms must continuously innovate and develop new products. New firms enter with similar products, compete away economic profits—the cycle continues.

Marketing expenditures on advertising and packaging (selling costs) are used to *create perception* of product differentiation even when actual product differences are small, and to **signal** quality.

- ♦ Selling costs are fixed costs that increase total costs, but average total cost might decrease if output increases enough.

- ♦ Selling costs might increase demand for a firm's product, but might also decrease demand by increasing competition.

Inefficiencies of monopolistic competition (selling costs and excess capacity) must be weighed against gain of greater product variety.

HELPFUL HINTS

1 Most industries are neither perfectly competitive nor pure monopolies; they lie somewhere between these two extremes. This does not mean that the last two chapters have been wasted. By examining firms under these extreme market structures, we now can discuss the wide range of industries between them in just two chapters.

The intermediate forms of market structure share many characteristics of perfect competition and/or monopoly. Consider the profit-maximizing rule of choosing the output where $MC = MR$. The rule applies not only in perfect competition and monopoly, but also in monopolistic competition and many of the oligopoly models we will see in Chapter 15. Free entry leads to zero long-run economic profit in both perfect competition and monopolistic competition. The downward-sloping demand and marginal revenue curves of monopoly also apply to monopolistic competition, a kinked demand curve, and dominant firm oligopoly models.

The extreme and unrealistic assumptions of models of perfect competition and monopoly allow us to isolate the impact of important forces like profit maximization and important constraints like competition and market demand. These forces and constraints also operate in more realistic market structures. But it was necessary to isolate these forces and constraints beforehand rather than attempt to immediately analyse "realistic" market structures like monopolistic competition and oligopoly, which would have been a confusing jumble of details and possible outcomes. It would have been like driving in a strange, large city without a road map.

2 In graphing a monopolistically competitive firm in long-run equilibrium, be sure that the ATC curve is tangent to the demand curve at the same level of output at which the MC and MR curves intersect. Also be sure that the MC curve intersects the ATC curve at the minimum point on the ATC curve.

SELF-TEST

True/False and Explain

What Is Monopolistic Competition?

1 Barriers to entry give monopolistically competitive firms some monopoly power.

2 Product differentiation gives monopolistically competitive firms some monopoly power.

3 Monopolistically competitive firms compete only on price.

4 Monopolistically competitive firms pay close attention to the actions of other individual firms.

5 Monopolistically competitive firms do not collude with other firms to fix higher prices.

Price and Output in Monopolistic Competition

6 In monopolistic competition, short-run profits attract new entry, shifting each individual firm's demand curve rightward.

7 Free entry is the key characteristic of monopolistic competition that produces excess capacity.

8 When a monopolistically competitive industry is in long-run equilibrium, economic profit is zero and price equals minimum average total cost.

9 In monopolistic competition, price exceeds marginal cost.

10 Monopolistically competitive firms can earn an economic profit in the long run.

Product Development and Marketing

11 Firms in monopolistic competition must innovate continuously to enjoy economic profits.

12 Selling costs always increase average total costs.

13 Advertising by monopolistic competitors is always efficient.

14 Advertising can signal product quality.

15 Advertising makes a monopolistically competitive firm's demand curve more elastic.

Multiple-Choice

What Is Monopolistic Competition?

1 In monopolistic competition, firms
   a can collude.
   b strategically interact with other firms.
   c have an element of monopoly power.
   d face a kinked demand curve.
   e do all of the above.

2 A monopolistically competitive firm is like a *monopoly* because
   a both face perfectly elastic demand.
   b both earn an economic profit in the long run.
   c both have *MR* curves that are below their demand curves.
   d neither is protected by high barriers to entry.
   e both are protected by high barriers to entry.

3 A monopolistically competitive firm is like a *perfectly competitive* firm because
   a both face perfectly elastic demand.
   b both earn an economic profit in the long run.
   c both have MR curves that are below their demand curves.
   d neither is protected by high barriers to entry.
   e both are protected by high barriers to entry.

4 With product differentiation
   a monopolistically competitive firms can compete on quality and marketing.
   b a firm makes a product that is slightly different from its competitors products.
   c a firm's demand curve is more inelastic compared to identical products.
   d a firm faces a downward-sloping demand curve.
   e all of the above are true.

5 In monopolistic competition,
   a the size of firms is small relative to the size of the industry.
   b the size of firms is large relative to the size of the industry.
   c the size of firms is the same as the size of the industry.
   d there are two firms in the industry.
   e there is one firm in the industry.

6 A monopolistically competitive firm can set the price of what it sells because of
   a barriers to entry.
   b economies of scale.
   c many buyers.
   d inelastic demand.
   e product differentiation.

7 Brand name products are an example of
   a economies of scope.
   b economies of scale.
   c product differentiation.
   d collusion.
   e none of the above.

Price and Output in Monopolistic Competition

8 For a monopolistically competitive firm in long-run equilibrium,
   a $P = MC$.
   b $MC = ATC$.
   c $AR = ATC$, but $P > MC$.
   d $MC = AR$, but $ATC > AR$.
   e none of the above is true.

9 Figure 14.1 represents a monopolistically competitive firm in short-run equilibrium. What is the firm's level of output?
   a Q_1
   b Q_2
   c Q_3
   d Q_4
   e zero

FIGURE **14.1**

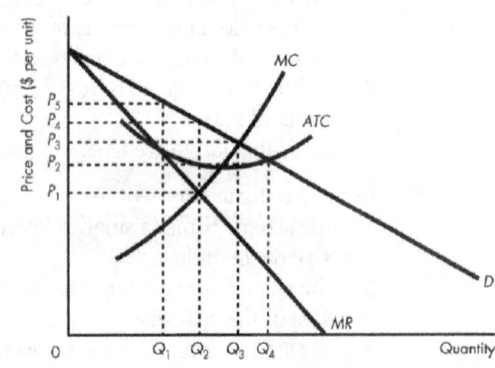

10 Figure 14.1 represents a monopolistically competitive firm in short-run equilibrium. What is the firm's economic profit *per unit*?
   a $P_4 - P_2$
   b $P_4 - P_1$
   c P_4
   d P_3
   e None of the above

11 Figure 14.1 represents a monopolistically competitive firm in short-run equilibrium. In the long run,
   a new firms will enter, and each existing firm's demand shifts leftward.
   b new firms will enter, and each existing firm's demand shifts rightward.
   c existing firms will leave, and each remaining firm's demand shifts leftward.
   d existing firms will leave, and each remaining firm's demand shifts rightward.
   e there will be no change from the short run.

12 Under monopolistic competition, long-run economic profit tends toward zero because of
   a product differentiation.
   b the lack of barriers to entry.
   c excess capacity.
   d inefficiency.
   e downward-sloping demand curves facing each firm.

13 In the long run, a monopolistically competitive firm will earn the same economic profit as
   a a monopolistically competitive firm in the short run.
   b a member of a cartel.
   c a pure price-discriminating monopolist.
   d a perfectly competitive firm.
   e none of the above.

14 Which of the following is true for perfect competition, monopolistic competition, and single-price monopoly?
   a homogeneous product
   b zero long-run economic profit
   c short-run profit-maximizing quantity where $MC = MR$
   d easy entry and exit
   e none of the above

15 In the long run, the firm in monopolistic competition will
   a face a perfectly elastic demand curve.
   b produce more than the quantity that minimizes ATC.
   c produce less than the quantity that minimizes ATC.
   d produce the quantity that minimizes ATC.
   e earn economic profit.

16 In the long run, a monopolistically competitive firm will produce the output at which price equals
    a marginal cost.
    b marginal revenue.
    c average variable cost.
    d average total cost.
    e **b** and **d**.

17 Which of the following characteristics is *not* shared by a single-price monopoly and monopolistic competition?
    a firms face a downward-sloping demand curve
    b profit-maximizing quantity where $MC = MR$
    c equilibrium ATC above minimum ATC
    d positive long-run economic profit
    e positive long-run normal profit

18 When firms in a monopolistically competitive industry incur economic losses, firms will
    a enter the industry, and demand increases for the original firms.
    b enter the industry, and demand decreases for the original firms.
    c exit the industry, and demand increases for the original firms.
    d exit the industry, and demand decreases for the original firms.
    e exit the industry, and supply increases for the original firms.

19 In the long run, all firms in a monopolistically competitive industry earn
    a zero accounting profit.
    b zero normal profit.
    c zero economic profit.
    d positive economic profit.
    e negative economic profit.

Product Development and Marketing

20 Selling costs
    a are variable costs that increase total cost.
    b always increase demand for a firm's product.
    c always decrease demand by increasing competition.
    d always provide consumers with valuable services.
    e include marketing expenditures on advertising and packaging.

21 Because consumers value product variety,
    a monopolistic competition is more efficient than perfect competition.
    b similar products will not have the same price.
    c the inefficiencies of monopolistic competition must be weighed against the benefits of variety.
    d monopolistically competitive firms earn long-run economic profits.
    e brand names are inefficient.

22 Monopolistically competitive firms constantly develop new products in order to
    a make the demand for their product more elastic.
    b increase demand for their product.
    c increase the quantity demanded of their product
    d increase supply of their product
    e do all of the above.

23 A firm's decision about how much to spend on product development depends on
    a only marginal revenue from product development.
    b only marginal cost of product development.
    c both marginal revenue from and marginal cost of product development.
    d both marginal social revenue from and marginal social cost of product development.
    e both average revenue from and average cost of product development.

24 In monopolistic competition, firms
    a have high selling costs.
    b have deficient capacity in the long run.
    c rarely advertise.
    d avoid brand names to keep costs down.
    e produce the efficient quantity of output.

25 An advantage of monopolistic competition over perfect competition is
    a economic profit.
    b product variety.
    c excess capacity.
    d efficiency.
    e economies of scale.

Short Answer Problems

1   Consider a single firm in a monopolistically competitive industry in the short run. Using axes like those shown in Fig. 14.2, draw a new graph for a firm making an economic profit.

FIGURE **14.2**

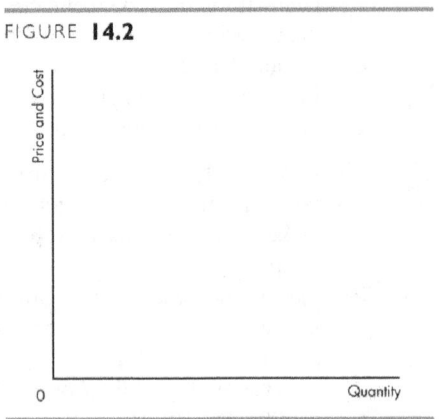

2   Consider a single firm in a monopolistically competitive industry in the short run. Using axes like those shown in Fig. 14.2, draw a new graph for a firm incurring a loss that will cause shutdown.

3   Consider a single firm in a monopolistically competitive industry in the short run. Using axes like those shown in Fig. 14.2, draw a new graph for a firm that is incurring a loss, but is still producing.

4   Starting from the situation in Short Answer Problem **3**, explain what will happen in this industry and how your graph in Problem **3** will be affected. (No new graph is required.)

5   Using axes like those shown in Fig. 14.2, draw a new graph for a firm in a monopolistically competitive industry in long-run equilibrium.

ⓔⓣ 6   Consider a monopolistically competitive industry in long-run equilibrium. Firm *A* in this industry attempts to increase profits by advertising.

   a   On the graph like the one in Fig. 14.3, show what will happen in the short run as a result of the decision to advertise. Briefly explain your graph.

   b   If the firm is successful in raising profits in the short run, what will happen in the long run?

FIGURE **14.3**

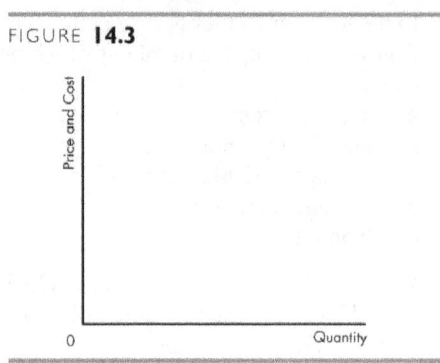

7   When all firms in a monopolistically competitive industry advertise, it makes the demand curve facing each firm more elastic. Explain why, using the concept of substitutes in consumption.

8   You are driving along an unfamiliar highway and you are hungry. There are many unfamiliar restaurants and a McDonald's. Even if you don't like McDonald's, explain why you might choose to eat there.

ANSWERS

True/False and Explain

1   **F**   Free entry and exit in monopolistic competition. (324–325)

2   **T**   Creates a downward-sloping demand curve; there is some ability to raise price without sales going to zero. (324–325)

3   **F**   With differentiated products, also compete on quality and marketing. (324–325)

4   **F**   Sensitive to average market price, but not individual competitors, as in oligopoly in Chapter 15. (324–325)

5   **T**   With many firms, coordination is difficult and collusion is not possible. (324–325)

6   **F**   New entry shifts individual firm demand (and marginal revenue) curves leftward. (326–329)

7   **F**   Product differentiation creates downward-sloping demand tangent to *ATC* below full capacity output. (326–329)

8   **F**   Zero economic profit, but $P \neq$ minimum *ATC*. (326–329)

9 T Difference between P and MC is markup (326–329)

10 F Without barriers to entry, new firms cause price to fall until economic profits = 0. (326–329)

11 T With existing products, new firms enter and compete away economic profits. (330–333)

12 F Selling costs are fixed costs that increase total costs, but if output increases enough, average total cost may decrease. (330–333)

⊕ 13 F Depends on information versus persuasion content of advertising and gains from increased product variety. (330–333)

14 T Advertising can be used to signal quality to consumers. (330–333)

15 T See Text Fig. 14.6. (330–333)

Multiple-Choice

1 c All other answers describe oligopoly, which is coming in Chapter 15. (324–325)

2 c Both have downward-sloping demand curves, so both have MR curves that are below demand curves. (324–325)

3 d Both have no entry barriers, which allows a large number of firms. (324–325)

4 e All are definitions or results of product differentiation. (324–325)

5 a Many firms, each with a small market share. (324–325)

6 e Product differentiation creates pricing power. Demand is not perfectly elastic. (324–325)

7 c See text discussion. (324–325)

⊕ 8 c Demand curve ($AR = P$) tangent to ATC and above MC. (326–329)

9 b Where $MC = MR$. (326–329)

⊕ 10 a At Q_2, $AR - ATC$. (326–329)

11 a With new entrants due to economic profit, industry demand is divided among more firms, so each firm's demand curve shifts leftward. (326–329)

12 b **a** and **e** create possibility of economic profit, **c** and **d** are outcomes, not forces leading to zero economic profit. (326–329)

13 d Zero economic profit. (326–329)

14 c **b** and **d** are false for monopoly. **a** is false for monopolistic competition. (326–329)

15 c Excess capacity at Q where demand is tangent to downward slope ATC. (326–329)

16 d Where demand curve is tangent to ATC. (326–329)

⊕ 17 d Zero long-run economic profit for monopolistic competition. (326–329)

18 c With exit, market demand is divided among a smaller number of firms. Demand and quantity supplied increase for originals. (326–329)

19 c Positive normal profits, positive accounting profits. (326–329)

20 e Selling costs are fixed costs that may increase or decrease demand, and may persuade consumers about exaggerated differences between products rather than provide valuable information. (330–333)

21 c Disadvantages of excess capacity and advertising costs versus gains from variety. (330–333)

22 b Increased demand allows short-run economic profit. New products make demand more inelastic. (330–333)

23 c Always compare MR and MC. Firms don't consider social costs or revenues. (330–333)

24 a Selling costs are used to differentiate products. Have inefficient, excess capacity and use brand names. (330–333)

25 b Variety provides choice. (330–333)

Short Answer Problems

1 Figure 14.2 Solution (a) illustrates a monopolistically competitive firm making an economic profit in the short run. The important feature of the graph is that at the profit-maximizing output, price is greater than average total cost. Economic profit is the shaded area.

FIGURE **14.2** SOLUTION

(a)

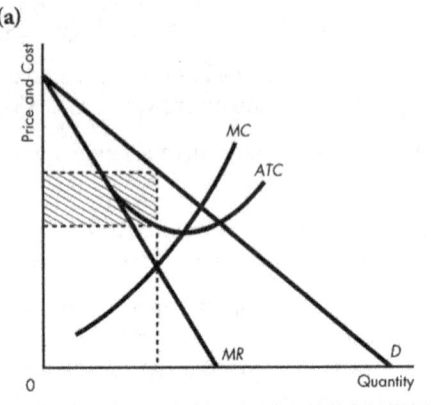

FIGURE **14.2** SOLUTION

(c)

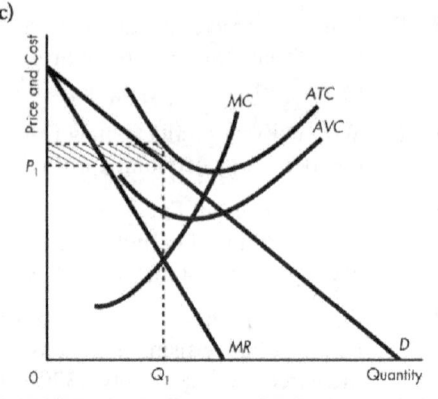

2   Figure 14.2 Solution (b) illustrates a firm that will shut down in the short run since price is less than average variable cost at the profit-maximizing (loss-minimizing) level of output.

FIGURE **14.2** SOLUTION

(b)

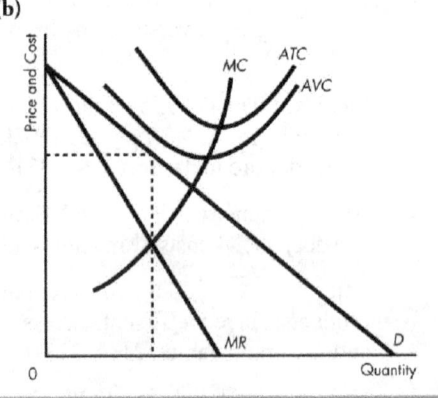

3   Figure 14.2 Solution (c) illustrates a firm incurring a loss but continuing to produce. The loss is the shaded area. Note that, at the profit-maximizing output, price is less than *ATC* but greater than *AVC*.

4   Since firms are incurring a loss, firms will leave the industry. The demand curves facing each remaining firm will shift rightward as they each attract some customers of departing firms. As firms' demand curves shift rightward, losses are reduced. Firms continue to have an incentive to leave until losses are eliminated. Thus remaining firms' demand curves continue to shift until they are tangent to the *ATC* curve.

5   Figure 14.2 Solution (d) illustrates a monopolistically competitive firm in long-run equilibrium. The demand curve facing the firm is tangent to the *ATC* curve at the profit-maximizing output. Thus the firm is making zero economic profit.

FIGURE **14.2** SOLUTION

(d)

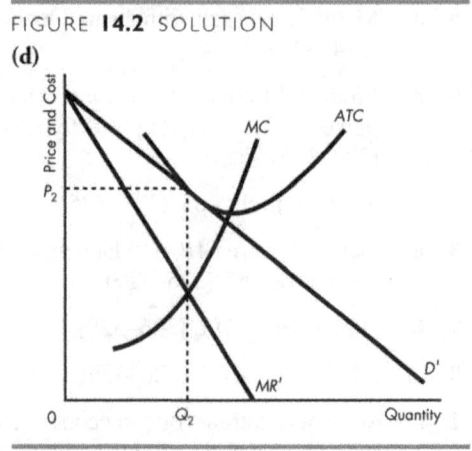

© **6 a** Advertising will increase firm A's cost, but also increase demand (it hopes). If the increase in demand (revenue) is greater than the increase in cost, firm A will increase its profit. Figure 14.3 Solution illustrates this situation. The initial curves are given by D_0, ATC_0, and MR_0.

Initially the firm is producing Q_0 and selling at price P_0 and making zero economic profit. Advertising, which is a fixed cost, raises the ATC curve to ATC_1 (MC does not shift), but also increases the demand and marginal revenue curves to D_1 and MR_1, respectively. The shift in the demand curve is sufficiently great that there is now positive economic profit at the new profit-maximizing level of output (Q_1). Economic profit is the shaded area.

FIGURE **14.3** SOLUTION

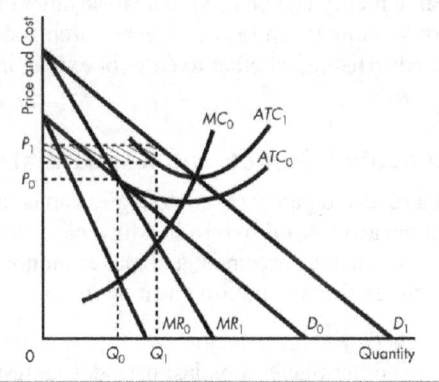

b Other firms will also begin to advertise to attempt to increase their profit (or recover lost profit). As all other firms advertise, the demand curve for our firm will shift back to the left as it loses some customers it gained. In the long run, once again, all firms will be making zero profit even after advertising.

7 Advertising by all firms in a monopolistically competitive industry makes consumers more aware of substitutes. From Chapter 4, we know that elasticity of demand depends on the substitute available for a product. The more substitutes consumers become aware of, the greater their choices, and the easier it is to switch to another product if the price rises.

8 McDonald's is a brand name, and you know from experience that, whatever you think of their food, the quality is consistent (and the washrooms are clean). You know what to expect. Since you have no information about the unfamiliar restaurants, you use the "information" provided by the brand name to make your choice.

Chapter 15
Oligopoly

What Is Oligopoly?

Oligopoly is a model of market structure where few firms compete and *strategically interact*. A firm considers the effects of its actions on behaviour of others and actions of others on its own profit.

- ♦ Natural or legal barriers prevent entry new firms.

- ♦ **Duopoly**—oligopoly market with two firms.

- ♦ **Cartel**—group of firms in collusive agreement.

Oligopoly Games

Game theory analyses strategic behaviour. Games have

- ♦ rules—specify permissible actions by players.

- ♦ **strategies**—actions such as raising or lowering price, output, advertising, or product quality.

- ♦ payoffs—profits and losses of players. A **payoff matrix** shows payoffs for every possible action by each player.

- ♦ outcome—determined by players' choices. In a **Nash equilibrium**, *A* takes best possible action given *B*'s action, and *B* takes best possible action given *A*'s action.

A "prisoners' dilemma" is a one-time, two-person game with a **dominant strategy equilibrium**. Each player has a dominant strategy (unique best strategy independent of other player's action) of cheating, that is, confessing.

- ♦ Prisoners' dilemma yields a Nash equilibrium outcome that is *not* in the best interests of the players.

In a duopoly game, each firm can *comply* with a **collusive agreement** to restrict output and raise price, or it can *cheat*.

- ♦ In one-time price-fixing game, prisoners' dilemma solution occurs—each firm has a dominant strategy of cheating, even though both firms would be better off if they could trust each other and comply.

- ♦ Unlike prisoners' dilemma game, a game of "chicken" has a Nash equilibrium that is *not* a dominant strategy equilibrium.

Game theory can be used to analyse other choices for firms—how much to spend on research and development, on advertising, whether to enter or exit an industry.

Repeated Games and Sequential Games

In a repeated game, other strategies can create **cooperative equilibrium** in which each firm complies with collusive agreement and makes monopoly profits. Requires firms to punish cheating in previous period.

- ♦ *Tit-for-tat strategy*—taking the same action the other player took last period. Lightest punishment.

- ♦ *Trigger strategy*—cooperating until the other player cheats, then cheating forever. Most severe punishment.

Game tree—shows decisions made at first and second stages of sequential game—can be used to analyse sequential entry-deterrence game. In a **contestable market** there are few firms but free entry and exit, so existing firms face competition from *potential* entrants. Existing firms may use strategies of

- ♦ set monopoly price, but risk entry of new firm.

- ♦ set competitive price and earn normal profit to keep out a potential competitor.

- ♦ **limit pricing**—set highest price that just inflicts loss on entrant. Compared to monopoly outcome, charge lower price and produce greater quantity to deter entry.

Anti-Combine Law

Anti-combine law regulates oligopolies; seeks to prevent them from becoming or behaving like monopolies.

Competition Act of 1986 distinguishes between

- ♦ criminal actions (conspiracy to fix prices, bid-rigging, false advertising), dealt with by courts.

- ♦ noncriminal actions (mergers, abuse of market position, exclusive dealing), dealt with by Competition Tribunal.

Evidence suggests anti-combine laws have served the social interest.

HELPFUL HINTS

1 This chapter uses elementary game theory to explain oligopoly. The prisoners' dilemma game illustrates the most important game theory concepts (rules, strategies, payoffs, outcome), which are then used in more complex game theory models like repeated and sequential games.

It is important to learn how to find the Nash equilibrium of a prisoners' dilemma–type game. Take the example of players *A* and *B*, where each player has to choose between two strategies—confess or deny. First set up the payoff matrix. Then look at the payoff matrix from *A*'s point of view. *A* does not know if *B* is going to confess or deny, so *A* asks two questions: (1) Assuming that *B* confesses, do I get a better payoff if I confess or deny? (2) Assuming that *B* denies, do I get a better payoff if I confess or deny?

If *A*'s best strategy is to confess, regardless of whether *B* confesses or denies, confessing is *A*'s dominant strategy. Next, look at the payoff matrix from *B*'s point of view. Let *B* ask the equivalent two questions, and find *B*'s dominant strategy. The combination of *A*'s dominant strategy and *B*'s dominant strategy comprises the Nash equilibrium outcome of the game.

2 The key insight of the prisoners' dilemma game is the *tension* between the Nash equilibrium outcome (where both players' best strategy is to confess because they can't trust each other) and the fact that both players could make themselves better off if only they would cooperate. All of the equilibrium situations we have examined up until now have been stable outcomes where all agents' self-interests (utility and profit) have been maximized. Remember, equilibrium is

defined as a situation where there is no tendency to change. The Nash equilibrium of the prisoners' dilemma is different. Even though both players confess, their individual self-interests are not maximized. It is the additional possibility of strategic interaction (to trust or not to trust the other player) that creates the instability of outcomes.

The instability of outcomes in this simple game helps us to understand more complex market phenomena such as gasoline price wars. When gasoline station owners trust each other, prices remain relatively high and profits are maximized. But there is always an incentive to cheat on a collusive agreement. Once cheating begins, trust breaks down and owners are driven to the equilibrium outcome where all owners cheat, prices fall, and profits are reduced. Eventually, reduced profits lead owners to take a chance on trusting each other again, since they figure it couldn't be worse than existing low prices and profits. All stations raise their prices, and the cycle begins again. This instability of price and profit outcomes stems from the cycle of trust and non-trust. In other words, instability arises from strategic interaction between station owners.

SELF-TEST

True/False and Explain

What Is Oligopoly?

1 An oligopolist will consider the reaction of other firms before it decides to cut its price.

2 There are no barriers to entry in oligopoly.

3 Cartels are legal associations of firms acting together to limit output, raise price, and increase economic profit.

4 The Herfindahl–Hirschman Index (HHI) that divides oligopoly from monopolistic competition is 1,000.

Oligopoly Games

5 A Nash equilibrium occurs when A takes the best possible action given the action of B, and B takes the best possible action given the action of A.

6 If duopolists agree to collude, they can (jointly) make as much profit as a single monopoly.

7 For colluding duopolists in a nonrepeated game, the equilibrium is always for both firms to cheat.

8 The Nash equilibrium in a game of "chicken" is a dominant strategy equilibrium.

Repeated Games and Sequential Games

9 For colluding duopolists in a repeated game, the equilibrium is always for both firms to cheat.

10 A limit-pricing strategy sets the price that inflicts the highest loss on a new entrant.

11 Repeated games are more likely to have a cooperative equilibrium than one-time only games.

12 If an oligopoly operates in a contestable market, one potential outcome is competitive prices and normal profits.

Anti-Combine Law

13 According to Canada's anti-combine laws, mergers and abuse of a dominant market position are criminal offences.

14 Anti-combine laws can work in the social interest or in the self-interest of producers.

15 The Competition Act distinguishes between business practices that are criminal and noncriminal.

Multiple-Choice

What Is Oligopoly?

1 If the efficient scale of production only allows three firms to supply a market, the market is called a
  a three-firm monopoly.
  b cost-based oligopoly.
  c natural oligopoly.
  d monopolistic competition.
  e competitive monopoly.

2 Each of the following is a characteristic of monopolistic competition. Which is *not* a characteristic of oligopoly?
  a Each firm faces a downward-sloping demand curve.
  b Firms are profit-maximizers.
  c The sales of one firm will not have a significant effect on other firms.
  d There is more than one firm in the industry.
  e Firms set prices.

3 A cartel is a group of firms that agree to
  a behave competitively.
  b raise the price of their products.
  c lower the price of their products.
  d increase the amount they produce.
  e cheat on each other.

4 Because an oligopoly has a small number of firms
  a each firm can act like a monopoly.
  b the firms may legally form a cartel.
  c the HHI for the industry is small.
  d the four-firm concentration ratio for the industry is small.
  e the firms are interdependent.

5 Figure 15.1 shows the daily demand (*D*) for limousine rides in Moose Jaw, Saskatchewan, and the average total cost (*ATC*) of a limousine company. The limousine market in Moose Jaw is
  a a natural duopoly.
  b a natural monopoly.
  c a natural oligopoly with three firms.
  d monopolistically competitive.
  e perfectly competitive.

FIGURE 15.1

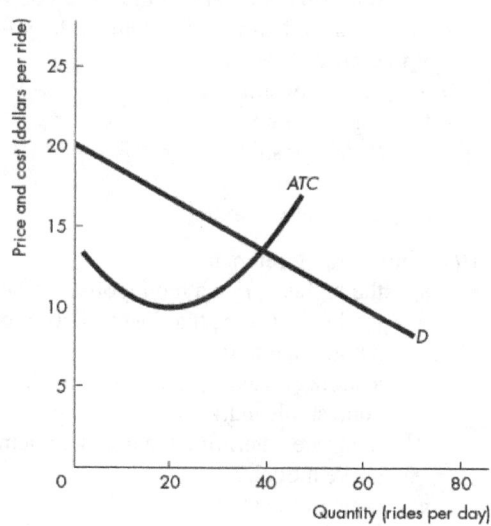

Oligopoly Games

6 Which of the following is *not* common to all games?
  a rules
  b collusion
  c strategies
  d payoffs
  e the analysis of strategic interaction

7 In the prisoners' dilemma with players Art and Bob, each prisoner would be best off if
  a both prisoners confess.
  b both prisoners deny.
  c Art denies and Bob confesses.
  d Bob denies and Art confesses.
  e none of the above occurs.

8 If a duopoly with collusion maximizes profit,
  a each firm must produce the same amount.
  b each firm must produce its maximum output possible.
  c industry marginal revenue must equal industry marginal cost at the level of total output.
  d industry demand must equal industry marginal cost at the level of total output.
  e total output will be greater than without collusion.

9 Table 15.1 gives the payoff matrix of profits for firms *A* and *B* when there are two strategies for each firm: (1) charge a low price or (2) charge a high price. The equilibrium in this game (played once) is a Nash equilibrium, because
  a firm *B* will reduce profit by more than *A* if both charge a lower price.
  b firm *B* is the dominant firm.
  c the best strategy for each firm does not depend on the strategy chosen by the other.
  d there is no credible threat by either firm to punish the other if it breaks the agreement.
  e all of the above are true.

TABLE 15.1

		Firm B			
		Low Price		High Price	
	Low Price	A:	$2	A:	$20
		B:	$5	B:	−$15
Firm A					
	High Price	A:	−$10	A:	$10
		B:	$25	B:	$20

10 Refer to the nonrepeated game in Table 15.1. In Nash equilibrium, what are firm *A*'s profits?
  a −$10
  b $2
  c $10
  d $20
  e indeterminate

11 Refer to the nonrepeated game in Table 15.1. If both firms could agree to collude, what would be firm *A*'s profits?
  a −$10
  b $2
  c $10
  d $20
  e indeterminate

12 Refer to the nonrepeated game in Table 15.1. The equilibrium of the game is called a

a dominant firm equilibrium.

b cooperative equilibrium.

c duopoly equilibrium.

d credible strategy equilibrium.

e Nash equilibrium.

13 The firms Trick and Gear form a cartel to collude to maximize profit. If this game is nonrepeated, the Nash equilibrium is

a both firms cheat on the agreement.

b both firms comply with the agreement.

c Trick cheats, while Gear complies with the agreement.

d Gear cheats, while Trick complies with the agreement.

e indeterminate.

14 If an R&D game between two firms is a game of chicken, then the equilibrium is

a both firms conduct R&D.

b neither firm conducts R&D.

c only one of the two firms conducts R&D.

d flawed because R&D must be done, but the game's equilibrium is that it might be done.

e none of the above.

15 Table 15.2 gives the payoff matrix of profits for Player One and Player Two. There are two strategies for each player. Player One can choose Up or Down. Player Two can choose Left or Right. In this nonrepeated game,

a Player One has a dominant strategy to choose Up.

b Player One has a dominant strategy to choose Down.

c Player Two has a dominant strategy to choose Left.

d Player Two has a dominant strategy to choose Right.

e neither player has a dominant strategy.

TABLE 15.2

Player Two

	Left	Right
Up	3 / 2	3 / 3
Down	4 / 4	2 / 3

(Player One on vertical axis)

Repeated Games and Sequential Games

16 Consider the same cartel consisting of Trick and Gear from Question 13. Now, however, the game is repeated indefinitely and each firm employs a tit-for-tat strategy. The equilibrium is

a both firms cheat on the agreement.

b both firms comply with the agreement.

c Trick cheats, while Gear complies with the agreement.

d Gear cheats, while Trick complies with the agreement.

e indeterminate.

17 The equilibrium in Question **16** is called a

a credible strategy equilibrium.

b dominant player equilibrium.

c duopoly equilibrium.

d trigger strategy equilibrium.

e cooperative equilibrium.

18 When a firm cooperates if the other cooperates, but plays the Nash equilibrium strategy forever if the other cheats, that is a

a dominant strategy.

b trigger strategy.

c tit-for-tat strategy.

d wimp's strategy.

e cooperative strategy.

19 Limit pricing refers to

a the highest price a monopolist can set.

b the highest price that just inflicts a loss on a potential entrant.

c a strategy used by entering firms in contestable markets.

d the price determined in a kinked demand curve model.

e none of the above.

20 Which of the following quotes illustrates a *contestable market* in the transporter industry?

a "I am producing extra transporters even though it results in lower short-run profits, to keep Tommy's Transporters from expanding into my market."

b "I am producing more transporters than Tommy and I agreed to in business negotiations last week."

c "If Tommy and I could agree on a higher transporter price, we would both make more profits."

d "I have been spending more on research and development of a new two-way transporter."

e None of the above.

21 A trigger strategy can be used
  a in a nonrepeated game or a repeated game.
  b in a nonrepeated game but not in a repeated game.
  c in a repeated game but not in a nonrepeated game.
  d only when there is no Nash equilibrium.
  e only in a contestable market.

Anti-Combine Law

22 Anti-combine laws attempt to
  a support prices.
  b establish Crown corporations.
  c prevent monopoly practices.
  d establish fair trade laws.
  e deregulate monopolies.

23 Canada's anti-combine law dates back to the
  a 1880s.
  b 1910s.
  c 1930s.
  d 1960s.
  e 1980s.

24 The Competition Act distinguishes between business practices that are criminal and noncriminal. Which of the following are criminal practices?
  a conspiracy to fix prices
  b bid-rigging
  c anti-competitive price-fixing actions
  d false advertising.
  e all of the above

25 Under the Competition Act, the Competition Tribunal may do all of the following *except*
  a force firms to lower prices.
  b prevent mergers.
  c dissolve mergers.
  d prohibit persons from controlling a class of business.
  e prohibit persons from practising anti-competitive acts.

Short Answer Problems

1 A small prairie town has two bakeries—Always Fresh and Never Stale. Transportation costs are high relative to the price of bread, so the bakeries do not get any out-of-town competition; the local bread industry is a duopoly. Always Fresh and Never Stale have the same cost curves, and each currently makes an annual profit of $2,000.

Suppose that a new advertising service, Philomena's Flyers, starts up. If one bakery advertises in Philomena's Flyers, its annual profits will increase to $5,000, while the other bakery will lose $2,000. If both advertise, each will make a zero profit. If neither advertises, each bakery will continue to make an annual profit of $2,000.

  a Represent this duopoly as a game by identifying the players, strategies, and possible outcomes.

  b Construct the payoff matrix.

  c What is the Nash equilibrium outcome? Explain.

2 Figure 15.2(a) on the next page gives the identical average total cost (*ATC*) curve for Always Fresh and Never Stale. Figure 15.2(b) gives the town's market demand curve for bread and the firms' joint marginal cost curve. Suppose that the two bakeries collude to maximize profit and agree to divide output equally for a single year.

  a How much will each bakery produce and what price per loaf will they charge?

  b What is each bakery's average total cost and profit?

FIGURE **15.2**

(a) *ATC* Curve for Each Bakery

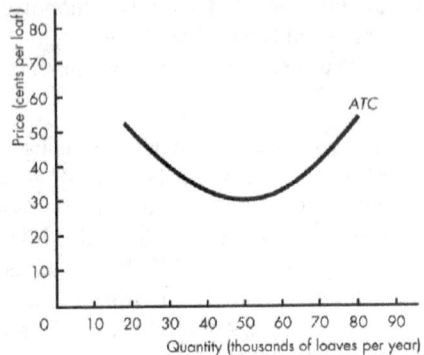

(b) **Market Demand for Bread and Firm's Joint *MC* Curve**

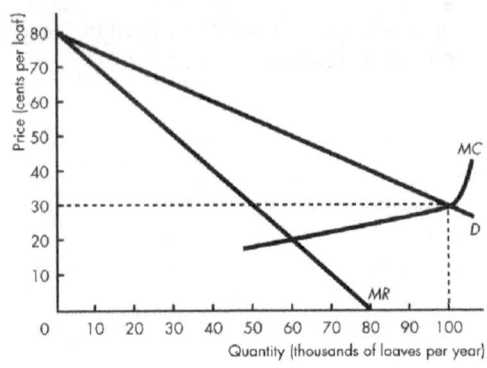

3 Now suppose that Never Stale convinces Always Fresh that demand has decreased and they must reduce their price by 10 cents per loaf in order to sell their agreed-upon quantity. Of course, demand has not decreased, but Always Fresh produces its agreed amount and charges 10 cents less per loaf. Never Stale, the cheater, also charges 10 cents less than before, but increases output sufficiently to satisfy the rest of demand at this price.

a How many loaves of bread does Never Stale produce?

b What is Always Fresh's average total cost and profit?

c What is Never Stale's average total cost and profit?

4 Return to the initial situation. The firms are preparing to enter into a *long-term* collusive agreement. Always Fresh credibly assures Never Stale that if Never Stale cheats in a repeated game, Always Fresh will undercut Never Stale's price as soon as the cheating is discovered. Would Never Stale want to cheat on the agreement now? Why or why not?

5 Two firms—Katie's Cabs and Madeleine's Movers—are the only two taxicab companies in a small town. These firms are playing a duopoly game. If they both comply with a collusive cartel agreement to restrict the number of their cabs and raise their prices, each can earn an economic profit of

$2 million. But if one firm cheats on the agreement—by cutting its prices just a little and quietly acquiring more taxis—and the other complies with the agreement, the cheater earns an economic profit of $2.5 million and the complier suffers an economic loss of $1 million. If both firms cheat, both earn only normal profits and $0 economic profit.

a Use this information to complete the payoff matrix of economic profits in Fig. 15.3. Put Katie's Cabs' payoffs in the shaded triangles and Madeleine's Movers' payoffs in the clear triangles.

b If this game is played only once, what is Katie's best strategy? What is Madeleine's best strategy? What will be the equilibrium outcome?

c When is the joint total profit the largest? When is Katie's profit the largest? Madeleine's profit?

FIGURE **15.3**

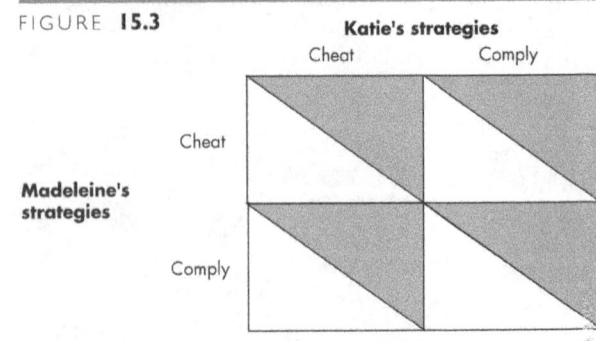

6 Suppose the taxi firm duopoly game in Short Answer Problem **5** changes. The payoffs are the same as before when both players choose the same strategy (both cheat or both comply). But when one player cheats and the other complies, the payoffs are now a $2.5 million economic profit for the cheater and a $0.5 million economic profit for the complier.

FIGURE **15.4**

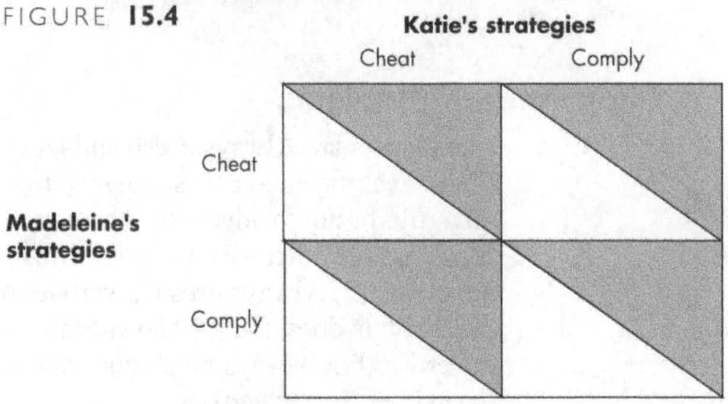

Katie's strategies
Cheat   Comply

Madeleine's strategies
Cheat

Comply

a Complete the payoff matrix in Fig. 15.4.

b Does Katie have a clear-cut best strategy? Does Madeleine? Is there a clear equilibrium outcome for this new game?

7 The taxi firm duopoly game changes again so that the payoff matrix is shown in Fig. 15.5. Madeleine and Katie now see that they will be playing a repeated game. Madeleine knows that Katie has adopted a tit-for-tat strategy. Last period, Madeleine complied with the cartel agreement.

FIGURE **15.5**

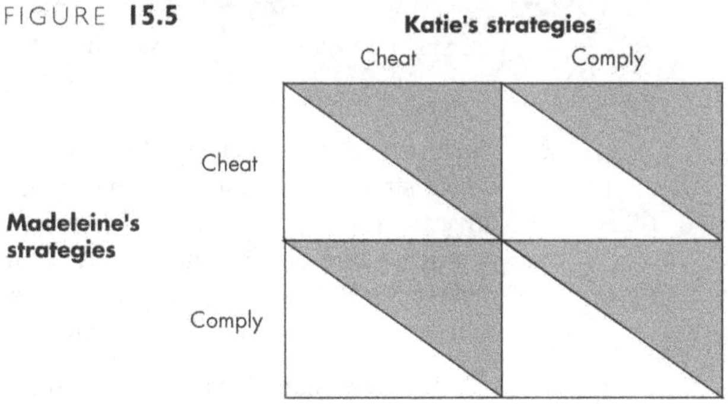

Katie's strategies
Cheat   Comply

Madeleine's strategies
Cheat

Comply

a If Madeleine cheats this period, what is her profit? If she cheats this period, what is the maximum profit she can earn next period? What is her maximum two-period profit if she cheats?

b If Madeleine complies with the agreement, what is her profit this period?

If she complies next period, what will be her profit? If she does not cheat in either period, what is the two-period profit she earns?

c Is Katie likely to cheat this period? Why?

8 After reading about the major anti-combine cases on pages 356–359 of the text, does it appear that Canada's anti-combine law works in the social interest or in the self-interest of producers?

ANSWERS

True/False and Explain

1 **T** Oligopoly involves strategic behaviour. (342–343)

2 **F** Small number of firms because of barriers to entry. (342–343)

3 **F** Cartels take those actions, but they are illegal. (342–343)

4 **T** Below 1,000 = monopolistic competition; above = oligopoly. (343)

5 **T** Definition. (346–347)

6 **T** With collusion, act exactly like monopoly. (348–349)

7 **T** True for nonrepeated game but may be false for repeated game. (349–352)

8 **F** Unlike prisoners' dilemma, *not* a dominant strategy equilibrium (346–354)

9 **F** Tit-for-tat strategy yields cooperative equilibrium in repeated game. (355–357)

10 **F** Sets highest price that just inflicts (smallest) loss, since any loss deters entry. (356–357)

11 **T** Extra strategies like tit-for-tat in repeated games support cooperative equilibrium. (354–357)

12 **T** Possible strategy to keep out competitors. (354–357)

13 **F** Noncriminal offences. Criminal offences include price fixing and false advertising. (358)

14 **T** See text discussion. (358–361)

15 T See text discussion. (358–361)

Multiple-Choice

1 c Economies of scale create natural oligopoly. (342–343)

2 c Oligopoly involves interdependence between firms. (342–343)

3 b Raise price and restrict output. (342–343)

4 e Each firm's actions affect the others. (342–343)

5 c Efficient scale of 1 firm is 20, so 3 firms satisfy market demand (60) at lowest price (10). (342–343)

6 b No collusion in prisoners' dilemma. (346–354)

7 b Both denying would yield lesser jail terms, but doesn't happen because players cannot trust each other enough to collude. (346–347)

8 c See Text Fig. 15.5(b). (349)

9 c Dominant strategy for each. (351–352)

10 b Both firms charge low price. (351–352)

11 c Both firms charge high price. (351–352)

12 e Each player takes the best possible action, given the action of the other player. (346–354)

13 a Similar to prisoners' dilemma outcome. (348–352)

14 c In the Nash equilibrium, one firm conducts R&D even though the non-R&D firm has higher profit. (354)

15 e Each player's strategy changes as the other player's strategy changes. (346–352)

16 b Cooperative equilibrium; each player responds rationally to the credible threat of the other. (355–357)

17 e Definition. (355–357)

18 b Definition. (355)

19 b Definition. c would be true for existing firms. (355–357)

20 a Produce greater quantity and charge lower price to deter entry. (355–357)

21 c Trigger strategy requires more than one game to change from cooperation to cheating. (355–357)

22 c See text discussion. (358–361)

23 a 1889—see text discussion. (358–361)

24 e See text discussion. (358)

25 a See Text Table 15.6. (358)

Short Answer Problems

1 a The players are Always Fresh and Never Stale. Each firm has two strategies: to advertise or not to advertise. There are four possible outcomes: (1) both firms advertise, (2) Always Fresh advertises but Never Stale does not, (3) Never Stale advertises but Always Fresh does not, and (4) neither firm advertises.

b The payoff matrix is given in Fig. 15.6. The entries give the profit earned by Always Fresh (clear triangles) and Never Stale (shaded triangles) under each of the four possible outcomes.

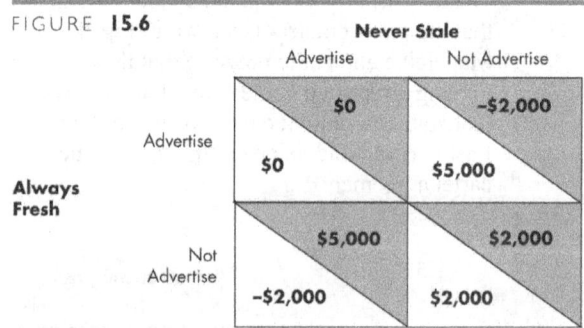

FIGURE **15.6**

c First, consider how Always Fresh decides which strategy to pursue. If Never Stale advertises, Always Fresh can advertise and make zero profit or not advertise and make a $2,000 loss. Thus Always Fresh will want to advertise if Never Stale does.

If Never Stale does not advertise, Always Fresh can advertise and make a $5,000 profit or not advertise and make a $2,000 profit. Therefore Always Fresh will want to advertise whether Never Stale advertises or not. Never Stale will come to the same conclusion. The Nash equilibrium is that both firms advertise.

2 a The firms will agree to produce 30,000 loaves each and sell at a price of 50 cents per loaf. We determine this by noticing (Fig. 15.2b) that the profit-maximizing (monopoly) output is 60,000 loaves for the industry ($MR = MC$ at 60,000), and the industry price is 50 cents per loaf. Since the firms have agreed to divide output equally, each will produce 30,000 loaves.

b From Fig. 15.2(a) we determine that, at 30,000 loaves, each firm's average total cost is 40 cents per loaf. Since price is 50 cents per loaf, profit will be $3,000 for each firm.

3 a At the new price of 40 cents per loaf, total quantity demanded is 80,000 loaves. Since Always Fresh continues to produce 30,000 loaves, this means that Never Stale will produce the remaining 50,000 loaves demanded.

b Since Always Fresh continues to produce 30,000 loaves, its average total cost continues to be 40 cents per loaf. With the new price also at 40 cents, Always Fresh will make a zero economic profit.

c Never Stale has increased output to 50,000 loaves, which implies average total cost of 30 cents per loaf. Thus, given a price of 40 cents, Never Stale's economic profit will be $5,000.

4 Given that the agreement is long term, Never Stale would almost surely not cheat. The reason is that, while Never Stale could increase short-term profit by cheating, it would lose much more future profit if Always Fresh retaliates in a repeated game.

The key point is that Never Stale's behaviour changes, not because cost or demand has changed, but rather because Always Fresh's behaviour has changed in the repeated game. In duopoly and oligopoly, the best strategy for any firm depends on the behaviour of other firms.

5 a The payoff matrix appears in Fig. 15.3 Solution.

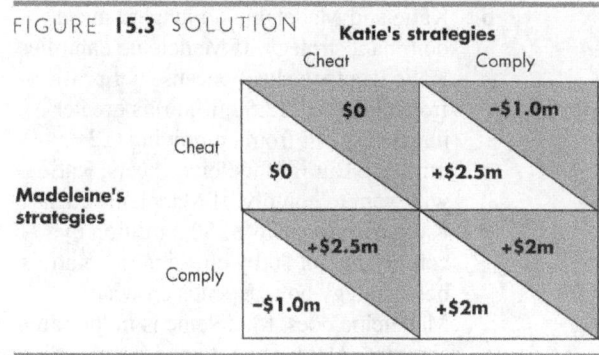

b Katie's best strategy is to cheat no matter what Madeleine does. If Madeleine complies with the agreement and does not cheat, Katie will cheat because her profit from cheating ($2.5 million) is greater than her profit from complying ($2 million). If Madeleine cheats, Katie will also cheat because her profit ($0) is higher than the loss she would incur by complying (–$1 million). Katie has a dominant strategy to cheat. Similarly, Madeleine's profits are higher if she cheats, no matter what Katie does. So Madeleine also has a dominant strategy to cheat. The Nash equilibrium outcome is for both players to cheat on the agreement.

c The taxicab industry's profits are highest ($4 million) when both Katie and Madeleine comply with the agreement. Katie's individual profit is highest if she cheats and Madeleine complies. Madeleine's individual profit is highest if she cheats and Katie complies. Though each player's *individual* interest is to cheat, their *joint* interest is to comply.

6 a The payoff matrix appears in Fig. 15.4 Solution.

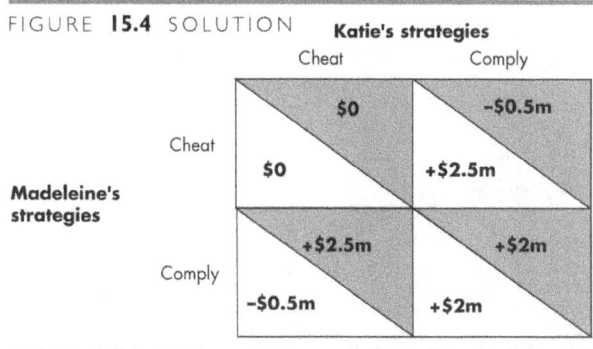

b Katie and Madeleine no longer have a dominant strategy. If Madeleine complies, Katie wants to cheat because her profit from cheating ($2.5 million) is greater than her profit from complying ($2 million). But if Madeleine cheats, Katie will want to comply. If Madeleine cheats, Katie earns a profit of $0.5 million by complying but $0 by cheating. So Katie's best strategy now depends on what Madeleine does. Madeleine is in the same situation. Her best strategy depends on what Katie does. Unlike the game in Short Answer Problem **5**, the outcome is not clear-cut. The equilibrium depends on which strategies Madeleine and Katie decide to pursue.

7 a Last period Madeleine complied, so Katie's tit-for-tat strategy means that Katie will comply this period. With Katie complying, Madeleine's profit this period by cheating is $2.5 million. Next period Katie will cheat because Madeleine cheated this period. So next period the most profit that Madeleine can earn is $0 by also cheating. (If Madeleine complied with the agreement when Katie cheated, Madeleine loses –$2 million.) Over two periods, Madeleine's total profit if she cheats in the first period is $2.5 million.

b Last period Madeleine complied, so Katie's tit-for-tat strategy means that Katie will comply this period. If Madeleine complies this period, she earns $2 million. Because Madeleine complies this period, Katie's tit-for-tat strategy means that next period Katie will comply. Then, if Madeleine also complies next period, she will earn $2 million. By complying each period Madeleine earns a total of $4 million over two periods.

c Madeleine is not likely to cheat. If she does, her total profits over the two periods are much less than if she complies over the two periods. Players in a repeated game are more likely to reach the cooperative equilibrium than are players in a one-time game.

8 Since the results of the cases are largely to increase competition and reduce prices to consumers, the Competition Act seems to work in the social interest. Most economists agree.

Part 4 Wrap Up
Understanding Firms and Markets

PROBLEM

FIGURE **P4.1**

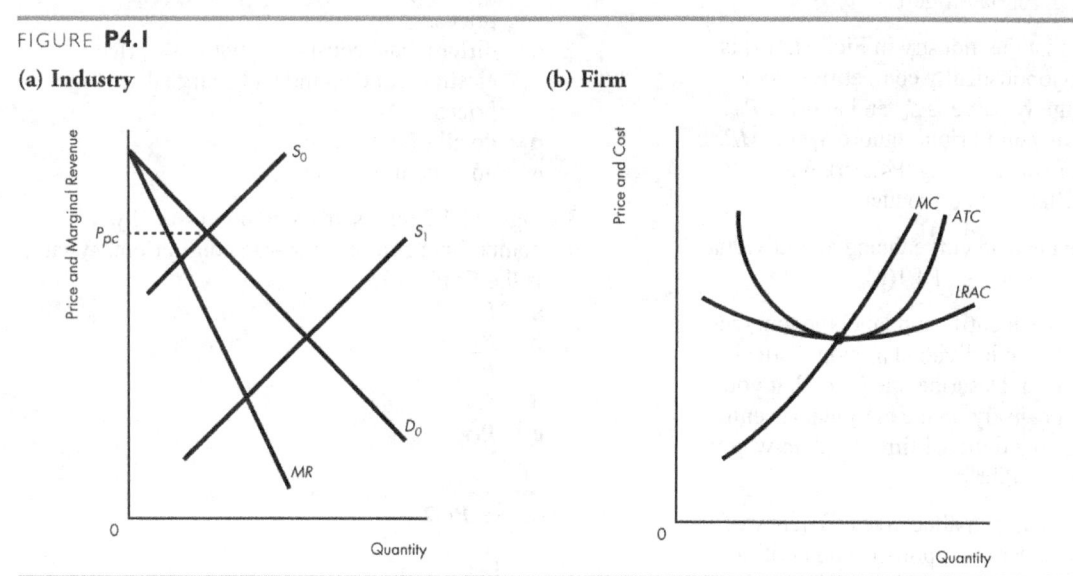

(a) Industry

(b) Firm

Despite significant differences between perfect competition, monopoly, and monopolistic competition, all of these market structures can be analysed using the diagrams in Fig. P4.1.

Figure P4.1(a) shows an industry in short-run equilibrium at the intersection of the demand (D_0) and supply (S_0) curves. Ignore for the moment the other supply curve (S_1) and the marginal revenue curve (MR). Long-run market demand is the same as short-run market demand. There are no external economies or diseconomies. Figure P4.1(b) shows the cost curves of one of many identical firms in the industry.

Let's first suppose this is a perfectly competitive (*pc*) industry.

a Describe the demand curve facing an individual firm; describe the marginal revenue curve.

b On Fig. P4.1, identify and label the industry short-run equilibrium price (P_{pc}) (this is a giveaway!), output (Q_{pc}), and individual firm output (q_{pc}). Is each individual firm making a profit or loss? Explain.

c What happens in the long run? On Fig. P4.1, identify and label the industry long-run equilibrium price (P^{LR}_{pc}), output (Q^{LR}_{pc}), and individual firm output (q^{LR}_{pc}).

Now suppose that the market in Fig. P4.1(a) is supplied by a single-price monopolist (*m*) with a legal monopoly. S_1 is the monopolist's marginal cost curve. Ignore S_0 and part (b) of the figure.

d Describe the demand curve facing the monopolist; describe the supply curve of the monopolist.

e On Fig. P4.1(a), identify and label the industry short-run equilibrium price (P_m) and output (Q_m).

f At Q_m, if the monopolist's average total cost is less than P_m, explain what happens in the long run. On Fig. P4.1(a), identify and label the industry long-run equilibrium price (P^{LR}_m) and output (Q^{LR}_m).

g Compare the long-run allocative efficiency of this industry under monopoly versus under perfect competition. Identify any deadweight loss on the appropriate figure.

Finally, suppose that the industry in Fig. P4.1(a) is supplied by many monopolistically competitive (*mc*) firms. The industry supply curve is S_0, and at price P_{pc}, each firm is in long-run equilibrium. Ignore S_1 and *MR*. Each firm has the cost curves in Fig. P4.1(b), but produces a slightly differentiated product.

h Describe the demand curve facing an individual firm and draw it on Fig. P4.1(b).

i On Fig. P4.1(b), identify and label the long-run output (q_{mc}) for an individual monopolistically competitive firm. Describe one point that you can identify precisely on the marginal revenue curve facing an individual firm. Explain why this is a long-run equilibrium.

j Compare the long-run allocative efficiency of this industry under monopolistic competition versus under perfect competition. What consideration must be taken into account that is not taken into account for a monopoly?

You should allocate 50 minutes for this examination (25 questions, 2 minutes per question). For each question, choose the one *best* answer.

1 The supply curve for a single-price monopoly is
a its marginal cost curve.
b its marginal cost curve above minimum average variable cost.
c its average variable cost curve.
d its marginal revenue curve.
e none of the above.

2 A successful price-discriminating firm must be able to
a prevent consumer resale.
b differentiate consumers with high price elasticity of demand and charge them low prices.
c differentiate consumers with low price elasticity of demand and charge them high prices.
d do all of the above.
e do none of the above.

3 Figure P4.2 represents a monopolistically competitive firm in short-run equilibrium. What is the firm's price?
a P_1
b P_2
c P_3
d P_4
e P_5

FIGURE **P4.2**

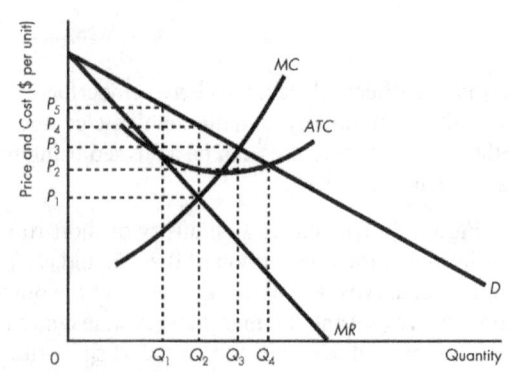

4 Figure P4.2 represents a monopolistically competitive firm in short-run equilibrium. In the long run, what is the firm's economic profit *per unit*?

a $P_4 - P_2$
b $P_4 - P_1$
c P_3
d P_2
e None of the above

5 For a single-price monopolist, which of the following statements is *false*?

a There is no unique one-to-one relationship between price and quantity supplied.
b For any output greater than zero, $MR < AR$.
c The industry demand curve is the monopolist's demand curve.
d The intersection of MR and MC provides all information necessary for identifying the profit-maximizing quantity and price.
e Total revenue is at a maximum where $MR = 0$.

6 A single-price monopoly never operates

a on an elastic portion of the demand curve.
b on a unit elastic portion of the demand curve.
c on an inelastic portion of the demand curve.
d at a quantity where marginal revenue is positive since total revenue is not at a maximum.
e under any of the above conditions.

7 In a perfectly competitive industry of 100 firms, the demand curve facing the individual firm is

a unit elastic.
b identical to the industry demand curve.
c 1/100 of the industry demand curve.
d one where $AR = MR$.
e none of the above.

8 If economic profits are being made by firms in a competitive industry, new firms will enter. This will shift

a the industry demand curve leftward, causing market price to fall.
b the industry demand curve rightward, causing market price to rise.
c the industry supply curve leftward, causing market price to rise.
d the industry supply curve rightward, causing market price to fall.
e none of the above curves.

9 When a firm spends $1,000 on advertising, the effect on its cost curves is

a ATC shifts up and MC does not change.
b ATC shifts up and MC shifts down.
c ATC and MC both shift up.
d MC shifts up and ATC does not change.
e AFC and MC both shift up.

10 In the prisoners' dilemma with players Art and Bob, the Nash equilibrium is

a both prisoners confess.
b both prisoners deny.
c Art denies and Bob confesses.
d Bob denies and Art confesses.
e indeterminate.

11 In a perfectly competitive industry, the market price is $5. An individual firm is producing the level of output at which marginal cost is $5 and is increasing, and average total cost is $25. What should the firm do to maximize its short-run profits?

a shut down
b expand output
c contract output
d leave output unchanged
e insufficient information to answer

12 The long-run competitive industry supply curve will be positively sloped if there are

a external economies.
b external diseconomies.
c no external economies or diseconomies.
d external costs.
e external benefits.

13 A perfectly competitive firm maximizes profit if

a marginal cost equals price and price is above minimum average variable cost.
b marginal cost equals price and price is above minimum average fixed cost.
c total revenue is at a maximum.
d average variable cost is at a minimum.
e average total cost is at a minimum.

14 The more perfectly a monopoly can price discriminate, the

a closer its output gets to the single-price monopoly output.
b more efficient is the outcome.
c more consumer surplus is converted to deadweight loss.
d more producer surplus is converted to deadweight loss.
e more producer surplus is captured as profit.

15 Selling costs in monopolistic competition
   a shift up the average total cost curve.
   b may be justified by the useful information provided to consumers.
   c may not provide benefits that justify the increased opportunity cost.
   d may attempt to increase product differentiation.
   e do all of the above.

16 The construction cost of a building is $100,000. The conventional depreciation allowance is 5 percent per year. At the end of the first year the market value of the building is $80,000. For the first year, the depreciation cost is
   a $20,000 to an accountant or an economist.
   b $5,000 to an accountant or an economist.
   c $5,000 to an accountant but $20,000 to an economist.
   d $20,000 to an accountant but $5,000 to an economist.
   e none of the above.

17 The marginal cost curve slopes upward because of
   a diminishing marginal utility.
   b diminishing marginal returns.
   c technological inefficiency.
   d economic inefficiency.
   e none of the above.

18 In economics, the long run is a time frame in which
   a one year or more elapses.
   b all resources are variable.
   c all resources are fixed.
   d there is at least one fixed resource and at least one variable resource.
   e all resources are variable but plant size is fixed.

19 A firm has $200 in explicit costs and sells the resulting output for $250. The normal rate of profit is 10 percent. Which of the following statements is *true*?
   a Implicit costs are $25.
   b Economic profits are $20.
   c Economic profits are $50.
   d Economic profits exceed accounting profits.
   e Explicit costs exceed implicit costs.

20 If *AFC* is falling, *MC* must be
   a rising.
   b falling.
   c above *AFC*.
   d below *AFC*.
   e none of the above.

21 If all inputs are increased by 10 percent and output increases by more than 10 percent, it must be the case that
   a average total cost is decreasing.
   b average total cost is increasing.
   c the *LRAC* curve is positively sloped.
   d there are economies of scale.
   e there are diseconomies of scale.

22 In Table P4.1, which method(s) of making a medical hologram is/are technologically efficient?
   a 1 only
   b 2 only
   c 3 only
   d 1, 2, and 3
   e 1 and 3 only

TABLE **P4.I** THREE METHODS OF MAKING ONE MEDICAL HOLOGRAM

	Quantities of Inputs	
Method	Labour	Capital
I	5	10
2	10	15
3	15	5

23 Refer to Table P4.1. If the price of labour is $20 per unit and the price of capital is $10 per unit, which method(s) is/are economically efficient?
   a 1 only
   b 2 only
   c 3 only
   d 2 and 3 only
   e 1 and 3 only

24 In a contestable market, the
   a Herfindahl–Hirschman Index is always low.
   b Herfindahl–Hirschman Index is always high.
   c firm in the market earns large economic profits.
   d firm in the market might play an entry deterrence game.
   e firm in the market will not use a limit-pricing strategy.

25 A strategy where a player matches in the current period the strategy the other player used in the previous period is called a
   a tit-for-tat strategy.
   b trigger strategy.
   c duopoly strategy.
   d dominant firm strategy.
   e golden rule strategy.

ANSWERS

Problem

a The individual firm's demand curve and marginal revenue curve is a horizontal line at P_{pc}.

b See Fig. P4.1(b) Solution. Each firm is making economic profit because at output q_{pc}, price (P_{pc} = average revenue) is greater than average total cost.

c See Fig. P4.1(a) Solution. In response to economic profit, new firms enter the industry, causing the industry supply curve to shift rightward until it reaches S_1. When price has fallen to P^{LR}_{pc}, economic profit has been eliminated and each firm is earning normal profit only.

d The monopolist's demand curve is the industry demand curve D_0. The monopolist does not have a supply curve since she can choose a combination of price and quantity.

e See Fig. P4.1(a) Solution.

f Even though the monopolist is earning economic profit, nothing happens in the long run because legal barriers prevent new entry. Long-run equilibrium price and output are the same as short-run price (P_m) and output (Q_m).

g Monopoly is less efficient than perfect competition, by the shaded area of deadweight loss indicated on Fig. P4.1(a) Solution.

h See Fig. P4.1(b) Solution. Since the firm is in long-run equilibrium, the downward-sloping demand curve must be tangent to the ATC curve at the equilibrium price P_{pc}.

i See Fig. P4.1(b) Solution. A profit-maximizing firm chooses the output (q_{mc}) where MC intersects MR. Hence the MR curve must intersect MC at q_{mc}. This is a long-run equilibrium because the firm is earning zero economic profit, so there is no incentive for entry or exit.

j Under monopolistic competition, ATC is higher (P_{pc}) than under perfect competition (P^{LR}_{pc}), implying less efficiency. However, the loss in allocative efficiency of monopolistic competition must be weighed against the gain in increased product variety.

Midterm Examination

1 e Monopoly has no supply curve. (302–305)

2 d See text discussion. (309–312)

3 d Highest possible price to sell Q_2. (326–329)

4 e Long-run economic profit per unit = zero. (326–329)

FIGURE **P4.1** SOLUTION

(a) Industry

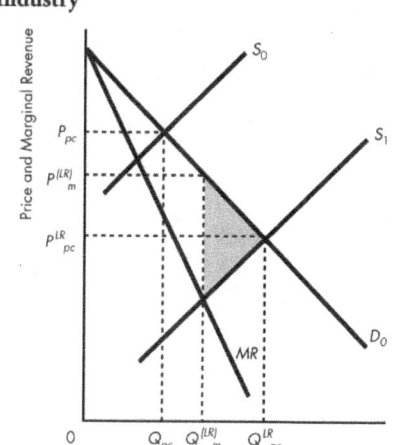

(b) Firm

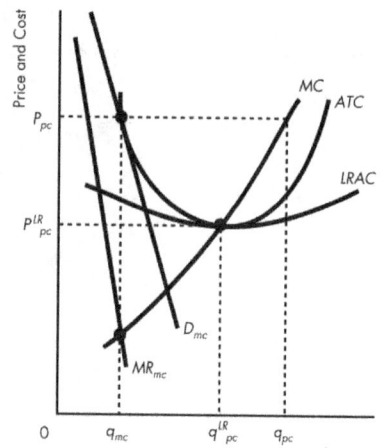

ⓔ **5 d** Need demand curve to identify price. (302–305)

6 c If demand is inelastic then $MR < 0$. But MR must always be > 0 to intersect (positive) MC. (302–305)

7 d Horizontal at market price. Infinite elasticity. (274–275)

8 d Economic profit/loss is a signal for supply shifts. Profit attracts entry of new firms. (280–283)

9 a Advertising affects fixed (and therefore total) costs, not marginal costs. (330–333)

10 a Outcome of game. (344–352)

ⓔ **11 e** Firm at Q where $P = MC$, but losing $ since $AR < ATC$. Need AVC information to determine if **a** or **d** is correct. (276–279)

12 b Increasing costs as industry Q increases. (286–289)

13 a AFC is irrelevant. Maximizing profit $\neq$ maximizing revenue. **d**, **e** might be true depending on P. (276–279)

14 b Perfect price discrimination has zero deadweight loss; all consumer surplus is captured as profit. (309–312)

15 e Enhanced information and variety may or may not justify increased (opportunity) cost of selling costs. (330–333)

16 c Accountant's depreciation = (5%) × $100,000. Economist's depreciation = Δ market value. (228–230)

17 b Diminishing marginal returns implies decreasing MP causing increasing MC. (257–261)

18 b Definition. All inputs and plant size are variable. (252)

19 e Implicit costs = 0.10 ($200) = $20; economic profit = $25; accounting profit = $50. (228–230)

20 e AFC is always falling; no necessary relation to MC. See Text Fig. 11.5. (257–261)

21 d Definition of downward-sloping $LRAC$. Since all inputs variable, **a** and **b** are irrelevant. (262–265)

22 e 2 uses more labour and more capital than 1. (231–232)

23 a 1 costs $200; 2 and 3 cost $350. (231–232)

24 d HHI may be high or low since it measures actual, not potential, competition. Firm may use entry deterrence or limit pricing and will not earn large profits. (353–355)

25 a Definition. (353–355)

KEY CONCEPTS

Externalities in Our Lives

Externality is cost or benefit from production activities or consumption activities that affects people who are not part of the original activity. Externalities may be negative or positive.

- ♦ **Negative externality**—imposes external cost.

  - Negative production externality (pollution)

  - Negative consumption externality (tobacco smoke)

- ♦ **Positive externality**—provides external benefit.

  - Positive production externality (honeybees pollinating nearby fruit orchard)

  - Positive consumption externality (flu vaccination)

- ♦ Externalities create market failure (*in*efficiency). Markets overproduce goods/services with negative externalities and underproduce goods/services with positive externalities.

Negative Externality: Pollution

Many people assume all pollution must be stopped. Economic analysis of pollution, however, evaluates costs and benefits to identify efficient amounts of pollution.

- ♦ **Marginal private cost** *(MC)*—cost of producing additional unit of good/service paid by producer.

- ♦ **Marginal external cost**—cost of producing additional unit of good/service that falls on people other than the producer.

- ♦ **Marginal social cost** *(MSC)*—MC incurred by entire society; MSC = MC + Marginal external cost.

Figure 16.1 (Text Fig. 16.2) shows the marginal private cost curve, which is also the supply curve ($S = MC$), and the marginal social cost curve (*MSC*). For any quantity produced, marginal external cost = vertical distance between $S = MC$ and *MSC* curves. Demand curve is the same as the marginal social benefit curve ($D = MSB$).

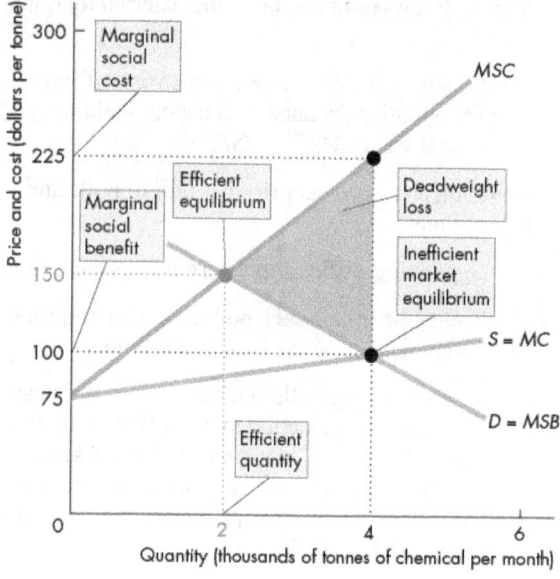

FIGURE 16.1 INEFFICIENCY WITH AN EXTERNAL COST

- ♦ Efficient equilibrium (where $D = MSB$ intersects *MSC*) takes into account all (private + external) costs.

- ♦ Private market equilibrium is inefficient (where $D = MSB$ intersects $S = MC$) because does not take into account marginal external cost.

♦ Private market equilibrium produces too much of a good with an external cost and creates deadweight loss (from $MSC > MSB$ for all units beyond efficient quantity).

Inefficiency from externalities can sometimes be reduced by establishing property rights.

  ♦ **Property rights** are a legally established title to ownership, use, and disposal of factors of production and goods and services.

  ♦ **Coase theorem**—If property rights exist and **transactions costs** (opportunity costs of conducting transactions) are low, there will be no externalities and private transactions are efficient. Who has property rights will *not* affect the efficiency of the outcome.

Where property rights cannot be established or transactions costs are high, other government actions can achieve efficiency even with negative externalities.

  ♦ Taxes—to create incentives for producers to cut back negative externalities, government can impose **Pigovian tax** equal to the external marginal cost.

    • This makes MSC curve the relevant MC curve for polluting producer's decision, yielding output where $MSC = MSB$.

  ♦ Emission charges—set price per unit of pollution that polluter pays.

    • In practice, difficult to determine correct price.

  ♦ Marketable permits—each polluter given pollution limit (permit) that can be bought and sold.

    • Firms reducing pollution below their limit can sell "excess" reduction to other firms who then can pollute more. In a competitive market for permits, price of permits = marginal external cost of pollution, yielding an efficient outcome where $MSC = MSB$.

Positive Externality: Knowledge

Knowledge from education and research creates private and social benefits.

  ♦ **Marginal private benefit** *(MB)*—benefit from one additional unit of good/service received by consumer.

  ♦ **Marginal external benefit**—benefit from one additional unit of good/service enjoyed by people other than the consumer.

♦ **Marginal social benefit** *(MSB)*—MB enjoyed by entire society; $MSB = MB +$ Marginal external benefit.

Figure 16.2 (Text Fig. 16.6) shows the marginal private benefit curve, which is also the demand curve ($D = MB$), and the marginal social benefit curve (MSB). For any quantity consumed, marginal external benefit = vertical distance between $D = MB$ and MSB curves. Supply curve is same as marginal social cost curve ($S = MSC$).

FIGURE 16.2 INEFFICIENCY WITH AN EXTERNAL BENEFIT

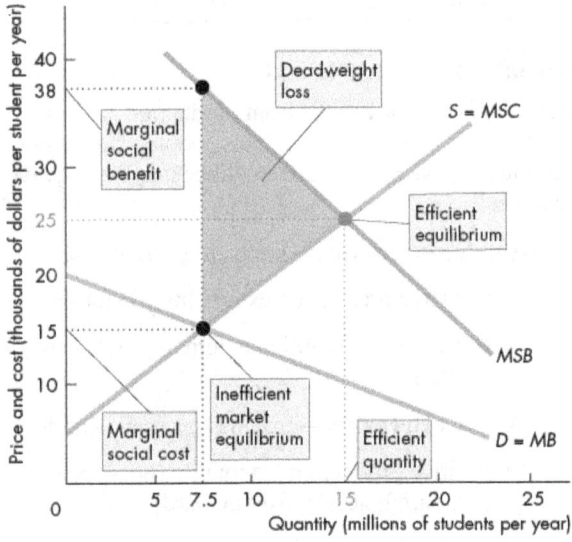

♦ Efficient equilibrium (where MSB intersects $S = MSC$) takes into account all (private + external) benefits.

♦ Private market equilibrium is inefficient (where $D = MB$ intersects $S = MSC$) because does not take into account marginal external benefit.

♦ Private market equilibrium produces too little of a good with external benefit and creates deadweight loss (from lost $MSB > MSC$ for all units below efficient quantity).

Government actions can achieve efficiency even with positive externalities.

  ♦ **Public provision**—government provides the good/service (public education) and charges price below cost that equals marginal private benefit at the efficient quantity.

    • Additional cost paid by taxpayers, to yield total cost = $S = MSC$.

◆ **Subsidies**—payment by government to private producers of goods/services.

• If subsidy is equal to external marginal benefit, supply curve becomes $S = MSC -$ subsidy, yielding efficient equilibrium quantity.

◆ **Vouchers**—government-provided tokens to households for buying specified goods/services.

• Value of voucher = marginal external benefit, making *MSB* curve the market demand curve and yielding efficient equilibrium outcome.

◆ **Patents** and **copyrights**—provide creators of knowledge with **intellectual property rights** in their discoveries; help ensure creator profits.

• Patents and copyrights encourage development of new knowledge, but create temporary monopoly, so gains from increased knowledge must be balanced against loss from monopoly.

HELPFUL HINTS

1 A competitive market will produce the quantity of output at which marginal private cost is equal to marginal private benefit. The allocatively efficient quantity is the quantity at which marginal social cost is equal to marginal social benefit.

The difference between *marginal social cost* and *marginal private cost* is marginal external cost, and the difference between *marginal social benefit* and *marginal private benefit* is marginal external benefit.

In most economic activities, people who are not part of the original activity are not affected, so there are no external costs or benefits. This means private and social costs and benefits coincide and competitive markets are efficient. However, when third parties are affected, there are external costs or benefits and competitive markets are *not* efficient. Markets overproduce goods/services with external costs (negative externalities) and underproduce goods/services with external benefits (positive externalities).

2 Competitive markets with externalities are not efficient because some of the costs or benefits are *external*. If those costs or benefits could be *internalized* somehow, then the market would be efficient. There are two main approaches to internalizing externalities discussed in this chapter.

The first is to establish and strictly enforce property rights. Then, costs imposed on people who are not part of the original activity can be recovered through the legal process and will be paid by those involved in the activity: the costs become internal (private).

The second approach to internalizing externalities is to tax activities that generate external costs and subsidize activities that generate external benefits. By charging a tax equal to the external costs, the entire cost becomes internal. Similarly, by paying a subsidy equal to the external benefits, the entire benefit becomes internal.

3 Figure 16.1 in the Key Concepts shows the production of a good with a negative externality (pollution). Note that *the efficient level of pollution is not zero*—efficient *Q* is *not Q* = 0. Generally, costs saved by reducing pollution to zero are less than the benefits lost (benefits from consuming goods whose production created pollution as a by-product).

SELF-TEST

True/False and Explain

Externalities in Our Lives

1 Externalities arise only from production.

2 Flu vaccination is an example of a positive production externality.

3 A negative production externality imposes an external cost.

Negative Externality: Pollution

4 If the production of a good involves no external cost, then marginal social cost is equal to marginal private cost.

5 If negative externalities exist, marginal social cost and marginal external cost are equivalent.

6 Externalities often arise from the absence of private property rights.

7 Assigning property rights always solves the problem of a negative externality.

8 Pigovian taxes create incentives for producers to cut back negative externalities.

9 Firms with a low marginal cost of reducing pollution will buy marketable pollution permits.

10 When external costs are present, the private market produces more than the efficient level of output.

11 The efficient quantity of pollution is zero.

Positive Externality: Knowledge

12 The existence of external benefits means that marginal social cost is greater than marginal private cost.

13 The private market equilibrium for goods with external benefits has deadweight loss, but the private market outcome with external costs has no deadweight loss because too many goods are produced.

14 Patents encourage invention and innovation.

15 Copyrights contribute to the development of knowledge, so they have no economic cost.

Multiple-Choice

Externalities in Our Lives

1 An externality is a cost or benefit arising from an economic activity that falls on
   a consumers but not producers.
   b producers but not consumers.
   c free riders.
   d rivals.
   e none of the above.

2 The production of too few goods with positive externalities is an example of
   a market failure.
   b government failure.
   c producer sovereignty.
   d consumer sovereignty.
   e external costs.

3 Which of the following illustrates the concept of external cost?
   a Bad weather reduces the size of the wheat crop.
   b A reduction in the size of the wheat crop causes income of wheat farmers to fall.
   c Smoking harms the health of the smoker.
   d Smoking harms the health of nearby nonsmokers.
   e Public health services reduce the transmission of disease.

Negative Externality: Pollution

4 The income elasticity of demand for a better environment is
   a negative.
   b zero.
   c positive.
   d trendy.
   e impossible to know without additional information.

5 Levels of acid rain caused by air pollution are
  a less than efficient levels due to external costs.
  b less than efficient levels due to external benefits.
  c more than efficient levels due to external costs.
  d more than efficient levels due to external benefits.
  e decreasing the earth's average temperature.

6 Figure 16.3 shows demand for good *A* as well as the marginal private cost (*MC*) and marginal social cost (*MSC*) associated with production of good *A*. Production of the sixth unit of output generates an *external*
  a cost of $1.50.
  b cost of $3.00.
  c cost of $6.00.
  d benefit of $3.00.
  e benefit of $6.00.

FIGURE **16.3**

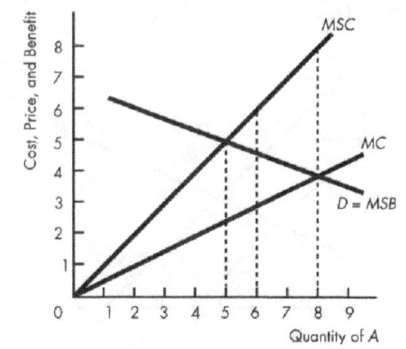

7 In Fig. 16.3, how many units of good *A* will be produced in an unregulated market?
  a 0 units
  b 5 units
  c 6 units
  d 8 units
  e impossible to calculate without additional information

8 In Fig. 16.3, what is the efficient quantity of good *A*?
  a 0 units
  b 5 units
  c 6 units
  d 8 units
  e impossible to calculate without additional information

9 At the current level of production of buckyballs, marginal social benefit is less than marginal social cost. To achieve allocative efficiency,
  a buckyballs should be taxed.
  b buckyballs should not be produced.
  c output of buckyballs should increase.
  d output of buckyballs should decrease.
  e property rights in buckyballs should be established.

10 The production of too many goods with negative externalities is an example of
  a redistribution.
  b consumer sovereignty.
  c producer sovereignty.
  d public failure.
  e market failure.

11 An externality is
  a the amount by which price exceeds marginal private cost.
  b the amount by which price exceeds marginal social cost.
  c the effect of government regulation on market price and output.
  d someone who consumes a good without paying for it.
  e a cost or benefit that arises from an activity but affects people not part of the original activity.

12 The marginal private cost curve (*MC*) is a positively sloped straight line starting at the origin. If marginal external costs per unit of output are constant, the marginal social cost curve is a positively sloped straight line
  a parallel to and above *MC*.
  b parallel to and below *MC*.
  c starting at the origin and above *MC*.
  d starting at the origin and below *MC*.
  e identical to *MC*.

13 A market economy tends to _____ goods with negative externalities and _____ goods with positive externalities.
  a overproduce; overproduce
  b overproduce; underproduce
  c underproduce; overproduce
  d underproduce; underproduce
  e produce; consume

14 Policies for correcting problems of negative externalities include all of the following *except*
  a emission charges.
  b patents.
  c quantitative limits.
  d Pigovian taxes.
  e marketable permits.

15 A battery acid producer pollutes the water upstream from nude swimmers belonging to the Polar Bear Club. If transactions costs are low, the quantity of pollution will be efficient
a only if Ronald Coase is a member of the Polar Bear Club.
b only if Ronald Coase is not a member of the Polar Bear Club.
c only if water property rights are assigned to the producer.
d only if water property rights are assigned to the Polar Bear Club.
e if water property rights are assigned either to the producer or the Polar Bear Club.

16 Refer to Table 16.1. If the fertilizer market is perfectly competitive and unregulated, output (in tonnes) is
a 1.
b 2.
c 3.
d 4.
e 5.

TABLE **16.1**   CHEMICAL FERTILIZER MARKET

Output (tonnes)	Marginal Private Benefit ($)	Marginal Social Benefit ($)	Marginal Private Cost ($)	Marginal Social Cost ($)
1	140	140	50	80
2	120	120	60	90
3	100	100	70	100
4	80	80	80	110
5	60	60	90	120

17 Refer to Table 16.1. Fertilizer has a per-unit marginal external
a cost of $100.
b benefit of $100.
c cost of $30.
d benefit of $30.
e cost of $0.

18 Refer to Table 16.1. The efficient output of fertilizer (in tonnes) is
a 1.
b 2.
c 3.
d 4.
e 5.

Positive Externality: Knowledge

19 The marginal private benefit curve (*MB*) is a negatively sloped straight line. If marginal external benefits per unit of output are positive and decreasing with additional output, the marginal social benefit curve is a negatively sloped straight line
a parallel to and above *MB*.
b parallel to and below *MB*.
c above and steeper than *MB*.
d above and flatter than *MB*.
e below and flatter than *MB*.

20 Figure 16.4 shows the demand curve for good *B*, the marginal social benefit (*MSB*) curve, and marginal private and social cost (*MC* = *MSC*) curve. How many units of good *B* will be produced and consumed in an unregulated market?
a 0
b 3
c 5
d 6
e 9

FIGURE **16.4**

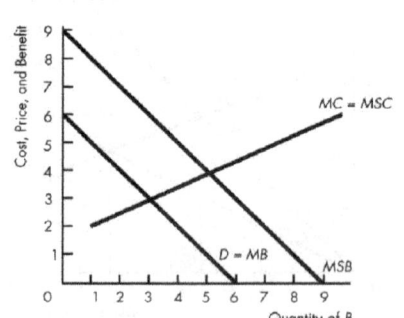

21 In Fig. 16.4, what is the efficient quantity (in units) of good *B*?
a 0
b 3
c 5
d 6
e 9

22 In Fig. 16.4, which of the following government policies would induce the market to achieve allocative efficiency?
a Tax the production of *B* at $3 per unit.
b Tax the production of *B* at $4 per unit.
c Provide vouchers for consumption of *B* at $1 per unit.
d Provide vouchers for consumption of *B* at $3 per unit.
e Provide vouchers for consumption of *B* at $4 per unit.

23 Policies to achieve allocative efficiency when there are external benefits include
  a intellectual property rights.
  b subsidies.
  c public provision.
  d all of the above.
  e none of the above.

24 Knowledge, as a factor of production,
  a displays diminishing marginal productivity.
  b creates external costs.
  c has costs totalling those paid to the patent holder.
  d is encouraged by intellectual property rights.
  e is all of the above.

25 When market failure occurs, government will act to reduce inefficiency. This is a prediction of a
  a fair results theory of government behaviour.
  b fair rules theory of government behaviour.
  c social interest theory of government behaviour.
  d public choice theory of government behaviour.
  e rent-seeking theory of government behaviour.

Short Answer Problems

1 Your roommate is an environmentalist who is appalled at the economic concept of an "efficient" level of pollution. She argues that since everyone agrees pollution is "bad," society must work toward eliminating all pollution. How would you, as an economics major, convince her that it is not in society's best interests to eliminate all pollution?

2 The production of steel also produces pollution and generates external costs. Suppose government attempts to solve the problem by imposing a tax on steel producers. At the after-tax level of output, we observe the original marginal social cost curve is below the demand curve. Is the after-tax level of output efficient? If not, should steel production, and therefore pollution production, be increased or decreased?

3 Two prairie pioneers, Jethro and Hortense, have adjacent fields. Because they get along so well and always work out any problems that arise, they have not bothered to put up a fence. Then one day Jethro buys a new pig, Babe. Babe sometimes wanders into Hortense's field and eats her corn. If Babe would only stay on Jethro's farm, he would eat valueless garbage. Suppose that Babe eats $500 worth of Hortense's corn per year (a negative externality imposed on

Hortense) and that to build a fence between the farms costs $300. No property rights to keep animals off the fields have been established yet.

  a If the property right is given to Jethro so Babe can continue to wander, will Hortense build a fence? Explain.

  b If, instead, the property right is given to Hortense, so that she can charge Jethro for the corn Babe eats, will Jethro build a fence? Explain.

  c Explain how this example illustrates the Coase theorem.

4 Lever Sisters Company produces Flatulost, a popular room deodorizer. Unfortunately, the production process releases sulphur dioxide into the atmosphere. The marginal private cost (*MC*) to Lever Sisters of producing Flatulost is

$$MC = 1Q_S$$

The marginal social cost (*MSC*) is

$$MSC = 3/2Q_S$$

The demand curve for Flatulost (there are no external benefits) is

$$P = 12 - 1/2Q_D$$

Q_S is the quantity of Flatulost supplied, P is the price of Flatulost in dollars, and Q_D is the quantity demanded.

  a In an unregulated market, what is the equilibrium quantity of Flatulost? the equilibrium price?

  b To achieve allocative efficiency, what should be the equilibrium quantity of Flatulost? the equilibrium price?

  c Compare the unregulated market quantity and price with the allocatively efficient quantity and price.

  d The government wants to impose a tax on Flatulost to achieve the allocatively efficient quantity of output. What should the tax be?

5 The first two columns of Table 16.2 give the demand schedule for education in Hicksville, while the third column gives the marginal social cost. Since education generates external benefits, marginal social benefit given in the last column is greater than marginal private benefit.

  a Represent the data in Table 16.2 graphically.

TABLE 16.2 EDUCATION IN HICKSVILLE

Quantity (number of students)	Marginal Private Benefit ($)	Marginal Social Cost ($)	Marginal Social Benefit ($)
100	500	200	800
200	400	250	700
300	300	300	600
400	200	350	500
500	100	400	400
600	0	450	300

b What equilibrium price and quantity would result if the market for education is unregulated?

c What is the allocatively efficient quantity of students in Hicksville?

6 In an attempt to address the inefficient level of education in Hicksville, the town council decides to publicly support schooling. The council offers a $200 voucher to each student who buys a year of education.

a Draw the new marginal private benefit curve, which includes the voucher, on your graph and label it MB_1.

b What are the approximate new equilibrium price and quantity?

7 The Hicksville town council increases the voucher to $400.

a Draw another marginal private benefit curve, which includes the voucher, on your graph and label it MB_2.

b What are the approximate corresponding equilibrium price and quantity?

c What level of voucher will achieve the efficient quantity of education?

8 What are the benefits and costs of creating intellectual property rights for the creation of new knowledge?

ANSWERS

True/False and Explain

1 F Externalities can arise from production or consumption and be negative or positive. (372–374)

2 F Positive consumption externality. (372–374)

3 T Positive production or consumption externality provides external benefit. (372–374)

4 T $MSC = MC$ + marginal external cost. (375–379)

5 F $MSC = MC$ + marginal external cost. (375–379)

6 T Property rights allow recovery of (external) costs. (375–379)

7 F True if transactions costs are low; false otherwise. (375–379)

8 T See text discussion. (375–379)

9 F Firms with low marginal cost of reducing pollution sell permits; firms with high marginal cost of reducing pollution buy. (375–379)

10 T Where MC (instead of MSC) intersects demand. (375–379)

11 F Efficient quantity where $D = MSB$ intersects MSC production (including pollution). (375–379)

ℂ **12 F** External benefits affect MSB, not MSC; $MSB = MB$ + marginal external benefit. (379–383)

ℂ **13 F** Both have deadweight loss; with external costs, deadweight loss is excess MSC over MSB for units produced beyond the efficient quantity. (379–383)

14 T Intellectual property rights overcome the positive externality problem of knowledge. (379–383)

15 F Copyrights are monopolies with associated inefficiencies; but the benefits of new knowledge are presumed to outweigh the costs of monopoly. (379–383)

Multiple-Choice

1 e Falls on people who are not part of the original activity. (372–374)

2 a Markets fail to produce efficient quantity of goods with positive externalities. (372–374)

3 d Cost falls on people who are not part of the original activity. (372–374)

4 c Better environment is a normal good, so $\eta_y > 0$. (375–379)

5 c   Market overproduction of good with negative externalities (external costs). (375–379)

6 b   Vertical distance between *MSC* and *MC* at $Q = 6$. (375–379)

7 d   Where *MC* intersects demand. (375–379)

8 b   Where *MSC* intersects demand. (375–379)

9 d   Draw graph. We don't know if positive, negative, or any externality. (375–379)

10 e   Failure to achieve allocative efficiency because external costs not taken into account in private, market decisions. (375–379)

11 e   Definition. (375–379)

12 a   *MC* shifts leftward by vertical distance equal to marginal external cost per unit. (375–379)

13 b   Outcomes of market failure. (375–379)

14 b   Patents correct problems of positive externalities. (375–379)

15 e   This is the Coase theorem. (375–379)

16 d   Where $MB = MC = 80$. (375–379)

17 c $MSC - MC$ is constant. (375–379)

18 c   Where $MSB = MSC$. (375–379)

19 c   Similar to Text Fig. 16.6. (379–383)

20 b   Where *MC* intersects demand. (379–383)

21 c   Where *MC* intersects *MSB*. (379–383)

22 d   Value voucher = marginal external benefit = vertical distance between *MB* and *MSB*. (379–383)

23 d   All move output to where $MSB = MSC$. (379–383)

24 d   No diminishing marginal productivity; creates external benefits; patent monopoly creates loss from restricted use. (379–383)

25 c   It is in the public interest to achieve efficiency. (379–383)

Short Answer Problems

1   We all want to eliminate pollution, *ceteris paribus*, but every action, including reducing pollution, has a cost. Once again, the key concept underlying the economic argument is opportunity cost. What is the opportunity cost of reducing pollution, or what does society have to give up to achieve a pollution-free environment?

Small reductions in pollution are relatively inexpensive—eliminating lead from gasoline and paint, conserving energy to reduce output from coal-fired electrical plants, etc. But to eliminate all pollution would mean eliminating all cars and airplanes, outlawing all power except solar and hydroelectric power, shutting down most factories, etc. The cost of eliminating *all* pollution is enormous, and that additional cost is far greater than the additional benefits from further reductions in pollution. Therefore some level of pollution is efficient. Pollution is part of the opportunity cost of the benefits we receive from driving or flying instead of walking, from enjoying the comfort of air conditioning in hot weather, and from enjoying goods produced in factories. The efficient level of pollution balances the marginal social cost of the pollution against the marginal social benefit of the production and consumption associated with that level of pollution.

2   Since the marginal social cost curve is below the demand curve at the after-tax output, marginal social cost is less than marginal benefit. This means that the tax has been set too high; it has been set at a level in excess of the external cost. As a result, the after-tax level of steel production will be less than the efficient level. The level of steel production and pollution production should be increased by decreasing the amount of the tax.

3 a   Hortense will build a fence. Although the fence costs $300 per year, it saves her the $500 in lost corn that Babe would otherwise eat.

b   Jethro will build a fence. $300 per year is less than the $500 per year he would have to pay Hortense for Babe's wanderings.

c   The Coase theorem states that if transactions costs are low, property rights are established and there are no externalities—an efficient outcome occurs regardless of who is assigned the property right. Because Jethro and Hortense can work out their problems amicably, transactions costs are low. Building a fence eliminates the negative externality of the wandering pig and occurs regardless of which pioneer is assigned the property right. The outcome is efficient because, for this one decision, the $300 cost to society of the fence is less than the $500 cost of consumed corn.

4 a In an unregulated market, the equilibrium quantity would be determined by the intersection of the supply (*MC*) and demand curves. In equilibrium, $Q_S = Q_D = Q^*$. Setting the *MC* equation equal to the demand equation yields

$$1Q^* = 12 - 1/2Q^*$$
$$3/2Q^* = 12$$
$$Q^* = 8$$

To solve for the equilibrium price (*P**), substitute *Q** into the demand (or into the *MC*) equation:

$$P^* = 12 - 1/2Q^*$$
$$P^* = 12 - 1/2\ (8)$$
$$P^* = 8$$

b In order to achieve efficiency, *MSC* must equal marginal social benefit (*MSB*). Since there are no external benefits, the demand curve is also the *MSB* curve. In equilibrium, $Q_S = Q_D = Q^*$. To find the equilibrium quantity, set the *MSC* equation equal to the demand equation:

$$3/2Q^* = 12 - 1/2Q^*$$
$$2Q^* = 12$$
$$Q^* = 6$$

To solve for the equilibrium price (*P**), substitute *Q** into the demand (or into the *MSC*) equation:

$$P^* = 12 - 1/2Q^*$$
$$P^* = 12 - 1/2\ (6)$$
$$P^* = 9$$

c Compared with the efficient outcomes, the unregulated market produces too much Flatulost (8 units versus 6) and the product sells at too low a price ($8 versus $9).

d The tax should be equal to the cost differential (*MSC* – *MC*) at the optimum output of 6 units. Since the *MSC* curve = $1.5 \times MC$ curve, the tax should be 50 percent.

5 a Figure 16.5 graphically represents the data in Table 16.2. The demand for education is given by the marginal private benefit curve (*MB*), the marginal social cost curve is *MSC*, and the marginal social benefit curve is *MSB*. Ignore the other curves for now.

b In an unregulated market, equilibrium price and quantity are determined by intersecting *MB* and *MC* curves. Equilibrium price is $300; equilibrium quantity is 300 students.

FIGURE **16.5**

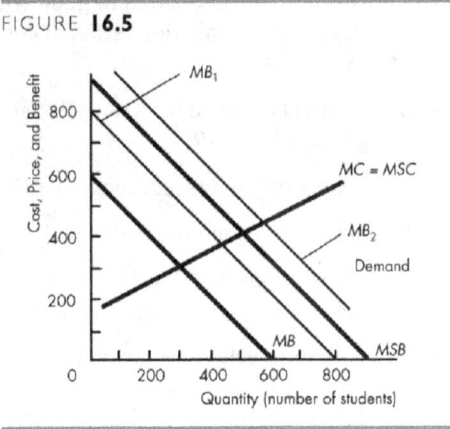

c Since there are no external costs, the efficient quantity is determined by the intersection of the *MSC* and *MSB* curves. Efficiency is attained at a quantity of 500 students.

6 a The voucher increases the marginal private benefit to each student by the amount of the voucher, $200. The new *MB* curve, labelled MB_1, is included in Fig. 16.5.

b The new equilibrium after the $200 voucher is at the intersection of the *MSC* and MB_1 curves. The price of a unit of education is approximately $370 and there are approximately 430 students.

7 a With a voucher of $400 per student, the *MB* curve shifts to MB_2 in Fig. 16.5.

b With this voucher the equilibrium is at the intersection of the *MSC* and MB_2 curves. The corresponding price of a unit of education is approximately $430 and the number of students is approximately 570.

c In order to achieve an efficient outcome, the voucher must make the *MB* curve coincide with the *MSB* curve. This requires a voucher of $300 per student.

8 Intellectual property rights create incentives for individuals to create new knowledge by granting the inventor a limited monopoly to benefit from the application of her idea. Without the property right, anyone could freely use the idea and there would be little profit to the inventor. The limited monopoly, although necessary as an incentive to produce knowledge, has a social cost—the restriction of knowledge-based output below the efficient, competitive quantity.

Chapter 17
Public Goods and Common Resources

Classifying Goods and Resources

A good/service/resource is either

- **excludable**—can prevent others from consuming it, or

- **nonexcludable**—can*not* prevent others from consuming it

and is either

- **rival**—one person's consumption decreases amount available for others, or

- **nonrival**—one person's consumption does *not* decreases amount available for others

These characteristics are used to classify all goods/services/resources into four types:

- **Private good**—rival and excludable. Example: a hot dog.

- **Public good**—nonrival and nonexcludable; can be consumed simultaneously by everyone; no one can be excluded. Example: national defence.

- **Common resource**—rival and nonexcludable; a unit can be used only once, but no one can be excluded from using other available units. Example: ocean fish.

- **Natural monopoly good**—nonrival and excludable; with economies of scale and low marginal cost, increased consumption reduces cost, but buyers can be excluded. Example: cable television.

Public Goods

Public goods create **free-rider** (someone who consumes without paying) **problem**—no one has an incentive to pay for a public good.

Efficient quantity of public good occurs at the quantity where marginal social benefit equals marginal social cost.

- Private provision of a public good creates a free-rider problem and provides less than the efficient quantity of the good.

- Government provision can provide an efficient quantity of a public good, where politicians compete for votes of well-informed voters.

The quantity of government provision of a public good generally depends on political marketplace and actions of voters, politicians, and bureaucrats.

- Politicians follow **principle of minimum differentiation**—tendency for competitors to make themselves identical to appeal to maximum number voters/clients.

- Voters may be **rationally ignorant**—deciding *not* to acquire information because cost of acquisition > expected benefit. Then politicians, influenced by bureaucrats and special interest lobbyists, may allow inefficient overprovision of a public good.

Types of political equilibrium:

- Social interest theory—predicts governments achieve efficiency because voters are fully informed.

- Public choice theory—predicts governments create inefficiency because voters are rationally ignorant.

Common Resources

Commonly owned resources create **tragedy of the commons**—overuse of a common resource because no one has an incentive to conserve and use it sustainably. Overfishing of Atlantic cod is an example.

◆ Sustainable catch is the quantity that can be caught year after year without depleting the stock.

◆ Overfishing occurs where maximum sustainable catch starts decreasing. Text Fig. 17.6 (p. 398) shows the maximum sustainable catch at 300,000 tonnes per year.

Figure 17.1 (Text Fig. 17.7) shows the tragedy of the commons outcome (overfishing equilibrium) and the efficient use outcome. The marginal cost curve (*MC*) shows the additional cost of keeping a boat and crew at sea long enough to catch an additional tonne of fish. The marginal social cost (*MSC*) curve shows the *MC* plus the external cost of stock depletion that makes it harder and more costly for others to catch fish. The marginal social benefit (*MSB*) curve shows the price consumers are willing to pay for an additional tonne of fish.

FIGURE 17.1

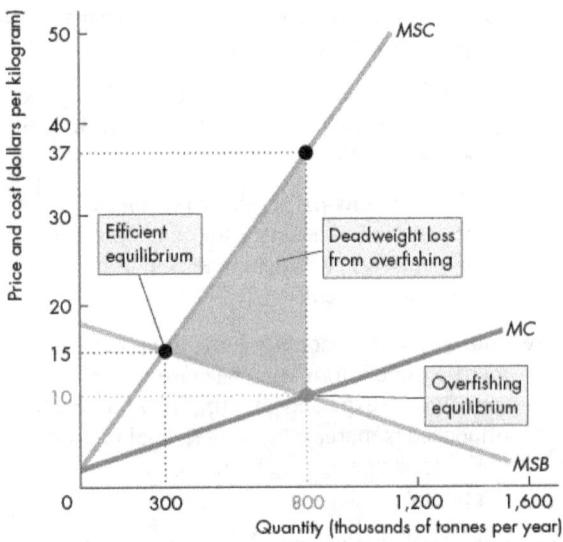

◆ Overfishing equilibrium—the unregulated equilibrium use of a common resource, is the quantity where *MC* = *MSB*. Overfishing occurs because the equilibrium of 800,000 tonnes is greater than the maximum sustainable production of 300,000 tonnes.

◆ Efficient equilibrium—the efficient use of a common resource is the quantity where *MSC* = *MSB*, or 300,000 tonnes.

Efficient use of a common resource requires incentives that confront users with marginal *social* consequences of their actions. Three main incentive methods:

◆ Property rights—assigning private property rights to a resource makes the *MSC* curve the same as the owner's *MC* curve, so owner will use the resource efficiently. But difficult to assign enforceable property rights to the ocean or the atmosphere.

◆ Quota—government sets quota at efficient quantity. Problems include incentives to cheat by increasing output and differing marginal costs among producers, so efficient producers might not get proper share of quotas.

◆ **Individual transferable quota (ITQ)**—production limit assigned to an individual, who can sell the quota to someone else. Market price of ITQ will equal marginal social benefit minus marginal cost at the efficient quantity, so producers with higher marginal costs will not produce.

HELPFUL HINTS

1 All goods provided by the government are not necessarily public goods. A public good is defined by being *nonrival* and *nonexcludable*, not by whether or not it is publicly provided. For example, many communities provide swimming pools and residential garbage pickup. Neither of these is a pure public good despite the fact that each may be provided by the government. In other communities, the same services are provided by the private market.

2 The nonrival and nonexcludable properties of pure public goods imply that we obtain the marginal benefit curve for the economy as a whole differently than for private goods.

For a private good, to obtain the demand curve for the whole economy, we sum the individual marginal benefit (demand) curves *horizontally*. For example, at a price of $7, suppose Max demands 5 units of a private good, Lisa demands 5 units, and total demand is 10 units. Because the private goods are rival and excludable, the units Max consumes must be different from the units Lisa consumes, and therefore must be added together to get total market demand.

But for a public good, to obtain the economy's marginal benefit curve we sum the individual marginal benefit curves *vertically*. For example, for the fifth unit of a public good, suppose Max is willing to pay $7 and

Lisa is willing to pay $7. Because public goods are nonrival and nonexcludable, both Max and Lisa can consume the fifth unit simultaneously. The total benefit from consuming the fifth unit is $7 + $7 = $14.

S E L F - T E S T

True/False and Explain

Classifying Goods and Resources

1 Cable television service is nonrival and excludable.

2 A movie you watch in a mostly empty theatre is both nonrival and nonexcludable.

3 Common resources are rival and nonexcludable.

Public Goods

4 Goods supplied by government are defined as public goods.

5 The excludability feature of goods leads to the free-rider problem.

6 The existence of public goods gives rise to the free-rider problem.

7 The economy's marginal benefit curve for a public good is obtained by adding the marginal benefits of each individual at each quantity of provision.

8 The private market will produce much less than the efficient quantity of pure public goods.

9 According to public choice theory, not only is there the possibility of market failure, there is also the possibility of "government failure."

10 Political parties tend to propose fundamentally different policies to give voters a clearer choice.

Common Resources

11 If the quantity of fish caught is less than the sustainable catch, the fish stock shrinks.

12 As the quantity of fish caught increases, the marginal social benefit of consuming fish decreases.

13 For a common resource, marginal social benefit is greater than marginal private benefit.

14 The efficient use of a common resource is the quantity where $MSC = MSB$.

15 Individual differences in marginal cost prevent an ITQ system from delivering an efficient outcome.

Multiple-Choice

Classifying Goods and Resources

1   When a city street is not congested, it is like a(n)
    a   external good.
    b   internal good.
    c   rival good.
    d   private good.
    e   public good.

2   A private good is
    1   rival.
    2   nonrival.
    3   excludable.
    4   nonexcludable.
    a   1 and 3
    b   1 and 4
    c   2 and 3
    d   2 and 4
    e   1 only

3   A common resource is
    1   rival.
    2   nonrival.
    3   excludable.
    4   nonexcludable.
    a   1 and 3
    b   1 and 4
    c   2 and 3
    d   2 and 4
    e   2 only

4   A public good is
    1   rival.
    2   nonrival.
    3   excludable.
    4   nonexcludable.
    a   1 and 3
    b   1 and 4
    c   2 and 3
    d   2 and 4
    e   4 only

5   Which of the following goods is nonexcludable?
    a   city bus
    b   toll bridge
    c   lighthouse
    d   art museum
    e   all of the above

Public Goods

6   Governments provide pure public goods like national defence because
    a   governments are more efficient than private firms at producing such goods.
    b   of free-rider problems that result in underproduction by private markets.
    c   people do not value national defence very highly.
    d   of the potential that private firms will make excess profits.
    e   of external costs.

7   The quantity of public goods produced by an unregulated market tends to be
    a   less than the efficient quantity.
    b   equal to the efficient quantity.
    c   greater than the efficient quantity.
    d   that which maximizes total public benefit.
    e   that which maximizes net public benefit.

8   The market demand curve for a *private* good is obtained by summing the individual marginal
    a   cost curves horizontally.
    b   cost curves vertically.
    c   benefit curves horizontally.
    d   benefit curves vertically.
    e   benefit curves diagonally.

9   The economy's total demand curve for a *public* good is obtained by summing the individual marginal
    a   cost curves horizontally.
    b   cost curves vertically.
    c   benefit curves horizontally.
    d   benefit curves vertically.
    e   benefit curves diagonally.

10 The efficient scale of provision of a public good occurs where
    a   total benefit is at a maximum.
    b   total benefit is at a minimum.
    c   marginal social benefit is at a maximum.
    d   marginal social benefit minus marginal social cost equals zero.
    e   marginal social cost is at a minimum.

11 Refer to Fig. 17.2, which shows the marginal social cost and marginal social benefit of defence satellites, which are a public good. The number of satellites a private market would supply is
a   0.
b   1.
c   2.
d   3.
e   4.

FIGURE **17.2**

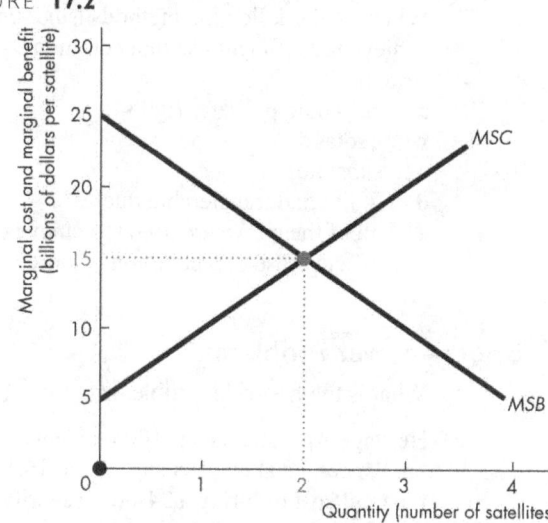

12 Refer to Fig. 17.2, which shows the marginal social cost and marginal social benefit of defence satellites, which are a public good. The efficient number of satellites is
a   0.
b   1.
c   2.
d   3.
e   4.

13 Refer to Fig. 17.2, which shows the marginal social cost and marginal social benefit of defence satellites, which are a public good. The number of satellites bureaucrats (who want to maximize their department's budget) would press for is
a   0.
b   1.
c   2.
d   3.
e   the efficient number.

14 According to public choice theory, a voter will favour a candidate whose political program is
a   perceived to offer the greatest personal benefit to the voter.
b   best for the majority of the people.
c   closest to the efficient use of resources.
d   favoured by the median voter.
e   all of the above.

15 Competitors who make themselves identical to appeal to the maximum number of voters illustrate the principle of
a   maximum differentiation.
b   minimum differentiation.
c   rational ignorance.
d   nonrivalry.
e   excludability.

16 Competition between two political parties will cause those parties to propose policies
a   that are quite different.
b   that are quite similar.
c   of rational ignorance.
d   that reduce the well-being of middle-income families and increase the well-being of the rich and the poor.
e   that equate total costs and total benefits.

17 Rational ignorance
a   results when the cost of information exceeds the benefits of having the information.
b   allows special interest groups to exert political influence.
c   combined with special interest groups can yield inefficient provision of public goods.
d   results in all of the above.
e   results in none of the above.

18 If voters have similar views and are well informed, the quantity of national defence provided by the government will tend to be
a   greater than the efficient quantity.
b   less than the efficient quantity.
c   the least costly quantity.
d   the quantity that maximizes net benefit.
e   the quantity that maximizes the Ministry of Defence budget.

19 On any given spending issue subject to a vote, the median voter is the one who favours
a the least spending.
b the most spending.
c the efficient level of spending.
d the average level of spending.
e spending more than the level favoured by half the voters and less than the level favoured by half the voters.

Common Resources

20 The tragedy of the commons is the absence of incentives to
a reduce marginal cost of common resources.
b prevent underuse of common resources.
c prevent overuse of common resources.
d discover new common resources.
e export wool in sixteenth-century England.

21 In the equilibrium for a common resource with no government regulation, marginal social
a benefit is greater than marginal benefit.
b cost is less than marginal cost.
c benefit equals marginal social cost.
d benefit is greater than marginal cost.
e benefit equals marginal cost.

22 In the equilibrium for a common resource, efficiency requires that marginal social
a benefit is greater than marginal benefit.
b cost is less than marginal cost.
c benefit equals marginal social cost.
d benefit is greater than marginal cost.
e benefit equals marginal cost.

23 ITQs are issued that will yield efficient output in the fishing market. ITQs will be traded at a market price equal to the marginal
a cost of producing the efficient output.
b social cost of producing the efficient output.
c social benefit of producing the efficient output minus the marginal cost.
d social benefit of producing the efficient output plus the marginal cost.
e social cost of producing the efficient output plus the marginal cost.

24 With a production quota for a common resource like fish,
a the common resources is always used efficiently.
b the marginal cost for each boat owner is the same.
c each boat owner has an incentive to stick to the production quota.
d each boat owner has an incentive to cheat on the production quota.
e none of the above.

25 Which of the following methods is *not* used to achieve the efficient use of a common resource?
a assigning property rights
b quotas
c subsidies
d individual transferable quotas
e all of the above are used to achieve the efficient use of a common resource

Short Answer Problems

1 What is the free-rider problem?

2 Heritage Apartments has 100 residents who are concerned about security. Table 16.1 gives the total cost of hiring a 24-hour security guard service as well as the marginal benefit to each of the residents

TABLE **17.1**

Number of Guards	Total Cost per Day ($)	Marginal Benefit per Resident ($)	Marginal Benefit to All Residents ($)
1	300	10	
2	600	4	
3	900	2	
4	1,200	1	

a Why is a security guard a public good for the residents of Heritage Apartments?

b Why will zero guards be hired if each of the residents must act individually?

c Complete the last column of Table 17.1 by computing the marginal benefit of security guards to all of the residents together.

3 Now suppose that the residents form an Apartment Council that acts as a governing body to address the security issue.

  a What is the optimal (allocatively efficient) number of guards? What is the net benefit at the optimal number of guards?

  b Show that net benefit is less for either one less guard or for one more guard than for the optimal number of guards.

  c How might the Apartment Council pay for the guards?

4 Two candidates are competing in an election for president of the Economics Club. The only issue dividing them is how much will be spent on the annual Economics Club party. It is well known that the seven voting members of the club (*A* through *G*) have the preferences in Table 17.2. These are strongly held preferences about exactly how much should be spent on the party.

TABLE **17.2** ECONOMICS CLUB PREFERENCES

Voting Member	Proposed Amount ($)
A	10
B	20
C	30
D	40
E	50
F	60
G	70

  a How much will each candidate propose to spend?

  b To demonstrate that your answer to part **a** is correct, consider the outcome of the following two contests:

    i Candidate 1 proposes the amount you gave in part **a** and candidate 2 proposes $1 less. Which candidate will win? Why?

    ii Candidate 1 proposes the amount you gave in part **a** and candidate 2 proposes $1 more. Which candidate will win? Why?

  c Suppose the Sociology Club is also electing a president and the same single issue prevails. It is well known that the seven voting members of the Sociology Club have the following strongly held preferences regarding exactly how much

should be spent on their party (see Table 17.3).

TABLE **17.3** SOCIOLOGY CLUB PREFERENCES

Voting Member	Proposed Amount ($)
T	0
U	0
V	0
W	40
X	41
Y	42
Z	43

How much will each of the two candidates propose in this case?

5 Explain why it may be rational for voters to be ignorant.

6 Table 17.4 gives three alternative income distributions for five individuals, *A* through *E*. Currently, income is distributed according to distribution 1 (the first column of the table). Consider alternative proposed distributions 2 and 3, one at a time.

TABLE **17.4**

Individual	Distribution 1 ($)	Distribution 2 ($)	Distribution 3 ($)
A	0	200	150
B	200	300	250
C	400	350	450
D	700	600	600
E	1,000	850	850

  a If distribution 2 is proposed as an alternative to distribution 1, will it have majority support? Why or why not?

  b If distribution 3 is proposed as an alternative to distribution 1, will it have majority support? Why or why not?

7 What is the tragedy of the commons problem, and why does it occur? Use the example of ocean fisheries to illustrate your explanation.

8 Figure 17.3 on the next page shows the marginal social cost, marginal private cost, and marginal social benefit curves for Atlantic Halibut fish, a common resource.

FIGURE **17.3**

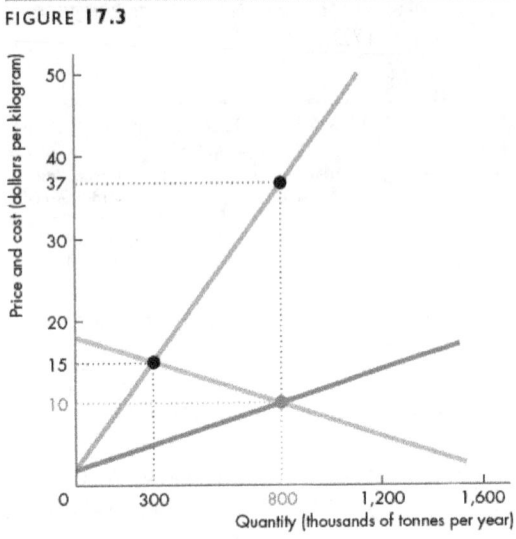

a   Label each curve.

b   What is the private equilibrium quantity of fish caught? What is the efficient quantity of fish caught? Illustrate the deadweight loss.

c   If the government were to set a production quota, what quota achieves the efficient outcome?

d   If the government issues individual transferable quotas (ITQs), what is the market price of an ITQ?

A N S W E R S

True/False and Explain

1   **T**   Your use of cable does not affect me, but buyers can be excluded from service. (392)

2   **F**   Nonrival because your attendance does not affect others' access to tickets, but those not paying can be excluded. (392)

3   **T**   Taking more fish from the ocean leaves less for others (rival), but no one can be prevented from fishing (nonexcludable). (392)

4   **F**   By definition, public goods are *nonrival* and *nonexcludable*. But governments also supply swimming pools, which are rival and excludable goods (see Helpful Hint 1). (393–397)

5   **F**   Nonexcludability creates a free-rider problem. (393–397)

6   **T**   Nonexcludability means there is no incentive for anyone to pay. (393–397)

7   **T**   See Helpful Hint **2**. (393–397)

8   **T**   Because there is no accounting for external benefits. (393–397)

9   **T**   Believe government agents act in own interest, not necessarily the public interest. (393–397)

10   **F**   Propose similar policies as vote-maximizing strategy appealing to the median voter. (393–397)

11   **F**   The fish stock grows. (398–403)

12   **T**   Consumers are willing to pay less for additional fish, according to the law of demand. (398–403)

13   **F**   Marginal social and private benefits from consuming fish are equal. Marginal social *cost* is greater than marginal private *cost*. (398–403)

14   **T**   Efficient use of a common resource is sustainable. (398–403)

15   **F**   Low cost producers are willing and able to pay more for quotas, so producers with higher marginal costs will not produce. (398–403)

Multiple-Choice

1   **e**   Nonrival and nonexcludable. Congestion creates rivalry. (392)

2   **a**   See Text Fig. 17.1. (392)

3   **b**   A unit of a common resource can be used only once, but no one can be excluded from using other available units. (392)

4   **d**   Can be consumed simultaneously by everyone; no one can be excluded. (392)

5   **c**   Can't prevent ships from seeing the light. (392)

6   **b**   Would not be profitable for private firms. (393–397)

7   **a**   Private production is unprofitable because of the free-rider problem. (393–397)

8   **c**   Because private goods are rival and excludable, quantities consumed by each individual at each price are different and must be added to get total market demand. (393–397)

9 d Because public goods are nonrival, can sum marginal benefit to each individual. (393–397)

10 d Equivalent to $MSB = MSC$. (393–397)

11 a Because of free-rider problem, no one is willing to pay for production. (393–397)

12 c Where MSB intersects MSC. (393–397)

13 d Best for bureaucrats, even though $MSC > MSB$. Possible only if voters are not well informed. (393–397)

14 a Voters, like consumers, are assumed to be concerned only with their own self-interest. (393–397)

15 b Definition of principle. (393–397)

16 b Vote maximizing by using principle of minimum differentiation. (393–397)

17 d a definition, b, c are outcomes of rational ignorance. (393–397)

18 d Government will respond to demands of voters. (393–397)

19 e Median = exactly halfway between. (393–397)

20 c Prevent overuse and depletion because common resources are rival and nonexcludable. (400–405)

21 e See Text Fig. 17.7; MSB and MB are the same. (398–403)

22 c See Text Fig. 17.7. (398–403)

23 c See Text Fig. 17.9. (398–403)

24 d MC is not the same for all. (398–403)

25 c Common resources are overused because they are too inexpensive, so subsidies would make overuse worse. (398–403)

Short Answer Problems

1 The free-rider problem is the problem of unregulated markets producing too little of a pure public good because there is little incentive for individuals to pay for the good. There is nothing to prevent the person from being excluded from consuming the good, or from getting a free ride.

2 a A security guard is a public good because, in this case, it is nonrival and non-excludable. It is nonrival because one resident's *consumption* of the security

provided by a guard does not reduce the security of anyone else. It is nonexcludable because once a security guard is in place, all residents enjoy the increased security; none can be excluded.

b If each resident must act individually in hiring a security guard none will be hired because each resident receives only $10 in benefit from the first guard, which costs $300 per day.

c The entries in the last column of Table 17.1 Solution are obtained by multiplying the marginal benefit per resident by the number of residents, 100. This multiplication is the numerical equivalent of summing the individual marginal benefit curves vertically for each quantity of guards.

TABLE **17.1** SOLUTION

Number of Guards	Total Cost per Day ($)	Marginal Benefit per Resident ($)	Marginal Benefit to All Residents ($)
1	300	10	1,000
2	600	4	400
3	900	2	200
4	1,200	1	100

3 a If the Apartment Council hires each guard for whom the marginal benefit exceeds the marginal cost, they will hire the optimal number of guards. The marginal cost of each additional guard is $300. The marginal benefit of the first guard is $1,000, so he will be hired. Similarly, the marginal benefit of the second guard is $400, and she will be hired.

The marginal benefit of the third guard is only $200, which is less than marginal cost. Therefore the efficient (optimal) number of guards is two. For two guards, the net benefit is $800: total benefit ($1,400) minus total cost ($600).

b For one guard, net benefit is $700: total benefit ($1,000) minus total cost ($300). For three guards, net benefit is also $700: total benefit ($1,600) minus total cost ($900). Thus the net benefit of $800 is greatest for two guards.

c The Apartment Council might pay for the guards by collecting a security fee of $6 per day from each of the 100 residents in order to hire two security guards.

4 a Each candidate will propose spending $40 since that is the preference of the median voter (voter *D*).

   b   **i** Candidate 1 will win because *D*, *E*, *F*, and *G* will vote for that candidate, because $40 comes closer to matching their preferences than the $39 proposed by candidate 2. Only *A*, *B*, and *C* will vote for candidate 2.

      ii Candidate 1 will win because *A*, *B*, *C*, and *D* will vote for that candidate; only *E*, *F*, and *G* will vote for candidate 2.

   c Candidates will both propose spending $40 on the party since that is what the median voter prefers. In this case, the median voter's view is not "average."

5 Most issues have only a small and indirect effect on most voters. In such cases it is irrational for a voter to spend much time and effort to become well informed because the additional cost would quickly exceed any additional benefit. Only if the voter is significantly and directly affected by an issue will it pay to become well informed. As a result, most voters will be rationally ignorant on any given issue.

6 a Only *A* and *B* are better off under distribution 2. Distribution 2 will receive the support of only *A* and *B* with *C*, *D*, and *E* opposed. Note that the median voter (*C*) is worse off under distribution 2.

   b Distribution 3 will receive majority support since it makes the median voter better off. It will be supported by *A*, *B*, and *C* and opposed by *D* and *E*.

7 The tragedy of the commons—the overuse and depletion of a common resource—occurs because no one has an incentive to conserve and use a shared resource sustainably. In the fishing example, each fisherman has an incentive to continue fishing until the marginal benefit (revenue from selling an additional tonne of fish) equals his marginal cost—the

additional cost of keeping a boat and crew at sea long enough to catch an additional tonne of fish. But for each tonne he catches, he doesn't take into account the external cost of stock depletion that makes it harder and more costly for others to catch fish.

8 a See Fig. 17.3 Solution. It shows the marginal social cost, marginal private cost, and marginal social benefit curves for Atlantic Halibut fish, a common resource.

FIGURE **17.3** SOLUTION

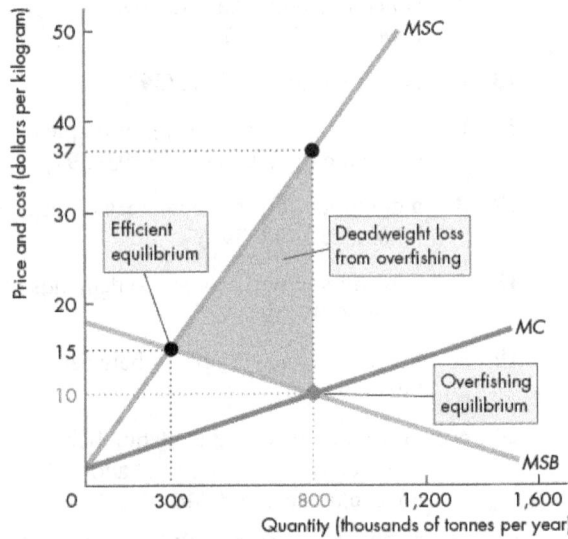

   b The private equilibrium quantity is determined by the intersection of the *MC* and *MSB* curves, 800,000 tonnes. The efficient sustainable catch, 300,000 tonnes, is determined by the intersection of the *MSC* and *MSB* curves. The deadweight loss is shaded.

   c The quota that achieves the efficient outcome is set for the quantity at which *MSC* equals *MSB*—300,000 tonnes.

   d The market price of an individual transferable quota (ITQ) equals the *MSC* – *MC* at the efficient level of fish, or $37 – $10 = $27 per tonne of fish.

Part 5 Wrap Up
Understanding Market Failure and Government

PROBLEM

Figure P5.1 illustrates an industry that produces the product *Arent'LecturesFun* together with a positive externality.

  a Label the three curves (some require more than one label). On the figure, identify the point of market equilibrium and the point of efficient equilibrium.

  b On the figure, shade in and identify the area of deadweight loss. Explain how that area represents deadweight loss.

  c Suppose the government decides to subsidize producers of *Arent'LecturesFun* to get them to produce the efficient quantity. On the figure, identify the amount of the public provision that will be paid by taxpayers, per unit of output. Explain how consumers and producers will now choose the efficient quantity of output.

FIGURE **P5.1**

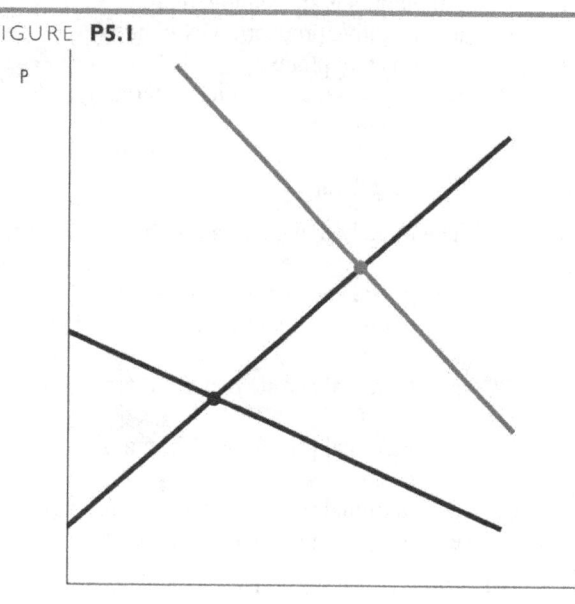

FIGURE **P5.2**   PAPER MARKET

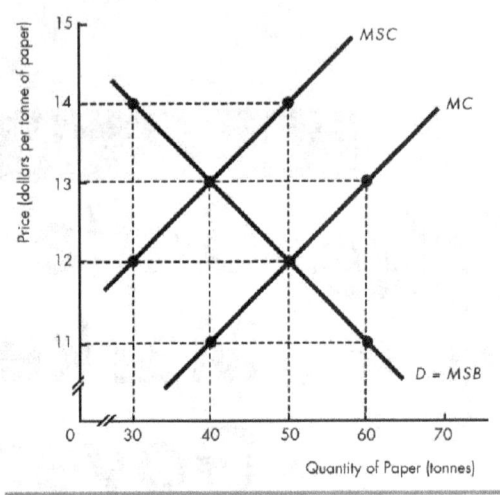

MIDTERM EXAMINATION

You should allocate 22 minutes for this examination (11 questions, 2 minutes per question). For each question, choose the one *best* answer.

1 The free-rider problem for a public good means that
  a the good is rival.
  b the good is excludable.
  c an unregulated market produces the efficient quantity.
  d an unregulated market produces less than the efficient quantity.
  e an unregulated market produces more than the efficient quantity.

2 Attending a noisy party that irritates the neighbours is an example of a
  a negative production externality.
  b positive production externality.
  c negative consumption externality.
  d negative production externality.
  e mistake for the host to not invite the neighbours.

3 The tragedy of the commons arises because _____ exceeds _____ at the unregulated equilibrium quantity.
  a marginal social benefit; marginal private benefit
  b marginal private benefit; marginal social benefit.
  c marginal private benefit; marginal social cost
  d marginal social cost; marginal social benefit.
  e marginal private cost; marginal social cost.

4 Refer to Fig. P5.2. The unregulated outcome in the paper market is
  a quantity = 40, price = 11.
  b quantity = 40, price = 13.
  c quantity = 50, price = 12.
  d quantity = 50, price = 14.
  e quantity = 60, price = 13.

5 Refer to Fig. P5.2. A tax of _____ per tonne is necessary to achieve the efficient output of _____ tonnes of paper.
  a $14; 50
  b $14; 30
  c $13; 40
  d $2; 50
  e $2; 40

6 According to the Coase theorem, if transactions costs are low and property rights exist,
  a negative externalities cause deadweight losses.
  b positive externalities cause deadweight losses.
  c private transactions are efficient.
  d public transactions are efficient.
  e the efficient level of pollution will be zero.

7 The market price at the quota quantity of an individual transferable quota (ITQ) equals the
  a marginal private benefit.
  b marginal social benefit.
  c marginal private benefit minus marginal cost.
  d marginal social benefit minus marginal cost.
  e marginal social benefit minus marginal private benefit.

8 Marketable permits for polluting the air
- **a** give firms a pollution limit that can be bought and sold.
- **b** overcome the need for the regulator to know the firms' own costs and benefits of pollution.
- **c** will be priced in a competitive market to yield efficient pollution outcomes where *MSC* = *MSB*.
- **d** can potentially achieve the same pollution outcome as Pigovian taxes.
- **e** are all of the above.

9 The *total benefit* of a given level of provision of a public good can be obtained by
- **a** adding the marginal benefit of each level of provision up to the given level.
- **b** adding the marginal benefit of each level of provision and then subtracting the marginal cost of each level of provision.
- **c** adding the net benefit of each level of provision up to the given level.
- **d** multiplying net benefit by the quantity of the public good provided.
- **e** none of the above methods.

10 Voters are asked to vote for either proposition *A* or proposition *B*. Proposition *A* will win if it
- **a** is closer the efficient use of resources.
- **b** is supported by bureaucrats.
- **c** is preferred by the median voter.
- **d** generates greater social benefits than social costs.
- **e** generates the fewest negative externalities.

11 Policies for correcting problems of positive externalities include
- **a** emission charges.
- **b** vouchers.
- **c** marketable permits.
- **d** Pigovian taxes.
- **e** all of the above

ANSWERS

Problem

a Figure P5.1 Solution shows the market equilibrium (quantity = 7.5, price = 15), the efficient equilibrium (quantity = 15, price = 25)

b The grey triangle represents the area of deadweight loss. For every unit between 7.5 and 15, the marginal social benefit (marginal private benefit plus positive externality) exceeds the marginal social cost.

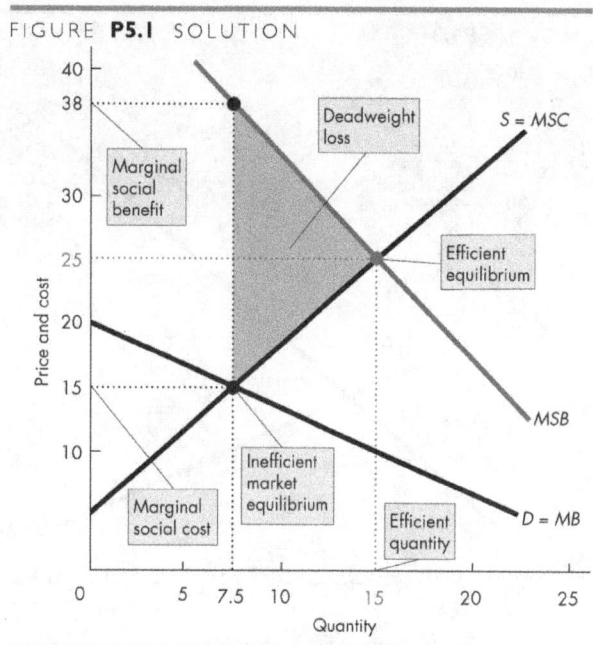

FIGURE **P5.1** SOLUTION

Both consumers and producers would be better off if these units were produced and sold at any price less than *MSB* and greater than *MSC*. But the private market outcome will not produce these units. In general, markets underproduce goods and services with positive externalities.

c Figure P5.3 on the next page shows the amount of public provision per unit, paid by taxpayers, required to induce producers to produce the efficient quantity. At that efficient quantity of 15, consumers are only willing to pay $10 per unit, equal to the marginal private benefit. With that $10 per unit plus the $15 per unit subsidy from the government (for a total of $25 per unit), producers are willing to supply the efficient quantity of 15.

FIGURE **P5.3**

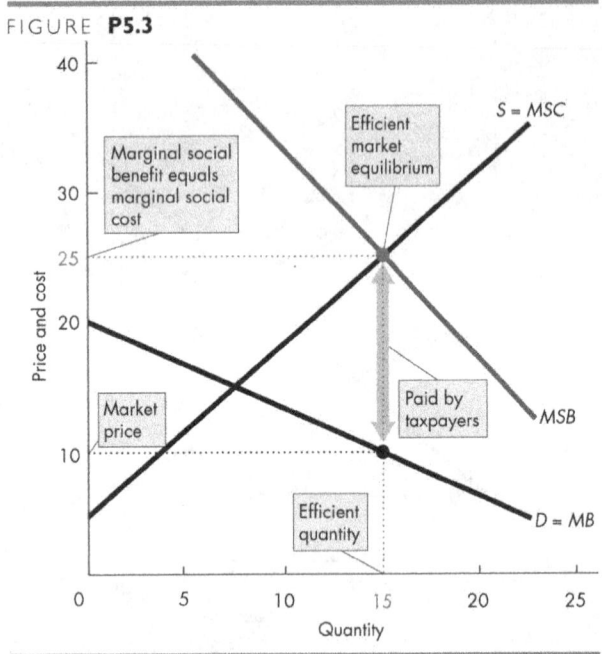

Midterm Examination

1 d Public goods are nonrival and nonexcludable. There is no incentive for people to pay, so there is no profitable private production. (392)

2 c Imposed by consumers of "party services." (392)

3 d See Text Fig. 17.7. (398–403)

4 c Where $D = MSB$ intersects MC. (375–379)

5 e $2 per tonne tax (vertical distance between MC and MSC) makes firm's MC equal to MSC. Output where $D = MSB$ intersects MSC. (375–379)

6 c There are no externalities. Level of pollution is where $MB = MSC$. (375–379)

7 c This makes the user pay the full opportunity cost of using the common resource. (398–403)

8 e See text discussion. (375–379)

9 a **b–d** involve irrelevant costs. (393–397)

10 c 50 percent of votes plus 1. (393–397)

11 b Others for negative externality problems. (375–379)

Chapter 18
Markets for Factors of Production

The Anatomy of Factor Markets

Factors of production, or resources (labour, capital, land, entrepreneurship) are hired by firms to produce output.

- ♦ Price of labour services (for **jobs**) is the wage rate.

- ♦ Price of capital services (for use of capital goods) is a rental rate.

- ♦ Price of land (all natural resources) services, including **nonrenewable natural resources**, is a rental rate.

- ♦ Entrepreneurs receive the economic profit/loss from their business decisions.

The Demand for a Factor of Production

Demand for factors is a **derived demand**, stemming from demand for goods and services produced by a factor and driven by a firm's profit-maximizing objective.

- ♦ **Value of marginal product** (*VMP*) is extra revenue from employing one more unit of factor.

  - $VMP = MP \times P_{output}$

- ♦ Profit-maximizing firm hires additional units of labour up to the quantity of factor where VMP = wage rate (W).

- ♦ Firm's demand curve for labour is downward-sloping value of marginal product curve of labour.

- ♦ Firm's long-run demand for labour curve (*VMP* curve) shifts rightward if

  - increased P_{output}.

  - technological change increases MP labour.

  - increased price of substitute factor of production.

  - decreased price of complement factor of production.

Labour Markets

Market demand curve for labour is the horizontal sum of quantities of labour demanded by all firms at each wage rate.

Supply of labour determined by households' decisions allocating time between labour supply (work) and leisure.

- ♦ Wage rate is *opportunity cost of leisure*.

- ♦ At wage rates above a household's *reservation wage*, household supplies labour.

- ♦ *Substitution effect* from higher wage induces increased quantity of labour supplied.

- ♦ *Income effect* from higher wage induces decreased quantity of labour supplied.

- ♦ When wage rises, quantity of labour supplied increases when substitution effect > income effect.

- ♦ Individual household labour supply curve is *backward bending* when income effect > substitution effect.

Market supply of labour curve is the horizontal sum of all household supply curves. Upward sloping over normal range of wage rates.

Labour unions are organized groups of workers, with objectives of increasing wage rate and influencing working conditions.

Methods of achieving objectives include

- ♦ restricting supply of labour.

- ♦ increasing demand for union labour by

  - increasing value of marginal product of union members.

  - encouraging import restrictions.

  - supporting minimum wage laws.

  - supporting immigration restrictions.

Monopsony—a market structure in which there is a single buyer. Firm that is the only employer in town is a monopsonist in the labour market.

- To hire more labour, a monopsonist must pay a higher wage. Marginal cost of labour curve (*MCL*) for monopsonist is upward sloping and above and steeper than the market supply curve of labour.

- Profit-maximizing rule for monopsonist is to hire quantity of labour where *MCL* curve intersects *VMP* curve, then offer lowest wage for which labour will work (on supply curve).

- For a monopsonist, employment and wage are lower than for competitive labour market. More elastic supply of labour means less *opportunity* for monopsony to cut wages, to reduce employment, or to increase economic profit.

Adding a union to a monopsony labour market can create **bilateral monopoly**, in which wage is determined by the relative bargaining strength of the firm and of the union.

- Highest possible wage where *MCL* intersects *VMP*. Lowest possible wage is pure monopsony wage.

- Adding a minimum wage law to a monopsony labour market can actually increase wages and increase employment.

Capital and Natural Resource Markets

Demand for capital is derived from value of marginal product of capital. Firms hire additional units of capital up to quantity where *VMP* of capital equals the rental rate of capital.

Firms decide whether to buy versus rent physical capital by evaluating present value.

- **Discounting** is conversion of a future amount of money to its present value.

- **Present value** of future amount of money is amount that, if invested today, will grow as large as future amount, taking account of earned interest.

$$\text{Present value} = \frac{\text{Amount money available } n \text{ years}}{(1 + r)^n}$$

- If present value of future rental payments exceeds cost of buying capital equipment, firm buys capital equipment.

- If present value of future rental payments is less than cost of buying capital equipment, firm rents capital equipment.

Economists call all natural resources *land*.

Supply of land is perfectly inelastic, so price is determined by demand alone. Demand for land is derived from value of marginal product of land. Firms hire additional units of land up to quantity where *VMP* of land equals the rental rate of land.

Price of nonrenewable natural resources depends on demand and supply.

- Demand is determined by value of marginal product (*VMP*) and expected future price.

- Supply is determined by marginal cost of extraction (*MC*), expected future price and scale of production facilities.

Hotelling Principle—price of natural resource expected to rise at rate = interest rate.

- If expected rate of price rise > interest rate, demand increases, supply decreases, and price of resource rises.

- If expected rate of price rise < interest rate, demand decreases, supply increases, and price of resource falls.

HELPFUL HINTS

1   Be careful to distinguish between the value of marginal product of a factor of production and the marginal revenue of a unit of output. The value of marginal product of a factor of production is calculated by multiplying marginal product and price of output ($VMP = MP \times P_{\text{output}}$). The intuition is this: marginal product tells us how much more output we receive from using more of a factor, and price of output tells us the value or revenue we receive from selling each unit of that additional output. Therefore MP times P_{output} tells us the value we receive (the *VMP*) from using more of the factor of production.

2   This chapter gives a broad overview of characteristics common to competitive markets for the factors of production labour, capital, and land. Profit-maximizing firms will hire factors up to the point where the value of marginal product (*VMP*) is equal to the price of the factor service.

3   The most important graph in this chapter appears in Text Fig. 18.1, reproduced here as Fig. 18.1. Using the example of Angelo's Bakery, the figure demonstrates that a firm's demand for labour curve is the same as its value of marginal product curve of labour.

FIGURE 18.1

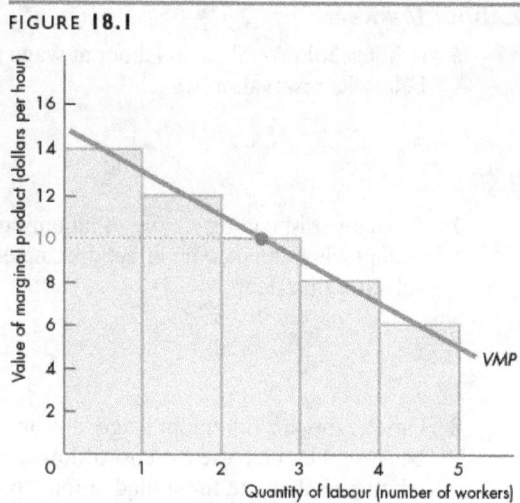

(a) Value of marginal product

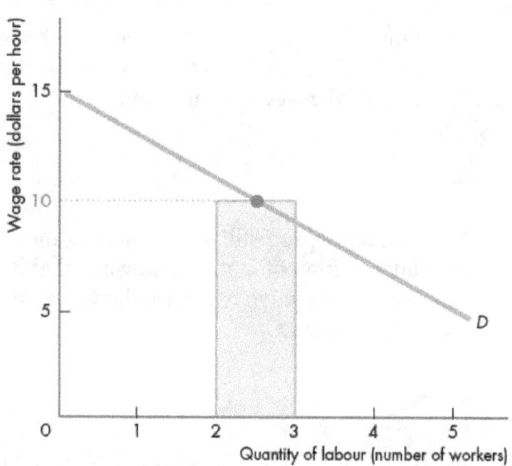

(b) Demand for labour

Part (a) shows the value of marginal product curve (*VMP*) based on the example in the textbook on page 418. Notice that the values for *VMP* are plotted midway between the labour inputs used in their calculation. For example, the *MRP* of moving from 0 to 1 labourer is 14, so the value of 14 on the *VMP* curve is plotted midway between 0 and 1 labourers.

Part (b) constructs Angelo's demand for labour by asking how much labour Angelo will hire at alternative wage rates. Since Angelo is a profit maximizer, he will hire labour up to the point where the value of marginal product of labour is equal to the wage rate. For example, if the wage rate is $10 per hour, Angelo will hire 3 workers since the value of marginal product is $10 when 3 workers are hired. Other points on

the labour demand curve can be obtained in similar fashion. The result is that the labour demand curve is the same as the *VMP* curve.

4   The concept of present value is essential in thinking about the value today of an investment or of future amounts of money. It gives us a method of comparing investments that have payments at different points in time. The intuition behind present value is a dollar today is worth more than a dollar in the future because today's dollar can be invested to earn interest. To calculate the value today of an amount of money that will be paid in the future, we must discount that future amount to compensate for the forgone interest. The present value of a future amount of money is the amount that, if invested today, will grow as large as the future amount, taking into account the interest that it will earn.

5   The profit-maximizing condition of hiring the services of a factor of production until *VMP* = price of factor service, must be adapted when a firm buys capital equipment instead of renting the equipment services.

    If the present value of future rental payments exceeds the cost of buying the capital equipment, the firm buys the capital equipment instead of renting. If the present value of the future rental payments is less than the cost of buying the capital equipment, the firm rents instead of buying.

6   This chapter introduces the concept of a monopsonist, a firm that is the only buyer in a market, such as labour. The monopsonist faces an upward-sloping supply curve of labour. As a result, its marginal cost of labour curve (*MCL*) is different from the labour supply curve.

    There is a close parallel between (a) the relationship between the labour supply curve and the *MCL* curve for the monopsonist and (b) the already familiar relationship (Chapter 13) between the demand curve and the marginal revenue curve (*MR*) for the monopolist. Both sets of relationships stem from the assumption of a single price for labour or output in the relevant market.

    The monopolist, as the only seller in an output market, faces a downward-sloping demand curve. The marginal revenue from the sale of an additional unit of output is *less* than the selling price because the monopolist must *lower* the price on all previous units as well.

Thus the *MR* curve lies *below* the demand curve for the single-price monopolist.

For the monopsonist in a labour market, the marginal cost of hiring an additional unit of labour is *higher* than the wage because the monopsonist must *raise* the wage on all previous units of labour as well. Thus the *MCL* curve lies *above* the supply of labour curve for the monopsonist.

Another way to think about this parallel is that the supply and *MCL* relationship (and the resulting wage versus *VMP* relationship) is just the demand and *MR* relationship (and the resulting price versus *MC* relationship) flipped upside-down.

S E L F - T E S T

True/False and Explain

The Anatomy of Factor Markets

1 Profit is the factor price of capital.

2 Farmland is a nonrenewable natural resource.

The Demand for a Factor of Production

3 A firm's average revenue product curve is also its demand for labour curve.

4 A factor's value of marginal product equals the marginal product of the factor multiplied by the price of output.

5 A firm's demand for labour decreases when the price of a substitute for labour rises.

Labour Markets

6 A household supplies no labour at wage rates below its reservation wage.

7 A backward-bending supply of labour curve occurs when the income effect dominates the substitution effect.

8 Unions support minimum wage laws in part because they increase the cost of low-skill labour, a substitute for skilled union labour.

9 For a firm that is a monopsonist in the labour market, the supply curve of labour is the marginal cost of labour curve.

10 In a monopsonistic labour market, the introduction of a minimum wage that is above the current wage will raise the wage but reduce employment.

11 In the case of bilateral monopoly in a labour market, the wage depends on the bargaining strength of the two traders.

Capital and Natural Resource Markets

12 If the present value of future rental payments for capital equipment is less than the cost of buying the capital equipment, the firm should buy the capital equipment.

13 The market supply of a particular piece of land is perfectly elastic.

14 For oil, the value of marginal product is the fundamental determinant of demand, and the marginal cost of extraction is the fundamental determinant of supply.

15 The Hotelling Principle states that the price of hotel stocks is expected to rise at a rate equal to the interest rate.

Multiple-Choice

The Anatomy of Factor Markets

1 Which price for a factor of production is determined differently from the rest?
- **a** wages for labour services
- **b** rental rates for capital services
- **c** rental rates for land services
- **d** profit rates for entrepreneurial services
- **e** none of the above—all are determined similarly

The Demand for a Factor of Production

2 An example of derived demand is the demand for
- **a** sweaters derived by an economics student.
- **b** sweaters produced by labour and capital.
- **c** labour used in the production of sweaters.
- **d** sweater brushes.
- **e** none of the above.

3 A profit-maximizing firm will continue to hire units of a factor of production until the
- **a** marginal cost of the factor equals its marginal product.
- **b** marginal cost of the factor equals its average revenue product.
- **c** average cost of the factor equals its value of marginal product.
- **d** marginal cost of the factor equals its value of marginal product.
- **e** factor's value of marginal product equals zero.

4 A firm's value of marginal product of labour curve is also its
- **a** marginal cost curve for labour.
- **b** labour demand curve.
- **c** labour supply curve.
- **d** output supply curve.
- **e** average revenue curve.

5 If the price of its output falls, a firm will employ
- **a** less labour, causing the wage to fall.
- **b** less labour, causing the marginal product of labour to rise.
- **c** less labour, causing the marginal product of labour to fall.
- **d** more labour, causing the marginal product of labour to rise.
- **e** more labour, causing the marginal product of labour to fall.

6 A technological change that increases the marginal product of labour will shift the labour
- **a** demand curve leftward.
- **b** demand curve rightward.
- **c** supply curve leftward.
- **d** supply curve rightward.
- **e** supply and demand curves rightward.

Labour Markets

7 If the wage rate increases, the *substitution* effect will give a household an incentive to
- **a** raise its reservation wage.
- **b** increase leisure and decrease work.
- **c** increase work and decrease leisure.
- **d** increase both work and leisure.
- **e** decrease both work and leisure.

8 If the wage rate increases, the *income* effect will give a household an incentive to
- **a** raise its reservation wage.
- **b** increase leisure and decrease work.
- **c** increase work and decrease leisure.
- **d** increase both work and leisure.
- **e** decrease both work and leisure.

9 As the wage rate rises, a household will have a backward-bending labour supply curve if
- **a** the income effect reinforces the substitution effect.
- **b** the wage rate rises above the reservation wage.
- **c** the substitution effect dominates the income effect.
- **d** the income effect dominates the substitution effect.
- **e** leisure is an inferior good.

10 The market supply curve of labour is
- **a** upward sloping.
- **b** backward bending.
- **c** first upward sloping and then backward bending as the wage increases.
- **d** vertical.
- **e** horizontal.

11 If the desire for leisure increased, the wage rate would
a rise and employment would fall.
b rise and employment would rise.
c fall and employment would fall.
d fall and employment would rise.
e fall and employment may rise or fall.

12 Which of the following would unions be *least* likely to support?
a increasing the legal minimum wage
b restricting immigration
c encouraging imports
d increasing demand for the goods their workers produce
e increasing the marginal product of union labour

13 A union is formed to restrict labour supply in a previously competitive labour market. If the union succeeds in raising the wage,
a employment will fall.
b employment will rise.
c employment will not change.
d the total wage bill will rise.
e the total wage bill will fall.

14 Figure 18.2 illustrates a monopsonist in the labour market (*MCL* = marginal cost of labour). The profit-maximizing wage rate and quantity of labour hired will be
a $4 per hour and 800 hours of labour.
b $4 per hour and 400 hours of labour.
c $7 per hour and 600 hours of labour.
d $9 per hour and 400 hours of labour.
e none of the above.

FIGURE **18.2**

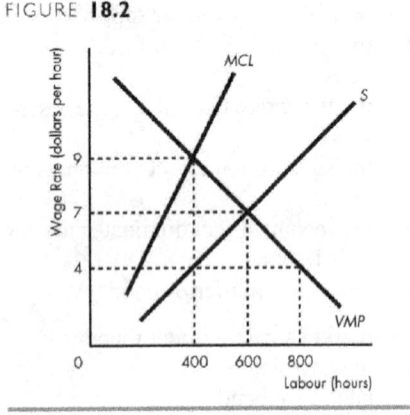

15 If the labour market illustrated in Fig. 18.2 became competitive, the equilibrium wage rate and quantity of labour hired would be
a $4 per hour and 800 hours of labour.
b $4 per hour and 400 hours of labour.
c $7 per hour and 600 hours of labour.
d $9 per hour and 400 hours of labour.
e none of the above.

18 If a union forms to face the monopsonist in Fig. 18.2, the situation is one of
a binding arbitration.
b derived demand.
c duopoly.
d collusive oligopoly.
e bilateral monopoly.

17 If a union and the monopsonist in Fig. 18.2 agree to collective bargaining, the outcome will be an hourly wage
a of $7.
b between $4 and $7.
c between $4 and $9.
d between $7 and $9.
e of $9.

18 Compared to a competitive labour market with the same value of marginal product and labour supply curves, a monopsonist market has a(n)
a lower wage and lower employment.
b lower wage and higher employment.
c higher wage and lower employment.
d higher wage and higher employment.
e indeterminate outcome.

19 For the monopsonist employer in Fig. 18.3, the profit-maximizing wage rate and quantity of labour hired will be
a $9 per hour and 300 hours of labour.
b $8 per hour and 350 hours of labour.
c $8 per hour and 500 hours of labour.
d $7 per hour and 400 hours of labour.
e $6 per hour and 300 hours of labour.

FIGURE **18.3**

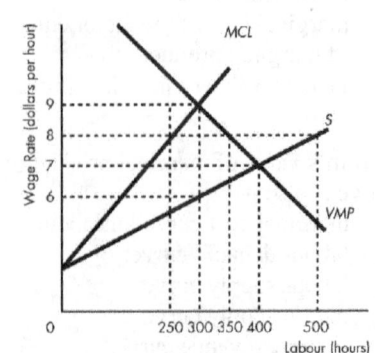

20 Suppose the government passes a minimum wage law that prohibits anyone from hiring labour at less than $8 per hour. In Fig. 18.3, the marginal cost of labour (*MCL*) for the monopsonist
a   is not affected.
b   equals $8 only from 0 to 250 hours of labour.
c   equals $8 only from 0 to 350 hours of labour.
d   equals $8 only from 0 to 500 hours of labour.
e   shifts up by a vertical distance of $8.

Capital Markets

21 The supply curve of capital is
a   upward sloping.
b   downward sloping.
c   perfectly elastic.
d   perfectly inelastic.
e   backward bending.

22 If the present value of $300 received one year from now is $200, what is the annual interest rate?
a   25 percent (0.25)
b   33.3 percent (0.333)
c   50 percent (0.5)
d   66.7 percent (0.667)
e   none of the above

23 Technological advances increase both the demand for capital and the supply of capital by the same amount. As a result, the rental rate _____ and the quantity of capital _____.
a   rises; increases
b   remains constant; increases
c   increases; remains constant
d   falls; increases
e   remains constant; decreases

Natural Resource Markets

24 Which of the following is a nonrenewable natural resource?
a   coal
b   land
c   water
d   trees
e   none of the above

25 If the market for a nonrenewable natural resource is currently in equilibrium, the price of the resource
a   is equal to the value of marginal product of the resource.
b   is expected to rise at a rate equal to the interest rate.
c   is expected to fall at a rate equal to the interest rate.
d   will actually rise at a rate equal to the interest rate.
e   will actually fall at a rate equal to the interest rate.

Short Answer Problems

1 Table 18.1 gives the total and marginal product schedules for a firm that sells its output and buys labour in competitive markets. Initially the price at which the firm can sell any level of output is $5 per unit and the wage rate at which it can purchase any quantity of labour is $15 per unit.

TABLE **18.1**

			P = $5		P = $3	
Quantity Labour (L)	Output (Q)	Marginal Product (MP$_L$)	Total Revenue (TR)	Value of Marginal Product (VMP$_L$)	Total Revenue (TR)	Value of Marginal Product (VMP$_L$)
0	0					
		... 12				
1	12					
		... 10				
2	22					
		... 8				
3	30					
		... 6				
4	36					
		... 4				
5	40					
		... 2				
6	42					

a   Complete the first two blank columns in Table 18.1 by computing the *TR* and *VMP$_L$* corresponding to a price of output = $5.

b   The value of marginal product of labour (*VMP$_L$*) can be computed by either of the following formulas:

$$VMP_L = \Delta TR/\Delta L$$
$$VMP_L = MP_L \times P_{output}$$

where ΔTR = the change in total revenue, ΔL = the change in labour, P_{output} = price of output, and MP_L = marginal product of labour. Show that these two formulas are equivalent for the case when the quantity of labour changes from 1 to 2 units.

c   If the firm maximizes profit, what quantity of labour will it employ? How much output will it produce?

d   If total fixed cost is $125, what is the amount of profit?

e   What is its profit if the firm hires one more unit of labour than the profit-maximizing quantity? one less unit of labour than the profit-maximizing quantity?

f   Draw a graph of the firm's demand for labour and the supply of labour to the firm and illustrate the profit-maximizing labour decision.

2   Now, suppose that the market demand for the output of the firm in Short Answer Problem **1** decreases, causing the price of output to decrease to $3 per unit. The total and marginal product schedules remain unchanged.

a   Complete the last two blank columns in Table 18.1 by computing the *TR* and *VMP_L* corresponding to price of output = $3.

b   If the wage remains at $15 per unit of labour, what is the profit-maximizing quantity of labour that the firm will hire? How much output will it produce?

c   Total fixed cost continues to be $125. What is the amount of profit?

d   Will the firm shut down in the short run? Explain.

e   Draw a new graph of the firm's demand for labour and supply of labour and illustrate the new profit-maximizing labour decision.

3   The price of output for the firm in Short Answer Problem **2** remains at $3, but the wage now rises to $21 per unit of labour. The total and marginal product schedules remain unchanged.

a   What happens to the demand curve for labour (the *VMP* of labour curve)?

b   Under these circumstances, what is the profit-maximizing quantity of labour that the firm will employ? How much output will it produce?

c   Total fixed cost continues to be $125. What is the amount of profit?

d   Draw a graph of the firm's demand for labour and supply of labour and illustrate the new profit-maximizing labour decision.

4   A perfectly competitive firm in long-run equilibrium produces flubits using only two factors of production—labour and capital. Each factor is sold in a perfectly competitive factor market. Labour costs $30 per unit and capital costs $50 per unit.

a   Assuming the firm has hired the profit-maximizing quantity of capital in part **b** of this question, the value of marginal revenue product of labour curve is

$$VMP_L = 110 - 8/5Q_L$$

where VMP_L is the value of marginal product of labour and Q_L is the quantity (in units) of labour employed. How many units of labour does the firm employ?

b   Assuming the firm has hired the profit-maximizing quantity of labour in part **a** of this question, the value of marginal product of capital curve is

$$VMP_K = 125 - 75/40Q_K$$

where VMP_K is the value of marginal product of capital and Q_K is the quantity (in units) of capital employed. How many units of capital does the firm employ?

c   The price of a flubit is $10.

   i   How many flubits is the firm producing? (*Hint:* Remember that the firm is in long-run equilibrium.)

   ii   What is the marginal (physical) product of the 25th unit of labour hired?

5   Initially we observe an industry facing a competitive labour market in which the supply of labour comes from two sources: domestic workers and foreign workers. All workers have similar skills. Also assume that the output of the industry competes with imported goods.

a   In Fig. 18.4 on the next page, graphically represent the initial competitive labour market. Draw the labour demand and supply curves and identify the equilibrium wage rate and level of employment.

FIGURE **18.4**

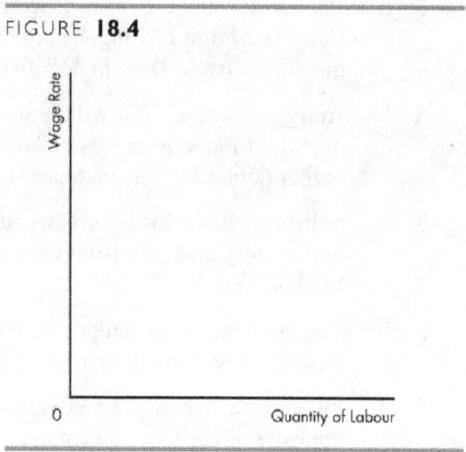

FIGURE **18.5**

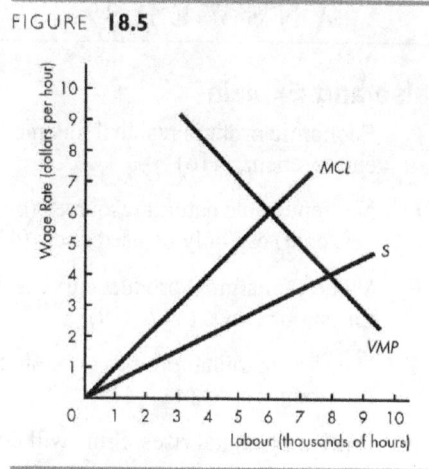

b   Now suppose a union consisting of domestic workers is formed. Through its support a law is passed that prohibits firms from hiring foreign workers. What effect will this have on employment and the wage rate? Illustrate graphically using the graph in part **a**.

c   Finally, the industry and union support the passage of a law that legally restricts imports that compete with industry output. Using the same graph, show the consequences for the wage rate and employment.

6   Pollutionless Paper is a pulp and paper mill that employs almost all of the labour in a small town in New Brunswick. The town's labour market, which approximates a monopsony, is illustrated in Fig. 18.5, where S is the supply curve of labour, and VMP and MCL are Pollutionless Paper's value of marginal product of labour and marginal cost of labour curves, respectively.

a   If Pollutionless Paper is a profit-maximizing monopsonist, what wage rate will it pay and how much labour will it employ? What is the VMP of labour at this level of employment?

b   If the town had a competitive labour market with the same VMP curve, what would the equilibrium wage rate and the level of employment be? Compare these outcomes with the monopsony outcomes in part **a**.

7   Consider the following alternatives for the labour market in Fig. 18.5.

a   Suppose the government imposes a minimum wage of $4 per hour. What wage rate will Pollutionless Paper pay and how much labour will it employ? Compare these outcomes with the monopsony outcomes in Short Answer Problem **6a**.

b   Suppose there is no legal minimum wage, but the workers form a union. If the union tries to negotiate a higher wage rate while maintaining employment at the monopsony level, what is the maximum wage rate that Pollutionless Paper will be willing to pay? What is the minimum wage rate that the union will accept?

8   Consider the negotiations between Pollutionless Paper and the union in Short Answer Problem **7b**.

a   What determines the wage rate that will actually be paid?

b   If Pollutionless Paper and the union are equally strong and realize it, what will the wage rate likely be?

c   If Pollutionless Paper and the union are equally strong, but the union mistakenly believes it is stronger, what is the likely outcome of negotiations?

d   If Pollutionless Paper and the union are equally strong, but Pollutionless Paper mistakenly believes it is stronger, what is the likely outcome of negotiations?

A N S W E R S

True/False and Explain

1 F Economic profit is residual income to the entrepreneur. (416)

2 F Nonrenewable natural resources (oil, natural gas, coal) can only be used once. (416)

3 F Value of marginal product curve is demand for labour curve. (417–419)

4 T Value of marginal product curve is demand for labour curve. (417–419)

5 F If price of capital rises, firms will demand more labour as a cheaper way of producing. (417–419)

6 T Reservation wage minimum needed for labour supply. (420–425)

7 T Versus upward sloping when substitution effect > income effect. (420–425)

8 T Increased price of substitute creates increased demand for union labour. (420–425)

9 F MCL curve is above supply curve of labour. (420–425)

10 F Wages and employment both increase; true for competitive labour market. (420–425)

11 F Firm should rent. (420–425)

12 F Reverse is true. (426–429)

13 F Perfectly inelastic. (426–429)

14 T Expected future prices are secondary determinant. (426–429)

15 F Definition applies to price of natural resources. (426–429)

Multiple-Choice

1 d Economic profit is a residual. Entrepreneurial services are not traded in markets. (416)

2 c Factor used as input to production. (417–419)

3 d Where supply curve of factor to firm (MC) intersects demand curve for factor (VMP). (417–419)

4 b Shows quantity of labour demanded at each wage rate. (417–419)

⊕ 5 b Labour demand curve shifts leftward. Because of diminishing MP, *decreased* quantity L causes *rise* in MP. (417–419)

6 b At a given wage, firm will demand increased quantity of labour because VMP is now higher (since MP has increased). (417–419)

7 c Substitute work for leisure because opportunity cost of leisure increases. (420–425)

8 b Consume more normal goods, including leisure, so working less. (420–425)

9 d Income and substitution effects work in opposite directions, so increase leisure dominates decrease work. (420–425)

10 a See text discussion. (420–425)

11 a Labour supply would shift leftward. (420–425)

12 c Increasing imports that are substitutes for domestically produced goods, decreasing demand for domestic, union labour. (420–425)

⊕ 13 a Leftward shift in supply decreases employment. Impact on wage bill depends on elasticity of demand for labour. (420–425)

14 b QL where MCL intersects VMP. Firm pays lowest wage required for labour to supply that QL (on supply curve). (420–425)

15 c Where S intersects VMP. (420–425)

16 e Firm is only buyer of labour, union is only seller of labour. (420–425)

17 c Between minimum firm can achieve ($4) and maximum union can achieve ($9). (420–425)

18 a See Text Fig. 18.3. (420–425)

19 e QL where MCL intersects VMP. Firm pays lowest wage required for labour to supply that QL (on supply curve). (420–425)

⊕ 20 d MCL is horizontal at minimum wage until it intersects S. Firm must then raise wage to get increased quantity supplied labour. (426)

21 a See Text Fig. 18.7. (426–429)

22 c Solve $200 = $300/(1 + r) for r. (426–429)

23 b Equal rightward shifts of both demand and supply curves. (426–429)

24 a Others are renewable natural resources. (426–429)

25 b This is the Hotelling Principle. For current equilibrium, *actual* future prices may or may not follow *expected* prices. (426–429)

Short Answer Problems

1 a The completed columns for *TR* and VMP_L corresponding to a price of output = $5 are shown in Table 18.1 Solution. The values for *TR* come from multiplying the quantity of output by the price of output ($5). The values for VMP_L between any two quantities of labour come from dividing the change in *TR* by the change in quantity of labour, or by multiplying the price of output ($5) by MP_L.

TABLE **18.1** SOLUTION

Quantity Labour (L)	MVMP Output (Q)	Marginal Product (MP_L)	P = $5 Total Revenue (TR)	P = $5 Value of Marginal Product (VMP_L)	P = $3 Total Revenue (TR)	P = $3 Value of Marginal Product (VMP_L)
0	0		0		0	
		... 12		... 60		... 36
1	12		60		36	
		... 10		... 50		... 30
2	22		110		66	
		... 8		... 40		... 24
3	30		150		90	
		... 6		... 30		... 18
4	36		180		108	
		... 4		... 20		... 12
5	40		200		120	
		... 2		... 10		... 6
6	42		210		126	

b From part **a**, the formula $VMP_L = \Delta TR/\Delta L$ yields a value of marginal product of labour of 50 when the quantity of labour changes from 1 to 2 units. To confirm that the second formula ($VMP_L = MP_L \times P_{output}$) gives the same answer when the quantity of labour changes from 1 to 2 units, substitute in the values for P_{output} ($5, the price of an additional unit of output) and MP_L (10 units of output). This yields the same value of marginal product of labour as above; $5 × 10 units = $50.

c The firm maximizes profit by employing labour up to the point where the *VMP* of labour is equal to the marginal cost of labour (the wage rate). That point occurs at 5 units of labour. The *VMP* of moving from 4 to 5

units of labour is 20, and the *VMP* of moving from 5 to 6 units of labour is 10. In moving from 4 to 5 units, *VMP* > *MC* so the firm should hire the 5th unit. But in moving from 5 to 6 units, *VMP* < *MC*, so the firm should not hire the 6th unit. Thus, by interpolation, the *VMP* at exactly 5 units of labour is 15 (midway between 20 and 10). So when 5 units of labour are employed, the *VMP* of labour is equal to the wage rate ($15). Given that 5 units of labour are employed, the profit-maximizing output will be 40 units (from Table 18.1 Solution).

d To calculate profit, first calculate total revenue and then subtract total cost. Total revenue is $200 (40 units of output × $5 per unit) and total cost is also $200—sum of total variable (labour) cost of $75 (5 units of labour × $15 per unit) and total fixed cost of $125. Thus profit is zero.

e If the firm employs one more unit of labour (6 units), total revenue will be $210 (42 units of output × the $5 price). Total cost will be the $125 fixed cost plus $90 in total variable cost (6 units of labour × $15 wage rate) or $215. Thus profit will be negative $5 ($5 loss).

If the firm employs one less unit of labour (4 units), total revenue will be $180 (36 units of output × the $5 price). Total cost will be the $125 fixed cost plus $60 in total variable cost (4 units of labour × $15 wage rate) or $185. Thus profit will be negative $5 ($5 loss).

f The graph of the firm's labour employment decision appears in Fig. 18.6. The demand for labour is the firm's VMP_L curve, which is labelled D_0 (D_1 will be discussed in Short Answer Problem **2**).

Notice that the values for *VMP* are plotted midway between the corresponding quantities of labour. For example, *VMP* of 60 is plotted midway between 0 and 1 units of labour.

Since the firm purchases labour in a perfectly competitive labour market, the supply of labour to the firm is perfectly elastic at the market wage rate. The labour supply curve is labelled $W = $15. The profit-maximizing decision is at the intersection of these curves, corresponding to a wage rate of $15 quantity of labour of 5 units.

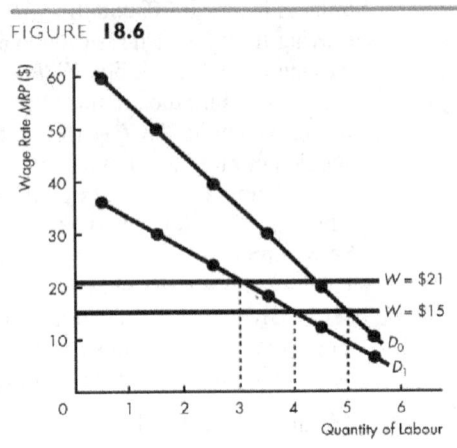

FIGURE **18.6**

2 a The completed columns for TR and VMP_L corresponding to price of output = $3 are shown in Table 18.2 Solution. The values for TR come from multiplying the quantity of output by the price of output ($3). The values for VMP_L between any two quantities of labour come from dividing the change in TR by the change in quantity of labour, or by multiplying the price of output ($3) by MP_L.

b If the wage rate remains at $15, the profit-maximizing quantity of labour will fall to 4 units since VMP_L equals the wage rate at 4 units of labour. The VMP of moving from 3 to 4 units of labour is 18, and the VMP of moving from 4 to 5 units of labour is 12. Thus, by interpolation, the VMP at exactly 4 units of labour is 15 (midway between 18 and 12). Given that 4 units of labour are employed, the profit-maximizing output will be 36 units (from Table 18.2 Solution).

c Profit equals total revenue minus total cost. Total revenue is $108 (36 units of output × $3 per unit) and total cost is $185—sum of total variable (labour) cost of $60 (4 units of labour × $15 per unit) and total fixed cost of $125. Thus profit is –$77, or a loss of $77.

d The firm will not shut down since total revenue ($108) is enough to cover total variable cost ($60) and part of fixed cost. If the firm shuts down, it would lose $125 of fixed cost rather than just $77.

e The graph of the firm's labour employment decision appears in Fig. 18.6. The new demand for labour is given by the firm's new VMP_L curve, labelled D_1. The supply of labour has not changed; it continues to be

horizontal at $15, the competitive market wage. The new profit-maximizing decision is at the intersection of these curves and corresponds to a wage rate of $15 and quantity of labour employed of 4 units.

3 a Since the price of output and the marginal product of labour are unaffected by a change in the wage rate, the demand curve for labour (the VMP of labour) will remain at D_1.

b If the wage rate rises to $21, the profit-maximizing quantity of labour will fall to 3 units since VMP_L equals the wage rate at 3 units of labour. Given that 3 units of labour are employed, the profit-maximizing output will be 30 units (from Table 18.2 Solution).

c Profit equals total revenue minus total cost. Total revenue is $90 (30 units of output × $3 per unit) and total cost is $188—sum of total variable (labour) cost of $63 (3 units of labour × $21 per unit) and total fixed cost of $125. Thus profit is –$98, or a loss of $98.

d See Fig. 18.6. The relevant labour demand curve continues to be D_1, but the labour supply curve reflects the rise in the competitive wage rate; it is now horizontal at a wage rate of $21 (labelled $W = $21). The new profit-maximizing decision is at the intersection of these curves and corresponds to a wage rate of $21 and a quantity of labour employed of 3 units.

4 a By assuming that the firm has already hired its capital, we know (in principle) fixed costs and can calculate the profit-maximizing quantity of the variable factor of production (labour) by setting the VMP_L equal to the wage rate ($30).

$$30 = 110 - 8/5Q_L$$
$$8/5Q_L = 80$$
$$Q_L = 50$$

b By assuming that the firm has already hired its labour, we can treat labour as the fixed cost and treat capital as the variable factor of production. Calculate the profit-maximizing quantity of the capital by setting the VMP_K equal to the cost of a unit of capital ($50).

$$50 = 125 - 75/40Q_K$$
$$75/40Q_K = 75$$
$$Q_K = 40$$

c **i** The fact that the firm is in long-run equilibrium provides the key to calculating the quantity of flubits produced. In long-run equilibrium, the firm earns zero economic profit, so total revenue is exactly equal to total cost.

We can calculate total cost by adding the costs of the (only) two factors of production. Labour cost is 50 units of labour × $30 per unit or $1,500. Capital cost is 40 units of capital × $50 per unit or $2,000. Total cost is therefore $3,500.

Total revenue must also be equal to $3,500. Since total revenue (TR) is just the price of output (P) times quantity sold (Q), we can calculate Q by substituting in the values we have for TR ($3,500) and P ($10).

$$TR = P \times Q$$
$$\$3,500 = \$10 \times Q$$
$$Q = 350$$

ii To calculate the marginal product of the 25th unit of labour, we begin by calculating the *value* of marginal product of the 25th unit of labour. Substituting $Q_L = 25$ into the equation for VMP_L yields

$$VMP_L = 110 - 8/5(25)$$
$$= 110 - 40$$
$$= 70$$

One definition of the value of marginal product of labour is the marginal product of labour (MP_L) times the price of output (P_{output}) or $VMP_L = MP_L \times P_{output}$. Rearranging to solve for MP_L yields

$$MP_L = VMP_L/P_{output}$$

Substituting in the values for the value of marginal product of the 25th unit of labour (70) and for the price of output ($10) yields

$$MP_L = 70/10$$
$$MP_L = 7$$

5 **a** The initial competitive demand for labour and supply of labour curves are D_C and S_C, respectively, in Fig. 18.4 Solution (ignore the other curves for now). The equilibrium wage rate is W_C and the competitive equilibrium level of employment is QL_C.

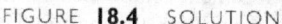

FIGURE **18.4** SOLUTION

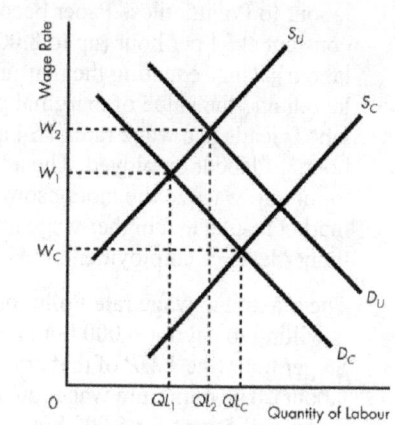

b If a law is passed prohibiting firms from hiring foreign workers, the labour supply curve (now under a union) will shift leftward (to S_U in Fig. 18.4 Solution). This will raise the wage rate to W_1 and decrease the quantity of labour employed to QL_1.

c Restrictions on imports will increase demand for the product produced in the industry and thus increase the derived demand (VMP) of labour in the industry. In Fig. 18.4 Solution this is a shift from D_C to D_U. The result is a further increase in the wage rate to W_2 and increase in employment to QL_2. Whether the quantity of labour hired now exceeds the initial competitive quantity depends on the magnitude of the shift in the labour demand curve.

6 **a** A profit-maximizing monopsonist will hire additional labour up to the point where MCL equals VMP. Referring to Fig. 18.5, this means that Pollutionless Paper will hire 6,000 hours of labour. To hire that quantity of labour, the labour supply curve S tells us that the wage rate must be $3 per hour. This is less than the $6 per hour value of marginal product of labour.

b In a competitive labour market, the wage rate would be $4 per hour and 8,000 hours of labour would be employed. The competitive labour market results in a higher wage rate and a higher level of employment than the monopsony outcomes.

7 a   If the government establishes a minimum wage at $4 per hour, the marginal cost of labour to Pollutionless Paper becomes constant at $4 per hour (up to 8,000 hours of labour). Thus, equating the marginal cost of labour and the value of marginal product of labour leads to a wage rate of $4 and 8,000 hours of labour employed. The addition of a minimum wage to the monopsony labour market results in a higher wage rate and a higher level of employment.

   b   The maximum wage rate Pollutionless Paper is willing to pay for 6,000 hours of labour is $6 per hour (the *VMP* of that amount of labour). The minimum wage rate that the union will accept for 6,000 hours of labour is $3 per hour (the supply price of that amount of labour).

8 a   The wage rate that will actually be paid as the outcome of bargaining depends on the relative bargaining strengths of the firm and the union. Bargaining strength depends on costs (from lockouts and strikes) that each side can inflict on the other if there is a failure to agree.

   b   Pollutionless Paper and the union will split the difference between $6 and $3 and agree on a wage rate of $4.50.

   c   If the union holds out for more than a $4.50 wage rate, Pollutionless Paper will likely lock out the workers.

   d   If Pollutionless Paper holds out for less than a $4.50 wage rate, the union will likely strike. When lockouts or strikes occur, it is usually because one side has misjudged the situation.

Chapter 19
Economic Inequality

Measuring Economic Inequality

Measures of economic inequality look at

- **market income**—wages, interest, rent, and profit before paying income taxes.

- **total income**—market income + cash payments to households by governments.

- **after-tax income**—total income – tax payments by households to governments.

Distribution of after-tax household income in Canada in 2009 was positively skewed.

- *Mode* (most common) income was $30,000–$34,999.

- *Median* income was $48,300.

- *Mean* income was $59,700.

There is a great deal of inequality of income and wealth. The degree of inequality is measured by the Lorenz curve.

- **Lorenz curve** for income (wealth) graphs the cumulative percentage of income (wealth) against the cumulative percentage of households.

- The 45° "line of equality" represents a hypothetically equal distribution of income (wealth).

- The farther the Lorenz curve from the line of equality, the more unequal the distribution.

- **Gini ratio** is the ratio of the area between the line of equality and the Lorenz curve, to the entire area beneath the line of equality. For equally distributed income, Gini ratio = 0. If 1 person has all income and others none, Gini ratio = 1.

- The distribution of wealth in Canada is even more unequal than the distribution of income.

Wealth is the *stock* of assets owned by an individual. Wealth includes *human capital* as well as financial assets. *Income* is the *flow* of earning received by an individual from his or her stock of wealth.

- Data used to construct wealth distributions do not include human capital and therefore overstate wealth inequalities.

- Distributions of annual income and wealth are more unequal than distributions of lifetime income and wealth.

- Even correcting for these factors, there are significant inequalities in distributions of income and wealth in Canada, with the income shares of the richest 20 percent of households rising since 1980.

Poverty exists when families cannot buy adequate food, shelter, and clothing.

- Poverty is a relative concept and is measured by the **low-income cutoff** (families spending 64 percent or more of their income on food, shelter, and clothing). On average in Canada since 1980, 17 percent of families have incomes below the low-income cutoff.

Inequality in the World Economy

Income inequality in Canada is

- more equal than distributions in Brazil and South Africa

- more unequal than distributions in Finland, Sweden, and many European countries.

Global distribution of income across countries is becoming more equal, while income distributions within countries are become more unequal.

The Sources of Economic Inequality

Income inequality arises from differences in human capital, or skill differentials in labour markets.

♦ Demand—high-skilled labour has higher value of marginal product (*VMP*) and demand curve than low-skilled labour.

♦ Supply—high-skilled labour has more *human capital*, which is costly to acquire. Supply curve for high-skilled labour is above the supply curve for low-skilled labour.

♦ Wages (equilibrium of demand and supply) are higher for high-skilled labour.

Wage differentials can be partly explained by

♦ human capital differences—differences in schooling, work experience, job interruptions, and effects of technological change and globalization.

♦ discrimination—results in lower wages and employment for those discriminated against.

♦ contests among superstars—result in extremely high incomes for winners. Globalization has increased the sizes of the talent pool and the income "prizes."

Wealth inequality increases between generations because

♦ assets can be inherited but debt cannot.

♦ of *assortative mating* (marrying within one's own socioeconomic class).

Income Redistribution

Income is redistributed by governments through income taxes, income maintenance programs, and subsidized services.

♦ Income taxes can be

• **progressive**—marginal tax rate increases with higher-level income.

• **regressive**—marginal tax rate decreases with higher-level income.

• **proportional** (*flat-rate tax*)—marginal tax rate is constant at all levels income.

♦ Income maintenance programs include social security, employment insurance, and welfare.

♦ Subsidized services (provision of goods and services below cost) such as education and health-care services reduce inequality.

Income distribution *after taxes and benefits* redistributes income to the very poor considerably, reducing the inequality of the *market income* distribution.

Income redistribution creates a **big tradeoff** between equity and efficiency. Redistribution uses scarce

resources and weakens incentives, so a more equally shared pie results in a smaller pie.

HELPFUL HINTS
---

1 Statistics used to construct Lorenz curves and Gini ratios do not always give an accurate picture of inequality. You should understand why a distribution of wealth that excludes the value of human capital gives a distorted picture relative to the distribution of income. You should also understand why the distribution of annual (static) income gives a distorted picture relative to the distribution of lifetime (dynamic) income. Finally, you should understand why the distribution of before-tax, before-benefits income gives a distorted picture relative to the distribution of after-tax, after-benefits income.

SELF-TEST

True/False and Explain

Measuring Economic Inequality

1 The farther the Lorenz curve from the 45° line, the more equal the distribution of income.

2 In Canada, measured income is more equally distributed than measured wealth.

3 Wealth distribution data exclude human capital and thus *overstate* inequality.

4 Income is a stock of earnings.

5 The lifetime distribution of income is more equal than the annual distribution of income.

Inequality in the World Economy

6 The global distribution of income across countries is becoming more equal, while income distributions within countries are become more unequal.

The Sources of Economic Inequality

7 The demand for low-skilled workers is to the left of the demand for high-skilled workers.

8 Globalization has increased the salary received by the "winner" of a contest to become the top executive of a large multinational company.

9 The larger the value of marginal product of skill and the more costly it is to acquire, the smaller the wage differential between high-skilled and low-skilled workers.

10 Assortative mating makes the distribution of wealth more unequal over time.

Income Redistribution

11 Under a proportional income tax, total taxes rise as income rises.

12 Under a progressive income tax, the marginal tax rate does not change as income rises.

13 A regressive income tax redistributes income from the rich to the poor.

14 Compared with the market distribution of income, government taxes and benefits reduce the inequality of income distribution.

15 In general, reducing income inequality by redistributing income from the rich to the poor will lead to greater production of goods and services.

Multiple-Choice

Measuring Economic Inequality

1 Which diagram is used by economists to illustrate the distribution of income or wealth?
   a   Lorenz curve
   b   normal bell-shaped distribution
   c   Sophia Loren curve
   d   low-income cutoff curve
   e   none of the above

2 In Fig. 19.1, the richest 20 percent of all households receive what share of all income?
   a   10 percent
   b   20 percent
   c   30 percent
   d   40 percent
   e   none of the above

FIGURE **19.1**

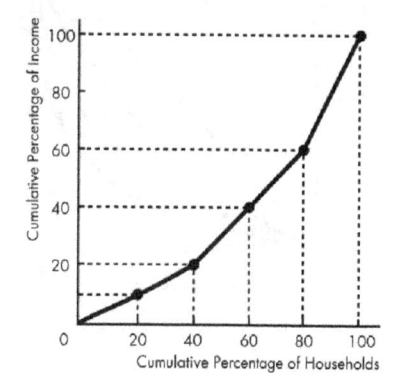

3 In Fig. 19.1, the poorest 20 percent of all households receive what share of income?
  a 10 percent
  b 20 percent
  c 30 percent
  d 40 percent
  e none of the above

4 In Fig. 19.1, the middle 20 percent of all households receive what share of income?
  a 10 percent
  b 20 percent
  c 30 percent
  d 40 percent
  e none of the above

5 The curve in Fig. 19.1 represents the
  a line of fairness.
  b line of equality.
  c learning curve.
  d wage differential curve.
  e Lorenz curve.

6 Consider the Lorenz curves in Fig. 19.2. Which Lorenz curve corresponds to the greatest income *inequality*?
  a *A*
  b *B*
  c *C*
  d *D*
  e impossible to tell without additional information

FIGURE **19.2**

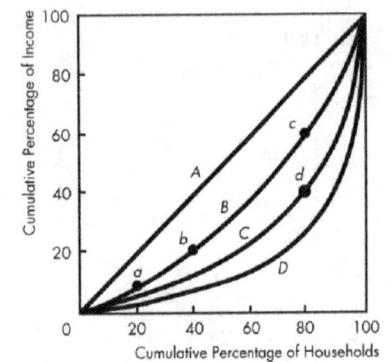

7 In Fig. 19.2, what is curve *A* (a straight line) called?
  a market distribution line
  b line of equality
  c fairness line
  d low-income cutoff line
  e none of the above

8 Which point in Fig. 19.2 indicates that the richest 20 percent of households earn 40 percent of the income?
  a *a*
  b *b*
  c *c*
  d *d*
  e none of the above

9 The distribution of *annual income*
  a understates inequality because it does not take into account the household's stage in its life cycle.
  b understates inequality because it does not take into account the distribution of human capital.
  c overstates inequality because it does not take into account the household's stage in its life cycle.
  d overstates inequality because it does not take into account the distribution of human capital.
  e is an accurate measure of inequality.

10 The distribution of *wealth*
  a understates inequality because it does not take into account the household's stage in its life cycle.
  b understates inequality because it does not take into account the distribution of human capital.
  c overstates inequality because it does not take into account the household's stage in its life cycle.
  d overstates inequality because it does not take into account the distribution of human capital.
  e is an accurate measure of inequality.

11 Which distribution would show the most *equality*?
  a stock of financial wealth
  b stock of human capital
  c annual income
  d lifetime income
  e all show the same degree of equality

12 Wealth differs from income in that
  a income is a stock, wealth is a flow.
  b wealth is derived from income.
  c income is what you earn, wealth is what you own.
  d income is what you own, wealth is what you earn.
  e wealth is preferable to income.

13 The Gini ratio for a perfectly equal distribution
of income is
a equal to zero.
b equal to 1.
c equal to 100.
d equal to infinity.
e named after Gini Lollobrigida

Inequality in the World Economy

14 Recently, the distribution of income within most
countries has become _____ equal and the
distribution of income in the world has become
_____ equal.
a less; less
b less; more
c more; less.
d more; more
e progressively; regressively

The Sources of Economic Inequality

15 Refer to Fig. 19.3. For any given quantity of
labour employed,
a the elasticity of demand is lower for high-
skilled workers than for low-skilled workers.
b wages will be lower for high-skilled workers
than low-skilled workers.
c wages will be higher for high-skilled
workers than low-skilled workers.
d the vertical distance between the curves is
the compensation for the cost of acquiring
skill.
e the vertical distance between the curves is
the present value of human capital.

FIGURE **19.3**

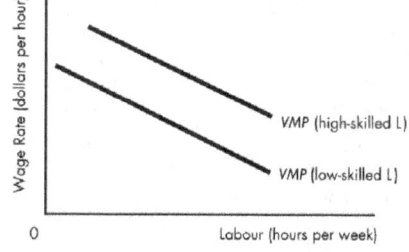

16 The vertical distance between the two supply
curves in Fig. 19.4
a is the compensation for the cost of acquiring
skill.
b is the *VMP* of skill.
c is the result of discrimination against low-
skilled workers.
d is the result of subsidies for high-skilled
workers.
e will disappear if there is free entry in the
high-skilled market.

FIGURE **19.4**

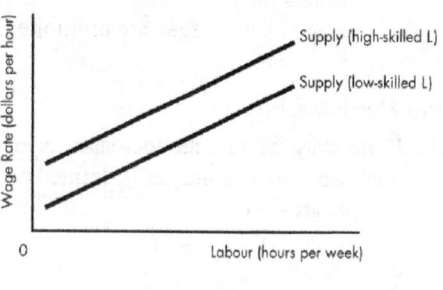

17 Refer only to the information in Fig. 19.4. For
any given wage rate, more hours of
a low-skilled labour will be demanded than
high-skilled labour.
b high-skilled labour will be demanded than
low-skilled labour.
c low-skilled labour will be supplied than
high-skilled labour.
d high-skilled labour will be supplied than
low-skilled labour.
e low-skilled labour will be supplied if the
VMP of skill increases.

18 Wage differentials between males and females
can be explained by
a educational differences.
b human capital differences.
c degree of specialization differences.
d discrimination.
e all of the above.

19 If discrimination restricts a group's access to
education and training, the effect will be to shift
their
a   *VMP* curve rightward and increase the wage.
b   *VMP* curve leftward and decrease the wage.
c   *VMP* curve rightward and decrease the
wage.
d   supply of labour curve up and decrease the
wage.
e   supply of labour curve down and decrease
the wage.

20 Assortative mating means that
a   poor men tend to marry rich women.
b   rich men tend to marry rich women.
c   rich men tend to marry poor women.
d   same-sex marriages occur because "like
attracts like."
e   same-sex marriages are prohibited.

Income Redistribution

21 If the marginal tax rate increases as income
increases, the income tax is defined as
a   progressive.
b   proportional.
c   negative.
d   regressive.
e   excessive.

22 In Table 19.1, which tax plan is proportional?
a   Plan *A*
b   Plan *B*
c   Plan *C*
d   Plan *D*
e   impossible to calculate without additional
information[

TABLE **19.1**

Current Market Income	Tax Payment Plan A	Tax Payment Plan B	Tax Payment Plan C	Tax Payment Plan D
0	0	0	0	200
1,000	100	100	200	200
2,000	200	400	200	200
4,000	400	1,600	200	200

23 In Table 19.1, which tax plan is progressive?
a   Plan *A*
b   Plan *B*
c   Plan *C*
d   Plan *D*
e   impossible to calculate without additional
information

24 Which of the following *reduces* the inequality of
income or wealth relative to the market
distribution?
a   government payments to the poor
b   a regressive income tax
c   large inheritances
d   assortative mating
e   all of the above

25 Redistribution of income from the rich to the
poor will lead to a reduction in total output. This
is known as the
a   market distribution.
b   Robin Hood principle.
c   inheritance principle.
d   big tradeoff.
e   capitalist dilemma.

Short Answer Problems

1 Consider the worlds of Vulcan and Klingon. The
Vulcan Lorenz curve is given in Fig. 19.5, and
the Klingon income distribution data are given in
Table 19.2.

FIGURE **19.5**

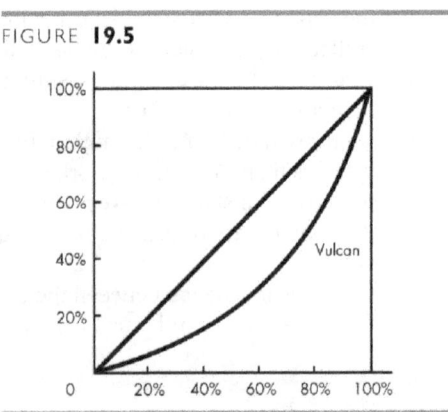

TABLE **19.2**   KLINGON INCOME
DISTRIBUTION

Household Income Rank	Percentage Share Total Income
Lowest 20%	10%
Second 20%	10%
Middle 20%	20%
Fourth 20%	30%
Highest 20%	30%

a   Label the axes of Fig. 19.5 and explain what
the diagonal line represents.

b   Using the data from Table 19.2, draw the
Klingon Lorenz curve on Fig. 19.5.

2 Chapter 5 describes two approaches to ideas about fairness—fair results and fair rules.

a Describe briefly each idea about fairness.

b Using only the information in Short Answer Problem **1**, which idea(s) about fairness can be used to judge Vulcan and Klingon? Which world is more fair according to the idea(s)?

3 Table 19.3 gives information regarding the distribution of income in an economy that generates $100 billion in total annual income.

TABLE **19.3** TOTAL HOUSEHOLD INCOME

Percentage of Households	Total Income (billions of $)	Income Share (%)	Cumulative Percentage of Households	Cumulative Percentage of Income
Poorest 20%	5			
Second 20%	10			
Third 20%	15			
Fourth 20%	20			
Richest 20%	50			

a Complete the last three columns in Table 19.3.

b Draw the Lorenz curve for income in this economy and label it *A*.

4 Now suppose a progressive income tax is levied on the economy. The distribution of after-tax income is given in Table 19.4. We assume none of the revenue is redistributed to families in the economy. Note that total after-tax income is $71 billion.

a Complete Table 19.4.

b Draw the Lorenz curve for after-tax income on the same graph you used for Short Answer Problem **3b** and label it *B*.

c What effect has the progressive income tax had on inequality?

d What is the size of the "big tradeoff" in this case?

TABLE **19.4** AFTER-TAX HOUSEHOLD INCOME

Percentage of Households	After-Tax Income (billions of $)	After-Tax Income Share (%)	Cumulative Percentage of Households	Cumulative Percentage of After-Tax Income
Poorest 20%	5			
Second 20%	9			
Third 20%	12			
Fourth 20%	15			
Richest 20%	30			

5 Finally, suppose that, in addition, the government redistributes all revenue so that the after-benefits (after-tax) income distribution is given in Table 19.5. For example, those in the poorest group receive benefits income of $10 billion so their after-benefits income becomes $15 billion.

TABLE **19.5** AFTER-BENEFITS HOUSEHOLD INCOME

Percentage of Households	After-Benefits Income Share (billions of $)	After-Benefits Income Share (%)	Cumulative Percentage of Households	Cumulative Percentage of After-Benefits Income
Poorest 20%	15			
Second 20%	16			
Third 20%	18			
Fourth 20%	20			
Richest 20%	31			

a Complete Table 19.5.

b Draw the Lorenz curve for after-benefits income on the same graph you used for Short Answer Problems **3b** and **4b** and label it *C*.

c What effect has income redistribution through benefits payments had on inequality?

6 Consider an economy consisting of 100 individuals who are identical in every way. Each lives to be 80 years of age and no older. Between birth and the age of 20 years they earn zero income; between the ages of 21 and 35 each earns an annual income of $30,000; between the ages of 36 and 50 each earns an annual income of $40,000; between the ages of 51 and 65 each receives an annual income of $60,000; and between the ages of 66 and 80 each receives an annual income of $20,000. At any given time there are 20 individuals in each of the five age groups. For simplicity, assume there are no bequests. This information is summarized in Table 19.6.

TABLE **19.6** LIFETIME INCOME PATTERNS

Age Group (years)	Number in Age Group	Individual Annual Income ($)
0–20	20	0
21–35	20	30,000
36–50	20	40,000
51–65	20	60,000
66–80	20	20,000

a Draw the Lorenz curve for lifetime income in this economy and label it *A*.

b Draw the Lorenz curve for annual income in this economy and label it *B*.

c Which of these is a better measure of the inequality among individuals in this economy? Why?

7 Figure 19.6 shows the demand and supply of low-skilled and high-skilled labour. D_L and D_H are the demand curves for low-skilled and high-skilled workers, respectively, and S_L and S_H are the supply curves for low-skilled and high-skilled workers, respectively.

FIGURE **19.6**

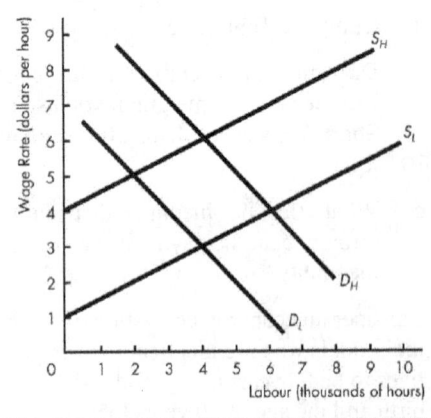

a What is the *VMP* of skill if 5,000 hours of each kind of labour are hired?

b What amount of extra compensation per hour is required to induce the acquisition of skill at the same level of hiring?

c What are the equilibrium wage and quantity of labour in the market for high-skilled labour?

d What are the equilibrium wage and quantity of labour in the market for low-skilled labour?

8 Why is there a "big tradeoff" between equity and efficiency?

A N S W E R S

True/False and Explain

1 **F** More unequal. (440–445)

2 **T** See text discussion. (440–445)

3 **T** Human capital wealth is more equally distributed than financial wealth. (440–445)

4 **F** Income is a flow of earning from a stock of wealth. (440–445)

5 **T** Differences in life cycle stages make annual income more unequal. (440–445)

6 **T** Because average incomes in poor countries are rising faster than average incomes in rich countries. (446–447)

7 **T** Because the value of marginal product of low-skilled workers is lower than that of high-skilled workers. (448–452)

8 **T** Globalization increases the size of the pool of job candidates, increasing the size of winner's "prize." (448–452)

9 **F** The larger the wage differential. (448–452)

10 **T** Wealthy people seek wealthy partners, increasing concentration of wealth. (448–452)

11 **T** Marginal tax rate is constant, but total taxes increase. (453–455)

12 **F** Marginal tax rate rises with higher incomes. (453–455)

13 **F** From poor to rich. (453–455)

14 **T** See text page 454. (453–455)

15 F   Lower production due to the big tradeoff.
(453–455)

Multiple-Choice

1 a   Definition. (440–445)

2 d   100 percent – 60 percent of cumulative
income. (440–445)

3 a   10 percent – 0 percent of cumulative
income. (440–445)

4 b   40 percent – 20 percent of cumulative
income. (440–445)

5 e   Definition. (440–445)

6 d   Curve farthest from 45° line. (440–445)

7 b   Definition. (440–445)

8 c   Moving from 80 percent to 100 percent of
households (richest 20 percent) moves
income from 60 percent to 100 percent of
total (40 percent). (440–445)

9 c   Human capital affects distribution of wealth,
not income. (440–445)

10 d   Life cycle biases distribution income, not
wealth. (440–445)

11 d   Lifetime income is more equally distributed
than annual income or than any wealth
distribution in a given year. (440–445)

12 c   Wealth is a stock, income is a flow derived
from wealth. (440–445)

13 a   Since no area inside the Lorenz curve.
(440–445)

14 b   See Text Fig. 19.8. (446–447)

15 c   Reverse of **a** is true. **d** applies to supply. **e** is
nonsense. (448–452)

16 a   See Text Fig. 19.9(b). (448–452)

17 c   No demand curves on figure. Increased
VMP skill shifts demand, not supply.
(448–452)

18 e   All can contribute to differentials. (448–452)

19 e   Education and training would increase
human capital and shift supply curve labour
up. (448–452)

20 b   Marriage within a socioeconomic class.
(448–452)

21 a   Definition. (453–455)

22 a   Taxes are always 10 percent of income.
(453–455)

23 b   With higher income, tax rate increases from
0 percent, to 10 percent, to 20 percent, to 40
percent. (453–455)

24 a   Others increase inequality. (453–455)

25 d   See text discussion. (453–455)

Short Answer Problems

1 a   See Fig. 19.5 Solution. The diagonal line
represents hypothetical income equality.

  b   See Fig. 19.5 Solution.

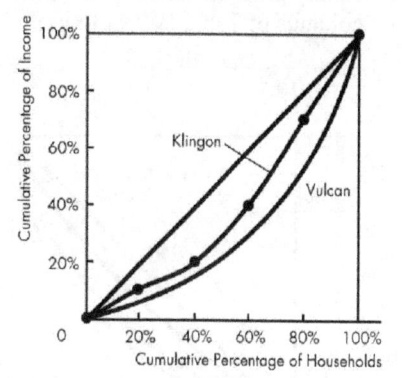

FIGURE **19.5** SOLUTION

2 a   According to the fair-results idea, there
should be equality of incomes. According to
the fair-rules idea, there should be equality
of opportunity.

  b   Since we have information only on income
outcomes and not on the processes or
opportunities leading to those incomes, only
the fair-results idea can be used to judge
Vulcan and Klingon. Since the Klingon
Lorenz curve is closer to the line of equality,
the Klingon world is more fair according to
the fair-results idea.

3 a   Table 19.3 is completed as Table 19.3
Solution. The income share for each group
of families is the total income of that group
as a percentage of total income in the
economy ($100 billion). The cumulative
percentage of income (last column) is
obtained by adding the percentage income
share of the group (from the third column) to
the total percentage income share of all
poorer groups of families.

TABLE **19.3**   SOLUTION
TOTAL HOUSEHOLD INCOME

Percentage of Households	Total Income (billions of $)	Income Share (%)	Cumulative Percentage of Households	Cumulative Percentage of Income
Poorest 20%	5	5	20	5
Second 20%	10	10	40	15
Third 20%	15	15	60	30
Fourth 20%	20	20	80	50
Richest 20%	50	50	100	100

b   The curve labelled *A* in Fig. 19.7 is the Lorenz curve for total family income. This simply plots the values in the last two columns of Table 19.3 Solution.

FIGURE **19.7**

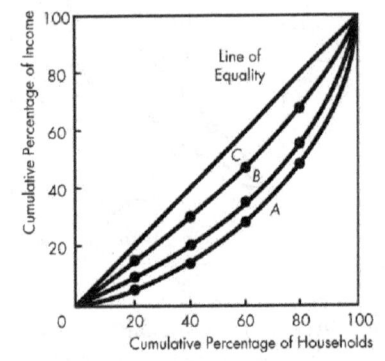

4   a   Table 19.4 is completed as Table 19.4 Solution.

TABLE **19.4**   SOLUTION
AFTER-TAX HOUSEHOLD INCOME

Percentage of Households	After-Tax Income (billions of $)	After-Tax Income Share (%)	Cumulative Percentage of Households	Cumulative Percentage of After-Tax Income
Poorest 20%	5	7	20	7
Second 20%	9	13	40	20
Third 20%	12	17	60	37
Fourth 20%	15	21	80	58
Richest 20%	30	42	100	100

b   The curve labelled *B* in Fig. 19.7 is the Lorenz curve for after-tax household income.

c   The progressive income tax has reduced inequality by taking a larger percentage of income from higher income groups.

d   The "big tradeoff" is the fact that a more equally shared pie results in a smaller pie. While the after-tax distribution is now more equal, total income has been reduced from $100 billion to $71 billion. The $29 billion loss is the cost of the big tradeoff, due to the costs of administering the redistribution program and the deadweight loss from weakened work incentives.

5   a   Table 19.5 is completed as Table 19.5 Solution.

TABLE **19.5**   SOLUTION
AFTER-BENEFITS HOUSEHOLD INCOME

Percentage of Households	After-Benefits Income Share (billions of $)	After-Benefits Income Share (%)	Cumulative Percentage of Households	Cumulative Percentage of After-Benefits Income
Poorest 20%	15	15	20	15
Second 20%	16	16	40	31
Third 20%	18	18	60	49
Fourth 20%	20	20	80	69
Richest 20%	31	31	100	100

b   The curve labelled *C* in Fig. 19.7 is the Lorenz curve for after-tax, after-benefits household income.

c   Income redistribution through benefits payments has reduced inequality.

6   a   Since each individual in the economy earns exactly the same lifetime income, the Lorenz curve for lifetime income coincides with the line of equality and is labelled *A* in Fig. 19.8.

FIGURE **19.8**

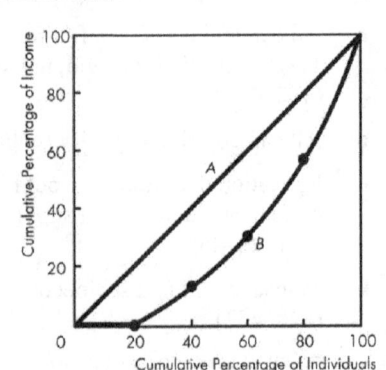

b The Lorenz curve for annual income is labelled *B* in Fig. 19.8. It reflects that the poorest 20 percent of individuals, those aged 0–20 years, receive 0 percent of the annual income; the second-poorest 20 percent, 60–80 years, 13 percent; the third-poorest 20 percent, 21–35 years, 20 percent; the fourth-poorest 20 percent, 36–50 years, 27 percent; and the richest 20 percent, 51–65 years, 40 percent.

c The distribution of lifetime income is a better measure of the degree of inequality. In this imaginary economy all individuals are identical (equal), a fact reflected in equal lifetime incomes. The only reason annual income distribution in this economy is not equal is because individuals are at different stages of identical life cycles.

7 a The *VMP* of skill is the difference between the *VMP* of high-skilled versus low-skilled labour; the vertical distance between the demand curves for high-skilled and low-skilled labour. In Fig. 19.6, the *VMP* of skill is $3 per hour when 5,000 hours of each kind of labour are employed.

b Since labour supply curves give the minimum compensation workers are willing to accept in return for supplying a given quantity of labour, the extra compensation for skill is the vertical distance between the supply curves of high-skilled and low-skilled labour. At 5,000 hours of employment for both kinds of labour, this is $3 per hour.

c In equilibrium in the market for high-skilled labour, the wage rate will be $6 per hour and employment will be 4,000 hours of labour. This occurs at the intersection of the D_H and S_H curves.

d In equilibrium in the market for low-skilled labour, the wage rate will be $3 per hour and employment will be 4,000 hours of labour. This occurs at the intersection of the D_L and S_L curves.

8 If greater equity means increasing the equality of income, it can only be achieved by income redistribution; the income of some must be taxed in order to make transfer payments to others. However, there are incentive effects that reduce the total amount of income available to be distributed.

If productive activities such as work are taxed, there will be a tendency to reduce time spent in those activities. Furthermore, any redistribution program would require resources to administer it and thus leave fewer resources for other productive activities. Thus we arrive at the insight that a more equally shared pie results in a smaller pie.

Part 6 Wrap Up
Understanding Factor Markets and Inequality

PROBLEM

FIGURE **P6.1**   LABOUR MARKETS FOR PROGRAMMERS

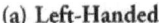

(a) Left-Handed

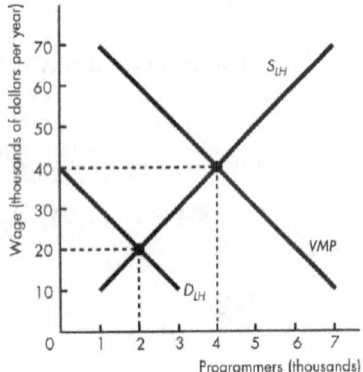

(b) Right-Handed

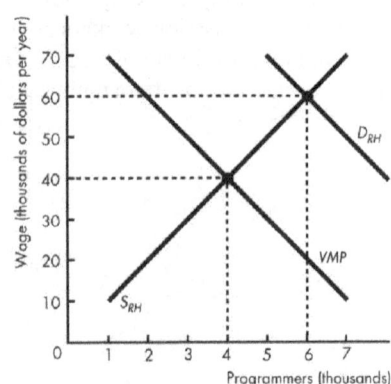

Suppose the computer software industry uses only two inputs—programmers (labour) and computers (capital). All programmers, whether left-handed or right-handed, have computer science degrees, are equally skilled and productive, and have the value of marginal product (*VMP*) curve in Fig. P6.1(a) and (b).

Software firms (run mostly by right-handers) discriminate against left-handed programmers, believing (wrongly) that left-handers are less productive than right-handers. Figure P6.1(a) shows the supply curve of

left-handed programmers and firms' demand curve for left-handed programmers.

Software firms also discriminate in favour of right-handed programmers, believing (wrongly) that right-handers are more productive than left-handers. Figure P6.1(b) shows the supply curve of right-handed programmers and firms' demand curve for right-handed programmers.

a What is the relationship between the wage and the value of marginal product for left-handed programmers? for right-handed programmers?

b Explain the competitive forces that would tend to eliminate this form of discrimination, even without government legislation.

c If owners of firms are so strongly prejudiced against left-handers that they are willing to accept lower profits rather than employ left-handers, will competitive forces eliminate this discrimination?

d The government introduces pay equity legislation, designed to equalize wages between left-handers and right-handers. The legislation includes an educational program to inform firms of the true and equal productivity of all programmers, regardless of their "handedness." If the program is successful, what will be the wage of programmers? the employment of left-handed programmers? the employment of right-handed programmers?

e With equalized programmer wages, what is now the relationship between the wage and the value of marginal product for left-handed programmers? for right-handed programmers? What other meaning does *pay equity* have besides paying different groups equal wages?

f As a result of the pay equity legislation, what has happened to the *average* wage of programmers?

g As a result of the pay equity legislation, what has happened to the average wage of *left-handed* programmers? Explain the impact on the decisions of left-handers to invest in human capital.

MIDTERM EXAMINATION

You should allocate 22 minutes for this examination (11 questions, 2 minutes per question). For each question, choose the one *best* answer.

1 Wealth is the
  a large flow of income earned by the rich.
  b large stock of income available to the rich.
  c stock of assets owned by an individual.
  d flow of assets to an individual from labour.
  e flow of assets to an individual from capital.

2 Refer to Fig. P6.2. For any given wage,
  a the elasticity of demand for high-skilled workers is greater than the elasticity of demand for low-skilled workers.
  b more high-skilled workers will be hired than low-skilled workers.
  c more low-skilled workers will be hired than high-skilled workers.
  d the horizontal distance between the curves is the compensation for the cost of acquiring skill.
  e the horizontal distance between the curves is the *MRP* of skill.

FIGURE **P6.2**

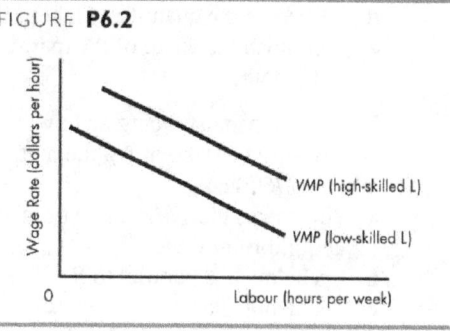

3 Consider the Lorenz curves in Fig. P6.3. Which point indicates that the richest 20 percent of families earn 60 percent of the income?
  a *a*
  b *b*
  c *c*
  d *d*
  e none of the above

FIGURE **P6.3**

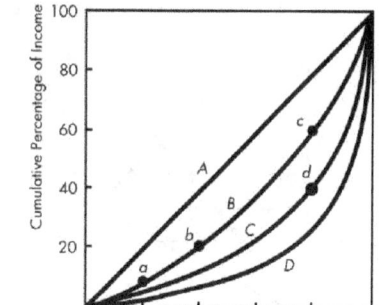

4 The demand curve for a factor of production will shift leftward as a result of a(n)
   a decrease in the price of the factor.
   b increase in the price of the factor.
   c increase in technology.
   d increase in the price of output.
   e decrease in the price of output.

5 A profit-maximizing firm hires labour in a competitive labour market. If the value of the marginal product of labour is greater than the wage, the firm should
   a increase the wage rate.
   b decrease the wage rate.
   c increase the quantity of labour it hires.
   d decrease the quantity of labour it hires.
   e diminish the value of the marginal product of labour.

6 For a monopsonist facing an upward-sloping supply curve of labour (S), the marginal cost of labour (MCL) curve
   a intersects the VMP curve of labour at the equilibrium wage.
   b is below and parallel to S.
   c is identical to S.
   d is above and parallel to S.
   e is none of the above.

7 Suppose the government passes a minimum wage law that prohibits anyone from hiring labour at less than $8 per hour. In Fig. P6.4, the monopsonist will hire
   a 250 hours of labour.
   b 300 hours of labour.
   c 350 hours of labour.
   d 400 hours of labour.
   e 500 hours of labour.

8 If the marginal tax rate decreases as income increases, the income tax is defined as
   a progressive.
   b proportional.
   c negative.
   d regressive.
   e redistributive.

9 Which of the following is *not* part of an individual's stock of wealth?
   a stock of assets
   b flow of earnings
   c human capital
   d physical assets
   e financial assets

10 "A more equally shared pie results in a smaller pie" is the
   a big tradeoff.
   b Robin Hood principle.
   c assortative mating principle.
   d capitalist dilemma.
   e socialist creed.

11 In a market for a nonrenewable natural resource, if the expected rate of price rise is less than the interest rate, then demand
   a increases, supply decreases, and the price of the resource rises.
   b increases, supply increases, and the price of the resource rises.
   c decreases, supply decreases, and the price of the resource may rise or fall.
   d decreases, supply increases, and the price of the resource rises.
   e decreases, supply increases, and the price of the resource falls.

FIGURE **P6.4**

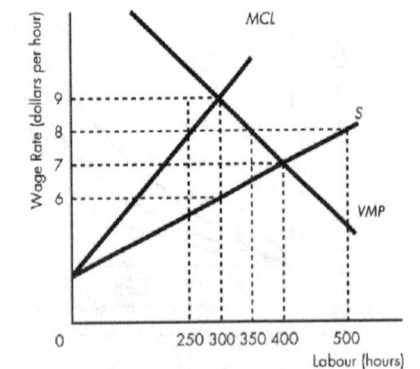

ANSWERS

Problem

a For the 2,000 left-handed programmers employed, the wage ($20,000 per year) is much less than the value of marginal product of $60,000 per year. For the 6,000 right-handed programmers employed, the wage ($60,000 per year) is much more than the value of marginal product of $20,000 per year.

b A nondiscriminating firm could earn higher profits by employing more left-handed programmers as long as their value of marginal product exceeds the wage. Similarly, profits will increase by employing fewer right-handed programmers as long as their wage exceeds their value of marginal product. The competitive outcome would be a wage of $40,000 per year for every programmer, and employment of 4,000 left-handed and 4,000 right-handed programmers.

c No. Firms can continue to discriminate if they "pay" for the discrimination in the form of lower profits.

d A successful education program alters firms' beliefs about left-handed and right-handed programmers and moves the demand curves to the true *VMP* curves. The outcome will be the same as the competitive outcome—a wage of $40,000 per year for every programmer, and employment of 4,000 left-handed and 4,000 right-handed programmers.

e The wage is equal to the value of marginal product for every programmer. Pay equity also means each labourer is being paid an amount *equal* to the value of his or her value of marginal product.

f Before legislation, the average yearly wage of programmers was a weighted (by employment) average of the wages of left-handers and right-handers.

$$\frac{(\$20,000 \times 2,000) + (\$60,000 \times 6,000)}{8,000} = \$50,000$$

After legislation, the average yearly wage has fallen to $40,000.

g The average yearly wage of left-handed programmers has increased from $20,000 to $40,000. This creates an incentive for more left-handers to invest in the necessary human capital (computer science degrees) to become programmers, increasing the quantity supplied of left-handed programmers.

Midterm Examination

1 c Wealth is a stock of assets. Assets are stocks, not flows (**d**, **e**); income is a flow, not stock (**b**). (440–445)

2 b Reverse of **a** is true. **d** is true for vertical distance between supply curves. **e** is true for vertical distance between demand curves. (448–452)

3 d Moving from 80 percent to 100 percent of families (richest 20 percent) moves income from 40 percent to 100 percent of total (60 percent). (440–445)

4 e Lower price of output lowers *VMP*. **a** and **b** move along the curve, **c** and **d** shift the curve rightward. (417–419)

5 c Hiring more labour increases profit since *VMP* > *MC*. **a** and **b** are wrong because a competitive firm can't change the wage; **e** is nonsense. (417–419)

6 e *MCL* is above but not parallel to *S*. *MCL* intersects *S* at equilibrium *QL*, not wage. (420–425)

7 c New *MCL* is flat at $8 until it hits the *S* curve, yielding *QL* where new *MCL* intersects *VMP*. (420–425)

8 d Definition. (453–455)

9 b Flow of earnings is *income* from an individual's stock of wealth. (440–445)

10 a Tradeoff between equity and efficiency arises because redistribution uses scarce resources and weakens incentives. (453–455)

11 e See text discussion of Hotelling Principle. (426–429)

Chapter 20
Measuring GDP and Economic Growth

Gross Domestic Product

Gross domestic product (GDP) is the market value of all final goods and services produced within a country in given time period.

- Total production measured by market value of each good.

- Only new **final goods** (bought by final users) are measured, not **intermediate goods** (bought by firms from firms, used as inputs in production).

- GDP measures total production *and* total income *and* total expenditure.

Circular flow of expenditure and income shows four economic sectors (firms, households, governments, rest of world) operating in factor markets and goods (and services) markets.

- Households sell factor services to firms in return for income—total household income = aggregate income (Y).

- Firms produce goods and services, and sell **consumption expenditure** (C) to households.

- Firms' expenditures on **investment** (I = purchase of *new* capital + additions to inventory).

- Governments buy goods and services from firms (**government expenditures** (G)). Governments also collect taxes and make financial transfers to households and firms, but these not part of the circular flow.

- Rest of world buys our **exports** (X) and sells us **imports** (M): **net exports** = exports – imports.

Circular flow shows that aggregate income = aggregate production = aggregate expenditure:

$$Y = C + I + G + X - M$$

Capital stock is plant, equipment, buildings, and inventories used to produce goods and services.

- Investment (I) = purchase of *new* capital.

- **Depreciation** = decrease in value of firm's capital because of wear and tear.

- **Gross investment** = net investment + replacing depreciated capital.

- Δ capital stock = **net investment** = gross investment – depreciation.

Measuring Canada's GDP

Statistics Canada measures GDP two ways on the basis of equality:

$$income = production = expenditure$$

- *Expenditure approach* measures $C + I + G + X - M$.

- *Income approach* adds up all incomes paid from firms to households (with some adjustments).

  - Net domestic income at factor cost = wages, salaries, and supplementary income + other factor income (profits + interest/investment income + farmers' income + nonfarm unincorporated business income).

  - Net domestic product at market prices = net domestic income + indirect taxes – subsidies.

  - GDP = net domestic product + depreciation.

- Gap between expenditure and income approaches is a statistical discrepancy, which arises due to measurement problems.

GDP increases from production of more goods and services, or from higher prices for goods and services.

- **Nominal GDP** is the value of final goods and services produced in a given year valued at that year's prices = sum of expenditures on goods and services.

♦ **Real GDP** is the value of final goods and services produced in given year when valued at prices of a reference base year. Real GDP measures changes in production only.

♦ Real GDP is calculated using quantities produced in each year, but valued with prices from the reference base year.

- In reference base year, real GDP = nominal GDP.

- To calculate real GDP in the current year, multiply current year quantity by base year price for each good, and sum resulting values.

The Uses and Limitations of Real GDP

Real GDP is used to compare standards of living over time and across countries.

♦ One method of comparison is **real GDP per person** (real GDP/population)—the value of goods and services enjoyed by the average person.

♦ Canada's real GDP per person over time shows growth of potential GDP per person (with slowdown after the 1960s) as well as fluctuations of real GDP around potential GDP.

- **Potential GDP** is the maximum level of real GDP that can be produced while avoiding shortages of labour, capital, land, and entrepreneurial ability that would bring rising inflation.

♦ Lower growth rates of real GDP per person after the 1970s lead to an accumulated gap in real GDP (known as the Lucas wedge).

♦ **Business cycles** are fluctuations of the pace of expansion of real GDP.

- Each cycle has two turning points (a peak and a trough), and two phases (**recession** when real GDP decreases for two or more quarters, and **expansion** when real GDP increases).

International comparisons of real GDP per capita are further flawed by currency conversion problems.

♦ Using market exchange rates, U.S. real GDP per person is 15 times that of China.

♦ Using purchasing power parity, or PPP, prices (prices prevailing in one country, such as the U.S.), U.S. real GDP per person is only 6.5 times China's.

Real GDP as a measure of economic well-being is flawed for the following reasons:

♦ Real GDP does not include factors increasing economic well-being (household production, underground economic activity, health, life expectancy, leisure, security, political freedom, social justice).

♦ Real GDP does not include factors that lower economic well-being (pollution).

♦ The Human Development Index is a broader measure of economic well-being that includes health and education measures, as well as real GDP per person.

Appendix: Graphs in Macroeconomics

Graphs in macroeconomics focus on changes in variables over time.

♦ **Time-series graphs** show the relationship between time (measured on x-axis) and other variable(s) (measured on y-axis).

♦ Reveals variable's level, direction of change, speed of change.

♦ Also reveals **cycle** (tendency to alternate between upward and downward movements), and **trend** (tendency to move in one general direction).

♦ A ratio scale is used on graphs to help see the growth rate of variables.

HELPFUL HINTS

1 Studying the circular flow and national accounts can be boring, but it is useful for several reasons. First, they provide crucial equalities that are the starting point for our economic model—studying this material will help you pass the course! Second, many current debates involve tradeoffs between economic growth and environmental damage. Understanding what GDP does and does not measure is crucial to this debate. Third, in macroeconomics we study how several markets operate simultaneously in a joint, interrelated equilibrium—the circular flow gives us our first taste of this interrelation.

2 One of the key equations in this and future chapters is

$$Y = C + I + G + X - M$$

which underlies Chapters 26 and 27.

Macroeconomics tries to understand what affects GDP, and we start by measuring production (GDP). However, we cannot directly measure production easily. The circular flow helps us measure it indirectly. In the circular flow, production is purchased by the four economic decision makers (measured by expenditure), and money earned from these sales is used to pay incomes. Therefore, production can be measured in three equivalent ways: income = expenditure = value of production (GDP). Therefore:

Y (income) $= C + I + G + X - M$ (expenditure).

3 Be sure to distinguish carefully between intermediate goods and investment goods. Both are goods sold by one firm to another, but they differ in terms of their use. Intermediate goods are processed and then resold, while investment goods are final goods. Also note that national income accounts include purchases of residential housing as investment because housing, like business capital stock, provides a continuous stream of value over time.

4 Note the difference between government expenditures on goods and services (G) and government transfer payments. Both involve payments by government, but transfer payments are not payments for currently produced goods and services. Instead, they are simply a flow of money, just like (negative) taxes.

5 It is important to understand the difference between real and nominal GDP. Nominal GDP is the value, *in current prices*, of the output of final goods and services in the economy in a year. Real GDP evaluates those final goods and services *at the prices prevailing in a base year (constant prices)*.

Nominal GDP can rise from one year to the next, either because prices rise or because output of goods and services rises. A rise in real GDP, however, means that output of goods and services has risen.

If we had a simple economy that produced only pizzas, this rise in real GDP would be easy to measure—are there more pizzas to eat? In a multiple-good economy, we have a more complex task and must turn to a weighted average of goods and services we produce.

SELF-TEST

True/False and Explain

Gross Domestic Product

1 GDP measures intermediate goods, not final goods.

2 Net investment gives the net addition to the capital stock.

3 In the aggregate economy, income is equal to expenditure and to GDP.

4 If exports currently equal imports, then GDP must equal consumption plus investment plus government expenditures.

5 Net exports are positive if expenditures by foreigners on goods and services produced in Canada are greater than expenditures by Canadian citizens on goods and services produced in other countries.

Measuring Canada's GDP

6 Real GDP is calculated by using the current year quantity and the base year price for each good.

7 If there were only households and firms and no government, market price and factor cost would be equal for any good.

8 Net exports are used in the income approach to measuring GDP.

9 If you are interested in knowing whether the economy is producing more output, you would look at real GDP rather than nominal GDP.

The Uses and Limitations of Real GDP

10 Potential GDP is the level of real GDP when labour, capital, land, and entrepreneurial ability are fully employed.

11 The Lucas wedge shows that business cycles lower economic well-being.

12 The Human Development Index shows the same ranking of countries as does real GDP per person.

13 If underground economic activity was included in GDP calculations, measured GDP levels would be higher.

Appendix: Graphs in Macroeconomics

14 A time-series graph shows the level of a variable across different groups at a point in time.

15 A ratio scale is used to distinguish a variable's level.

Multiple-Choice

Gross Domestic Product

1 For the aggregate economy, income equals
  a expenditure, but these are not generally equal to GDP.
  b GDP, but expenditure is generally less than these.
  c expenditure equals GDP.
  d expenditure equals GDP only if there are no government or foreign sectors.
  e expenditure equals GDP only if there is no depreciation.

2 Which of the following is a consumption expenditure?
  a spending by the CBC on children's programs
  b welfare payments to single mothers
  c the purchase of a new car by the IPSCO steel company
  d the purchase of a new car by the Singh household
  e the purchase of a computer by the IPSCO steel company

3 Danielle's Deliveries had $200,000 worth of delivery vans in 2012. During 2013, Danielle scrapped $20,000 worth of worn-out vans and bought $45,000 worth of new vans. What was Danielle's net investment in 2013?
  a $20,000
  b $25,000
  c $45,000
  d $65,000
  e $225,000

4 Which of the following would be counted as investment expenditure in GDP calculations?
  a The government builds a new building.
  b The Hong household buys a computer.
  c IPSCO Steel adds 1 million sheets to inventory.
  d IPSCO Steel sells pipe to Alaska.
  e Fred's Pizza Joint sells an old oven to Velma's Pizza Haven.

5 Which of the following adds to Canadian GDP?
  a I shovel my own driveway
  b I sell my used Honda
  c the production and sale of flour to a bakery
  d the purchase of a CD made in China
  e the ice cream I buy from my grocery store

Measuring Canada's GDP

6 To obtain the factor cost of a good from its market price,
- **a** add indirect taxes and subtract subsidies.
- **b** subtract indirect taxes and add subsidies.
- **c** subtract both indirect taxes and subsidies.
- **d** add both indirect taxes and subsidies.
- **e** subtract depreciation.

7 From the data in Table 20.1, what is net investment in Eastland?
- **a** −$160
- **b** $160
- **c** $240
- **d** $400
- **e** $500

TABLE **20.1** DATA FROM EASTLAND

Item	Amount ($)
Wages, salaries, and supplementary labour income	800
Government expenditures on goods and services	240
Depreciation	240
Gross private domestic investment	400
Personal income taxes net of transfer payments	140
Indirect taxes	120
Net exports	80
Consumption expenditures	640

8 From Table 20.1, what additional data are needed to compute net domestic income at factor cost?
- **a** income of nonfarm unincorporated businesses
- **b** transfer payments
- **c** subsidies
- **d** depreciation
- **e** net taxes

9 From the data in Table 20.1, what is GDP in Eastland?
- **a** $1,120
- **b** $1,180
- **c** $1,360
- **d** $1,420
- **e** cannot be calculated with the given data

10 From the data in Table 20.2, compute Southton's nominal GDP in the current year.
- **a** $197
- **b** $198
- **c** $208
- **d** $209
- **e** cannot be calculated with the given data

TABLE **20.2** DATA FROM SOUTHTON

Item	Price ($) Base	Price ($) Current	Quantity Base	Quantity Current
Rubber ducks	1.00	1.25	100	100
Beach towels	7.00	6.00	12	14

11 From the data in Table 20.2, compute Southton's nominal GDP in the base year.
- **a** $184
- **b** $197
- **c** $198
- **d** $209
- **e** cannot be calculated with the given data

12 From the data in Table 20.2, compute Southton's real GDP in the base year.
- **a** $184
- **b** $197
- **c** $198
- **d** $209
- **e** cannot be calculated with the given data

13 From the data in Table 20.2, compute Southton's real GDP in the current year.
- **a** $184
- **b** $197
- **c** $198
- **d** $209
- **e** cannot be calculated with the given data

The Uses and Limitations of Real GDP

14 The underground economy is all economic activity that
- **a** produces intermediate goods or services.
- **b** is not taxed.
- **c** is legal but unreported or is illegal.
- **d** has negative social value.
- **e** is conducted underground.

15 Given that pollution is a byproduct of some production processes,
- **a** GDP accountants adjust GDP downward.
- **b** GDP accountants adjust GDP upward.
- **c** GDP accountants do not adjust GDP unless pollution is a serious problem.
- **d** GDP tends to overstate economic well-being.
- **e** GDP tends to understate economic well-being.

16 Which of the following is *not* a reason for GDP incorrectly measuring the value of total output?
a leisure time
b household production
c underground economic activity
d depreciation
e environmental quality

17 Which of the following is the major reason China's measured GDP might be underestimated?
a It includes replacement of depreciated capital stock.
b It includes production processes that create pollution as a side-effect.
c It ignores decreases in health and life expectancy.
d It does not use purchasing power parity prices.
e It ignores human rights and political freedoms.

18 Which of the following statements by politicians is talking about the business cycle?
a "Canadian unemployment is falling due to the upturn in the economy."
b "Crime rates increase every spring as the school year ends."
c "An average of 220,000 new jobs are created each year in Canada."
d "More capital investment will create more jobs."
e "Business always rises just before Christmas."

19 In New Adanac, the average growth rates of potential GDP per capita were 4 percent in the 1980s, but fell to 1 percent in the 1990s. Which of the following statements about this change is true?
a A strong recession must have started in the 1990s.
b 1990 was a peak year for the business cycle.
c The Lucas wedge equals 3% of GDP per person for each of the 10 years.
d The Lucas wedge equals 1% of GDP per person for each of the 10 years.
e The Lucas wedge equals 4% of GDP per person for each of the 10 years.

20 From the data in Table 20.3, in which year did Sudland's business cycle reach a peak?
a 2009
b 2010
c 2011
d 2012
e 2013

TABLE 20.3 DATA FROM SUDLAND

Year	Actual Real GDP	Potential Real GDP
2007	100	100
2008	107	105
2009	114	111
2010	113	118
2011	114	126
2012	122	134
2013	140	140

21 From the data in Table 20.3, in which year did Sudland's business cycle hit a trough?
a 2009
b 2010
c 2011
d 2012
e 2013

22 From the data in Table 20.3, in which year(s) did Sudland have a recession?
a 2010
b 2010 and 2011
c 2009, 2010, 2011
d 2010, 2011, 2012
e 2010, 2011, 2012, 2013

23 Why is the Human Development Index thought to be a better measure of economic well-being than real GDP per person?
a It includes a measure of resource depletion.
b It ignores health, which is hard to measure.
c It includes leisure time and household production.
d It includes health and education measures, as well as real GDP per person.
e It includes only health and education measures, ignoring real GDP per person.

Appendix: Graphs in Macroeconomics

24 Figure 20.1 on the next page is a time-series graph. The horizontal axis measures _____ and the vertical axis measures _____.
a time; the variable of interest
b time; slope
c the variable of interest in one year; the variable of interest in another year
d the variable of interest; time
e slope; time

FIGURE **20.1**

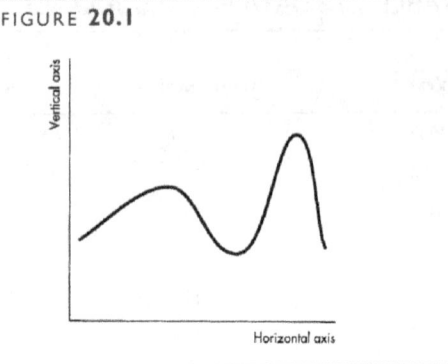

25 The tendency for a variable to rise or fall over
time is called its
a   slope.
b   trend.
c   *y*-coordinate.
d   level.
e   correlation.

Short Answer Problems

Ct **1** How can we measure gross domestic product by
using either the expenditure or the income
approach, when neither of these approaches
actually measures production?

2 Suppose nominal GDP rises by 75 percent
between year 1 and year 2.

a   If the average level of prices has also risen
by 75 percent between year 1 and year 2,
what has happened to real GDP?

b   If the average level of prices has risen by
less than 75 percent between year 1 and year
2, has real GDP increased or decreased?

3 What *productive* activities are *not* measured and
thus are *not* included in GDP? Is this lack of
measurement a serious problem?

4 Use the data for Northland given in Table 20.4 to
compute the following:

a   GDP

b   net investment

c   net exports

TABLE **20.4** DATA FOR NORTHLAND

Item	Amount (billions of $)
Consumption expenditure (*C*)	600
Taxes (*Tax*)	400
Transfer payments (*TR*)	250
Exports (*X*)	240
Imports (*M*)	220
Government expenditure on goods and services (*G*)	200
Gross investment (*I*)	150
Depreciation (*Depr*)	60

5 Consider the data in Table 20.5 on potential and
real GDP in $ for the country of Dazedland.

a   Identify the peaks and troughs of the
business cycle for this economy.

b   In which years is this economy in recession?

c   What happened to productivity in 2011?

d   Calculate the Lucas wedge that resulted after
2011. (Assume the population stays
constant, so that the changes in real GDP
and potential GDP would be reflected in
changes in real GDP per person and
potential GDP per person.)

TABLE **20.5** DATA FOR DAZEDLAND

Year	Actual Real GDP	Potential Real GDP
2007	200	200
2008	212	210
2009	211	220
2010	209	230
2011	240	240
2012	240	240
2013	248	248
2014	258	256
2015	254	264
2016	266	272

6 Figure 20.2 on the next page shows the circular
flow for Northweston. Aggregate income is $450
billion, exports are $40 billion, imports are $30
billion, consumption expenditure is $275 billion,
government expenditure is $100 billion.

a Identify what each label A, B, C, D, and E represents as an economic value.

b What is aggregate expenditure? Explain your steps.

c What is GDP? Explain your steps.

d What is investment? Explain your steps.

Figure **20.2**

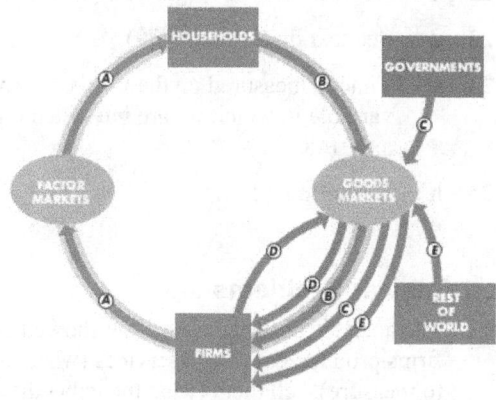

7 Consider the following economic activities. Identify to which of the markets in the circular flow each activity belongs. Give a one-line reason for each answer.

a Fred of the Forest buys a new loincloth in preparation for his date with Angela.

b Fred goes back to school at the University of Sandhurst to get his BA in Vine Swinging.

c While in school, Fred goes on a Spring Break vacation in Florida.

d Fred has graduated and is getting paid to knock down trees by Treetop City.

e Fred buys his first house.

f Fred and Angela open up Treetop Bed and Breakfast, catering only to Europeans.

8 Consider the list of economic activities in Short Answer Problem **7**. Identify whether the activity involves expenditures and, if so, to which component of expenditures each activity belongs (*C, I, G, X, M*).

ANSWERS

True/False and Explain

1 **F** The opposite is true. (468)

2 **T** Net investment nets out depreciation (replacement of worn-out capital), leaving only new capital additions. (470)

3 **T** From the circular flow, firm production is sold (expenditure) and earnings are used to pay out incomes. (469)

4 **T** If $X = M$, then $X - M = 0$, and $Y = C + I + G + 0$. (469)

5 **T** By definition of exports (goods and services sold to the rest of the world) and imports (goods bought from the rest of the world), net exports = exports − imports. (468)

6 **T** Definition. (473)

7 **T** Market price = factor cost + taxes − subsidies. (471–472)

8 **F** They are an expenditure, used in the expenditure approach. (471)

9 **T** Real GDP measures the quantity of goods and services, while nominal GDP measures current dollar value and includes price level increases. (473)

10 **F** Shows impact of productivity slowdown. (474)

11 **F** There is a correlation between real GDP per person and real GDP per person, but rankings are different. (479)

12 **T** Since they are omitted, and they are a productive activity, real GDP would be higher if they were included. (478)

13 **F** Real GDP is an imperfect measure of standard of living; answer depends on factors such as exchange rates between each country's currency. (476–477)

14 **F** Definition of a cross-section graph. A time-series graph shows the relationship between time (on *x*-axis) and other variable(s) (on *y*-axis). (482)

15 **F** Shows when the *growth rate* changes. (483)

Multiple-Choice

1 c Expenditure = money earned by sales of produced goods, which is used to pay incomes (including profits). (470)

2 d **a** is government expenditure, **b** is transfer payment, **c** and **e** are investment. (468–470)

3 b Net investment = gross investment ($45,000) – replacement of depreciated capital ($20,000). (470)

4 c **a** is government expenditure, **b** is consumption, **d** is an export, and **e** is not current production. (468–470)

5 e **a** is household production, **b** is previous production, **c** is an intermediate good, **d** was produced outside Canada. (468)

6 b Market price = factor cost + indirect taxes – subsidies, so factor cost = market price – indirect taxes + subsidies. (471–473)

7 b Net investment = gross investment – capital consumption. (471–473)

8 a Table lists the other four components of factor incomes. (471–473)

9 c $Y = C + I + G + X - M = 640 + 400 + 240 + 80 = 1,360$. (471–473)

10 d Nominal GDP = sum of dollar value (= current price × current quantity) of all goods = ($1.25 × 100) + ($6 × 14) = 209. (473)

11 a Nominal GDP = sum of current price × current quantity of all goods = ($1 × 100) + ($7 × 12) = 184. (473)

12 a In base year, real GDP = nominal GDP. (473)

13 c Real GDP = sum of base price × current quantity of all goods = ($1 × 100) + ($7 × 14) = 198. (473)

14 c Definition. (477)

15 d No such adjustment occurs, so GDP overstates economic well-being. (478)

16 d Depreciation is part of GDP. (477–479)

17 d See text discussion. (476–477)

18 a Upturn implies expansion, which implies unemployment falls. **b** and **e** are irrelevant and seasonal, **c** is the average over the cycle, **d** is growth in potential GDP. (475–476)

19 c We cannot tell when year was, and low growth is not a recession. Lucas wedge = accumulated loss of output from slowdown in real GDP growth = 4% – 1% = 3%. (474–476)

20 a Growth turns from positive to negative. (475–476)

21 b Real GDP hits its lowest point. (475–476)

22 a Negative real GDP growth. (475–476)

23 d See text discussion. (479)

24 a Time is measured on the x-axis and the variable in which we are interested on the y-axis. (482)

25 b Definition. (482)

Short Answer Problems

1 The analysis of the circular flow showed that firms produce goods and services (what we wish to measure), sell them (what the expenditure approach measures), and then use the proceeds to pay for factor incomes, rents, profits, etc. (what the income approach measures). Therefore expenditure = production = income.

2 a Real GDP is unchanged. The increased value of goods and services is only because of increased prices.

   b The fact that prices have risen less in proportion to the increase in nominal GDP means that real GDP has increased.

3 Activities that produce goods and services not included in GDP are underground economic activity and household production. Underground activities are not reported, because they are illegal or are legal but are not reported to circumvent taxes or government regulations. Household production includes productive activities that households perform for themselves. Because they do not hire someone else to mow the lawn or wash the car, they are not included in GDP. The seriousness of the problem depends on the actual size of the activity. The underground economy is estimated at about 5 to 15 percent of the Canadian economy.

4 a GDP = $C + I + G + (X - M)$ = $970 billion.

   b Net $I = I - Depreciation$ = $90 billion.

   c Net exports = $X - M$ = $20 billion.

5 a Peaks occur the year before percentage change in real GDP turns from positive to negative, 2008 and 2014. Troughs occur when percentage change in real GDP turns from negative to positive, 2010 and 2015.

b The economy is in recession when the growth rate of real GDP is negative, 2009, 2010, and 2015.

c Since growth in potential GDP slowed initially to zero and then continued at a slow rate, there is a productivity slowdown.

d The Lucas wedge calculates the amount of difference between actual real GDP and what it would have been if real GDP had grown at the rate of potential GDP after the productivity slowdown. Since potential GDP was initially growing at $10 per year, that means the potential GDP would have been:
$250 in 2012
$260 in 2013
$270 in 2014
$280 in 2015
$290 in 2016
The shortfalls compared to actual real GDP are:
$10 in 2012
$12 in 2013
$12 in 2014
$26 in 2015
$24 in 2016
for a total Lucas wedge of $84.

6 a A is aggregate income, B is consumption expenditure, C is government expenditure, D is investment, and E is net exports.

b Aggregate income = aggregate expenditure = $450 billion.

c Aggregate income = aggregate expenditure = GDP = $450 billion.

d Investment is the only missing component of aggregate expenditure, and can be deduced from the equation $Y = C + I + G + X - M$, or $450 = $275 + I + $100 + $40 - $30, implying $I = $65 billion. (Note that components of aggregate expenditure must all flow through the goods market.)

7 a Goods and service market—purchase of a good.

b Goods and service market—purchase of an educational service.

c This is an expenditure, but money flows to the United States. Therefore, part of the domestic market.

d Factor market—Fred is working for wage income.

e Goods and service market—purchase of a good.

f Goods and services market—purchase of a service.

8 a Expenditure (C).

b Expenditure (C).

c Not a domestic expenditure (M).

d Not an expenditure, a factor service purchase.

e Expenditure (I—house purchases count as investment).

f Expenditure (X).

Chapter 21
Monitoring Jobs and Inflation

Employment and Unemployment

Unemployment rises in recessions and falls in expansions.

♦ Unemployment creates problems from lost production/incomes of unemployed and damaged job prospects from lost human capital.

Statistics Canada surveys households on their job status.

♦ **Working-age population** = Number of people age 15 years and over.

♦ **Labour force** = employed + unemployed

• Employed = those with full-time or part-time jobs.

• Unemployed = without work, actively seeking within last four weeks, waiting to be called back after layoff, or waiting to start new job within four weeks.

♦ **Unemployment rate** = percentage of labour force unemployed. Increases during recessions.

♦ **Labour force participation rate** = percentage of working-age population in labour force. Strong upward trend until 1990; decreases during recessions, increases during expansions.

♦ **Employment-to-population ratio** = percentage of working-age population with jobs. Increased from 1960s to 1990 (many new jobs created); decreases during recessions, increases during expansions.

Measured unemployment rate excludes some underutilized labour (because they have not looked for a job within the last four weeks).

♦ **Marginally attached workers**—neither working nor looking for work, but available and want work.

♦ **Discouraged workers**—stopped looking for jobs because of repeated job search failures.

The most costly unemployment is long-term (it lasts more than 14 weeks), which fluctuates with the business cycle.

Unemployment and Full Employment

There is always some unemployment due to frictions, structural change, and cycles.

Frictional unemployment—due to normal labour turnover. Depends on the number of entrants/re-entrants and job creation/destruction.

♦ People become unemployed when they are laid off, voluntarily quit, or enter or re-enter the labour force to search for jobs.

♦ People end unemployment when they are hired, recalled, or withdraw from the labour force.

Structural unemployment—job losses due to technological change or international competition changing the skills need to perform jobs or the location of jobs.

♦ Lasts longer than frictional unemployment and is higher in slow-growing eastern provinces.

Cyclical unemployment—higher than normal unemployment at a business cycle trough and lower than normal at a peak.

Natural employment—only frictional and structural unemployment (no cyclical unemployment).

♦ **Natural unemployment rate** = natural unemployment as a percentage of the labour force.

♦ **Full employment**—unemployment rate equals natural unemployment rate.

♦ The natural unemployment rate is influenced by

  • the population age distribution—more younger workers means more frictional unemployment.

  • the scale of technological change.

  • the level of the real wage rate.

  • the level of unemployment benefits—higher benefits encourage more job search.

♦ Economists agree there is natural unemployment, but disagree about the size of the natural rate and the amount it fluctuates.

Actual unemployment rate fluctuates around the natural rate, as real GDP fluctuates around potential GDP over the business cycle.

♦ **Output gap**—the gap between real GDP and potential GDP.

  • When the output gap is positive, unemployment rate < the natural rate.

  • When the output gap is negative, unemployment rate > the natural rate.

♦ The natural unemployment rate is trending downward in Canada.

The Price Level, Inflation, and Deflation

Changes in **price level** (average level of prices) determines the value of future payments (loans, savings).

♦ **Inflation rate**—percentage change in price level.

♦ Unpredictable inflation

  • creates winners/losers by creating unpredictable changes in the value of money, redistributing income and wealth.

  • lowers real GDP and employment.

  • leads to resources diverted from productive activities to predicting inflation.

♦ **Hyperinflation**—rapid inflation where money loses its value very quickly.

Consumer Price Index (CPI) measures average of prices paid for a fixed basket of consumer goods and services.

♦ CPI = 100 for reference base period (2002).

♦ CPI basket is constructed from monthly surveys of consumers' spending habits.

$$CPI = \frac{\text{Cost of CPI basket at current prices}}{\text{Cost of CPI basket at base-period prices}} \times 100.$$

Inflation rate = percentage change in CPI.

♦ CPI overstates inflation rate (biased upward) because

  • new goods replace old goods.

  • quality improvements create some of price rises.

  • consumers change consumption toward cheaper goods not reflected in the fixed-basket price index.

  • consumers substitute toward discount outlets not covered in CPI surveys.

♦ Magnitude of CPI bias is probably low in Canada, but leads to distorted contracts, more government outlays, and incorrect wage bargaining.

Alternative price indexes include

♦ **GDP deflator** [(nominal GDP/real GDP) × 100], which measures all goods and controls for biases.

♦ **chained price index for consumption** [(nominal consumption/real consumption) ×100], which does not use fixed quantities.

Core inflation rate excludes volatile elements of CPI to reveal underlying trends.

Real variables (nominal variables divided by GDP deflator) are used to see what is "really" happening to key macroeconomic variables.

HELPFUL HINTS

1 In a dynamic economy, some unemployment is efficient. There are economic benefits of frictional unemployment to individuals and to society. Younger workers typically experience periods of unemployment trying to find jobs that match their skills and interests. The benefit of the resulting frictional unemployment is a more satisfying and productive work life. Society benefits because the frictional unemployment that accompanies such a job search allows workers to find jobs in which they are more productive. As a result, total production of goods and services increases. (Compare this case with the case for graduates in the Republic of China up until the 1990s. They were assigned jobs upon graduation, with very little personal input about the type of job or location.)

On the other hand, structurally unemployed workers will not get a new job without retraining or relocation. There is a greater cost to the worker and society—structurally unemployed workers are typically unemployed for longer time periods. These workers bear much of the cost of restructuring industries in our economy, although society gains in the long run from shifts of labour and other resources to new industries.

2 The term "full employment," or its equivalent "natural rate of unemployment," does not mean that everyone has a job. Rather, it means that the only unemployment is frictional and structural—there is no cyclical unemployment.

It is possible for the actual rate of unemployment to be less than the natural rate of unemployment because it is possible for employment to exceed full employment levels. In these situations, people are spending too little time searching for jobs, and therefore less-productive job matches are being made.

3 There are three different types of unemployment, but defining these types does not explain them. Explanations of how unemployment occurs are a goal of the remaining chapters in the textbook!

S E L F - T E S T

True/False and Explain

Employment and Unemployment

1 The employment-to-population ratio is the percentage of the working-age population in the labour force.

2 If the employment-to-population ratio increases, unemployment always decreases.

3 George was laid off last month, and is waiting to be recalled to his old job, so he is not actively seeking work. George is *not* counted as unemployed.

4 If the working-age population is 600,000, employment is 400,000, and unemployment is 30,000, then the unemployment rate is 7.0%.

5 A university student seeking a job is counted as unemployed.

6 If the number of discouraged workers decreases, the employment-to-population ratio decreases as they begin to look for jobs.

7 Discouraged workers are counted as unemployed but probably should not be.

Unemployment and Full Employment

8 Being unemployed for a few months after graduating from university always hurts the graduate.

9 A decline in the number of jobs in the automobile sector matched by an equal increase in the number of jobs offered in the banking sector will not alter the unemployment rate.

10 At full employment, there is no unemployment.

11 Bill has just graduated from high school and is looking for his first job. Bill is frictionally unemployed.

12 Fluctuations in unemployment over the business cycle create frictional unemployment.

The Price Level, Inflation, and Deflation

13 The CPI overstates the inflation rate because it ignores substitution toward higher-quality goods by households.

14 The market basket used in calculating the CPI changes each year.

15 The magnitude of the CPI bias in Canada is high.

Multiple-Choice

Employment and Unemployment

1 In a country with a working-age population of 20 million, 13 million are employed, 1.5 million are unemployed, and 1 million of the employed are working part time, half of whom wish to work full time. The size of the labour force is
a 20 million.
b 15.5 million.
c 14.5 million.
d 13 million.
e 11.5 million.

2 In a country with a working-age population of 20 million, 13 million are employed, 1.5 million are unemployed, and 1 million of the employed are working part time, half of whom wish to work full time. The labour force participation rate is
a 75.5%.
b 72.5%.
c 65%.
d 57.5%.
e none of the above.

3 In a country with a working-age population of 20 million, 13 million are employed, 1.5 million are unemployed, and 1 million of the employed are working part time, half of whom wish to work full time. The unemployment rate is
a 10%.
b 10.3%.
c 11.5%.
d 15.4%.
e none of the above.

4 Who of the following would be counted as unemployed in Canada?
a Doris only works five hours a week, but is looking for a full-time job.
b Kanhaya has stopped looking for work, since he was unable to find a suitable job during a two-month search.
c Sharon is a university student with no job.
d Maurice has been laid off from his job for 20 weeks, but expects a call back soon.
e Bogdan has been laid off from his job, but does not expect a call back and is not looking.

5 If the employment-to-population ratio increases,
a the unemployment rate *must* decrease.
b the labour force participation rate *must* increase.
c the labour force participation rate will be unaffected.
d aggregate hours worked *must* increase.
e none of the above.

6 The economic costs of unemployment include
a workers quitting and going to university.
b political problems for government.
c lost human capital of the unemployed.
d the creation of winners and losers due to job creation/destruction.
e the diversion of resources from productive activities to predicting unemployment.

7 Including discouraged workers in the measured unemployment rate would
a not change the measured unemployment rate.
b lower the measured unemployment rate.
c raise the natural rate of unemployment.
d raise the full employment rate.
e raise the measured unemployment rate.

8 If the number of discouraged workers increases, all else unchanged, the
a unemployment rate will increase.
b employment-to-population ratio will decrease.
c labour force participation rate will increase.
d labour force participation rate will decrease.
e employment-to-population ratio will increase.

Unemployment and Full Employment

9 Which of the following events would raise cyclical unemployment?
   a Real GDP growth slows down or turns negative.
   b Unemployment benefits increase.
   c The pace of technological change increases.
   d Both job destruction and job creation increase.
   e All of the above

10 Unemployment will increase if there is an increase in the number of people
   a retiring.
   b withdrawing from the labour force.
   c recalled from layoffs.
   d leaving jobs to go to school.
   e leaving school to find jobs.

11 Who of the following would be considered structurally unemployed?
   a a Saskatchewan farmer who has lost her farm and is unemployed until retrained
   b a Nova Scotia fishery worker who is searching for a better job closer to home
   c a steelworker who is laid off but who expects to be called back soon
   d an office worker who has lost her job because of a general economic slowdown
   e none of the above

12 Who of the following would be considered cyclically unemployed?
   a a Saskatchewan farmer who has lost her farm and is unemployed until retrained
   b a Nova Scotia fishery worker who is searching for a better job closer to home
   c a steelworker who is laid off but who expects to be called back soon
   d an office worker who has lost her job because of a general economic slowdown
   e none of the above

13 Who of the following would be considered frictionally unemployed? A steelworker who
   a loses her job because of technological change.
   b is laid off but expects to be called back within a week.
   c gives up her job because she retires.
   d decides to leave the labour force and become a full-time ballet student.
   e becomes discouraged and stops looking for jobs.

14 In a recession, what is the largest source of the increase in unemployment?
   a people quitting jobs
   b people getting laid off
   c new entrants to the labour force
   d re-entrants to the labour force
   e involuntary part-time workers

15 At full employment, there is no
   a natural unemployment.
   b unemployment.
   c cyclical unemployment.
   d structural unemployment.
   e frictional unemployment.

16 Unemployment caused by permanently decreased demand for horse-drawn carriages is an example of
   a cyclical unemployment.
   b marginal unemployment.
   c frictional unemployment.
   d structural unemployment.
   e discouraged unemployment.

17 The natural rate of unemployment is
   a the rate at which unemployment equals 0%.
   b the same as cyclical unemployment.
   c the rate at which cyclical unemployment equals 6%.
   d the rate at which cyclical unemployment equals 0%.
   e none of the above.

The Price Level, Inflation, and Deflation

18 Comparing the core inflation rate to the Consumer Price Index, the core inflation rate
   a controls for the biases of the CPI.
   b measures all goods produced, not just consumer goods.
   c uses current-period quantities, not base-period quantities.
   d excludes the volatile elements of the CPI.
   e includes volatile elements not in the CPI.

19 If the inflation rate is positive, the price level in an economy is
   a falling rapidly.
   b rising.
   c constant.
   d falling slowly.
   e zero.

20 From the data in Table 21.1, what is Southton's Consumer Price Index for the current year?

TABLE **21.1** DATA FROM SOUTHTON

	Price ($)		Quantity	
Item	Base	Current	Base	Current
Rubber ducks	1.00	1.25	100	100
Beach towels	9.00	6.00	12	14

a 112
b 105.6
c 100.5
d 100
e 94.7

21 Refer to the data in Table 21.1. Between the base year and the current year, the relative price of rubber ducks
a remained unchanged.
b fell.
c rose.
d cannot be determined with the given information.
e depends on whether overall inflation was positive.

22 Which of the following is *not* a reason the Consumer Price Index overstates inflation?
a New goods of higher quality and prices replace old goods.
b Quality improvements create some part of price rises in existing goods and services.
c Consumers change their consumption basket toward cheaper goods not reflected in the fixed-basket price index.
d Consumers substitute toward using discount outlets not covered in CPI surveys.
e It does not measure the underground economy.

23 The technique used to calculate the CPI implicitly assumes that consumers buy
a relatively more of goods with relative prices that are increasing.
b relatively less of goods with relative prices that are decreasing.
c the same relative quantities of goods as in a base year.
d goods and services whose quality improves at the rate of growth of real GDP.
e more computers and CD players and fewer black-and-white TVs.

24 How does an unpredictable inflation rate cause problems?
a Business cycles become more variable.
b The stock market falls in value.
c The value of money rises.
d Resources are diverted from productive activities to tax evasion.
e Resources are diverted from productive activities to forecasting inflation.

25 In 2009 the Consumer Price Index measured 114.3. In 2010 it measured 118.0. What was inflation in 2010?
a 1.18%
b 3.1%
c 3.2%
d 3.7%
e 18%

Short Answer Problems

🄲🄽 **1** Explain why an economy does not have 0 percent unemployment when it has full employment.

🄲🄽 **2** Should the government try to force the unemployment rate down as close to zero as possible? Discuss some problems such a policy might create.

3 Consider the following information about an economy: working-age population—20 million; full-time employment—8 million; part-time employment—2 million (1 million of whom wish they had full-time jobs); unemployment—1 million.

  a What is the labour force in this economy? What is the labour force participation rate?
  b What is the unemployment rate?
  c What is the involuntary part-time rate?
  d What is the employment-to-population ratio?
  e If 0.6 million of those unemployed are frictionally and structurally unemployed, what is the natural rate of unemployment?
  f What is the amount of cyclical unemployment?
  g Can you tell if this economy is in recession or expansion? Is the output gap positive or negative?

4 Are the costs of unemployment more severe for frictional or structural unemployment? Why?

5 Explain the difference between cyclical and structural unemployment. How would you tell a cyclically unemployed person from a structurally unemployed person?

6 Table 21.2 gives data for Southland, where there are three consumption goods: bananas, coconuts, and grapes.

TABLE **21.2** DATA FOR SOUTHLAND

Goods	Quantity in Base-Period Basket	Base Period Price ($)	Base Period Expenditure ($)	Current Period Price ($)	Current Period Expenditure ($)
Bananas	120	6		8	
Coconuts	60	8		10	
Grapes	40	10		9	

a Complete the table by computing expenditures for the base period and expenditures for the same quantity of each good in the current period.

b What is the value of the basket of consumption goods in the base period? in the current period?

c What is the Consumer Price Index for the current period?

ⓒ d On the basis of the data in this table, would you predict consumers would make any substitutions between goods between the base period and the current period? If so, what kind of problems would this create for your measurement of the CPI?

7 Examine each of the following changes in John Carter's labour market activity, and explain whether they constitute unemployment, employment, or being out of the labour force. If unemployment, which of the three types of unemployment is represented?

a John graduates from Barsoom High and starts looking for a job.

b John has no luck finding the full-time job he wants and takes a part-time job cleaning out the canals.

c Canal-cleaning doesn't work out for John because of unforeseen allergies, so he quits.

d Discouraged by the lack of work, John stops looking and stays home watching his favourite soap opera, *As Mars Turns*.

e John sees an advertisement on TV for the Barsoom Swordfighter School, and enrols to get his BSF.

f John graduates at the top of his class and joins the Princess Dejah Thoris guards.

g Barsoom University invents a new laser personal defence system, and the Princess disbands her guards—John spends a long time looking for work.

h John sees an advertisement seeking someone to help explore the ruins of the lost city of Rhiannon and signs up as security—the six-armed tribes are particularly ferocious there.

ⓒ 8 Consider the data from 1995 in Table 21.3 on Canada as a whole and Newfoundland specifically.

TABLE **21.3**

Economy	Labour Force Participation Rate	Unemployment Rate	Employment-to-Population Ratio
Canada	64.8	9.5	58.6
Newfoundland	53.1	18.3	43.3

Source: Statistics Canada, *Labour Force Review.*

Newfoundland has twice the unemployment of Canada, as well as a radically lower employment-to-population ratio and labour force participation rate. By examining these, can you get any insight into the impact of a high unemployment rate on the labour market in Newfoundland? Why is the gap in the employment-to-population ratio (15.3 points) so much bigger than the unemployment gap (8.8 points)?

A N S W E R S

True/False and Explain

1 F Percentage of working-age population with jobs. (494–495)

2 F True if participation decreases or doesn't increase much, otherwise false. (494–495)

3 F Since he is waiting for recall, he is counted. (493)

4 **T** Unemployment rate = [unemployment/ (unemployment + employed)] × 100 = (30,000/430,000) × 100 = 7.0%. (494–495)

5 **F** Counted as out of labour force (not actively seeking work). (494–5)

6 **F** This change will only change the labour force participation. (495–496)

7 **F** Not counted as unemployed, but probably should be. (495–496)

8 **F** Depends on whether the time unemployed leads to a better job. (497)

9 **F** Workers retrain/relocate, leading to more structural unemployment. (497)

10 **F** Full employment still has frictional and structural unemployment. (497–498)

11 **T** Searching for jobs = frictionally unemployed. (497)

12 **F** Create *cyclical* unemployment. (497)

13 **T** See text discussion. (503–504)

14 **F** Changed every 10 years. (500)

15 **F** Low due to Statistics Canada's corrections. (504)

Multiple-Choice

1 **c** Employed + unemployed. (494–495)

2 **b** Labour force/working-age population = 14.5/20 = 72.5%. (494–495)

3 **b** Unemployed/labour force = 1.5/14.5 = 10.3%. (493–495)

4 **d** Doris is employed, Kanhaya isn't looking for work, Sharon is out of the labour force, Bogdan does not expect to be called back. (493)

5 **e** Any of **a** to **d** *might* occur, but they do not *have* to occur. (493–495)

6 **c** **a** is a gain, **b** is a real but not an economic cost, **d** is normal activity, **e** is nonsense. (492)

7 **e** It would add extra unemployed workers to the measured rate. (495–496)

8 **d** Discouraged workers were unemployed, but stop looking and exit the labour force, so unemployment rate decreases, labour force participation decreases, employment-to-population ratio is unchanged. (495–496)

9 **a** **b** to **d** raise frictional or structural unemployment, but if real GDP growth slows down, cyclical unemployment increases. (497)

10 **e** Others all lower unemployment. (497)

11 **a** Structural unemployment includes having the wrong skills. Others are frictional or cyclical unemployment. (497)

12 **d** Cyclical unemployment is due to economy-wide slowdowns. (497)

13 **b** **a** is structural and the rest are not officially unemployed. (497)

14 **b** See text discussion. (497)

15 **c** Definition. (497–498)

16 **d** Definition—unemployment caused by structural change. (497)

17 **d** Definition. (497–498)

18 **d** By construction. (504–505)

19 **b** Positive inflation implies current price level – past price level > 0, by definition. (503)

20 **e** CPI = [(sum of current prices × base quantities)/(sum of base prices × base quantities)] × 100. (500–502)

21 **c** Ratio P(ducks)/P(towels) has risen. (500–502)

22 **e** This problem is for real GDP. (503–504)

23 **c** Because assumes a fixed basket. (503–504)

24 **e** Forecasting inflation becomes important because unpredictable inflation leads to unpredictable winners and losers because the value of money *falls*. (500)

25 **c** Inflation = (Δ price level/past price level) × 100 = [(118 – 114.3)/114.3] × 100 = 3.2%. (502)

Short Answer Problems

1 An economy always has some unemployment, of people searching for jobs—frictional and structural unemployment. We define full employment as when there is zero cyclical unemployment, but still some frictional and structural unemployment.

2 Pushing down the unemployment rate would eliminate frictional unemployment (which would reduce the number of good job matches) and structural unemployment (which would prevent the structural readjustment the economy needs). Therefore, it does not seem like a good idea to get unemployment as close to zero as possible!

3 a The labour force is 11 million, the sum of employment and unemployment. Labour force participation rate = percentage of the working-age population who are in the labour force = 11/20 or 55 percent.

b The unemployment rate is 9.1 percent, the number of unemployed as a percentage of the labour force.

c It is 9.1 percent, the percentage of the labour force who are part time and want full time.

d It is 50 percent, the percentage of the working-age population with a job.

e Natural unemployment is frictional plus structural unemployment = 0.6 million. Natural rate of unemployment is 5.45% = (0.6 million/11 million) × 100.

f Cyclical unemployment is actual unemployment minus natural unemployment, or 0.4 million.

g Since there is positive cyclical unemployment, real GDP is below potential GDP and the output gap is negative. It is possible we have a recession (negative real GDP growth), but the economy could be expanding out of the recession.

4 The costs of unemployment include lost output of the unemployed, and deterioration of skills and abilities; in other words, human capital erodes. These costs are higher for structural unemployment because it lasts longer, and often workers' human capital becomes worthless in the marketplace.

5 Cyclical unemployment is caused by a downturn in the economy, when there is a decrease in demand for all products. Structural unemployment is caused by structural changes in a specific industry or region and there is a decrease in demand for a certain type of labour whose skills are no longer desired.

Cyclical unemployment will end when the economy turns up. Structural unemployment will end when the workers retrain or move.

6 a Table 21.2 is completed here as Table 21.2 Solution. Note that the base-period quantities are evaluated at current prices to

find the value of quantities in the current period.

TABLE **21.2** SOLUTION

Goods	Quantity in Base-Period Basket	Base Period Price ($)	Base Period Expenditure ($)	Current Period Price ($)	Current Period Expenditure ($)
Bananas	120	6	720	8	960
Coconuts	60	8	480	10	600
Grapes	40	10	400	9	360

b The value of the basket of consumption goods in the base period is the sum of expenditures in that period: $1,600. The value of the basket of consumption goods in the current period is obtained as the sum of values of quantities in that period: $1,920.

c The Consumer Price Index is the ratio of the value of quantities in the current period to the base period expenditure, times 100:

CPI = (1,920/1,600) × 100 = 120.

d Since the price of grapes has fallen relative to the prices of bananas and coconuts, we expect consumers to substitute toward the cheaper grapes and away from bananas and coconuts. This substitution means our CPI measure will be biased upward.

7 a He is an entrant and is frictionally unemployed.

b He is now employed, although he is also involuntarily part time.

c He is a job leaver, and is frictionally unemployed.

d He is a discouraged worker, but technically out of the labour force.

e He is still out of the labour force.

f He is employed.

g He is structurally unemployed.

h He is employed again.

8 The higher unemployment rate in Newfoundland has pushed many workers out of the labour force—they have become discouraged workers and are not even attempting to find work. (We can see this in the lower participation rate.) The bigger gap in the employment-to-population ratio reflects this exiting, because it includes measured unemployed and discouraged workers.

Part 7 Wrap Up
Monitoring Macroeconomic Performance

PROBLEM

a Consider the following data for the economy of Autoland for 2012 and 2013. Calculate the value of nominal GDP for each year.

TABLE P7.1 2012

Item	Amount (billions of $)
Government expenditures on goods and services	60
Government transfer payments	30
Income taxes	80
Wages, etc., paid to labour	200
Export earnings	30
Consumption expenditure	180
Import payments	25
Net investment expenditure	15
Depreciation	5

TABLE P7.2 2013

Item	Amount (billions of $)
Wages, etc., paid to labour	200
Indirect taxes	20
Profits	20
Subsidies	5
Interest income	5
Depreciation	10
Farmers' income	10
Income of nonfarm unincorporated business	10

b Using your data from **a**, complete the following table:

TABLE P7.3

Year	Nominal GDP (billions of $)	Price Level	Real GDP (billions of 2002 $)
2012		132.5	
2013		140.0	

c What is the inflation rate in 2013?

d If real GDP = potential GDP in 2012, and potential GDP is unchanged in 2013, what has happened to the output gap and cyclical unemployment between 2012 and 2013?

MIDTERM EXAMINATION

You should allocate 16 minutes for this examination (8 questions, 2 minutes per question). For each question, choose the one *best* answer.

1   Which of the following people would be counted as unemployed in Canada?
    a   Doris only works 20 hours a week and is not looking for a full-time job.
    b   Kanhaya has stopped looking for work since he has had no luck finding a job.
    c   Sharon is a university student with no job.
    d   Maurice is working in his garden while looking for work.
    e   Taylor is on disability leave.

2   Which of the following is *not* an example of investment in the expenditure approach to measuring GDP? General Motors
    a   buys a new auto stamping machine.
    b   adds 500 new cars to inventories.
    c   buys Canadian government bonds.
    d   builds another assembly plant.
    e   replaces worn-out stamping machines.

3   The capital stock in the year 2013 equals the capital stock in the year 2012
    a   minus depreciation.
    b   plus net investment plus depreciation.
    c   plus gross investment.
    d   plus net investment.
    e   plus net investment minus depreciation.

4   In a country with a working-age population of 20 million, 13 million are employed, 1.5 million are unemployed, and 1 million of the employed are working part time, half of whom wish to work full time. The employment-to-population ratio is
    a   57.5%.
    b   65%.
    c   72.5%.
    d   75.5%.
    e   none of the above.

5   A business cycle is the
    a   increase in real GDP for more than two periods.
    b   decrease in real GDP for more than two periods.
    c   increase in the economic potential to produce goods and services.
    d   irregular fluctuation of potential GDP around real GDP.
    e   irregular fluctuation of real GDP around potential GDP.

6   Which of the following is a reason why normal measurement of real GDP is too high as an estimate of economic well-being?
    a   It excludes expenditures on health.
    b   It excludes the impact of pollution.
    c   It excludes leisure time.
    d   It excludes household production.
    e   It uses purchasing power parity prices.

7   Unpredictable inflation creates problems for society because
    a   it makes it difficult for consumers to switch to cheaper goods when relative prices are rising.
    b   it creates a negative output gap.
    c   consumers are unable to tell quality changes in goods from price changes.
    d   it leads to society diverting resources from productive activities to predicting inflation.
    e   discount outlets become too important in the overall consumption decisions of households.

8   If a price index was 150 at the end of 2013 and 165 at the end of 2014, what was the rate of inflation for 2014?
    a   9.1%
    b   10%
    c   15%
    d   50%
    e   65%

ANSWERS

Problem

a For 2012, calculate nominal GDP as the sum of $C + I + G + X - M$. For G, you must use only expenditures on goods and services, and you need to calculate gross investment (= net investment + depreciation, or $20 billion). Thus nominal GDP = 180 + 20 + 60 + 30 − 25 = $265 billion for 2012.

For 2013 you need to use the income approach. First, calculate net domestic income at factor cost = wages, etc. + other factor income (profits + interest income + farmers' income + income of nonfarm unincorporated business) = 200 + 20 + 5 + 10 + 10 = $245 billion. Next, to get net domestic product add indirect taxes and subtract subsidies from net domestic income, or 245 + 20 − 5 = $260 billion. Finally, to get gross domestic product, add depreciation to net domestic product, or 260 + 10 = $270 billion for 2013.

b Table P7.3 is completed here as Table P7.3 Solution, using the formula real GDP = (nominal GDP/price level) × 100.

TABLE P7.3 SOLUTION

Year	Nominal GDP (billions of $)	Price Level	Real GDP (billions of 2002 $)
2012	265	132.5	200.0
2013	270	140.0	192.9

c The inflation rate is equal to

$$5.7\% = \frac{140.0 - 132.5}{132.5} \times 100$$

d If potential GDP = $200 billion in 2012 and 2013, then in 2013 real GDP was less than potential GDP by $7.1 billion and the output gap has gone from $0 in 2012 to −$7.1 billion in 2013. The decrease in real GDP to below potential GDP means the unemployment rate must be above the natural rate in 2013, so that cyclical unemployment is positive in 2013.

Midterm Examination

1 d Doris is employed part time, Kanhaya is not looking for work (discouraged worker), and Sharon and Taylor are out of the labour force. (493–49)

2 c This is a purchase of financial assets, not capital stock. (470)

3 a Definition. (470)

4 b Employed/working-age population × 100 = 13/20 × 100 = 65%. (494–495)

5 e Definition. (474–476)

6 b Pollution would lower economic well-being. (477–479)

7 d See text discussion. (500)

8 b 10% = [(165 − 150)/150] × 100. (502)

Chapter 22
Economic Growth

The Basics of Economic Growth

Economic growth is a sustained expansion of production possibilities, measured as the increase in real GDP.

- ♦ **Economic growth rate** = annual percentage change in real GDP =
$$\frac{\text{Real GDP this year} - \text{Real GDP last year}}{\text{Real GDP last year}} \times 100$$

- ♦ Standard of living depends on **real GDP per capita** (real GDP/population).

- ♦ Compounding leads to rapid growth—**rule of 70** states that the number of years it takes a variable to double in value = 70/(percentage growth rate).

Economic Growth Trends

Canada's growth rate was low in the 1950s, higher in the 1960s, average in the 1970s, slower in the 1980s, and below average after 1996.

- ♦ Internationally, between 1960 and now, Canada's real GDP per person has been similar to the United States, but Japan and other Asian countries have been catching up to both countries.

How Potential GDP Grows

Economic growth requires a sustained increase in potential GDP.

- ♦ More real GDP produced requires less leisure and more time spent working.

- ♦ Potential GDP is the level of real GDP at full-employment quantity of labour (with fixed amounts of land, entrepreneurial ability, capital).

- ♦ **Aggregate production function** (*PF*) shows the relationship between real GDP and the quantity of labour employed, all other influences constant.

- • Increase in quantity of labour employed creates movement up along the *PF*.

Aggregate labour market determines the quantity of labour hours employed and real GDP supplied.

- ♦ Demand for labour (*LD*)—quantity of labour demanded at each **real wage rate** = (money or nominal wage rate)/price level.

  - • Firms hire labour as long as marginal product of labour > real wage rate.

  - • Law of diminishing returns says that firms will hire more labour only if real wage rate falls.

- ♦ Supply of labour (*LS*)—quantity of labour supplied at each real wage rate.

  - • Increase in real wage rate increases quantity of labour supplied because more people work and more people choose to work longer hours.

- ♦ Real wage rate adjusts to create full-employment labour market equilibrium where *LD* = *LS*, with real GDP = potential GDP.

Potential GDP increases if the labour supply increases or **labour productivity** (real GDP per hour of labour) increases.

- ♦ Labour supply increases if hours per worker increase, or employment-to-population ratio increases, or working-age population increases.

  - • Labour supply curve shifts right, real wage rate decreases, increasing hiring, causing movement along the *PF*, increasing potential GDP.

- ♦ Increase in labour productivity increases demand for labour—therefore, real wage rate increases, quantity of labour supplied increases, *PF* shifts upward, and potential GDP increases.

- ♦ Increases in population lower real GDP per person, but increases in labour productivity increase it.

Why Labour Productivity Grows

A fundamental precondition for labour productivity growth is an appropriate *incentive* system created by firms, markets, property rights, and money.

Given these preconditions, the pace of growth is affected by three things that increase labour productivity:

- Physical capital growth increases capital per worker.

- Human capital growth from education and training (including learning by repetitively doing tasks).

- Discovery of new technologies (often embodied in new capital).

Growth Theories, Evidence, and Policies

Classical growth theory argues that real GDP growth is temporary because it leads to population explosions that bring real GDP back to subsistence levels.

- It is also called Malthusian theory.

- Modern-day Malthusians argue that high population growth and climate change will eventually lower real GDP per person.

Neoclassical growth theory says that real GDP per person grows due to technological change inducing growth in capital per hour of labour.

- Assumes population growth rate is independent of economic growth.

- Driving force of economic growth is technological change and its interaction with capital accumulation.

- Ongoing *exogenous* technological advances increase the rate of return on capital, increasing saving and investment, increasing capital per person, creating real GDP growth.

- As capital per hour of labour increases, the rate of return on capital decreases due to diminishing returns, so capital accumulation and growth end unless new technological advances occur.

- Predicts growth rates and income levels per person in different countries should converge, but this convergence doesn't happen empirically.

New growth theory holds that real GDP per person grows indefinitely because of choices people make in pursuit of growth.

- New discoveries are sought for (temporary) profits, but once made discoveries are copied and benefits

are dispersed throughout the economy *without* diminishing returns.

- Knowledge is a special kind of capital not subject to diminishing returns or decreasing rate of return.

- Inventions increase the rate of return to knowledge capital, resulting in increased capital per person and real GDP growth with *no automatic slowdown* because rate of return to capital does not diminish.

- New growth theory seems to fit the facts best (but not perfectly) with evidence that political stability, investment, and trade help economic growth.

Different growth theories lead to five main suggestions for increasing economic growth rates:

- Stimulate saving (and investment in capital) by tax incentives.

- Subsidize research and development and new technology.

- Improve education quality.

- Provide international aid to developing countries (but this suggestion has poor results empirically).

- Encourage international trade.

HELPFUL HINTS

1 Economic growth is a powerful force in raising living standards. Countries become rich by achieving high rates of growth in per person GDP and maintaining them over long periods of time. Compounding income can create startling effects. Consider the post-1973 productivity growth slowdown. Growth between 1960 and 1973 averaged 3.3 percent per year, but after 1973 was less than 2.1 percent per year. Between 1973 and 2007, real GDP per person rose by about 103 percent $(= [(1.021)^{34} - 1] \times 100)$. However, if growth had continued at the pre-1973 rate of 3.3 percent, real GDP per person would have increased by about 202 percent $(= [(1.033)^{34} - 1] \times 100)$. Even the worst recession over this period lowered real GDP per person by about 5 percent (see the discussion of the Lucas wedge in Chapter 20). Avoiding the productivity growth slowdown would clearly have had a big payoff!

2 The key to understanding different theories of growth is the role of "the law of diminishing returns" in each theory. This law states that adding more of one input, other inputs held

constant, eventually leads to a diminishing returns to adding extra inputs.

In neoclassical theory, the discovery of a new technology increases the rate of return on capital, increasing saving and investment, and increasing the amount of capital used. However, the increase in capital eventually leads to diminishing returns. Think of the introduction of new, more powerful computers. As the number of computers increases, holding constant the number of workers, the extra output of the nth computer will not be as high as the productivity of the first computer. Eventually, productivity of extra capital must decrease (decreasing the rate of return), and economic growth automatically slows down.

New growth theory has a different idea of technology and capital, with no diminishing returns and no slowdown in economic growth. New growth theory examines "knowledge capital," a concept of technology that is not embodied in capital, but in ideas. These ideas might include new management techniques or new production processes (such as assembly lines) that can be copied from business to business without diminishing returns. Consider the introduction of new and better software (such as word processing software). As more copies of the software are introduced into different businesses around the country, we do not run into diminishing returns until the entire country has access to the new knowledge. Even then, improved software will be continually developed and introduced without diminishing returns (so that the rate of return does *not* decrease), and economic growth need not automatically slow down.

SELF-TEST

True/False and Explain

The Basics of Economic Growth

1   The standard of living depends on the level of real GDP.

Economic Growth Trends

2   Canada's growth sped up in the 1990s, which was unusual in Canadian history.

3   Asian countries are catching up with Canada's real GDP per person.

How Potential GDP Grows

4   The aggregate production function shows the relationship between real GDP and labour inputs.

5   As the real wage rate increases, the quantity of labour demanded decreases, other things remaining constant.

6   An increasing population decreases the real wage rate and potential GDP.

7   An increase in labour productivity decreases real wages and increases potential GDP.

Why Labour Productivity Grows

8   Higher levels of human capital with the same physical capital per person will not raise per person income.

9   Rapid changes in technology create growth without the need for new capital.

10   The only way labour productivity can increase is if there is more physical capital.

Growth Theories, Evidence, and Policies

11 The empirical evidence is strongly in favour of classical growth theory.

12 Neoclassical growth theory argues that economic growth eventually slows down because the rate of return on capital diminishes as the amount of capital increases.

13 Classical growth theory argues that economic growth leads to a smaller population growth rate.

14 High economic growth has typically been accompanied by high saving rates.

15 In new growth theory, there are no diminishing returns for knowledge capital.

Multiple-Choice

The Basics of Economic Growth

1 Growthland's real GDP per capita was $112 billion in 2012 and $117 billion in 2013. What is the growth rate of Growthland's real GDP per capita?
a 4.3%
b 4.5%
c 5%
d 12%
e 17%

2 If Amazonia's growth rate of real GDP per capita is 7%, how many years before real GDP per capita doubles?
a Impossible to calculate without more data
b 3.5
c 7
d 10
e 14.3

Economic Growth Trends

3 Canada's economic growth rates were highest in which of the following decades?
a 1930s
b 1960s
c 1970s
d 1980s
e 1990s

4 Compared to growth in other countries, between 1960 and 2010 Canada
a fell behind most other countries.
b dramatically caught up to and passed other countries.
c worsened dramatically versus the United States, but did better versus other countries.
d did as well as or better than most countries except certain Asian countries.
e did none of the above.

5 Which of the following statements about Canada's long-term growth trends is *false*?

a Economic growth rates have been steady, except for the business cycle.
b Economic growth rates show periods of slow and high growth.
c Economic growth rates were faster in the 1990s than in the 1980s.
d Economic growth rates have generally been faster in Japan than in Canada.
e African countries have fallen further behind Canada in recent years.

How Potential GDP Grows

6 The aggregate production function shows
a how much real GDP changes as capital stock changes, all else remaining the same.
b how much real GDP changes as the price level changes, all else remaining the same.
c how much labour demand changes as the real wage rate changes, all else remaining the same.
d how much labour demand changes as the money wage rate changes, all else remaining the same.
e none of the above.

7 The labour demand curve is
  a positively sloped and shifts with changes in the capital stock.
  b positively sloped and shifts with changes in the quantity of labour employed.
  c negatively sloped and shifts with changes in the capital stock.
  d negatively sloped and shifts with changes in the quantity of labour employed.
  e negatively sloped and shifts with changes in the real wage rate.

8 If the money wage rate is $12 per hour and the GDP deflator is 150, what is the real wage rate per hour?
  a $18
  b $15
  c $12
  d $8
  e $6

9 Which of the following quotations describes the upward-sloping labour supply curve?
  a "Recent higher wage rates have led to more leisure."
  b "The recent lower price level has induced people to work fewer hours."
  c "The recent higher real wage rate has induced people to work more hours."
  d "The recent high investment in capital equipment has raised hiring by firms."
  e "Adding extra workers leads to lower productivity of each additional worker."

10 *Ceteris paribus*, an increase in labour productivity results in a
  a higher real wage rate and higher potential GDP per hour of work.
  b lower real wage rate and higher potential GDP per hour of work.
  c higher real wage rate and lower potential GDP per hour of work.
  d lower real wage rate and lower potential GDP per hour of work.
  e constant real wage rate in the long run.

11 *Ceteris paribus*, an increase in population results in a
  a higher level of labour employed and higher potential GDP per hour of work.
  b lower level of labour employed and higher potential GDP per hour of work.
  c higher level of labour employed and lower potential GDP per hour of work.
  d lower level of labour employed and lower potential GDP per hour of work.
  e constant level of labour employed and constant potential GDP per hour of work.

12 If the real wage rate is higher than the equilibrium wage rate,
  a the real wage rate increases due to the labour surplus.
  b the real wage rate decreases due to the labour surplus.
  c labour supply decreases due to the high real wage rate.
  d labour demand increases due to the high real wage rate.
  e labour demand decreases due to the labour surplus.

13 If the capital stock increases, which of the following happens?
  a The demand for labour increases.
  b The supply of labour increases.
  c Technology will improve.
  d The level of real GDP decreases.
  e The real wage rate decreases.

Why Labour Productivity Grows

14 Which of the following is *not* a source of economic growth?
  a increasing stock market prices
  b better-educated workers
  c growing stock of capital equipment
  d an appropriate incentive system
  e advances in technology

15 Which of the following occurs with an improvement in technology?
  a The labour supply increases.
  b The capital stock increases.
  c The human capital stock decreases.
  d Real GDP growth decreases.
  e The real wage rate decreases.

16 Which of the following is an example of human capital?
a The use of a laptop instead of pen and paper to take class notes.
b A student being better at note-taking at the end of the fourth year than in the first year of university.
c A student who records economics classes is doing better in a third-year business class than a student who does not.
d Installing a software upgrade on your computer.
e Falling asleep on your economics text while studying.

17 Which of the following would shift the aggregate production function upward?
a a decrease in the stock of capital
b a decrease in the real wage rate
c an increase in labour employed
d an increase in the price level
e a technological discovery

Growth Theory, Evidence, and Policies

18 Which of the following is a suggestion for increasing Canadian economic growth rates?
a Stimulate saving by taxing consumption.
b Reduce the time period for patent protection to increase replication.
c Put less public research funds into universities.
d Protect our industries from foreign competition.
e Tax education.

19 Government subsidies for research and development are justified
a because there is too little private saving.
b because it is too expensive for small firms.
c because there are external benefits to research and development that firms ignore.
d in order to take advantage of gains from specialization and exchange.
e in order to overcome diminishing returns.

20 In neoclassical growth theory, if the rate of return on capital increases due to a technological advance, then
a the rate of return on capital will eventually decline.
b capital per hour of labour will decrease.
c real GDP per hour of labour will decrease.
d the rate of return on capital will never decline.
e population growth will explode.

21 In new growth theory, if the rate of return on capital increases due to a technological advance, then
a the rate of return on capital will eventually decline.
b capital per hour of labour will decrease.
c real GDP per hour of labour will decrease.
d the rate of return on capital will never decline.
e population growth will explode.

22 Incentives are important in the new growth theory because they
a imply there are no diminishing returns.
b lead to higher rates of saving.
c imply that economic growth does not lead to population growth.
d create specialization and exchange.
e lead to profit-seeking searches for new discoveries.

23 In classical growth theory, economic growth eventually stops after a technological advance because
a of diminishing returns.
b knowledge capital is easily replicated.
c the rate of return on capital decreases back down to the target rate of savers.
d real GDP per person becomes too high.
e of high population growth resulting from increasing real GDP per person.

24 Compared to physical capital, knowledge capital
a can be replicated without diminishing returns.
b can be held in your hand.
c leads to an automatic slowdown in growth.
d cannot be replicated without diminishing returns.
e is none of the above.

25 The key difference between neoclassical growth theory and new growth theory is that
a capital is not subject to diminishing returns under new growth theory.
b capital is subject to diminishing returns under new growth theory.
c increases in technology increase the population, which drives workers' incomes back down to subsistence levels in neoclassical theory.
d technological advances are exogenous in new growth theory.
e the rule of 70 only holds in new growth theory.

Short Answer Problems

1 Pinkland has a population of 500 in 2012 and 525 in 2013. Its real GDP is $5,500,000 in 2012 and $6,050,000 in 2013.

    a   Calculate Pinkland's real GDP per capita in each year.

    b   Calculate the growth rates of real GDP and real GDP per capita between 2012 and 2013.

    c   If Pinkland's economic growth rate of real GDP per capita continues at this level, how many years will it take to double real GDP per capita?

2 Blueland's real GDP per capita is $100 and growing at 7% per year. Redland's real GDP per capita is $1,000 and growing at 3.5% per year. Use the rule of 70 to construct a table showing how many years it will take Blueland's real GDP per capita to catch up to Redland's if these growth rates remain constant.

3 Some economists speculate that the Asian miracle economies have achieved such fast growth at least partially because of their adeptness at replicating new technology from other countries. Explain how and why replicating is a good source of growth.

4 Paul Krugman and others argue that the Asian miracle economies' extra-high economic growth is mostly due to the mobilization of capital and labour resources that were previously underutilized, and that North American worries that these countries will surpass Canada and the United States are unfounded. Assuming it is true, explain why this argument implies these worries are unfounded.

5 Use an aggregate production function to explain why an increase in the amount of capital per hour of labour leads to economic growth.

6 An economy starts with the 2009 aggregate production function in Table 22.1, with 120 hours of labour hired in 2009.

    a   Graph this economy's 2009 aggregate production function.

    b   A technological innovation in 2010 increases labour productivity by 10%. Show the impact of this change in the remaining columns of Table 22.1, and on your graph from part **a**.

    c   Where is the likely new 2010 production point for this economy? Explain briefly.

TABLE 22.1

Labour (hrs/yr)	Real GDP (2009)	Real GDP per hour of labour (2009)	Real GDP (2010)	Real GDP per hour of labour (2010)
100	500	5.00		
110	540	4.91		
120	570	4.75		
130	590	4.54		
140	600	4.29		
150	605	4.03		

7 Consider the economy from Short Answer Problem **6**. The 2009 labour market equilibrium was at a real wage rate of $15, with 120 hours of labour hired. After the technological innovation, assuming no population increase, explain using a graph of the labour market for this country what has happened to labour demand, labour supply, amount of labour hired, and the real wage rate in 2010. Exact numbers are not needed, just an indication of the types of changes.

8 Some commentators argue that, until recently, Japan had a higher growth rate than Canada or the United States because the Japanese people care more about the future and less about present consumption, leading to a higher Japanese saving rate. Explain within the context of growth theory whether this argument seems correct.

ANSWERS

True/False and Explain

1 **F**   Depends on real GDP *per capita*. (518)

2 **F**   Growth was higher in the 1960s. (520)

3 **T**   See text discussion. (521–522)

4 **T**   Definition. (523)

5 **T**   Definition of labour demand curve. (524)

6 **F**   Increasing population increases the labour supply, decreases the real wage, but more labour is hired so potential GDP increases. (525–526)

7 **F**   Shifts *LD* curve rightward, and increases real wage rate. (527)

8 **F**   Human capital growth is part of advances in technology. (529)

9 F Rapid technological change is embodied in new human and physical capital. (530)

10 F Technological advances or increases in human capital also raise labour productivity. (521)

11 F New growth theory explains it better. (534–535)

12 T Due to law of diminishing returns. (532)

13 F Economic growth increases real GDP per hour, which increases population growth. (531)

14 T See discussion of East Asian economies. (535)

15 T Because knowledge capital can be duplicated at zero marginal cost. (532–534)

Multiple-Choice

1 b Growth rate = [(Δ real GDP per capita)/original level] × 100 = (5/112) × 100 = 4.5%. (518)

2 d By rule of 70: 70/7 = 10. (519)

3 b See text discussion. (520)

4 d See text discussion. (521–522)

5 a Growth rates have fluctuated. (521–522)

6 e Definition: how much real GDP changes as labour hired changes. (523–525)

7 c Negatively sloped due to diminishing marginal product. **d** and **e** imply movements along the demand curve. (523–525)

8 d Real wage = (money wage/price level) × 100. (519–523)

9 c Higher wages, higher quantity of labour supplied. **a** and **b** are opposite relationships, **d** and **e** refer to labour demand. (523–528)

10 a A productivity increase increases labour demand, raising the real wage rate. Potential GDP per hour of work = productivity, so it must have increased. (525–528)

11 c Labour supply shifts rightward, real wage falls, more people hired, but potential GDP per hour of work falls due to diminishing marginal productivity. (525–528)

12 b The labour surplus pushes down real wages. (524)

13 a Labour is more productive and therefore firms demand more. (526–527)

14 a Prices have no impact on productivity, others increase it. (526–527)

15 b New technology is typically embodied in new capital. (530)

16 b The student has learned (raised their human capital) by repetition. (529)

17 e Technological discovery increases the productivity of labour. (528–530)

18 a **b** would lower return to and number of inventions, **c** would lower research and number of inventions, and trade and education should be encouraged. (535)

19 c See text discussion. (535)

20 a If rate of return on capital is high, saving increases supply of capital, increasing capital per hour of labour (and more real GDP per hour of labour). Eventually rate of return on capital decreases due to the law of diminishing returns. (531–532)

21 d If rate of return on capital is high, saving increases supply of capital, increasing capital per hour of labour (and more real GDP per hour of labour), but no change in rate of return on capital since the law of diminishing returns doesn't apply to knowledge capital. (532–534)

22 e This assumption makes technological change endogenous and continuous. (532–534)

23 e This growth leads to a decrease in real GDP per hour of labour. (531)

24 a Due to its nature—see text discussion. (534)

25 a Due to the different nature of knowledge capital. (531–534)

Short Answer Problems

1 a Real GDP per capita = real GDP/population. In 2012, this equals $5,500,000/500 = $11,000. In 2013, this equals $6,050,000/525 = $11,524.

 b Growth rate of real GDP = $\frac{6,050,000 - 5,500,000}{5,500,000} \times 100\% = 10\%$.

Growth rate of real GDP per capita =
$$\frac{11,524 - 11,000}{11,000} \times 100\% = 4.8\%.$$

c From the rule of 70, 70/4.8 = 17.5 years.

2 The rule of 70 means that Blueland's real GDP per capita doubles every 10 years (= 70/7) while Redland's doubles every 20 years (= 70/3.5). Table 22.2 below shows the progress of each country's real GDP over several decades, and shows that Blueland will catch up to Redland in about 70 years.

TABLE **22.2**

Year	Blueland Real GDP per Capita	Redland Real GDP per Capita
0	100	1,000
10	200	
20	400	2,000
30	800	
40	1,600	4,000
50	3,200	
60	6,400	8,000
70	12,800	
80	25,600	16,000

3 Knowledge capital can be replicated without diminishing returns, so that the rate of return on capital increases after replication, which in turn brings more saving and investment. Capital per hour of labour can increase without limit, implying growth can increase without limit.

4 If Asian growth is due to increasing amounts of capital and labour, eventually these countries will run into diminishing returns to each of these inputs, so increases in productivity will slow down, meaning economic growth will also slow.

5 The aggregate production function illustrates how output increases as the amount of labour hired increases, holding constant labour productivity. Labour productivity increases with more physical capital, more human capital, or technological advances. If capital per hour of labour increases, the productivity of workers is increasing, so output per hour of labour is increasing—there is faster economic growth. This is illustrated graphically by an upward shift in the aggregate production function, reflecting more output for each amount of labour used.

6 a Figure 22.1 below shows the graph of the 2009 production function, labelled PF_{2009}.

Figure 22.1

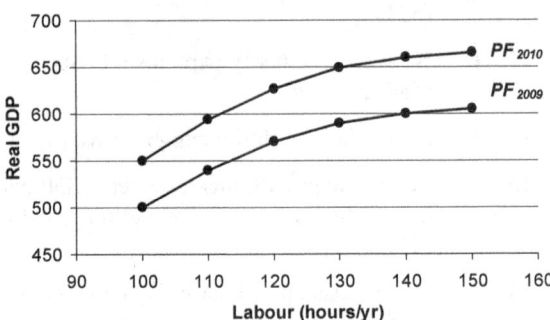

b Table 22.1 Solution below shows the impact of the 10% increase in productivity as 10% higher real GDP at each level of labour, which translates into 10% higher real GDP per hour of labour hired.

TABLE **22.1** Solution

Labour (hrs/yr)	Real GDP (2009)	Real GDP per Hour of Labour (2009)	Real GDP (2010)	Real GDP per Hour of Labour (2010)
100	500	5.00	550	5.5
110	540	4.91	594	5.4
120	570	4.75	627	5.23
130	590	4.54	649	4.99
140	600	4.29	660	4.71
150	605	4.03	665.5	4.44

The new 2010 production function in Fig. 22.1 is labelled PF_{2010}.

c If the original labour hired was 120, we know that the higher productivity (5.23 > 4.75) means firms want to hire more labour, not less. Therefore, we can assume labour hired is at least 120, if not higher. Reading off the PF_{2010} curve, production will at least be at real GDP of 627, if not higher.

7 Figure 22.2 on the next page shows the original labour demand curve (LD_{2009}), labour supply curve (LS), and the original wage and quantity labour hired. As in the answer to Short Answer Problem 6c, labour demand will rise due to higher productivity. Labour supply is initially unchanged due to unchanged population, so the higher labour demand leads to a higher real wage rate, inducing a higher quantity of labour supplied, shown as a movement along the labour supply curve to a new, higher level of labour hired in the market equilibrium. Figure 22.2 shows this change. We cannot tell exactly how much the real wage rate increases, or how much more labour is hired, but it will be higher than the original levels for both.

8 If the Japanese people had a higher saving rate, this meant the increase in the supply of capital in Japan is higher in any situation. In general, Japan would have a higher capital stock per person than Canada, and it would be increasing each year at a higher rate, in turn leading to a higher growth rate of real GDP per person in Japan than in Canada. Thus this argument seems to hold true.

Figure **22.2**

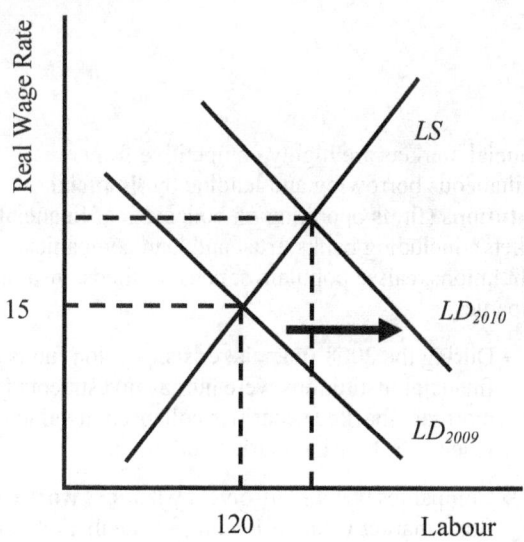

Chapter 23

Finance, Saving, and Investment

Financial Institutions and Financial Markets

Financial markets channel saving from households to firms, who invest in new capital.

- ♦ *Finance*—activity of providing funds for capital expenditures. *Money*—used to pay for items and make financial expenditures.

- ♦ Physical capital is tools, instruments, machines, buildings used to produce goods and services. **Financial capital** is funds firms use to buy physical capital, which produces real GDP.

- ♦ **Gross investment** = amount spent on new capital. **Net investment** = Δ value of capital stock = gross investment – depreciation.

- ♦ **Wealth** = value of things people own. Δ wealth = **saving** (= income – net taxes – consumption) + capital gains/losses.

Three types of financial markets:

- ♦ Loan markets involve businesses or households borrowing from banks, including household **mortgages**—legal lending contracts giving lender ownership of house if borrower defaults.

- ♦ **Bond markets** involve firms, governments issuing/selling **bonds** (promise to make specified payments on specified dates).
  - • Bond terms can be months up to decades.
  - • **Mortgage-backed securities** are bonds paying income from a package of mortgages.

- ♦ Firms' **stock** shares (certificate of ownership and claim to profits) are traded in **stock markets**.

Financial markets are highly competitive from simultaneous borrowing and lending by **financial institutions** (firms operating on both sides of financial markets), including banks, trust and loan companies, credit unions, caisse populaires, pension funds, insurance companies.

- ♦ During the 2008 financial crisis, pension funds and financial institutions were hurt as investments in mortgage-backed securities collapsed in value when U.S. housing market collapsed.

- ♦ Companies become insolvent when **net worth** (total market value of lending – total market value of borrowing) is negative.

- ♦ Companies become illiquid if they are solvent but have insufficient cash to meet debt payments.

- ♦ Insolvent companies are forced to merge or are taken over by government.

- ♦ Interest rate on asset $= \dfrac{\text{interest received}}{\text{price of asset}} \times 100$

- ♦ Price of asset and interest rate are inversely related.

The Loanable Funds Market

Loanable funds market—aggregate of all financial markets.

- ♦ Adding financial flows from loanable funds to circular flow shows how investment is financed.

- ♦ Households' income spent on consumption or saving or **net taxes** (T = taxes – transfer payments received from governments): $Y = C + S + T$.

- ♦ Circular flow from Chapter 20 shows: $Y = C + I + G + X - M$.

♦ Combining above, I financed by private saving (S) + government saving ($T - G$) + borrowing from rest of world ($M - X$):

$$I = S + (T - G) + (M - X)$$

♦ If $T > G$, government can lend some of its surplus.

♦ If foreigners sell Canadians more goods than they buy from us ($M > X$), we must borrow from them to finance the difference, so foreign savings flows to Canada for investment purposes.

♦ I financed by **national saving** $[= S + (T - G)] +$ foreign borrowing.

Nominal interest rate = dollars paid yearly in interest by borrower to lender as percent of dollars borrowed.

♦ **Real interest rate**—nominal rate adjusted for inflation ($\approx$ nominal interest rate – inflation rate).

♦ Real interest rate is the opportunity cost of loanable funds—determined in the market for loanable funds.

Quantity of loanable funds *demanded* to finance investment, government budget deficit, international lending.

♦ The higher the real interest rate, the lower is the quantity of loanable funds demanded—**demand for loanable funds** (DLF curve) has a negative relationship between the real interest rate and the quantity demanded.

♦ DLF shifts rightward if expected profit increases.

Quantity of loanable funds *supplied* from saving, government budget surplus, international borrowing.

♦ The higher the real interest rate, the higher is the quantity of loanable funds supplied—**supply of loanable funds** (SLF curve) has a positive relationship between the real interest rate and the quantity supplied.

♦ SLF curve shifts rightward if disposable income increases, expected future income falls, wealth falls, or default risk falls.

Real interest rate adjustments achieve equilibrium where quantity of loanable funds demanded = quantity supplied.

♦ Factors shifting DLF rightward lead to new equilibrium with higher real interest rate, and more loanable funds are supplied.

♦ Factors shifting SLF rightward lead to new equilibrium with lower real interest rate, and more loanable funds are demanded.

♦ Real interest rate has no trend over time.

Starting in 2001, U.S. Federal Reserve (the Fed) provided loanable funds (increasing SLF), leading to lower interest rates and large increases in house prices.

♦ In 2006, the Fed slowed SLF growth, interest rates rose, and many mortgage holders defaulted, pushing financial institutions into insolvency.

Government in the Loanable Funds Market

Government budget surplus increases the supply of loanable funds, lowering the real interest rate— investment increases more than private saving decreases.

♦ The **crowding-out effect** is when the budget deficit increases the real interest rate and investment decreases.

♦ The **Ricardo–Barro effect** holds that the government budget has no effect on the real interest rate or investment because rational taxpayers know increases in budget deficit (surplus) imply higher (lower) future taxes, so they adjust saving by an equivalent amount—no change in real interest rate.

The Global Loanable Funds Market

Loanable funds market is global—suppliers move to national markets with the highest real interest rates, demanders to markets with the lowest real interest rate.

♦ Flows in funds mean there will be one real interest rate globally (for assets with equal risk).

♦ Riskier assets will pay interest rate = rate on safe loan + risk premium.

♦ A country with a higher interest rate than the global rate will be a net borrower globally and have negative net exports as a result.

♦ A country with a lower interest rate than the global rate will be a net lender globally and have positive net exports as a result.

♦ Changes in demand and supply for small countries like Canada have no effect on the global interest rate. Changes for larger countries shift world DLF or SLF and affect the global interest rate.

HELPFUL HINTS

1 Financial markets and financial institutions are at the centre of many economic activities. In Chapter 22 on economic growth, investment in physical capital plays a key role in creating economic growth. This chapter explains how household saving, government saving, and investment from foreigners are channelled via financial markets and institutions to firms that purchase capital goods to carry out investment.

   These concepts will reappear in Chapter 24 ("Money, the Price Level, and Inflation") and Chapter 30 ("Monetary Policy"), where we will see the role of the central bank in setting interest rates in financial markets (affecting investment and overall economic activity). Chapter 25 will highlight key relationships between interest rates, exchange rates, and the overall economy. Chapter 28 illustrates the impact of financial market problems on the business cycle, and Chapter 29 explains how government fiscal policy interacts with the financial markets to affect interest rates and investment.

   Financial markets and institutions are the key to understanding many other economic activities and policies. In the 2007–2008 financial crisis, a combination of external forces and loose monetary policy created a housing bubble. When the bubble started collapsing in 2007, this led to difficulties with financial institutions, difficulties that have spread to the goods and services markets and to the labour market. Over the next four years, governments of the western economies carried out massive monetary expansions and the largest fiscal stimuli in history in an attempt to avert a long recession. We will explore how these policies work in Chapters 29 and 30.

2 Although Canada is a strong developed country with a high standard of living, it is still a relatively small player on world financial markets. This means that the (risk-adjusted) real interest rate in Canada is set in the world market. Consequently, even though Canada has a strong financial sector without a housing crisis, we can still be affected by a U.S.-born financial crisis. The U.S. crisis has led to higher U.S. real interest rates (and higher aversion to risk), and these higher interest rates have spread to Canadian financial markets, creating negative effects for the Canadian economy.

SELF-TEST

True/False and Explain

Financial Institutions and Financial Markets

1 When a household buys stock in a company, this is an example of gross investment.

2 A company is illiquid when it has negative net worth.

3 A mortgage is a bond paying income based on a package of house loans.

4 If a household has saving of $2,000 and a capital loss of $3,000, its net wealth will decrease.

5 If the interest rate on an asset increases, the price of the asset increases.

The Loanable Funds Market

6 The higher a household's expected future income, the more loanable funds they will supply.

7 If the nominal interest rate is 6% and the inflation rate is 4%, the real interest rate is 10%.

8 With no government and no international sector, if the demand for loanable funds is greater than the supply of loanable funds at the current real interest rate, the real interest rate will increase.

9 With no government and no international sector, an increase in the profits firms expect to earn will lead to a higher real interest rate in the loanable funds market.

10 $I = S + (G - T) + (M - X)$.

11 If the inflation rate increases and the nominal interest rate has increased, the real interest rate must be constant.

Government in the Loanable Funds Market

12 If there is no Ricardo–Barro effect, a higher government deficit lowers investment, other things being equal.

13 If there is a Ricardo–Barro effect, a higher government deficit lowers investment, other things being equal.

The Global Loanable Funds Market

14 If Calonia is a net lender to the rest of the world, it will have positive net exports.

15 Calonia is a small part of the global loanable funds market. If Calonia's demand for loanable funds is greater than Calonia's supply of loanable funds at the current real interest rate, the real interest rate will increase.

Multiple-Choice

Financial Institutions and Financial Markets

1 The capital stock does *not* include the
a inventory of raw cucumbers ready to be made into pickles by the Smith Pickle Company.
b Smith family holdings of stock in the Smith Pickle Company.
c pickle factory building owned by the Smith family.
d pickle-packing machine in the pickle factory building owned by the Smith family.
e pickle inventories in the pickle factory building owned by the Smith family.

2 Eel Electronics has lent $10 million and borrowed $8 million. It has cash earnings per month of $100,000 and debt payments per month of $120,000. Eel Electronics is
a solvent and liquid.
b insolvent and illiquid.
c solvent and illiquid.
d insolvent and liquid.
e solvent if interest rates are low enough.

3 On January 1, 2013, Bobcat Excavations had $50,000 worth of bobcat machines. During 2013, these machines fell in value by 50%. Bobcat also bought $35,000 worth of new machines. What was Bobcat's net investment in 2013?
a $10,000
b $25,000
c $35,000
d $60,000
e $85,000

4 In which market would you find mortgage-backed securities?
a stock market
b bond market
c housing market
d capital market
e loan market

5 Elena starts the year with $2,500 worth of stock and no other wealth. Her grandmother gives her a $5,000 Canada Savings Bond. Elena earns $15,000 in income, pays $1,000 in taxes, and spends $15,000 on consumption goods. Her stocks rise in value to $3,000. What is Elena's wealth at the end of the year?
 a $6,500
 b $7,000
 c $7,500
 d $8,000
 e $9,000

6 Elena owns a Canada Savings Bond initially worth $5,000, which pays $500 per year. The value of the bond rises in the bond market to $7,500. What is the new interest rate on the bond?
 a 5%
 b 6.67%
 c 10%
 d 20%
 e 500%

7 The key characteristic of financial institutions is that they
 a are always liquid.
 b will lend to anyone.
 c buy a diversified portfolio of assets.
 d simultaneously borrow and lend.
 e provide risk-sharing services.

The Loanable Funds Market

8 Which of the following shifts the supply curve of loanable funds leftward?
 a increase in current disposable income
 b decrease in current disposable income
 c decrease in expected future income
 d increase in the real interest rate
 e decrease in the real interest rate

9 Which of the following is *false*?
 a $Y = C + I + G + M - X$
 b $I = S + (T - G) + (M - X)$
 c $Y = C + S + T$
 d $Y + M = C + I + G + X$
 e $Y = C + I + G + X - M$

10 Saving can be measured as income minus
 a taxes.
 b transfer payments.
 c net taxes minus consumption expenditure.
 d consumption expenditure.
 e net taxes plus subsidies.

11 In Canada's economy, investment is financed by
 a $C + I + G + X - M$.
 b $C + S + T$.
 c $S + T + M$.
 d $S + (T - G) + (X - M)$.
 e $S + (T - G) + (M - X)$.

12 Which of the following causes a household to increase the amount it saves?
 a decrease in current disposable income
 b increase in expected future income
 c increase in net taxes
 d decrease in expected future income
 e none of the above

13 Investment will be higher if
 a the government deficit is higher.
 b national saving is higher.
 c net exports are higher.
 d the real interest rate is higher.
 e government spending is higher.

14 Southton has investment of $100, household saving of $90, net taxes of $25, government spending of $30, exports of $25, and imports of $10. What is national saving?
 a $85
 b $90
 c $95
 d $100
 e $105

15 If the inflation rate increases by 3 percent and the nominal interest rate increases by 2 percent, the
 a real interest rate increases.
 b opportunity cost of borrowing increases.
 c opportunity cost of borrowing decreases.
 d opportunity cost of spending increases.
 e level of spending decreases.

16 Table 23.1 on the next page shows the initial market for loanable funds in Northland. The prime minister of Northland gives a brilliant speech, convincing firms in Northland of future strong economic growth in the country. The likely new equilibrium has a real interest rate of ___ with a quantity of loanable funds of ___.
 a 6%; $100 billion
 b 7%; $100 billion
 c 7%; $120 billion
 d 5%; $120 billion
 e 5%; $80 billion

TABLE **23.1** DATA FROM NORTHLAND

Real Interest Rate	Demand for Loanable Funds ($ billions)	Supply of Loanable Funds ($ billions)
3%	160	40
4%	140	60
5%	120	80
6%	100	100
7%	80	120
8%	60	140

17 Table 23.1 shows the initial market for loanable funds in Northland. Disposable income then increases. The likely new equilibrium has a real interest rate of ___ with a quantity of loanable funds of ____.
a 6%; $100 billion
b 7%; $100 billion
c 7%; $120 billion
d 5%; $120 billion
e 5%; $80 billion

Government in the Loanable Funds Market

18 Table 23.1 shows the initial market for loanable funds in Northland. There is no Ricardo–Barro effect. If the government moves from a balanced budget to a surplus of $20 billion, the new equilibrium has a real interest rate of ___ and quantity of loanable funds traded equal to ____.
a 6.5%; $110 billion
b 6.5%; $90 billion
c 5.5%; $90 billion
d 5.5%; $110 billion
e 6%; $120 billion

19 In the market for loanable funds, if the Ricardo–Barro effect does not hold, a higher government surplus leads to
a increased real interest rate and increased investment.
b increased real interest rate and decreased investment.
c decreased real interest rate and increased investment.
d decreased real interest rate and decreased investment.
e no effect on real interest rate or investment.

20 Figure 23.1 shows the loanable funds market for a country that is not part of the global market. Currently the country has a government budget balance = 0. There is no Ricardo–Barro effect. If the government introduces a deficit of $20 billion, the new real interest rate = ___ and the new level of investment = ___.
a 7%; $40 billion
b 5%; $60 billion
c 7%; $50 billion
d 5%; $50 billion
e 6%; $50 billion

Figure **23.1**

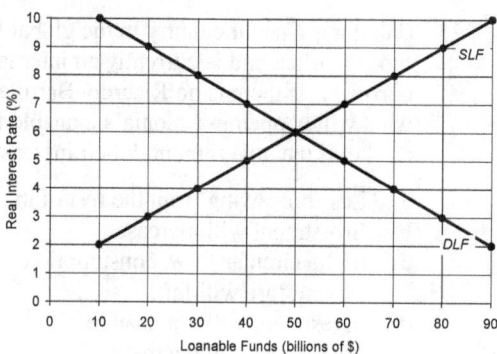

The Global Loanable Funds Market

21 Figure 23.1 shows the loanable funds market for a country that is part of the global market, with no government budget deficit or surplus. If the world interest rate is 4%, we have net _____ and investment of ____.
a lending of $40 billion; $40 billion
b borrowing of $40 billion; $30 billion
c borrowing of $0 billion; $50 billion
d borrowing of $40 billion; $70 billion
e lending of $40 billion; $70 billion

22 Which of the following newspaper quotations describes a situation where Canada would end up with lower investment?
a "A rise in the U.S. government budget deficit is forcing up world interest rates."
b "World lenders are worried about Canada's government budget deficit."
c "The booming Chinese economy is dramatically raising its spending on new investment projects."
d All of the above
e None of the above

23 In the global economy, investment is financed by

a $S + (T - G)$.

b $S + (T - G) - (X - M)$.

c $S + (G - T)$.

d $S + (T - G) + (X - M)$.

e $S + (T - G) + (M - X)$.

24 In Canada's economy, the real interest rate is determined by

a national investment.

b national saving.

c the government budget deficit/surplus.

d all of the above.

e none of the above.

25 Calonia is a small country in the global loanable funds market, and is currently an international borrower. If there is no Ricardo–Barro effect, what will happen in Calonia's loanable funds market if the government deficit increases?

a Less borrowing from the rest of the world.

b Investment will increase.

c In the circular flow, consumption expenditure will fall.

d Investment will not change.

e Investment will decrease.

Short Answer Problems

1 The Athabasca Oil Exploration Company starts the year with $1 million worth of equipment. It has debts of $500,000, for a beginning net worth of $500,000. During the year, the following events occur:

- Athabasca borrows $2.5 million to buy $2 million worth of new equipment plus $500,000 worth of stock in another company.

- The stock in the other company increases in value to $600,000.

- Athabasca's old equipment depreciates in value to a worth of $250,000.

a Calculate Athabasca's gross and net investment for the year, and the end of year value of its physical capital stock.

b At the end of the year, what is Athabasca's net worth? Is it solvent?

2 In an interview in the late 1990s, the Governor of the Bank of Canada argued that Canada's interest rates had fallen drastically in the late 1990s because the federal and provincial governments had drastically reduced the size of their budget deficits, and that this would increase investment spending. Assume initially that Canada does not participate in the global loanable funds market. With the help of a graph, explain if the explanation makes sense.

3 Return to the statements made by the governor in question **2**. In reality, Canada does participate in the global loanable funds market and was a net borrower in the late 1990s. In this case, would Canada's lower budget deficits lead to lower interest rates? Once again, draw a (new) graph of the loanable funds market as part of your answer.

4 Consider the following data on Calonia:

TABLE **23.2** DATA FOR CALONIA

Item	Amount (billions of $)
Consumption expenditure (C)	600
Net taxes (T)	300
Exports (X)	240
Imports (M)	220
Government expenditure on goods and services (G)	200
Net investment (I)	150
Depreciation	60
Household income (Y)	1030

Use this data to calculate Calonia's:

a Gross investment

b Net exports and foreign borrowing or lending

c Government deficit or surplus

d Household saving

e National saving

f Total funds available for investment

5 Marie started the year with $100,000 of stock. During the year, the following events occurred:

- Marie's stocks rose in value to $128,000. She sold $20,000 of stock at the end of the year to use as a down payment on her new house.

- Marie borrowed $172,000 from the bank, and with her stock sale proceeds as the difference, bought a house for $192,000.

- Marie earned $35,000 and paid $12,000 in taxes.

- Marie consumed $22,000.

Showing all steps, calculate Marie's wealth at the end of the year.

6 Opar is an isolated economy that does not trade with the world. It has constant real GDP of 100 million opals, government expenditure is constant at $12 million opals, and the government deficit is constant at 2 million opals. Consider the values of consumption and investment shown in Table 23.3.

TABLE **23.3** DATA FROM OPAR

Real Interest Rate	C	Supply of Loanable Funds (Saving)	I	Demand for Loanable Funds
3%	75		22	
4%	70		18	
5%	65		14	
6%	60		10	
7%	55		6	
8%	50		2	

a Calculate and fill in the two blank columns of the table. What is the real interest rate and quantity of loanable funds in Opar in equilibrium?

b Pellucidar is another isolated economy that does not trade with the world. It has constant real GDP of 120 million opals, government expenditure is constant at 15 million opals, and the government deficit is constant at 4 million opals. Consider the values of consumption and investment shown in Table 23.4.

Calculate and fill in the two blank columns of the table. What is the real interest rate and quantity of loanable funds in Pellucidar in equilibrium?

TABLE **23.4** DATA FROM PELLUCIDAR

Real Interest Rate	C	Supply of Loanable Funds (Saving)	I	Demand for Loanable Funds
3%	100		32	
4%	95		28	
5%	90		24	
6%	85		20	
7%	80		16	
8%	75		12	

7 An enterprising entrepreneur builds a machine that drills through the earth and connects Opar to Pellucidar. International trade opens up, and so does a loanable funds market between the two countries.

Table 23.5 below shows the total *world* loanable funds market.

TABLE **23.5** WORLD DATA

Real Interest Rate	C	Supply of Loanable Funds (Saving)	I	Demand for Loanable Funds
3%	175		54	
4%				
5%				
6%				
7%				
8%				

a Using your data from Tables 23.3 and 23.4, fill in the remaining information and find the world equilibrium real interest rate and quantity of loanable funds traded.

b For Opar after world trade, what is the level of domestic saving, domestic investment, net exports, and international lending or borrowing?

c For Pellucidar after world trade, what is the level of domestic saving, domestic investment, net exports, and international lending or borrowing?

8 Suppose that a technological innovation dramatically raises expected profits in Canada. Assuming that Canada is initially neither a net lender nor a net borrower on the global loanable funds market, draw a graph of Canada's loanable funds market and show the impact (if any) of the innovation on the demand for loanable funds, the supply of loanable funds, the real interest rate, investment, net exports, and foreign borrowing or lending.

ANSWERS

True/False and Explain

1 **F** Example of financial capital, not physical capital. (544)

2 **F** Insolvent = negative net worth. Illiquid = solvent (positive net worth) but insufficient cash to meet debt payments. (547)

3 **F** Mortgage is a contract giving lender house ownership if borrower defaults. (545–546)

4 **T** Δ Net wealth = saving – capital loss = $2,000 – $3,000 = –$1,000. (544–545)

5 **F** With constant interest payment, interest rate and asset price are inversely related. (548)

6 **F** Higher future income, less saving, less loanable funds supplied. (551–552)

7 **F** Real ≈ nominal – inflation = 6% – 4% = 2%. (549–550)

8 **T** Excess demand pushes up real interest rate, decreasing quantity demanded, increasing quantity supplied until equal at new equilibrium real interest rate. (552)

9 **T** Higher expected profits lead to higher demand for loanable funds, creating a shortage and raising real interest rates. (552–553)

10 **F** $I = S + (T – G) + (M – X)$. (548–549)

11 **F** Real = nominal – inflation. Depends on how much nominal rate and inflation rate have increased. (549–550)

12 **T** Higher deficit means more government borrowing, shifting *DLF* rightward, increasing real interest rate, and lowering investment. (556)

13 **F** Effect from True/False **12** is countered by rational taxpayers saving for higher future tax payments—*SLF* shifts rightward. (556)

14 **T** When Calonia lends, the rest of the world is using the funds to pay for Calonia's positive net exports = rest of world's negative net exports. (557)

15 **F** Real interest rate is determined by the global rate. If Calonia's demand is greater than supply, Calonia borrows from the rest of world. (557–558)

Multiple-Choice

1 **b** Definition. (544)

2 **c** Net worth = $10 million – $8 million > 0 (solvent), and cash payments < debt payments (illiquid). (547)

3 **a** Net investment = gross investment – depreciation = $35,000 – $25,000 (0.50 × $50,000) = $10,000. (544)

4 **b** Bonds paying income from package of mortgages. (545)

5 **b** New wealth = original wealth + Δ wealth = original wealth + saving + capital gain/loss + stock gift = original wealth + after-tax income – consumption + capital gain/loss + stock gift = $2,500 + $15,000 – $1,000 – $15,000 + $500 + $5,000 = $7,000. (544)

6 **b** Interest rate = (interest payment)/value × 100 = $500/$7,500 × 100 = 6.67%. (548)

7 **d** Definition. (546)

8 **b** Less income available for saving. (551–552)

9 **a** Should be $X – M$ and not $M – X$. (548–549)

10 **c** From $S = (Y – T) – C$. (548–549)

11 **e** Definition. (548–549)

12 **d** Lower future income means more saving for future. (551–552)

13 **b** $I = S + (T – G) + (M – X)$ tells us **a, c, e** are false and **b** is true. Higher real interest rate discourages investing; **d** is false. (548–551)

14 **a** National saving = $S + (T – G) = $90 + $25 – $30 = $85. (548–549)

15 **c** Real interest rate decreases since increase in inflation rate > increase in nominal interest rate. Opportunity cost of spending decreases, so spending increases. Real interest rate decreases, opportunity cost of borrowing decreases. (549–550)

16 **c** Expected future profits increase and shifts *DLF* rightward, raising real interest rate and quantity of loanable funds. (552–553)

17 **d** Higher disposable income shifts *SLF* rightward, real interest rate falls, quantity of loanable funds increases. (552–553)

18 **a** Deficit shifts *DLF* rightward by $20 billion at every level. New equilibrium is where new *DLF* and old *SLF* intersect. (556)

19 c   *SLF* shifts rightward— real interest rate decreases, increasing investment. (556)

20 a   *DLF* shifts rightward by $20 billion— real interest rate increases to 7%, decreasing investment along old *DLF*. (556)

21 d   Imagine a flat *SLF* at 4%, borrow difference between domestic *DLF* and *SLF*. (557–559)

22 d   **a** shifts world *SLF* leftward, **b** raises the risk premium (adds a risk premium to the world interest rate when Canada borrows), **c** shifts world *DLF* rightward. (557–559)

23 a   In global economy $X = M$. (557–559)

24 e   It is determined by the world real interest rate. (557–558)

25 d   *SLF* is horizontal at global real interest rate. More funds will flow in to finance the deficit. With no change in real interest rate, there is no change in investment. (557–558)

Short Answer Problems

1 a   Gross investment = total spending on (physical) capital equipment = $2 million. Net investment = gross investment − depreciation = $2 million − $750,000 = $1.25 million. Capital stock = old capital stock + net investment = $1 million + $1.25 million = $2.25 million.

b   Net worth = total market value of (physical and financial) assets − total market value of borrowing = $2.25 million + $600,000 − $3 million = −$150,000. It has negative net worth; it is insolvent.

2   Figure 23.2 shows the effects the governor is talking about in action. DLF_0 is the original demand for loanable funds, with r_0 the original real interest rate.

Deficit reduction causes a decline in the demand for loanable funds—a shift to DLF_1. With no global markets, this leads to a lower real interest rate, r_1. The lower real interest rate increases the quantity of investment demand, shown as the movement along the *DLF* curve. Assuming deficits are now zero, the quantity of investment demand goes from I_0 to I_1. (Assuming no Ricardo–Barro effect.)

Figure **23.2**

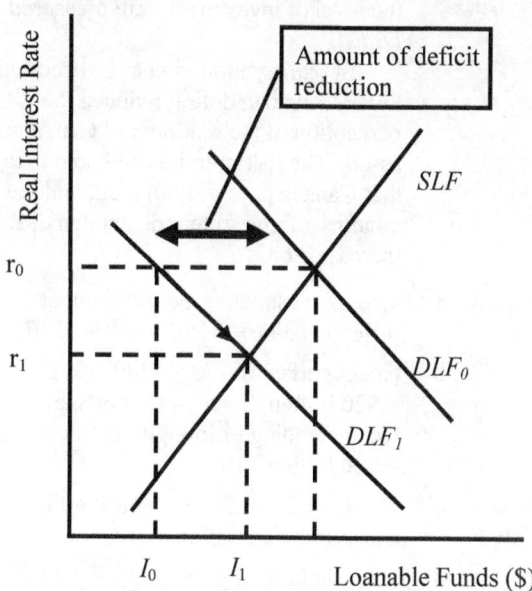

3   Figure 23.3 shows the situation with a global market. Since Canada was initially a net borrower, we know the world interest rate (r_{WORLD}) is initially lower than a Canadian-only equilibrium, and at this interest rate the demand for loanable funds is greater than the supply.

Figure **23.3**

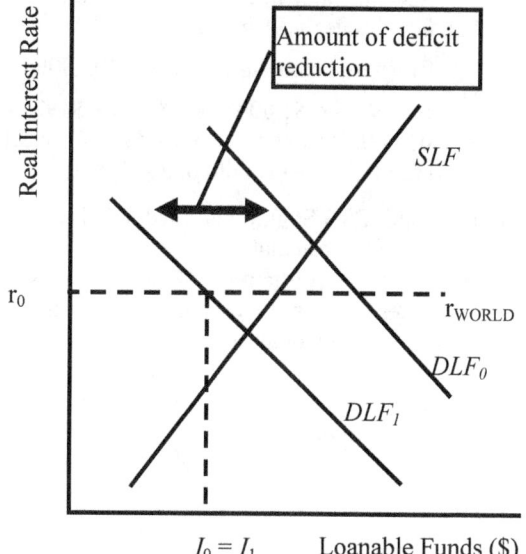

With the deficit reduction comes a decline in the demand for loanable funds, the leftward shift to DLF_1. With global markets, this does not change the real interest rate, and there is also no change in the level of investment (still measured on DLF_1).

In reality, another change occurred. The lower Canadian deficit reduced the perception of the riskiness of Canadian assets. The risk premium fell, and the r_{WORLD} that Canada pays did fall a bit, and the quantity of investment demanded did increase a bit.

4 **a** Gross investment = net investment + depreciation = $150 + $60 = $210 billion.

   b Net exports = $X - M$ = $240 − $220 = $20 billion. Since net exports are positive, we are lending to foreigners; foreign lending = $20 billion.

   c $G - T$ = $200 − $300 = −$100 billion, a government surplus.

   d Household saving = $Y - C - T$ = $1,030 − $600 − $300 = $130 billion.

   e National saving = $S + (T - G)$ = $130 + $100 = $230 billion.

   f I = national saving − foreign lending = $230 −$20 = $210 billion.

5 First, we must calculate Marie's saving, which is income − consumption − net taxes = $35,000 − $12,000 − $22,000 = $1,000. This will be added to her wealth.

Second, value of the stocks = $128,000 − $20,000 in sales = $108,000.

Third, she has a house worth $192,000.

So, assets = $1,000 + $108,000 + $192,000 = $301,000. However, we must deduct her debts of $172,000 for net wealth of $129,000.

6 **a** Table 23.3 Solution is filled in below. Saving is calculated as $S = Y - C - T$, where income is constant at 100 million opals, and taxes are 10 million opals given the deficit of 2 million opals and government expenditure of 12 million opals. The demand for loanable funds = I + the deficit of 2 million opals.

TABLE 23.3 SOLUTION

Real Interest Rate	C	Supply of Loanable Funds (Saving)	I	Demand for Loanable Funds
3%	75	15	22	24
4%	70	20	18	20
5%	65	25	14	16
6%	60	30	10	12
7%	55	35	6	8
8%	50	40	2	4

Equilibrium occurs when quantity demanded equals quantity supplied of 20 million opals at 4%.

   b Table 23.4 Solution is filled in below, using the same method as in Short Answer Problem **6a**. Equilibrium occurs at an interest rate of 6% with 24 million opals traded.

TABLE 23.4 SOLUTION

Real Interest Rate	C	Supply of Loanable Funds (Saving)	I	Demand for Loanable Funds
3%	100	9	32	36
4%	95	14	28	32
5%	90	19	24	28
6%	85	24	20	24
7%	80	29	16	20
8%	75	34	12	16

7 **a** Table 23.5 Solution on the next page is calculated first by adding the consumption of each country at each real interest rate, etc. The world real interest rate occurs when world quantity supplied equals world quantity demanded at 44 million opals and real interest rate of 5%.

TABLE **23.5** SOLUTION

Real Interest Rate	C	Supply of Loanable Funds (Saving)	I	Demand for Loanable Funds
3%	175	24	54	60
4%	165	34	46	52
5%	155	44	38	44
6%	145	54	30	36
7%	135	64	22	28
8%	125	74	14	20

b At a real interest rate of 5%, in Opar the quantity supplied of loanable funds is 25 million opals and the quantity demanded is 16 million opals. This leaves a surplus of 9 million opals that are lent internationally (foreigners borrow 9 million opals), so that net exports equal +9 million opals.

c At a real interest rate of 5%, in Pellucidar the quantity supplied of loanable funds is 19 million opals, the quantity demanded is 28 million opals. This leaves a shortage of 9 million opals that are borrowed internationally (foreigners lend 9 million opals), so that net exports equal −9 million opals.

8 Figure 23.4 shows the loanable funds market. Since Canada is neither a net lender nor a net borrower, the Canadian quantity demanded and supplied of loanable funds is initially equal at the world real interest rate.

Figure **23.4**

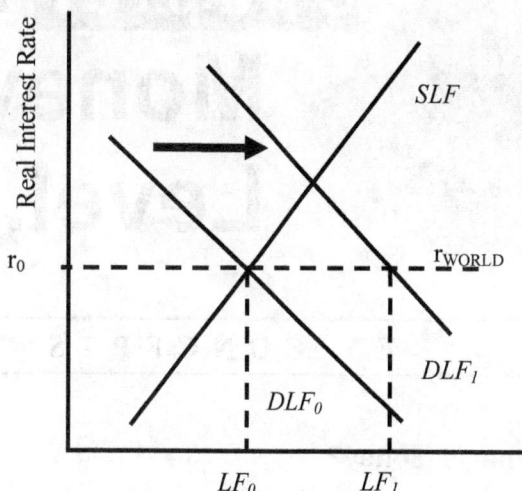

Loanable Funds ($)

The initial impact of the increased profits is increased investment by firms, leading to a rightward shift in the demand for loanable funds to DLF_1, with a resulting increase in the quantity of loanable funds traded from LF_0 to LF_1 (the difference equals the additional investment) and no change in the real interest rate. There is no change in the Canadian supply, so extra loanable funds come from the global market by borrowing internationally, the difference between LF_0 and LF_1. As a net international borrower, Canada must now have negative net exports equal to that amount.

Chapter 24
Money, the Price Level, and Inflation

What Is Money?

Money is something acceptable as a **means of payment** (method of settling a debt) and has three functions:

- Medium of exchange—accepted in exchange for goods and services.
  - Better than **barter** (direct exchange of goods for goods)—guarantees double coincidence of wants.
- Unit of account—agreed measure for prices.
- Store of value—exchangeable at a later date.

Two official measures of money:

- **M1**—currency held by individuals and businesses + chequable deposits of individuals and businesses.
- **M2**—M1 + all other deposits.

Money is **currency** (coins + Bank of Canada notes) and deposits (convertible into currency, used to pay debts).

- Cheques are only an instruction to banks.
- Credit cards are ID cards for loans, not money.
- Currency plus some deposits are means of payments; other deposits are not, but have liquidity.

The Banking System

The banking system consists of depository institutions and the Bank of Canada.

- **Depository institutions** take deposits from households and firms and make loans to others.

- **Chartered banks** (chartered under the Bank Act), **credit unions** and caisses populaires, and **trust and mortgage loan companies**.

- Banks and other depository institutions provide services for fees and earn income lending out deposits. Banks have four assets:

  - **reserves** (cash + deposits at Bank of Canada), held to meet demand for currency
  - liquid assets (short-term government and commercial bills)
  - securities (longer-term bonds)
  - loans to corporations and households

- Banks make profits by paying depositors low interest rates and lending at high rates in return for services of

  - creating liquidity
  - pooling risks
  - lowering cost of borrowing funds
  - lowering cost of monitoring borrowers

Bank of Canada is Canada's **central bank**—supervises financial institutions, markets, payments system, and conducts monetary policy.

- Acts as banker to other banks and government, and as **lender of last resort** (makes loans to the banking system when there is a reserve shortage).

- Bank of Canada is the sole issuer of bank notes.

- Bank of Canada balance sheet shows assets (government securities and loans to banks, usually zero) and liabilities (bank notes and deposits of banks and government).

- **Monetary base** (Bank of Canada notes/coins + depository institutions' deposits at the Bank) can be changed using **open market operation** (purchase or sale of government securities by Bank).

♦ If Bank of Canada buys government bonds, this increases banking system reserves, increasing the monetary base.

♦ If Bank of Canada sells government bonds, this decreases banking system reserves, decreasing the monetary base.

How Banks Create Money

Banks create money (deposits) when they lend out excess reserves (**reserves** = notes/coins in vaults + deposits at the Bank of Canada).

♦ Quantity of deposits that can be created is limited by the monetary base, the level of desired reserves, and the desired currency holding.

♦ People desire to hold some money as currency—**currency drain ratio** = currency/deposits.

♦ If a bank gets a new deposit, it creates **excess reserves** (actual reserves – desired reserves).

  • **Desired reserve ratio** = ratio of reserves to total deposits banks wish to hold.

♦ Banks loan out excess reserves.

  • Borrower spends loan (and keeps some as currency), recipient of spent money deposits it at her bank.

  • New bank has more reserves, some are desired but some are excess reserves, leading to further steps in the deposit multiplier process.

♦ Total Δ quantity of money = increase in currency + increase in deposits.

♦ **Money multiplier** = (Δ quantity of money)/(Δ monetary base).

The Market for Money

People choose money holdings based on price level, nominal interest rate, real GDP, financial innovation.

♦ People hold money for its buying power.

  • Increase in price level (P) causes equal increase in nominal money demanded (M), so no change in real money demanded (M/P).

♦ Interest rate = opportunity cost of holding money.

  • Higher interest rate decreases quantity of real money demanded.

  • **Demand for money** is the relationship between the quantity of real money demanded and the nominal interest rate, holding constant other factors.

♦ Increase in real GDP shifts MD curve rightward.

♦ Financial innovation has an ambiguous effect on MD curve—decreases demand for currency and some deposits, increases demand for other deposits.

Money market equilibrium occurs when the quantity of money demanded equals the quantity of money supplied.

♦ Short-run equilibrium is determined by the quantity of money supplied (determined by actions of banks and the Bank of Canada).

♦ Changes in interest rate create a new equilibrium in the money market.

  • If the Bank of Canada increases the quantity of money, people find themselves with excess money holdings.

  • Therefore, they buy financial assets, increasing the price of financial assets and decreasing the interest rate toward equilibrium.

♦ In the long run, supply and demand of loanable funds determines real interest rate, nominal interest rate = real interest rate + expected inflation rate.

The Quantity Theory of Money

Quantity theory of money predicts an increase in quantity of money leads to equal percentage increase in price level.

♦ Quantity theory starts with **velocity of circulation** (the average number of times a dollar is used annually to buy goods and services).

♦ ($V = PY/M$), which leads to equation of exchange: ($MV = PY$).

  • Assumes velocity is unaffected by ΔM.

  • Then, $\% \Delta P = \% \Delta M - \% \Delta Y$.

♦ Historical evidence suggests the money growth rate is correlated with the inflation rate, but greater than the inflation rate.

Mathematical Note: The Money Multiplier

The money multiplier (mm) is the ratio of money (M) to the monetary base (MB): $mm = M/MB$.

♦ M = deposits + currency = $D + C$.

♦ MB = bank reserves + currency = $R + C$.

♦ Therefore $mm = (D + C)/(R + C)$.

♦ Divide all variables on right-hand side by D to get $mm = (1 + C/D)/(R/D + C/D)$.

♦ C/D is the currency ratio, R/D is the banks' reserve ratio.

HELPFUL HINTS

1 What is money? Whatever meets the functions of money is money. For example, cigarettes functioned as money in prisoner-of-war camps. However, you should be able to answer this question on several levels. First, as a general definition, money is a medium of exchange. Second, as a classification, chequable deposits are money but savings deposits are not. Third, as more specific definitions, M1 and M2 are official definitions of money.

We refer to our income earnings as the "money we make working." However, in economics, money means the *stock* of money we are holding in currency plus deposits (M1 or M2). Money does *not* mean the *flow* of income earnings—be careful of this distinction.

Distinguish between the act of holding money and the act of consumption spending. Holding money means dealing with money markets, not goods and services markets. The choice for households in this chapter is between holding bonds and holding money. The choice for consumer spending involves saving versus spending.

2 Become thoroughly familiar with the money multiplier process by which banks create money.

Two fundamental facts allow banks to create money. First, banks create money by creating new chequable deposits. Second, banks hold fractional reserves. Fractional reserves mean that when a bank receives a deposit, it only holds part of it as reserves and lends the rest. The bank is not indulging in a scam—it is still maintaining assets (reserves plus loans) to match its liabilities (deposits). When that loan is spent, at least part of the proceeds will likely be deposited in another bank, creating a new deposit (money).

The deposit multiplier process follows from this last fact: banks make loans when they receive new deposits. These loans are spent—some leaves the process as currency drain, and the rest returns to another bank, creating another new deposit. The process repeats itself, adding more deposits (but in progressively smaller amounts) in each round. Practise going through examples until the process becomes second nature. As you go, note the role played by the profit-seeking behaviour of banks. Profit-seeking leads them to turn reserves, which earn no revenues, into loans, which earn revenues.

3 Be careful to avoid a common error when working through open market operations. When the Bank of Canada buys or sells securities, private bank reserves at the Bank of Canada change. Many students automatically put the changed bank reserves at the Bank of Canada under assets in the Bank's balance sheet, because they are an asset on the *private bank's balance sheet*. However, this is an error—the reserves are a deposit at the Bank of Canada, and therefore a *liability* to the Bank of Canada.

4 The important equation of exchange states:

$$\text{Quantity of money} \times \text{Velocity of circulation} = \text{Price level} \times \text{Real GDP}$$

The quantity of money times the average number of times each dollar is spent (equalling total expenditure) is equal to the dollar value of the goods and services on which it was spent. The equation is always true by definition—it is an identity. By further assuming that both the velocity of circulation and potential GDP are independent of the quantity of money in the long run, we get the quantity theory of money. The assumptions imply that when the quantity of money increases by 10 percent, in the long run the price level increases by 10 percent to maintain equality between the two sides of the equation.

SELF-TEST

True/False and Explain

What Is Money?

1 Money is anything generally acceptable as a means of payment.

2 A fixed term deposit at a chartered bank is part of M1.

3 If the public shifts deposits from chequing accounts to nonchequing accounts, M1 will decrease and M2 increase.

The Banking System

4 One of the key economic functions of banks is acting as a lender of last resort.

5 Individual households are generally better at pooling risk than are depository institutions.

6 A bank's reserves consist of cash in its vault plus its deposits at the Bank of Canada.

How Banks Create Money

7 The size of the monetary base limits the amount of deposit creation in the money creation process.

8 If a depositor uses a debit card to buy something, her bank's reserves decline.

The Money Market

9 If the price level increases, the quantity of real money people want to hold increases.

10 If interest rates increase, the quantity of real money demanded decreases.

11 The development of near-money deposits and growth in the use of credit cards in the 1970s caused the demand for M1 to shift leftward.

12 If households or firms have more money than they want to hold, they will buy financial assets, causing asset prices to increase and the interest rate to decrease.

13 If the price of a bond increases, the interest rate earned on the bond decreases.

The Quantity Theory of Money

14 If the quantity of money is $50 billion and nominal GDP is $200 billion, the velocity of circulation is 1/4.

15 The international data does not support the quantity theory of money.

Multiple-Choice

What Is Money?

1 Which of the following is a function of money?
   a   medium of exchange
   b   measure of liquidity
   c   pooling risk
   d   store of exchange
   e   reducing transactions costs

2 Which of the following is a component of M2 but *not* of M1?
   a   currency in circulation
   b   personal chequing deposits
   c   personal nonchequing deposits
   d   currency in bank vaults
   e   Canada Savings Bonds

3 Which of the following is *most* liquid?
   a   chequing deposits
   b   real estate
   c   government bonds
   d   savings deposits
   e   cheques

4   Which of the following is *not* a store of value?
    a   credit cards
    b   personal chequing deposits
    c   term deposits
    d   other chequable deposits
    e   nonchequing deposits

The Banking System

5   Which of the following statements about depository institutions is *false*?
    a   They maximize their owner's wealth, ignoring all else.
    b   They keep reserves to meet cash withdrawals.
    c   A credit union is a depository institution.
    d   They pool and therefore reduce risk.
    e   They borrow at low interest rates and lend at higher interest rates.

6   Which of the following is an economic service provided by a depository institution?
    a   borrowing low and lending high
    b   keeping cash reserves
    c   pooling liquidity
    d   lowering the cost of borrowing funds
    e   creating liquid liabilities

7   When a bank receives short-term deposits and issues long-term loans, this is an example of
    a   being a lender of last resort.
    b   lowering the cost of borrowing.
    c   creating liquidity.
    d   taking unnecessary risks.
    e   pooling risk.

8   Which of the following is an asset of the Bank of Canada?
    a   currency in circulation
    b   government securities held in the Bank of Canada
    c   deposits of chartered banks at the Bank of Canada
    d   coins in circulation
    e   deposits of governments at the Bank of Canada

9   Which balance sheet in Table 24.1 shows the initial impact on the banking sector of an open market purchase by the Bank of Canada of $100 million of government securities from the banking sector?
    a   (a)
    b   (b)
    c   (c)
    d   (d)
    e   none of the above

TABLE 24.1 BANKING SYSTEM BALANCE SHEET (MILLIONS)

(a)

Assets		Liabilities
Reserves	+100	
Securities	−100	

(b)

Assets		Liabilities
Reserves	−100	
Securities	+100	

(c)

Assets		Liabilities	
Reserves	+100	Deposits	+100

(d)

Assets		Liabilities	
		Deposits	+100
		Securities	−100

How Banks Create Money

10 The Bank of Speedy Creek currently has actual (and desired) reserves of $40, loans of $460, and deposits of $500. What is its desired reserve ratio?
    a   4%
    b   8%
    c   12.5%
    d   25%
    e   40%

11 The Bank of Speedy Creek currently has actual (and desired) reserves of $40, loans of $460, and deposits of $500. Huck Finn comes along and deposits $10. After Huck's deposit, but before any other actions have occurred, the total amount of *monetary base* in the economy
    a   is unchanged, with currency $10 higher and deposits $10 lower.
    b   has increased by $10.
    c   has decreased by $10.
    d   is unchanged, with deposits $10 higher and currency $10 lower.
    e   depends on if Huck deposited his money in a savings deposit or a demand deposit.

12 The Bank of Speedy Creek currently has actual (and desired) reserves of $40, loans of $460, and deposits of $500. Huck Finn comes along and deposits $10. After Huck's deposit, but before any other actions have occurred, the total amount of *money* in the economy has

   a stayed the same, with currency and deposits unchanged.

   b stayed the same, with currency falling and deposits rising.

   c decreased, with currency falling and deposits staying the same.

   d increased, with currency unchanged and deposits rising.

   e decreased, with currency falling and deposits unchanged.

13 The Bank of Speedy Creek currently has actual (and desired) reserves of $40, loans of $460, and deposits of $500. Huck Finn comes along and deposits $10. After Huck's deposit, but before any other actions have occurred, the Bank of Speedy Creek will have excess reserves of

   a zero.

   b $9.

   c $9.20.

   d $10.

   e $40.

14 The Bank of Speedy Creek currently has actual (and desired) reserves of $40, loans of $460, and deposits of $500. Huck Finn comes along and deposits $10. After Huck's deposit, given that the Bank of Speedy Creek is profit-seeking, what amount of new loans will it make?

   a zero

   b $9

   c $9.20

   d $10

   e $40

15 The Bank of Speedy Creek currently has actual (and desired) reserves of $40, loans of $460, and deposits of $500. Huck Finn comes along and deposits $10. After Huck's deposit, and after the Bank of Speedy Creek has lent the amount it wishes to lend, the total amount of reserves in the bank will be $_____, the total amount of loans will be $_____, and the total amount of deposits will be $_____.

   a 40.80; 469.20; 510

   b 40; 460; 500

   c 50; 470; 520

   d 41; 469; 510

   e 42.50; 467.50; 510

16 If new deposits are made in the banking system, which of the following will limit the amount of the new money created?

   a the desired reserve ratio only

   b the currency drain ratio only

   c the monetary base only

   d the desired reserve ratio and the currency drain ratio, but not the monetary base

   e the desired reserve ratio, the currency drain ratio, and the monetary base

17 Which of the following steps in the description of the money multiplier process is *wrong*?

   a Banks lend out excess reserves.

   b Bank deposits increase.

   c The deposits are spent.

   d Some new spending returns as deposits, and currency comes in as new deposits.

   e Banks once again have excess reserves, and the process continues.

The Market for Money

18 Consider Fig. 24.1. Which of the following best describes the response of this household to an *increase* in their annual income?

   a movement from *a* to *f*

   b movement from *a* to *c*

   c movement from *e* to *a*

   d movement from *b* to *a*

   e movement from *a* to *e*

FIGURE **24.1** THE DEMAND FOR REAL MONEY BALANCES BY AN INDIVIDUAL HOUSEHOLD

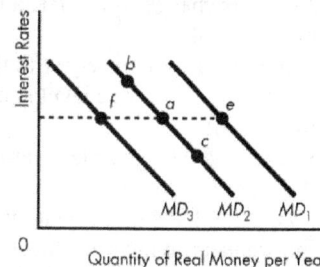

19 Which of the following could cause the demand curve for M1 to shift leftward?

   a increase in real GDP

   b decrease in interest rates

   c expanded use of credit cards

   d increase in quantity of money supplied

   e increase in the price level

20 Real money is equal to nominal money
a divided by real GDP.
b minus real GDP.
c divided by the price level.
d minus the price level.
e divided by velocity.

21 If the interest rate is above the equilibrium rate, how is equilibrium achieved in the money market?
a People buy goods to get rid of excess money, lowering the price of goods, and lowering the interest rate.
b People sell goods to get rid of excess money, lowering the price of goods, and lowering the interest rate.
c People sell bonds to get rid of excess money, lowering the price of bonds, and lowering the interest rate.
d People sell bonds to get rid of excess money, raising the price of bonds, and lowering the interest rate.
e People buy bonds to get rid of excess money, raising the price of bonds, and lowering the interest rate.

22 Money market equilibrium occurs
a when interest rates are constant.
b when the level of real GDP is constant.
c when quantity of real money supplied equals quantity of real money demanded.
d only under a fixed exchange rate.
e when bond prices are constant.

The Quantity Theory of Money

23 The quantity theory of money begins with the equation of exchange, $MV = PY$, and then adds the assumptions that
a velocity varies inversely with the rate of interest, and the price level is independent of the quantity of money.
b velocity and the price level are independent of the quantity of money.
c potential GDP and the quantity of money are independent of the price level.
d potential GDP and the price level are independent of the quantity of money.
e velocity and potential GDP are independent of the quantity of money.

24 According to the quantity theory of money, in the long run
a V/M is constant.
b Y/M is constant.
c Y/P is constant.
d M/P is constant.
e M/V is constant.

25 According to the quantity theory of money, an increase in the quantity of money will increase the price level
a but will have no effect on real GDP or velocity of circulation.
b as well as increase both real GDP and velocity of circulation.
c as well as increase real GDP but decrease velocity of circulation.
d as well as decrease real GDP but increase velocity of circulation.
e but have no effect on real GDP while decreasing velocity of circulation.

Short Answer Problems

1 Banks can no longer issue their own paper money, but can create deposit money by crediting people's deposits. Since there is no paper money deposited to back up this creation, is this created money real? Is it acceptable in society? Why or why not?

2 Briefly explain how and why banks create new money during the deposit multiplier process (in a multibank system).

3 Why do people care about the quantity of real money they hold rather than the quantity of nominal money?

4 There is only one chartered bank in the country of Adanac, and it has the following assets and liabilities:

Currency reserves	$20 million
Reserves held at the Bank of Adanac	$10 million
Loans	$700 million
Securities	$20 million
Deposits	$750 million

a Assuming that the bank has freely chosen its reserves, what is its desired reserve ratio?

b If the amount of currency in circulation is $50 million, what is the monetary base? What is the money supply?

c What is the currency drain ratio?

5 Consider the balance sheets in Table 24.2 on the next page for the Bank of Canada and the Bank of Speedy Creek:

TABLE **24.2**

Bank of Speedy Creek

Assets		Liabilities	
Reserves	60	Deposits	1,000
Securities	100		
Loans	840		
	1,000		

Bank of Canada

Assets		Liabilities	
Government securities	9,000	Bank of Canada notes	10,000
Loans to banks	500	Chartered banks' deposits	1,000
Other net assets	2,000	Government deposits	500
	11,500		11,500

Suppose that the Bank of Canada buys all $100 of securities from the Bank of Speedy Creek. Show what happens to the balance sheets of the Bank of Speedy Creek and the Bank of Canada as a result of this action, explaining as you go. What does this action do to the reserves in the banking system?

6 Assume the central bank adjusts the quantity of money to keep the quantity of real money supplied constant.

   a Describe what happens to the money supply in this situation.

      Show on a graph and briefly explain what each of the following will do (in sequence) to the demand for real money (defined as M1) and therefore the equilibrium interest rate. Assume that the real money supply remains constant.

   b The price level rises.

   c There is a financial innovation (widespread adoption of electronic funds transfers) that reduces the need to use chequing accounts.

   d Real GDP falls during a recession.

7 Briefly explain the role of the Bank of Canada in the banking system.

8 We observe an economy in which the price level is 1.5, real GDP equals potential GDP at $240 billion, and the quantity of money is $60 billion.

   a What is the velocity of circulation?

   b According to the quantity theory of money, what is the long-run result of an increase in the quantity of money to $80 billion?

ANSWERS

True/False and Explain

1   T   Basic function of money. (568)

2   F   See definition of M1. (569–570)

(ct) 3   F   M1 decreases as chequing accounts decrease, but chequing and nonchequing accounts are both part of M2, so no change in M2. (569–570)

4   F   This is function of a central bank. (572–573)

5   F   Large size allows banks to pool risk. (571–572)

6   T   Definition. (571)

7   T   Limits the amount available for desired reserves and desired currency holdings. (576)

8   T   Withdrawal decreases deposits = decrease in reserves. (576–577)

9   F   Real money demand is independent of the price level. (578–579)

10   T   Increase in interest rate increases the opportunity cost of holding money and decreases the quantity of money demanded. (578–579)

11   T   Shift toward M2—see text discussion. (580)

12   T   Agents substitute toward bonds, increasing bond demand and bond prices, which implies a decrease in bond interest rate. (581)

13   T   Price of bond and its interest rate are inversely related. (581)

14   F $V = PY/M = 200/50 = 4$. (582)

15   F   Correlation between money growth and inflation is not perfect, but it is strong. (583)

Multiple-Choice

1   a   See text discussion. (568)

2   c   Definition. (569)

3   a   Most readily changed into currency. (570)

4 a Credit cards are not guaranteed for future purchases—credit card company might cancel your card. (569)

5 a Must be prudent about risk, too. (571)

6 d See text discussion. (572)

7 c Short-term deposits are more liquid for depositors than lending long-term themselves. (572)

8 b Definition. (573)

9 a Buying government bonds increases reserves. (575)

10 b Desired reserve ratio = chosen reserves/deposits = 40/500 = 0.08. (576)

11 d Decrease in currency in circulation = increase in bank reserves. (576–577)

12 b Decrease in currency as deposit made = increase in deposits. (576–577)

13 c Excess = actual ($50) – desired ($40.80 = 0.08 × $510). (576–577)

14 c Banks will lend the amount of excess reserves. (576–577)

15 a The $10 deposit is divided between the new desired reserves (0.08 × $10) and new loans. (576–577)

16 e The monetary base limits possible amount of new reserves and new currency in circulation. The higher the desired reserve ratio, the more money banks hold back at each stage. The higher the currency drain ratio, the more households hold back at each stage. (576)

17 d Some of the new spending is kept back as currency and not deposited. (579)

18 e *a* to *f*, *e* to *a* are decreases in income, others are Δ interest rates. (579)

19 c Financial innovation means people use less money. Other changes create rightward shift or no shift. (579)

20 c Definition. (578)

21 e If interest rate > equilibrium, this implies too much money, which implies buying bonds, leading to increase in price of bonds and therefore decrease in interest rates. (581)

22 c Definition. (581)

23 e See text discussion. (582–583)

24 d Because theory assumes $Y/V (= M/P)$ is constant. (582–583)

25 a Due to assumption that neither GDP nor velocity affected by Δ quantity of money. (582–583)

Short Answer Problems

1 This created money is real, because it is backed by the assets of the bank, which consist of the bank's reserves, loans, and holdings of securities.

Deposit money is generally accepted in society (you can buy goods, pay debts, etc., with it) because people know that the banks will provide currency upon demand.

2 Banks create money by making new loans. When banks get a new deposit, this leaves them with excess reserves. The desire to make profits leads banks to lend out excess reserves, creating a matching deposit, which is new money. When these loans are spent, the person receiving the money deposits much of it in a bank deposit, creating excess reserves, and the process continues.

3 Nominal money is simply the number of dollars, while real money is a measure of what money will buy. Real money decreases if the price level rises while the number of dollars is constant. What matters to people is the quantity of goods and services that money will buy, not the number of dollars. If the price level rises by 10 percent, people will want to hold 10 percent more dollars (given a constant real income and interest rates) to keep the same purchasing power.

4 a Desired reserve ratio = desired reserves/deposits = 30/750 = 0.04.

b Monetary base = reserves + currency in circulation = $80 million. Money supply = currency in circulation + deposits = $800 million.

c Currency drain ratio = currency in circulation/deposits = 50/750 = 1/15 = 0.0667.

5 The impact of the purchase on the balance sheets is shown in Table 24.3 on the next page.

The Bank of Canada increases its securities by 100, and pays for it by increasing the Bank of Speedy Creek's deposits at the Bank of Canada by 100, which is an increase in this bank's reserves by 100 (matching the decrease in security holdings). The balance sheets in Table 24.3 show the changes, and then the new positions.

The increase in banks' deposits of 100 also increases the reserves of the banking system by 100.

TABLE 24.3

Changes in Balance Sheets
Bank of Speedy Creek

Assets		Liabilities	
Reserves	+100	Deposits	0
Securities	−100		
Loans	0		
	0		

Bank of Canada

Assets		Liabilities	
Government securities	+100	Bank of Canada notes	0
Loans to banks	0	Ch. banks' deposits	+100
Other net assets	0	Government deposits	0
	+100		+100

6 a   If the central bank is targeting the quantity of money, quantity of money supplied is fixed and money supply curve is vertical (at *MS* in Fig. 24.2).

FIGURE **24.2**

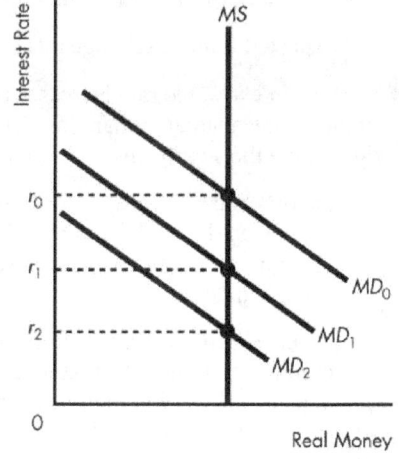

b   A change in price level has no impact on real money demand, so no impact on equilibrium interest rate (*r*). In Fig. 24.2, demand for real money remains at MD_0, and interest rate remains at r_0.

c   This financial innovation reduces the need to use chequing accounts, which are part of M1. Therefore demand for real money falls to MD_1, and equilibrium interest rate falls to r_1 in Fig. 24.2.

d   Decrease in real GDP lowers demand for real money to MD_2, and the equilibrium interest rate falls to r_2 in Fig. 24.2.

7   The Bank of Canada supervises financial institutions and markets and the financial system, and conducts monetary policy. It acts as banker to other banks and to the government, and acts as lender of last resort by making loans to the banking system when there is a shortage of reserves. It is also the sole issuer of bank notes.

8 a   The velocity of circulation is

$$\text{Velocity of circulation} = \frac{\text{Price level} \times \text{Real GDP}}{\text{Quantity of money}}$$

With the given values for the price level, real GDP, and quantity of money, we have

$$\text{Velocity of circulation} = \frac{1.5 \times 240}{60} = 6$$

b   The quantity theory of money predicts that in the long run an increase in quantity of money causes an equal percentage increase in the price level. An increase in money from $60 billion to $80 billion is a one-third (33%) increase. Thus the quantity theory of money predicts the price level will increase by a third (33%). Since the initial price level is 1.5, the predicted price level will be 2.0. (Can also be calculated using the equation of exchange.)

Chapter 25

The Exchange Rate and the Balance of Payments

The Foreign Exchange Market

To buy foreign goods/assets, Canadians need **foreign currency** (foreign notes, coins, bank deposits); to buy Canadian goods/assets, foreigners need Canadian dollars.

- ♦ Currencies of one country are exchanged for the currency of another in the **foreign exchange market**.

- ♦ **Exchange rate** = price at which one currency exchanges for another.

- ♦ Currency depreciation (appreciation) is the decrease (increase) in value of the Canadian dollar in terms of another currency.

The exchange rate is determined by supply and demand in the foreign exchange market.

- ♦ Demand for Canadian dollars = supply of foreign currency; supply of Canadian dollars = demand for foreign currency.

- ♦ Quantity of Canadian dollars demanded in foreign exchange market = planned amount to buy at a given price, based on demands for Canadian exports and assets; depends on:

  - exchange rate

  - world demand for Canadian exports

  - interest rates in Canada and other countries

  - expected future exchange rate

- ♦ Increase in exchange rate decreases quantity demanded of Canadian dollars (movement up to the left along the demand curve), because

  - exports become more expensive for foreigners, decreasing demand for exports and therefore demand for dollars.

  - expected profits decrease from buying Canadian dollars to hold until they appreciate.

- ♦ Quantity of Canadian dollars supplied in foreign exchange market = planned amount to sell at a given price = planned purchases of foreign currencies to buy imports and foreign assets; depends on:

  - exchange rate

  - Canadian demand for imports

  - interest rates in Canada and other countries

  - expected future exchange rate

- ♦ Increase in exchange rate increases the quantity supplied of Canadian dollars (movement up to the right along the supply curve), because

  - imports become cheaper for Canadians, increasing demand for imports/demand for foreign currency = increase in supply of Canadian dollars.

  - expected profits increase from buying foreign currency to hold until it appreciates, increasing demand for foreign currency = increase in supply of Canadian dollars.

- ♦ Market equilibrium is determined by demand and supply—exchange rates adjust instantly as required to achieve equilibrium for all exchange rates.

Exchange Rate Fluctuations

Demand curve for Canadian dollars shifts *rightward* if

- ◆ world demand for Canadian exports increases.

- ◆ **Canadian interest rate differential** (Canadian interest rate – foreign interest rate) increases, increasing demand for Canadian assets.

- ◆ expected future exchange rate increases, increasing expected profits from buying Canadian dollars and holding them until they appreciate.

Supply curve of Canadian dollars shifts *leftward* if

- ◆ Canadian demand for imports decreases.

- ◆ Canadian interest rate differential increases.

- ◆ expected future exchange rate increases.

Expected changes in exchange rates are strongly affected by arbitrage behaviour (buying in one market and selling at a higher price in another), which in turn creates

- ◆ **purchasing power parity** (two currencies have the same value or purchasing power)—if no parity, and a Canadian dollar buys more than a U.S. dollar, demand for the Canadian dollar increases, supply decreases, and Canadian dollar appreciates.

- ◆ **interest rate parity** (two currencies earn the same rate of return, adjusted for expected Δ exchange rate)—if parity does not hold (adjusted for risk), and if returns are higher in Canada, increased demand for Canadian dollar instantly increases the exchange rate.

Real exchange rate (*RER*) is the relative price of Canadian-produced goods and services versus foreign-produced—$RER = (E \times P)/P^*$ where $P/P^* =$ Canadian/foreign price level and $E =$ nominal exchange rate = foreign currency per Canadian dollar.

- ◆ Nominal exchange rate is determined by purchasing power parity and interest parity, and in the short run this also determines the real exchange rate.

- ◆ In the long run the nominal exchange rate and price levels are determined together, and the real exchange rate does not change.

Exchange Rate Policy

Three different exchange rate policies:

- ◆ Current policy is **flexible exchange rate**— exchange rate is determined by supply and demand, changes in interest rates influence exchange rate.

- ◆ **Fixed exchange rate** policy pegs the exchange rate at a target value—if Δ exchange rate, Bank of Canada must buy/sell Canadian dollars to change demand/supply—works only as long as foreign currency reserves last.

- ◆ **Crawling peg** policy intervenes to meet selected target *path* for the exchange rate.

Financing International Trade

Balance of payments accounts measure Canada's international trading, borrowing, and lending.

- ◆ **Current account** = net exports + net interest income + net transfers.

- ◆ **Capital account** = foreign investment in Canada – Canadian investment abroad.

- ◆ **Official settlements account** = net changes in Canada's **official reserves** (government's holdings of foreign currency). If official reserves increase, official settlement balance is negative.

- ◆ Current account balance + capital account balance + official settlements balance = 0.

- ◆ To pay a current account deficit we must borrow from abroad or decrease official reserves.

Net borrower country borrows more from rest of world than lends in current year (capital account surplus).

- ◆ **Net lender**—lending more to rest of world than borrowing in current year (capital account deficit).

- ◆ **Debtor nation**—has borrowed more than lent to rest of world over history; **creditor nation** is the reverse.

Current account balance is primarily determined by **net exports** $(X - M)$.

- ◆ From circular flow, net exports = **private sector balance** $(S - I)$ + **government sector balance** $(T - G)$.

- ◆ In the short run, the nominal exchange rate affects net exports; in the long run it has no effect.

HELPFUL HINTS

1 There is an important difference between trade within a single country and trade between countries—currency. Individuals trading in the same country use the same currency, and trade is straightforward. International trade (to be examined in detail in Chapter 31) is complicated by the fact that individuals in different countries use different currencies. A Japanese vendor selling goods wants payment in Japanese yen, but a Canadian buyer is likely holding only Canadian dollars. This chapter addresses this complication by examining the foreign exchange market.

2 The exchange rate is volatile because supply and demand often shift in a reinforcing manner, since they are both affected by the same changes in expectations. These changes in expectations are driven by two forces: purchasing power parity and interest rate parity. Each of these is a version of the law of one price, which states that anytime there is a difference in the price of the same good in two markets, natural economic forces (unless restricted) will eliminate that discrepancy and establish a single price. Suppose that the price in market 1 increases relative to the price in market 2. Individuals will now buy in market 2 (lower price) and not in market 1 (higher price). This increase in demand in market 2 and decrease in demand in market 1 will cause the two prices to come together. This principle also applies to international markets: natural market forces result in a single world price for the same good (allowing for effects of tariffs, transport costs, etc.).

Suppose that purchasing power parity does not hold. For example, suppose that the wholesale price of an MP3 player in Canada is $100, and in Japan it is 10,000 yen, and that the exchange rate is currently 125 yen per dollar. The dollar price of the player in Japan is $80 (10,000 yen/125 yen per dollar). People expect the demand for the player in Canada to decrease (= a decrease in demand for Canadian dollars) and the demand for the player in Japan to increase (= supply of dollars rising), which would lead to the exchange rate depreciating toward 100 yen per dollar (purchasing power parity level). Expectations will lead to a decrease in demand for the Canadian dollar and an increase in supply of the Canadian dollar, so that the exchange rate will depreciate even before demand for the player adjusts!

The law of one price also holds for prices of assets like bonds. Recall from Chapter 23 that bond prices are inversely related to interest rates; interest rate parity is a version of the law of one price. Consider a situation where, taking into account the expected depreciation of the Canadian dollar, the Canadian interest rate was higher than the U.S. rate (which implies the price of bonds is lower in Canada). Buyers would demand Canadian bonds, raising their price and lowering Canadian interest rates. In addition, they would be selling U.S. bonds, lowering their price and raising U.S. interest rates. These actions occur until the interest rate differential between the two countries has shrunk to a level where it just reflects the expected depreciation of the Canadian dollar—interest rate parity holds.

SELF-TEST

True/False and Explain

The Foreign Exchange Market

1 If the exchange rate between the Canadian dollar and the Japanese yen changes from 130 yen per dollar to 140 yen per dollar, the Canadian dollar has appreciated.

2 If the Canadian dollar can buy $0.75 U.S., the U.S. dollar can buy $1.25 Canadian.

3 The demand for Canadian dollars by foreigners is automatically matched by Canadian demand for foreign currency.

4 A decrease in the exchange rate increases the quantity demanded for Canadian dollars because exports become cheaper for foreigners.

5 The expected profits effect says that an increase in the exchange rate will decrease the quantity supplied of Canadian dollars.

Exchange Rate Fluctuations

6 An increase in Canadian interest rates increases demand for the Canadian dollar.

7 The demand and supply of Canadian dollars tend to move independently of each other.

8 Countries with currencies expected to appreciate will have higher interest rates than countries with currencies expected to depreciate.

9 If the yen price of the dollar is 100 yen per dollar and the price of a traded good is $10 in Canada, purchasing power parity implies that the price in Japan will be 1,000 yen.

10 If the foreign exchange value of the Canadian dollar is expected to increase, the supply of Canadian dollars increases.

Exchange Rate Policy

11 If the Bank of Canada sets a target exchange rate and demand for the Canadian dollar increases, the Bank of Canada will sell Canadian dollars.

12 Under a flexible exchange rate, Bank of Canada policy will not affect the exchange rate.

Financing International Trade

13 There can be no such thing as a balance of payments surplus/deficit, because by definition a *balance* of payments must always *balance*.

14 If a nation is a net borrower from the rest of the world it must be a debtor nation.

15 If Canada borrows more from the rest of the world than it lends to the rest of the world, Canada has a capital account surplus.

Multiple-Choice

The Foreign Exchange Market

1 The exchange rate between the Canadian dollar and the British pound is 0.5 pounds per dollar. If a radio sells for 38 pounds in Britain, what is the dollar price of the radio?
 a $19
 b $25
 c $38
 d $57
 e $76

2 Consider Table 25.1. Between 2009 and 2010, the Canadian dollar _____ versus the euro and _____ versus the yen.
 a appreciated; depreciated
 b appreciated; appreciated
 c depreciated; depreciated
 d depreciated; appreciated
 e has not changed; has not changed

TABLE **25.1**

Currency	2009 Exchange Rate	2010 Exchange Rate
EU euro	2 euros/dollar	3 euros/dollar
Japanese yen	120 yen/dollar	90 yen/dollar

3 Consider Table 25.1. Between 2009 and 2010, the yen
   a must have depreciated in value versus the euro.
   b must have appreciated in value versus the euro.
   c may or may not have appreciated in value versus the euro.
   d will have appreciated in value versus the euro if the euro has a high weight in CERI.
   e will have appreciated in value versus the euro if the euro has a lower weight in CERI.

4 If the demand for Canadian dollars increases, this is matched by a(n)
   a increase in demand for foreign exchange.
   b increase in supply of foreign exchange.
   c increase in supply of Canadian dollars.
   d decrease in demand for foreign exchange.
   e decrease in supply of foreign exchange.

5 The quantity of Canadian dollars demanded depends on all of the following *except*
   a the exchange rate.
   b the interest rate in Canada.
   c interest rates in the rest of the world.
   d the Canadian demand for imports.
   e the expected future exchange rate.

6 A decrease in the exchange rate increases the quantity demanded of Canadian dollars because
   a exports become more expensive for foreigners.
   b imports become more expensive for Canadians.
   c expected profits from buying Canadian dollars increase.
   d expected profits from buying foreign currency decrease.
   e cross exchange rates adjust quickly.

7 Which of the following best describes the expected profit effect?
   a A lower exchange rate leads to importers using the forward market to lower exchange rate risk.
   b A lower exchange rate leads to buying foreign currency to hold until it appreciates.
   c A higher exchange rate leads to buying foreign currency to hold until it appreciates.
   d A higher exchange rate leads to buying Canadian dollars to hold until they appreciate.
   e A higher exchange rate leads to exporters using the forward market to lower exchange rate risk.

8 An increase in the exchange rate increases the quantity supplied of Canadian dollars because
   a imports become cheaper for Canadians, increasing demand for imports and therefore demand for foreign currency, which equals an increase in quantity supplied of Canadian dollars.
   b imports become more expensive for Canadians, increasing demand for imports and therefore demand for foreign currency, which equals an increase in quantity supplied of Canadian dollars.
   c our exports become cheaper for foreigners, increasing demand for exports and therefore demand for foreign currency, which equals an increase in quantity supplied of Canadian dollars.
   d expected profits increase from buying and holding Canadian dollars until they appreciate in value, which increases the quantity supplied of Canadian dollars.
   e expected profits increase from selling and holding foreign currency until it appreciates in value, which increases the quantity supplied of Canadian dollars.

9 If the exchange rate is too high in the foreign exchange market,
   a there is a surplus and the exchange rate will increase.
   b there is a surplus and the exchange rate will decrease.
   c exports are cheap, and the demand curve for Canadian dollars will shift rightward.
   d there is a shortage and the exchange rate will decrease.
   e there is a shortage and the exchange rate will increase.

Exchange Rate Fluctuations

10 Which of the following quotations best describes purchasing power parity?
   a "The recent high Canadian interest rate has increased demand for the Canadian dollar."
   b "The market feeling is that the Canadian dollar is overvalued and will likely depreciate."
   c "The price of bananas is the same in Canada and the United States, adjusting for the exchange rate."
   d "The expected depreciation of the Canadian dollar is currently lowering demand for it."
   e None of the above.

11 When would the exchange rate decrease in value the most?
    a   Supply and demand of dollars both increase.
    b   Supply of dollars increases, and demand decreases.
    c   Supply of dollars decreases, and demand increases.
    d   Supply and demand of dollars both decrease.
    e   When the Bank of Canada intervenes.

12 Which of the following shifts the supply curve of Canadian dollars rightward?
    a   Increase in demand for foreign goods by Canadian citizens.
    b   Decrease in demand for Canadian goods by foreigners.
    c   The dollar is expected to appreciate.
    d   U.S. interest rates decrease.
    e   None of the above

13 Which of the following shifts the demand curve for Canadian dollars rightward?
    a   Increase in demand for foreign goods by Canadian citizens.
    b   Decrease in demand for Canadian goods by foreigners.
    c   The dollar is expected to appreciate.
    d   The dollar is expected to depreciate.
    e   U.S. interest rates increase.

14 If interest rates in Canada are greater than interest rates in Japan, interest rate parity implies that
    a   the inflation rate is higher in Japan.
    b   Japanese financial assets are poor investments.
    c   the yen is expected to depreciate against the dollar.
    d   the yen is expected to appreciate against the dollar.
    e   Canadian financial assets are poor investments.

15 Consider Fig. 25.1. Which graph best shows the impact of an increase in demand for Canadian exports?
    a   (a)
    b   (b)
    c   (c)
    d   (d)
    e   (e)

FIGURE **25.1**

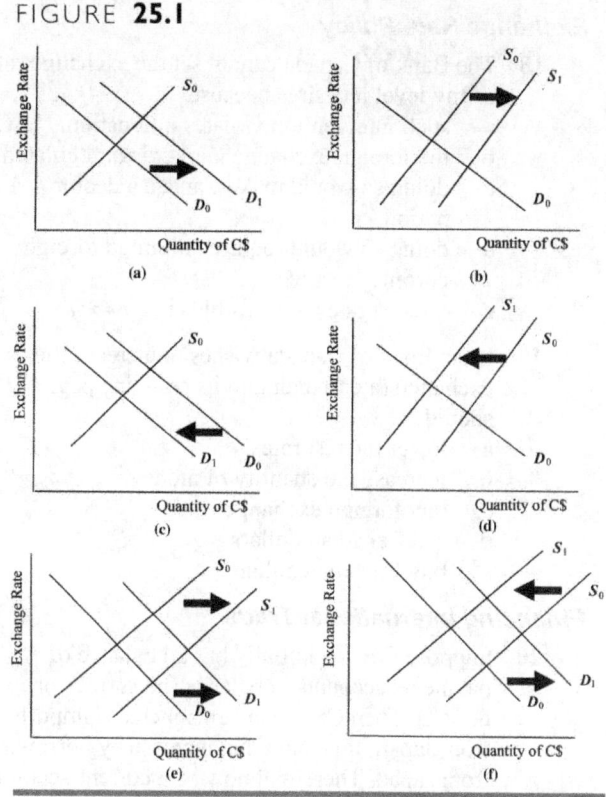

16 Consider Fig. 25.1. Which graph best shows the impact of an increase in the Canadian interest rate differential?
    a   (a)
    b   (c)
    c   (d)
    d   (e)
    e   (f)

17 Consider Fig. 25.1. Which graph best shows the impact of a decrease in Canadian demand for imports?
    a   (a)
    b   (b)
    c   (c)
    d   (d)
    e   (f)

Exchange Rate Policy

18 The Bank of Canada cannot set the exchange rate at any level it desires because
  a such intervention violates international law.
  b the foreign exchange market is unregulated.
  c doing so would make Canada a debtor nation.
  d doing so would require unlimited foreign currency reserves.
  e interest rate parity forbids it.

19 If the Bank of Canada wishes to increase the exchange rate to maintain its crawling peg, it should
  a lower interest rates.
  b increase the quantity of money.
  c buy foreign exchange.
  d sell Canadian dollars.
  e buy Canadian dollars.

Financing International Trade

20 Suppose Canada initially has all balance of payments accounts in balance (no surplus or deficit). Then Canadian firms increase imports from Japan, financing that increase by borrowing from Japan. There will now be a current account
  a surplus and a capital account surplus.
  b surplus and a capital account deficit.
  c deficit and a capital account surplus.
  d deficit and a capital account deficit.
  e deficit and a capital account balance.

21 The country of Mengia came into existence at the beginning of year 1. Given the information in Table 25.2, in year 4 Mengia is a
  a net lender and a creditor nation.
  b net lender and a debtor nation.
  c net borrower and a creditor nation.
  d net borrower and a debtor nation.
  e net lender and neither a creditor nor a debtor nation.

TABLE **25.2**

Year	Borrowed from Rest of World (billions of dollars)	Lent to Rest of World (billions of dollars)
1	60	20
2	60	40
3	60	60
4	60	80

22 Assuming that Mengia's official settlement account is always in balance, in which year or years in Table 25.2 did Mengia have a current account surplus?
  a year 1
  b year 2
  c years 1, 2, and 3
  d years 1 and 2
  e year 4

23 If Mengia's official settlement balance was in deficit every year, for which year or years in Table 25.2 can you say for sure there was a current account surplus?
  a year 1
  b year 2
  c years 2 and 3
  d years 1 and 2
  e years 3 and 4

24 Suppose a country's government expenditures are $400 billion, net taxes are $300 billion, saving is $300 billion, and investment is $250 billion. This country has a government budget
  a surplus and a private sector surplus.
  b surplus and a private sector deficit.
  c deficit and a private sector surplus.
  d deficit and a private sector deficit.
  e surplus and a private sector balance.

25 The distinction between a debtor or creditor nation and a net borrower or net lender nation depends on the distinction between
  a the level of saving and the saving rate.
  b the level of saving and the rate of borrowing.
  c the stock of net debt and the flow of net borrowing.
  d exports and imports.
  e nothing really; they are the same.

Short Answer Problems

1 Suppose there is an increase in demand for Canadian exports. Illustrate and explain with a graph of the foreign exchange market what this change will do when there is a

  a flexible exchange rate.

  b fixed exchange rate.

2 What determines the value of the nominal exchange rate in the short run, in a market with no government intervention?

ⓒ 3 Consider this headline from the December 12, 1997, issue of *The Globe and Mail*: "Dollar Hits New 11-½ Year Low: Interest Rate Hike Expected After Recurrence of Asian Flu Forces Bank of Canada to Intervene." Clearly the Canadian dollar's exchange rate was decreasing in value during December 1997. Explain why an increase in interest rates by the Bank of Canada would help reverse this decrease.

ⓒ 4 Explain how an expected increase in the exchange rate can be a self-fulfilling prophecy.

5 Table 25.3 shows some exchange rates for the Canadian dollar.

TABLE **25.3** EXCHANGE RATES

	USD	JPY	CAD
USD	—	0.78	?
JPY	?	—	?
CAD	1.06	0.83	—

Note: USD = U.S. dollar, JPY = 100 Japanese yen, CAD = Canadian dollar.

a Fill in the missing values in the table, showing all calculations.

b If you were a trader, could you make money by starting with $100 Canadian, buying some USD, using your USD to buy some Japanese yen, and then use your yen to buy Canadian dollars? (Ignore minor rounding errors of 1% or less.)

6 Suppose that the nominal exchange rate between the Canadian dollar and the euro is 2 euros per dollar, that the price level in Canada is 122.7, and the price level in Europe is 200.5.

a What is the real exchange rate expressed as units of Eurozone real GDP per unit of Canadian real GDP?

b Does purchasing power hold?

c If purchasing power does not hold, explain what will happen in the foreign exchange market in the long run to create purchasing power parity.

7 You are trying to decide whether to buy some laptops for your business in either Canada or the United States. Looking at identical machines on the Dell Canada and the Dell U.S. websites, you find that they sell for US$750 in the United States and CAD$1,000 in Canada.

a Where would you buy the laptop if the exchange rate between the Canadian dollar and the U.S. dollar was US$0.80 per C$?

b If there is a profit opportunity, where would you resell it if you wanted to make a profit? (Ignore any taxes, tariffs, transportation costs, and differences in quality.)

c Does purchasing power parity hold?

8 The international transactions of a country for a given year are reported in Table 25.4.

TABLE **25.4**

Transaction	Amount (billions of dollars)
Exports of goods and services	100
Imports of goods and services	130
Transfers to the rest of the world	20
Loans to the rest of the world	60
Loans from the rest of the world	?
Increases in official reserves	10
Net interest income	0

a What is the official settlements balance?

b What is the amount of loans from the rest of the world?

c What is the current account balance?

d What is the capital account balance?

ANSWERS

True/False and Explain

1 T Dollar is more valuable—takes more yen to buy one dollar. (594)

2 F Inverting $0.75 USD/CAD yields $1.33 = 1/0.75. (594)

3 F Automatically matched by the *supply* of foreign currency. (595)

4 T If $CAD is cheaper, takes less foreign currency to buy each $CAD, making our exports cheaper, increasing demand for exports, which increases quantity demanded of $CAD. (595–596)

5 F The expected profits lead to *increased* selling of Canadian dollars. (597)

6 T Increases the interest rate differential, making Canadian assets more attractive to foreigners. (599)

7 F Both are affected by expected future exchange rate and interest rates, so they move together. (599–601)

⊕ 8 F Expected appreciation implies increased earnings in foreign currency terms, which increases demand for foreign bonds, which decreases interest rates until interest rate parity holds. (602)

9 T Under purchasing power parity, the yen price is identical in each country. $10 × 100 yen/$ = 1,000 yen. (602)

10 F Expected increase in foreign exchange value of dollar implies a profit opportunity from holding dollars, which increases demand for dollars. (599–602)

11 T Shifts supply curve of $CAD rightward, offsetting shift in demand. (604–605)

12 F Will not affect it intentionally, but might unintentionally, since changes in monetary policy affect interest rates, which affect demand and supply of Canadian dollars. (604)

⊕ 13 F Overall flow of money in/out of country = sum of the three balances of payment must balance. Each of the three balances may be in deficit/surplus/balance. (607–609)

14 F May or may not be true. For net borrower, *current* net borrowing > 0. For debtor nation, sum of *all* net borrowing > 0. (609)

15 T Definition—note which way the money is flowing. Surplus = net $ flow in. (607–609)

Multiple-Choice

1 e $76 = £38 × ($2 per £). (594)

2 a Takes more euros to buy CAD$1 (increase in value) and less yen (decrease in value). (594)

⊕ 3 b 2009: 1/60 euro/yen = (2 euros/$)/ (120 yen/$). 2010: 1/30 euro/yen = (3 euros/$)/(90 yen/$). Takes more euros in 2010 to buy 1 yen, so yen has appreciated. (594)

4 b Buyers of Canadian $ must supply foreign exchange to buy it. (595)

5 d Affects supply of Canadian $. (595–597)

6 c Expected profits effect—low Canadian $ is likely to appreciate. (596)

7 c High Canadian $ value = low foreign currency value, which is then more likely to appreciate and make a profit. (597)

8 a Imports effect. (596–597)

9 b If exchange rate is high, there is a surplus (quantity supplied > quantity demanded) and therefore downward pressure on price (exchange rate). (598)

10 c Two currencies have the same purchasing power. (602)

11 b Draw a graph. (599–601)

12 a Increased demand for foreign currency increases supply of Canadian dollars. (600)

13 c **a** has no impact on demand, **b**, **d**, and **e** shift demand leftward. (599)

14 d Therefore Canadian dollar expected to depreciate, offsetting the interest rate differential. (601–602)

15 a Greater demand for exports = greater demand for Canadian $ to buy exports. (599–602)

16 e Higher interest rate differential makes Canadian assets more desirable, increasing demand for these assets (and therefore increasing demand for Canadian $) and decreasing demand for foreign assets (and therefore decreasing demand for foreign currency = decrease in supply of Canadian currency). (602)

17 d Lower Canadian demand for imports means lower Canadian demand for foreign currency = decrease in supply of Canadian currency. (599–600)

18 d Such intervention requires buying/selling Canadian dollars, which changes foreign currency reserves, which cannot occur forever. (604–606)

19 e This increases demand for CAD. **a** decreases demand, **b–d** increase supply. (605–606)

⊕ 20 c Imports > exports implies current account deficit. Borrowing > lending implies capital account surplus. (Think about which direction money is flowing.) (607–609)

21 b Current lending > borrowing implies net lender. Sum of past borrowing > sum of lending implies debtor nation. (609)

22 e Official settlements balance = 0 implies current account surplus = capital account deficit, which occurs only when lending > borrowing. (607–609)

Ⓒ **23 e** Since current account + capital account + official settlements account = 0, when official settlements is a deficit, to be sure current is a surplus, it must be the case that capital is 0 or a deficit. (607–609)

24 c Government sector deficit = $T - G = 300 - 400 = -100$. Private sector surplus = $S - I = 300 - 250 = +50$. (610–611)

25 c Debtor/creditor depends on stock of accumulated net debt. Borrower/lender depends on current year flow. (609)

Short Answer Problems

1 a Under a flexible exchange rate, the government does not intervene. Therefore, the exchange rate will adjust to find the new equilibrium. An increase in demand for Canadian exports leads to an increase in demand for Canadian dollars to buy those exports, shown in Fig. 25.2 as a rightward shift in the demand curve. The result is a new equilibrium with a higher exchange rate (ER_1) and a higher quantity of Canadian dollars exchanged ($C\$_1$) each day in the foreign exchange market.

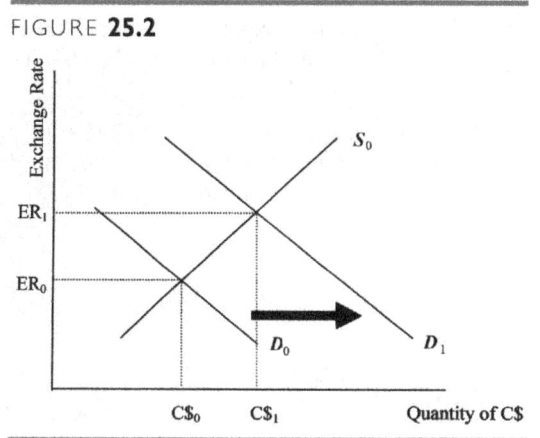

FIGURE **25.2**

b Under a fixed exchange rate, the government intervenes to keep the exchange rate fixed at the target (original) value. Therefore, the exchange rate will *not* adjust to find the new equilibrium. As above, an increase in demand for Canadian exports leads to an increase in demand for Canadian dollars to buy those exports, shown in Fig. 25.3 as a rightward shift in the demand curve. However, now the Bank of Canada supplies Canadian dollars to match this increase (buying foreign currency), so there is also a rightward shift in the supply curve. The result is a new equilibrium with the same exchange rate (ER_0) and an even higher quantity of Canadian dollars exchanged ($C\$_2$) each day in the foreign exchange market.

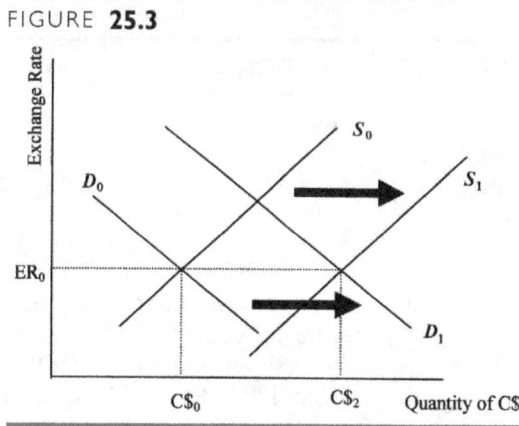

FIGURE **25.3**

2 The value of the exchange rate is determined by supply and demand. The supply of the Canadian dollar is affected by three things—changes in the Canadian interest rate differential, changes in the expected future exchange rate, and the Canadian demand for imports. The demand for the Canadian dollar is also affected by the first two factors, as well as by the world demand for Canadian exports. Finally, changes in the interest rate differential and in the expected future exchange rate are driven by purchasing power parity and interest rate parity.

Ⓒ **3** An increase in Canadian interest rates increases the Canadian interest rate differential, which increases the desirability of Canadian assets relative to foreign assets. This increases demand for Canadian dollars by foreigners, and decreases demand for foreign exchange by Canadians, which decreases the supply of the Canadian dollar. These shifts in demand and supply increase the exchange rate.

4 If the exchange rate is expected to increase, there will be an increase in demand for Canadian dollars to try and make a profit from the increase. In addition, there will be a decrease in supply of Canadian dollars because the expected increase implies a decrease in the value of foreign currency and therefore a decrease in the demand for foreign currency, which is matched by a decrease in supply of Canadian dollars. The impact of these two changes is a shift leftward in the supply curve and a shift rightward in the demand curve for Canadian dollars, which both put upward pressure on the Canadian exchange rate!

5 a Table 25.3 Solution shows the appropriate values. Values are calculated by inverting the existing values: e.g., 1.28 = 1/0.78.

TABLE 25.3 SOLUTION

	USD	JPY	CAD
USD	—	0.78	0.94
JPY	1.28	—	1.21
CAD	1.06	0.83	—

b The columns for each currency tell us what they buy. CAD$100 will buy US$94. Going to the USD column, we can see that US$94 will buy 120 (= 94 × 1.28) hundreds of yen. Going to the JPY column, we can see that 120 hundreds of yen can buy CAD$100 (= 120 × 0.83). Therefore, there is no profit opportunity; the rates are aligned.

6 a The real exchange rate is calculated with the formula

$$RER = E \times (P_{CAN}/P_{EURO})$$
$$= 2 \times (122.7/200.5) = 1.224$$

The real exchange rate is 1.224 units of Eurozone real GDP per unit of Canadian real GDP.

b No, purchasing power parity does not hold. When it holds, the real exchange rate = 1. If we bought the "average" Eurozone good at 200.5 euros, this converts to CAD$100.25 (= 200.5/2), which is less than the price of the average Canadian good (122.7).

c There is a profit opportunity to be made by moving relatively cheaper Eurozone goods from Europe to Canada. Traders carrying out this arbitrage will be buying up European goods and demanding euros to do so. The extra demand for euros will raise the value of the euro and lower the value of the Canadian dollar (lower the nominal exchange rate) to something less than 2 euros per CAD. This in turn will eventually erase the profit opportunity, as the real exchange rate converges on 1.

7 a The Canadian laptop costs US$800 = CAD$1,000 × US$0.80 per CAD. Therefore, it is cheaper to buy from the U.S. website.

b It is profitable to buy it in the United States for US$750 and sell it in Canada for US$800.

c No, the two currencies do not have the same purchasing power—U.S. dollars buy more.

8 a Because official reserves increased, the official settlements balance is –10.

b Current account balance + capital account balance + official settlements balance = 0, or (100 – 130 – 20) + (Loans from rest of world – 60) + (–10) = 0, so loans from rest of world = 120.

c Current account balance is a $50 billion deficit: exports – imports – transfers to the rest of the world + net interest income to the rest of the world.

d Capital account balance is a surplus of $60 billion: loans from the rest of the world – loans to the rest of the world.

Part 8 Wrap Up
Understanding Macroeconomic Trends

PROBLEM

Most countries in the world reacted to the financial crisis of 2008 with a variety of expansionary fiscal policies (increasing worldwide government deficits) and expansionary monetary policies (increasing the supply of loanable funds). We will not study fiscal and monetary policies and their short-term impacts on the economy until Chapters 29 and 30, but we can examine the impact of these policies on the global market for loanable funds.

a In a graph of the global loanable funds market, show the impact of the theoretical policies on the loanable funds market.

b Canada is a relatively small country in the world market, which in 2008 had net international lending and government deficits both roughly equal to 0. Next, we had the changes in part **a** above (assume the deficit effect in part **a** is *stronger* than the monetary policy effect) changing the world real interest rate. Second, the Canadian government also increased the size of its government deficit. Show the impact of these two changes on a new graph of the Canadian loanable funds market. Explain what happens to net international borrowing, Canadian investment, saving, and the government deficit.

c What will be the impact of the changes from part **b** on the Canadian balance of payments? Assume that the official settlements account

stays with a balance of 0 throughout your analysis.

d What is the impact of the changes in part **b** on the level of domestic investment in Canada? (Assume no Ricardo–Barro effect.) Under neoclassical growth theory, explain what this change would do to long-term economic growth.

MIDTERM EXAMINATION

You should allocate 32 minutes for this examination (16 questions, 2 minutes per question). For each question, choose the one *best* answer.

1 The key difference between neoclassical growth theory and classical growth theory is that
   a capital is not subject to diminishing returns under classical growth theory.
   b capital is subject to diminishing returns under classical growth theory.
   c increases in technology lead to increases in population that drive workers' incomes back down to the subsistence level in classical theory.
   d technological advances are exogenous in classical growth theory.
   e the rule of 70 only holds in the neoclassical growth theory.

2 In the market for loanable funds, if the Ricardo–Barro effect holds, a higher government deficit leads to
   a an increase in interest rates and an increase in investment.
   b an increase in interest rates and a decrease in investment.
   c a decrease in interest rates and an increase in investment.
   d a decrease in interest rates and a decrease in investment.
   e no effect on interest rates or investment.

3 A bank can create money by
   a selling some of its investment securities.
   b increasing its reserves.
   c lending its excess reserves.
   d printing more cheques.
   e converting reserves into securities.

4 If the current account is in deficit, and the capital account is also in deficit, the change in official reserves is
   a negative.
   b positive.
   c probably close to zero, but might be either negative or positive.
   d zero.
   e not affected.

5 Which of the following shifts the supply curve of loanable funds rightward?
   a increase in current disposable income
   b decrease in current disposable income
   c increase in expected future income
   d increase in the real interest rate
   e decrease in the real interest rate

6 Which of the following quotations describes a movement along the labour demand curve?
   a "Recent higher wage rates have led to more leisure being consumed."
   b "The recent lower price level has induced people to work more hours."
   c "The recent higher real wage rate has induced people to work more hours."
   d "The recent high investment in capital equipment has raised hiring by firms."
   e None of the above

7 Consider the following data on the economy of Adanac:

Currency reserves of private banks	$ 5 billion
Currency in circulation	15 billion
Personal + nonpersonal chequing deposits	40 billion
Personal nonchequing deposits	25 billion
Nonpersonal nonchequing deposits	25 billion
Fixed term deposits	125 billion
Canada Savings Bonds	200 billion

In this economy, what is the value (in billions of dollars) of M1? of M2?
   a 105; 230
   b 110; 235
   c 55; 430
   d 55; 230
   e 60; 430

8 Which of the following quotations best describes the interest rate parity effect?
   a "The recent high Canadian interest rate has increased the demand for the Canadian dollar."
   b "The market feeling is that the Canadian dollar is overvalued and will likely appreciate."
   c "The price of bananas is the same in Canada and the United States, adjusting for the exchange rate."
   d "The expected appreciation of the Canadian dollar is currently lowering demand for it."
   e None of the above

9 Which of the following will *not* increase labour productivity?
   a an increase in population
   b more physical capital
   c a better-educated workforce
   d more learning-by-doing
   e more on-the-job training

10 Which of the following would cause the dollar to depreciate against the yen?
   a increase in the Canadian money supply
   b increase in interest rates in Canada
   c decrease in interest rates in Japan
   d increase in the expected future exchange rate
   e increase in the current exchange rate

11 The amount of real money people want to hold will increase if either real income increases or the
  a price level increases.
  b price level decreases.
  c interest rate increases.
  d interest rate decreases.
  e price of bonds decreases.

12 Figure P8.1 shows the loanable funds market for an economy that is part of the global market, with no government budget deficit or surplus. If the world interest rate is 7%, what is net lending or borrowing on the world market, and what is investment?
  a Net lending is $20 billion and investment is $40 billion.
  b Net borrowing is $20 billion and investment is $40 billion.
  c Net borrowing is $0 billion and investment is $50 billion.
  d Net borrowing is $20 billion and investment is $60 billion.
  e Net lending is $20 billion and investment is $60 billion.

FIGURE **P8.1**

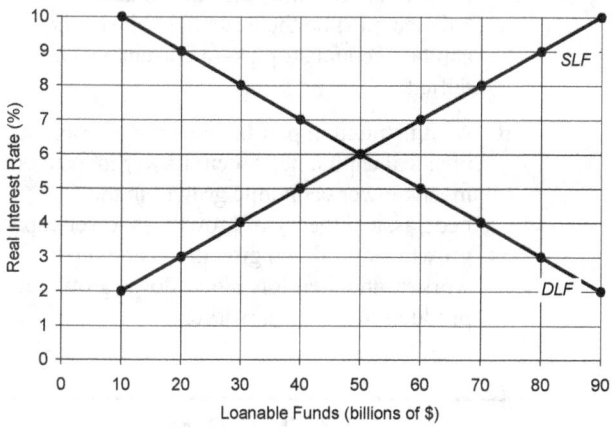

13 The Bank of Canada is following a flexible exchange rate policy. What happens if the demand for Canadian dollars increases?
  a The Bank of Canada will buy Canadian dollars.
  b The Bank of Canada will sell Canadian dollars.
  c The Bank of Canada will buy foreign currency.
  d The Bank of Canada will sell foreign currency.
  e The Bank of Canada will do nothing.

14 Which theory of economic growth concludes that, in the long run, people do not benefit from growth?
  a classical theory
  b neoclassical theory
  c new growth theory
  d old growth theories
  e none of the theories

15 Anglers' Fishing has lent $12 million and borrowed $18 million. It has cash earnings per month of $140,000 and debt payments per month of $120,000. Anglers' Fishing is
  a solvent and liquid.
  b insolvent and illiquid.
  c solvent and illiquid.
  d insolvent and liquid.
  e solvent as long as interest rates are low enough.

16 If households and firms find that their holdings of real money are less than desired, they will
  a sell financial assets, causing interest rates to increase.
  b sell financial assets, causing interest rates to decrease.
  c buy financial assets, causing interest rates to increase.
  d buy financial assets, causing interest rates to decrease.
  e buy goods, causing the price level to increase.

ANSWERS

Problem

  a The deficits mean governments of the world will be borrowing more, increasing the demand for loanable funds, shown as a shift rightward in *DLF* in Fig. P8.2 on the next page. The monetary policies will shift *SLF* rightward. The net effect is an increase in the amount of loanable funds traded, with an unclear effect on the world real interest rate, depending on whether the shift in demand or supply is stronger. In Fig. P8.2, the demand shift is shown as stronger, as assumed in part **b** below, leading to a rise in the world real interest rate.

FIGURE **P8.2**

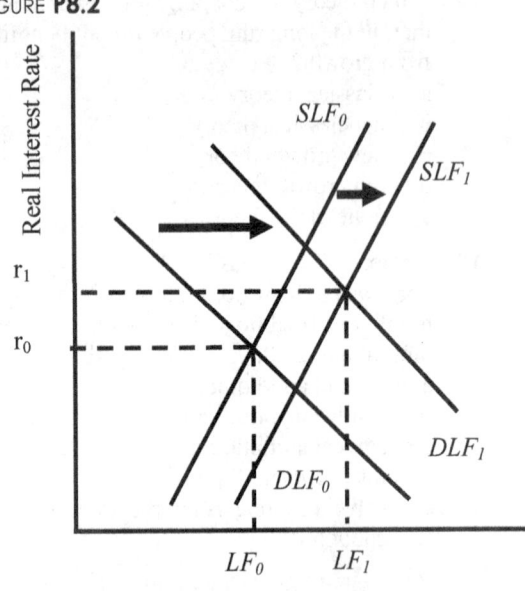

FIGURE **P8.3**

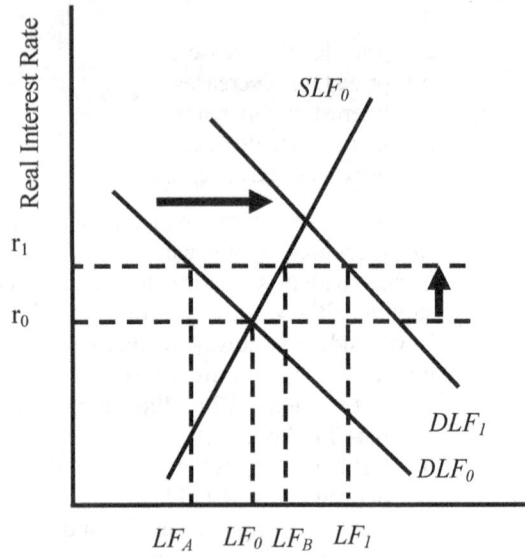

b As a small player in the world market, Canada faces a given world real interest rate. Figure P8.3 shows the Canadian market. At the initial equilibrium with SLF_0, DLF_0, and r_0, Canada has no government deficit or international borrowing/lending, so quantity supplied of loanable funds is equal to quantity demanded at LF_0.

When the world rate rises to r_1, this is as if the effective SLF shifts upward to r_1. In addition, the new Canadian government deficit means a shift rightward in the DLF to DLF_1 in Canada. In the new equilibrium, the total amount of loanable funds traded in Canada is now LF_1. Of this amount, only LF_B is generated from internal savings (the higher interest rate has encouraged some increase in domestic saving), so net international borrowing by Canada is $LF_1 - LF_B$. In addition, the higher interest rate causes a decline in domestic investment to LF_A. Finally, the size of the government deficit is the difference between DLF_1 and DLF_0, the amount $LF_1 - LF_A$.

c If Canada has net international borrowing, there is a net inflow of funds and a capital account surplus. Since the official settlements balance is zero, then the current account balance must be the exact opposite of the capital account surplus—a current account deficit.

d As illustrated in part **b**, domestic investment in physical capital has fallen. Lower investment means lower economic growth in the neoclassical theory of growth, as lower capital growth slows down growth in capital per worker, and therefore slows down growth in productivity of each worker.

MIDTERM EXAMINATION

1 **c** In neoclassical theory, population growth is not driven by economic growth. In both theories, capital is subject to diminishing returns and technology is exogenous. (531–535)

2 **e** If there is a government deficit, households increase saving in anticipation of higher future taxes. (556)

3 **c** Lending reserves is done by crediting borrowers' deposits, creating more deposits = more money. (566–577)

4 a Official settlements balance = –(capital account + current account) > 0, which implies change in official reserves < 0. (607–609)

5 a Households save some of their disposable income. (551–552)

6 e **a, b, c** are *LS* effect; **d** is shift in *LD* curve. (523–528)

7 d M1 = currency in circulation + chequing deposits, M2 = M1 + personal nonchequing deposits + nonpersonal nonchequing deposits + fixed term deposits. (569)

8 a If two currencies do not have the same interest rate, market conditions will change demand for assets and the dollar. (602)

9 a This creates more labour supply and lowers productivity. (528–530)

10 a **a** decreases interest rates, which decrease demand for Canadian dollars. **b–d** are an increase in demand, **e** is a move along the curve, not a shift. (599–603)

11 d Real money demand is not affected by Δ price level, decrease in price of bonds increases interest rate, lowering quantity of real money demanded. (578–579)

12 a At 7%, quantity supplied is $60 billion and quantity demanded (investment) is $40 billion, for net international lending of $20 billion. (557–558)

13 e Under a flexible exchange rate regime, the Bank ignores the exchange rate market. (604)

14 a In the long run, technological advances increase demand for labour and real GDP per capita, but population increases lower real GDP *per capita* back to original level. (531–535)

15 d Net worth = $12 million – $18 million < 0 (insolvent), and cash payments > debt payments (liquid). (547)

16 a They sell bonds for money, extra sales decrease price of bonds and increases interest rates. (581)

Chapter 26
Aggregate Supply and Aggregate Demand

Aggregate Supply

The *AS–AD* model explains how equilibrium real GDP and the price level are determined and fluctuate.

Quantity of *real GDP supplied* depends on quantities of labour, physical and human capital, state of technology.

- ◆ At a given time, only quantity of labour can vary.

- ◆ Labour market can be at full employment, above full employment, or below full employment.

- ◆ Potential GDP is the quantity of real GDP supplied at full employment.

    - • Over the business cycle, employment fluctuates around full employment, as real GDP fluctuates around potential GDP.

Two *AS* concepts: long-run (*LAS*) and short-run (*SAS*).

- ◆ **Long-run aggregate supply (*LAS*)** is relationship between quantity of real GDP supplied (*Y*) and price level when money wage rate changes in step with price (*P*) level to achieve full employment.

    - • *LAS* curve is vertical at potential GDP— increase in *P* leads to equivalent percentage increase in resource prices, which means profits and real wages remain constant—no Δ employment, no Δ quantity supplied *Y*.

    - • *LAS* shifts rightward when potential GDP increases due to increase in full employment quantity of labour, increase in capital stock, and technological advance.

- ◆ **Short-run aggregate supply (*SAS*)** is relationship between quantity of real GDP supplied and price level when the money wage rate, other resource prices, and potential GDP are held constant.

    - • *SAS* curve is upward sloping—increase in *P* leads to an increase in profits and employment and an increase in quantity supplied *Y*.

- ◆ *SAS* shifts along with *LAS*, but also shifts if Δ resource prices.

- ◆ Money wage changes due to expected changes in inflation and departures from full employment creating changes in labour market.

Aggregate Demand

Quantity of real GDP demanded is the total amount of final goods and services produced in Canada that economic agents plan to buy. It depends on price level, expectations, fiscal/monetary policy, and world economy.

- ◆ **Aggregate demand (*AD*)** is total quantity of real GDP demanded ($Y = C + I + G + X - M$) at a given price level (*P*).

- ◆ Increase in *P* decreases quantity of real GDP demanded, represented by movement up along the *AD* curve because of *wealth* and *substitution effects*.

- ◆ Changes in other factors shift the *AD* curve.

    - • If **fiscal policy** cuts taxes (which increases **disposable income**) or increases government expenditure, *AD* increases.

    - • If monetary policy decreases interest rates or increases quantity of money, *AD* increases.

- If exchange rate decreases or foreign income increases, *AD* increases.

- Increase in expectations of future disposable income or future inflation or future profits increases *AD*.

Explaining Macroeconomic Trends and Fluctuations

There are two different types of macroeconomic equilibrium. Long-run equilibrium is the state toward which the economy is heading. Short-run equilibrium is the normal state of the economy, and occurs at each point in time along the path to long-run equilibrium.

♦ **Long-run macroeconomic equilibrium** occurs when real GDP = potential GDP—when *AD* = *SAS* = *LAS*.

♦ **Short-run macroeconomic equilibrium** occurs when real GDP demanded = real GDP supplied (where *AD* = *SAS*), with *P* adjusting to achieve equilibrium.

♦ Economic growth results from *LAS* shifting rightward on average, due to increase in labour, capital, and technology advances.

♦ Persistent inflation occurs when *AD* grows faster than *LAS*—quantity theory of money says money supply growth is the most likely source.

♦ Growth in *Y* is not steady, but goes in cycles because *AD* and *SAS* do not shift at the same pace.

♦ Over the business cycle, short-run equilibrium may occur at

- **full-employment equilibrium**, where real GDP = potential GDP.

- **below full-employment equilibrium**— *AD* = *SAS* left of *LAS*; real GDP < potential GDP by amount of **recessionary gap** (= **output gap**—gap between real GDP and potential GDP).

- **above full-employment equilibrium**— *AD* = *SAS* right of *LAS*; real GDP > potential GDP by amount of **inflationary gap**.

♦ Economy fluctuates in the short run because of fluctuations in *AD* and *SAS*.

♦ If *AD* increases so *Y* > potential, the economy does not stay in above full-employment equilibrium— upward pressures on the money wage rate shifts *SAS* leftward toward long-run equilibrium.

♦ If resource prices increase so *SAS* shifts leftward and *Y* < potential, then **stagflation** results (inflation and falling real GDP).

Macroeconomic Schools of Thought

Economist have different views about business cycles.

♦ **Classical** macroeconomists believe the economy is self-regulating and always at full employment.

- **New classical** economists believe business cycles are efficient responses of the economy to uneven technological change.

♦ **Keynesian** macroeconomists believe the economy is rarely at full employment and needs active monetary and fiscal policy.

- **New Keynesian** economists agree with Keynesians that money wage is sticky *and* other prices are, too.

♦ **Monetarists** believe the economy is self-regulating and normally at full employment, provided monetary policy is not erratic.

HELPFUL HINTS

1 The aggregate demand and aggregate supply model introduced in this chapter (and developed throughout this book) is an insightful method of analyzing complex macroeconomic events. To sort out these complex events, it is helpful if you *always draw a graph*—even a small graph in the margin of a multiple-choice question. Graphs are powerful and effective tools for analyzing economic events.

2 When using graphs, two factors often confuse students:

a Sometimes graphs are based on explicit numerical or algebraic models, where the intercepts, slopes, sizes of shifts, etc., have explicit values. Often these numbers are based on real-world values, but sometimes they are just "made-up" numbers that the instructor has picked to illustrate the point (although they are still economically logical). Do *not* get caught up in the exact values of the numbers. Concentrate on the basic economic results—for example, an increase in *AD* leads to an increase in the price level and real GDP.

b One common student mistake is failing to *distinguish between a shift in a curve versus a movement along a curve*. This distinction is crucial in understanding the factors that influence *AD* and *AS*, and you can be sure that your instructor will test you on it! The slope of the *AD* curve reflects the impact of a change in the price level on aggregate demand. A change in the price level produces a *movement along* the *AD* curve. A change in one of the factors affecting the *AD* curve other than the price level *shifts* the entire *AD* curve. Similarly, a change in the price level produces a *movement along* the *SAS* or the *LAS* curve and does not lead to a shift in the curves.

3 A change in the price level will not shift the *AD* or the *AS* curves. To cement the previous point, consider Fig. 26.1. The initial long-run equilibrium is at the point *a*. (For the moment, ignore the SAS_1 curve.)

FIGURE **26.1**

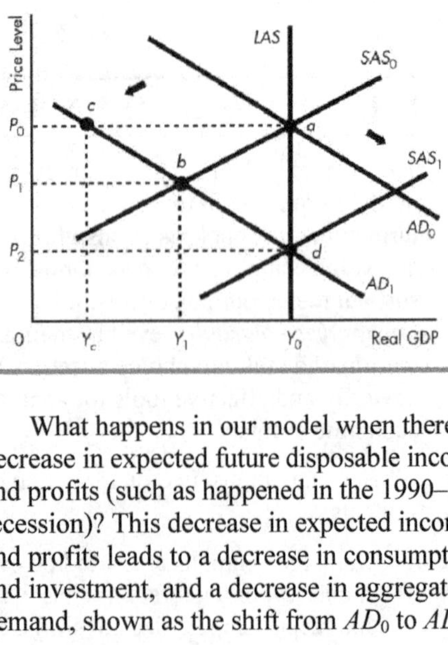

What happens in our model when there is a decrease in expected future disposable income and profits (such as happened in the 1990–1991 recession)? This decrease in expected income and profits leads to a decrease in consumption and investment, and a decrease in aggregate demand, shown as the shift from AD_0 to AD_1.

To understand what happens next, imagine that the AD_0 and SAS_1 curves are peeled off the page (remember, we are ignoring SAS_1 for the moment). This removal leaves us with the curves SAS_0 and AD_1, and with a price level of P_0. At P_0, there is a surplus of goods and services (the quantity of real GDP supplied is Y_0 [at *a*], greater than the quantity of real GDP demanded of Y_c [at *c*]). Firms find their inventories piling up, so they cut prices and decrease production.

This decrease in price eliminates the surplus in two ways. First, as price decreases, firms supply fewer goods and services: a movement down along the *SAS* curve from *a* to *b*. (Be careful—the price change does *not* shift the *SAS* curve.) Second, the decrease in price increases the quantity demanded: a movement down along AD_1 from *c* to *b*. (Note there is no shift in the *AD* curve as price changes.)

The result is the new, below full-employment equilibrium at *b*, with a lower price level (P_1) and a lower level of real GDP (Y_1).

4 In Fig. 26.1, point *b* is a short-run, below full-employment equilibrium, but it is not a long-run equilibrium, since $Y_1 < Y_0$ (potential). There are two possible adjustments back from Y_1 to Y_0. First, the government or central bank could intervene with an expansionary fiscal or monetary policy, raising *AD* back to AD_0—the economy will move back to a full-employment, long-run equilibrium at *a* with $Y = Y_0$ (potential). Second, if the government does nothing, the unemployment at *b* will lead to downward pressures on the money wage rate and other resource prices (although this adjustment can be very slow). As the money wage rates decrease, the *SAS* curve shifts slowly rightward, eventually reaching SAS_1, with a full-employment, long-run equilibrium at *d* with $Y = Y_0$ (potential).

SELF-TEST

True/False and Explain

Aggregate Supply

1 As the price level increases, in the long run the aggregate quantity of goods and services supplied increases.

2 Any factor that shifts the short-run aggregate supply curve rightward also shifts the long-run aggregate supply curve rightward.

3 A technological advance (other things remaining unchanged) shifts the long-run aggregate supply curve rightward, but the short-run aggregate supply curve will not shift.

4 If the wage rate decreases (other things remaining unchanged), both the long-run aggregate supply curve and the short-run aggregate supply curve shift rightward.

Aggregate Demand

5 An increase in the foreign exchange value of the dollar will increase aggregate demand in Canada.

6 An increase in the expected rate of inflation will decrease aggregate demand.

7 An increase in the quantity of money increases the quantity of real GDP demanded.

8 If the price level increases, the quantity of real GDP demanded will decrease.

Explaining Macroeconomic Trends and Fluctuations

9 A shift rightward in the aggregate demand curve increases the price level, which in turn shifts the short-run aggregate supply curve rightward in the short run.

10 If the aggregate demand curve and the short-run aggregate supply curve both shift rightward at the same time, but the aggregate demand curve shifts further rightward, the price level increases.

11 An economy is initially in short-run equilibrium and then expected future profits decrease. The new short-run equilibrium will always be a below full-employment equilibrium.

12 If the economy is in an above full-employment equilibrium, the long-run aggregate supply curve will shift rightward until the economy is at full-employment equilibrium.

13 If real GDP is higher than potential GDP, the money wage rate will rise.

Macroeconomic Schools of Thought

14 If the economy slows down, a Keynesian would argue this is the efficient response of the economy to a technological shock.

15 Under the monetarist view of the business cycle, the main cause of recessions is changes in the money supply.

Multiple-Choice

Aggregate Supply

1 A technological advance will shift
  a both *SAS* and *AD* rightward.
  b both *SAS* and *LAS* leftward.
  c *SAS* rightward but leave *LAS* unchanged.
  d *LAS* rightward but leave *SAS* unchanged.
  e both *SAS* and *LAS* rightward.

2 An increase in the money wage rate will shift
  a both *SAS* and *LAS* rightward.
  b both *SAS* and *LAS* leftward.
  c *SAS* leftward, but leave *LAS* unchanged.
  d *LAS* rightward, but leave *SAS* unchanged.
  e *SAS* rightward, but leave *LAS* unchanged.

3 Long-run aggregate supply will increase for all of the following reasons *except*
  a a fall in the money wage rate.
  b a rise in human capital.
  c the introduction of new technology.
  d more aggregate labour hours.
  e more capital stock.

4 Potential GDP is the level of real GDP at which
  a aggregate demand equals short-run aggregate supply.
  b there is full employment.
  c there is a recessionary gap.
  d there is over full employment.
  e prices are sure to increase.

5 The short-run aggregate supply curve is the relationship between the price level and the quantity of real GDP supplied, holding constant
  a the wage rate only.
  b the quantities of resource inputs.
  c the level of government expenditures.
  d the price level.
  e the prices of resource inputs.

6 Consider Fig. 26.2. Which graph illustrates what happens when resource prices decrease?
  a (a)
  b (b)
  c (c)
  d (d)
  e none of the above

FIGURE **26.2**

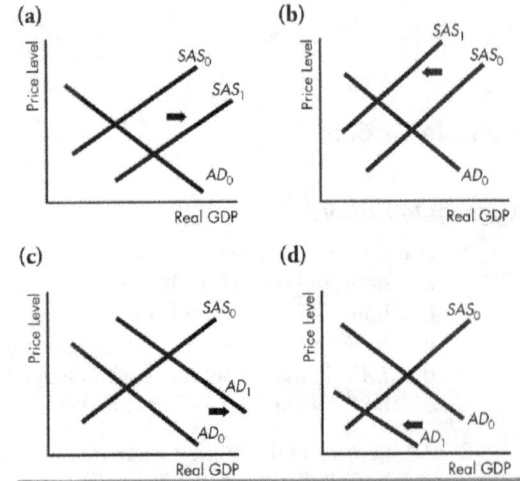

Aggregate Demand

7 Consider Fig. 26.2. Which graph illustrates what happens when government expenditures increase?
  a (a)
  b (b)
  c (c)
  d (d)
  e none of the above

8 Consider Fig. 26.2. Which graph illustrates what happens when the quantity of money decreases?
  a (a)
  b (b)
  c (c)
  d (d)
  e none of the above

9 Consider Fig. 26.2. Which graph illustrates what happens when expected future disposable income increases?
  a (a)
  b (b)
  c (c)
  d (d)
  e none of the above

10 Which of the following is a reason for the downward slope of the aggregate demand curve?
  a the wealth effect
  b the expectations effect
  c the expected inflation effect
  d the nominal balance effect
  e none of the above

11 Which of the following will cause the aggregate demand curve to shift rightward?
  a an increase in interest rates (at a given price level)
  b an increase in expected inflation
  c an increase in taxes
  d a decrease in the price level
  e an increase in the price level

Explaining Macroeconomic Trends and Fluctuations

12 Short-run macroeconomic equilibrium *always* occurs when the
  a economy is at full employment.
  b economy is below full employment.
  c economy is above full employment.
  d quantity of real GDP demanded equals the quantity of real GDP supplied.
  e *AD* curve intersects the *LAS* curve.

13 We observe an increase in the price level and a decrease in real GDP. Which of the following is a possible explanation?
    a   The expectation of future profits has increased.
    b   The expectation of future disposable income has increased.
    c   The price of raw materials has increased.
    d   The stock of capital has increased.
    e   The money supply has increased.

14 Consider the economy represented in Table 26.1. In short-run macroeconomic equilibrium, the price level is _____ and the level of real GDP is _____ billion.
    a   120; $600
    b   120; $500
    c   125; $550
    d   130; $600
    e   130; $500

TABLE **26.1**

Price Level	Aggregate Demand (billions of 2002 $)	Short-Run Aggregate Supply (billions of 2002 $)	Long-Run Aggregate Supply (billions of 2002 $)
100	800	300	600
110	700	400	600
120	600	500	600
130	500	600	600
140	400	700	600

15 Consider the economy represented in Table 26.1. The economy is in a(n)
    a   full-employment equilibrium and resource prices will not change.
    b   above full-employment equilibrium and resource prices will increase.
    c   above full-employment equilibrium and resource prices will decrease.
    d   below full-employment equilibrium and resource prices will decrease.
    e   below full-employment equilibrium and resource prices will increase.

16 Consider the economy represented in Table 26.1. There is
    a   an inflationary gap equal to $100 billion.
    b   an inflationary gap equal to $50 billion.
    c   a recessionary gap equal to $50 billion.
    d   a recessionary gap equal to $100 billion.
    e   no gap; the economy is at full employment.

17 The economy cannot remain at a level of real GDP above long-run aggregate supply (*LAS*) because prices of productive resources will
    a   decrease, shifting *LAS* rightward.
    b   decrease, shifting *SAS* rightward.
    c   increase, shifting *LAS* leftward.
    d   increase, shifting *SAS* leftward.
    e   increase, shifting *SAS* rightward.

18 Consider an economy starting from a position of full employment. When aggregate demand decreases, which of the following changes does *not* occur?
    a   The price level decreases.
    b   The level of real GDP decreases in the short run.
    c   A recessionary gap arises.
    d   Resource prices decrease in the long run, shifting the short-run aggregate supply curve rightward.
    e   The long-run aggregate supply curve shifts leftward to create the new full-employment equilibrium.

19 If resource prices remain constant, an increase in aggregate demand will cause a(n)
    a   increase in the price level and an increase in real GDP.
    b   increase in the price level and a decrease in real GDP.
    c   decrease in the price level and an increase in real GDP.
    d   decrease in the price level and a decrease in real GDP.
    e   increase in the price level but no change in real GDP.

20 If real GDP is greater than potential GDP, the economy is
    a   not in short-run equilibrium.
    b   in a recessionary equilibrium.
    c   in an above full-employment equilibrium.
    d   in a below full-employment equilibrium.
    e   in full-employment equilibrium.

21 Which of the graphs in Fig. 26.3 on the next page illustrates a below full-employment equilibrium?
    a   (a) only
    b   (b) only
    c   (c) only
    d   (d) only
    e   both (c) and (d)

FIGURE **26.3**

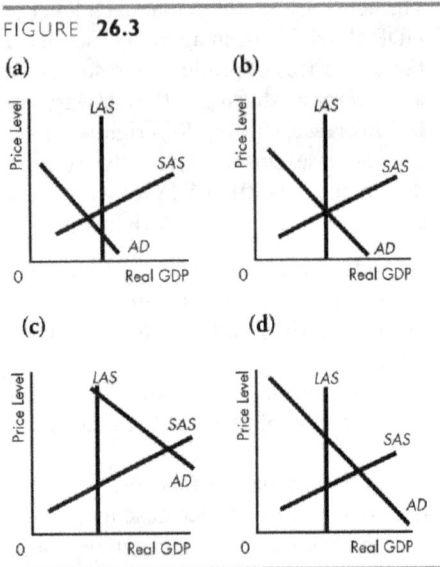

(a)

(b)

(c)

(d)

22 Which of the graphs in Fig. 26.3 illustrates an above full-employment equilibrium?
   a   (a) only
   b   (b) only
   c   (c) only
   d   (d) only
   e   both (c) and (d)

23 Which one of the following newspaper quotations best describes a movement along an *SAS* curve?
   a   "The decrease in consumer spending may lead to a recession."
   b   "The increase in consumer spending is expected to lead to inflation, without any increase in real GDP."
   c   "Recent higher wage settlements are expected to cause higher inflation this year."
   d   "Growth has been unusually high the last few years due to more women entering the workforce."
   e   "The recent tornadoes destroyed many factories in Calgary and Edmonton."

Macroeconomic Schools of Thought

24 Which of the following news quotes *best* describes a *Keynesian* view of a recession?
   a   "Rapid computerization is creating obsolete workers and higher unemployment."
   b   "The unexpectedly tight fiscal policy is raising spending and lowering unemployment."
   c   "The anti-inflationary policy of the Bank of Canada is increasing spending."
   d   "The cuts in government spending have helped lower consumer spending and created unemployment."
   e   "Businesses are very worried about future sales and have lowered their purchases of capital equipment."

25 Which of the following news quotes *best* describes a *new classical* view of a recession?
   a   "Rapid computerization is creating obsolete workers and higher unemployment."
   b   "The unexpectedly tight fiscal policy is raising spending and lowering unemployment."
   c   "The anti-inflationary policy of the Bank of Canada is increasing spending."
   d   "The cuts in government spending have helped lower consumer spending and created unemployment."
   e   "Businesses are very worried about future sales and have lowered their purchases of capital equipment."

Short Answer Problems

1 The substitution effects imply that an increase in the price level will lead to a decrease in the aggregate quantity of goods and services demanded. Explain.

2 Why is the *LAS* curve vertical?

3 Why is the *SAS* curve positively sloped?

4 What are the most important factors in explaining the steady and persistent increases in the price level over time in Canada?

5 Suppose the economy is initially in full-employment equilibrium. Graphically illustrate the short-run effects of an increase in the money wage rate. What happens to the price level and the level of real GDP?

6 Consider an economy that is in above full-employment equilibrium due to an increase in *AD*. Prices of productive resources have not changed. With the help of a graph, discuss how the economy returns to full-employment equilibrium with no government intervention.

7 Table 26.2 shows the aggregate demand and short-run aggregate supply schedule for an economy. Long-run aggregate supply is equal to 1.1 trillion 2002 $.

TABLE **26.2**

Price Level	Aggregate Demand (trillions of 2002 $)	Short-Run Aggregate Supply (trillions of 2002 $)
100	1.3	0.9
105	1.2	1.0
110	1.1	1.1
115	1.0	1.2
120	0.9	1.3

a Graph this economy's *AD*, *SAS*, and *LAS* curves, and show the original macroeconomic equilibrium. What kind of equilibrium is this—below full employment, above full employment, or full employment? If there is an inflationary or recessionary gap, identify how large it is.

b Next, suppose that at every price level, the quantity of real GDP demanded falls by $200 billion. Plot the new aggregate demand curve on your graph, and show the new short-run equilibrium. What kind of equilibrium is this—below full employment, above full employment, or full employment? If there is an inflationary or recessionary gap, identify how large it is.

c Suppose that the government does not take any action and that the cause of the decrease in aggregate demand remains unchanged. What kind of adjustment occurs in the long run? Explain what happens to the price level, real GDP, *AD*, and *AS* during this adjustment, illustrating the changes on your graph.

8 Consider an economy for which economists have estimated that last year's real GDP was $800 billion, equal to potential GDP. The price level was 105. Suppose that this year the economists estimate that potential GDP has increased by

10 percent. However, actual real GDP has decreased by 5 percent, while the price level has also decreased by 5 percent.

Draw an *AD–AS* graph showing last year's equilibrium, as well as last year's aggregate demand, aggregate supply (short run and long run), price level, and real GDP level. Next, given this information, show what has happened to the price level and the level of real GDP this year (show this year's equilibrium), plus what has happened to aggregate demand, short-run aggregate supply, and long-run aggregate supply since last year.

ANSWERS

True/False and Explain

1 **F** In the long run, the money wage rates increase as well, leaving profits, real wages, and production unchanged. (624–625)

2 **F** Changes in resource prices shift only *SAS* and not *LAS*. (626–627)

3 **F** Anything that shifts *LAS* also shifts *SAS*. (626–627)

4 **F** Only the *SAS* shifts in response to a wage change. (626–627)

5 **F** Increase in the value of the dollar makes Canadian exports more expensive and imports cheaper, decreasing demand for Canadian goods. (629–632)

6 **F** If individuals expect an increased inflation rate, they will spend more today to avoid higher future prices. (629–632)

7 **T** Higher quantity of money increases spending. (629–632)

8 **T** Movement along the *AD* curve due to wealth and substitution effects. (628–629)

9 **F** Increase in *P* leads to movement along the *SAS* curve, not a shift in it. (636–637)

10 **T** Try drawing a graph. (636–637)

11 **F** Depends on where initial short-run equilibrium is relative to *LAS*, and on the size of the decrease in *AD* from the decrease in future profits—try drawing graphs. (636–637)

12 **F** *SAS* shifts, not *LAS*. (633–637)

13 **T** Unemployment is below the natural rate, which puts upward pressure on the money wage rate. (636–637)

14 **F** This is a new classical argument. (638–639)

15 **T** Monetarists believe the main source of *AD* shocks is change in money supply. (638–639)

Multiple-Choice

1 **e** Technological advances means the same inputs can produce more output, leading to an increase in quantity supplied in both the short and long run. (624–632)

2 **c** Wage rate is held constant along given *SAS*; if money wage rate increases, production is less at every price level, shifting *SAS* leftward. (626–627)

3 **a** Changes in the money wage rate change *SAS* only, not *LAS*. (626–627)

4 **b** Definition. (624)

5 **e** Short run is defined as a time period where resource prices are constant. (625)

6 **a** When resource prices decrease, firms produce more at every price level, shifting *SAS* rightward. (626–627)

7 **c** Increase in government expenditures increases aggregate spending, shifting *AD* rightward. (628–632)

8 **d** Decrease in quantity of money decreases aggregate spending, shifting *AD* leftward. (628–632)

9 **c** Increase in expected future disposable income increases household consumption, shifting *AD* rightward. (628–632)

10 **a** **b** and **c** shift *AD* curve, **d** doesn't exist. (628–632)

11 **b** Answers **a** and **c** cause a shift leftward; **d** and **e** are movements along the *AD* curve. (628–632)

12 **d** Short-run macroeconomic equilibrium always occurs where *AD = SAS*; equilibrium *may* occur at answers **a**–**c** and **e**, but doesn't *always* occur there. (636–637)

ⓒ⓽ 13 **c** Answers **a**, **b**, and **e** increase *AD*, increasing real GDP, while **d** shifts *LAS* rightward, increasing real GDP. **c** shifts *SAS* leftward, increasing *P* and decreasing real GDP (try drawing a graph). (636–637)

14 **c** Short-run equilibrium where *AD = SAS*, at *P* = 125 and real GDP = 550—halfway between *P* = 120 and *P* = 130. (632–633)

15 **d** Real GDP = $550 billion < potential (full employment) GDP of $600 billion, so unemployed workers eventually offer to work for less. (632–637)

16 **c** Actual real GDP = $550 billion, $50 billion less than potential GDP of $600 billion. (632–633)

17 **d** Above *LAS*, extra demand for resources increases their prices, increasing cost of production, so *SAS* shifts leftward. (632–637)

18 **e** Decrease in *AD* creates recession, decreasing resource prices, shifting *SAS* rightward, pushing economy back to *LAS*. (636–637)

19 **a** Rightward shift in *AD* and movement up along the *SAS* curve (636–637)

20 **a** Below full-employment equilibrium occurs when *AD = SAS* to left of *LAS*. (632–633)

21 **e** Above full-employment equilibrium occurs when *AD = SAS* to right of *LAS*. (632–633)

22 **c** Equilibrium is with *AD = SAS*; if *Y* is > *LAS* then there is an above full-employment equilibrium. (632–633)

ⓒ⓽ 23 **a** Decrease in consumer spending leads to shift leftward in *AD*, movement down *SAS* curve in the short run, decreasing *P*, and decreasing *Y*. (632–637)

24 **e** Expectations (animal spirits) primary cause of recession for Keynesians. (638–639)

25 **a** Fluctuations in technological advances primary cause of recession for new classicals. (638–639)

Short Answer Problems

1 There are two substitution effects. First, if the prices of domestic goods increase and foreign prices remain constant, domestic goods become relatively more expensive, so households will

buy fewer domestic goods and more foreign goods. This decline in spending decreases the quantity of real GDP demanded. Thus, an increase in the price level (prices of domestic goods) decreases the aggregate quantity of (domestic) goods and services demanded.

Second, the increase in the price level increases the rate of interest, which increases saving and decreases spending. This decline in spending also decreases the quantity of real GDP demanded.

2 Long-run aggregate supply is the level of real GDP supplied when the money wage rate changes in step with the price level to achieve full employment. Since this level of real GDP equals potential GDP and is independent of the price level, the long-run aggregate supply curve is vertical. Potential GDP is the level of real GDP when resource prices freely adjust to clear resource markets.

3 The short-run aggregate supply curve is positively sloped because it holds resource prices constant. When the price level increases, firms see the prices of their output (revenues) increasing, but the prices of their input (costs) remain unchanged. With profits increasing, each firm has an incentive to increase output, and so aggregate output increases.

4 The price level increases either from an increase in aggregate demand or from a decrease in aggregate supply. Both of these forces have contributed to periods of an increasing price level. The steady and persistent increases in the price level, however, have been the result of a tendency for aggregate demand to increase faster than aggregate supply, due principally to increases in the growth rate of the quantity of money.

5 In Fig. 26.4, the economy is initially at point a on the SAS_0 curve. An increase in the money wage rate will shift the SAS curve leftward to SAS_1. At the new equilibrium, point b, the price level has increased and the level of real GDP has decreased.

FIGURE **26.4**

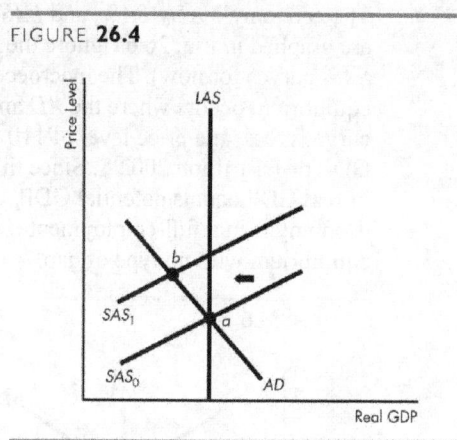

6 In Fig. 26.5, the increase in AD from AD_0 to AD_1 results in above full-employment equilibrium at point b and causes the price level to increase. Since money wage rates have not changed, the real cost of labour to firms decreases, profits rise, and output is stimulated as indicated by the movement along the SAS_0 curve from point a to point b. Furthermore, the purchasing power of workers' money wage rates decreases.

FIGURE **26.5**

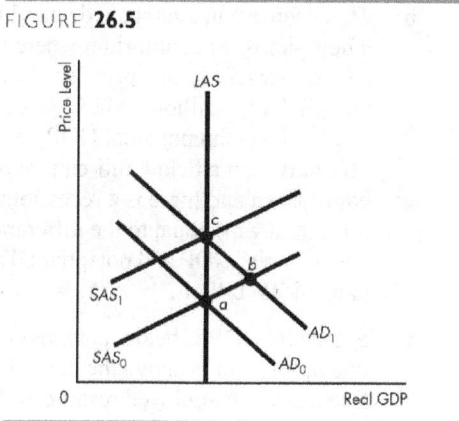

Workers eventually demand higher money wage rates and firms will be willing to pay them. Similarly, other prices of productive resources will increase. This increase in prices of productive resources shifts the SAS curve leftward, resulting in a new equilibrium. There will continue to be pressure for money wage rates and other prices of productive resources to increase until the SAS curve shifts all the way to SAS_1, where the purchasing power of the money wage rates and other prices of productive resources has been restored and the economy is again at full employment, point c.

7 a The economy's AD_0, SAS_0, and LAS curves are graphed in Fig. 26.6 (ignore the AD_1 and SAS_1 curves for now). The macroeconomic equilibrium occurs where the AD and SAS curves cross, at a price level of 110 and real GDP of 1.1 trillion 2002 \$. Since this level of real GDP equals potential GDP, this economy is in a full-employment equilibrium with no type of gap.

FIGURE **26.6**

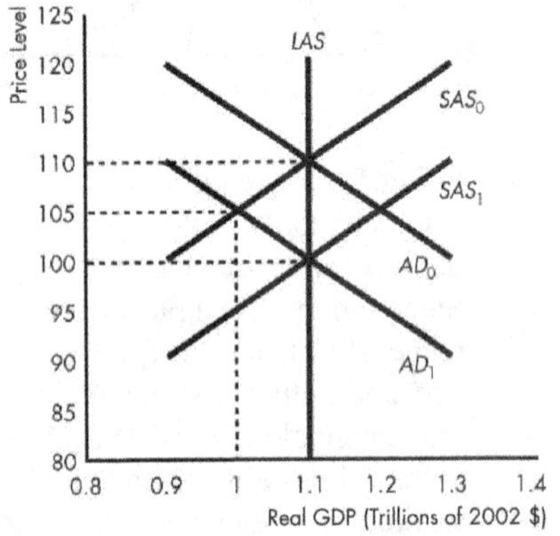

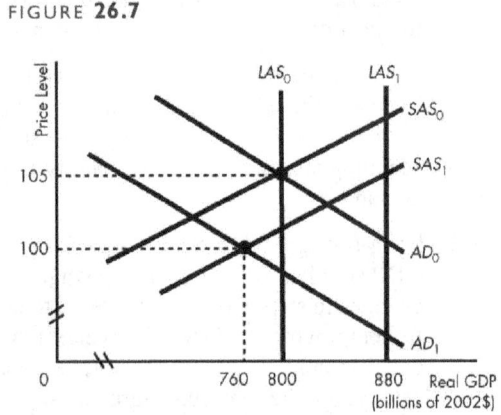

Real GDP (Trillions of 2002 \$)

b This decrease in aggregate demand leads to a new short-run equilibrium where the new AD_1 crosses SAS_0, at a price level of 105 and real GDP of 1 trillion 2002 \$. Since real GDP is less than potential GDP, the economy is in a below full-employment equilibrium and there is a recessionary gap (or output gap) equal to the difference between real GDP and potential GDP. The gap is \$100 billion.

c Since real GDP is below potential GDP, unemployment is above the natural rate. Eventually unemployed resources start offering to work for lower resource prices, shifting the SAS curve rightward to SAS_1, raising aggregate supply, lowering prices even more, and leading to a new long-run equilibrium where SAS_1 crosses AD_1 and LAS where the price level is 100 and real GDP is back at potential GDP (\$1.1 trillion).

8 Figure 26.7 shows the original full-employment equilibrium, at last year's equilibrium price level of 105 and income level of 800.

FIGURE **26.7**

For the current year, the LAS curve has shifted rightward to LAS_1, a value of 880, and the SAS curve shifts with it to SAS_1, all else equal. The new short-run equilibrium must be along the intersection of SAS_1 and an AD curve. Since prices are 5 percent lower at 100, and real GDP is 5 percent lower at 760, the new AD curve must have shifted leftward as shown.

(*Hint:* To decide where AD_1 should be, first find the intersection of $P = 100$ and $Y = 760$ on the new SAS curve, then draw in the AD curve to go through this point.)

Chapter 27
Expenditure Multipliers: The Keynesian Model

Fixed Prices and Expenditure Plans

In the very short term, price level is fixed—aggregate demand determines aggregate quantity sold.

- ◆ To understand AD, we study the aggregate expenditure model.

- ◆ **Aggregate planned expenditure** (AE) = planned consumption (C) + planned investment (I) + planned government expenditures (G) + planned exports (X) – planned imports (M) = real GDP (Y).

- ◆ C, M depend on real GDP (Y), so that increases in Y increase AE, and increases in AE increase Y.

Consumption and saving depend primarily on **disposable income** (YD) = real GDP – taxes + transfer payments.

- ◆ **Consumption function** shows the relationship between disposable income and consumption—increase in YD leads to increase in C.

- ◆ **Saving function** shows the relationship between disposable income and saving—increase in YD leads to increase in S, with $\Delta C + \Delta S = \Delta YD$.

- ◆ **Marginal propensity to consume** (MPC) = fraction of ΔYD that is consumed = $\Delta C/\Delta YD$ = slope of consumption function.

- ◆ **Marginal propensity to save** (MPS) = fraction of ΔYD that is saved = $\Delta S/\Delta YD$ = slope of saving function.

- ◆ $MPC + MPS = 1$.

Influences other than ΔYD *shift* the functions.

- ◆ Increase in *expected future disposable income* or decrease in *real interest rate* or increase in *wealth* shifts S function downward, C function upward.

- ◆ Consumption and saving are a function of real GDP, since increase in real GDP increases YD.

Import function relates imports and real GDP.

- ◆ **Marginal propensity to import** is fraction of ΔY spent on imports = $\Delta M/\Delta Y$.

Real GDP with a Fixed Price Level

Components of aggregate expenditure interact to determine Y, and AE is influenced by Y.

- ◆ AE can be represented by a graph or schedule. Increase in Y leads to increase in AE.

- ◆ Aggregate planned expenditure has two parts:

  - • **Autonomous expenditure** (A) = $I + G + EX$ = part of AE that does *not* vary with income.

  - • **Induced expenditure** (N) = $C – I$ = part of AE that *does* vary with income.

- ◆ Actual aggregate expenditure may not equal planned expenditure if level of real GDP is not consistent with plans.

- ◆ **Equilibrium expenditure** is the level of aggregate expenditure when AE = real GDP.

  - • On a graph, where AE curve crosses 45° line.

  - • If real GDP is above equilibrium value, AE < real GDP. Firms cannot sell all their production, increasing unplanned inventories. Firms lower production, leading to a decrease in real GDP and convergence to equilibrium.

- If real GDP is below equilibrium value, AE > real GDP. Firms sell all production and more, leading to unplanned decrease in inventories. Firms increase production to restore inventories, leading to increase in real GDP and convergence to equilibrium.

The Multiplier

The **multiplier** is the amount by which change in autonomous expenditure is multiplied to determine change in equilibrium expenditure and real GDP.

- ♦ Increase in autonomous expenditure increases real GDP, leading to a further (secondary) increase in aggregate planned expenditure, leading to further increases in real GDP, etc.

- ♦ Secondary, *induced* effects means total Δ real GDP > initial Δ autonomous expenditure.

- ♦ Multiplier = (Δ real GDP)/(Δ autonomous expenditure) = 1/(1 − slope of AE function).

  - Multiplier > 1 because of induced effects.

  - Higher slope of AE function implies larger induced effects and larger multiplier.

  - Multiplier is higher if MPC is higher, or marginal tax rate is lower, or marginal propensity to import is lower.

- ♦ Recessions and depressions begin with expenditure fluctuations magnified by the multiplier effect.

The Multiplier and the Price Level

Aggregate demand curve shows the relationship between real GDP demanded and the price level, other things remaining the same, and can be derived from AE curve.

- ♦ Increase in price level shifts AE curve downward (due to wealth and substitution effects), lowers equilibrium real GDP, and is shown by movement up and to left on AD curve.

- ♦ Δ non-price variables (autonomous expenditures) shift both AE and AD curves.

- ♦ In the short run, an increase in AE leads to a shift rightward in the AD curve, increasing the price level, which lowers AE somewhat, offsetting the increase in Y somewhat, so multiplier is smaller.

- ♦ In the long run, vertical LAS means there is a large enough increase in the price level to cause a decrease in AE that totally offsets the initial increase, so multiplier = 0.

HELPFUL HINTS

1   The 45° line is important for understanding the consumption function and the expenditure function. It is a *reference line* on a graph, showing the points where the two variables on the axes of the graph have the same value.

Consider the graph of consumption and disposable income in Fig. 27.1. Along the 45° line, consumption equals disposable income at all points. For example, at point *a*, $C = YD = $300 billion.

FIGURE **27.1**

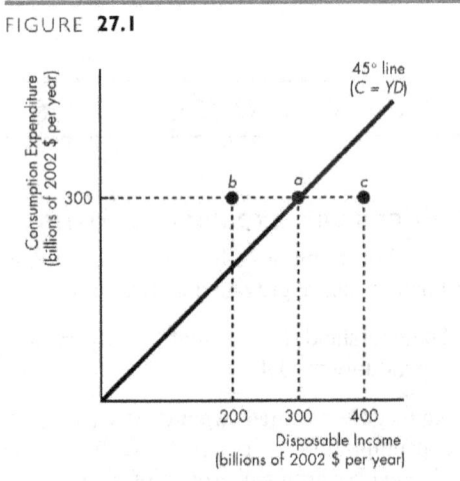

Consider point *b*. Consumption is still equal to $300 billion, but now disposable income is only $200 billion. To the left of the 45° line, variables measured on the vertical axis (here, consumption) are greater than variables measured on the horizontal axis (here, disposable income).

Next, consider point *c*. Consumption is still equal to $300 billion, but now disposable income is $400 billion. To the right of the 45° line, variables measured on the vertical axis are less than variables measured on the horizontal axis.

To summarize, consider the consumption function (*CF*) shown in Fig. 27.2 on the next page. Using the 45° line as our reference, any point on the consumption function to the left of the 45° line has consumption greater than disposable income (and therefore saving [= YD − C] is negative). Any point on the consumption function to the right of the 45° line has consumption less than disposable income (and saving is positive).

FIGURE **27.2**

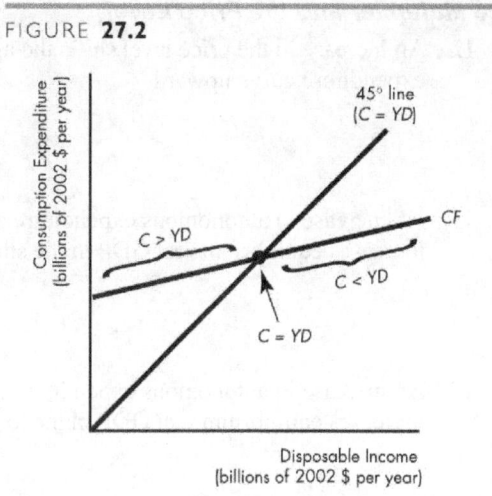

To make sure you understand, draw the graph of the aggregate expenditure function, with a 45° line, and identify the points on your graph where aggregate expenditure is greater than income, equal to income, or less than income. *Note:* For the consumption function, the 45° line is a pure reference line—it is possible in equilibrium for consumption to be greater than, less than, or equal to disposable income. However, for the aggregate expenditure function, the point on the 45° line where $AE = Y$ is more than just a reference point; it shows the point of *equilibrium expenditure*.

2 Aggregate demand is the relationship between the price level and the quantity of goods and services demanded; in other words, it is the relationship between the price level and the level of planned aggregate expenditure. One purpose of this chapter is to help you understand planned aggregate expenditure by separating and examining its individual components. In particular, we examine consumption expenditure, investment, and net exports—the three components of private aggregate expenditure. As you put the discussion of this chapter and the next in perspective, remember that the ultimate objective is a more complete understanding of aggregate demand (and what shifts it), which combines these expenditure components with government expenditure on goods and services. This understanding of the components will help you in later chapters to understand the potential causes of past and future recessions.

Be sure you can distinguish the *AD* curve from the *AE* curve—they are based on different thought experiments. Each *AE* curve holds constant the price level, and represents only a single point on an *AD* curve. The *AD* curve allows the price level to vary. Changing the price level will shift the *AE* curve, but create a movement along the *AD* curve.

3 This chapter distinguishes between *autonomous* expenditure and *induced* expenditure. Autonomous expenditure is independent of changes in real GDP, whereas induced expenditure will vary as real GDP varies. In general, a change in autonomous expenditures creates a change in real GDP, which in turn creates a change in induced expenditure. As the flow graph in Fig. 27.3 illustrates, these changes are at the heart of the multiplier effect.

FIGURE **27.3**

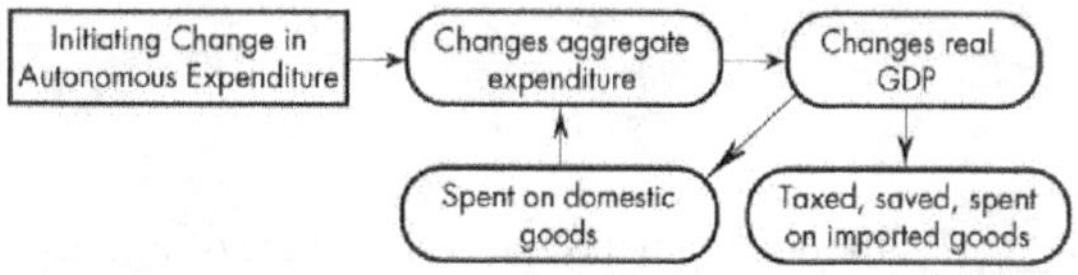

| Initiating Change in Autonomous Expenditure | → | Changes aggregate expenditure | → | Changes real GDP |

| Spent on domestic goods | | Taxed, saved, spent on imported goods |

(Even though autonomous expenditure may be independent of changes in real GDP, it will not be independent of changes in other variables—for example, the price level.)

S E L F - T E S T

True/False and Explain

Fixed Prices and Expenditure Plans

1 The sum of the marginal propensity to consume and the marginal propensity to save equals 1.

2 A change in disposable income will shift the consumption function.

3 An increase in expected future disposable income will shift both the consumption and saving functions upward.

4 Net taxes increase as real GDP increases.

Real GDP with a Fixed Price Level

5 When aggregate planned expenditure exceeds real GDP, inventories will increase more than planned.

6 Equilibrium expenditure occurs when aggregate planned expenditure equals real GDP.

7 Induced expenditure is that part of aggregate expenditure that varies as real GDP varies.

8 The aggregate expenditure schedule lists the level of aggregate planned expenditure that is generated at each level of real GDP.

The Multiplier

9 If the slope of the *AE* function is 0.75, the multiplier is equal to 3.

10 If the marginal tax rate increases, the multiplier will be higher.

11 If the marginal propensity to import decreases, the multiplier will be higher.

The Multiplier and the Price Level

12 An increase in the price level shifts the aggregate expenditure curve upward.

13 An increase in autonomous expenditure always increases equilibrium real GDP in the short run.

14 An increase in autonomous expenditure always increases equilibrium real GDP in the long run.

15 The higher the marginal propensity to consume, the higher the multiplier in the long run.

Multiple-Choice

Fixed Prices and Expenditure Plans

1 The fraction of the last dollar of disposable income saved is the
  a marginal propensity to consume.
  b marginal propensity to save.
  c marginal propensity to dispose.
  d marginal tax rate.
  e saving function.

2 Consider Table 27.1. Autonomous consumption is equal to
  a $0.
  b $65.
  c $100.
  d $260
  e $400.

TABLE **27.1**

Disposable Income (2002 $)	Consumption Expenditure (2002 $)
0	100
100	165
200	230
300	295
400	360

3 Consider Table 27.1. The marginal propensity to consume is
   a 0.35.
   b 0.65.
   c 1.15.
   d 1.65.
   e not calculable with the information given.

4 In Table 27.1, at which of the following level(s) of *YD* is there positive saving?
   a 0
   b 100
   c 200
   d 300
   e all of the above levels

5 Which of the following events would shift the consumption function upward?
   a increase in disposable income
   b decrease in disposable income
   c decrease in the real interest rate
   d decrease in expected future disposable income
   e increase in wealth

Real GDP with a Fixed Price Level

6 The aggregate expenditure curve shows the relationship between aggregate planned expenditure and
   a disposable income.
   b real GDP.
   c the interest rate.
   d consumption expenditure.
   e the price level.

7 If there is an unplanned increase in inventories, aggregate planned expenditure is
   a greater than real GDP and firms will increase output.
   b greater than real GDP and firms will decrease output.
   c less than real GDP and firms will increase output.
   d less than real GDP and firms will decrease output.
   e less than real GDP and firms will decrease investment.

8 If $AE = 50 + 0.6Y$ and $Y = 200$, unplanned inventory
   a increases are 75.
   b increases are 30.
   c decreases are 75.
   d decreases are 30.
   e changes are 0 and equilibrium exists.

9 Autonomous expenditure is *not* influenced by
   a the interest rate.
   b the foreign exchange rate.
   c real GDP.
   d the price level.
   e any variable.

10 In Fig. 27.4, the marginal propensity to consume is
   a 0.3.
   b 0.6.
   c 0.9.
   d 1.0.
   e none of the above.

FIGURE **27.4**

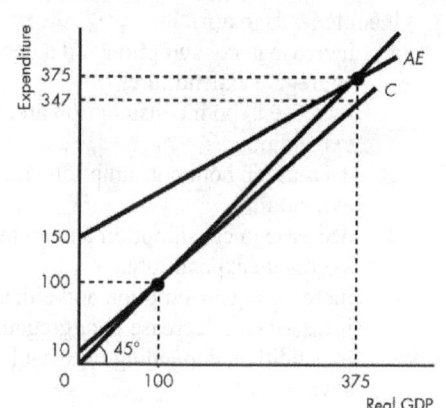

Note: There are no taxes in this economy.

11 In Fig. 27.4, *autonomous* aggregate expenditure is
   a 10.
   b 100.
   c 150.
   d 347.
   e 375.

12 In Fig. 27.4, *equilibrium* expenditure is
   a 10.
   b 100.
   c 150.
   d 347.
   e 375.

13 In Fig. 27.4, at the equilibrium level of real GDP, *induced* expenditure is
   a 28.
   b 150.
   c 225.
   d 347.
   e 375.

14 In Fig. 27.4, the marginal propensity to import is
  a 0.
  b 0.1.
  c 0.25.
  d 0.3.
  e 0.6.

The Multiplier

15 In Fig. 27.4, the multiplier is
  a 0.25.
  b 1.
  c 1.60.
  d 2.50.
  e 10.

16 An increase in expected future disposable income leads to a(n)
  a increase in consumption and a decrease in aggregate expenditure.
  b increase in both consumption and aggregate expenditure.
  c decrease in both consumption and aggregate expenditure.
  d decrease in consumption and an increase in aggregate expenditure.
  e increase in consumption and either an increase or a decrease in aggregate expenditure, depending on what happens to saving.

17 Which of the following quotations illustrates the idea of the multiplier?
  a "The new stadium will generate $200 million in spinoff spending."
  b "Higher expected profits are leading to higher investment spending by business and will lead to higher consumer spending."
  c "The projected cuts in government jobs will hurt the local retail industry."
  d "Taking the grain elevator out of our small town will destroy all the jobs."
  e All of the above

18 The value of the multiplier increases with a(n)
  a increase in the marginal propensity to import.
  b increase in the marginal tax rate.
  c decrease in the marginal propensity to consume.
  d decrease in the marginal propensity to save.
  e increase in the marginal propensity to save.

19 If the slope of the *AE* curve is 0.75, what is the value of the multiplier?
  a 0.25
  b 0.75
  c 1.33
  d 2.50
  e 4.0

The Multiplier and the Price Level

20 An increase in the price level will
  a shift the *AE* curve upward and increase equilibrium expenditure.
  b shift the *AE* curve upward and decrease equilibrium expenditure.
  c shift the *AE* curve downward and increase equilibrium expenditure.
  d shift the *AE* curve downward and decrease equilibrium expenditure.
  e have no impact on the *AE* curve.

21 A decrease in the price level will
  a increase aggregate expenditure and thus produce a movement along the aggregate demand curve.
  b increase aggregate expenditure and thus produce a rightward shift in the aggregate demand curve.
  c increase aggregate expenditure and thus produce a leftward shift in the aggregate demand curve.
  d have no effect on aggregate expenditure.
  e increase aggregate expenditure but produce no effect on the aggregate demand curve.

22 Suppose that investment increases by $10 billion. If the multiplier is 2, the *AD* curve will
  a shift rightward by the horizontal distance of $20 billion.
  b shift rightward by a horizontal distance greater than $20 billion.
  c shift rightward by a horizontal distance less than $20 billion.
  d not be affected.
  e shift upward by a vertical distance equal to $20 billion.

23 Suppose the multiplier is 2 and the short-run aggregate supply curve is positively sloped. If investment increases by $10 billion, equilibrium real GDP will
  a increase by $20 billion.
  b increase by more than $20 billion.
  c decrease by less than $20 billion.
  d be unaffected.
  e increase by less than $20 billion.

24 Suppose the multiplier is 2 and investment increases by $10 billion. Starting at potential GDP, in the long run equilibrium real GDP will
  a increase by $20 billion.
  b increase by more than $20 billion.
  c decrease by less than $20 billion.
  d be unaffected.
  e increase by less than $20 billion.

25 What will happen in the short run to real GDP and prices if exports increase?
  a The AE curve will shift rightward by an amount determined by the size of the multiplier, and the increase in real GDP will be the same size.
  b The AE curve will shift leftward by an amount determined by the size of the multiplier, and the decrease in real GDP will be the same size.
  c The AE curve will shift rightward by an amount determined by the size of the multiplier, and the increase in real GDP will be larger.
  d The AE curve will shift rightward by an amount determined by the size of the multiplier, and the increase in real GDP will be smaller.
  e The AE curve will shift rightward by an amount determined by the size of the multiplier, and the increase in real GDP will be 0.

Short Answer Problems

1 Explain how studying the circular flow in Chapters 20 and 23 helps us to understand the multiplier process of Chapter 27.

2 Suppose aggregate planned expenditure is greater than real GDP. Explain how equilibrium expenditure is achieved.

3 Define and explain autonomous expenditure, induced expenditure, and what role each plays in the multiplier process.

4 Explain (without algebraic expressions) why the multiplier is larger if the marginal propensity to consume is higher.

5 Explain how the effects of price level changes on the AE curve will generate an AD curve.

6 Table 27.2 illustrates the consumption function for a very small economy.

TABLE **27.2**

Disposable Income (2002 $)	Consumption Expenditure (2002 $)	Saving (2002 $)
0	3,000	
3,000	5,250	
6,000	7,500	
9,000	9,750	
12,000	12,000	
15,000	14,250	

  a Compute the economy's saving at each level of disposable income by completing Table 27.2.

  b Compute the economy's MPC and MPS.

  c From the information given and computed, draw the economy's consumption and saving functions.

7 Consider an economy with the following components of aggregate expenditure:
  • Consumption function: $C = 20 + 0.8Y$
  • Investment function: $I = 30$
  • Government expenditures: $G = 8$
  • Export function: $X = 4$
  • Import function: $M = 2 + 0.2Y$

(There are no taxes, so $YD = Y$.)

  a What is the marginal propensity to consume in this economy?

  b What is the equation of the aggregate expenditure function in this economy?

  c Find this economy's equilibrium aggregate expenditure and real GDP by completing the columns of Table 27.3.

TABLE **27.3**

Y	C	I	G	X	M	AE
0						
30						
60						
90						
120						
150						
180						

8 Explain carefully what an increase in expected future disposable income will do to the consumption function, the saving function, the aggregate expenditure curve, and the aggregate demand curve.

ANSWERS

True/False and Explain

1 T Last dollar of YD is either spent or saved. (650)

2 F Change in YD leads to movement along consumption function. (648–651)

3 F Shifts upward consumption function—more consumption expenditure at each level of current YD, but given constant current YD, this increase in consumption means less saving. (650–651)

4 T Due to induced income taxes. (651)

5 F AE > real GDP creates excess sales, leading to falling inventories. (654–655)

6 T Definition. (654–655)

7 T Definition. (653)

8 T Definition. (653)

9 F Multiplier = $1/(1 - $ slope of AE function) = $1/(1 - 0.75) = 1/0.25 = 4$. (658)

ⓒⓣ **10 F** Higher marginal tax rate lowers slope of AE curve and size of multiplier. (658–659)

11 T Lower marginal propensity to import increases slope of AE curve and size of multiplier. (658–661)

12 F Increase in price level lowers AE through wealth and substitution effects. (661–663)

13 T Increase in AE shifts AD curve rightward, movement along SAS in short run with an increase in real GDP. (663–665)

14 F Same initial effect as for **13**, but if start at potential GDP, given vertical LAS curve, there is no increase in real GDP. (663–665)

15 F In long run, multiplier is zero due to vertical LAS curve. (663–665)

Multiple-Choice

1 b Definition. (650)

2 c Level of consumption when disposable income is zero. (648)

3 b $MPC = \Delta C/\Delta YD = (165 - 100)/(100 - 0) = 0.65$. (650)

4 d $YD > C$. Also true at $YD = 400$. (648–651)

5 e **a** and **b** are movements along curve, **c** and **d** shift it downward. (650–651)

6 b Definition. (653)

ⓒⓣ **7 d** Increase in inventories means $AE <$ real GDP. Firms' sales decrease, so they decrease production in response. (654–655)

ⓒⓣ **8 b** $Y = 200$ implies $AE = 50 + 0.6(200) = 170$. Unplanned inventories = $Y - AE = +30$. (654–655)

9 c Definition. (653)

10 c MPC = slope of consumption function = $\Delta C/\Delta Y = 90/100 = 0.9$. (650)

11 c Intercept of AE function. (653)

12 e Where AE curve crosses 45° line. (654–655)

13 c Induced = aggregate – autonomous = 375 – 150 = 225. (654–655)

ⓒⓣ **14 d** Marginal propensity to import = MPC – slope of AE curve = $0.9 - 0.6 = 0.3$, where slope of AE curve = $\Delta AE/\Delta Y = 225/375 = 0.6$. (653–655)

15 d Multiplier = $1/(1 - $ slope of AE function) = $1/(1 - 0.6) = 1/0.4 = 2.5$. (658)

16 b Increase in expected future disposable income leads to more consumption spending, less saving, and an increase in autonomous expenditure. (650–657)

17 e All of the choices discuss secondary, induced effects. (656–657)

ⓒⓣ **18 d** This change raises the MPC and multiplier. Others lower the multiplier. (657–659)

19 e Multiplier = $1/(1 - $ slope of AE function) = $1/(1 - 0.75) = 1/0.25 = 4.0$. (658)

20 d Increase in price level decreases aggregate expenditure due to wealth and substitution effects. New equilibrium at lower real GDP = equilibrium expenditure. (661–663)

21 a Decrease in price level increases aggregate expenditure due to three effects, leading to movement along the AD curve. (661–663)

22 a Multiplier effect raises AE and Y by 2 times original Δ autonomous expenditure, which leads to a shift rightward by the same amount in the AD curve. (661–663)

23 e Multiplier effect of Question **22** is reduced by the increase in price level due to positively sloped *SAS* curve. (661–663)

24 d Vertical *LAS* curve means that there is no increase in real GDP after shift rightward in *AD*. (661–663)

25 d More autonomous expenditure, *AD* shifts rightward, but positive slope to *SAS* means price level increases and reduces the size of the increase in real GDP. (662–663)

Short Answer Problems

1 The circular flow shows us that firms produce goods and services, sell them to consumers, investors, governments, and the rest of the world, and use the money earned to pay factors of production, who in turn buy goods and services. The circular flow thus shows us the secondary, induced effects of the multiplier process in action. An initial increase in autonomous expenditure increases sales for firms, increasing household income, increasing consumption expenditure, etc.

2 If aggregate planned expenditure is greater than real GDP, inventories decrease more than planned, and firms increase output to replenish those depleted inventories. As a result, real GDP increases. This continues as long as real GDP is less than aggregate planned expenditure. It will stop only when equilibrium is attained—when real GDP equals aggregate planned expenditure.

3 Autonomous expenditure is the part of aggregate expenditure that does not vary with real GDP, but varies as a result of changes in other variables such as the real interest rate. Induced expenditure is the part of aggregate expenditure that varies with real GDP. The multiplier process starts out with a change in autonomous expenditure that changes aggregate expenditure, which in turn changes real GDP. This change in real GDP creates secondary effects by changing induced expenditure in the same direction, which in turn changes aggregate expenditure and real GDP, leading to a total effect that is a multiple of the initial change in autonomous expenditure.

4 Any initial stimulus to autonomous expenditure generates a direct increase in real GDP. The basic idea of the multiplier is that this initial increase in real GDP generates further increases in real GDP as increases in consumption expenditure are induced. At each round of the

multiplier process, the increase in spending, and thus the further increase in real GDP, are partially determined by the marginal propensity to consume. A larger marginal propensity to consume means a larger increase in real GDP at each round, so the total increase in real GDP will be greater. Thus the multiplier will be larger if the marginal propensity to consume is larger.

5 The aggregate demand curve illustrates the relationship between the price level and aggregate expenditures. The aggregate expenditure diagram shows the level of equilibrium expenditure holding the price level constant. If the price level changes, the *AE* curve shifts resulting in a new level of equilibrium expenditure. Thus, for each price level, there is a different level of equilibrium expenditure. These combinations of price level and corresponding aggregate expenditure are points on the aggregate demand curve. For example, if the price level increases, autonomous expenditure will decline and the *AE* curve shifts downward. This shift decreases equilibrium expenditure. Since an increase in the price level is associated with a reduction in equilibrium expenditure, the *AD* curve is negatively sloped.

6 a The answers to **a** are shown in Table 27.2 Solution, where saving = $YD - C$.

TABLE **27.2** SOLUTION

Disposable Income (2002 $)	Consumption Expenditure (2002 $)	Saving (2002 $)
0	3,000	–3,000
3,000	5,250	–2,250
6,000	7,500	–1,500
9,000	9,750	–750
12,000	12,000	0
15,000	14,250	+750

b The $MPC = (\Delta \text{ consumption})/(\Delta \text{ disposable income})$. Using the first two entries in the table, we can see that change in consumption is 2,250, and the change in disposable income is 3,000, so that the $MPC = 0.75 = 2,250/3,000$.

The $MPS = (\Delta \text{ saving})/(\Delta \text{ disposable income})$. Using the first two entries in the table, we can see that Δ saving is +750, and Δ disposable income is 3,000, so that the $MPS = 0.25 = 750/3,000$. Using any other two adjacent entries in the table will yield the same result.

c The consumption function is shown in Fig. 27.5, and the saving function is illustrated in Fig. 27.6.

FIGURE **27.5**

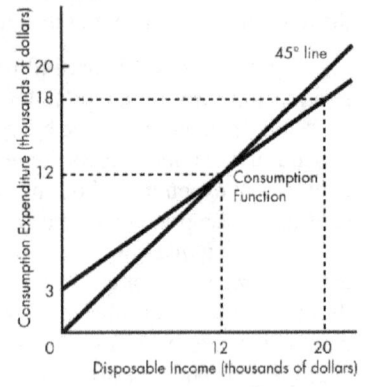

FIGURE **27.6**

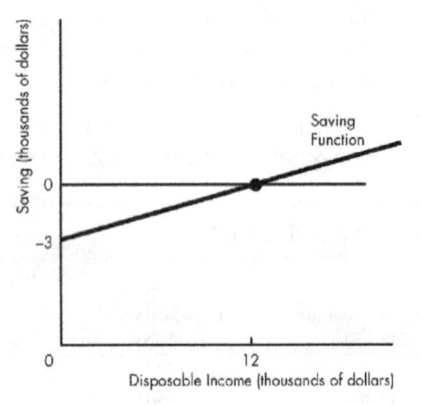

7 a From the consumption function equation we know this value is $0.8 = \Delta C/\Delta Y$.

b Substitute the various equations into:

$$AE = C + I + G + X - M,$$

$$AE = 20 + 0.8Y + 30 + 8 + 4 - 2 - 0.2Y,$$

$$AE = 60 + 0.6Y.$$

c The answer is presented in Table 27.3 Solution below. The table is constructed by substituting the various values of Y into the equations. Note that equilibrium occurs when $AE = Y$ at a value of 150.

TABLE **27.3** SOLUTION

Y	C	I	G	X	M	AE
0	20	30	8	4	2	60
30	44	30	8	4	8	78
60	68	30	8	4	14	96
90	92	30	8	4	20	114
120	116	30	8	4	26	132
150	140	30	8	4	32	150
180	164	30	8	4	38	168

8 An increase in expected future disposable income leads to less saving (so that the saving function shifts downward at each level of disposable income) and more consumption out of current disposable income (so that the consumption function shifts upward). This is an increase in autonomous consumption, and also an increase in aggregate expenditure, leading to a shift upward in the aggregate expenditure function. This shift creates multiplier effects and a shift rightward in the aggregate demand curve at the current price level.

Chapter 28

Canadian Inflation, Unemployment, and Business Cycle

Inflation Cycles

Inflation is caused by two sources in the short run.

Demand-pull inflation arises from increasing aggregate demand due to tax cuts or increases in quantity of money, government expenditures, exports, or investment.

- ♦ Short-run result is increased P (inflation), increased Y, and decreased unemployment to below natural rate.

- ♦ Unemployment less than the natural rate creates a labour shortage, increasing wages and costs. *SAS* shifts leftward, price level increases even more, but real GDP falls back to original level.

- ♦ If *AD* shifts rightward again, and wages increase again, a *demand-pull inflation spiral* may result.

- ♦ Persistent inflation requires persistent increases in the quantity of money.

Cost-push inflation arises from increases in costs (increases in money wage rates and money prices of raw materials).

- ♦ *SAS* shifts leftward, firms decrease production, creating **stagflation** (increased price level, decreased real GDP).

- ♦ If the government or the Bank of Canada shifts *AD* rightward in response, price level increases again, so that input owners raise input prices again, and a *cost-push inflation spiral* may result.

- ♦ If there is no government or Bank response—economy remains with high unemployment in the short run.

If inflation is expected, then money wages adjust to keep up with anticipated inflation, Δ price level only, no Δ real GDP or employment.

- ♦ Expected inflation creates actual inflation.

- ♦ To anticipate inflation, people must forecast it.

- ♦ People forecast inflation in different ways, including hiring specialists.

- ♦ Best possible forecast on basis of all available relevant information is a **rational expectation**.

Inflation and Unemployment: The Phillips Curve

The **Phillips curve** shows the relationship between inflation and unemployment.

- ♦ **Short-run Phillips curve** (*SRPC*) shows the relationship between inflation and unemployment for a given expected inflation rate and natural rate of unemployment. It is negatively sloped.

- ♦ In the short run, if actual inflation > expected, then movement up and leftward along *SRPC*.

- ♦ **Long-run Phillips curve** (*LRPC*) shows the relationship between inflation and unemployment when actual inflation = expected. It is vertical at the natural rate of unemployment.

- ♦ Decrease in expected inflation rate shifts *SRPC* downward.

- ♦ Increase in natural rate of unemployment shifts both *LRPC* and *SRPC* rightward.

The Business Cycle

Two approaches to understanding the business cycle.

Mainstream theory states potential GDP grows steadily, but aggregate demand grows at fluctuating rate and causes cycles.

♦ If money wage rate is sticky and if aggregate demand grows faster than potential GDP, inflationary gap results.

♦ If aggregate demand grows slower than potential GDP, recessionary gap results.

Four mainstream theories with different sources of aggregate demand shocks and money wage stickiness:

♦ **Keynesian cycle theory**—fluctuations in business confidence create fluctuations in investment and aggregate demand; money wage assumed sticky.

♦ **Monetarist cycle theory**—fluctuations in investment and consumption driven by fluctuations in money growth create fluctuations in aggregate demand; money wage assumed sticky.

♦ **New classical cycle theory**—unexpected fluctuations in aggregate demand come from incorrect expectations; money wage sticky due to incorrect expectations.

♦ **New Keynesian cycle theory**—unexpected fluctuations in aggregate demand come from incorrect expectations due to the fact that money wages were negotiated over several past dates.

Real business cycle (RBC) theory regards random fluctuations in productivity (due to Δ pace of technological change) as main source of the cycle.

♦ RBC recession starts with technological change that makes existing capital obsolete—temporary decrease in productivity.

♦ Fall in productivity decreases demand for labour and capital (which decreases real rate of interest).

♦ Decreasing real rate of interest decreases labour supply (intertemporal substitution effect), leading to a small decrease in the real wage rate and a large decrease in employment—recession begins.

Critics of RBC theory argue that instead money wages are sticky, intertemporal substitution is weak, and technological shocks are *caused by AD* fluctuations.

♦ Defenders of RBC theory reply that it is consistent with facts (explains both growth *and* cycles) and microeconomic theory.

HELPFUL HINTS

1 An important concept introduced in this chapter is that of a *rational expectation*—the best possible forecast on the basis of all available relevant information. Text Fig. 28.5 applies this concept to forecasting the price level. The *actual* price level occurs in the short run at the intersection of the *AD* curve and the *SAS* curve, and in the long run at the intersection of the *AD* curve and the *LAS* curve. In Fig. 28.5, when *AD* is expected to increase to AD_1, the best (most likely to be correct) *forecast* of the new price level is at the intersection of AD_1 and *LAS*, yielding a wage demand leading to SAS_1.

Note that the rational expectation of the price level will be at the intersection of the *expected* aggregate demand curve and the *expected short-run* aggregate supply curve in the short run, and the *expected long-run* aggregate supply curve in the long run. The *actual* equilibrium, which determines the *actual* price level, is at the intersection of the *actual* aggregate demand curve and the *actual short-run* aggregate supply curve.

2 This chapter contains competing theories for explaining real-world events. There is no dispute over the facts such as the level of prices or real GDP. The dispute centres on what changes in the economy created the facts, and what government policies might affect the economy.

To help you remember and understand these theories, use Table 28.1 on the next page. It highlights the similarities and differences between the theories, and how radically different real business cycle theory is.

Theories differ based on two primary factors: the source of the cycle (*AD* versus *AS*) and the responsiveness of the labour market (sticky versus flexible wages). Be sure you can catalogue and understand these theories.

Remember, these are theories, *not* statements of facts, and their explanations could be incorrect. Only proper empirical investigation over time will cast light on their validity.

TABLE **28.1** BUSINESS CYCLE THEORIES

Labour Market Structure	Theory	Primary Source of the Cycle
Wages are sticky, U above natural rate	Keynesian	Investment (*AD* shocks)
	Monetarist	Investment, consumption, growth rate of money (*AD* shocks)
	New classical	Unexpected fluctuations in *AD*
	New Keynesian	Unexpected *and* expected fluctuations in *AD*
Wages are flexible, U = natural rate always	Real business cycle	Productivity (*AS*) shocks

S E L F - T E S T

True/False and Explain

Inflation Cycles

1 If people expect aggregate demand to increase but it does not, the price level will increase and real GDP will decrease.

2 Increases in government expenditures alone can create persistent inflation.

3 An increase in exports cannot create demand-pull inflation.

4 Inflation resulting from expansionary monetary policy is an example of cost-push inflation.

5 Stagflation occurs when real GDP decreases and the price level increases.

6 If an increase in aggregate demand is correctly anticipated, inflation will not occur.

7 A rational expectation is a forecast that is always correct.

Inflation and Unemployment: The Phillips Curve

8 The short-run Phillips curve shows that if there is an increase in the inflation rate, unemployment will decrease.

9 The long-run Phillips curve shows a tradeoff between inflation and unemployment.

10 If there is an increase in the expected rate of inflation, the long-run Phillips curve shifts rightward.

11 If there is a decrease in the natural rate of unemployment, only the long-run Phillips curve shifts.

The Business Cycle

12 Unanticipated decreases in aggregate demand cause recessions only in new Keynesian theory, not in new classical theory.

13 A decrease in aggregate demand will cause a recession in Keynesian theory.

14 Real business cycle theorists believe that wages are flexible and adjust quickly.

15 In real business cycle theory, most fluctuations in real GDP are the best possible responses of the economy to the uneven pace of technological change.

Multiple-Choice

Inflation Cycles

1 Which one of the following is a cause of demand-pull inflation?
  a a sharp increase in the price of oil
  b higher wages negotiated by unions
  c an increase in exports
  d a decrease in the money supply
  e a decrease in exports

2 Demand-pull inflation occurs when
  a aggregate demand increases.
  b aggregate supply decreases.
  c input costs increase.
  d people incorrectly forecast inflation.
  e unemployment is above the natural rate.

3 Which of the following would cause the aggregate demand curve to keep shifting rightward year after year?
  a a one-time tax cut
  b a one-time increase in government expenditures on goods and services
  c inflation
  d continuous excess wage demands
  e a positive rate of money growth

4 An increase in the price level due to an increase in the price of oil
  a will create stagflation in the short run and *will* trigger a cost-push inflation spiral.
  b will create stagflation in the short run and *may* trigger a cost-push inflation spiral.
  c will raise output above potential GDP.
  d must lead to an increase in the wage rate.
  e must lead to a decrease in the wage rate.

5 Figure 28.1 illustrates an economy initially in equilibrium at point *a*. What would cause the short-run aggregate supply curve to shift from SAS_0 to SAS_1?
  a increase in the price of oil
  b increase in the price level
  c increase in the marginal product of labour
  d increase in the demand for money
  e decrease in wages

FIGURE **28.1**

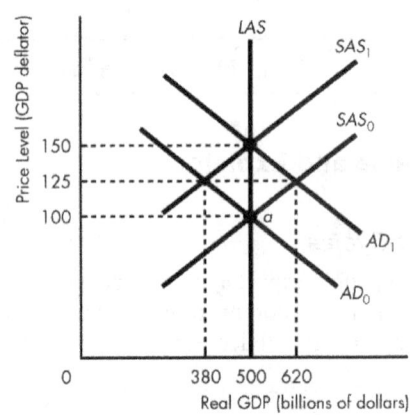

6 If the AD curve in Fig. 28.1 is correctly expected to shift from AD_0 to AD_1, what will be the new equilibrium real GDP (Y) and price level (P)?
  a $Y = \$380$ billion, $P = 125$
  b $Y = \$500$ billion, $P = 150$
  c $Y = \$500$ billion, $P = 100$
  d $Y = \$620$ billion, $P = 125$
  e $Y = \$500$ billion, $P = 125$

7 If the AD curve in Fig. 28.1 is expected to shift from AD_0 to AD_1 but, in fact, remains at AD_0, what will be the new equilibrium real GDP (Y) and price level (P)?
  a $Y = \$380$ billion, $P = 100$
  b $Y = \$500$ billion, $P = 150$
  c $Y = \$500$ billion, $P = 100$
  d $Y = \$620$ billion, $P = 125$
  e $Y = \$380$ billion, $P = 125$

8 If the *AD* curve in Fig. 28.1 is expected to remain at AD_0 but, in fact, shifts to AD_1, what will be the new equilibrium real GDP (*Y*) and price level (*P*)?

  a   *Y* = $380 billion, *P* = 125
  b   *Y* = $500 billion, *P* = 150
  c   *Y* = $500 billion, *P* = 100
  d   *Y* = $620 billion, *P* = 125
  e   *Y* = $500 billion, *P* = 125

9 Which of the following is *not* true of a rational expectation forecast?
  a   It uses all available information.
  b   It can be wrong.
  c   It is always correct.
  d   It is the best possible forecast.
  e   Sometimes economic agents purchase their forecasts from specialists.

10 Stagflation results directly from a shift of the aggregate
  a   demand curve leftward.
  b   demand curve rightward.
  c   supply curve leftward.
  d   supply curve rightward.
  e   demand curve rightward, followed by a shift leftward in the aggregate supply curve.

Inflation and Unemployment: The Phillips Curve

11 The short-run Phillips curve shows the relationship between
  a   the price level and real GDP in the short run.
  b   the price level and unemployment in the short run.
  c   unemployment and real GDP in the short run.
  d   inflation and unemployment, when inflation expectations can change.
  e   inflation and unemployment, when inflation expectations do not change.

12 Figure 28.2 illustrates an economy's Phillips curves. What is the natural rate of unemployment?
  a   9%
  b   6%
  c   4%
  d   depends on the actual inflation rate
  e   cannot be determined without more information

FIGURE **28.2**

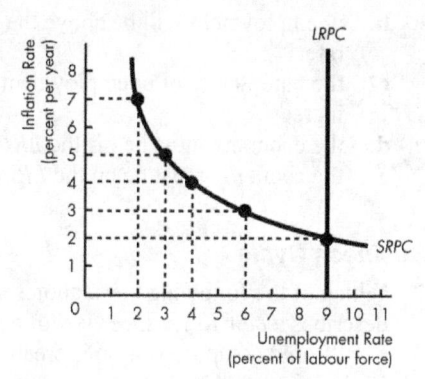

13 Figure 28.2 illustrates an economy's Phillips curves. What is the expected inflation rate?
  a   9%
  b   4%
  c   2%
  d   depends on the actual inflation rate
  e   cannot be determined without more information

14 Figure 28.2 illustrates an economy's Phillips curves. If the current inflation rate is 4 percent, what is the current unemployment rate?
  a   9%
  b   6%
  c   4%
  d   3%
  e   cannot be determined without more information

15 If the inflation rate is lower than the expected inflation rate,
  a   unemployment will be above the natural rate.
  b   the natural rate of unemployment will increase.
  c   the expected inflation rate will increase.
  d   unemployment will be below the natural rate.
  e   the economy must off the *SRPC*.

16 If there is a fully anticipated increase in the inflation rate,
  a unemployment will be below the natural rate.
  b unemployment will be above the natural rate.
  c the natural rate of unemployment will increase.
  d the economy must be off the *LRPC*.
  e the economy must be on the *LRPC*.

The Business Cycle

17 Which of the following news quotes *best* describes a *new Keynesian* view of a recession?
  a "Rapid computerization is creating obsolete workers and higher unemployment."
  b "The unexpectedly tight fiscal policy is raising spending and lowering unemployment."
  c "The promised anti-inflationary policy of the Bank of Canada is increasing spending."
  d "The promised cuts in government spending have helped lower consumer spending and created unemployment."
  e "Businesses are very worried about future sales and have lowered their purchases of capital equipment."

18 Which of the following news quotes *best* describes a *new classical* view of a recession?
  a "Rapid computerization is creating obsolete workers and higher unemployment."
  b "The unexpectedly tight fiscal policy is lowering spending and creating unemployment."
  c "The promised anti-inflationary policy of the Bank of Canada is lowering spending as promised."
  d "The promised cuts in government spending have helped lower consumer spending and created unemployment."
  e "Businesses are very worried about future sales and have lowered their purchases of capital equipment."

19 What is the key impulse in the Keynesian theory of the business cycle?
  a changes in expected future sales and profits
  b changes in the quantity of money
  c unanticipated changes in aggregate demand
  d anticipated changes in aggregate demand
  e changes in the pace of technological change

20 An increase in aggregate demand causes real GDP to increase by the least amount in the
  a Keynesian theory.
  b monetarist theory.
  c new Keynesian theory.
  d new classical theory.
  e real business cycle theory.

21 If the intertemporal substitution effect is weak, then RBC theory will have problems explaining
  a a large decrease in employment in a recession.
  b how a recession begins.
  c why aggregate demand decreases in a recession.
  d the automatic adjustment to full employment.
  e what creates technological change.

22 The intertemporal substitution effect states that
  a in a recession, investment is low and the capital stock increases slowly, leading to a rising marginal product of capital.
  b money wages are based on a rational expectation of the price level.
  c a decrease in productivity leads to a decrease in the demand for capital, and a decrease in the real interest rate.
  d when current real wages and real interest rates are high, people decrease their labour supply strongly.
  e when current real wages and real interest rates are high, people increase their labour supply strongly.

23 According to the real business cycle theorists, increased unemployment rate during a recession is due to an increase in the
  a deviation of the unemployment rate from the natural rate, resulting from a real wage rate that is too high to clear the labour market.
  b deviation of the unemployment rate from the natural rate, resulting from increased job market turnover.
  c natural rate of unemployment resulting from a real wage that is too high to clear the labour market.
  d natural rate of unemployment resulting from increased job market turnover.
  e rate of new entries into the labour market.

24 Which of the following news quotes *best* describes a *real business cycle* view of a recession?
- **a** "Rapid computerization is creating obsolete workers and higher unemployment."
- **b** "The unexpectedly tight fiscal policy is lowering spending and creating unemployment."
- **c** "The promised anti-inflationary policy of the Bank of Canada is lowering spending as promised."
- **d** "The promised cuts in government spending have helped lower consumer spending and created unemployment."
- **e** "Businesses are very worried about future sales and have lowered their purchases of capital equipment."

25 According to real business cycle theory, if the Bank of Canada increases the money supply when real GDP declines, real GDP
- **a** will increase, but only temporarily.
- **b** will increase permanently.
- **c** and the price level will both be unaffected.
- **d** will be unaffected, but the price level will increase.
- **e** will decrease due to the inefficiencies introduced into production as a result.

Short Answer Problems

1 What happens to the price level and real GDP if the government increases expenditures on goods and services and that increase is not anticipated (the price level is not expected to change)?

2 Explain how the events in Short Answer Problem **1** might lead to a demand-pull inflation spiral.

3 List the four important features of the Canadian economy that make severe depression less likely today.

4 Explain the differences between the short-run Phillips curve and the long-run Phillips curve.

5 Sometimes politicians or other commentators say: "Unemployment is a more serious economic and social problem than inflation. Increasing inflation by a small amount in order to lower unemployment is therefore worthwhile." Briefly evaluate this statement.

6 Why does inflation start? Why does it persist?

7 Table 28.2 gives data for a hypothetical economy in years 1 and 2.

TABLE **28.2**

	Year 1	Year 2
Real GDP (billions of dollars)	800	750
Price level (GDP deflator)	100	105

- **a** If the real business cycle theory is true, what happened to aggregate demand and aggregate supply in this economy?
- **b** If the new Keynesian theory is true, what happened to aggregate demand and aggregate supply in this economy?

8 Consider the labour market in the economy from Short Answer Problem 7.
- **a** If the real business cycle theory is true, what happened in the labour market? Is the overall unemployment natural or not?
- **b** If the new Keynesian theory is true, what happened in the labour market? Is the overall unemployment natural or not?

ANSWERS

True/False and Explain

1 T If expected increase in aggregate demand, it increases wage demands, leading to leftward shift in *SAS* curve, but no ΔAD curve, resulting in stagflation. (682)

2 F Persistent inflation requires persistent increases in quantity of money. (678–679)

3 F Increase in exports shift *AD* rightward, which can create demand-pull inflation. (678–679)

4 F Cost-push inflation is due to an increase in input costs. (678–679)

5 T Definition. (680–681)

6 F *AD* shifts rightward, *SAS* shifts leftward due to higher wage demands, so price level increases. (682)

7 F Correct on *average*. (683)

8 T Movement up and leftward along the *SRPC*. (684–686)

9 F Vertical at the natural rate of unemployment. (684–686)

10 F Movement upward along the *LRPC*. (684–686)

11 F Both SRPC and LRPC shift when the natural rate shifts. (684–686)

12 F In both theories, unanticipated decrease means wages are set too high, creating unemployment and recession. (687)

13 T Due to sticky money wages, SAS curve does not adjust quickly. (687)

14 T See text discussion. (688–691)

15 T See text discussion. (688–691)

Multiple-Choice

1 c Increase in demand. (678–679)

2 a Definition. (678–679)

3 e **a** and **b** have one-time effects, **c** caused by Δ*AD*, and **d** is supply-side effect. (678–679)

4 b Increase in price of oil leads to leftward shift in *SAS* curve, creating cost-push inflation (stagflation), which *may* trigger a cost-push inflation spiral if government raises aggregate demand. (680–681)

5 a Increase in price of crucial input leads to increase in costs of production and leftward shift of *SAS*. (680–681)

6 b Expected *P* at intersection of *LAS* and expected $AD = AD_1$, and actual new *SAS* is set here, and new equilibrium is where actual *AD* and new *SAS* cross. (682–683)

7 e Expected *P* at intersection of expected $AD = AD_1$, and actual new *SAS* is set here, and new equilibrium is where actual *AD* and new *SAS* cross. (682–683)

8 d Expected *P* at intersection of *LAS* and expected $AD = AD_1$, and actual new *SAS* is set here, and new equilibrium is where actual *AD* and new *SAS* cross. (682–683)

9 c Correct on *average*. (682–683)

10 c Definition. (680–681)

11 e Definition. (684)

12 a *LRPC* is at natural rate. (685)

13 c Expected inflation rate is where *SRPC* crosses *LRPC*. (685)

14 c Found by reading off the *SRPC*. (684–685)

15 a Draw a Phillips curve. (684–685)

16 e Economy just moves up *LRPC*. (684–685)

17 b One of the key impulses in new Keynesian theory is unexpected change in *AD*. (687)

18 b Key impulse in new classical theory is unexpected change in *AD*. (687)

19 a See text discussion. (687)

20 e Vertical *AS* curve. (687–691)

21 a Intertemporal substitution means Δ current real wage or real interest rate leads to big Δ labour supply. (687–691)

22 e Definition. (687–691)

23 d All unemployment is natural, and real wage rate is always correct. (687–691)

24 a Key impulse is Δ pace of technological change. (687–691)

25 d Because *LAS* is vertical. (687–691)

Short Answer Problems

1 An increase in government expenditures on goods and services shifts the aggregate demand curve rightward. If the price level is not expected to change, the short-run aggregate supply curve remains unchanged, and the increase in aggregate demand causes the price level to increase and real GDP to increase.

2 The higher price level leads to demands for higher wages, which push up the costs of production and shift the *SAS* curve leftward, leading to a further increase in the price level and a decrease in real GDP. A demand-pull inflation spiral could result *if* the government once again raises the level of their purchases or if the government continues to run a deficit (financed by printing money). *AD* will then continue to shift rightward, triggering leftward shifts in *SAS*, leading to the demand-pull inflation spiral.

3 The four important features of the Canadian economy that make severe depression less likely today are (1) bank deposits are insured; (2) the Bank of Canada is prepared to be the "lender of last resort"; (3) taxes and government spending

play a stabilizing role; and (4) multi-income families are more economically secure.

4   The short-run Phillips curve assumes that the expected inflation rate is constant, and is therefore downward sloping. Therefore, an increase in the inflation rate (and therefore a decrease in real wages), will create a decrease in unemployment to a rate below the natural rate. The long-run Phillips curve is constructed assuming that the expected inflation rate adjusts fully to reflect changes in the actual inflation rate, and is therefore vertical at the natural rate of unemployment. If there is an increase in the actual inflation rate, there is an equivalent increase in the expected inflation rate (so that the real wage rate stays constant), and the rate of unemployment stays constant at the natural rate.

5   Partially this statement is a value judgment, based on the tradeoff of a higher cost to society from the higher inflation versus the gain to society from a lower inflation rate. In this case, we would need to evaluate the costs of inflation vis-à-vis the costs of unemployment. However, there is also an objective (positive) problem with this statement. In the short run, such a tradeoff does exist, represented by the downward-sloping short-run Phillips curve. In the long run, there is no such tradeoff. As a result, a higher inflation rate leads to a lower unemployment rate in the short run, but eventually inflation expectations will increase, shifting upward the short-run Phillips curve, and unemployment returns to the natural rate. Therefore, in the long run, increasing inflation will have no impact on the unemployment rate, but will increase the costs to society that come from the higher inflation.

6   Inflation is an increase in the price level, and starts with either a shift rightward in the *AD* curve due to increases in the quantity of money, government spending, or exports (demand-pull inflation), or with a shift leftward in the *SAS* curve due to increases in wages or raw materials prices (cost-push inflation). However, the increase in the price level in either case can only persist if an inflation spiral results from the initial shock. A demand-pull or cost-push inflation spiral starts when increases in aggregate demand and shifts leftward in *SAS* chase each other up the long-run aggregate supply curve.

7   a   Since real GDP has decreased, the *LAS* curve must have shifted leftward, since the only *AS* curve is a vertical *LAS* in an RBC world. For the price level to have increased, it must be the case that either the *AD* curve increased, or decreased so little that in combination with the *LAS* curve shift the price level has increased.

    b   In order to get both the price level rising and real GDP decreasing, it must be that the *SAS* curve shifted leftward by more than the shift rightward in the *AD* curve (if there was one), indicating that people anticipated an increase in *AD* (leading to an increase in wages and a shift leftward in the *SAS*), but the actual increase was less than anticipated.

8   a   A real business cycle recession starts with a temporary decrease in productivity, which leads to a decrease in the marginal product of capital, and a decrease in the demand for capital (and therefore a decrease in the real interest rate), a decrease in the demand for investment, and a shift leftward in the *AD* curve. In addition, there is a decrease in the demand for labour because of the decrease in productivity, and a shift leftward in the supply of labour because of the lower real interest rate. These two shifts lead to a decrease in employment and a shift leftward in the *LAS* curve. All unemployment is natural.

    b   In the new Keynesian labour market, money wages are based on wrong expectations, so that real wages are too high since the increase in money wages is more than the increase in the price level. Labour supply is greater than labour demand, creating the unemployment. All the extra unemployment is cyclical, not natural.

CHAPTERS
26–28

Part 9 Wrap Up
Understanding Macroeconomic Fluctuations

PROBLEM

You have been hired as an economic consultant for the premier of the country of Nova Calenia. The economy of Nova Calenia is in recession, reflected in Table P9.1.

TABLE P9.1

	Year 1	Year 2
Price level (GDP deflator)	125	130
Inflation Rate	7%	4%
Real GDP (billions of constant dollars)	200	190
Real wages (billions of constant dollars)	15.00	15.45
Employment (billions of hours)	100	90
Unemployment (%)	8	11

One set of advisors (who are mainstream business cycle theorists) have told the premier that the recession has been caused by an unexpected decrease in aggregate demand (due to an unexpected decrease in exports), combined with sticky wages (inflation was expected to remain constant at 7 percent).

a Explain briefly to the premier what these advisors think is happening to the market for goods and services. Explain what happens to aggregate expenditure as part of your answer. In addition, draw an *AD–AS* graph illustrating what happens in this market. Explain what happens in the labour market (just describe what is going on in the labour market, but do draw a graph of what has happened to the Phillips curve).

Another set of advisors (real business cycle theorists) have argued that these events are due solely to an aggregate supply shock, driven by technological change.

b Explain briefly to the premier what these advisors think is happening to the market for goods and services (draw an *AD–AS* graph as part of your answer) and in the labour market (just describe what is going on, do not draw a graph of the labour market).

MIDTERM EXAMINATION

You should allocate 24 minutes for this examination (12 questions, 2 minutes per question). For each question, choose the *best* answer.

1 The consumption function shows the relationship between consumption expenditure and
   a the interest rate.
   b the price level.
   c disposable income.
   d saving.
   e nominal income.

2 If the money wage rate decreases,
   a *AD* shifts rightward.
   b firms hire less labour.
   c only *LAS* shifts rightward.
   d only *SAS* shifts rightward.
   e both *SAS* and *LAS* shift rightward.

3 The changes represented in Fig. P9.1 *must*
a not occur in the real world, because *AD* and *SAS* cannot change at the same time.
b create an inflationary gap.
c create a recessionary gap.
d create inflation.
e do none of the above.

FIGURE **P9.1**

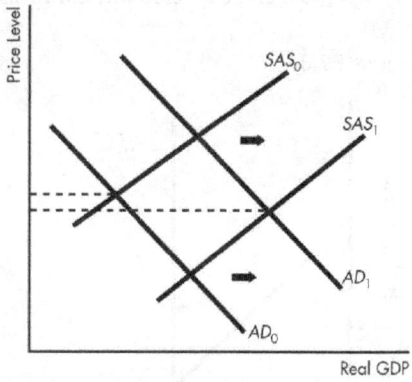

4 If real GDP is less than aggregate planned expenditure,
a aggregate planned expenditure will increase.
b real GDP will decrease.
c the price level must decrease to restore equilibrium.
d imports must be too large.
e aggregate planned expenditure will decrease.

5 We observe an increase in the price level and an increase in real GDP. A possible explanation is that the
a quantity of money has fallen.
b expectation of future disposable income has decreased.
c price of raw materials has increased.
d stock of capital has increased.
e expectation of future profits has increased.

6 What is the key impulse in the new Keynesian theory of the business cycle?
a changes in animal spirits
b changes in the money supply
c unanticipated changes in aggregate demand
d anticipated changes in aggregate demand
e changes in the pace of technological change

7 Suppose that investment increases by $10 billion. Which of the following *reduces* the effect of this increase in autonomous expenditure on equilibrium real GDP?
a increase in the marginal propensity to consume
b decrease in the marginal propensity to import
c decrease in the marginal tax rate
d steeper *SAS* curve
e flatter *SAS* curve

8 In a recent study, the University of Underfunded argued that it created four times as many jobs as people it hired directly. This argument illustrates the idea of
a the marginal propensity to consume.
b the multiplier.
c government spending.
d the tax multiplier.
e universities wasting taxpayers' dollars.

9 What is the key impulse in the real business cycle theory of the business cycle?
a changes in expected future sales and profits
b changes in the money supply
c unanticipated changes in aggregate demand
d anticipated changes in aggregate demand
e changes in the pace of technological change

10 The aggregate demand curve illustrates that as the price level decreases, the
a quantity of real GDP demanded increases.
b quantity of real GDP demanded decreases.
c quantity of nominal GDP demanded increases.
d quantity of nominal GDP demanded decreases.
e value of assets decrease.

11 A rise in the natural rate of unemployment is shown as a
a rightward shift in only the long-run Phillips curve only.
b leftward shift in only the long-run Phillips curve only.
c rightward shift in only the short-run Phillips curve only.
d leftward shift in both the short-run and long-run Phillips curves.
e rightward shift in both the short-run and long-run Phillips curves.

12 Suppose OPEC unexpectedly collapses, decreasing the price of oil. This is a positive aggregate supply shock. As a result, in the short run the price level will
   a   increase and real GDP will increase.
   b   increase and real GDP will decrease.
   c   decrease and real GDP will increase.
   d   decrease and real GDP will decrease.
   e   increase and real GDP will stay the same.

ANSWERS

Problem

a   Figure P9.2 shows the Year 1 equilibrium at a price level of 125 and real GDP of 200. The fall in exports is a fall in planned aggregate expenditure. There will be unplanned increases in inventories and firms will reduce production in response, leading to a fall in real GDP, price level held constant. This is shown as a shift leftward in the AD curve to AD_1 in Fig. P9.2. Under mainstream theory, with sticky wages and expected inflation of 7 percent, firms and workers had expected a price level of 134 (= 125 × 1.07), which determines the shift in the SAS curve to SAS_1. The resulting below-full-employment equilibrium is shown in Fig. P9.2.

Figure **P9.2**

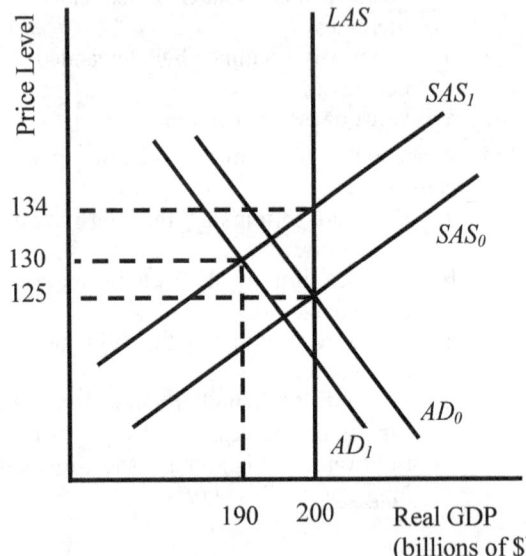

The labour market has rising real wages and rising unemployment, implying that the real wage is too high (nominal wages were based on the expected inflation of 7 percent, but since AD was unexpectedly low, the actual inflation is only 4 percent, creating high real wages), creating (cyclical) unemployment above the natural rate. Figure P9.3 shows the short-run and long-run Phillips curves for this economy, assuming that the natural rate of unemployment is 8 percent and expected inflation was 7 percent.

Figure **P9.3**

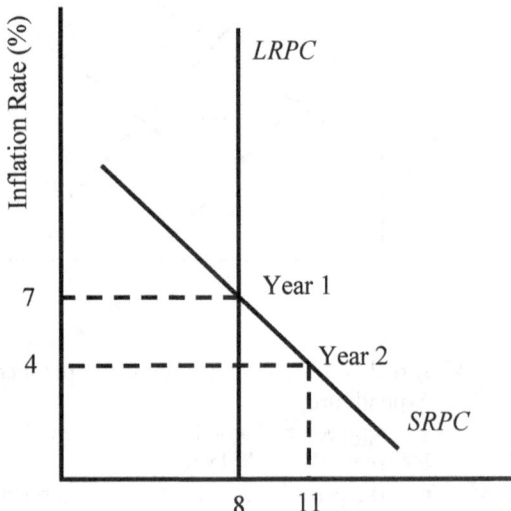

b   The real business cycle graph of the market for goods and services is shown in Fig. P9.4 on the next page. Note that aggregate demand is assumed constant, and that a shift leftward in long-run aggregate supply causes all the changes. This shift is due to a decrease in productivity, because of the technological change, which lowers the demand for labour and capital (lowering the real interest rate). There is also a decrease in the supply of labour, because of the lower real interest rate, creating a big decrease in labour hired, and therefore a shift leftward in the LAS curve. The extra unemployment is due to a rise in natural unemployment—the turnover rate has risen in the labour market.

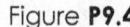

Figure **P9.4**

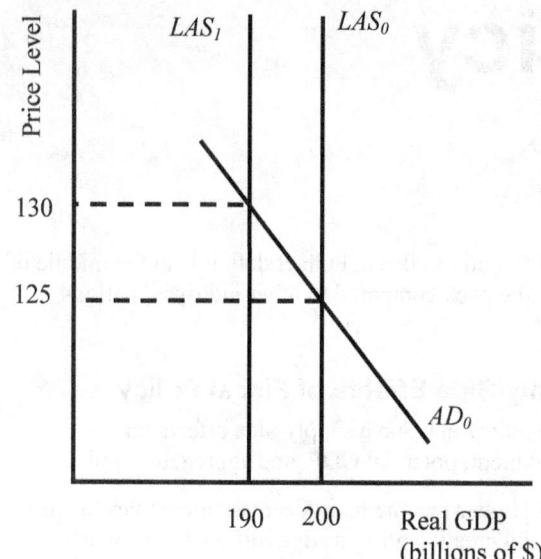

Midterm Examination

1 **c**   Definition. (648–651)

2 **d**   If the money wage rate decreases, the cost of production decreases, firms hire more labour, supply more goods and services, represented by (only) *SAS* shifting rightward. (632–637)

3 **e**   These changes could occur. Gaps cannot be determined without *LAS* curve. (636–637)

4 **a**   Firms' sales > production decreases inventories, leading to increased production. New equilibrium has higher real GDP = higher *AE*. (652–653)

5 **e**   **e** shifts *AD* rightward, increasing *P* and real GDP. **a** and **b** shift *AD* leftward, while **c** shifts *SAS* leftward, decreasing *Y*, and **d** shifts *LAS* rightward, decreasing *P* (draw a graph). (632–637)

6 **c**   Anticipated changes are not as important— see text discussion. (687–691)

7 **d**   Leads to more ΔP, less ΔY. All others make the effect larger. (661–665)

8 **b**   University spending creates multiplier effects. (658–660)

9 **e**   See text discussion. (687–691)

10 **a**   *AD* curve is downward sloping due to wealth and substitution effects. Real GDP by definition, not nominal, and asset values increase here. (6328–631)

11 **e**   *LRPC* is vertical at new higher natural rate, and *SRPC* shifts with it since it crosses the *LRPC* at the natural rate. (684–686)

12 **c**   Fall in the cost of production and a rightward shift in *SAS*. (680–681)

Chapter 29
Fiscal Policy

The Federal Budget

The **federal budget** is an annual statement of revenue and outlays of the government of Canada (provincial budget is for provincial governments).

♦ Budgets finance government activities and achieve macroeconomic policy objectives (**fiscal policy**).

♦ Fiscal policy is made by government and Parliament, in consultation with bureaucrats, provincial governments, and business and consumer groups.

♦ Budgetary revenues—personal income taxes, corporate income taxes, indirect taxes (GST and HST), investment income.

♦ Budgetary outlays—transfer payments, expenditures on goods and services, debt interest payments.

♦ Budget balance = revenues − outlays

  • **Budget surplus** when revenues > outlays.

  • **Budget deficit** when revenues < outlays.

  • **Balanced budget** when revenues = outlays.

♦ **Government debt** = total borrowing by governments = sum of past deficits − sum of past surpluses.

  • Persistent deficits of the 1980s increased borrowing, which increased interest payments and increased deficit, etc.

  • Balanced budget of 1997 stopped this cycle—government debt is falling.

♦ Provincial government outlays are almost as large as federal; focused on hospitals, schools, and colleges/universities.

♦ Canada's current budget deficit is in the middle of the pack compared to other industrial nations.

Supply-Side Effects of Fiscal Policy

Fiscal policy may have supply-side effects on employment, potential GDP, and aggregate supply.

♦ Higher income taxes decrease incentives to work by creating a **tax wedge** (difference between before-tax wage rate and after-tax wage rate), decreasing labour supply and potential GDP.

♦ Taxes on consumption increase the wedge by increasing consumption prices, effectively lowering the real wage rate and labour supply.

♦ Taxes on interest income weaken incentives to save, reduce quantity of saving (quantity supplied of loanable funds), and therefore reduce investment and growth rate of real GDP.

♦ Since nominal interest rate is taxed, extra strong impact of tax on real *after-tax* interest rate.

♦ **Laffer curve** is the relationship between the tax rate and tax revenue collected. Claims high tax rate may collect less taxes than a lower tax rate due to negative incentives.

♦ Most economists note incentive effects of tax cuts, but believe tax cuts will reduce tax revenues and potentially increase budget deficits.

Fiscal Stimulus

Fiscal stimulus is the use of fiscal policy to increase production and employment, and can be **discretionary** (initiated by Parliament, involves changing government outlays, taxes) or **automatic** (triggered by state of economy).

♦ If real GDP decreases, tax revenues decrease and transfer payments increase—this *automatically* provides stimulus that shrinks a recessionary gap.

♦ If real GDP increases, tax revenues increase and transfer payments decrease—this *automatically* provides restraint that shrinks an inflationary gap.

Budget deficits fluctuate with business cycle due to cyclical fluctuations in net taxes, providing automatic stimulus and restraint.

♦ **Structural surplus or deficit** is budget balance when the economy is at full employment.

♦ **Cyclical surplus or deficit** = actual balance – structural balance.

♦ Cyclical surplus or deficit is due only to the fact that real GDP ≠ potential.

♦ Currently, Canada has a cyclical deficit *and* a structural deficit.

Discretionary fiscal policy works to affect *AD*, both directly and via multiplier effects.

♦ **Government expenditure multiplier** = quantified effect of a change in government expenditures on real GDP.

♦ Initial increase in *G* increases real GDP, which leads to secondary, induced effects.

♦ **Tax multiplier** = quantified effect of change in autonomous taxes on real GDP.

♦ Increase in *T* decreases *YD*, decreases *C*, and decreases real GDP, leading to secondary, induced effects.

♦ Increases in *G* or cuts in *T* increase government borrowing, raise interest rates, which cuts investment, partially offsetting the initial effect.

If real GDP < potential GDP, discretionary fiscal policy can be used to restore full employment.

♦ Increases in *G*, decreases in *T* increase aggregate expenditure and shift the *AD* curve rightward.

♦ Multiplier effect shifts the *AD* curve even further right, movement along the *SAS* curve in short run toward full-employment equilibrium.

♦ Reducing government expenditures or increasing taxes reduces aggregate expenditure, shifts *AD* leftward, reducing an inflationary gap.

♦ Tax cuts may work better due to reinforcing supply-side effects.

Discretionary fiscal policy is limited by

♦ recognition lag—recognizing fiscal policy is needed.

♦ law-making lag—slowness of the legislative process.

♦ impact lag—time it takes policy to have an impact.

HELPFUL HINTS

1 It is crucial to distinguish between two types of autonomous shocks. One type adds to the instability of the economy; it includes changes in autonomous consumption, investment, and exports. The other is planned to (hopefully) reduce the instability of the economy; it includes fiscal policy—changes in government expenditures and taxes. Because the two shocks work through the same multiplier process, the same process that creates instability can also help to reduce instability.

2 The size of the fiscal policy multipliers depends on the sizes of the *MPC*, the marginal tax rate, and the marginal propensity to import. Figure 29.1 below shows why. A crucial part of the multiplier process is the change in induced expenditure in the second round of the multiplier. These induced expenditures are reduced as income is siphoned off for saving, to pay for taxes, or to buy imported goods!

FIGURE **29.1**

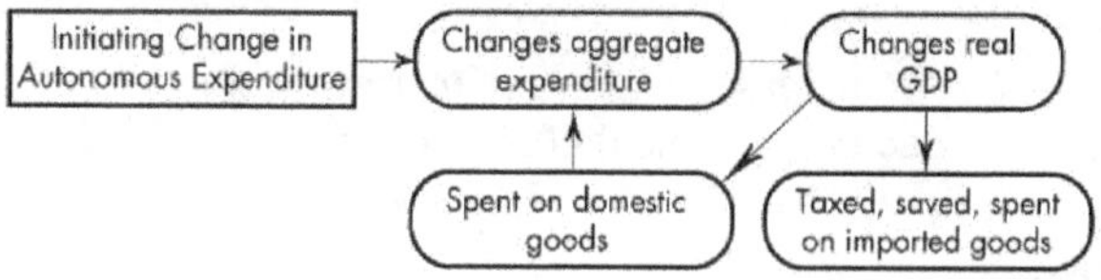

SELF-TEST

True/False and Explain

The Federal Budget

1 The federal deficit is the total amount of borrowing the federal government has undertaken.

2 Only government expenditures on goods and services, not transfer payments, are crucial in analysing the federal deficit.

3 A government starts with a balanced budget. In the next year, if the percentage growth in outlays is higher than the percentage growth in revenues, the government will have a deficit.

4 Government investment income is an example of a budgetary outlay.

5 The federal government had budget deficits from 1997 to 2008.

Supply-Side Effects of Fiscal Policy

6 Cutting income taxes will shift the *AD* curve rightward, but will reduce potential GDP.

7 An increase in taxes on interest income will decrease potential GDP growth.

8 The Laffer curve claims that a cut in the tax rate always increases tax revenue.

9 If the nominal interest rate is 10 percent, the tax rate is 5 percent, and the inflation rate is 4 percent, then the real after-tax interest rate is 1 percent.

Fiscal Stimulus

10 An increase in autonomous transfer payments matched by an increase in autonomous taxes will increase real GDP by the size of the increase in transfer payments.

11 Taxes and transfer payments that vary with income automatically reduce fluctuations in real GDP.

12 If real GDP increases, so do tax revenues.

13 If an economy has a structural deficit, the budget balance at potential GDP is negative.

14 A cut in tax rates will increase equilibrium real GDP in the short run.

15 An increase in government expenditures shifts the *AD* curve rightward.

Multiple-Choice

The Federal Budget

1 Provincial government outlays
  a are small and irrelevant to the economy.
  b are an important source of fiscal policy.
  c are always equal to provincial government revenues.
  d are focused on transfer payments to individuals, such as employment insurance.
  e tend to fluctuate with federal outlays.

2 Which of the following would *not* increase the budget deficit?
  a an increase in interest on the government debt
  b an increase in government expenditures on goods and services
  c an increase in government transfer payments
  d an increase in indirect business taxes
  e a decrease in government investment income

3 The budget deficit grew as a percentage of GDP after 1974 because
  a government expenditures on goods and services rose, while tax revenues remained constant.
  b government expenditures on goods and services remained constant, while tax revenues fell.
  c transfer payments rose, while tax revenues remained constant.
  d debt interest payments rose, while tax revenues fell.
  e none of the above.

4 Which of the following groups does *not* influence federal fiscal policy?
  a government bureaucrats
  b provincial governments
  c Parliament
  d business and consumer groups
  e government unions

5 Which of the following is a budgetary outlay?
  a personal income taxes
  b government investment income
  c debt interest payments
  d indirect taxes
  e corporate income taxes

6 The government of Ricardia's budget lists the following projected collections and spending: $25 million in personal income taxes, $15 million in corporate income taxes, $5 million in indirect taxes, $2 million in investment income, $30 million in transfer payments, $12 million in government expenditures, and $8 million in debt interest. Ricardia has a government budget
  a surplus of $3 million.
  b surplus of $57 million.
  c surplus of $13 million.
  d deficit of $13 million.
  e deficit of $3 million.

7 The largest source of revenues for the federal government is
  a transfer payments.
  b expenditures on goods and services.
  c personal income taxes.
  d corporate income taxes.
  e indirect taxes such as the GST.

8 Compared to the other major industrial economies, in recent years Canada
  a is one of the heaviest borrowers.
  b is the only one of these economies running a surplus.
  c is the only one of these economies running a deficit.
  d is the only economy with provincial/state governments that play a significant role.
  e is in the middle of the pack for deficit levels.

Supply-Side Effects of Fiscal Policy

9 Which of the following quotations correctly refers to the effects of fiscal policy in the *long run*?
  a "The increase in taxes will increase real GDP."
  b "The increase in taxes will raise prices only."
  c "A change in the budget has no impact on real GDP unless it changes aggregate supply."
  d "A change in the budget has no impact on real GDP."
  e "An increase in government expenditures on goods and services will increase real GDP."

10 Which of the following quotations correctly refers to the effects of fiscal policy in the *short run*?
  a "The increase in taxes will increase real GDP."
  b "The increase in taxes will raise prices only."
  c "A change in the budget has no impact on real GDP unless it changes aggregate supply."
  d "A change in the budget has no impact on real GDP."
  e "The increase in government expenditures on goods and services will increase real GDP."

11 If the nominal interest rate is 11 percent, the inflation rate is 4 percent and the tax rate is 25 percent, what is the real after-tax interest rate?
   a   −1.25%
   b   4.25%
   c   5.25%
   d   8%
   e   10%

12 An increase in the tax rate on interest income will lead to
   a   less saving, more spending, and more economic growth.
   b   less saving, less investment, and lower economic growth.
   c   more saving, more investment, and higher economic growth.
   d   a strong intertemporal substitution effect, leading to more labour supplied.
   e   higher real after-tax interest rates.

13 Which of the following is *not* a problem created for an economy by a higher tax wedge?
   a   It lowers after-tax real interest rates.
   b   It raises before-tax wage rates and lowers employment.
   c   Potential GDP decreases.
   d   Saving decreases.
   e   The government's deficit rises.

14 Which of the following would lower potential GDP?
   a   increased tax rate on interest income
   b   increased tax rate on consumption spending
   c   increased tax rate on labour income
   d   all of the above
   e   only **a** and **c**

15 The Laffer curve has been criticized by mainstream economists because
   a   there is no theoretical possibility of higher tax rates leading to lower tax revenues.
   b   higher tax rates do not create negative incentive effects.
   c   tax cuts are just spent, not saved as predicted by the theory.
   d   savers look only at real interest rates, not nominal interest rates.
   e   empirically, tax cuts have not led to higher tax revenues.

Fiscal Stimulus

16 Suppose that the tax multiplier is −2. If taxes decrease by $4 billion and incentives to work and save are affected, in the long run real GDP will
   a   decrease by $8 billion.
   b   increase by $8 billion.
   c   be unaffected.
   d   increase, but by how much is unclear.
   e   decrease, but by how much is unclear.

17 Short-run fiscal policy is limited by the fact that
   a   the *LAS* curve is vertical.
   b   the legislative process is slow.
   c   real GDP is typically not equal to potential GDP.
   d   the policy might shift the *SAS* curve to the right.
   e   the policy might shift the *SAS* curve to the left.

18 Which of the following is an example of a fiscal policy designed to counter a recessionary gap?
   a   increasing debt interest payments
   b   increasing taxes
   c   decreasing transfer payments
   d   increasing transfer payments
   e   decreasing government expenditures on goods and services

19 During an expansion, tax revenue
   a   and government outlays decline.
   b   declines and government outlays increase.
   c   increases and government outlays decline.
   d   and government outlays increase.
   e   stays constant and government outlays increase.

20 Which of the following happens *automatically* if the economy goes into a recession?
   a   Only government outlays increase.
   b   Only net taxes increase.
   c   The deficit increases.
   d   The deficit decreases.
   e   Both government outlays and net taxes increase, and the deficit stays the same.

21 Which of the following policies will *not* shift the *AD* curve rightward?

a increasing government expenditures on goods and services

b decreasing autonomous taxes

c increasing autonomous transfer payments

d increasing government expenditures on goods and services *and* increasing autonomous taxes by the same amount

e decreasing government expenditures on goods and services *and* decreasing autonomous taxes by the same amount

22 Consider the economy of NoTax, where the multiplier is 2.5. If the government desires to shift the *AD* curve rightward by $5 billion, the correct increase in government expenditures is

a $2 billion.

b $2.5 billion.

c $3 billion.

d $7.5 billion.

e $8.33 billion.

23 If supply-side effects are strong, which of the following statements is true?

a The government expenditure multiplier is likely stronger than the tax multiplier.

b The tax multiplier is likely stronger than the government expenditure multiplier.

c Both the government expenditure and the tax multiplier are zero.

d Both the government expenditure and the tax multiplier are equally strong.

e Fiscal policy affects aggregate demand more than it affects aggregate supply.

24 A cyclical deficit is when

a government outlays are greater than revenues.

b government outlays are less than revenues.

c there is a deficit due to the fact that real GDP is greater than potential GDP.

d there is a deficit due to the fact that real GDP is less than potential GDP.

e there is a deficit even when real GDP equals potential GDP.

25 The country of Ricardia has a budget plan with constant government outlays equal to $100 billion and taxes related positively to real GDP by the equation: Taxes = $25 billion + 0.1*Y*. If the structural deficit is $10 billion, what is potential GDP in this economy?

a $65 billion

b $75 billion

c $650 billion

d $750 billion

e $850 billion

Short Answer Problems

1 What changes in the components of the federal government budget after 1974 were the principal causes of continuing large government deficits?

2 During the summer of 1995, Saskatchewan had a provincial election. A central plank of the Saskatchewan Liberal Party's election strategy was a promise to cut taxes dramatically, stating that these cuts would create 50,000 new jobs (about 10 percent of the labour force) over the next five years. Critics claimed that this policy would have only a small effect in Saskatchewan, that most of the new jobs from the tax cuts would show up in other provinces.

a What economic concept underlies the Liberals' promise?

b What economic concept underlies the critics' argument?

c The Liberals lost the election, so we did not see if the tax cuts would have had the promised effect. What do you think would have happened?

3 Suppose you are visiting the town of Elbow, Saskatchewan, which is suffering a depressed economy due to low wheat prices. You spend $100 on accommodation and another $100 golfing and dining at the excellent local golf club.

a What factors will influence how much extra real GDP will be generated within Elbow by your $200 of expenditure? (Treat Elbow as if it were a separate economy.)

b What does your answer imply for the argument made by the Elbow town council that the Saskatchewan government should shift a government department to the town to stimulate the town's economy?

4 Explain why the multiplier effect of a tax cut on real GDP is smaller once we consider the aggregate supply curve. Second, what happens if there are incentive effects from the tax cuts?

5 Table 29.1 gives some information on the real interest rates, inflation rates, and tax rates from three different countries.

TABLE **29.1**

	Ricardia	Barroland	Lafferia
Nominal interest rate	12%	10%	10%
Inflation rate	6%	5%	6%
Tax rate	40%	50%	50%
Real, before-tax interest rate			
Real, after-tax interest rate			
Tax wedge			

a Complete Table 29.1.

b Assuming all other factors are equal, which country has the biggest negative incentive effects for lenders?

c Assuming all other factors are equal, which country has the lowest costs for investors?

6 Some politicians and economists argue that tax cuts are beneficial for the government budget balance and are also beneficial for the economy in the short run *and* the long run. Explain their arguments and evaluate them briefly.

7 As finance minister for the government of Adanac, you have decided that to get re-elected next year, your government needs to raise real GDP by $200 billion.

a What possible fiscal policies would work to achieve your goal?

b Your crack team of economists has estimated the economy's government expenditure multiplier to be 4. You are confident that this estimate is correct, since you threatened to exile the economists to the North Pole should they err. If you decide to change only government expenditures, how much change is required to accomplish your goal?

c Having carried out the increase in government expenditures, you find that the increase in real GDP is less than $200 billion, jeopardizing your chance for re-election. Before you exile the poor economists to the North Pole, is there any excuse for their mistake? (In other words, what went wrong?)

d You were focused on the short run, but what other factors could have been important for long-run considerations in picking your appropriate policy?

8 During the fall of 2008 and early 2009, Canada faced the possibility of recession as an outcome of the credit crunch. The government of Canada and the opposition parties debated what the appropriate fiscal policy might be in light of this danger. The Conservative government was worried about the potential recession, but was also worried about the long-term effects of having a deficit, and were also worried that the proposed fiscal policies might not work well to reverse a recession.

a What are the potential dangers of having a new, larger deficit?

b Why might fiscal policy not work to prevent or reduce the effects of a recession?

c What are the dangers of *not* carrying out an anti-recessionary fiscal policy?

d Which danger do you think is higher—carrying out an anti-recessionary policy that doesn't work or creates deficits, or not carrying out such a policy?

ANSWERS

True/False and Explain

1 F Deficit is when outlays > revenues in the current year. (704–705)

2 F Government expenditures on goods, transfers payments, and interest payments are all part of outlays. (704)

3 T If outlays grow faster than taxes, outlays > taxes next year and there is a deficit. (704–705)

4 F Example of revenue. (704)

5 F It ran surpluses. (705–709)

6 F An income tax cut raises *YD* and shifts *AD* rightward, and raises incentives to work and save, raising labour supply and *raising* potential GDP. (710–711)

7 T Due to negative incentive effects reducing investment and GDP growth. (712)

8 F Only if the tax rate is high enough to be past the peak of the Laffer curve. (713)

9 T Real after-tax rate = nominal rate × (1 – tax rate) – inflation rate = (10% × 0.5) – 4% = 1%. (712–713)

10 F They exactly offset each other (Δ net taxes = 0), so Δ real GDP = 0. (715–719)

11 T If income decreases, this decreases taxes + increases transfers, and increases disposable income, which increases aggregate expenditure, increasing income, potentially offsetting the initial decrease. (714–715)

12 T More is spent by households, so there is more income and indirect taxes (like GST/HST). (714–715)

13 T Definition. (714–715)

14 T Shifts *AD* rightward. (715–719)

15 T Increase in government expenditures = increase in quantity of goods and services demanded, so higher level of *AD*, same price level. (715–719)

Multiple-Choice

1 e May have a deficit, not really used for fiscal policy, almost as large as federal government outlays, *federal* government does employment insurance. (704–709)

2 d This is an increase in revenue. (704–705)

3 c See text discussion. (705–709)

4 e See text discussion. (704)

5 c Others are sources of revenue. (704–705)

6 e Budget balance = revenue – outlays = ($25 + $15 + $5 + $2) – ($30 + $12 + $8) = –$3 million. (704–705)

7 c See text discussion. (704–705)

8 b See text discussion. (709)

9 c In the long run, changes in fiscal policy have an impact only if they change potential GDP (aggregate supply). (710–713)

10 e A shift rightward in *AD* increases real GDP in the short run. (710–719)

11 b 11 × (1 – 0.25) – 4 = 4.25%. (712)

12 b Lower return to saving, less saving (lower quantity supplied of loanable funds), raising before-tax real interest rate, leading to lower investment and lower economic growth. (712–713)

13 e Deficit may or may not rise. (710–713)

14 d **a**, **b**, and **c** raise the tax wedge, lowering employment and saving, lowering potential GDP. (710–713)

15 e See text discussion. (713)

16 d Only the incentive effects on potential GDP matter for the long run, but size is uncertain. (710–719)

17 b Others are irrelevant or are not limitations. (719)

18 d Shifts the *AD* curve rightward. (715–719)

19 c Increase in real GDP increases tax revenue. Decrease in unemployment decreases transfer payments. (714–715)

20 c In a recession, decrease in *Y* decreases taxes and increases spending on employment insurance, etc., increasing deficit. (714–715)

21 e Decrease in *G* shifts *AD* leftward by government expenditure multiplier; decrease in taxes shifts *AD* rightward by tax multiplier, which has a smaller impact. (718–720)

22 a Invert Δ*Y* = multiplier × Δ*G*: Δ*G* = Δ*Y*/multiplier = 5/2.5 = 2. (718)

23 b Likely that the incentives effects on *AS* are strong and important, and therefore the tax multiplier is stronger. (714–719)

24 d Definition. (714–715)

25 c $10 billion = *G* – *T* = $100 billion – $25 billion – 0.1 (potential GDP), therefore potential GDP = (100 – 25 – 10)/0.1 = $650 billion. (714–715)

Short Answer Problems

1 The deficit increased because government outlays as a percentage of GDP increased, while taxes as a percentage of GDP fell during the late 1970s and then slowly increased. The components of spending that showed the most consistent growth were transfer payments and interest payments on government debt.

2 a The Liberals were counting on the tax multiplier to boost aggregate expenditure and create new jobs.

b The critics argued that most of the new expenditure would be on products from outside the province—that the marginal propensity to import for a province is very high, so that the multipliers are very low.

c It is likely that fiscal policy multipliers are low for individual provinces due to high marginal propensities to import. For your information, imports in Saskatchewan were about 62 percent (= 15.14 billion/29.28 billion) of provincial real GDP in 1995. (*Source:* Statistics Canada, CANSIM matrices D21425 and D31874.)

3 a Your $200 will trigger a multiplier process—the owners of the factors of production at the golf course will spend their extra income, for example. This spending induces second-round increases in consumption expenditure, leading to a final change in real GDP in Elbow that is a multiple of $200. The size of the multiplier effect will be determined by two things. First, the larger the marginal propensity to consume in Elbow and the smaller the marginal propensity to import (from outside Elbow), the larger the multiplier will be. In a small town, the marginal propensity to import from outside the town is likely to be quite high, making the multiplier much smaller. Second, the effect is smaller if the aggregate supply curve is steeper—the increase in aggregate demand gets reduced by an increase in the price level.

b Such a shift might stimulate the town's economy, since the annual increase in government expenditures will create multiplier effects. The usefulness of this shift is limited by the factors that might reduce the size of the multiplier. (This was actual government policy in Saskatchewan until the Conservatives were defeated in

1991, at least partially because of this policy.)

4 The multiplier tells us the size of the change in real GDP relative to the size of an initial change in government expenditure or taxes. Once we consider the *AS* curve, we know the price level will increase as aggregate demand increases—the increase in the price level being higher, the steeper the *AS* curve. This increase in the price level lowers aggregate expenditure, shown by the movement up the *AD* curve, leading to a smaller increase in real GDP compared to the case with no price effect.

The tax cut would reduce the tax wedge, creating incentive effects that would increase labour supply (lowering the before-tax wage rate and increasing labour demand) and the quantity supplied of loanable funds (lowering real interest rates and increasing investment). These incentive effects would increase potential GDP.

5 a Table 29.1 Solution shows the answers. The real, after-tax interest rate is solved using the formula: Nominal rate × (1 − tax rate) − inflation rate. The tax wedge is the difference between the before-tax real rate (nominal rate − inflation rate) paid by borrowers and the after-tax real rate received by lenders.

TABLE **29.1** SOLUTION

	Ricardia	Barroland	Lafferia
Nominal interest rate	12%	10%	10%
Inflation rate	6%	5%	6%
Tax rate	40%	50%	50%
Real, before-tax interest rate	6%	5%	4%
Real, after-tax interest rate	1.2%	0%	−1%
Tax Wedge	4.8%	5%	5%

b Based on having the highest tax wedge, Lafferia and Barroland have the biggest negative incentive effect for lenders.

c Lafferia has the lowest before-tax real interest rate (4%), and therefore would have the lowest costs for investors.

6   The Laffer curve claims a tax cut could potentially have such strong incentive effects that total tax revenues would rise, helping the government budget balance. However, when the U.S. cut its tax rates under Reagan, the result was a fall in tax revenue and a rise in the budget deficit.

With respect to the economy, a cut in taxes increases disposable income and shifts the *AD* curve rightward in the normal multiplier manner, increasing real GDP in the short run. If the *LAS* curve does not shift, in the long run the economy will return to potential GDP. However, supply-side economists argue that tax cuts will also increase the after-tax returns to work and saving, which in turn will increase labour supply and saving, increasing potential GDP and shifting the *AS* curves rightward. An evaluation is still somewhat premature. As the text points out, it is still a matter of political opinion whether the *AS* effects are small or large. So far, there is no hard empirical evidence one way or the other.

7 a   You would need to increase aggregate demand, which means that you would need to either increase government expenditures on goods and services, or increase transfer payments, or cut taxes.

   b   If the government expenditure multiplier equals 4, to raise real GDP by $200 billion you need to increase government expenditures by $50 billion = $200/4 billion.

   c   The multiplier effects we have been analysing are based on the assumption that the price level is constant. In the real world, the stimulation of aggregate demand that you have carried out would raise the price level, which lowers aggregate expenditure and partially (or completely) offsets the increase in real GDP from your policy. In addition, there was likely crowding-out effects from the higher interest rates caused by the higher deficit.

   d   If you had chosen a tax cut for your policy, this might have had positive incentive effects on labour supply and saving, leading to a higher level of potential GDP in the long run.

8 a   A larger deficit increases the demand for loanable funds (see Chapter 23), and potentially increases real interest rates, crowding out private investment, and lowering long-term economic growth. In addition, a deficit increases the size of the government debt, and therefore increases the required debt payments by the government. Looking at the history of the government's deficits between 1971 and 1997, debt payments can create a vicious circle of rising debt, rising debt payments, rising deficits, rising debt, etc.

   b   Fiscal policy might not work due to lags in the system. The recognition lag would not be an issue (the problem was recognized!), but the law-making lag (getting the legislation passed) is a possible problem, as is the impact lag (the time it takes the policy to have an impact). If the policy arrives after the economy has started to readjust to full employment, we may create inflationary pressures.

   c   The dangers of not carrying out an anti-recessionary fiscal policy would be a longer and deeper recession, with more lost jobs and bankrupt businesses.

   d   This choice depends on your personal evaluation of the pros and cons listed above, as well as your judgement on which negatives to avoid!

Chapter 30
Monetary Policy

Monetary Policy Objectives and Framework

Bank of Canada Act sets objectives of monetary policy.

- ◆ Bank controls quantity of money and interest rates to avoid inflation and prevent excessive swings in GDP growth and unemployment.

- ◆ Current policy is **inflation rate targeting**—explicit inflation rate target range (1 to 3 percent a year, trend of 2 percent), clear explanation of actions.

  - Inflation is measured by CPI, but Bank also focuses on *core inflation* (CPI excluding the eight most volatile prices and indirect taxes).

  - Since range was set in mid-1990s, actual inflation rate has usually been within target range.

- ◆ Benefits of a target range are clear understanding by financial markets and as anchor for inflation expectations.

  - Critics argue Bank should pay more attention to unemployment rate and real GDP growth.

- ◆ Governing Council of Bank of Canada is responsible for conduct of monetary policy, with briefings by Bank economists.

- ◆ Governor of Bank of Canada consults with Minister of Finance.

The Conduct of Monetary Policy

The Bank of Canada can control only one policy instrument: either quantity of money (monetary base) *or* exchange rate *or* short-term interest rate.

- ◆ The Bank targets the short-term interest rate, specifically the **overnight loans rate** (interest rate on overnight loans big banks make to each other).

- ◆ The Bank announces its interest rate target eight times a year.

- ◆ The tools used to achieve the chosen target are the operating band and overnight operations.

- ◆ **Operating band** is the target overnight rate plus or minus 0.25 percentage points.

  - Top of operating band = **bank rate** (overnight rate + 0.25%)—interest rate the Bank of Canada charges big banks on loans. Since a bank can always borrow at the bank rate, the overnight rate never goes higher than this.

  - Bottom of band = **settlement balances rate**— interest rate the Bank of Canada pays for reserves banks hold at the Bank of Canada. Since a bank can always earn the settlement balances rate, the overnight rate never goes lower than this.

  - The Bank of Canada can always make the overnight loans rate fall within target range.

- ◆ Open market operations move the overnight rate to the target rate.

  - If the Bank of Canada buys government bonds, this increases banking system reserves (= increased supply of overnight funds), increasing loans, lowering the overnight rate.

  - If the Bank of Canada sells government bonds, this decreases banking system reserves (= decreased supply of overnight funds), decreasing loans, raising the overnight rate.

Monetary Policy Transmission

Changing overnight rate affects aggregate demand (*AD*), real GDP growth, and inflation through several channels.

- ◆ With a lower overnight rate, other interest rates fall, quantity of money and supply of loanable funds increase, real interest rates fall.

- With lower interest rates, exchange rate falls, increasing net exports and *AD*.

- With lower real interest rates, consumption and investment increase, increasing *AD*.

- Increasing *AD* increases real GDP growth and inflation, although takes up to two years for full effects.

♦ Higher overnight rate has opposite effects, decreasing *AD*, real GDP growth, and inflation.

♦ Historical evidence shows changes in the overnight rate create different effects on long-term and short-term interest rates.

- Because banks can easily choose between overnight loans and Treasury bills as short-term assets, they are close substitutes and the two rates move together.

- 10-year government bond rate and long-term corporate bond rate are close substitutes (although corporate rate is slightly higher on average), so these two rates move together.

- Short-term and long-term bond rates usually move together, but are not close substitutes, and sometimes move in different directions.

♦ Exchange rate responds to interest rate differential (gap between Canadian and U.S. rates), but relationship is weak since many other factors determine exchange rates.

Expenditure plans are affected by real interest rate.

♦ Lower real interest rate, lower opportunity cost of spending, greater consumption expenditure and investment.

♦ Lower real interest rate, lower Canadian dollar exchange rate, greater net exports.

Final link in transmission chain is a change in *AD* changing real GDP and price level.

♦ With real GDP < potential GDP, lowering the overnight rate increases the quantity of money and the supply of loanable funds. This lowers real interest rates and increases *AD*, increasing real GDP and price level, leading to faster convergence to potential GDP.

♦ If real GDP > potential GDP (inflationary pressure), increasing the overnight rate lowers the quantity of money and the supply of loanable funds, increasing the real interest rate and decreasing *AD*, lowering inflationary pressure.

♦ Monetary policy is sometimes wrong due to time lags before policy takes effect.

♦ When the Bank of Canada changes overnight rates, real GDP growth changes, but there is a loose link because real interest rates react to the overnight rate *and* inflation expectations, and because of time lags in the adjustment process.

Extraordinary Monetary Stimulus

The financial crisis and recession of 2008–2009 led to some extraordinary monetary policies.

♦ The crisis created three problems in various banks and countries:

- Widespread falls in asset prices created solvency problems for banks if their equity became close to or below zero.

- Some banks faced significant currency drains, creating liquidity problems.

- For some banks, depositors lost confidence and a bank run began.

♦ Banks began calling in loans, and the national and global loanable funds markets dried up.

♦ Policymakers carried out five key policy actions:

- Open market purchases worked to increase bank liquidity.

- Extending deposit insurance works to reassure depositors and prevent withdrawals.

- Governments and central banks swapped government assets for toxic bank assets, as well as buying shares in banks—both of these actions worked to reduce the solvency problem.

- Changing accounting standards reduced problems with solvency as well.

♦ Despite these strong efforts, the recovery has been very slow.

♦ Critics argue that this slowness is due to the U.S. Fed pursuing a confusing and uncertain monetary policy, and that it should instead have a clear monetary rule such as Canada's inflation rate targeting strategy or the Taylor rule.

HELPFUL HINTS

1 Let's use a numerical example to review how the Bank of Canada can get the overnight rate to be in the middle of the target range. Suppose that the Bank wishes the overnight rate to be 3.5 percent, which means the operating band will be 3.25 to 3.75 percent.

How can the Bank guarantee that the overnight rate will be within the 0.5 percent target range? Two key factors keep the rate in the range. One is that the Bank of Canada is willing to lend as much money as the banks want to borrow at the bank rate (which is set at the upper end of the target, 3.75%). If the overnight rate was 4 percent, no bank would borrow at this rate as they could borrow at the (lower) bank rate. Therefore, the overnight rate is less than or equal to the bank rate. The second factor is that the Bank of Canada is willing to allow the banks to hold as many deposits at the Bank of Canada as they want, and to earn the settlement balances rate of 3.25 percent. If the overnight rate was 3 percent, no bank would lend at this rate as they could earn 3.25 percent. Therefore, the overnight rate is greater than or equal to the settlements balances rate. In sum:

Settlement balances rate ≤ overnight rate ≤ bank rate

3.25% ≤ overnight rate ≤ 3.75%

As long as the Bank of Canada is willing to meet all borrowing/lending requirements implied by the rates it sets, it can force the *actual* overnight rate to be in this range. However, if the actual rate gets stuck at one end, it would be difficult for the Bank to continuously accept deposits or loan out money. In that case it must use open market operations to affect the amount of reserves and the overnight rate.

2 Open market operations affect the overnight rate via their impact on banking system reserves. One liability of the Bank of Canada is banks' deposits at the Bank of Canada (which are part of the banks' reserves). In addition, the largest class of assets of the Bank of Canada is its holdings of government securities. Finally, recall that if total assets increase, due to the conventions of double-entry bookkeeping, total liabilities must increase by the same amount.

An open market purchase by the Bank of Canada of government securities is an increase in its assets paid for by an increase in its liabilities, principally an increase in the deposits of banks at the Bank of Canada. This increase in deposits at the Bank of Canada is an increase in banks' reserves, leaving them with excess reserves they will lend out, initially in the overnight market, pushing down the overnight rate.

SELF-TEST

True/False and Explain

Monetary Policy Objectives and Framework

1 The monetary policy objective of the Bank of Canada is to avoid inflation and prevent excessive swings in the exchange rate.

2 The Bank of Canada's current inflation target is a range of 1 to 3 percent per year for core inflation.

3 The benefits of a target range include creating an anchor for inflation expectations.

The Conduct of Monetary Policy

4 Increasing the bank rate will increase the amount of lending by the banking system.

5 If the Bank of Canada sells government securities in the open market, bank reserves decrease.

6 To tighten monetary policy, the Bank of Canada raises the overnight rate target.

Monetary Policy Transmission

7   A decrease in the overnight rate shifts the *AD* curve rightward.

8   An increase in the overnight rate decreases the exchange rate.

9   A decrease in the overnight rate reduces inflationary pressures.

10   An increase in the overnight rate will increase the quantity of money and lower money demand.

11   The overnight rate and the 10-year government bond rate move very closely together.

12   A lower real interest rate creates more consumption spending.

Extraordinary Monetary Stimulus

13   A fall in the prices of the assets held by a bank creates a liquidity problem for the bank.

14   Extending deposit insurance has the goal of reducing deposit withdrawals and bank runs.

15   Inflation targeting is the sole component of the Taylor rule.

Multiple-Choice

Monetary Policy Objectives and Framework

1   Why does the Bank of Canada pay close attention to the core inflation rate in addition to the overall CPI inflation rate?
   a   The core rate is more volatile and therefore a better predictor of trend inflation.
   b   The core rate includes taxes, while the overall CPI rate does not.
   c   The core rate has a lower average value and therefore makes the Bank look better.
   d   The core rate is less volatile and a better predictor of future CPI inflation.
   e   The core rate excludes eight volatile prices and is therefore more likely to stay within the target band.

2   One criticism of the Bank of Canada's focus on an inflation control target is that
   a   if inflation falls below the target range a recession will result.
   b   if inflation edges above the target range, the Bank decreases aggregate demand and could create a recession.
   c   the Bank pays too much attention to unemployment and real GDP growth and not enough to inflation control.
   d   it makes setting expectations of inflation difficult.
   e   the Bank rarely achieves its target.

3   Who is responsible for setting monetary policy in Canada?
   a   the government of Canada
   b   the Governor of the Bank of Canada
   c   the Bank of Canada's economists
   d   the Governing Council of the Bank of Canada
   e   the Governing Council of the Bank of Canada, after consultation with the government of Canada

The Conduct of Monetary Policy

4   The bank rate is the interest rate
   a   banks charge their very best loan customers.
   b   banks pay on term deposits.
   c   the Bank of Canada pays on reserves held by banks.
   d   the Bank of Canada charges when it lends reserves to banks.
   e   received for holding Government of Canada Treasury bills.

5 The Bank of Canada's current decision-making rule
   a uses the overnight loans rate target to affect the current state of the economy.
   b uses open market operations to affect the current state of the economy.
   c uses the overnight loans rate target to hit the inflation rate target.
   d uses open market operations to try and affect the exchange rate.
   e uses the growth rate of the monetary base to affect lending.

6 If the Bank of Canada aims to lower the overnight rate, it will
   a lower the bank rate and settlement balances rate, as well as buy government securities.
   b lower the bank rate, increase the settlement balances rate, as well as buy government securities.
   c lower the bank rate and settlement balances rate, as well as sell government securities.
   d raise the bank rate and settlement balances rate, as well as buy government securities.
   e raise the bank rate and settlement balances rate, as well as sell government securities.

7 Why does the Bank of Canada use open market operations together with overnight rate targeting?
   a to ensure the overnight rate hits the target
   b to offset the impact of the overnight rate
   c to provide liquidity for banks
   d to lower interest rates
   e to raise interest rates

8 In an open market operation aimed at increasing expenditure, the Bank of Canada
   a sells government bonds, decreasing bank reserves, decreasing lending, decreasing the overnight rate.
   b sells government bonds, decreasing bank reserves, decreasing lending, increasing the overnight rate.
   c sells government bonds, decreasing bank reserves, increasing lending, increasing the overnight rate.
   d buys government bonds, increasing bank reserves, increasing lending, decreasing the overnight rate.
   e buys government bonds, increasing bank reserves, increasing lending, increasing the overnight rate.

9 The current overnight loans rate is 3 percent, with the Bank of Canada's operating band set at 2.75 to 3.25 percent. If the Bank of Canada lowers their operating band to 2.25 to 2.75 percent, which of the following is one of the reasons the overnight rate will fall to within this new range?
   a Since the banking system can now borrow from the Bank of Canada at 2.75 percent, no bank would borrow on the overnight loan market at 3 percent.
   b Since the banking system can now borrow from the Bank of Canada at 2.25 percent, no bank would borrow on the overnight loan market at 3 percent.
   c Since the banking system can now earn 2.75 percent from the Bank of Canada, no bank would lend on the overnight loan market at 3 percent.
   d Since the banking system can now earn 2.25 percent from the Bank of Canada, no bank would lend on the overnight loan market at 3 percent.
   e There is a legal requirement that the overnight rate must be within the Bank of Canada's operating band.

10 The current overnight loans rate is 3 percent, with the Bank of Canada's operating band set at 2.75 to 3.25 percent. If the Bank of Canada lowers their operating band to 2.25 to 2.75 percent, what open market operation might be used to move the overnight rate to the middle of the target?
   a buying foreign exchange in the foreign exchange market
   b buying Canadian dollars in the foreign exchange market
   c selling foreign exchange in the foreign exchange market
   d buying government securities in the open market
   e selling government securities in the open market

Monetary Policy Transmission

11 Why is the exchange rate a key monetary variable?
   a It is one of the four main policy rules.
   b It is a key policy objective.
   c It is a barometer of monetary policy.
   d It shows how much the monetary base must be multiplied to measure the resulting increase in the quantity of money.
   e It is part of the channel by which a change in the overnight rate affects aggregate demand.

12 The headline "The Bank of Canada Has Cut the Bank Rate" suggests that the Bank of Canada is trying to
 a lower inflationary pressures.
 b increase the overnight loans rate.
 c stimulate aggregate demand.
 d raise the value of the Canadian dollar.
 e help banks make profits.

13 In a situation of unemployment, a decrease in the overnight rate will lead to a(n)
 a increase in real GDP and the price level.
 b increase in real GDP, but a decrease in the price level.
 c increase in real GDP, but no change in the price level.
 d increase in the price level, but no change in real GDP.
 e decrease in the price level and real GDP.

14 A monetary policy aimed at increasing domestic expenditure will
 a increase interest rates and decrease the exchange rate.
 b have no impact on interest rates, but increase the exchange rate.
 c have no impact on interest rates nor on the exchange rate.
 d decrease interest rates and increase the exchange rate.
 e decrease interest rates and the exchange rate.

15 Which of the following statements about historical evidence on monetary policy is *true*?
 a The overnight interest rate moves inversely with short-term interest rates.
 b The overnight interest rate is not related to short-term interest rates.
 c When the Bank of Canada lowers the overnight rate, real GDP rises immediately.
 d When the gap between Canadian and U.S. interest rates increases, the exchange rate decreases.
 e When the gap between Canadian and U.S. interest rates increases, the exchange rate increases.

16 Consider Fig. 30.1. Which graph represents an anti-inflationary monetary policy?
 a (a)
 b (b)
 c (c)
 d (d)
 e none of the above

FIGURE **30.1**

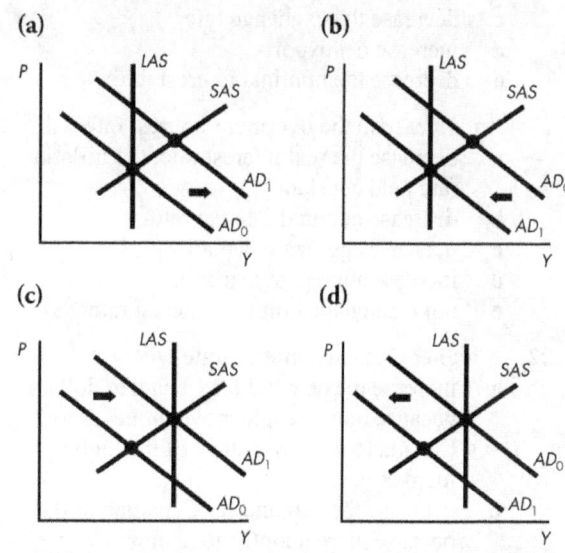

17 Consider Fig. 30.1. Which graph represents an attempt to lower unemployment with monetary policy?
 a (a)
 b (b)
 c (c)
 d (d)
 e none of the above

18 Which of the following statements *correctly* describes an anti-inflationary monetary policy?
 a "The Bank of Canada's purchases of government securities is stimulating the housing sector."
 b "The Bank of Canada's moves to lower interest rates are behind the decrease in the value of the Canadian dollar."
 c "The Bank of Canada's moves to increase the overnight loans rate are leading to less lending and less consumer spending."
 d "The Bank of Canada's sales of government securities are stimulating the housing sector."
 e "The Bank of Canada's moves to decrease the value of the Canadian dollar are leading to more spending in the economy."

19 If the inflation rate increases by 3 percent and the nominal interest rate increases by 2 percent,
 a the real interest rate increases.
 b money demand increases.
 c money demand decreases.
 d investment decreases.
 e consumption expenditure decreases.

20 An increase in the real interest rate will
    a decrease consumption expenditure.
    b increase investment.
    c decrease the exchange rate.
    d increase net exports.
    e decrease the nominal interest rate.

21 An increase in the overnight interest rate will
    a decrease the real interest rate, the inflation rate held constant.
    b decrease nominal interest rates.
    c decrease aggregate demand.
    d increase aggregate demand.
    e not change the nominal interest rate.

22 A higher Canadian interest rate will
    a increase the demand for Canadian dollars because more people move money into Canada to take advantage of the higher interest rate.
    b decrease the demand for Canadian dollars because more people move money out of Canada to take advantage of the higher interest rate.
    c increase the demand for Canadian dollars because more people move money out of Canada to take advantage of the higher interest rate.
    d decrease the demand for Canadian dollars because more people move money into Canada to take advantage of the higher interest rate.
    e not affect the demand for Canadian dollars.

23 Changing the overnight rate affects aggregate demand through several channels. Which of the following is *not* one of those channels?
    a Higher real interest rates lower net exports.
    b Higher real interest rates raise consumption expenditure.
    c Higher real interest rates lower investment spending.
    d Lower real interest rates raise consumption expenditure.
    e Lower real interest rates raise investment spending.

Extraordinary Monetary Stimulus

24 Which of the following policy actions increases bank reserves?
    a an open market purchase
    b an increase in interest rates
    c buying toxic assets from banks
    d buying shares in banks
    e accounting changes that allow banks to revalue their assets

25 How does a bank run put a bank under stress?
    a It creates a decrease in asset prices and creates liquidity problems.
    b Deposits enter the bank creating cash surpluses.
    c Deposits leave the bank and equity falls below zero, creating liquidity and solvency problems.
    d Loans are paid off by borrowers and the bank cannot make profits.
    e Loans are not repaid and the bank suffers a solvency problem.

Short Answer Problems

1 How does an open market purchase of government securities lead to a decrease in the overnight rate? What are the ripple effects of this policy on the different components of aggregate expenditure?

2 Explain what the policy action in Short Answer Problem **1** does to aggregate demand, real GDP, and the price level in the short run. How is it different in the long run?

3 Suppose there is an increase in the overnight rate and therefore in other interest rates. Using a graph of the aggregate demand–aggregate supply model, show what happens to the price level and the level of real GDP in the short run and in the long run.

4 Consider the following data, from the imaginary country of Sarconia:

Current inflation rate	3% per year
Current overnight rate	4% per year
Current growth rate of real GDP	3% per year
Estimated (long-term) growth rate of potential GDP	3% per year
Current unemployment rate	5%
Estimate of natural unemployment rate	7%
Current growth rate of monetary base	12% per year

    a Is Sarconia suffering from an inflationary gap, a recessionary gap, or is it right at potential GDP? How do you know?

    b If the Bank of Sarconia has an inflationary target of 2 to 4 percent per year, what would be the appropriate policy strategy?

    c If the Bank of Sarconia follows a Taylor rule with an inflationary target of 2 to 4 percent per year, what should be its policy strategy?

5 In Short Answer Problem **4**, you should have found different policy conclusions for each of the rules in parts **b** and **c**. Explain what differences in the crucial factors underlying each rule lead to the different policy conclusions.

6 "If banking system reserves are increasing, this is a sign that loans and deposits will soon expand." Evaluate this statement.

7 Consider the following "quotation" from the *Regional Post*:

Interest Rates Crash after Bank of Canada Action

by J. S. Smith

The Bank of Canada cut interest rates dramatically yesterday. ... [T]he bank cut its target for overnight rates to 3.25% from 4.00%. The major banks quickly followed suit, cutting the cost of borrowing for their best customers (the prime rate) to 5.50% from 6.25%. This change was followed by reductions in other rates, including mortgage rates.

Explain the link from the overnight rate target to the prime rate that the major banks charge their best customers.

8 If the Bank of Canada wishes to reduce inflationary pressure, explain briefly what steps it will have to carry out in the overnight loans market.

ANSWERS

True/False and Explain

1 **F** Avoid inflation and prevent excessive swings in real GDP growth and unemployment. (728)

2 **F** 1 to 3 percent for overall inflation. (728–729)

3 **T** See text discussion. (729)

4 **F** Higher bank rate increases cost of borrowing reserves, so banks wish to hold more reserves, and *decrease* loans. (730–732)

5 **T** People buy securities with deposits that are transferred to the Bank of Canada, decreasing reserves. (731–732)

6 **T** They must raise the bank rate and the settlement balances rate, and potentially carry out an open market operation. (731)

7 **T** A lower overnight rate pushes down short-term and long-term interest rates, which increases consumption, investment, and net exports, shifting *AD* curve rightward. (735)

8 **F** A higher overnight rate pushes up interest rates, raising Canadian interest rate differential, raising demand for Canadian dollar, and therefore the exchange rate. (735)

9 **F** A lower overnight rate pushes down short-term and long-term interest rates, increasing consumption, investment, and net exports, shifting the *AD* curve rightward, pushing up price level. (733–740)

10 **F** A higher overnight rate leads to lower bank reserves, lower loans, less deposits, and lower quantity of money. Lower quantity of money raises interest rate and lowers money demand. (735)

11 **F** They move together, but not that closely. See Text Fig. 30.5. (733–734)

12 **T** A lower real rate leads to less saving and more consumption. (741)

13 **F** Creates solvency problem. (741)

14 **T** Depositors have less incentive to withdraw. (742)

15 **F** It looks at both inflation and the output gap. (747)

Multiple-Choice

1 **d** See text discussion. (728)

2 **b** Anti-inflationary policy leads to decreased *AD*, which can lead to recession and unemployment. (728)

3 **e** See text discussion. (730)

4 **d** Definition. (731)

5 **c** Overnight loan rate is a policy instrument aimed at policy objective of inflation rate. (731–732)

6 **a** Lowering two rates will force the overnight rate down in between these two rates (see Helpful Hint **1**), and buying securities increases banking system reserves, leading to more overnight loans, pushing rate down. (731–732)

7 a   The target range will guarantee the overnight rate is within the range, but not at the desired level unless open market operations support the target range. (731–732)

8 d   Buying bonds increases reserves to pay for them, which creates excess reserves, leading to an increase in funds available for lending in the overnight loans market, pushing down the overnight rate. (732)

9 a   Upper end of band is the bank rate—the rate the Bank of Canada charges for borrowing from it. No profit-seeking bank will pay more than this rate to borrow, forcing down the actual overnight rate to less than or equal to this rate. (731–732)

10 d   They need to buy securities to raise banking system reserves to increase funds for lending in the overnight market to push down the overnight rate. (731–732)

11 e   Δ overnight rate leads to Δr, which Δ demand for Canadian dollar and exchange rate, which ΔX, ΔM, and AD. (735)

12 c   Lowering the bank rate lowers costs of borrowing to replenish reserves, so banking system will maintain lower reserves, lend out more money, lowering interest rates and stimulating consumption, investment, net exports, and AD. (733–740)

13 a   Decrease in the overnight rate shifts AD rightward, increasing real GDP and the price level if initial equilibrium is left of full employment (draw a graph). (736–740)

14 e   Decrease in overnight rate decreases interest rates, decreasing demand for the Canadian dollar and therefore exchange rate. (733–735)

15 e   See text discussion. (733–740)

16 b   Output is above natural rate (inflationary gap). Policy is attempting to reduce AD to reduce the gap. (736–740)

17 c   Output is below natural rate (recessionary gap). Policy is attempting to increase AD to reduce the gap. (736–740)

18 c   All other changes lead to lower interest rates and higher aggregate expenditure, shifting AD rightward. (733–740)

19 c   Nominal interest rate increases, money demand decreases. Real interest rate decreases since increase in inflation rate > increase in nominal interest rate, so investment and consumption expenditure increase. (735)

20 a   Higher cost of borrowing decreases borrowing and spending. (735)

21 c   Higher overnight rate increases other interest rates and decreases consumption, investment, and net exports. (735)

22 a   People trying to earn more on their money buy Canadian assets and must buy Canadian dollars to buy Canadian assets. (735)

23 b   Higher real interest rates lower borrowing and spending. (733–740)

24 a   Bank of Canada buys government securities from banks (crediting their reserves held at the Bank). (742)

25 c   Withdrawals create cash shortages and the bank has to use up reserves and its equity to match withdrawals. (741)

Short Answer Problems

1   An open market purchase of government securities by the Bank of Canada increases the reserves of the banking system by increasing one of its components—banks' deposits at the Bank of Canada. When the securities are purchased from banks, the Bank of Canada pays for the securities by crediting the bank's deposit at the Bank of Canada, which directly increases their reserves. The banks now have more reserves, and will try to lend more on the overnight market (and will need to borrow less), putting downward pressure on overnight rates.

The lower overnight rates create substitution effects, pushing down other interest rates, increasing consumption expenditure and investment spending. The lower interest rates also lower demand for the Canadian dollar, which lowers the value of the exchange rate and increases net exports.

2   The impact of the extra consumption, investment, and net exports is that the aggregate demand curve shifts rightward. In the short run, this increases real GDP and the price level, as in Text Fig. 30.6(d). In the long run, if the economy started out in recession (as in the Text Figure) it will converge towards potential GDP without other effects. However, if it started out at potential GDP, the increase in aggregate demand will create inflationary pressures, which in turn will create wage increases. Short-run aggregate supply shifts leftward, creating further increases in the price level and decreases in real GDP as the economy moves back towards potential GDP.

3 Figure 30.2 illustrates the consequences of an increase in the overnight rates. The economy is initially in long-run equilibrium at point a, the intersection of AD_0 and SAS_0 (and LAS). The price level is P_0 and GDP is at potential, Y^*. An increase in the overnight rate lowers consumption, investment, and net exports and shifts the AD curve leftward, from AD_0 to AD_1. The new short-run equilibrium is at point b. The price level decreases to P_1 and real GDP decreases to Y_1. In the long run, however, input prices also decrease, which shifts SAS rightward, from SAS_0 to SAS_1. A new long-run equilibrium occurs at point c. In the long run, the price level decreases further to P_2, while real GDP returns to potential, Y^*.

FIGURE **30.2**

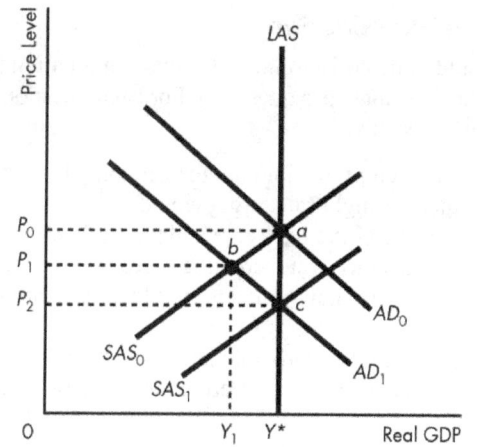

4 a Since unemployment is below the natural rate, real GDP is above potential GDP and there is an inflationary gap.

   b Since inflation is exactly in the middle of the inflationary target range, the appropriate policy would be to do nothing different.

   c A Taylor rule follows the following formula:

   $$R = 2 + INF + 0.5(INF - 2) + 0.5GAP$$

   R is the overnight rate, INF is the inflation rate, and GAP is an estimate of the output

gap. Substituting in the information from the question, we see:

$$R = 2 + 3 + 0.5(3 - 2) + 0.5GAP, \text{ or}$$

$$R = 5.5 + 0.5GAP$$

We do not know what GAP is, but if there is an inflationary gap, $GAP > 0$. Therefore, the overnight rate should be higher than 5.5 percent. Since it is currently 4 percent, it needs to be raised.

5 The simple inflationary rule of part **b** only focuses on the inflation target, which was currently being met, and not on any future problems. The Taylor rule (which also looks at the output gap as a source of future inflationary pressures) tries to forecast future pressures and offset them before they occur.

6 Banking system reserves might be increasing for two reasons, which will have opposite future effects on loans and deposits. It might be as a result of an open market operation, where the Bank of Canada is buying securities and pumping up the reserves of the banking system. This creates *excess* reserves, which will be lent out, creating deposits expansion.

   A second reason might be because the Bank of Canada has raised the overnight loan rate, making it more expensive for banks to be short of reserves. Then, banks will raise their *desired* reserves in order to avoid being short. In this case, they will be shrinking their loans (and therefore deposits) to increase their desired reserves.

7 The overnight rate is the rate banks in the banking system charge each other when there are shortages in reserves at the end of the day. If this rate climbs dramatically, banks will want to hold more reserves. To do this, they will call in loans to their other customers and raise loan rates, since these are substitutes for overnight loans.

8 To reduce inflationary pressure, the Bank of Canada needs to reduce aggregate demand. To do this, the Bank must raise nominal and real interest rates. To raise the overnight rate, the Bank would raise its target range for the overnight rate. In addition, they would probably carry out an open market sale of government securities. If they sell securities to the banking system, these securities will be paid for out of reserves, reducing the amount of reserves.

Part 10 Wrap Up
Understanding Macroeconomic Policy

PROBLEM

Due to a recession in the United States, the Canadian economy now has a large recessionary gap. You are working as a special economic advisor to the Prime Minister. She has two policy options to evaluate.

a The Governor of the Bank of Canada suggests carrying out an anti-recessionary *monetary* policy. The Prime Minister would like you to explain such a policy. Give an example of the changes to the overnight rate target and the type of open market operation the Bank of Canada would carry out. What is the overall impact of expansionary monetary policy on bank reserves and the overnight rate? Explain what this policy will do to real interest rates, consumption, investment, net exports, aggregate demand, the price level, and real GDP in the short run.

b The Minister of Finance suggests carrying out an anti-recessionary *fiscal* policy. The Prime Minister would like you to explain how this policy would work. Give an example of the changes to taxes and/or government expenditures that would be needed to make this work. (The government currently has a balanced budget.) Explain how this policy would work through the economy to affect government expenditures, consumption, investment (hint: think of the impact on real interest rates), net exports, aggregate demand, the price level, and real GDP in the short run.

c Now that you have explained the two policies, the Prime Minister has to pick between them.

She turns to you, and asks you to give her a quick summary of some of the potential indirect impacts of each policy on the economy, as well as issues around loose links and timing lags. Which policy would you recommend?

Midterm Examination

You should allocate 16 minutes for this examination (8 questions, 2 minutes per question). For each question, choose the *best* answer.

1 An attempt to stimulate the economy by using the overnight rate target would
a lower the bank rate and the settlement balances rate, creating more excess reserves, creating more loans, and lowering interest rates on loans.
b raise the bank rate and the settlement balances rate, creating more excess reserves, creating more loans, and lowering interest rates on loans.
c raise the bank rate and the settlement balances rate, creating less excess reserves, creating less loans, and increasing interest rates on loans.
d lower the bank rate and the settlement balances rate, creating less excess reserves, creating less loans, and increasing interest rates on loans.
e lower the bank rate and the settlement balances rate, creating more excess reserves, creating more loans, and increasing interest rates on loans.

2 An increase in income tax rates leads to
  a only a rightward shift in the *AD* curve.
  b only a leftward shift in the *AD* curve.
  c only a leftward shift in the *SAS* curve.
  d only a rightward shift in the *SAS* curve.
  e both a leftward shift in the *AD* curve and the *SAS* curve.

3 An open market purchase of government securities by the Bank of Canada will
  a increase bank reserves and increase the overnight rate.
  b decrease bank reserves and decrease the overnight rate.
  c increase bank reserves and decrease the overnight rate.
  d decrease bank reserves and increase the overnight rate.
  e decrease bank reserves but increase the overnight rate if banks have excess reserves.

4 An increase in the tax rate on wages will lead to
  a less labour hired, more production, and higher potential GDP.
  b less saving, less investment, and lower economic growth.
  c more labour hired, more production, and higher potential GDP.
  d a strong intertemporal substitution effect, leading to more labour supplied.
  e higher real before-tax wage rates.

5 Which of the following quotations *correctly* describes the impact of monetary policy on the economy?
  a "House sales are down a lot, due to the lower interest rates."
  b "The lower interest rates created by the central bank are creating lower exports."
  c "The tightening of monetary policy is helping sell goods abroad."
  d "Businesses are investing more, now that interest rates have become higher."
  e "The lower interest rates created by the central bank are creating more jobs."

6 The presence of income taxes in an economy means that
  a fiscal policy multipliers are made stronger.
  b discretionary fiscal policy is eliminated.
  c there will always be a structural deficit.
  d there will always be a cyclical deficit.
  e fluctuations in aggregate expenditure are reduced.

7 Whenever the inflation rate is above the target, or there is a positive output gap, the Bank of Sarconia raises the overnight rate target. The Bank of Sarconia is
  a following an inflation targeting rule.
  b carrying out an expansionary policy.
  c following a Taylor rule.
  d carrying out an extraordinary stimulus.
  e worried about bank insolvency.

8 Which of the following is *not* a source of budgetary revenues?
  a personal income taxes
  b transfer payments
  c corporate income taxes
  d indirect taxes
  e investment income

ANSWERS

Problem

a The Bank of Canada wants to lower interest rates, and will do so by lowering the overnight target range (lowering the bank rate and the settlements balance rate) and by purchasing government securities. The Bank of Canada buys these securities from private banks and pays for them by crediting the banks' deposits at the Bank of Canada (which are reserves).

The lower overnight target rate and the open market operation lead to excess reserves in the banking system. The banks will try to increase their overnight lending and reduce their overnight borrowing, which pushes down overnight rates. The banks will also lend out their excess reserves, leading to an expansion of loans, deposits, and therefore the money supply.

The lower overnight rates create substitution effects, lowering other interest rates. The increase in loanable funds also lowers real interest rates in the short run, which increases consumption expenditure and investment, and decreases the demand for Canadian dollars and therefore decreases the value of the Canadian dollar and increases net exports.

The increase in consumption, investment, and net exports increases aggregate demand, which translates into a shift rightward in the *AD* curve, which increases the price level, triggering a movement along the short-run aggregate supply curve, increasing real GDP.

b An appropriate tax policy would be a tax cut. This would increase disposable income, which would increase consumption expenditure and therefore aggregate demand. An increase in government expenditures would lead directly to an increase in aggregate demand.

The increase in consumption or government expenditures increases aggregate demand, which translates into a shift rightward in the aggregate demand curve, which increases the price level, triggering a movement along the short-run aggregate supply curve, increasing real GDP.

One complication is that the fiscal policy, by either cutting taxes or raising government expenditures, would create a budget deficit. A budget deficit increases the demand for loanable funds and increases real interest rates. The higher real interest rates will lower investment spending. The higher real interest rates will also increase the demand for the Canadian dollar, increasing the exchange rate, lowering exports, and raising imports. The decrease in investment and net exports will somewhat offset the impact of the original increase in aggregate demand.

c Indirect impacts on the economy might flow from two factors. First, the budget deficit and higher interest rates will potentially lower investment and therefore have a negative impact on capital accumulation and economic growth. Second, if tax cuts are used for the fiscal policy, this would reduce the tax wedge and potentially have positive incentive effects, helping increase potential GDP.

Fiscal policy suffers from three potential lags: the recognition lag (not an issue in this case), the law-making lag (the changes to tax or spending policy must pass Parliament), and the impact lag (the policies take time to have an impact on the economy). Monetary policy also suffers from timing lags in the monetary policy transmission process. In addition, monetary policy affects aggregate demand via the real interest rate, which is affected by a variety of other factors, including inflation expectations. Therefore, monetary policy only has a "loose link" to aggregate demand.

Your policy recommendation depends on your judgment of the speed and effectiveness of each policy. It's a value judgment!

MIDTERM EXAMINATION

1 a Decrease in bank rate and settlement balances rate decreases cost of borrowing from central bank, decreasing desired reserves, creating excess reserves, creating increase in loans, etc. (730–732)

2 b Tax increase reduces YD and AD via multiplier effects, and also reduces incentive effects so shifts SAS left. (710–719)

3 c Bank of Canada pays for securities by crediting banks' reserves, which creates excess reserves and more lending, lowering the overnight rate. (731–732)

4 b Lower return to working, lower quantity supplied of labour, raising before-tax wage rates, reducing labour hired, production, and therefore potential GDP. (712–713)

5 e Decrease in r leads to increase in C (so **a** is wrong), increase in I (so **d** is wrong), increase in NX (so **b** and **c** are wrong), and all increase AD, which creates more jobs. (737–740)

6 e Income taxes act to automatically stabilize the economy. Multipliers are weaker, can still do discretionary policy, and there may or may not be a cyclical/structural deficit depending on other factors. (714–715)

7 c See Taylor rule formula. Other formulas ignore output gap. (741–743)

8 b Outlay. (704–705)

Notes

Notes

Notes

Notes